Computer Systems Organization & Architecture

Computer Systems Organization & Architecture

JOHN D. CARPINELLI

New Jersey Institute of Technology

Addison
Wesley

Boston San Francisco New York
London Toronto Sydney Tokyo Singapore Madrid
Mexico City Munich Paris Cape Town Hong Kong Montreal

Senior Acquisitions Editor	Susan Hartman
Assistant Editor	Lisa Kalner
Executive Marketing Manager	Michael Hirsch
Production Services	Marilyn Lloyd/ Pre-Press Company, Inc.
Composition and Art	Pre-Press Company, Inc.
Copyeditor	Carol Noble
Text Design	Joyce Cosentino
Cover Design	Regina Hagen
Cover Photograph	© 2000, PhotoDisk, Inc.
Design Manager	Regina Hagen
Prepress and Manufacturing	Caroline Fell
Media Producer	Jennifer Pelland

Access the latest information about Addison-Wesley Computer Science titles from our World Wide Web site: http://www.awl.com/cs

The programs and applications presented in this book have been included for their instructional value. They have been tested with care, but are not guaranteed for any particular purpose. The publisher does not offer any warranties or representations, nor does it accept any liabilities with respect to the programs or applications.

Library of Congress Cataloging-in-Publication Data

Carpinelli, John D.
   Computer systems organization and architecture / John D. Carpinelli.
      p. cm.
   Includes bibliographical references and index.
   ISBN 0-201-61253-4
      1. Computer organization. 2. Computer architecture. I. Title.

QA76.9.C643 C37 2001
004.2'2—dc21   00-055836

1 2 3 4 5 6 7 8 9 10-MA-0403020100

To Mary and Maria

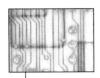

Table of Contents

PART 3   Advanced Topics

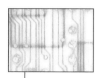

Preface

Introduction

This book is designed for use in a computer organization or computer architecture course typically offered by computer engineering, computer science, electrical engineering, or information systems departments. Such a course would typically be at the junior or senior level, or at an advanced sophomore level. This book is also appropriate for bridge courses for graduate students in computer engineering, computer science, electrical engineering, or information systems.

There are no formal prerequisites for this book. Many students will have taken a course in digital circuits before using this book; although helpful, this is not absolutely necessary. I have included two chapters of background material on digital circuits and finite state machines for students lacking this background. Students do not need to know any specific programming language, but they should be able to follow an algorithm written in pseudo-code.

My Approach

In the past, I've taught the topics in this book using different texts. No text was perfect. Some started at too high a level of complexity, losing students in minutiae and details before they could grasp the fundamental concepts. Others covered material without cohesion between topics. These issues, and others, caused problems for my students. I wrote this book to address these problems and to improve student learning. It is my hope that I've successfully resolved some of the problems found in other texts.

Writing this book made me think about a lot more than the material it covers. I considered different ways to present the material, and different design methods. The methods I use in this book are primarily those that worked best for my students.

I like to include a lot of design work in my courses. Students learn by doing; they gain a better understanding of why things work the way they do. Accrediting boards, especially in engineering, require design work in the curriculum. This book includes a strong design component, starting with relatively simple designs and progressing to more complex designs.

Students seem to prefer a top-down approach to system design; however, studies show that they learn the material better when it is taught bottom-up. To balance these two, I first describe systems top-down. This gives students an overall perspective on the design process, since they know where each piece ultimately fits into the final design. However, I design the systems bottom-up, designing small parts of the system and then integrating them together to form the desired system. I feel that the bottom-up approach provides a better foundation for students to build on concepts learned earlier.

I like to illustrate concepts using simple examples. This allows me to introduce concepts without too many other details that confuse the presentation. For example, the book introduces CPU design with a 4-instruction, Very Simple CPU. After students have gone through this design, the book presents the more complex, 16-instruction Relatively Simple CPU that builds on the design techniques used for the Very Simple CPU while also introducing some more advanced techniques. This CPU is used in other design examples throughout the book.

This book uses the Relatively Simple CPU as a running theme. I start by specifying its instruction set architecture, and then design a simple computer using this CPU. The book then presents the design of the CPU itself, using both hardwired and microcoded control. Later in the book, I use this CPU to illustrate other topics, such as how interrupts are processed within the CPU. Such continuity minimizes the amount of extraneous material that students must learn, allowing them to concentrate on the concepts being taught.

For the topic of CPU design, specifically the control unit of the CPU, I use a finite state machine approach. By specifying the operations necessary to fetch, decode, and execute instructions as a straightforward sequence, I believe this gives students a better understanding of how the CPU processes instructions. It also offers the advantage of partitioning the design into two parts: specifying operations and implementing them.

Finally, I think students learn better when they can relate concepts to real-world systems. I've included real-world examples, both historical and current, in each chapter to meet this student need.

Scope of Coverage

This book covers a wide range of topics, from basic digital circuits through parallel processing. First, let's look at the topics covered in each chapter; then we'll describe possible paths through the text. This book is divided into three parts, each described below.

Digital Logic and Finite State Machines

The first part, *Digital Logic and Finite State Machines*, contains the first two chapters. Chapter 1, *Digital Logic Fundamentals*, introduces the basics of Boolean algebra and digital components, using both combinatorial and sequential logic. It introduces some of the more complex components used in the designs found throughout the text. This chapter includes a real-world section on programmable logic devices. Students use this material in their designs throughout the book.

Chapter 2 provides an *Introduction to Finite State Machines*. Such a chapter isn't typically found in a book on computer organization and architecture, but I felt it was important to have it in this book. The control unit of a microprocessor is a finite state machine; learning the basics of finite state machines makes it easier to understand how microprocessors work and why they work the way they do. Finite state machines are used extensively in the designs of CPUs in Chapters 6 and 7.

Computer Organization and Architecture

The second part of this book, *Computer Organization and Architecture*, covers the following eight chapters. Chapter 3 covers the *Instruction Set Architecture* (ISA) of a microprocessor. When you set out to design a microprocessor, you first determine the tasks it must perform, and then specify the instructions, internal registers, and other ISA components it needs to perform these tasks. The ISA is the first step in the design process.

The text looks at *Computer Organization* in Chapter 4. It examines how the processor connects to memory and input/output devices in a computer. This chapter also examines how physical memory is constructed. It provides a strong foundation on which the rest of this book is built. Two simple computer organizations are presented in this chapter. The first is based on the Relatively Simple CPU, an instructional aid used throughout this text; the other is a real-world design based on Intel's 8085 microprocessor.

Chapter 5 examines *Register Transfer Languages*. RTLs are used throughout the book to design microprocessors and other computer system components. This chapter presents the basic syntax of RTL and some typical designs. This gives students the knowledge needed to design systems found in this book, as well as systems beyond this text. This chapter also introduces VHDL, a hardware description language widely used in digital design.

The next five chapters examine the design of different portions of computer systems in detail. *CPU Design with Hardwired Control* is introduced in Chapter 6. First, this chapter presents the design of a Very Simple CPU from scratch. This illustrates some of the standard CPU design concepts without flooding the students with too many details. Then a more complex but still relatively simple CPU design is presented. The Relatively Simple CPU design uses many of the design techniques used for the Very Simple CPU and also introduces more advanced techniques.

A CPU can have one of two types of control units. Hardwired control was introduced in Chapter 6. In Chapter 7 this book presents *Microsequencer Control Unit Design*. This type of control is used in many advanced microprocessors available today. First, this chapter presents the design of a microsequencer for the Very Simple CPU developed earlier. As in the previous chapter, this introduces the fundamentals of microsequencers without too many extraneous details. Then this chapter presents the design of a microsequencer for the Relatively Simple CPU, again building on the foundation established by the earlier, simpler example while introducing more advanced design techniques. This chapter also examines the internal organization of a microcoded CPU, the Pentium microprocessor.

Chapter 8 examines *Computer Arithmetic*. It looks at different numeric formats and the algorithms to perform arithmetic operations on data in these formats. This chapter examines the hardware to implement these algorithms as well. This chapter also looks at specialized hardware to perform arithmetic operations and the IEEE 754 floating point standard used by all modern processors.

Chapter 9 covers the *Memory Organization* in computer systems. It introduces the memory hierarchy, and examines cache and virtual memory in detail. To illustrate their configuration in a typical computer system, this chapter examines the memory hierarchy of a computer with a Pentium microprocessor which runs Windows NT.

Input/Output Organization is covered in Chapter 10. It examines the basic input/output (I/O) functions, as well as some methods to improve I/O data transfers. Although this chapter covers interrupts, the section on interrupts may be covered earlier without any loss of continuity.

Advanced Topics

The last two chapters comprise the third part of the book, *Advanced Topics*. Chapter 11 covers *Reduced Instruction Set Computing*, or RISC processing. It introduces the rationale for RISC and its main features. As with interrupts in the previous chapter, the material on instruction pipelines in this chapter was written so that it may be covered earlier in the text without any loss of continuity. This chapter also introduces Intel's Itanium microprocessor.

Finally, Chapter 12 provides an *Introduction to Parallel Processing*. It presents the basic organizations and topologies of multiprocessor systems. It examines interprocessor communication and memory organization, and presents parallel algorithms for common functions.

FEATURES

This book includes several features designed to make the material more accessible to students. Some of the features are listed below.

- *Practical Perspectives.* These perspectives help students understand why systems are designed the way they are, and show students how the concepts are applied to real systems. Examples of these perspectives include why LED displays are designed active low, and how cache memory is organized in the Itanium microprocessor.

- *Historical Perspectives.* These perspectives describe components, systems, or events from the past. They help students gain an understanding by introducing timelines and important events in computer design. Examples of these perspectives include the timeline of Intel's early microprocessors and how the Pentium microprocessor got its name.

- *Real-World Examples.* Each chapter ends with an example of a real-world component or system, or a commonly used standard. This gives the students a better understanding of the concepts covered in the book. These sections examine the internal organization of several microprocessors, ranging from the 25-year-old 8085 to the latest Itanium. They also look at how the topics covered in the chapter are implemented in real-world systems, such as cache and virtual memory management in Pentium/Windows computers. Finally, these sections examine standards used in computer design, such as the IEEE 754 Floating Point Standard and the Universal Serial Bus Standard.

Paths Through the Book

The path an instructor uses for this book depends on the background of the students in the class. If the students have no background in digital logic, they should start at the beginning of the book. They would typically begin by covering Chapters 1, 2, 3, and 4. They could then study all of Chapter 5, or only the sections on RTL, and some or all of Chapter 6. The course can include Chapters 7 and 8, or exclude them without a loss of continuity. Most courses would then cover Chapters 9 and 10. Time permitting, the instructor could cover Chapters 11 and/or 12, or selected topics from these chapters.

If the students have already taken a course in digital design, they can skip Chapter 1 and probably Chapter 2. Some digital design courses do not cover finite state machines, or do so at a cursory level. If this is the case, Chapter 2 can be included in the course or assigned to students as a self-study topic or reference. From here, the course would normally cover Chapters 3 to 7. Chapter 8 is optional, depending on the preference of the instructor. The course would then cover Chapters 9, 10, and 11, and, as an option, some or all of Chapter 12.

Regardless of the path used, the instructor may wish to make some modifications. An instructor may wish to replace some of the real-world sections with other material. For example, Chapter 5 introduces VHDL. If the course using this book is a pre-requisite or co-requisite for a lab which uses Verilog, it would be appropriate to introduce material on Verilog rather than cover the VHDL section. Instructors should note that some of the real-world sections build on earlier sections. Chapters 3, 4, and 6 all use the 8085 microprocessor in their real-world sections, and the Pentium microprocessor introduced in Chapter 7 is used in the real-world computer discussed in Chapter 9.

A couple of topics could fit well in several places in the text. This is especially true for the material on interrupts in Chapter 10 and instruction pipelines in Chapter 11. I wrote this material to be self-contained, so that instructors can cover it along with earlier chapters without breaking the flow of the material. Instructors can cover these topics after Section 6.4, or with their present chapters in the book.

Supplements

There is a variety of supplemental material available for use with this book. Some are available to everyone; others are only available to instructors. All of the following supplements are available at the book's companion web site at http://www.awl.com/carpinelli.

Supplements Available to Everyone

- *Relatively Simple CPU Simulator.* This simulator allows students to enter a program, assemble it, and simulate its execution. The simulator animates the flow of data within the CPU to give students a better feel for how the CPU works. The simulator is written as a Java applet that can be run using any Java-enabled web browser on any computing platform. Additional simulators will be regularly added to the book's companion web site.
- *Figures.* All figures in this book have been converted to image files. Instructors may download these files for use in preparing their classroom presentations.

Supplements Available Only to Instructors

- *Solutions Manual.* A solutions manual containing solutions for every problem in this book is available. This manual is for qualified instructors only. It is available through your Addison Wesley sales representative or by sending an e-mail message to aw.cse@awl.com.
- *Instructor's Manual.* An instructor's manual is available for this book. It includes prerequisite topics, outcomes, and a summary for each chapter, as well as author's comments. As with the solutions manual, this manual is for qualified instructors only. It is available through your Addison Wesley sales representative or by sending an e-mail message to aw.cse@awl.com.

Acknowledgments

There is only one author listed for this book, but many people influenced its development and final form. Perhaps the greatest influence on this book is the students who have taken my undergraduate computer organization and architecture courses during the past 15 years. They have given me great feedback about what works and what does not when explaining the topics in this book. I've tried to use their feedback as much as possible in preparing this book because I trust their opinions. I especially thank the students who have tested preliminary versions of some chapters during the past few semesters.

Although I specified the basic functions of the Relatively Simple CPU simulator, it was implemented by four of my students, Aamish Kapadia, Ray Bobrowski, Leo Hendriks, and Benedicto Catalan. They did much more than simply code the simulator; they suggested and implemented several of its features. The simulator has more features and is much more user-friendly because of their efforts.

My colleagues at the New Jersey Institute of Technology were extremely helpful while preparing this book. Sol Rosenstark, who has written several books, provided invaluable advice from the beginning that made writing this book much easier. Tony Lambiase, Ken Sohn, and Joe Strano were always available to discuss the topics in this book, teaching and writing styles, and matters completely unrelated to this book. Our off-campus lunches broke many instances of writer's block.

I developed most, but not all, of the figures in this book. Thanks to Intel Corporation for granting permission to reprint several of their figures, and to Michelle Evans for arranging reprint permissions.

The publishing team at Addison Wesley has been terrific right from the start of this project. My editor, Susan Hartman Sullivan, and assistant editor, Lisa Kalner, provided the guidance and encouragement I needed to complete this book. As a first-time textbook author, I'm sure that I needed more help than more seasoned authors; I could not have completed this book without them. (And thanks for the iguana, Lisa.) Thanks also to Pat Mahtani, Michael Hirsch, Mary Boucher, Jennifer Pelland, Regina Hagen, and Joyce Cosentino of Addison Wesley, and Marilyn Lloyd of Pre-Press Company.

The reviewers for this book were very helpful. Their critiques and suggestions were an important factor in improving the manuscript, both in correcting errors and clarifying the presentation. The reviewers for this book are listed below.

- Murray R. Berkowitz (Towson University)
- Jose G. Delgado-Frias (University of Virginia)
- Ata Elahi (Southern Connecticut State University)
- Hassan Farhat (University of Nebraska)
- John C. Kelly, Jr. (North Carolina A&T State University)
- Rabi Mahapatra (Texas A&M University)
- Robert McIlhenny (California State University, Northridge)
- Paliath Narendran (University at Albany—SUNY)
- Yusuf Ozturk (San Diego State University)
- Ralph L. Place (Ball State University)
- John B. Zuckerman (Texas A&M University)

Finally, I'd like to thank my family and friends for their support and encouragement throughout the writing of this book. Thanks to my wife, Mary, for her love, understanding, and undying support. And thanks to my daughter, Maria, whose arrival during the writing of this book was a most welcome distraction.

1

Digital Logic and Finite State Machines

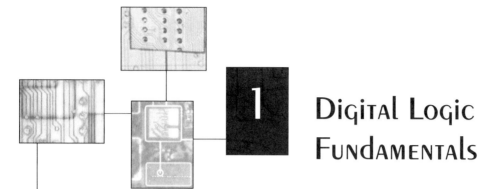

1 Digital Logic Fundamentals

Digital logic is the basis for computer design. Digital logic gates, latches, memories, and other components are used to design computer systems and their subsystems, including the central processing unit/microprocessor. A good understanding of the basics of digital logic is necessary in order to learn the fundamentals of computer design.

There are two classes of digital logic: combinatorial logic and sequential logic. The values output by a combinatorial logic circuit depend solely on its current inputs. When certain input values are set, a combinatorial circuit generates output values corresponding to those input values. When the inputs to a combinatorial circuit are changed, the output values change to correspond to the new input values. Previous values of the inputs and outputs do not matter; the current outputs depend solely on the current inputs.

In contrast, the outputs of a sequential circuit depend on both the current inputs and on previous inputs and outputs of the circuit. Sequential circuits have storage elements that record the state of the circuit. It is actually this state information that is combined with the circuit inputs to generate the outputs of the circuit. The state and inputs also combine to generate the new state of the circuit. The same inputs to a sequential circuit may generate different outputs and different new states, depending on the circuit's current state.

Neither combinatorial nor sequential logic is better than the other. In practice, both are used as appropriate in system design. In fact, most sequential circuits include some combinatorial logic (although the reverse is not true).

In this chapter we present a brief overview of digital logic. First, however, we introduce the basics of boolean algebra. This is the mathematical basis for digital system design; it is presented independent of its implementation in digital logic.

Combinatorial logic is covered next. First, we describe the basic combinatorial components, simple logic gates. These gates directly correspond to simple boolean functions. Then more complex digital components, which are commonly used in system design, are described. Finally, we examine a couple of combinatorial circuits.

Next, this chapter examines sequential digital logic. It first introduces latches and flip-flops, the basic building blocks of sequential circuits. Then more complex sequential components are introduced.

Finally, we examine programmable logic devices, or PLDs, and Field Programmable Gate Arrays, FPGAs. These devices are individual chips that contain a large number of combinatorial and sequential components. They can be programmed to implement combinatorial and/or sequential circuits. A large PLD or FPGA can be programmed to implement several circuits simultaneously, or one complex circuit—even something as complex as a very simple microprocessor.

1.1 Boolean Algebra

From a logic standpoint, a boolean value can be either true or false; "maybe" is not allowed. In digital logic, 1 is usually used to represent true and 0 to represent false; for that reason, we use 1 and 0 throughout this book. This section first introduces the basic boolean functions and then examines the fundamental methods used to combine, manipulate, and transform these functions.

1.1.1 Basic Functions

Any digital system must be able to process its digital data in order to perform its prescribed operations. The most fundamental of these capabilities are **boolean functions**. These functions produce a boolean output based on one or more boolean inputs.

One of the most common functions is the **AND** function. Its output is 1 if and only if every input has a value of 1. In expression form, the AND of boolean values x and y could be represented as $x \wedge y$, $x \cdot y$, or simply xy. More than two values can be "ANDed" together. For example, $xyz = 1$ only if $x = 1$, $y = 1$, and $z = 1$. In an extreme, perhaps absurd, example, consider a function in which one million values are ANDed together. The output is 1 only if all one million inputs are 1. If 999,999 inputs are 1 and one input is 0, the output is 0.

Table 1.1(a) is the truth table for the function $x \wedge y$. As with all truth tables, the left-most columns represent the inputs to the logic function, one column per input. Every possible combination of inputs is listed, one combination per row. The right-most column shows the output for each combination. In this case, the output is 1 only when both inputs are 1.

Table 1.1

Boolean functions for (a) AND, (b) OR, (c) XOR, and (d) NOT

x	y	$x \wedge y$	x	y	$x \vee y$	x	y	$x \oplus y$	x	x'
0	0	0	0	0	0	0	0	0	0	1
0	1	0	0	1	1	0	1	1	1	0
1	0	0	1	0	1	1	0	1		
1	1	1	1	1	1	1	1	0		
	(a)			(b)			(c)		(d)	

The **OR** function produces an output of 1 if any of its inputs is equal to 1. It does not matter if more than one input is equal to 1; the output is the same whether only one or all inputs are 1. The logical OR is represented as $x \vee y$ or $x + y$, and its truth table is shown in Table 1.1(b). As with the AND function, more than two values can be "ORed" together. For instance, $(u + v + w + x + y + z) = 1$ if at least one of the six values is 1.

The **exclusive OR**, or **XOR**, function is based on the OR function. Unlike the OR, however, in the exclusive OR the number of inputs that are 1 does matter. If two inputs are equal to 1, their XOR is 0, not 1. This function is represented as $x \oplus y$, and its truth table is shown in Table 1.1(c). More than two values can be XORed together. In general, the output is equal to 1 if an odd number of input values are 1, and 0 if an even number of inputs are 1.

Unlike these functions, the **NOT** function operates on a single boolean value. Its output is the complement of its input. An input of 1 produces an output of 0, and an input of 0 generates an output of 1. The NOT function is represented as x', $\bar{x}$, or $/x$. Its truth table is shown in Table 1.1(d).

The AND, OR, and XOR functions have complementary counterparts. The **NAND** (NOT AND) function outputs a 1 if not all of its inputs are 1. The **NOR** function produces a 1 if no inputs are equal to 1. The **XNOR** function, sometimes called the **equivalence** function, outputs a 1 if an even number of inputs are 1. Their truth tables, for two inputs, are shown in Table 1.2. Like their counterparts, they may have more than two inputs.

Table 1.2

Boolean functions for (a) NAND, (b) NOR, and (c) XNOR

x	y	NAND
0	0	1
0	1	1
1	0	1
1	1	0

(a)

x	y	NOR
0	0	1
0	1	0
1	0	0
1	1	0

(b)

x	y	XNOR
0	0	1
0	1	0
1	0	0
1	1	1

(c)

These are only a few of the possible functions of two boolean values. In fact, there are 16 valid functions, as shown in Table 1.3. However, those presented in this section directly correspond to digital logic components. We present these components in Section 1.2, Basic Combinatorial Logic.

Table 1.3

All possible binary boolean functions

x	y	0	$\wedge$	xy'	x	$x'y$	y	$\oplus$	$\vee$	NOR	XNOR	y'	$x + y'$	x'	$x' + y$	NAND	1
0	0	0	0	0	0	0	0	0	0	1	1	1	1	1	1	1	1
0	1	0	0	0	0	1	1	1	1	0	0	0	0	1	1	1	1
1	0	0	0	1	1	0	0	1	1	0	0	1	1	0	0	1	1
1	1	0	1	0	1	0	1	0	1	0	1	0	1	0	1	0	1

1.1.2 Manipulating Boolean Functions

The simple boolean functions presented so far are useful in and of themselves. However, digital systems often must implement functions that are more complex than these basic operations. These complex boolean functions can be created by combining the AND, OR, NOT, and other boolean operations introduced in this chapter. For example, consider a function that must be 1 if either $x = 1$ and $y = 0$, or $y = 1$ and $z = 1$. This can be expressed as $xy' + yz$. The first term, xy', is equal to 1 only if $x = 1$ and $y' = 1$, or $y = 0$. The latter term is 1 if $y = 1$ and $z = 1$. Its truth table is shown in Table 1.4.

Table 1.4

Truth table for the function $xy' + yz$

x	y	z	xy'	yz	$xy' + yz$
0	0	0	0	0	0
0	0	1	0	0	0
0	1	0	0	0	0
0	1	1	0	1	1
1	0	0	1	0	1
1	0	1	1	0	1
1	1	0	0	0	0
1	1	1	0	1	1

We can also combine values by "ANDing" together the results of OR operations. For example, the function that must be 1 if either $x = 1$ or $y = 0$, and either $y = 1$ or $z = 1$, could be expressed as $(x + y')(y + z)$. Its truth table is given in Table 1.5.

Table 1.5

Truth table for the function $(x + y')(y + z)$

x	y	z	$x + y'$	$y + z$	$(x + y')(y + z)$
0	0	0	1	0	0
0	0	1	1	1	1
0	1	0	0	1	0
0	1	1	0	1	0
1	0	0	1	0	0
1	0	1	1	1	1
1	1	0	1	1	1
1	1	1	1	1	1

Note that the distributive property applies to boolean equations. In this case, the function $(x + y')(y + z)$ could also be expressed as $x(y + z) + y'(y + z)$ or as $xy + xz + y'y + y'z$. (Since $y'y$ must be 0, this becomes $xy + xz + y'z$.) The reader may verify that each representation produces the same result for all values of x, y, and z.

An interesting property for generating equivalent functions is **DeMorgan's Law**. DeMorgan's Law allows a digital designer to convert an AND function to an equivalent OR function and vice versa. By using DeMorgan's Law to generate equivalent functions, a digital designer may be able to simplify complex functions. This, in turn, can simplify the designs of the digital circuit to realize the function. In equation form, DeMorgan's Law can be expressed by the following two equivalent equations.

$$(ab)' = a' + b'$$
$$(a + b)' = a'b'$$

To verify this, simply construct a truth table for each function. This is left as an exercise for the reader.

In addition to being used for minimizing logic, DeMorgan's Law is useful for generating the complement of a function. For example, the complement of the function $xy' + yz$ can be calculated by setting $a = xy'$ and $b = yz$, so in the second DeMorgan's Law equation, this becomes

$$(xy' + yz)' = (xy')'(yz)'$$

Further applying DeMorgan's Law to the individual terms yields

$$(xy')'(yz)' = (x' + y)(y' + z') = x'y' + x'z' + yy' + yz' = x'y' + x'z' + yz'$$

The truth table in Table 1.6 shows that all of these functions are equivalent. Comparing the functions with those of Table 1.4 shows that they are the desired complement.

Table 1.6

Equivalent functions for $(xy' + yz)'$

x	y	z	$(xy')'$	$(yz)'$	$(xy')'(yz)'$	$(x' + y)$	$(y' + z')$	$(x' + y)(y' + z')$	$x'y'$	$x'z'$	yz'	$x'y' + x'z' + yz'$
0	0	0	1	1	1	1	1	1	1	1	0	1
0	0	1	1	1	1	1	1	1	1	0	0	1
0	1	0	1	1	1	1	1	1	0	1	1	1
0	1	1	1	0	0	1	0	0	0	0	0	0
1	0	0	0	1	0	0	1	0	0	0	0	0
1	0	1	0	1	0	0	1	0	0	0	0	0
1	1	0	1	1	1	1	1	1	0	0	1	1
1	1	1	1	0	0	1	0	0	0	0	0	0

Each possible set of input values is called a **minterm**. For a function with three inputs, say x, y, and z, there are eight possible minterms: $x'y'z'$, $x'y'z$, $x'yz'$, $x'yz$, $xy'z'$, $xy'z$, xyz', and xyz. We can express a function as the logical OR of all minterms for which its value is true. Consider the function shown in Table 1.6. The three representations of the function are true when $x = 0$, $y = 0$, and $z = 0$ $(x'y'z')$; $x = 0$, $y = 0$, and $z = 1$ $(x'y'z)$; $x = 0$, $y = 1$, and $z = 0$ $(x'yz')$; and $x = 1$, $y = 1$, and $z = 0$ (xyz'). In addition to the three representations in the table, we could also represent this function as $x'y'z' + x'y'z + x'yz' + xyz'$.

Another useful device for minimizing logic is the **Karnaugh map**, or **K-map**. A Karnaugh map is set up as a grid and is used to represent the values of a function for different input values. The rows and columns of the K-map correspond to the possible values of the function's inputs. Each cell in the K-map represents a minterm; the entry in each cell of the Karnaugh map corresponds to the output for its minterm. To illustrate this, consider the three-input Karnaugh map shown in Figure 1.1(a). Since there are three inputs, x, y, and z, and each input can have the value 0 or 1, there are $2^3 = 8$ possible combinations of input values, and eight cells in the K-map. The upper-left cell of this map would contain the value of the function when input $x = 0$ (row) and $y = 0$ and $z = 0$ (column); this corresponds to minterm $x'y'z'$. Similarly, the lower-right cell contains the value of the function when $x = 1$, $y = 1$, and $z = 0$. Figure 1.1(b) shows a four-input Karnaugh map.

FIGURE 1.1
Three- and four-input Karnaugh maps

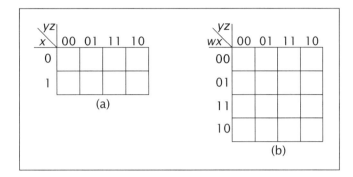

Notice in these Karnaugh maps that the input values do not follow the linear progression 00, 01, 10, 11. Rather, they are ordered 00, 01, 11, 10. This ordering is called the **Gray code** order. Before describing Karnaugh maps further, we need to first describe Gray code ordering and why it is used in Karnaugh maps.

A Gray code is a reflected code whose order depends on the number of bits in its value. Figure 1.2 illustrates the process of deriving a Gray code. The 1-bit Gray code is trivial; it is the sequence 0, 1, as shown in Figure 1.2(a).

FIGURE 1.2
Gray code sequence generation

0	0 ⇒	0 ⇒	00	000
1	1	1	01	001
		1	11	011
		0	10	010
(a)				110
		(b)		111
				101
				100
				(c)

This 1-bit Gray code sequence serves as the basis for the 2-bit Gray code. To derive the 2-bit sequence, we start by listing the 1-bit sequence. Then we list the 1-bit sequence again, but in reverse (reflected) order. We append a leading bit of 0 to the values in the original 1-bit sequence and a leading 1 to the values in the reflected sequence; this gives us the 2-bit Gray code. Figure 1.2(b) illustrates this process. This same process is used to derive the $(n + 1)$-bit Gray code sequence from the n-bit Gray code. Figure 1.2(c) shows the 3-bit Gray code sequence as derived from the 2-bit sequence.

All Gray code sequences are cycles. The next element in the sequence after the last is the first. For the 3-bit Gray code, its sequence is

$$000\rightarrow001\rightarrow011\rightarrow010\rightarrow110\rightarrow111\rightarrow101\rightarrow100\rightarrow000\rightarrow\ldots$$

An important property of Gray codes is that adjacent values differ by only one bit. In the 3-bit Gray code, for example, value 110 is adjacent to 010 (only the most significant bit is different) and 111 (only the least significant bit is different). This is why Gray codes are used in Karnaugh maps. As we will see shortly, this eases the task of simplifying functions using K-maps. Since these functions (presumably) will be implemented in hardware, simplifying the functions usually results in simpler hardware.

To illustrate how to minimize functions using Karnaugh maps, consider the expression shown in Table 1.6, $(xy' + yz)' = x'y' + x'z' + yz'$. Its Karnaugh map is shown in Figure 1.3(a). The minimization process starts by grouping together adjacent 1s; the values can be adjacent horizontally or vertically. For example, the two left-most 1s in the top row of this map are adjacent; the circle around the two values indicates that they are grouped together. In the same manner, the two values in the right-most column are grouped together. Although not so obvious, there is a third grouping in this map. Recall that Gray codes wrap around; the last element in a Gray code sequence is adjacent to the first. The two 1s in the upper corners of the K-map are adjacent and must be grouped together. Figure 1.3(b) shows the Karnaugh map with these groupings. Note that these groupings are allowed to overlap.

FIGURE 1.3

Karnaugh map for the function $(xy' + yz)'$ without and with groupings

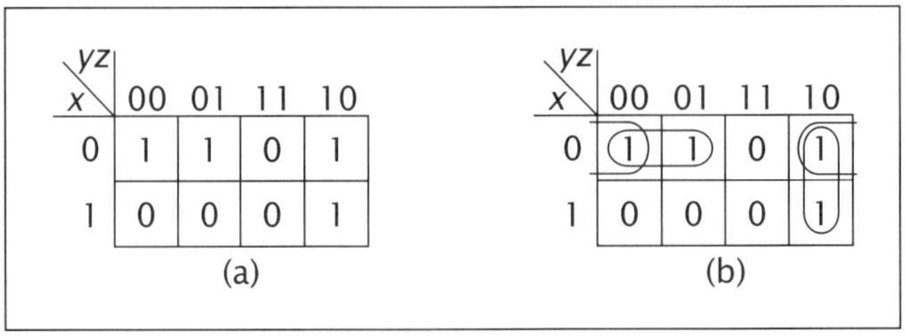

(a)   (b)

Sometimes a Karnaugh map will have a 1 that is not adjacent to any other 1, and thus cannot be grouped with any other terms. When this happens, there isn't anything you can do about it. Simply treat this term as its own group of one.

Why should we bother grouping together 1s in the Karnaugh map? Consider the first group we formed. The left-most element of this group represents the input values $x = 0$, $y = 0$, and $z = 0$, or $x'y'z'$. The other element has $x = 0$, $y = 0$, and $z = 1$, or $x'y'z$. Combining these two terms yields the following.

$$x'y'z' + x'y'z = x'y'(z + z') = x'y'(1) = x'y'$$

Together, these two terms can be expressed as one simpler term. This is why 1s are grouped together; the groups correspond to simpler expressions, which ultimately simplifies the design of the hardware to realize the function. The other two groups correspond to the terms $x'y'z + x'yz' = x'z'$ and $x'yz' + xyz' = yz'$. Thus, the original expression can be represented as

$$(xy' + yz)' = x'y' + x'z' + yz'$$

Once all groups of size 2 are created, these groups are combined into groups of size 4, if possible. The groups of size 2 can be grouped together if they are entirely within the same row or column, are adjacent, and do not overlap. They can also be grouped together if they span the same columns or rows, and their elements are *all* adjacent to one another without overlapping. In turn, the groups of size 4 are combined into groups of size 8, and so on, until no more groups can be combined. The final groups, regardless of size, are called **prime implicants**. In this example, the groups of size 2 cannot be combined.

To derive a minimal expression, we must select the fewest groups that cover all active minterms (cells with a value of 1) in the Karnaugh map. We start by checking for cells that are covered by only one group. The groups covering these cells are **essential prime implicants**, and must be included in the final expression. In this example, we have two essential prime implicants. One covers the left two cells on the top row of the Karnaugh map; it corresponds to minterms $x'y'z'$ and $x'y'z$, or the function $x'y'$. The other covers the last column of the Karnaugh map. Its minterms are $x'yz'$ and xyz'; this group corresponds to the function yz'.

Next we would look for groups covering other 1s in the K-map. Although there are systematic methods for selecting the groups to cover these additional cells, this can usually be done by inspection for such small Karnaugh maps. In this example, all 1s were covered by the essential prime implicants, so no other terms are needed. The function has a minimal expression of $x'y' + yz'$.

Now consider a more complex example, the Karnaugh map shown in Figure 1.4(a). It contains several groups of size 2, circled in this figure. Notice that the four groups corresponding to $w'x'z'$, $wx'z'$, $x'y'z'$, and $x'yz'$ wrap around the edges of the K-map. Also note that the cell for $w'xyz$ cannot be grouped with any other value. Sometimes this happens, and nothing can be done to minimize the term. This term is its own prime implicant.

Karnaugh map for a more complex function

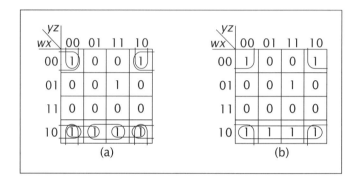

(a)   (b)

Next, the groups of size 2 are combined in the same manner to produce groups of size 4. In this example, two such groups exist. The group representing wx' is the combination of $wx'y'$ and $wx'y$, and also of $wx'z'$ and $wx'z$. The group encompassing the four corners of the map, $x'z'$, is also the combination of two groups, $w'x'z'$ and $wx'z'$, and also $x'y'z'$ and $x'yz'$. If any groups of size 2 could not be included in a larger group, they would be kept as components of the final function, just as $w'xyz$ was kept in the previous step.

This process would continue with groups of size 4 being combined into groups of size 8, and so on until no larger groups could be created. In this example, no groups larger than size 4 exist. The prime implicants for this function are wx', $x'z'$, and $w'xyz$. As it turns out, each is also an essential prime implicant for this function. The final function can be expressed as $wx' + x'z' + w'xyz$. Note that wx' and $x'z'$ overlap. Unlike the previous example, though, neither is fully contained in other groups. Overlap is allowable as long as each term of the final function contains at least one value not represented in the other terms.

Sometimes a designer doesn't care what value is output for given input values. This happens when some patterns of input values will never occur. This is called a **don't care condition** and is represented as X in the Karnaugh map. When forming groups to minimize a function, we can treat the don't care values as either 0 or 1, whichever makes it easier to group the minterms. For example, consider the Karnaugh map in Figure 1.5. This is the map for segment a of a 7-segment LED display. The inputs $wxyz$ represent a decimal digit for values 0000 to 1001, 0 to 9. The remaining input patterns, 1010 to 1111, are not used since they do not correspond to decimal digits. They are treated as don't cares in the K-map. Using the don't cares as shown in Figure 1.5 generates the minimal function $w + xy' + x'y + yz'$. (The function $w + xy' + x'y + xz'$ is another valid minimal function for this example. Sometimes a K-map can produce more than one minimal function, all of which are valid.)

Karnaugh map for one segment of a 7-segment LED driver

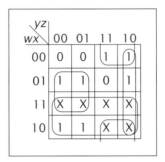

1.2   Basic Combinatorial Logic

Logic gates are digital components that implement the logic functions described in the previous section. The functions AND, OR, XOR, NOT, NAND, NOR, and XNOR are represented in digital schematics by the symbols shown in Figure 1.6. In this figure, every gate except the NOT gate has two inputs and generates an output that is the desired function. It is possible for each of these types of gates (except the NOT gate) to have more than two inputs.

Logic symbols for the (a) AND, (b) OR, (c) XOR, (d) NOT, (e) NAND, (f) NOR, and (g) XNOR gates

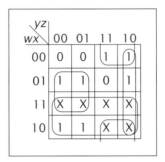

Note that the NOT, NAND, NOR, and XNOR gates have small circles on their outputs. This indicates that the output of the gate is complemented, that is, inverted. Comparing the AND and NAND gates, we see that, except for the inverted output, they appear the same. Also note that the output of the NAND gate is the complement of the AND gate. Logically, one can consider the NAND gate to be an AND gate that sends its output to a NOT gate. (In terms of chip fabrication, it's really the other way around; the AND gate is actually a NAND gate that sends its output to a NOT gate.)

These gates can be combined to realize more complex functions. Consider the function $wx' + x'z' + w'xyz$. Two different realizations of this function are shown in Figure 1.7. The first uses only NOT gates and two-input logic gates, while the latter uses gates with more than two inputs. Notice that the order of the inputs to a gate does not matter. For example, the inputs to the four-input AND gate of Figure 1.7(b) can be arranged in any of 24 (= 4!) possible orders, but the output will always be $w'xyz$.

FIGURE 1.7

Two realizations of the function $wx' + x'z' + w'xyz$

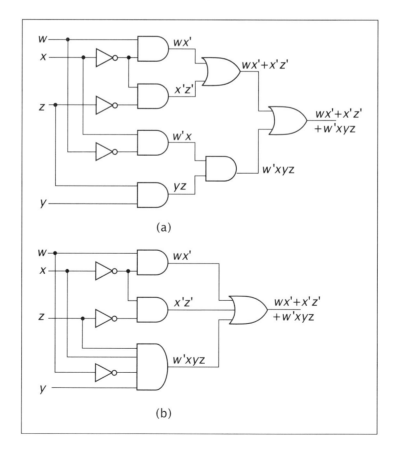

(a)

(b)

One class of digital components not yet covered is **buffers**. A buffer does not perform any operation on its input value; its output is the same as its input. Although they may not appear to have a logical purpose, buffers play an important role in computer design.

There are two primary types of buffers: regular buffers (or simply buffers) and **tri-state buffers**. Both are shown in Figure 1.8. The regular buffer always passes its input directly to its output, as shown in its truth table, Table 1.7(a). Its purpose is to boost the current of the input to a higher level. When implemented in digital logic, boolean values 0 and 1 have specific voltage and current values; buffers maintain these values to ensure that the system performs properly.

Logic symbols for (a) regular buffer, (b) tri-state buffer with active high enable, and (c) tri-state buffer with active low enable

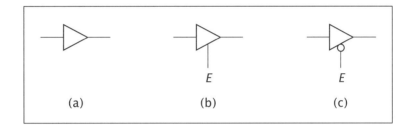

Truth tables for (a) regular buffer, (b) tri-state buffer with active high enable, and (c) tri-state buffer with active low enable

INPUT	OUTPUT	INPUT	E	OUTPUT	INPUT	E	OUTPUT
0	0	X	0	Z	0	0	0
1	1	0	1	0	1	0	1
		1	1	1	X	1	Z
(a)		(b)			(c)		

The tri-state buffer is more complex. As shown in Figure 1.8(b), it has a data input, just like the regular buffer, but also an **enable** input E. If $E = 1$, the buffer is enabled and the input is passed directly to the output. However, if $E = 0$, the buffer is disabled. Regardless of the input, denoted by a don't care X in Table 1.7(b), the output is a **high impedance** state, **Z**. The tri-state buffer can also have an inverted enable signal, as shown in Figure 1.8(c). As Table 1.7(c) shows, $E = 0$ enables the buffer and $E = 1$ disables it, again producing a high impedance output.

To understand high impedance, recall from Ohm's law that *current = voltage ÷ resistance*, or $I = V/R$. Impedance works like resistance, but accounts for inductance and capacitance as well as resistance. For a constant voltage, current decreases as impedance increases. The high impedance state reduces current to levels so low that it is almost as if the output of the buffer isn't connected to anything. This is the role of tri-state buffers; they can be disabled to essentially break connections. We examine their role in digital design in greater detail in Chapters 4 and 6.

1.3 More Complex Combinatorial Components

We can use the logic gates introduced in the previous section to construct any possible logic circuit; no additional components are needed. However, some logic functions are used frequently and have been designed as higher level components. They have been fabricated as individual integrated circuit chips (ICs) and as macrofunctions for custom IC designs. In this section we introduce some of the most frequently used components.

1.3.1 Multiplexers

A **multiplexer**, or **MUX**, is a selector. It chooses one of its data inputs and passes it through to its output. To illustrate its operation, consider the 4-to-1 multiplexer shown in Figure 1.9. Four binary data values are passed to the inputs of the multiplexer. Two select signals determine which of the four inputs is passed through to the output. Note that the four AND gates include the following pairs of inputs, in addition to the data input: $S_1'S_0'$; $S_1'S_0$; S_1S_0'; and S_1S_0. If $S_1 = 0$ and $S_0 = 0$, the inputs to the top AND gate are input 0, S_1' (= 1) and S_0' (= 1); the output is the value of input 0. The other three gates each input either S_1 or S_0 (or both). Since both are 0, these AND gates produce 0 results. The inputs to the OR gate are the value of input 0, and three 0s, so its output is the value of input 0. Setting S_1 and S_0 to 01, 10, or 11 produces outputs of the value of input 1, 2, and 3, respectively. Finally, the output passes to a tri-state buffer. If the buffer is enabled ($E = 1$), the value is passed as the output of the multiplexer. Otherwise, the output is the high impedance value Z. Note that some multiplexers have an active low enable signal, that is, $E = 0$ passes the output through and $E = 1$ generates a high-impedance output of Z. Figure 1.9(b) and (c) show the schematic representations of the 4-to-1 multiplexer with active high and active low enable signals, and their truth tables.

FIGURE 1.9

A 4-to-1 multiplexer: (a) its internal configuration, (b) its schematic representation with an active high enable signal, and (c) its schematic representation with an active low enable signal

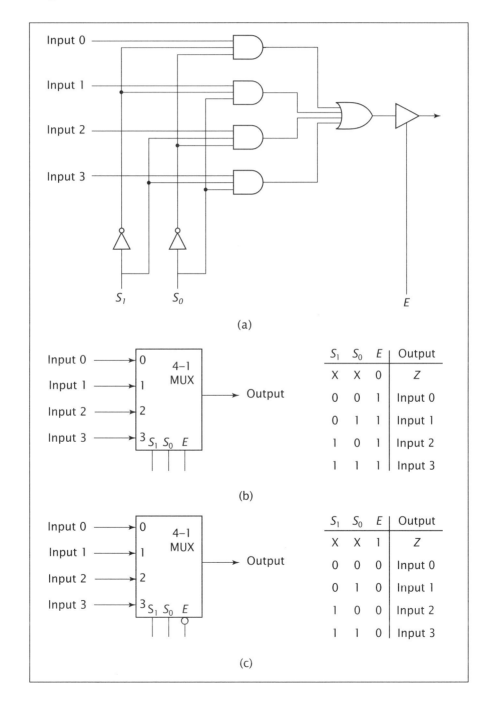

Multiplexers can be cascaded to select from a large number of inputs. Figure 1.10 shows a 4-to-1 multiplexer constructed from 2-to-1 multiplexers. The two left-most multiplexers use the same control signal. These two MUXs generate the two inputs to the final MUX, which chooses the value to output. This circuit performs exactly the same function as the 4-to-1 multiplexer of Figure 1.9.

FIGURE 1.10

A 4-to-1 multiplexer constructed using 2-to-1 multiplexers

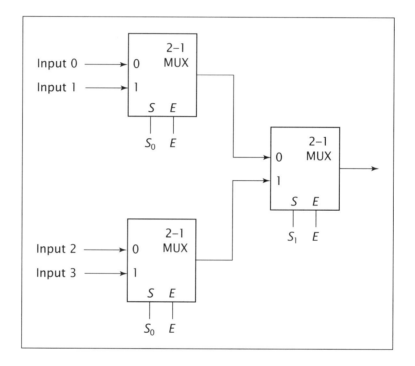

1.3.2 DECODERS

A **decoder**, as its name implies, accepts a value and decodes it. It has n inputs and 2^n outputs, numbered from 0 to $2^n - 1$. Each output represents one minterm of the inputs. The output corresponding to the value of the n inputs is activated. For example, a decoder with three inputs and eight outputs will activate output 6 when the input values are 110.

Figure 1.11 shows a 2-to-4 decoder. For inputs $S_1S_0 = 00, 01, 10$, and 11, outputs 0, 1, 2, and 3, respectively, are active. As with the multiplexer, an output enable can tri-state all outputs.

Figure 1.11

A 2-to-4 decoder: (a) its internal configuration, (b) its schematic representation with an active high enable signal, and (c) its schematic representation with an active low enable signal

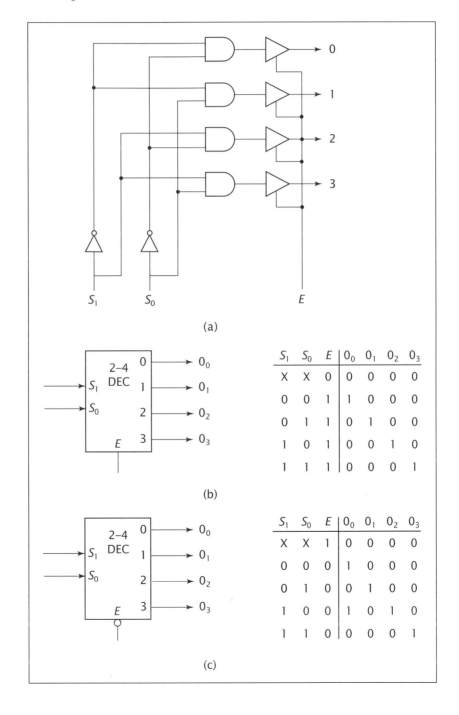

As shown in Figure 1.11, decoders can have active high or active low enables. In addition, other variants have active low outputs (the selected output has a value of 0 and all others are set to 1), or output all 0s when not enabled instead of state Z.

1.3.3 ENCODERS

The **encoder** is the exact opposite of the decoder. It receives 2^n inputs and outputs an n-bit value corresponding to the one input that has a value of 1. The 4-to-2 encoder and its schematic representations are shown in Figure 1.12. Notice that there is a third output, V. This value indicates whether any of the inputs are active. As shown in Figure 1.12(a), the encoder will output $S_1 S_0 = 00$ if either input 0 is active or no input is active. The V signal distinguishes between these two cases.

This encoder works if exactly zero or one inputs are active, but fails if more than one is high. For instance, if inputs 1 and 2 are high, the encoder sets $S_1 S_0 = 11$, which represents neither input. When more than one input can be active, a different type of encoder must be used. This is the role of the **priority encoder**.

A priority encoder works just like a regular encoder, with one exception. Whenever more than one input is active, the output is set to correspond to the highest active input. For example, if inputs 0, 1, and 3 are active, the output is set to $S_1 S_0 = 11$, corresponding to input 3. Two possible circuit diagrams for a 4-to-2 priority encoder (without an enable input) are shown in Figure 1.13 on page 22, along with their truth table. The first disables an input if a higher-numbered input is active. This guarantees that no more than one active signal is passed to the rest of the decoder, which can be the same as the regular encoder. The second passes all inputs to the decoding circuitry, but modifies that circuitry to create priority. For instance, input 1 only sets S_0 to 1 if input 2 is not active. We have optimized this circuit to eliminate unnecessary prioritization. In this circuit, $S_1 = 1$ if input 2 is set, even if input 3 is high, since both require S_1 to be 1.

1.3.4 COMPARATORS

A **comparator** compares two n-bit binary values to determine which is greater, or if they are equal. To illustrate its design, consider the simple 1-bit comparator in Figure 1.14 on page 23. Bits X_i and Y_i are compared, and exactly one of the three outputs, $X > Y$, $X = Y$ or $X < Y$, is set high. The only conditions under which $X > Y$ are $X_i = 1$ and $Y_i = 0$. Similarly, $X < Y$ only if $X_i = 0$ and $Y_i = 1$. $X = Y$ if $X_i = Y_i = 1$ or $X_i = Y_i = 0$; both are realized by the XNOR gate.

FIGURE 1.12

A 4-to-2 encoder: (a) its internal configuration, (b) its schematic representation with an active high enable signal, and (c) its schematic representation with an active low enable signal

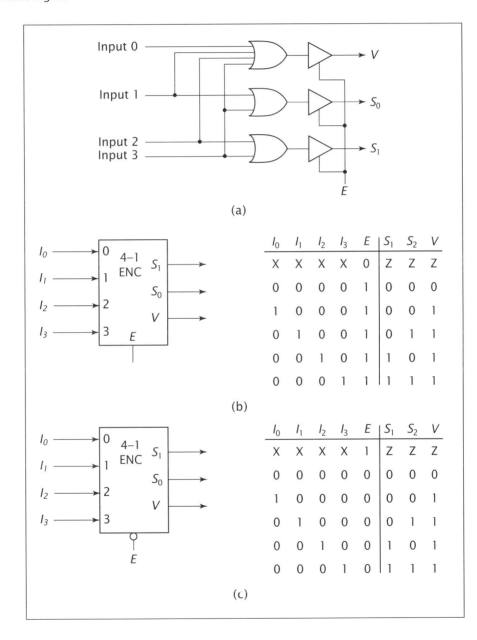

(a)

(b)

I_0	I_1	I_2	I_3	E	S_1	S_2	V
X	X	X	X	0	Z	Z	Z
0	0	0	0	1	0	0	0
1	0	0	0	1	0	0	1
0	1	0	0	1	0	1	1
0	0	1	0	1	1	0	1
0	0	0	1	1	1	1	1

(c)

I_0	I_1	I_2	I_3	E	S_1	S_2	V
X	X	X	X	1	Z	Z	Z
0	0	0	0	0	0	0	0
1	0	0	0	0	0	0	1
0	1	0	0	0	0	1	1
0	0	1	0	0	1	0	1
0	0	0	1	0	1	1	1

Figure 1.13

Two implementations of a 4-to-2 priority encoder (a) and (b) and their truth tables (c)

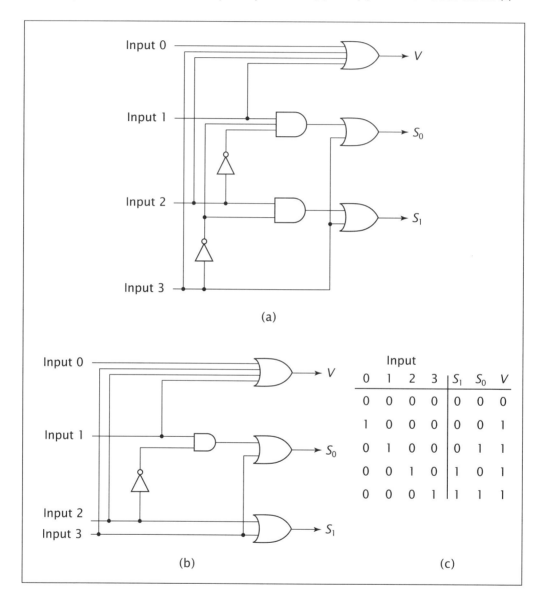

Input				S_1	S_0	V
0	1	2	3			
0	0	0	0	0	0	0
1	0	0	0	0	0	1
0	1	0	0	0	1	1
0	0	1	0	1	0	1
0	0	0	1	1	1	1

(b)   (c)

It is possible to extend this design for multibit numbers. Consider the process of comparing two *n*-bit numbers. We would start by comparing the most significant bits. If they are not equal, the number that has 1 as its bit value must be larger than the other, regardless of the values of the less significant bits; 1XXX is always greater than

Figure 1.14

A 1-bit comparator (a) and its truth table (b)

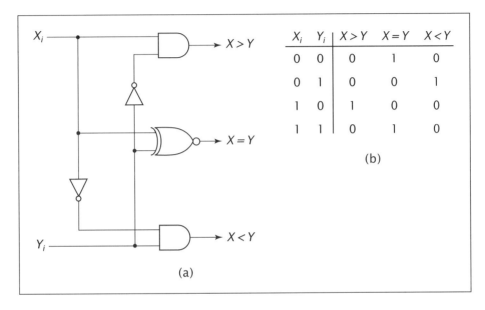

0XXX. If they are equal, we must check the next bit, and so on until one number is found to be greater than the other, or all bits are checked and the numbers are found to be equal.

To do this, the comparator of Figure 1.14 must be modified to include information from previous bit comparisons. If $X = Y_{in}$ is 1, the numbers are equal so far, and the same operations as in the original comparator are performed. However, if either $X > Y_{in}$ or $X < Y_{in}$ is active, that value is simply passed through. This corresponds to the case where we have checked the high-order bits and already know which value is larger. This modified comparator is shown in Figure 1.15 on page 24. Figure 1.16 shows how these 1-bit comparators are cascaded to form an n-bit comparator.

1.3.5   Adders and Subtracters

The circuits used to perform arithmetic operations are constructed using combinatorial logic. Of these circuits, **adders** are the most commonly used, not only to perform addition, but also to perform subtraction, multiplication, and division.

The most basic of the adders is the **half adder**. It inputs two 1-bit values, X and Y, and outputs their 2-bit sum as bits C and S. Bit C is the carry and bit S is the sum. One implementation of the half adder, along with its schematic symbol and its truth table, are shown in Figure 1.17 on page 25.

FIGURE 1.15

A 1-bit comparator with propagated inputs

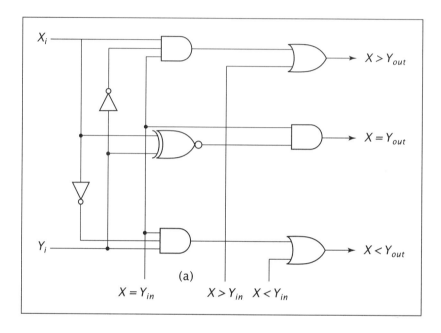

(a)

FIGURE 1.16

An *n*-bit comparator constructed using 1-bit comparators with propagated inputs

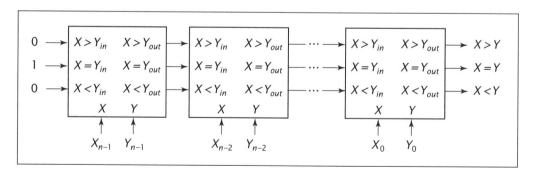

In the real world, circuits must add numbers that are more than one bit wide. Such a circuit cannot use half adders because there is no way to input carry information from previous bits. For this reason, the **full adder** was developed. It has three inputs: the two data inputs and a carry input. It has the same outputs as the half adder. One possible circuit design for the full adder, its schematic representation, and its truth table are shown in Figure 1.18. It implements the functions $C = X_i Y_i \vee X_i C_{in} \vee Y_i C_{in}$ and $S = X_i \oplus Y_i \oplus C_{in}$.

FIGURE 1.17

A half adder: (a) its internal configuration, (b) its schematic representation, and (c) its truth table

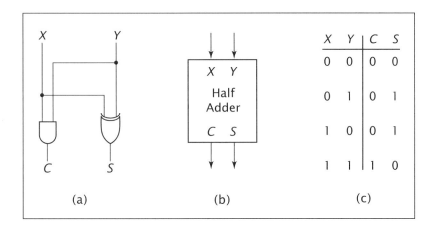

FIGURE 1.18

A full adder: (a) its internal configuration, (b) its schematic representation, and (c) its truth table

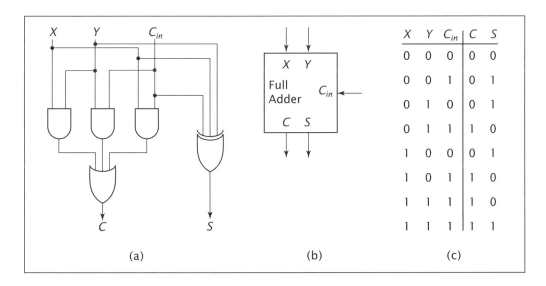

With the carry input, full adders can be cascaded to produce an n-bit adder by connecting output C of an adder to C_{in} of the next adder. This configuration is called a **ripple adder**. A 4-bit ripple adder is shown in Figure 1.19, along with its schematic symbol. Note that the least significant adder is a full adder with an externally generated carry input. In Chapter 8, we will see that most CPUs require this carry input for some operations. If it was not needed, this full adder either could have its carry input set to 0, or it could be replaced by a half adder.

FIGURE 1.19

A 4-bit adder constructed using full adders and its schematic representation

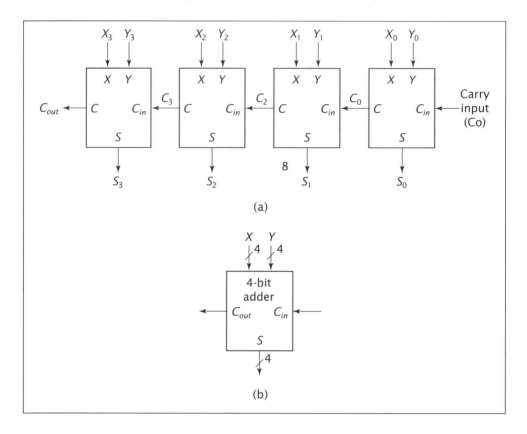

The reason this circuit is called a ripple adder is because the carry bits ripple through the adder. Consider the worst-case scenario, $X = 1111$, $Y = 0001$, and the carry input = 0. The right-most full adder outputs $C = 1$ and $S = 0$. This C is then input to the next adder, which also outputs $C = 1$ and $S = 0$. Only after this computation is complete is the C value output to the next adder, and so on. Each full adder has a small **propagation delay**; these delays add up as the carry bits are propagated, or ripple, from right to left.

One solution to the delay problem is the **carry lookahead adder**. This adder breaks the implementation of the carry into two parts. The **generate** part, **g**, is set to 1 when the inputs of the adder produce a carry, regardless of the value of the carry input. This only occurs when both inputs are 1; therefore, $g = X \wedge Y$. (See the truth table in Figure 1.17(c) to verify this.) The second part is the **propagate**, **p**. This is set to 1 when exactly one of the two inputs is 1; $p = X \oplus Y$. This value is then ANDed with the input carry. If $p = 1$, the result of this AND operation is the same as the value of the input carry, which is thus propagated unchanged. In general, this can be expressed by the equation

$$C_{i+1} = g_i + p_i C_i$$

For the 4-bit adder, these values are

$$C_1 = g_0 + p_0 C_0$$
$$C_2 = g_1 + p_1 C_1 = g_1 + p_1(g_0 + p_0 C_0)$$
$$C_3 = g_2 + p_2 C_2 = g_2 + p_2(g_1 + p_1(g_0 + p_0 C_0))$$
$$C_4 = g_3 + p_3 C_3 = g_3 + p_3(g_2 + p_2(g_1 + p_1(g_0 + p_0 C_0)))$$

Recalling that $g_i = X_i \wedge Y_i$ and $p_i = X_i \oplus Y_i$, C_1 and C_2 can be expressed as

$$C_1 = X_0 Y_0 + (X_0 \oplus Y_0)C_0$$
$$C_2 = X_1 Y_1 + (X_1 \oplus Y_1)(X_0 Y_0 + (X_0 \oplus Y_0)C_0)$$

The equations for C_3 and C_4, as well as the logic diagrams for the carry outputs, are left as exercises for the reader.

Although not used as frequently as adders, there are logic components that directly subtract two values. A **full subtracter** has three inputs: two data inputs and a borrow input. (Just as adding two numbers column by column generates carries, subtracting numbers generates borrows from one bit position to the next.) Figure 1.20 on page 28 shows the full subtracter and its truth table. It implements the functions $B_{i+1} = X_i'Y_i \vee X_i'C_{in} \vee Y_i C_{in}$ and $D = X_i \oplus Y_i \oplus C_{in}$.

It is possible to use **two's complement** addition to implement subtraction. The two's complement of a value is essentially the negative of that value. It is generated by complementing the value and adding 1; the two's complement of X is $X' + 1$. Two's complement addition implements the operation $X - Y$ as $X + (-Y)$. By doing this, a CPU may use a parallel adder for both addition and subtraction. Not including a separate subtracter saves hardware while still allowing the CPU to perform the same functions. We describe this in more detail in Chapter 8.

1.3.6 MEMORY

Memory is a group of circuits used to store data. Although not strictly combinatorial in design, memory can be used as combinatorial components in digital circuits; for that reason, we include memory in this section.

A memory component has some number of memory locations, each of which stores a binary value of some fixed length. The number of locations and the size of each location vary from memory chip to memory chip, but they are fixed within an individual chip. The size of

FIGURE 1.20

A full subtracter: (a) logic diagram and (b) truth table

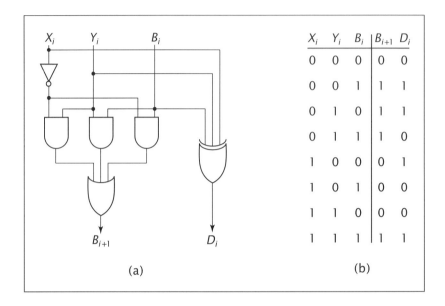

X_i	Y_i	B_i	B_{i+1}	D_i
0	0	0	0	0
0	0	1	1	1
0	1	0	1	1
0	1	1	1	0
1	0	0	0	1
1	0	1	0	0
1	1	0	0	0
1	1	1	1	1

(a)   (b)

the chip is denoted as the number of locations times the number of bits in each location. For example, a memory chip of size 512×8 has 512 memory locations, each of which has eight bits.

The **address** inputs of a memory chip choose one of its locations. A memory chip with 2^n locations requires n address inputs, usually labeled $A_{n-1}A_{n-2} \ldots A_0$. The 512×8 memory has address lines $A_8 A_7 \ldots A_0$.

The **data** pins on a memory chip are used to access the data. There is one pin per bit in each location. For chips with m bits per location, these pins are $D_{m-1}D_{m-2} \ldots D_0$. The 512×8 memory chip has eight data pins, $D_7 D_6 \ldots D_0$.

In addition to these pins, memory chips may have several other inputs, as shown in Figure 1.21. A chip enable signal, labeled CE, enables or disables the entire chip. Many digital systems include more than one memory chip, so it is often necessary to select the correct chip as well as the correct address. When disabled, the data pins output the high impedance Z. As with the control input of the tri-state buffer, CE may be active high or active low.

So far, the input and output signals presented are the same for all types of memory chips. Now we must describe the two primary classes of chips, **ROM** and **RAM**. ROM stands for **read only memory**. Data is programmed into the chip using a separate ROM programmer. Then the programmed chip is used as a component in the circuit. The circuit does not change the contents of the ROM. As discussed in Chapter 8, ROMs can be used as lookup tables to implement various

FIGURE 1.21

Memory chips: (a) ROM and (b) RAM

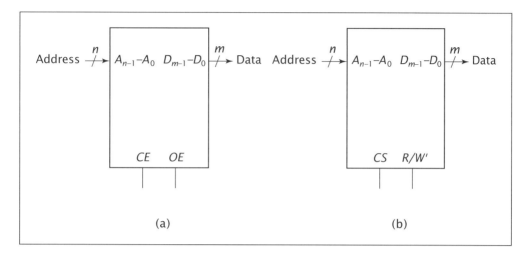

(a)   (b)

functions. Personal computers use ROMs to store the instructions that constitute their **basic input/output system**, or **BIOS**. When power is removed from a ROM chip, it still maintains its data; ROM is called **nonvolatile** because it has this property.

RAM stands for **random access memory**. This is often referred to as read/write memory. Unlike the ROM, it initially contains no data. The digital circuit in which it is used stores data at various locations in the RAM and retrieves data from these locations. For this reason, its data pins are bidirectional (data can flow in to or out of the chip via these pins) as opposed to those of the ROM, which are output only. Also unlike the ROM, a RAM chip loses its data once power is removed; it is a **volatile** memory.

This explains the difference between the final control signals on these chips. The ROM has an output enable signal, *OE*. Both *OE* and *CE* must be active for a ROM to output data; otherwise its outputs are tri-stated. The RAM has a directional select signal, *R/W'*. When $R/W' = 1$, the chip inputs data from the rest of the circuit; when $R/W' = 0$, it outputs data just like the ROM. RAM is most commonly used for temporary storage in digital circuits and for working memory in personal computers.

1.4 Combinatorial Circuit Designs

Many useful circuits can be designed using the gates and components presented in the previous sections. This section presents two of these designs. The first is a **binary coded decimal** (**BCD**) to 7-segment decoder, which is used in digital displays; it uses only combinatorial logic gates. The second is a simple **data sorter**. It sorts four 4-bit binary values in descending order using some of the more complex combinatorial components introduced in Section 1.3.

1.4.1 BCD TO 7-SEGMENT DECODER

The **BCD to 7-segment decoder** performs a common function: it converts the binary representation of a decimal digit, 0000 to 1001, to the signals needed to show the digit on a 7-segment LED display. Figure 1.22 shows the 7-segment LED with its segment labels, the pattern for each digit, and the truth table for the decoder.

FIGURE 1.22

A 7-segment LED display: (a) segment labels, (b) patterns, and (c) truth table

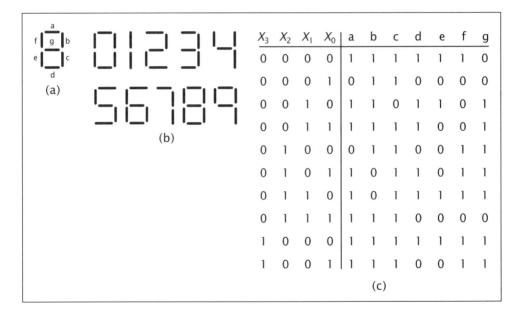

X_3	X_2	X_1	X_0	a	b	c	d	e	f	g
0	0	0	0	1	1	1	1	1	1	0
0	0	0	1	0	1	1	0	0	0	0
0	0	1	0	1	1	0	1	1	0	1
0	0	1	1	1	1	1	1	0	0	1
0	1	0	0	0	1	1	0	0	1	1
0	1	0	1	1	0	1	1	0	1	1
0	1	1	0	1	0	1	1	1	1	1
0	1	1	1	1	1	1	0	0	0	0
1	0	0	0	1	1	1	1	1	1	1
1	0	0	1	1	1	1	0	0	1	1

(c)

This circuit is actually seven distinct circuits, one for each segment, *a* through *g*. The design process for each is the same. For each segment, we create a Karnaugh map with X_3-X_0 as the inputs and the value of the segment as the cell value; we use don't cares for the remaining cells. Segment *a* was already calculated in Section 1.1, so we do not repeat it here. Segments *b* and *c* have the Karnaugh maps shown in Figure 1.23(a). Their final equations are $b = X_2' + X_1'X_0' + X_1X_0$, and $c = X_2 + X_1' + X_0$. Logic circuits to implement these equations are shown in Figure 1.23(b). The remaining segments are left as exercises for the reader.

For many applications, it is preferable to use **active low** LED displays—that is, a 0 lights the display and a 1 blanks the display. (See the Practical Perspective on page 32 for the reason this is done.) To do

FIGURE 1.23

Design for segments: (a) Karnaugh maps and (b) circuits to implement segments b and c

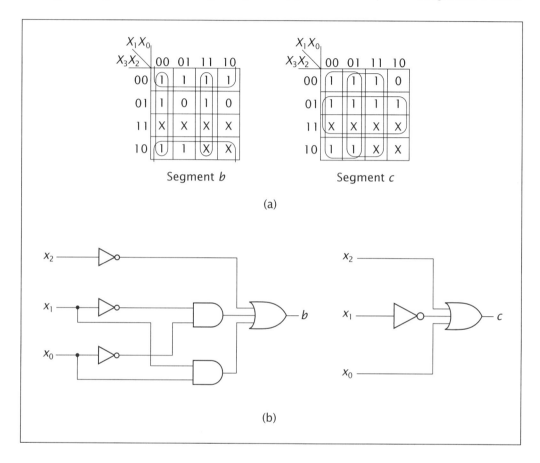

Segment b

Segment c

(a)

(b)

this, we would complement every entry in the truth table of Figure 1.22. Then we would follow the same procedure as for active high outputs: A K-map would be constructed for each segment and its entries grouped, then a final circuit would be designed. An alternative is to simply invert the outputs derived for the active high case, but the circuitry might be more complex than necessary. This design is left as an exercise for the student.

1.4.2 DATA SORTER

A simple data sorter will input four 4-bit values and output them in descending order. It implements a procedure similar to a bubble sort in that it compares adjacent entries and swaps them if necessary.

The basic building block of this circuit is the compare-and-swap module shown in Figure 1.24(a). It receives two data inputs and compares them using the 4-bit comparator described in Section 1.3. The

PRACTICAL PERSPECTIVE: Why LEDs Are Usually Active Low

LEDs can be wired so they are lit by a logic 1 (active high) or by a logic 0 (active low). Both configurations are shown in Figure 1.A, both unlit and lit. The LED is lit if current is flowing through it. This only happens if there is a potential difference; that is, the voltage at the input of the LED is greater than the voltage at its output. A logic 1 typically corresponds to a voltage of about 5V for TTL digital logic; a logic 0 represents a voltage of 0V. (The LEDs in this figure always have an input voltage greater than or equal to their output voltage. If this was not the case—for example if the LEDs were reversed—they still would not be lit.)

Figure 1.A
LEDs: (a) active high and (b) active low

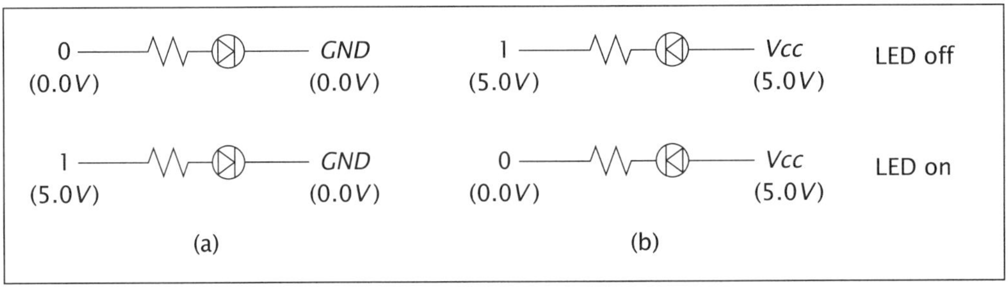

0 (0.0V)	⎓⎓⊗	GND (0.0V)	1 (5.0V)	⎓⎓⊗	Vcc (5.0V)	LED off
1 (5.0V)	⎓⎓⊗	GND (0.0V)	0 (0.0V)	⎓⎓⊗	Vcc (5.0V)	LED on
	(a)			(b)		

In Figure 1.A(a), the active high LED is lit when its logic input is 1. When its input is 0, both the input and output of the LED are at 0V; there is no potential difference and thus no current. When the input is 1, there is a 5V potential difference, which causes current to flow through the LED and light it up. The resistor limits the current, typically to 5 to 15mA.

Figure 1.A(b) shows the active low LED. Here, a logic 1 results in no potential difference (and thus no current), while logic 0 produces a potential difference, along with its associated current and a lit LED.

Notice that the current to light the active high LED is sourced by the logic component, which generates the logic 1. However, the active low LED receives its current from the circuit's power supply. The logic component sinks, rather than sources the current. This is one reason to use active low LEDs: It is preferable to source the current to light the LEDs directly from the power supply rather than from a logic component.

A second reason to use active low LEDs has to do with speed. The logic signal to light the LED often comes from the output of a gate, usually an AND or OR gate. For active low signals, the faster NAND or NOR gate is used instead. Thus, active low LED signals are often generated faster than their active high counterparts.

FIGURE 1.24

Design of (a) a two-input compare-and-swap module, and (b) four-input data sorter

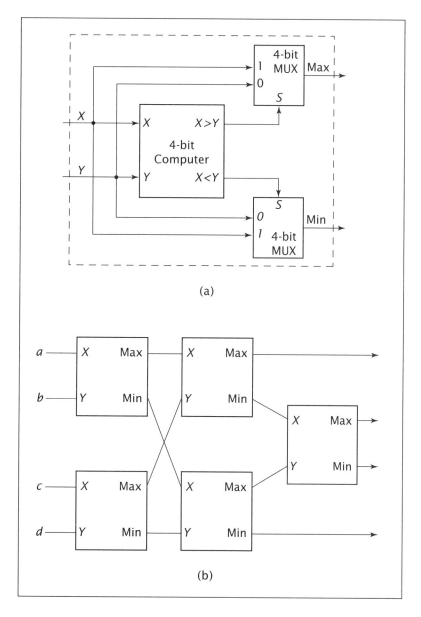

(a)

(b)

comparator output $X > Y$ is used to select one of the two inputs to the upper multiplexer. If $X > Y$, it selects the X input and passes it through. If not, then either $X < Y$ or $X = Y$; in either case, it passes input Y through. The result is that the output of this multiplexer is the greater of X and Y. Following similar logic, the $X < Y$ output of the comparator selects the lesser of X and Y and outputs it from the lower multiplexer.

Notice that the multiplexers each have 4-bit inputs and outputs. This is allowable and often used for multibit values. It is equivalent to having four 1-bit multiplexers in parallel. Since one entire value or the other should be passed through, the four 1-bit multiplexers would have the same control input.

Using this building block, the entire network can be constructed to sort the input values. One minimal network is shown in Figure 1.24(b).

1.5 Basic Sequential Components

Except for memory, the components presented so far in this chapter are combinatorial. Once their inputs are changed, their outputs may also change. When values must be stored for later use, sequential logic is needed. Unlike combinatorial logic, **sequential components** can retain their output values even when their inputs change.

The most fundamental sequential components are the **latch** and **flip-flop**. They store one bit of data and make it available to other components. There are various ways of defining these two components. In this text, the main difference between the two is that flip-flops are edge triggered and latches are level triggered; this is explained shortly. There are several types of latches and flip-flops.

Most flip-flops and latches have a **clock input**. The clock input is usually derived from an oscillator or other circuit that alternates its output between 0 and 1. It is used to synchronize the flow of data in a digital system. Figure 1.25 shows a typical clock sequence.

Figure 1.25
A typical clock sequence

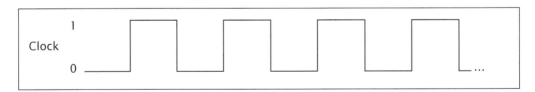

The simplest types of sequential components are the **D latch** and the **D flip-flop**. The flip-flop has one data input, D, and a clock input. When the clock input changes from 0 to 1, the data on the D input is loaded in to the flip-flop. The data is made available via output Q, and its complement via output Q'. Some variants also have a load signal (LD), which must be high as the clock changes from 0 to 1 in order for data to be loaded into the flip-flop. The D flip-flop is shown in Figure 1.26(a).

There are a couple of symbols in the truth tables in Figure 1.26 that must be explained. First, note the symbol $\uparrow$. This is a standard notation for the rising edge of the clock; that is, when the clock makes its transition from 0 to 1. Also note the value Q_0. It indicates that Q

Figure 1.26

The (a) positive edge triggered D flip-flop and (b) positive level triggered D latch and their truth tables

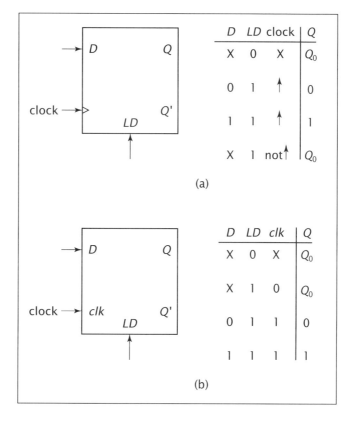

(a)

(b)

retains its previous value, regardless of whether that value was 0 or 1. As in the Karnaugh map, X is don't care.

This type of flip-flop is called **positive edge triggered** because its output changes only on the rising (positive) edge of the clock. A type of D latch is the **positive level triggered** latch. As shown in Figure 1.26(b), it loads data as long as both its clock and load signals are 1. If both are 1, the value of the D input is passed to the Q output. If D changes while the load and clock signals are 1, Q also changes. Once either the load or clock signal goes to 0, the Q value is latched and held.

Some variants of this flip-flop and latch have asynchronous set and clear capabilities. They can be set to 1 or cleared to 0 regardless of the other inputs to the latch, including the clock and load inputs. Figure 1.27 shows a positive level triggered D latch with set and clear, along with its truth table.

The **SR latch**, sometimes called the **RS latch**, has two data inputs. The S input sets the latch to one, and the R input resets it to zero. When both are zero, the output of the latch remains unchanged. Unlike the D

FIGURE 1.27

A positive level triggered D latch with set and clear, and its truth table

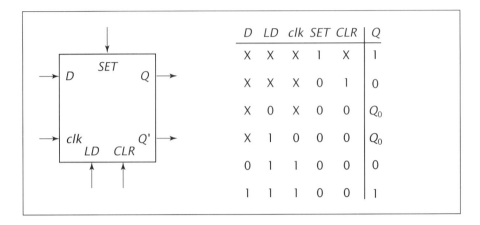

D	LD	clk	SET	CLR	Q
X	X	X	1	X	1
X	X	X	0	1	0
X	0	X	0	0	Q_0
X	1	0	0	0	Q_0
0	1	1	0	0	0
1	1	1	0	0	1

FIGURE 1.28

An SR latch and its truth table

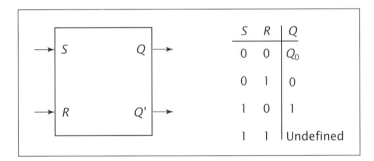

S	R	Q
0	0	Q_0
0	1	0
1	0	1
1	1	Undefined

latch, the SR latch does not have a clock input; its *S* and *R* inputs are always active. The SR latch and its truth table are shown in Figure 1.28. Notice that the output of the latch is undefined when *SR* = 11. This represents the case when the latch is being set to 1 and reset to 0 simultaneously. The circuit designer must ensure that the *S* and *R* inputs are never set to 1 at the same time or the circuit may exhibit unpredictable behavior.

The **JK flip-flop** resolves the problem of undefined outputs associated with the SR latch. As with the SR latch, *J* = 1 sets the output to 1 and *K* = 1 resets the output to 0. However, *JK* = 11 inverts the current value. Since all states are defined, this flip-flop is often used instead of the SR latch. The JK flip-flop and its truth table are shown in Figure 1.29.

One other type of flip-flop is the **T**, or **toggle**, **flip-flop**. The *T* input does not specify a value for this flip-flop's output, only whether or not it should be changed. On the rising edge of the clock, if *T* = 0, the

FIGURE 1.29

A JK flip-flop and its truth table

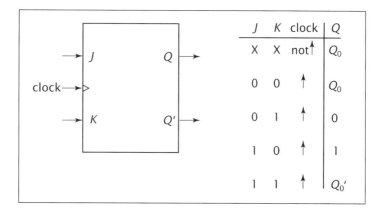

J	K	clock	Q
X	X	not↑	Q_0
0	0	↑	Q_0
0	1	↑	0
1	0	↑	1
1	1	↑	Q_0'

FIGURE 1.30

A T flip-flop and its truth table

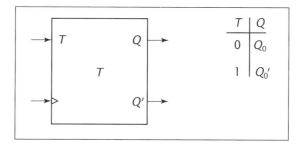

T	Q
0	Q_0
1	Q_0'

output of the flip-flop is unchanged. However, if $T = 1$, the output is inverted. The T flip-flop and its truth table are shown in Figure 1.30.

All of the flip-flops and latches shown so far are positive edge triggered or positive level triggered. They also have active high load, set, and clear inputs. It is possible for these components to have negative edge triggered, negative level triggered, and active low control signals. As with the enable signal of the tri-state buffer, the signal inversion is denoted by a small circle at the base of the signal input. This does not apply to the D, S, R, J, K, and T inputs. These data inputs cannot be active low.

Flip-flops and latches may be combined in parallel to store data with more than one bit. To illustrate this, consider the 4-bit D flip-flop shown in Figure 1.31. The control signals for all four flip-flops are tied together. This ensures that all four bits are loaded, set, or cleared together, so that the flip-flops act as one unified data register. There are specific ICs and VLSI macrocells to implement registers of four, eight, or more bits. Unlike the 1-bit flip-flops, however, they usually output only the stored value, not its complement.

FIGURE 1.31

A 4-bit D flip-flop: (a) internal configuration, and (b) its schematic representation

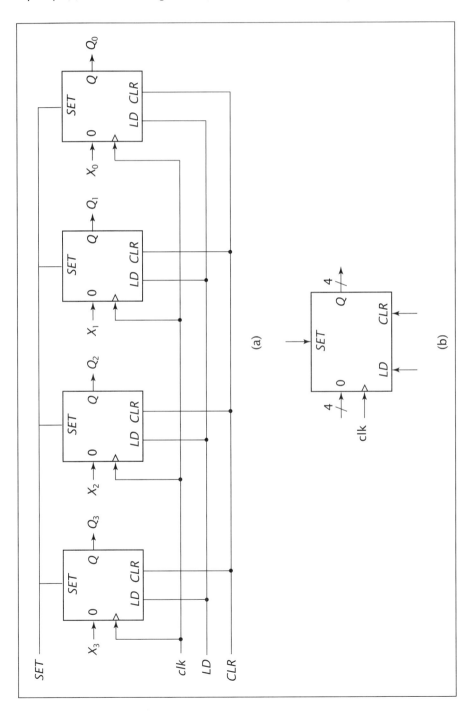

1.6 MORE COMPLEX SEQUENTIAL COMPONENTS

As was the case with combinatorial logic, some frequently used sequential functions have been fabricated as higher-level components and VLSI macrofunctions. This section examines two classes of these components: counters and shift registers.

1.6.1 COUNTERS

A **counter** does exactly what its name implies—it counts. It stores a binary value and, when signaled to do so, arithmetically increments or decrements its value. (Some counters do only one or the other, while other counters can do both.) Like other registers, counters can be loaded with an externally supplied value. Some counters can also be cleared.

Figure 1.32 shows one implementation of a 4-bit up counter, along with its truth table. It uses D flip-flops to store the 4-bit value. The *CLR* control signal clears the counter. Setting *INC* = 1 increments the counter on the leading edge of the clock. Signal C_{out} is set to 1 as the count increments from 1111 to 0000.

To see how this counter works, assume that it contains the value 1111. The increment signal is then set to 1. On the rising edge of the clock, the AND gate that drives the clock of the right-most flip-flop goes from 0 to 1, causing it to load its data. This data is the flip-flop's inverted value—0 in this case—so X_0 goes from 1 to 0. This also causes Q' to change from 0 to 1. Since this output serves as the clock for the second flip-flop, that flip-flop loads its data, which is also 0. This causes the third flip-flop to load a value of 0, which in turn causes the left-most flip-flop to load a value of 0. Since X_3 was 1 before this flip-flop was clocked, C_{out} is briefly set to 1.

This is a **ripple counter**. Just as carry bits could ripple through the 4-bit adder of Figure 1.18, the clock signals ripple through this counter. This produces propagation delays, just as with the ripple adder. It is possible to use a lookahead scheme so that all four flip-flops are clocked virtually simultaneously, thus eliminating the ripple effect. This design is left as an exercise for the student.

There are several variants of this counter. One is the down counter. It decrements its value instead of incrementing it and generates a borrow rather than a carry out. Otherwise it works exactly the same as the up counter. Another variant allows the counter to count up or down; a direction signal determines which the counter will do. Finally, any of these counters may have the ability to load external data as well as count. This is referred to as **parallel load capability**. Figure 1.33 shows the schematic symbol and truth table for a 4-bit up/down counter with parallel load.

Figure 1.32
A 4-bit counter and its truth table

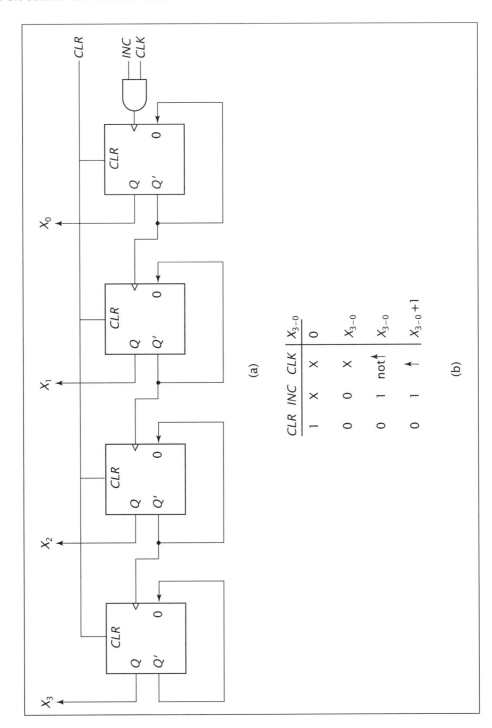

FIGURE 1.33
A 4-bit up/down counter with parallel load and its truth table

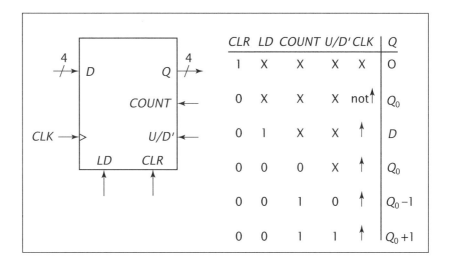

CLR	LD	COUNT	U/D'	CLK	Q
1	X	X	X	X	O
0	X	X	X	not↑	Q_0
0	1	X	X	↑	D
0	0	0	X	↑	Q_0
0	0	1	0	↑	$Q_0 - 1$
0	0	1	1	↑	$Q_0 + 1$

1.6.2   Shift Registers

A **shift register** can shift its data one bit position to the right or left. It is particularly useful for certain hardware multipliers and dividers, which use a shift-add or shift-subtract methodology. (See Chapter 8 for a description of these algorithms and their hardware implementations.)

A 4-bit left-shift register is shown in Figure 1.34. When the shift left (*SHL*) signal is high, data is shifted one position to the left on the rising edge of the clock. An externally supplied bit value is shifted in to the right-most bit. The left-most bit is overwritten and lost.

This register has several variants. Instead of shifting left, it may shift right, or it may shift in either direction under external control (similar to the *U/D'* signal of the up/down counter). Each register may also be able to load data in parallel and/or clear its data.

The linear shift is one of only three types of shifts used in arithmetic operations. The circular shift works the same as the linear shift, except the bit that would be lost in the linear shift is instead circulated and shifted back into the register. The arithmetic shift appends an extra bit to the left of the shift register. Unlike the other bits, its value is not changed by the shift operation. These operations are summarized in Table 1.8 on page 43.

Each of these operations can be realized by properly configuring a linear shift register and a 1-bit flip-flop for the arithmetic shifts. Their designs are left as exercises for the student.

FIGURE 1.34

A 4-bit left-shift register and its truth table

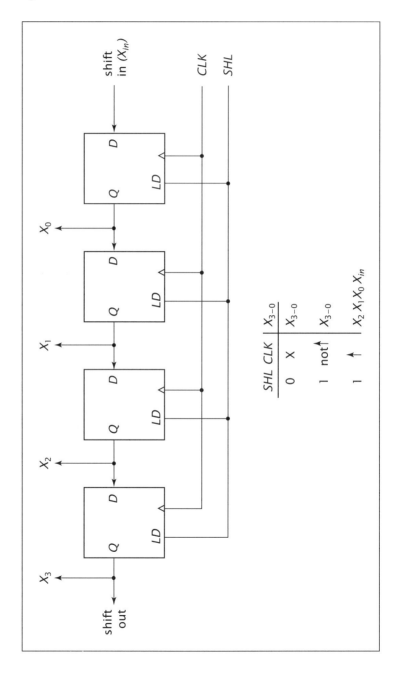

Table 1.8

Shift operations

Shift type	Mnemonic	X
Linear shift left	shl	$X_2 X_1 X_0 X_i$
Linear shift right	shr	$X_{in} X_3 X_2 X$
Circular shift left	cil	$X_2 X_1 X_0 X_3$
Circular shift right	cir	$X_0 X_3 X_2 X_1$
Arithmetic shift left	ashl	$X_3 X_1 X_0 X_i$
Arithmetic shift right	ashr	$X_3 X_3 X_2 X_1$

1.7   Real World Example: Programmable Logic Devices

Each of the components introduced in this chapter is available on a TTL IC chip. Circuits can be constructed using these chips and wiring them together. An alternative is to program the components into a single chip. This reduces wiring, space, and power requirements for the circuit. (See the following Historical Perspective for a description of how digital circuits have been implemented through the years.)

One such device, the **Programmable Logic Array**, or **PLA**, contains one or more AND-OR arrays, shown in Figure 1.35. In the array, the inputs and their complements are made available to several AND gates. An X indicates that the value is input to the AND gate. The

---

HISTORICAL PERSPECTIVE: Digital Circuit Implementation

Digital circuits have been implemented using a number of technologies. In the 1940s, vacuum tubes and relays were used to construct the earliest computers. After the invention of the transistor, these devices were used to construct digital circuits; the transistors were used as switches, which were on or off. As digital design became more common, manufacturers developed specific integrated circuit chips that contained logic components; the designer simply connected the inputs and outputs of the chips to construct digital circuits.

More recently, manufacturers have created chips that hold a large number of logic components. The user can program connections within the chip instead of wiring connections between chips. Using design software, a digital designer can create a design, simulate it to make sure that it will work, and program it into a single chip. At the extreme end of the design process, a designer can create a design and then fabricate a custom chip for that design.

outputs of the AND gate are then input to OR gates, which produce the chip's outputs. The user selects the inputs to the AND and OR gates, basically setting the Xs on the inputs to these gates, to realize the desired functions. The PLA in this figure realizes the functions $b = X_2' + X_1'X_0' + X_1X_0$ and $c = X_2 + X_1' + X_0$.

The **Programmable Array of Logic**, or **PAL**, is similar to the PLA. However, its OR block is not programmable; certain AND gates serve as inputs to specific OR gates. The AND inputs are programmable, as in the PLA. Figure 1.36 shows the internal configuration of a PAL set to realize the same function for b and c as in the previous example.

FIGURE 1.35

PLA programmed for the functions $b = X_2' + X_1'X_0' + X_1X_0$ and $c = X_2 + X_1' + X_0$

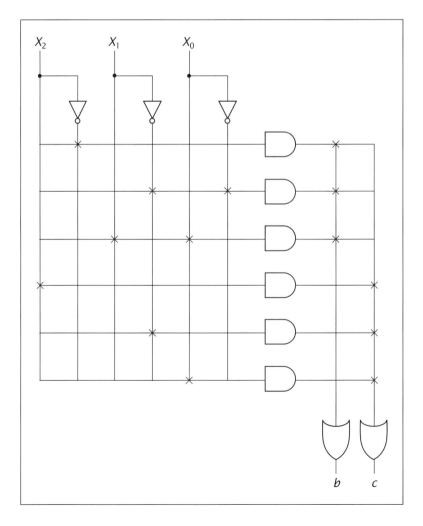

FIGURE 1.36

PAL programmed for the functions $b = X_2' + X_1'X_0' + X_1X_0$ and $c = X_2 + X_1' + X_0$

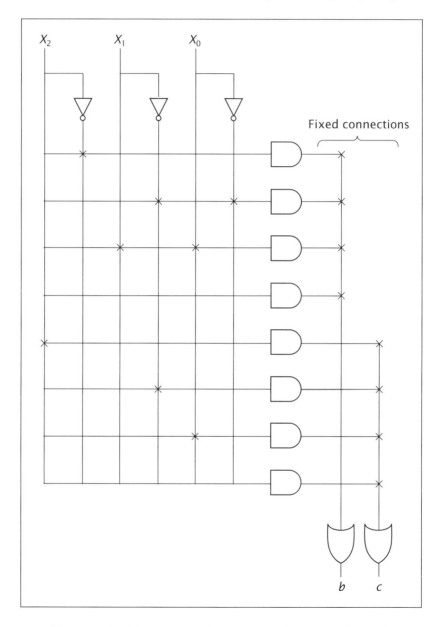

Real PLAs and PALs are much more complex than those shown in Figures 1.35 and 1.36, but they follow the same general organization. They usually have more AND and OR gates, and can support a greater number of inputs. The BCD to 7-segment decoder can easily be programmed into a single PLA or PAL.

PLAs and PALs are somewhat limited. Because they do not contain any latches nor flip-flops, they can only realize combinatorial logic designs. A more complex component, the **Programmable Logic Device**, or **PLD**, is needed to realize sequential circuits.

Programmable Logic Devices encompass PLAs and PALs, and much more. A PLD may contain several logic blocks. Each logic block in turn contains several macrocells, each of which may be equivalent to a PLA with an output flip-flop. In addition, an internal interconnection array can be configured to connect signals between logic blocks. Unlike PLAs and PALs, the input/output pins of the PLD's IC can usually be programmed for the desired function. They are fixed on PLAs and PALs. As one might guess, PLDs are usually used for more complex designs than PLAs or PALs.

Field Programmable Gate Arrays, **FPGAs**, are among the most complex PLDs available. They contain an array of cells, each of which can be programmed to realize a function. There are also programmable interconnects between cells, allowing them to connect to each other. FPGAs typically include flip-flops, allowing a designer to create a complex sequential circuit on a single chip. FPGAs often contain the equivalent of 10,000 or more simple logic gates on a single chip.

1.8 Summary

Digital logic is the base upon which computers are built. Computers use digital components to interact with memory and peripheral devices. Even the computer's microprocessor is just a very complex digital circuit.

Digital logic is based on boolean algebra, a system in which every variable has one of two values, usually represented as 0 and 1. We can create boolean functions to model any system we want to build using digital logic.

Digital logic can be divided into two categories: combinatorial logic and sequential logic. Combinatorial logic generates outputs that are based solely on its current input values. The basic building blocks of combinatorial logic are the AND, OR, XOR, and NOT gates. Using only these gates, and tools like Karnaugh maps, it is possible to construct any combinatorial logic circuit. To simplify the task of the digital designer, manufacturers have designed IC chips and VLSI macrofunctions to implement commonly used components, such as multiplexers, decoders, and adders.

Unlike combinatorial logic, the outputs of sequential logic depend on its current state as well as its input values. The same sequential circuit may generate different output values for the same inputs, depending on its current state. Latches and flip-flops are the fundamental building blocks of sequential logic, and they come in several varieties, including the *D*, *SR*, *JK*, and *T* types. As with combinatorial logic, designers have created components for commonly used functions, such as counters and shift registers.

About 25 years ago, digital designers constructed circuits using individual IC chips; each chip contained a few logic gates or some digital component. Now designers use programmable logic devices that can hold many components on a single chip. These PLDs allow designers to reduce the circuit size, and thus cost, while providing the same or better functionality.

Problems

1 Verify that the functions $(x + y')(y + z)$ and $xy + xz + y'z$ are equivalent.

2 Show the truth tables for the following functions:

a) $wx + xz + y'$
b) $w + x + y + z$
c) $w'x'yz + w'xyz + w'x'yz' + w'xyz'$

3 Verify DeMorgan's Law, as presented in Section 1.1.2.

4 Using DeMorgan's Law, give equivalent functions for the following.

a) $(wxyz)'$
b) $(wx)' + (y + z')'$
c) $(wx)' + (wy)' + (wz)' + (xy)' + (xz)' + (yz)'$

5 For the following Karnaugh maps, show the maximum groupings and minimal logic equation.

$wx\backslash yz$	00	01	11	10
00	1	1	0	0
01	0	1	1	0
11	0	0	1	1
10	1	0	0	1

(a)

$wx\backslash yz$	00	01	11	10
00	1	1	0	1
01	1	1	1	0
11	1	1	1	0
10	1	0	0	1

(b)

6 For the following Karnaugh maps, show the maximum groupings (including don't cares if appropriate) and minimal logic equation.

$wx\backslash yz$	00	01	11	10
00	1	0	0	1
01	1	X	1	1
11	0	1	X	0
10	0	X	X	0

(a)

$wx\backslash yz$	00	01	11	10
00	X	1	1	X
01	0	X	X	0
11	0	0	X	0
10	X	X	X	X

(b)

7 For the following equations, construct the Karnaugh map, group terms, and generate equivalent minimal equations.

    a) $w'y'z + wxy' + w'xz + wxy$

    b) $w'x'y'z' + w'xy' + wy'z' + wxy'z + wyz'$

    c) $w'x'yz' + w'x'y'z + w'xy'z' + w'xyz + wx'y'z' + wx'yz + wxy'z + wxyz'$

8 Draw the circuit that implements each of the following equations.

    a) $w + xz + w'xy'$

    b) $(wx + xy + yz)'$

    c) $((w'x)' + (yz'))'$

9 For the following circuit, determine the equation it implements, minimize the equation using a Karnaugh map, and develop the circuit to realize the minimal equation.

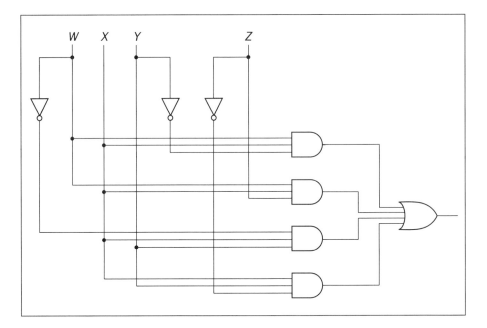

10 Design an 8-to-1 multiplexer using

    a) one 2-to-1 MUX and two 4-to-1 MUXs

    b) one 4-to-1 MUX and four 2-to-1 MUXs

11 Modify the decoder of Figure 1.11 so that its outputs are active low.

12 Modify the decoder of Figure 1.11 so that its outputs are all low, instead of state Z, when not enabled.

13 Design an 8-to-1 encoder using two 4-to-1 encoders and any necessary additional logic gates.

14 Design an 8-to-1 priority encoder using two 4-to-1 priority encoders and any necessary additional logic components.

15 Design a 2-bit comparator that compares two 2-bit values in whole, rather than one bit at a time. The circuit has inputs X_1X_0 and Y_1Y_0, and outputs $X > Y$, $X = Y$, and $X < Y$.

16 For the 4-bit carry lookahead adder, express C_3 and C_4 solely in terms of X, Y, and the input carry C_0.

17 Show the logic circuits to realize C_1 and C_2 of the 4-bit carry lookahead adder.

18 Show the Karnaugh maps, logic equations, and logic circuits to implement segments d, e, f, and g of the BCD to 7-segment decoder.

19 Design the BCD to 7-segment decoder for active low outputs. Do not simply invert the outputs of the active high decoder.

20 Prove that at least five sorters are needed to sort four input values.

21 Construct a T flip-flop using
   a) a D flip-flop
   b) a JK flip-flop

22 Redesign the counter of Figure 1.32 to incorporate a lookahead mechanism to eliminate the ripple effect.

23 Modify the counter of Figure 1.32 so that it functions as a down counter.

24 Design a 3-bit Gray code up counter with lookahead using JK flip-flops. The counter should traverse the sequence 000→001→011→010 →110→111→101→100→000→. . .

25 Design the following circular shift registers:
   a) a left circular shift register using a left-shift register
   b) a right circular shift register using a right-shift register

26 Design the following arithmetic shift registers:

    a) an arithmetic left-shift register using a left-shift register and a 1-bit D flip-flop

    b) an arithmetic right-shift register using a right-shift register and a 1-bit D flip-flop

27 Some arithmetic algorithms require a decimal shift left, dshl (see Chapter 8). This operation shifts a register's value four bits to the left; 0000 is shifted into the four right-most bits. Design a 16-bit register that can perform the dshl function.

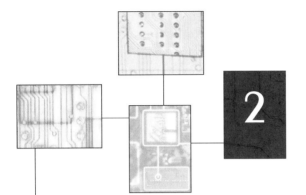

2 INTRODUCTION TO FINITE STATE MACHINES

The combinatorial circuits described in Chapter 1 can be designed in a relatively straightforward manner. We create functions and then minimize them using Karnaugh maps or some other method, such as a logic design computer program. We then implement the minimized function in hardware. It is not so easy, however, to design sequential circuits. A **finite state machine** is a tool to model the desired behavior of a sequential system. The designer first develops a finite state model of the system behavior and then designs a circuit to implement this model.

A finite state machine consists of several **states**. **Inputs** to the machine are combined with the current state of the machine to determine the new state, or **next state** of the machine. Depending on the type of machine, **outputs** are generated based on either the state of the machine, or the state of the machine and the machine inputs. This is illustrated in Figure 2.1(a).

FIGURE 2.1

State machine models: (a) generic and (b) alarm clock system

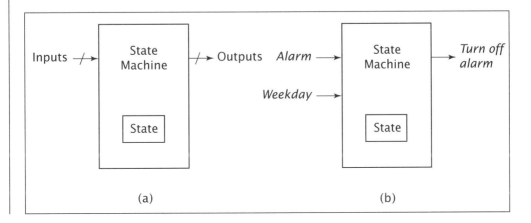

Consider a greatly simplified example. As a student, you wake up at 6 a.m. every weekday so you won't miss your first class. On weekends, however, you like to catch up on the sleep you lost while studying late, and do not need to wake up that early. You are asleep, your alarm clock goes off at 6 a.m., and you wake up. If this is a weekday, you turn off the alarm clock, get out of bed, and get ready for the day ahead. However, if it is a weekend, you set the alarm by mistake. You angrily turn off the alarm clock (throw it across the room, flush it down the toilet, or otherwise disable it), and go back to sleep.

We can model this sequence of events by the finite state machine illustrated in Figure 2.1(b). The state machine is actually you. You can be in one of three states: asleep, awake but still in bed, or awake and up. You receive two inputs: the alarm, which wakes you up, and whether or not the current day is a weekday, which determines how you react to the alarm. In this example, the only output is to turn off the alarm clock. (This assumes that you don't really destroy the clock; if you do, then this example would also need a "destroy alarm clock" output.)

This is the first step in going from a description of the behavior of a system to its implementation as a sequential circuit. Next, this behavior would be encoded in a state table and diagram, then designed and implemented as a sequential digital circuit.

Although finite state machines can be used for very simple digital circuits, such as one for this example, they are especially useful for designing more complex systems. In computer architecture, they are well suited to the task of designing microprocessors. (See the following Historical Perspective for more information.) Chapters 6 and 7 apply the finite state machine approach to the design of microprocessor control units.

This chapter is organized as follows. First, we introduce the basics of finite state machines, with state diagrams and state tables. We show how to develop these from the specification of system behavior. Next, the two main types of finite state machines, Mealy and Moore machines, are described. We look at their specifications as state tables and diagrams, as well as typical implementations in hardware. We examine the process of converting the state diagram to its sequential circuit implementation. Finally, some practical issues, including how to handle unused states and machine conversion, are discussed.

2.1 State Diagrams and State Tables

State diagrams and **state tables** are convenient mechanisms for specifying the behavior of sequential systems. The state table is similar to the truth tables presented in Chapter 1. Unlike a truth table, however, a state table does not consider the system clock in specifying its transitions. It is implicit that transitions occur only when allowed by

---

HISTORICAL PERSPECTIVE: Finite State Machines and Microprocessors

A microprocessor contains three main sections: a register section; an arithmetic/logic unit; and a control unit (see Chapter 4). The control unit inputs the instructions to be executed, as well as other information, such as the values in flag registers. (See Chapter 3.) The control unit outputs the control signals to load and modify the contents of registers, to perform arithmetic and logical functions, and to access memory and input/output devices. It outputs these signals in the proper sequence so that the microprocessor fetches, decodes, and executes each instruction correctly.

The control unit of a microprocessor is, in essence, a finite state machine. The instruction and flag values are the machine inputs, and the control signals are the machine outputs. Each state represents one step in the process of fetching or executing an instruction. By going through the states in the correct sequence, the control unit outputs the control signals in the order needed to process each instruction.

---

the clock, typically on the leading edge of the clock. In this chapter, all circuits change their states and outputs only on the leading edge of the clock.

To illustrate state tables, consider the alarm clock example at the beginning of this chapter. A state table is set up as shown in Table 2.1(a). The present state and all inputs occupy the left half of the table. The next state and outputs to be generated by each combination of the present state and inputs are listed on the right half of the table.

Table 2.1(b) shows the state table for this example. The state table has two inputs, *Alarm* and *Weekday*, and one output, *Turn off alarm*. When you are asleep and the alarm is on, you go from being asleep to being awake in bed. You also turn off the alarm. These are represented by the first row of Table 2.1(b). The other two rows encode your actions after turning off the alarm; either you get up or go back to sleep.

This table covers everything you would do but does not indicate what you would not do. For instance, if you are asleep at 4 a.m. and the alarm does not go off, you remain asleep. Table 2.1(c) shows the state table for this example, including these conditions of inaction. The first row of the table covers the situation in which you are asleep, the alarm does not go off, and you remain asleep. The last row indicates that, once you are awake and up, you stay awake and up. (This doesn't mean you never sleep again; this model only covers waking up with the alarm.) The other new row is the third row; it is included for completeness. You should never be awake in bed while the alarm is going off; you should shut it off as you wake up. However, the alarm could malfunction or, in a semiconscious state, you might miss the off switch. This extra line in the table accounts for these conditions. With

Table 2.1

State tables: (a) generic, (b) for the alarm clock problem, and (c) for the alarm clock problem with inaction states

Present state	Inputs	Next state	Outputs

(a)

Present state	Alarm	Weekday	Next state	Turn off alarm
Asleep	On	X	Awake in bed	Yes
Awake in bed	Off	Yes	Awake and up	No
Awake in bed	Off	No	Asleep	No

(b)

Present State	Alarm	Weekday	Next state	Turn off alarm
Asleep	Off	X	Asleep	No
Asleep	On	X	Awake in bed	Yes
Awake in bed	On	X	Awake in bed	Yes
Awake in bed	Off	Yes	Awake and up	No
Awake in bed	Off	No	Asleep	No
Awake and up	X	X	Awake and up	No

(c)

this line included, the table specifies actions for every possible set of input values for every state.

A state table may be represented graphically by a state diagram. To derive this state diagram, each state is represented by a circled **vertex**, and each row of the state table is shown as a directed **arc** from the present state vertex to the next state vertex. Figure 2.2 shows the state diagram for the alarm clock example twice, each with a different representation of the outputs. In the first state diagram, the outputs are associated with the states. In Figure 2.2(b), the outputs are associated with the arcs; an output of 1 signifies that "Turn off alarm" is Yes. By convention, inputs which are don't care and inactive outputs are not shown.

As another example, consider the state table for the JK flip-flop shown in Table 2.2(a). The flip-flop has two states, Y and Z, and two inputs, J and K. Each row of the table gives a present state, values of the J and K inputs, the next state to occur under these conditions, and the output value, Q. For example, when the flip-flop is in state Z, and the inputs are $J = 1$ and $K = 1$, the next state is state Y.

State transitions may be combined to present a more compact state table. The state table shown in Table 2.2(b) is an equivalent representation of the state table of Table 2.2(a). The first row, with Present State = Y, $J = 0$, $K = X$ (don't care) and Next State = Y, is a

FIGURE 2.2
State diagrams for the alarm clock example

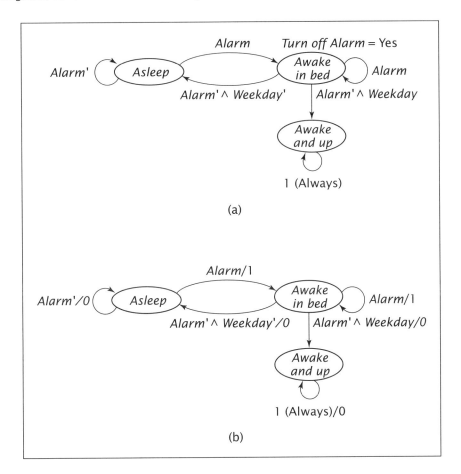

(a)

(b)

TABLE 2.2
State tables for the JK flip-flop

Present State	J	K	Next State	Q
Y	0	0	Y	0
Y	0	1	Y	0
Y	1	0	Z	1
Y	1	1	Z	1
Z	0	0	Z	1
Z	0	1	Y	0
Z	1	0	Z	1
Z	1	1	Y	0

(a)

Present State	J	K	Next State	Q
Y	0	X	Y	0
Y	1	X	Z	1
Z	X	0	Z	1
Z	X	1	Y	0

(b)

combination of the first two rows of the previous table. The other rows are derived in a similar manner. Regardless of which representation is used, a complete state table must include each possible combination of present states and input values, and no such combination may match more than one row of the table.

The state diagram for the state tables of Table 2.2 is shown in Figure 2.3. In Figure 2.3(a), the pertinent conditions of J and K are shown. The same finite state machine is shown in Figure 2.3(b) with an alternate representation of the inputs. Here the values of J and K are shown explicitly.

FIGURE 2.3

State diagrams for the JK flip-flop: (a) conditions in terms of J and K, and (b) conditions as values of J and K

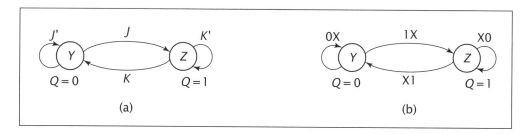

(a)   (b)

Just as the state table must include each possible input value exactly once, so must the state diagram. To verify that this is the case in this example, look at all arcs coming out of one vertex. Their conditions should be **mutually exclusive**, that is, no input values should meet the conditions of more than one arc. Together, the conditions on the arcs should cover all possible input values. It can be seen that this is the case for each state in the state diagram of Figure 2.3.

By convention, **self-arcs** are sometimes not shown. It is implicit that all conditions not covered by an arc cause the machine to remain in the same state. In Figure 2.3, the arcs that go from state Y back to itself, and from state Z back to itself, could be removed. (As will be seen in the next section, this can only be done for certain types of state diagrams.)

2.2 MEALY AND MOORE MACHINES

The whole purpose of a finite state machine, or just about any digital circuit, is to generate output data. This data can be the result of computations, or signals to control other circuitry. A system must generate outputs or it can serve no useful purpose.

A finite state machine can represent outputs in one of two ways. A **Moore machine**, named after Edward Moore, associates its outputs with the states. The outputs are represented either within the vertex corresponding to a state or adjacent to the vertex. In contrast, a **Mealy machine**, named after George Mealy, associates outputs with the transitions. In addition to the input values, each arc also shows the output values generated during the transition. The format of the label of each arc is INPUTS/OUTPUTS. In Figure 2.2, state diagram (a) is the Moore machine representation of the alarm clock system; the Mealy machine is state diagram (b).

Notice that the self-arcs must be shown for Mealy machines, but not for Moore machines. Since the Mealy machine shows output values on the arcs, it is necessary to show the self-arcs to provide the output values. The Moore machine does not need to show these arcs since its outputs are associated with the states, not with the arcs.

Both Mealy and Moore machines can be used to represent any sequential system, and each has its advantages. The Mealy machine can be more compact than the Moore machine, particularly when two arcs with different output values go to the same state. Figure 2.4 shows the state table and state diagrams for a JK flip-flop with a modified output value. In this example, the output is 1 if the state changes and 0 if the machine remains in the same state. An equivalent Moore machine would have to include additional states to represent this system. These additional states also increase the hardware needed to implement the system.

The Moore machine offers a simpler implementation when the output values depend only on the state and not on the transitions. A Moore machine requires less hardware to produce the output values

FIGURE 2.4

JK flip-flop with modified outputs: (a) state table and (b) state diagram

Present State	J	K	Next State	Q
Y	0	X	Y	0
Y	1	X	Z	1
Z	X	0	Z	0
Z	X	1	Y	1

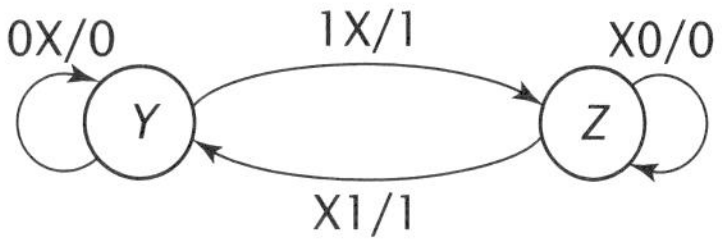

than does a Mealy machine, since its outputs depend only on its state; the outputs of a Mealy machine depend on both its state and its input values. The Moore machine is well suited for representing the control units of microprocessors and central processing units. This is examined more closely in Chapters 6 and 7.

2.3   Designing State Diagrams

To illustrate the process of developing state tables and state diagrams from system specifications, this section presents three examples of varying complexity: a counter, a string checker, and a toll booth controller.

2.3.1   Modulo 6 Counter

A modulo 6 counter is a 3-bit counter that counts through the sequence

$$000{\to}001{\to}010{\to}011{\to}100{\to}101{\to}000 \;...\; (0{\to}1{\to}2{\to}3{\to}4{\to}5{\to}0{\to}\;...)$$

Unlike a regular 3-bit counter, it does not use the values 110 (6) nor 111 (7). Its input U controls the counter. When $U = 1$, the counter increments its value on the rising edge of the clock. When $U = 0$, it retains its current value regardless of the value of the clock. The value of the count is represented as the 3-bit output $V_2 V_1 V_0$. There is an additional output, C, which is 1 when going from 5 to 0, and 0 otherwise. (To simplify this example, the C output remains at 1 until the counter goes from 0 to 1.)

The finite state machine for this counter must have six states, arbitrarily labeled S_0, S_1, S_2, S_3, S_4, and S_5. State S_i corresponds to counter output i; the states follow the sequence

$$S_0{\to}S_1{\to}S_2{\to}S_3{\to}S_4{\to}S_5{\to}S_0{\to}\;...$$

To derive the state table for this counter, look at each state individually; for each state, examine what happens for all possible values of the inputs. For example, in state S_0, input U can be either 0 or 1. If $U = 0$, the state machine remains in state S_0 and outputs $C = 1$ and $V_2 V_1 V_0 = 000$. However, if $U = 1$, the machine goes to state S_1 and outputs $C = 0$ and $V_2 V_1 V_0 = 001$. We derive the state table values for the other states in the same way. Table 2.3 shows the state table for this counter. As already described, each state goes to the next state in the sequence if $U = 1$ and remains in the same state if $U = 0$.

This state table can be represented as either a Mealy machine or a Moore machine without any additional states. Notice in this table that, whenever the next state is the same as the current state, the outputs are also the same as their present values. The state diagram for the Mealy machine for this state table is shown in Figure 2.5(a). The outputs are ordered C, V_2, V_1, V_0. Figure 2.5(b) shows the Moore machine state diagram for this system. Note that each arc in these state diagrams corresponds to one row of the state table.

State table for the modulo 6 counter

Present State	U	Next State	C	$V_2 V_1 V_0$
S_0	0	S_0	1	000
S_0	1	S_1	0	001
S_1	0	S_1	0	001
S_1	1	S_2	0	010
S_2	0	S_2	0	010
S_2	1	S_3	0	011
S_3	0	S_3	0	011
S_3	1	S_4	0	100
S_4	0	S_4	0	100
S_4	1	S_5	0	101
S_5	0	S_5	0	101
S_5	1	S_0	1	000

FIGURE 2.5

State diagrams for the modulo 6 counter: (a) Mealy and (b) Moore

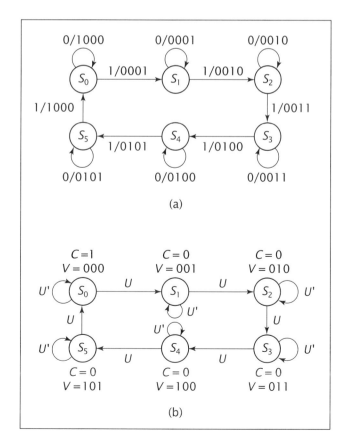

(a)

(b)

2.3.2 STRING CHECKER

A string checker inputs a string of bits, one bit per clock cycle. When the previous three bits form the pattern 110, it sets output $M = 1$; otherwise $M = 0$. The pattern is checked continuously throughout the entire bit stream. The system does not check the first three bits, then the next three, and so on. Rather, it checks bits 1, 2, and 3, then 2, 3, and 4, then 3, 4, and 5, and so on forever.

One way to design this system is to have the last three bits received represent the state of the system. This would result in eight states, S_0 to S_7. State S_i is active when the last three bits form the binary equivalent of i. For example, if the last three bits read in are 011, then S_3 is active. The last bit read in is the least significant bit. When it is read in, the other bits are shifted left in the binary representation of i; the most significant bit is shifted out and lost.

As shown in the state table of Table 2.4, each state goes to one of two possible next states, depending on whether input bit I is 0 or 1. For example, state S_2 corresponds to the condition in which the last three input bits are 010. When bit I is input, these bits are shifted left. The leftmost zero is lost and the new binary value is $10I$, which corresponds to state S_4 (100) if $I = 0$ or S_5 (101) if $I = 1$.

Table 2.4

State table for the string checker

Present State	I	Next State	M
S_0	0	S_0	0
S_0	1	S_1	0
S_1	0	S_2	0
S_1	1	S_3	0
S_2	0	S_4	0
S_2	1	S_5	0
S_3	0	S_6	1
S_3	1	S_7	0
S_4	0	S_0	0
S_4	1	S_1	0
S_5	0	S_2	0
S_5	1	S_3	0
S_6	0	S_4	0
S_6	1	S_5	0
S_7	0	S_6	1
S_7	1	S_7	0

The Mealy and Moore machines for this system are shown in Figure 2.6.

State diagrams for the string checker: (a) Mealy and (b) Moore

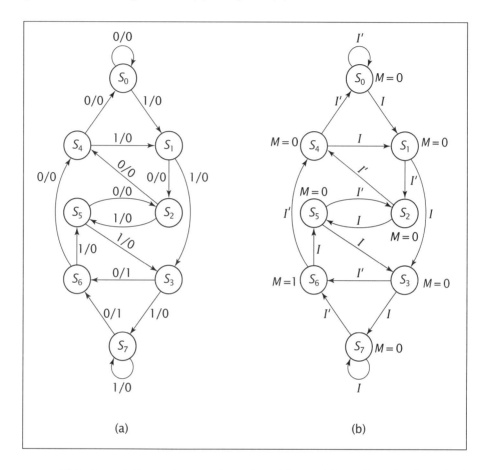

(a)

(b)

This is not the only way to solve this problem. See the Practical Perspective for another solution.

2.3.3 Toll Booth Controller

A toll booth controller has two external sensors. The first indicates whether a car is at the toll booth; $C = 1$ when a car is present and $C = 0$ otherwise. The second sensor indicates whether a coin has been deposited in the toll booth's collection basket and its value. This sensor sets $I_1 I_0 = 00$ if no coin has been deposited, $I_1 I_0 = 01$ if a nickel has been deposited, $I_1 I_0 = 10$ if a dime has been deposited and $I_1 I_0 = 11$ if a quarter has been deposited. (This toll booth does not accept pennies nor coins with values above 25 cents.)

PRACTICAL PERSPECTIVE: Different Models for the Same Problem

Sometimes the most obvious model of a problem is not the most efficient and does not yield the optimal solution. For example, the eight-state solution is only one possible way to define the states for the string checker. One alternative is to define four states, each specifying a different amount of the string as being matched so far. One such assignment is as follows.

S_0:   No bits matched
S_1:   One bit matched (--1)
S_2:   Two bits matched (-11)
S_3:   All three bits matched (110)

In each state, consider both possible values of the input bit and determine which next state is appropriate. Doing this for each state yields the state table shown in Table 2.A. Notice that each state takes into account partial patterns that it may input even if it does not progress toward the desired string. For example, if the machine is in state S_2 (-11) and inputs a 1, it remains in S_2, since its last two bits are still 1.

Table 2.A

State table for the string checker with revised state assignments

Present State	I	Next State	M
S_0 (---)	0	S_0 (---)	0
S_0 (---)	1	S_1 (--1)	0
S_1 (--1)	0	S_0 (---)	0
S_1 (--1)	1	S_2 (-11)	0
S_2 (-11)	0	S_3 (110)	1
S_2 (-11)	1	S_2 (-11)	0
S_3 (110)	0	S_0 (---)	0
S_3 (110)	1	S_1 (--1)	0

Figure 2.A shows the Mealy and Moore machines for this state table. As with the state tables, these machines are much simpler than those in the original design because they have only half the number of states. These state diagrams would require less complex hardware designs than the original state diagrams in Figure 2.6. Most important, they generate the same outputs for the same sequence of inputs as in the original design, thus meeting the system specification.

(continued)

State diagrams for the string checker with revised state assignments: (a) Mealy and (b) Moore

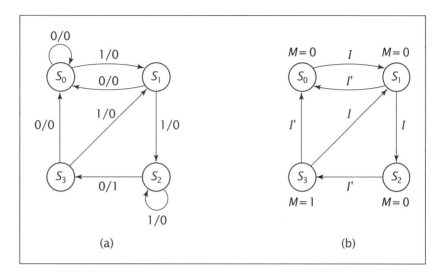

(a)   (b)

The toll booth has two output lights and an output alarm. When a car pulls in to the toll booth, a red light (R) is lit. It remains lit until the driver deposits at least 35 cents, at which point the red light goes off and the green light (G) is lit. The green light remains lit until the car leaves the toll booth; when this happens, the red light is lit again. If the car leaves the toll booth without paying the full toll, the red light remains lit and the alarm (A) is activated. The alarm remains active until another car enters the toll booth, when it is turned off.

This system requires several states, corresponding to the listed conditions. In addition, it requires several more states to keep track of how much money has been deposited. Table 2.5 shows the states that are sufficient to specify the finite state machine, along with their outputs.

To develop the state table, we again look at each individual state and determine all possible actions that can occur. In state S_{NOCAR}, for example, there is no car in the toll booth. The only two things that can happen are (1) a car enters the toll booth ($C = 1$) and the state machine goes to state S_0, or (2) no car arrives ($C = 0$) and the state machine remains in state S_{NOCAR}. Other states are more complicated. For example, during state S_5 (car in toll booth, 5 cents paid), any of the following can occur.

Table 2.5

States for the toll booth controller

State	Condition	R	G	A
S_{NOCAR}	No car in toll booth	1	0	0
S_0	Car in toll booth, 0 cents paid	1	0	0
S_5	Car in toll booth, 5 cents paid	1	0	0
S_{10}	Car in toll booth, 10 cents paid	1	0	0
S_{15}	Car in toll booth, 15 cents paid	1	0	0
S_{20}	Car in toll booth, 20 cents paid	1	0	0
S_{25}	Car in toll booth, 25 cents paid	1	0	0
S_{30}	Car in toll booth, 30 cents paid	1	0	0
S_{PAID}	Car in toll booth, full toll paid	0	1	0
S_{CHEAT}	Car left toll booth without paying full toll	1	0	1

- The car leaves the toll booth ($C = 0$) and the state machine goes to state S_{CHEAT}.
- The car remains in the toll booth ($C = 1$) and a nickel is paid ($I_1 I_0 = 01$), and the state machine goes to state S_{10}.
- The car remains in the toll booth ($C = 1$) and a dime is paid ($I_1 I_0 = 10$), and the state machine goes to state S_{15}.
- The car remains in the toll booth ($C = 1$) and a quarter is paid ($I_1 I_0 = 11$), and the state machine goes to state S_{30}.
- The car remains in the toll booth ($C = 1$) and nothing new is paid ($I_1 I_0 = 00$), and the state machine remains in state S_5.

Table 2.6

State table for the toll booth controller

Present State	C	$I_1 I_0$	Next State	R	G	A	Present State	C	$I_1 I_0$	Next State	R	G	A
S_{NOCAR}	1	XX	S_0	1	0	0	S_{15}	0	XX	S_{CHEAT}	1	0	1
S_{PAID}	0	XX	S_{NOCAR}	1	0	0	S_{15}	1	01	S_{20}	1	0	0
S_{CHEAT}	1	XX	S_0	1	0	0	S_{15}	1	10	S_{25}	1	0	0
S_0	0	XX	S_{CHEAT}	1	0	1	S_{15}	1	11	S_{PAID}	0	1	0
S_0	1	01	S_5	1	0	0	S_{20}	0	XX	S_{CHEAT}	1	0	1
S_0	1	10	S_{10}	1	0	0	S_{20}	1	01	S_{25}	1	0	0
S_0	1	11	S_{25}	1	0	0	S_{20}	1	10	S_{30}	1	0	0
S_5	0	XX	S_{CHEAT}	1	0	1	S_{20}	1	11	S_{PAID}	0	1	0
S_5	1	01	S_{10}	1	0	0	S_{25}	0	XX	S_{CHEAT}	1	0	1
S_5	1	10	S_{15}	1	0	0	S_{25}	1	01	S_{30}	1	0	0
S_5	1	11	S_{30}	1	0	0	S_{25}	1	10	S_{PAID}	0	1	0
S_{10}	0	XX	S_{CHEAT}	1	0	1	S_{25}	1	11	S_{PAID}	0	1	0
S_{10}	1	01	S_{15}	1	0	0	S_{30}	0	XX	S_{CHEAT}	1	0	1
S_{10}	1	10	S_{20}	1	0	0	S_{30}	1	01	S_{PAID}	0	1	0
S_{10}	1	11	S_{PAID}	0	1	0	S_{30}	1	10	S_{PAID}	0	1	0
							S_{30}	1	11	S_{PAID}	0	1	0

FIGURE 2.7
State diagram for the Moore machine for the toll booth controller

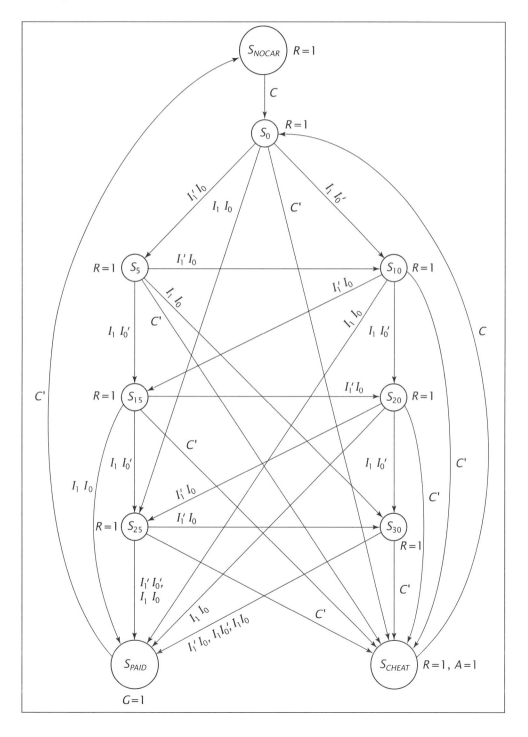

Table 2.6 summarizes the transitions that can occur between states. Impossible conditions, such as having money deposited while no car is in the toll booth, are not considered here. Also, transitions that lead back to the same state are not shown.

The state diagram for the Moore machine for this system is shown in Figure 2.7. Because of its large number of states and input values, it is much more complex than the previous examples. The design of the state diagram for the Mealy machine is left as an exercise for the reader.

2.4 FROM STATE DIAGRAM TO IMPLEMENTATION

Converting a problem specification to an equivalent state table and state diagram is essential, but it is only the first step in this process. The next step is to design the system hardware to implement the state machine. Note that we are not concerned with the original problem specification at this point in the design process, at least not directly. We are implementing the finite state machine, and how we develop the state machine does not affect how we implement it.

This section examines the process of designing the digital logic to implement a finite state machine. The first step is to assign a unique binary value to each state. Since the digital circuit must be able to read the current state as part of its operation, the state must be encoded in binary. Next, we design the hardware to go from the current state to the correct next state. This logic converts the current state and input values to the next state value, and stores that value. At this point, the logic design correctly traverses the states of the state diagram for all states and input values. Our final task is to generate the outputs of the state machine. This is done using combinatorial logic. The state, and sometimes the input values, are the inputs to this logic; the combinatorial logic's outputs are the system outputs.

2.4.1 ASSIGNING STATE VALUES

When implementing a state machine, each state must be assigned a unique binary value. For a machine with n states, the state value will have $\lceil \log_2 n \rceil$ bits.

Consider, for example, the modulo 6 counter. This counter has six states, S_0 to S_5. We need three bits to encode state values for these states. For now, we will assign state value 000 to S_0, 001 to S_1, and so on, up to 101 to S_5. Figure 2.8 shows the Mealy and Moore state diagrams for the modulo 6 counter. Other than the state values, the state diagrams of Figure 2.8 are identical to the original state diagrams of Figure 2.5.

FIGURE 2.8

State diagrams for the modulo 6 counter with values shown: (a) Mealy and (b) Moore

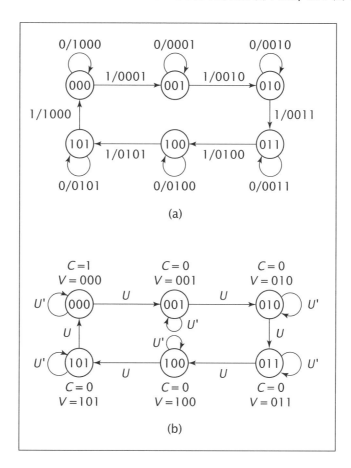

Although any values can be assigned to the states, some assignments are better than others. As mentioned earlier, the state values are used to generate two groups of values: the state machine outputs and the next state. A primary goal is to assign state values so as to minimize the logic needed to generate the output and next state values.

This is often an iterative process, with the designer first selecting state values, then creating a preliminary design to generate the outputs and next state, then modifying the state values and repeating the process. There is a good heuristic that simplifies this process. Whenever possible, have the state value be the same as the output values for that state. When this is the case, the same combinatorial logic can be used to generate both the next state and the system outputs. (This is the reason we chose the assignments 000 to 101 for states S_0 to S_5 in the modulo 6 example.)

2.4.2 Mealy and Moore Machine Implementations

Once the state values have been defined, we are ready to design the digital logic to implement the system. Mealy and Moore machines each have generally used standard implementations. The generic Mealy machine implementation is shown in Figure 2.9(a). The current state value is stored in the register. The state value, along with the machine inputs, are input to a logic block, which generates the next state value and the machine outputs. The next state is loaded into the register on the leading edge of every clock cycle.

FIGURE 2.9

(a) Generic Mealy machine and (b) its implementation of a modulo 6 counter

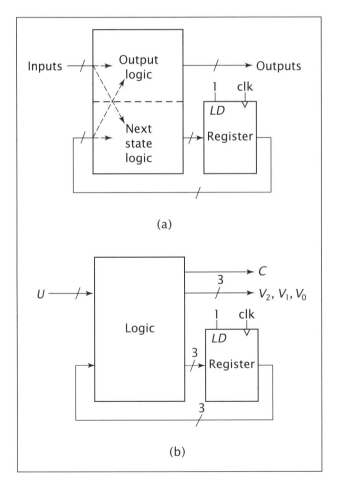

The logic block is designed to meet the digital specifications and will be different for every system. It may consist of combinatorial logic gates, multiplexers, lookup ROMs, and other logic components.

The logic block cannot include any sequential components, since it must generate its values within one clock cycle.

The logic block itself contains two parts. One part generates the next state, based on the present state and the system inputs, and the other produces the system outputs, also based on the present state and system inputs. (These parts may share hardware if doing so simplifies the design.) Figure 2.9(b) shows the logical configuration of the Mealy machine for the modulo 6 counter, which has the state diagram shown in Figure 2.8(a).

The outputs of a Moore machine depend only on its present state and not on its inputs. For this reason, its configuration is different from that of a Mealy machine. The generic Moore machine is shown in Figure 2.10(a). As with the Mealy machine, the present state is stored

FIGURE 2.10

(a) Generic Moore machine and (b) its implementation of a modulo 6 counter

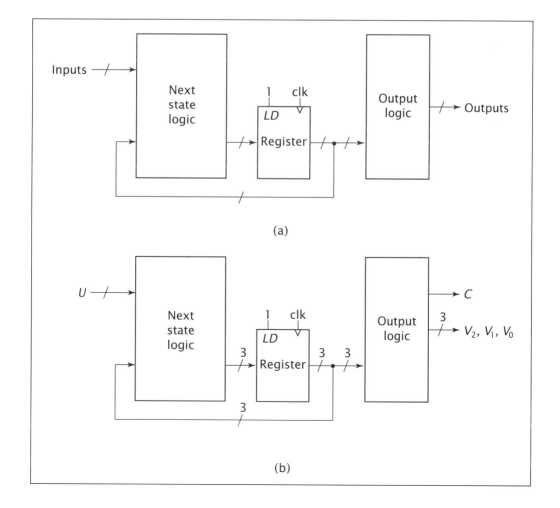

in the register, and this value is fed back to a logic block. The logic block also receives the system inputs and generates the next state value. Since the system outputs depend only on the present state, only the state value is input to a logic block that generates the outputs. The two logic blocks are equivalent to the one combined block of the Mealy machine; in fact, the next state logic section is the same in both systems. However, the output logic block does not use the system inputs to generate the system outputs, so it may be simpler than its counterpart in the Mealy machine. The system to implement the Moore machine for the modulo 6 counter, which has the state diagram of Figure 2.8(b), is shown in Figure 2.10(b).

2.4.3   GENERATING THE NEXT STATE

Since both the Mealy machine and the Moore machine must traverse the same states under the same conditions, their next state logic is identical. This section presents three methods for designing the next state logic: using combinatorial logic gates, using multiplexers, and using a lookup ROM.

To implement the next state logic using combinatorial logic, we begin by setting up a truth table. The system inputs and present state value are the inputs of the truth table, and the next state bits are the outputs. We construct a Karnaugh map for each output bit and derive its equation. Then we design the digital logic to match each equation.

Table 2.7 shows the truth table needed for the modulo 6 counter. It is essentially the same as Table 2.3, with the state names replaced

Table 2.7

State table for the modulo 6 counter with values shown

Present State $(P_2 P_1 P_0)$	U	Next State $(N_2 N_1 N_0)$
000	0	000
000	1	001
001	0	001
001	1	010
010	0	010
010	1	011
011	0	011
011	1	100
100	0	100
100	1	101
101	0	101
101	1	000

by their values and the system outputs eliminated. $P_2P_1P_0$ is the present state value and $N_2N_1N_0$ is the next state value.

Once the table has been created, we draw the Karnaugh maps and generate the equations for N_2, N_1, and N_0 as a function of the present state bits P_2, P_1, P_0, and input U. The Karnaugh maps are shown in Figure 2.11. They yield the following equations.

$$N_2 = P_2P_0' + P_2U' + P_1P_0U$$
$$N_1 = P_1P_0' + P_1U' + P_2'P_1'P_0U$$
$$N_0 = P_0'U + P_0U'$$

FIGURE 2.11

Karnaugh maps for the next state of the modulo 6 counter

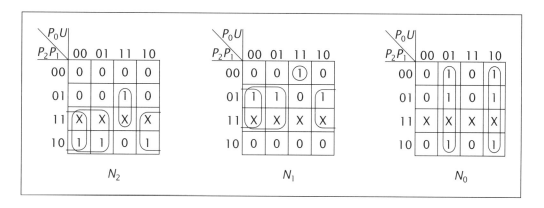

Once we have derived these equations, it is straightforward to develop the combinatorial logic that implements the next state logic. The logic for this system is shown in Figure 2.12.

A different approach to designing the next state logic uses multiplexers. Each input to the multiplexer corresponds to the next state under one possible value of the system inputs. The inputs drive the select signals of the multiplexer. As shown in Figure 2.13 for the modulo 6 counter, this approach uses input U to select one of two possible next states, the next state if $U = 0$, or the next state if $U = 1$.

To determine the inputs to the multiplexer, we begin by splitting the truth table into multiple tables, one for each possible value of the system inputs. Then we follow the procedure as used to derive the next state using combinatorial logic gates.

For the modulo 6 counter, there is only one input, U. As shown in Table 2.8, the initial state table is broken into two separate tables, one for $U = 0$ and the other for $U = 1$.

FIGURE 2.12

Implementation of the next state logic for the modulo 6 counter

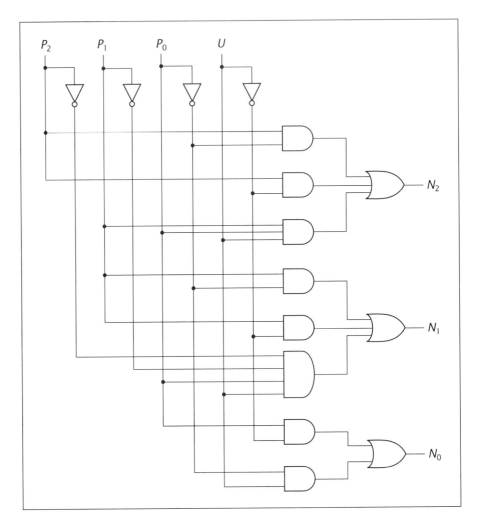

TABLE 2.8

State tables for the modulo 6 counter with values shown

$P_2P_1P_0$	$N_2N_1N_0$	$P_2P_1P_0$	$N_2N_1N_0$
000	000	000	001
001	001	001	010
010	010	010	011
011	011	011	100
100	100	100	101
101	101	101	000
$U = 0$		$U = 1$	

FIGURE 2.13

Preliminary implementation of the next state logic for the modulo 6 counter using a multiplexer

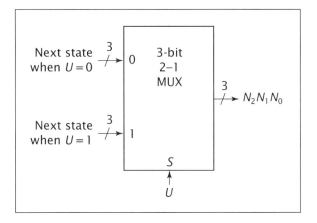

We then create Karnaugh maps from these tables to derive equations for N_2, N_1, and N_0 when $U = 0$ and $U = 1$. These values are as follows.

Next state when $U = 0$: $N_2 = P_2$
$N_1 = P_1$
$N_0 = P_0$

Next state when $U - 1$: $N_2 - P_2P_0' + P_1P_0$
$N_1 = P_1P_0' + P_2'P_1'P_0$
$N_0 = P_0'$

Finally, we implement these values using combinatorial logic, as shown in Figure 2.14.

A third approach to generating the next state of a finite state machine is to use a lookup ROM. In this method, the present state value and all system inputs are connected to the address inputs of the ROM; the next state is derived from the ROM outputs. The correct value must be stored in each location of the ROM to ensure proper operation. Figure 2.15(a) shows the next state generator for the modulo 6 counter using a lookup ROM. The three bits that encode the present state, P_2, P_1, and P_0, are connected to the three high-order address inputs of the ROM. The one condition bit, U, drives the low-order address bit A_0. The data in each location is the value of the next state for the present state and input values which generate its address. For example, when the current state is S_4 ($P_2P_1P_0 = 100$) and $U = 1$, the next state should be S_5 ($N_2N_1N_0 = 101$). These values of P_2, P_1, P_0, and U generate address 9 (1001) to the lookup ROM; the ROM must have the value 5 (101) stored at this location. The values in the other locations

Final implementation of the next state logic for the modulo 6 counter using a multiplexer

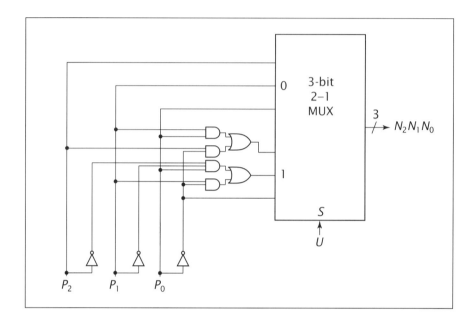

are generated in the same way. Figure 2.15(b) shows the data stored in each location in the lookup ROM.

The order of the inputs to the lookup ROM shown in Figure 2.15 are not the only allowable configuration. The inputs could have been arranged in any order, as long as the correct values were stored in the proper locations of the ROM. In general, however, keeping the present state bits in order and assigning them to the high-order address inputs simplifies the design process. This assignment keeps all locations associated with a given state at adjacent locations, which makes it easier to design and debug the system.

2.4.4 Generating System Outputs

Although Mealy and Moore machines use different values to generate system outputs, both follow the same design procedure to develop their output logic. Two approaches to output logic design, using combinatorial logic gates and using a lookup ROM, are similar to the techniques used to create the next state logic.

As before, the combinatorial logic technique begins by creating a truth table. For the Mealy machine, the table inputs are the present state and the system inputs, and the table outputs are the system outputs. For the Moore machine, only the present state bits are table in-

FIGURE 2.15

Implementation of the next state logic for the modulo 6 counter using a lookup ROM:
(a) logic diagram and (b) lookup ROM data

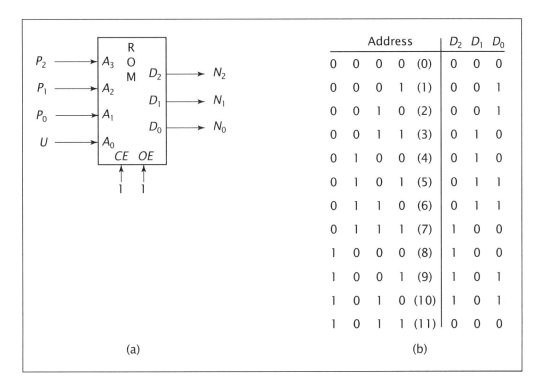

Address					D_2	D_1	D_0
0	0	0	0	(0)	0	0	0
0	0	0	1	(1)	0	0	1
0	0	1	0	(2)	0	0	1
0	0	1	1	(3)	0	1	0
0	1	0	0	(4)	0	1	0
0	1	0	1	(5)	0	1	1
0	1	1	0	(6)	0	1	1
0	1	1	1	(7)	1	0	0
1	0	0	0	(8)	1	0	0
1	0	0	1	(9)	1	0	1
1	0	1	0	(10)	1	0	1
1	0	1	1	(11)	0	0	0

(a)   (b)

puts, since only these bits are used to generate the system outputs. The system outputs are still the table outputs. Table 2.9 shows the tables for the Mealy and Moore machines for the modulo 6 counter. The data in these tables is taken from Table 2.3 in the original problem specification. Recall that V_2, V_1, and V_0 are the system outputs.

As with the next state logic, we construct Karnaugh maps from these tables and derive equations for the outputs. For the Mealy machine, these values are

$$C = P_2'P_1'P_0'U' + P_2P_0U$$
$$V_2 = P_2P_0' + P_2U' + P_1P_0U$$
$$V_1 = P_1P_0' + P_1U' + P_2'P_1'P_0U$$
$$V_0 = P_0'U + P_0U'$$

Note that the equations for V_2, V_1, and V_0 are exactly the same as those for N_2, N_1, and N_0 of the next stage logic. This is the result of optimally assigning state values to states S_0 through S_5. In this case, we can use the same combinatorial logic to generate both sets of signals.

Table 2.9

Tables of outputs for the (a) Mealy and (b) Moore machines for the modulo 6 counter

$P_2 P_1 P_0$	U	C	$V_2 V_1 V_0$	$P_2 P_1 P_0$	C	$V_2 V_1 V_0$
000	0	1	000	000	1	000
000	1	0	001	001	0	001
001	0	0	001	010	0	010
001	1	0	010	011	0	011
010	0	0	010	100	0	100
010	1	0	011	101	0	101
011	0	0	011			
011	1	0	100			
100	0	0	100			
100	1	0	101			
101	0	0	101			
101	1	1	000			
	(a)				(b)	

The logic for the Moore machine is even simpler. It is not necessary to construct Karnaugh maps to see that the following equations generate the system outputs.

$$C = P_2' P_1' P_0'$$
$$V_2 = P_2$$
$$V_1 = P_1$$
$$V_0 = P_0$$

In either machine, we would construct any additional logic necessary to generate the outputs. The complete designs for the Mealy and Moore machine implementations of the modulo 6 counter are shown in Figures 2.16 and 2.17, respectively.

It is also possible to generate system outputs using a lookup ROM. Just as was the case for the next state generator, the inputs of the lookup ROM are the present state and the system inputs. The outputs of the ROM are the system outputs. A significant advantage of this approach is that we can use the same ROM to generate both the next state and the system outputs. Figure 2.18 shows the lookup ROM implementation of the Moore machine of the modulo 6 counter. Since $V_2 = N_2$, $V_1 = N_1$, and $V_0 = N_0$, only one output is used for each pair. If the outputs were not the same as the next state, which is usually the case, separate output bits would be needed. (This is a direct result of optimally assigning values to the states.) Also note that, although it may appear otherwise, the system inputs are not used to generate the system outputs. Here, V_2, V_1, and V_0 are derived directly from the present state. For each present state, the outputs are the same regardless of the value of input U. Also, output C is calculated solely from the

Mealy machine implementation of the modulo 6 counter

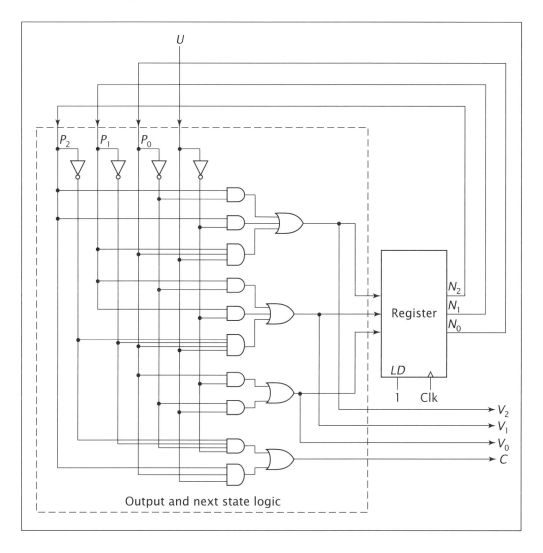

current state and stored in the lookup ROM. We can see in the truth table of Figure 2.18 that, for a given state, C also has the same value for all values of U.

2.4.5 AN ALTERNATIVE DESIGN

There are other methods of implementing finite state machines. One method uses a counter to store the current state and a decoder to generate signals corresponding to each state. The counter can be

FIGURE 2.17

Moore machine implementation of the modulo 6 counter

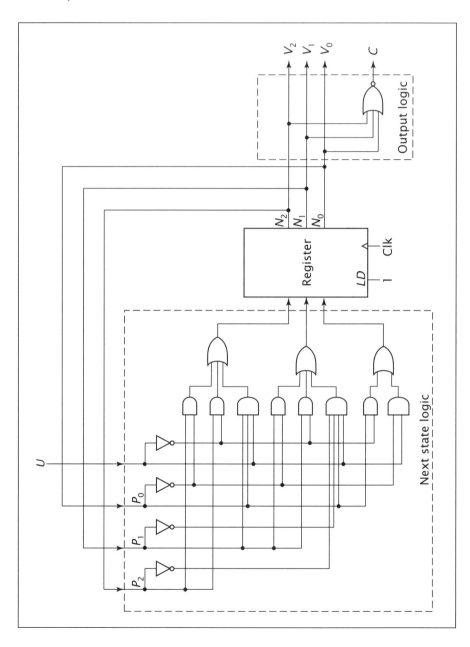

FIGURE 2.18

Moore machine implementation of the modulo 6 counter using a lookup ROM

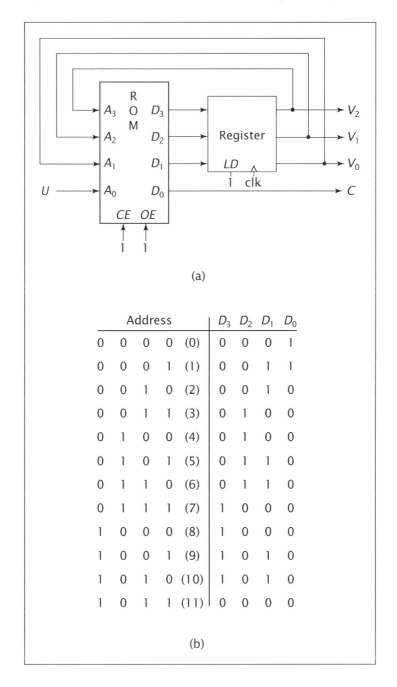

(a)

Address	D_3	D_2	D_1	D_0
0 0 0 0 (0)	0	0	0	1
0 0 0 1 (1)	0	0	1	1
0 0 1 0 (2)	0	0	1	0
0 0 1 1 (3)	0	1	0	0
0 1 0 0 (4)	0	1	0	0
0 1 0 1 (5)	0	1	1	0
0 1 1 0 (6)	0	1	1	0
0 1 1 1 (7)	1	0	0	0
1 0 0 0 (8)	1	0	0	0
1 0 0 1 (9)	1	0	1	0
1 0 1 0 (10)	1	0	1	0
1 0 1 1 (11)	0	0	0	0

(b)

incremented, cleared, or loaded with a value to go from one state to another. Unlike the previous implementations, it is not necessary to regenerate the same state value in order to remain in the same state. This can be accomplished by neither incrementing, clearing, nor loading the counter.

Figure 2.19(a) shows the generic logic design for this methodology. The counter plays the role of the register in the Mealy and Moore machines, as well as a portion of the next state logic. The state value is input to a decoder; each outputs of the decoder represents one state. The decoder outputs and system inputs are input to the logic block, which generates the system outputs and the information needed to generate the next state value. If the system inputs are used to generate both the next state and the system outputs, this design can be used to implement a Mealy machine. However, if the system outputs are generated solely by using the state value, and the system inputs are used only to generate the next state, then it implements a Moore machine.

Figure 2.19(b) shows the implementation of the Moore machine for the modulo 6 counter using this methodology. The 3-bit counter holds the present state and sends its value to the decoder. The outputs of the decoder represent the states: output 0 is state S_0, output 1 is state S_1, and so on. Since this is a Moore machine, only these signals are combined to produce outputs V_2, V_1, V_0, and C. (In this example, the decoder is not necessary since V_2, V_1, and V_0 are the same as the outputs of the counter, and C can be realized as $V_2'V_1'V_0'$, but this is not usually the case.)

The next state control is also straightforward. When $U = 1$, the modulo 6 counter is incremented. When the output is 000, 001, 010, 011, or 100, this can be accomplished by incrementing the state counter. However, when the output is 101, incrementing the state counter produces an output of 110, while 000 is the desired value. In this case, the counter is cleared. When $U = 0$, no signal is activated and the counter retains its previous value, thus remaining in the same state.

2.4.6 The Eight-State String Checker

In this subsection we present the design of the finite state machine for the eight-state string checker of Section 2.2.3. Only the Moore machine is implemented here; the Mealy machine implementation is left as an exercise for the reader. The state diagram for this machine is shown in Figure 2.5(b).

As before, the first step is to assign binary values to the states. For this example, S_0 through S_7 are set to 000 through 111, respectively. These values can replace S_0 through S_7 in the state diagram.

FIGURE 2.19

Alternative state machine hardware design: (a) generic hardware and (b) Moore machine implementation of the modulo 6 counter

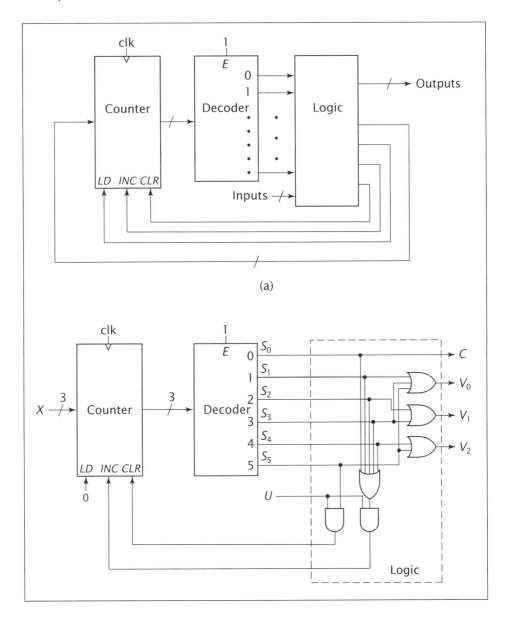

Next, the hardware to implement this state diagram is designed. Starting with the generic hardware shown in Figure 2.10(b), the primary task is to design the next state and output logic.

To create the next state logic, we first modify the state table of Table 2.4 to include the state value assigned to each state; this is shown in Table 2.10. As before, $P_2P_1P_0$ is the present state value and $N_2N_1N_0$ is the next state value.

Table 2.10

State table for the string checker with state values shown

$P_2P_1P_0$	I	$N_2N_1N_0$
000	0	000
000	1	001
001	0	010
001	1	011
010	0	100
010	1	101
011	0	110
011	1	111
100	0	000
100	1	001
101	0	010
101	1	011
110	0	100
110	1	101
111	0	110
111	1	111

Constructing Karnaugh maps and grouping terms yields the following equations to generate the next state value.

$$N_2 = P_1$$
$$N_1 = P_0$$
$$N_0 = I$$

The output logic is also straightforward. Whenever the machine is in state S_6, output M is 1; otherwise it is zero. This can be implemented as

$$M = P_2P_1P_0'$$

The complete logic design for this machine is shown in Figure 2.20.

FIGURE 2.20

Moore machine hardware implementation of the eight-state string checker

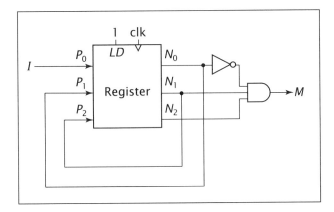

2.5   REAL WORLD EXAMPLE: PRACTICAL CONSIDERATIONS

Several issues regarding finite state machines not covered in the previous sections include handling unused states, asynchronous designs, and machine conversion.

2.5.1   UNUSED STATES

The designs presented so far in this chapter all work properly once they are in a known state. However, there may be a problem if the machine enters an **unused state**, also called an **unknown state** or an **undefined state**. This could be caused by a flaw in the design, but most often occurs when the state machine circuitry is powered up.

To illustrate the meaning of an unused state, consider the Moore machine implementation of the modulo 6 counter. First, recall that the state diagram for this counter, shown in Figure 2.8(b), has six states with binary state values 000 to 101. The state value is stored in the register of the finite state machine hardware, shown in Figure 2.17. An unused state is entered when an unused state value is stored in this register, whether as the result of circuit power up or a design flaw. For this example, the unused state values are 110 and 111.

By examining the circuit, we can determine the system's behavior under these conditions. When the present state is 110, the next state is 110 if $U = 0$ or 111 if $U = 1$. For present state value 111, the next state is 111 if $U = 0$ and 000 if $U = 1$. The revised state diagram, including the unused states, is shown in Figure 2.21(a).

FIGURE 2.21

State diagrams for (a) the Moore implementation of the modulo 6 counter including unused states and (b) an invalid implementation

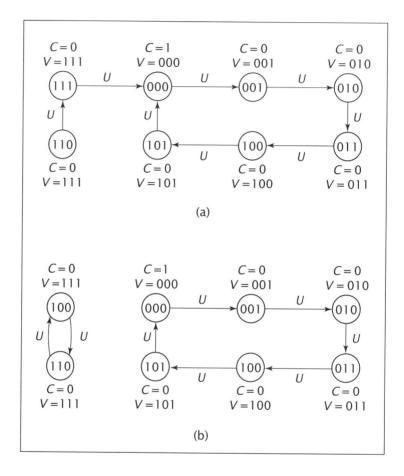

This circuit might still be considered acceptable. It is possible to reach a known state from any unknown state; however, the user must set $U = 1$ for up to two clock cycles to guarantee that this happens. Whether or not this is acceptable is up to the designer. In contrast, Figure 2.21(b) presents an unacceptable implementation. If a circuit that realizes this state diagram powers up with a state value of 110 or 111, it can never reach a valid state.

A more common approach is to create dummy states for all unused state values. Each dummy state would go to a known state at the next clock cycle, usually to a reset state. In this example, we create two dummy states for the unused values 110 and 111. This guarantees that the state machine will be functional after at most one clock cycle. Figure 2.22 shows a revised state diagram for the modulo 6 counter. By convention, the value 1 on the arcs from states 110 and 111 to 000 in-

dicate that the transfer is unconditional—that it is always taken. Also
note that the outputs for these states are $C = 0$ and $V = 111$. This is a
design decision; the value of V is set to 111 to show the user that the
state machine is in an invalid state. Depending on the user's requirements, it could have been set to 000 or some other value, if desired.

Revised state diagram for the Moore implementation of the modulo 6 counter with
dummy states for unused state values

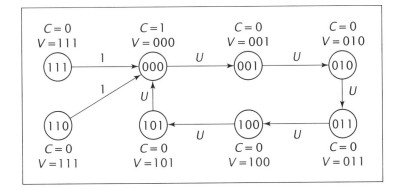

Given the revised state diagram, we can design this finite state
machine using the proceudre we used for the original design. The revised state table, including outputs, is shown in Table 2.11.

State table for the modulo 6 counter with unused states

$P_2 P_1 P_0$	U	$N_2 N_1 N_0$	C	$V_2 V_1 V_0$
000	0	000	1	000
000	1	001	1	000
001	0	001	0	001
001	1	010	0	001
010	0	010	0	010
010	1	011	0	010
011	0	011	0	011
011	1	100	0	011
100	0	100	0	100
100	1	101	0	100
101	0	101	0	101
101	1	000	0	101
110	0	000	0	111
110	1	000	0	111
111	0	000	0	111
111	1	000	0	111

We use this table to construct Karnaugh maps, which yield the following values for the next state and output signals.

$$N_2 = P_2 P_1' P_0' + P_2 P_1' U' + P_1 P_0 U$$
$$N_1 = P_2' P_1 P_0' + P_2' P_1 U' + P_2' P_1' P_0 U$$
$$N_0 = P_2' P_0' U + P_1' P_0' U + P_2' P_0 U' + P_1' P_0 U'$$
$$C = P_2' P_1' P_0'$$
$$V_2 = P_2$$
$$V_1 = P_1$$
$$V_0 = P_0 + P_2 P_1$$

The circuit to implement this finite state machine is similar to that of Figure 2.17, with the logic modified to realize the revised values of N_2, N_1, N_0, C, V_2, V_1, and V_0.

2.5.2 Asynchronous Designs

Almost all finite state machines are synchronous; the state value is stored in a register that is loaded on the rising edge of the system clock. However, it is possible to design a finite state machine that is asynchronous. This design would consist entirely of combinatorial logic. There would be no registers in the circuit, nor would there be a system clock. As a result, asynchronous designs are usually faster than their synchronous counterparts. A generic design for an asynchronous Moore machine is shown in Figure 2.23.

Figure 2.23

Generic asynchronous Moore machine

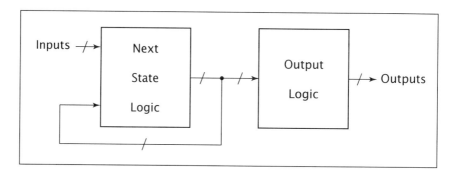

To illustrate this design method, again consider the Moore machine for the original modulo 6 counter. Since this is a methodology for implementing the machine, the state diagram shown in Figure 2.8(b) is used without modification. The next state and output logic are also the same since the machine traverses the same state sequence. A preliminary asynchronous design for this circuit is shown in Figure 2.24. This circuit does not implement the finite state machine properly.

There are two major problems with asynchronous circuit implementations, and this circuit has both of them. The first is the non-uniformity of gate delays. Consider the case when the machine is in state 011 and $U = 0$. When U becomes 1, the machine should generate a next state value of 100. If the propagation delays of the portions of

---

FIGURE 2.24

Preliminary asynchronous Moore machine implementation of the modulo 6 counter

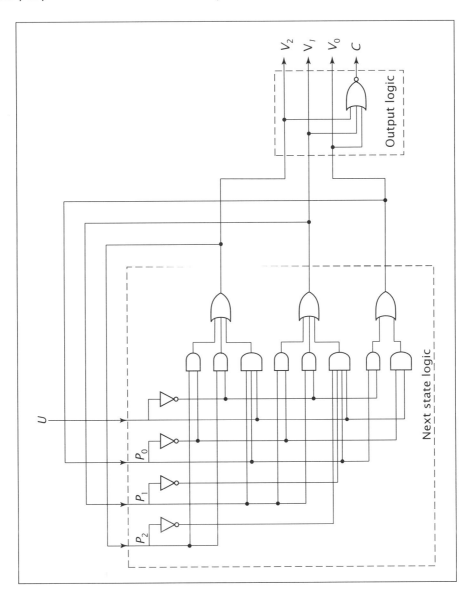

the circuit which generate P_2, P_1, and P_0 are always exactly the same, this would work. However, this is almost never the case.

Assume that P_0 is calculated slightly faster than P_1 and P_2. When P_0 changes from 1 to 0, the machine enters state 010 (since P_1 and P_2 have not changed yet). The new value of P_0 is fed back as an input to the portions of the circuit which generate P_2 and P_1 (and P_0). Clearly this will not yield the desired state value. If the circuitry to set P_1 is fastest, the next state will be 001. If P_2 is fastest, the machine would produce an invalid next state value of 111.

This problem can be alleviated by assigning state values so that each state transition results in a change to only one bit of the state value. (Gray codes are often used in asynchronous circuits for this reason.) Figure 2.25 shows one such state assignment for the asynchronous Moore machine for the modulo 6 counter, along with the revised state diagram.

Revised state values and state diagram for the modulo 6 counter

State	Value
S_0	0 0 0
S_1	0 0 1
S_2	0 1 1
S_3	1 1 1
S_4	1 1 0
S_5	1 0 0

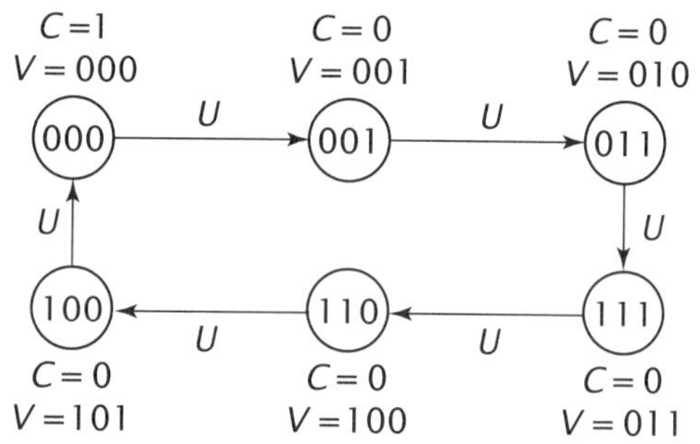

The revised state table, based on these state values, is shown in Table 2.12.

Following the same design procedure as before, we use this table to generate the following values for the next state and output signals.

$$N_2 = P_2 U' + P_1 U$$
$$N_1 = P_1 U' + P_0 U$$
$$N_0 = P_2' U + P_0 U'$$
$$C = P_2' P_1' P_0'$$
$$V_2 = P_2 P_0'$$
$$V_1 = P_1 P_0$$
$$V_0 = P_2 P_1' + P_2 P_0 + P_1' P_0$$

Table 2.12

State table for the modulo 6 counter with revised state values

$P_2 P_1 P_0$	U	$N_2 N_1 N_0$	C	$V_2 V_1 V_0$
000	0	000	1	000
000	1	001	1	000
001	0	001	0	001
001	1	011	0	001
011	0	011	0	010
011	1	111	0	010
111	0	111	0	011
111	1	110	0	011
110	0	110	0	100
110	1	100	0	100
100	0	100	0	101
100	1	000	0	101

The circuitry to implement this machine is shown in Figure 2.26. This circuit properly moves from one state to the correct next state, but it exhibits the second major problem inherent to asynchronous state machine implementations: It doesn't stop. For example, assume the machine is in state 000 and the value of input U goes from

Figure 2.26

Hardware implementation of the modulo 6 counter with revised state values

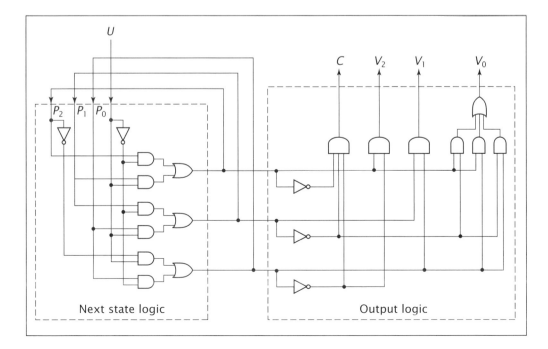

0 to 1. The machine generates a next state value of 001 and the correct system outputs in a few nanoseconds. This new value is fed back into the circuit and, if U is still set to 1, proceeds to generate the next state value of 011, continuing until U is set to 0. In its present form, the circuit acts more like a random number generator than a modulo 6 counter.

This problem can also be resolved, but at the expense of increased system complexity. The state diagram must be modified so that each state is split in two. The first of each state pair is entered when $U = 1$. The machine stays in this state until U becomes 0; then it enters the second state of the pair. This holds the machine in the same state until the value of U changes, thus causing the state transitions to occur on the rising and falling edges of U rather than whenever $U = 1$. Figure 2.27 shows the state diagram incorporating the extra states. The design of the hardware to implement this state machine is left as an exercise for the student.

FIGURE 2.27

Revised state diagram for the modulo 6 counter with additional states

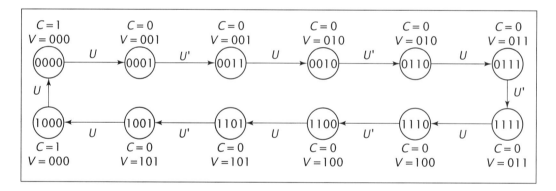

One final physical problem must be fixed. Presumably, input U will be generated using a mechanical switch. In the real world, the input will not make a clean transition from 0 to 1 or from 1 to 0; rather, the voltage level will bounce a bit as it reaches its desired value. This could cause one or more extra, unintended transitions of U to be recognized by the circuit. The input may have to be **debounced** to avoid these extraneous transitions. (This is done within the switch; the state machine circuitry is not changed.) Once this is done, the circuit will work properly.

As illustrated here, implementing the state diagram as an asynchronous circuit adds a significant amount of complexity to the hardware. As digital logic becomes faster, synchronous finite state machines have become fast enough to handle most tasks that formerly required asynchronous implementations. For this reason, asynchronous designs are not generally used to implement finite state machines.

2.5.3   Machine Conversion

There are standard methods for converting between Mealy and Moore state diagrams. This may become necessary when the desired implementation is changed during the design process, or to compare equivalent implementations before choosing a final design.

The process of converting a Mealy state diagram to a Moore state diagram is relatively straightforward. First, we replace each state with a set of m states, where all of the arcs which go into the original state have a total of m different output values. We associate one of the m output patterns with each new state. To illustrate this, consider the state diagram of Figure 2.4, the JK flip-flop with modified outputs; it is redrawn as Figure 2.28(a). Since state Y has two different output values on arcs which are input to it, 0 and 1, we replace it with two states, Y_0 and Y_1. Output value 0 is associated with Y_0 and output value 1 is assigned to Y_1. Similarly, state Z is split into two states. These states and their outputs are shown in Figure 2.28(b).

Figure 2.28

Converting a Mealy state diagram to a Moore state diagram: (a) original Mealy state diagram, (b) new states and output values, and (c) final Moore state diagram

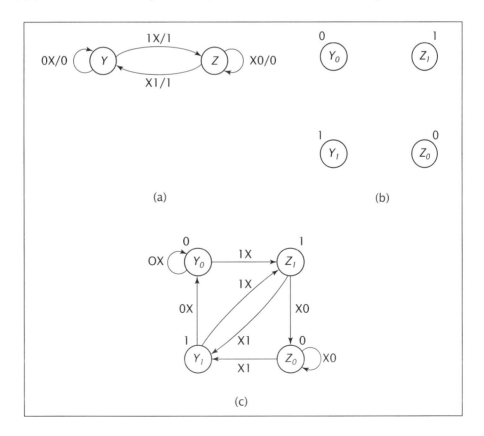

The final task is to convert the arcs from the Mealy representation to the Moore representation. Each arc from a state in the Mealy state diagram is replaced by one arc from each state in the Moore state diagram that was derived from that state. In this case, each arc from state Y is replaced by two arcs, one from Y_0 and the other from Y_1. The destination of each arc is the state corresponding to the destination state of the arc in the Mealy machine which has the desired output value. Since outputs are now associated with the states, they are not included in the arcs. For example, the arc from Y to Z in the Mealy state diagram is replaced by arcs labeled "1X" from Y_0 to Z_1 and from Y_1 to Z_1. Note that these arcs go to Z_1 rather than to Z_0 because Z_1 has the desired output value of 1. Repeating this process yields the Moore state diagram of Figure 2.28(c). The arcs from states Y_0 and Z_1 to themselves are shown for clarity; they may be excluded by convention.

Once the state diagram has been converted, the state machine hardware can be designed using the techniques presented earlier in this chapter.

By comparison, the process of converting from a Moore state diagram to a Mealy state diagram is trivial. We simply add the output of a state to all arcs that go to that state and remove the output values from the states themselves. Once the conversion is done, we design the hardware as before.

2.6 SUMMARY

Finite state machines provide a systematic method for designing sequential digital systems. A designer converts a problem specification to a set of possible states and defines the transitions from one state to another. These states and transitions, along with the inputs and outputs, are expressed as a state table or state diagram. The state table or diagram can then be implemented using digital logic. Finite state machines are the basis for the control unit of microprocessors.

There are two types of finite state machines. The outputs of a Mealy machine are defined with respect to the transitions from one state to another (or from one state back to itself). For Moore machines, on the other hand, the outputs are a function of only the current state. It is possible to convert a state machine from one type to the other.

There are several things to consider when designing a finite state machine. Among these, assigning values to states is crucial. A good assignment can significantly reduce the digital logic needed to implement the state machine, while a bad assignment introduces unnecessary complexity that provides no benefit in the final product.

Another important consideration is how to handle unused states when implementing a finite state machine. A digital circuit could find itself in an unused state, for instance, when power is first applied to the circuit. A well-designed state machine must recover from such a situation and return to normal functioning if it is to be useful.

Problems

1 Create the state table and draw the state diagram for

    a) a D flip-flop
    b) a T flip-flop

2 Create the state table and draw the state diagram for the SR flip-flop. Include a third state, U, for the state in which the output is undefined.

3 Modify the state table and state diagram for the toll booth controller example in Section 2.3.3 so that all states, even those that cannot physically occur, are accounted for in the design.

4 Develop the state diagram for the Mealy machine implementation of the toll booth controller example in Section 2.3.3.

5 Design the Mealy machine implementation of the eight-state string checker of Section 2.3.2 using combinatorial logic.

6 Design the eight-state string checker of Section 2.3.2 using a lookup ROM.

7 Design the Moore machine implementation of the four-state string checker of Section 2.3.2 using combinatorial logic.

8 Design the Mealy machine implementation of the four-state string checker of Section 2.3.2 using combinatorial logic.

9 Design the four-state string checker of Section 2.3.2 using a lookup ROM.

10 Design the Moore machine implementation of the toll booth controller in Section 2.3.3 using combinatorial logic.

11 Design the Mealy machine implementation of the toll booth controller in Section 2.3.3 using combinatorial logic.

12 Design the toll booth controller of Section 2.3.3 using a lookup ROM.

13 Verify the functions for the next state and output values for the Moore machine implementation of the modulo 6 counter including unused states.

14 Redesign the Mealy machine implementation of the modulo 6 counter to include unused states.

15 Why isn't it necessary to include unused states in the designs of the four- and eight-state string checkers?

16 Redesign the Moore machine implementation of the toll booth controller to include unused states.

17 Design the asynchronous circuit that corresponds to the state diagram of Figure 2.28.

18 In a classic problem, a farmer, a fox, a chicken, and a sack of corn are on the left bank of a river. There is a small boat that will hold the farmer and at most one of the other three. Using as many trips as needed, the farmer must transfer the other three and himself to the right bank of the river. However, if he leaves the fox and chicken on one bank of the river while he is on the other bank, the fox will eat the chicken. Likewise, if he is on one bank and the chicken and corn are on the other bank, the chicken will eat the corn.

Design a Moore finite state machine using combinatorial logic to simulate this situation. Each state value has four bits, A, B, C, D, representing the farmer, fox, chicken, and corn, respectively. Each bit is 0 if its item is on the left bank and 1 if it is on the right bank. Two input bits, YZ, encode the action. IF $YZ = 00$, the farmer crosses the river alone. For $YZ = 01$, 10, or 11, the farmer crosses the river with the fox, chicken, or corn, respectively. There are two outputs. Output L is set to 1 whenever the fox eats the chicken or the chicken eats the corn. Output W is set to 1 when all four reach the right bank of the river. Otherwise, no output is active. When either $L = 1$ or $W = 1$, the machine resets to state 0000 on the next clock cycle.

Include all unused states in your design.

19 Repeat Problem 18, but design a Mealy machine instead of a Moore machine.

20 A certain television game show has three contestants, A, B, and C. Each player has a signaling button which goes to a circuit that outputs YZ. The circuits sets YZ to 00 when no player has pressed his or her button, and sets $YZ = 01$, 10, or 11 when the first player to press the signaling button is player A, B, or C, respectively. A clue is displayed and one of the players presses the signaling button; this locks out the other players from being recognized, and activates the player's output light, A_o, B_o, or C_o. The player then gives an answer. If the answer is correct, the host presses the R (for right/reset) button, enabling all contestants' buttons. If not, the host presses the W (for wrong) button. This disables that player's button and turns off his or her output light, but doesn't affect the other player's buttons. They can ring in and are processed in the same manner. (Thus, if a second player presses the button but answers incorrectly, only the third player's button is active.) At any time that no player is answering a question, the host can reset the game by pressing the *R* button, as when, for example, time expires.

Design the Moore machine signal button controller for this game show. Implement the finite state machine using a lookup ROM. Show the contents of the ROM.

21 Repeat Problem 20, but design a Mealy machine instead of a Moore machine.

22 Show the state diagram that corresponds to the following hardware. *X* and *Y* are system inputs. Ignore states for which decoder outputs are not shown.

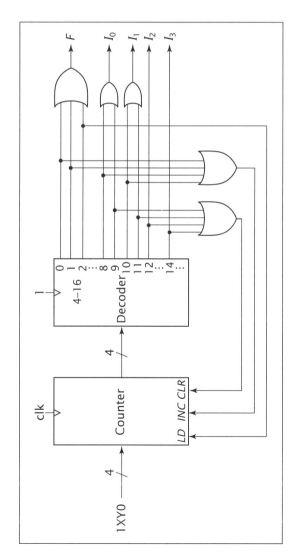

23 Show the state diagram realized by the following circuit and data.

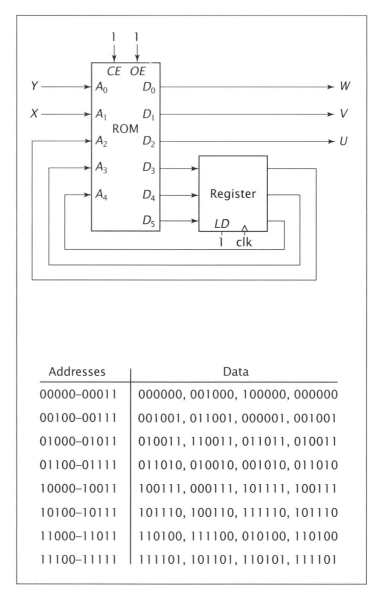

Addresses	Data
00000–00011	000000, 001000, 100000, 000000
00100–00111	001001, 011001, 000001, 001001
01000–01011	010011, 110011, 011011, 010011
01100–01111	011010, 010010, 001010, 011010
10000–10011	100111, 000111, 101111, 100111
10100–10111	101110, 100110, 111110, 101110
11000–11011	110100, 111100, 010100, 110100
11100–11111	111101, 101101, 110101, 111101

24   Show the state diagram realized by the following circuit.

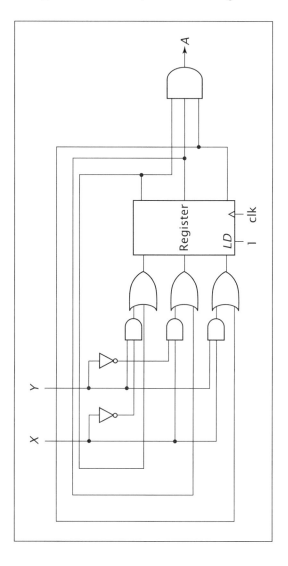

25 The following state diagram is supposed to be implemented by the circuit shown below. Find and correct the errors in the hardware.

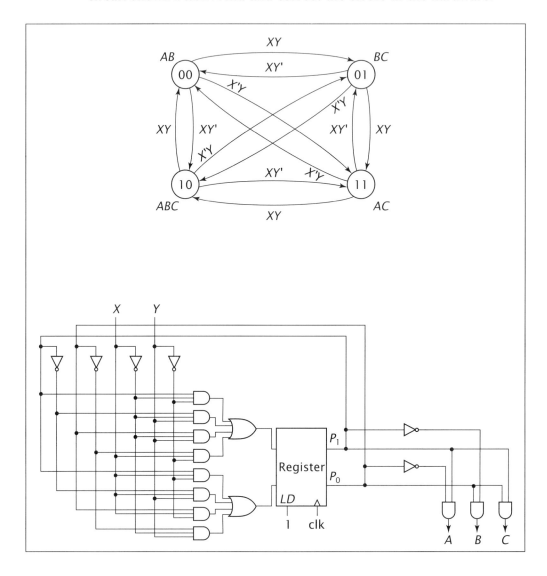

26 The state diagram of problem 25 is supposed to be implemented by the following hardware. Find and correct the errors in the hardware.

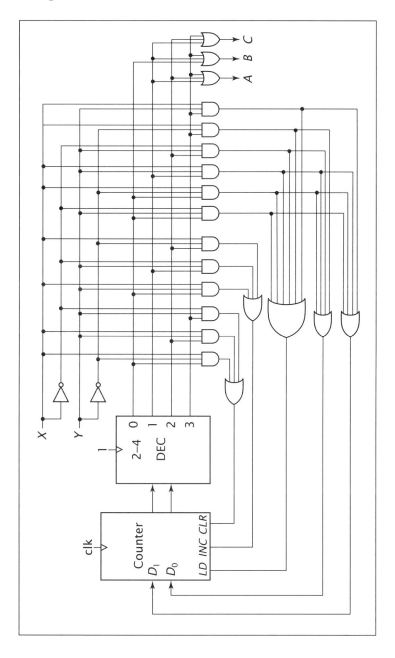

27 The state diagram of problem 25 is supposed to be implemented by the following circuit with the ROM data shown beside it. Find and correct the errors in the data; do not modify the circuit hardware.

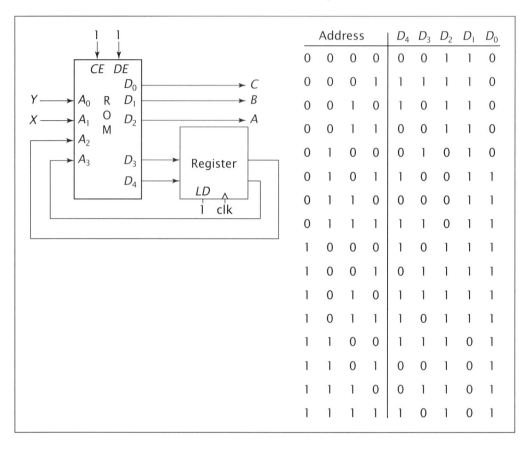

Address				D_4	D_3	D_2	D_1	D_0
0	0	0	0	0	0	1	1	0
0	0	0	1	1	1	1	1	0
0	0	1	0	1	0	1	1	0
0	0	1	1	0	0	1	1	0
0	1	0	0	0	1	0	1	0
0	1	0	1	1	0	0	1	1
0	1	1	0	0	0	0	1	1
0	1	1	1	1	1	0	1	1
1	0	0	0	1	0	1	1	1
1	0	0	1	0	1	1	1	1
1	0	1	0	1	1	1	1	1
1	0	1	1	1	0	1	1	1
1	1	0	0	1	1	1	0	1
1	1	0	1	0	0	1	0	1
1	1	1	0	0	1	1	0	1
1	1	1	1	1	0	1	0	1

2

Computer
Organization and
Architecture

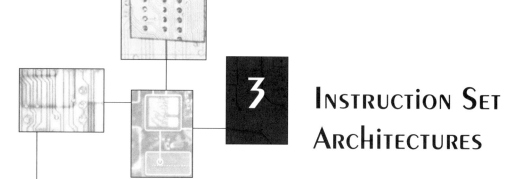

3 INSTRUCTION SET ARCHITECTURES

It is not necessary to know every detail of how something works in order to use it. For example, you do not have to know the specifics of how an internal combustion engine works in order to drive a car. Of course the engine designer must know these details, but the driver does not. However, the driver must know how to interact with the engine and car, how to use the steering wheel, gas and brake pedals, the clutch (if the car has a standard transmission), the turning signals and lights, and so on. It is sufficient for the driver to know how to interface with the car in order to drive it.

The **instruction set architecture**, or **ISA**, is much like the car interface, but for microprocessors instead of automobiles. A microprocessor's ISA includes the information needed to interact with the microprocessor, but not the details of how the microprocessor itself is designed and implemented. It is essentially a programmer's view of the microprocessor. It provides the details a programmer would need to know in order to write a program for the microprocessor, or the details a compiler would need in order to compile a program written in C++, or some other high-level programming language, so that it could be run by the microprocessor.

As its name implies, an instruction set architecture includes the microprocessor's instruction set, the set of all assembly language instructions that the microprocessor can execute. But there is more to an ISA than the instruction set. A programmer would also need to know the details of the programmer-accessible **registers** within the microprocessor. (As described in Chapter 6, a microprocessor also has some registers that it uses to perform operations that cannot be directly accessed by the programmer. These registers are not a part of the ISA.) These programmer-accessible registers store and perform operations on data. The instruction set architecture must specify these registers, their sizes, and the instructions in the instruction set that can use each register. The ISA also includes information necessary to interact with memory. Certain microprocessors require instructions to start only at specific memory locations; this alignment of instructions would be part of the instruction set architecture. Some processors have interrupts, which cause the microprocessor to stop what it is doing and perform some other, preprogrammed function. How the microprocessor reacts to interrupts, from a programming point of view, is part of the ISA. The physical actions that are necessary to recognize that an external interrupt has occurred, however, are not a part of the ISA. (Program instructions within the instruction set that enable and disable interrupts are definitely included in the instruction set architecture.)

Before we describe instruction set architectures, we need to discuss programming languages. This chapter begins by describing different levels of programming languages. We look at the tools used to convert programs from each level to their equivalent binary machine code, which is the actual code executed by the microprocessor. We then examine assembly language instructions in more detail. We introduce the different types of assembly language instructions and the data formats they work with. We describe the different addressing modes a microprocessor may have and its possible instruction formats.

With this background, we can examine instruction set architectures. We next examine the factors to be considered when designing the instruction set and register set of a microprocessor's ISA. This chapter also examines the instruction set architectures of two microprocessors. The Relatively Simple CPU is an instructional aid created for this book. It is used throughout this text to illustrate computer design principles. The 8085 microprocessor is an older Intel microprocessor that predates the IBM-compatible personal computer. Although much less powerful than current microprocessors, it is still used in applications that don't require too much processing power. Sojourner, the Mars Pathfinder robot that explored the Martian surface in 1997, used this microprocessor.

3.1 Levels of Programming Languages

In this section, we describe the various levels of programming languages, how they are related to each other, and how they are converted to a form that can be executed by a microprocessor. We do not delve into the specifics of any of these languages. This section also introduces the process of converting a Java applet to run on a computer.

Java applets follow a different procedure than most other languages, so they are examined separately.

3.1.1 LANGUAGE CATEGORIES

Traditionally, computer programming languages are divided into three categories. Appropriately, languages with the highest level of abstraction are collectively referred to as **high-level languages**. These languages hide the details of the computer and operating system on which they will run from the programmer. They are said to be **platform-independent**; the same program code can be converted and run on computers with different microprocessors and operating systems without modification. Languages such as C++, Java, and Fortran are high-level languages.

Assembly languages are at a much lower level of abstraction. Each microprocessor has its own assembly language. A program written in the assembly language of one microprocessor cannot be run on a computer that has a different microprocessor—with one very important exception. A company that develops microprocessors will usually design new processors so that they are **backward compatible** with its previous microprocessors. For example, Intel's Pentium III microprocessor can run programs written in the assembly languages of its Pentium II, Pentium Pro, Pentium, 80486, 80386, 80286, and 8086 microprocessors—basically any code ever written for an IBM-compatible personal computer. With backward compatibility, someone can buy a new computer with a state-of-the-art microprocessor and still use the same software (which they've already paid for and know how to use) that they used on their old computer. Such cost and time savings are an important marketing consideration in microprocessor and assembly language instruction set design.

Unlike high-level languages, instructions in assembly languages can directly manipulate the data stored in a microprocessor's internal components. Assembly language instructions can load data from memory into a microprocessor's registers, add values, and perform many other operations. Assembly languages are not platform-independent.

The lowest level of programming languages are **machine languages**. These languages contain the binary values that cause the microprocessor to perform certain operations. When a microprocessor reads and executes an instruction, it is a machine language instruction. Programmers do not write programs in machine language. Rather, programs written in a high-level language or assembly language are converted to machine language, which is then executed by the microprocessor. As with assembly languages, machine languages are platform-specific; each microprocessor has its own machine language that may be backward compatible with the machine languages of its predecessor processors.

3.1.2   Compiling and Assembling Programs

Once a programmer has written a program in a high-level or assembly language, the program must be converted to machine code. High-level language programs are **compiled**, and assembly language programs are **assembled**. We now look at these processes from a high-level perspective. We examine the processes themselves, but not the internal workings of compilers and assemblers.

Let's start with compilers. A program written in a high-level language is input to a compiler. The compiler checks to make sure every statement in the program is valid (the dreaded syntax error check). When a program has no syntax errors, the compiler finishes compiling the program, the **source code**, and generates an **object code** file. The object code is the machine language equivalent of the source code.

At this point the program has been compiled successfully, but it is not yet ready to be executed. Some programs use the object code of other programs in addition to their own. A **linker** combines your object code with any other required object code. This combined code is stored as an **executable file**. It is actually the code in this file that the computer runs. A loader copies the executable file into memory; the microprocessor then runs the machine code contained in that file.

As noted earlier, high-level languages are platform-independent. The same high-level source code can be compiled to run on different microprocessors and operating systems, or computing platforms. In practice, each platform has a separate compiler, although it is theoretically possible to have a single compiler that produces different object code for different platforms. Figure 3.1 illustrates the relationship between the different types of code in the compilation process.

A high-level language statement is usually converted to a sequence of several machine code instructions. Furthermore, there may be more than one valid conversion for a statement, which can complicate the design of a compiler. This is not the case with assembly language. Each assembly language instruction corresponds to one unique machine code instruction. For this reason, assemblers are much less complex than compilers.

Figure 3.2 shows the process of converting an assembly language program to an executable form. (Recall that each assembly language is specific to one microprocessor; we don't need assemblers for different platforms because assembly language programs usually run on only one platform.) The assembler, like the compiler, converts its source code to object code. From there, it follows the linking and loading procedure that was used for compiled code.

FIGURE 3.1

Compilation process for high-level programs. Loaders are included within the computing platforms.

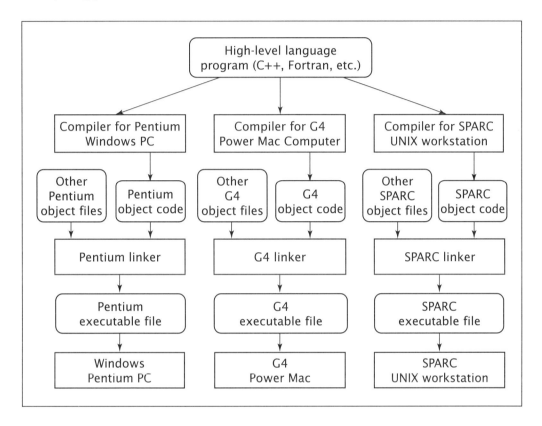

Figures 3.1 and 3.2 show the process of converting a program to a machine readable form for personal computers and workstations. Many computers, however, are much simpler than these systems. The microprocessor systems used to control consumer appliances, for example, generally consist of a microprocessor and a small amount of memory (or a microcontroller) and some circuitry to interact with a keypad and a digital display. In such a system, an assembly language program would be assembled to generate object code, but that might be the end of the process. These control programs are relatively small, and no other object files may be needed. These computer systems do not have an operating system per se because they are so simple that one is not needed. (My microwave oven works just fine without Windows 2000 and it hasn't crashed yet.) The original assembly language program may be all the software the system has and needs. In this case, the object code generated from the assembly language program is the final executable code.

FIGURE 3.2

Assembly process for assembly language programs

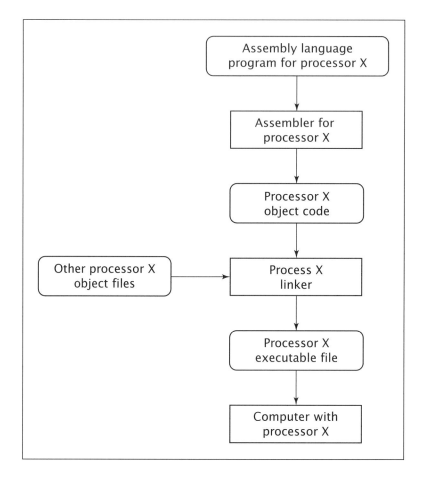

Most software for personal computers is written in a high-level language. More programmers know C++, for example, than know the Pentium assembly language. There are also many support tools for high-level languages.

Assembly language is sometimes used in conjunction with high-level languages to optimize code. For instance, a large program might be written in C++, but the programmer may write a few of its functions in assembly language. Since assembly language instructions specify direct interactions with the microprocessor's registers, a well-written assembly language routine will be smaller and run faster than a compiled version of the same routine written in a high-level language. There is a tradeoff, however, in including assembly language routines in a high-level language program. Since the assembly

PRACTICAL PERSPECTIVE: Java Applets—A Different Way of Processing Programs

Java applets are computer programs written in the Java programming language. Unlike other high-level language programs, however, they are not compiled to machine code that can be executed by a microprocessor. Instead, as shown in Figure 3.A, they are compiled to a format called **bytecode**. The bytecode is input to a **Java Virtual Machine**, or **JVM**, which interprets and executes the code. The JVM can be a hardware chip, but it is usually a program itself, often a part of a Web browser. You can think of the bytecode as the machine code of the JVM.

FIGURE 3.A
Compilation process for Java applets

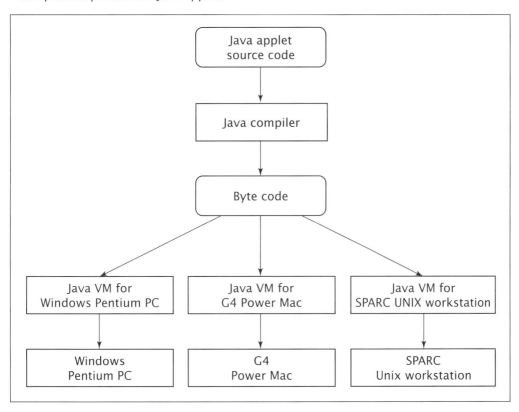

Unlike a standard compiler, which produces object code for a particular computer system, the Java compiler produces bytecode that is platform-independent. The Java Virtual Machine for each platform interprets the bytecode so that it can run on its specific platform. This is useful for applets that are accessed over the World

(continued)

Wide Web. Only one set of bytecode needs to be available; the server doesn't have to supply different bytecode to different platforms. However, the down side of this is that the bytecode must be interpreted by the JVM, rather than directly executed by the microprocessor. This results in the code running much slower. There are **just-in-time compilers**, which compile the bytecode to an executable file, but they introduce overhead and delay the initial execution of the program.

language routine is written for a specific microprocessor, the program is no longer platform-independent.

The code for small computer systems, such as the microwave oven controller, are often written in assembly language. For these applications, the speed of the routine usually is not important. (You can only push the buttons on your microwave oven so fast; even a slow microprocessor routine will be much faster than you.) Instead, the smaller size of the routine translates into less memory required in the system, which reduces overall cost.

3.2 Assembly Language Instructions

A microprocessor's assembly language instruction set is an important part of its instruction set architecture. This section introduces the attributes of assembly language instructions. Assembly language instructions can be divided into types based on the functions they perform. Instructions may work on different types of data, and they may use different methods to access system memory. These topics are all discussed in this section. In addition, this section reviews the format of assembly language and machine code instructions. Examples of assembly language instructions are examined later in this chapter.

3.2.1 Instruction Types

Assembly language instructions can be grouped together based on the types of operations they perform. The exact groups may vary, but in general they contain the types shown in this subsection. Every textbook author has his or her own way of classifying assembly language instructions; here's mine.

3.2.1.1 Data Transfer Instructions

The most common operation a microprocessor performs is to move data from one place to another. (Technically, the microprocessor actually copies the data, since the data is not removed from its original location when it is copied to the new location, but the term *move* is commonly, though incorrectly, used.) The assembly language instructions that do this are the data transfer instructions. These instructions do not modify the data; they only copy the value to its destination. These instructions typically perform one of the following transfers.

- *Load data from memory into the microprocessor.* A microprocessor usually contains several registers to store data that it is using. (You can think of the registers as a group of flip-flops.) These instructions copy data from memory into a microprocessor register.
- *Store data from the microprocessor into memory.* This is similar to loading data, except data is copied in the opposite direction, from a microprocessor register to memory.
- *Move data within the microprocessor.* These operations copy data from one microprocessor register to another.
- *Input data to the microprocessor.* In computer systems, a microprocessor may need to obtain data from an external device. For example, in the microwave oven controller, the microprocessor must know which key was pressed on the keypad in order to perform the correct function. The microprocessor inputs data from the input device, the keypad in this case, into one of its registers.
- *Output data from the microprocessor.* The microprocessor copies data from one of its registers to an output device, such as the digital display of the microwave oven.

In addition to these types of data transfer instructions, some assembly language instruction sets contain specialized data transfer instructions. These instructions may transfer a block of data from one area of memory to another, or between memory and an input or output device.

3.2.1.2 DATA OPERATION INSTRUCTIONS

Unlike data transfer instructions, data operation instructions do modify their data values. They typically perform some operation using one or two data values (**operands**) and store the result.

Arithmetic instructions make up a large part of the data operation instructions. Instructions that add, subtract, multiply, or divide values fall into this category. Instructions that increment or decrement (add one to or subtract one from) a value are also in this class. A clear instruction, which sets a value to zero, may be either an arithmetic instruction or a logic instruction.

A special class of arithmetic instructions are floating point instructions. General arithmetic instructions operate on integer values. Floating point operations perform the same operations, but on floating point data.

Logic instructions perform basic logical operations on data. They AND, OR, or XOR two data values, or complement a single value. These operations are done in a bit-wise manner. For example, consider an instruction that ANDs two 8-bit values, *A* and *B.* They consist of the bits

$A_7, A_6, A_5, A_4, A_3, A_2, A_1, A_0$ and $B_7, B_6, B_5, B_4, B_3, B_2, B_1, B_0$, respectively. The AND operation sets the result to $A_7 \wedge B_7, A_6 \wedge B_6, A_5 \wedge B_5, A_4 \wedge B_4, A_3 \wedge B_3, A_2 \wedge B_2, A_1 \wedge B_1, A_0 \wedge B_0$. The other logic operations work in a similar manner.

Shift instructions, as their name implies, shift the bits of a data value. For example, the left shift of a value moves each bit one position to the left; the most significant bit may be lost or shifted around to the least significant position, depending on the type of left shift. There are several types of shifts, which are described in greater detail in Chapter 1.

3.2.1.3 PROGRAM CONTROL INSTRUCTIONS

One of the mantras of high-level programming is to (almost) never use GOTO statements. High-level languages have constructs, such as FOR...DO and DO...WHILE to control the flow of a program without resorting to the dreaded GOTO statement. Assembly languages do not have this option. A jump or branch instruction is commonly used to go to another part of the program. These jumps can be absolute (always taken) or conditional (taken only if some condition is met). Conditional jumps are particularly useful for implementing program loops.

Assembly language programs may include subroutines, just as high-level language programs may have subroutines, procedures, and functions. An assembly language instruction set may include instructions to call and return from subroutines. As with jumps, the instruction set may also include conditional calls and returns.

A microprocessor can be designed to accept interrupts. An interrupt basically causes the microprocessor to stop what it is doing and start executing other instructions. In this respect, it is somewhat similar to handling a subroutine. An assembly language instruction set may include specific instructions to generate interrupts; these are called **software interrupts**. There are also interrupts that are not part of the instruction set. **Hardware interrupts** are triggered by devices outside of the microprocessor. **Exceptions**, or **traps**, are triggered when valid instructions perform invalid operations, such as dividing by zero.

One final type of program control instruction is the halt instruction. This instruction causes a microprocessor to stop executing instructions, such as at the end of a program.

3.2.2 DATA TYPES

A microprocessor may have to operate on more than one type of data. As a result, its instruction set may include different instructions to perform the same operation on different data types. This subsection reviews the most common of these data types.

Numeric data can often be represented as integers. In unsigned integers, an n-bit value can range from 0 to $2^n - 1$. An n-bit signed integer can have any value between -2^{n-1} and $2^{n-1} - 1$, inclusive. Both formats can be used in arithmetic algorithms; we cover this in detail in Chapter 8. An instruction set may include arithmetic instructions that operate on either or both types of integers.

Some numeric data cannot be represented as integers. These values, which typically include fractional portions, are represented in floating point format in computers. A microprocessor may have special registers and instructions exclusively for floating point data. Floating point data, operations, and standards, are discussed in more detail in Chapter 8.

The boolean values TRUE and FALSE are used often enough to warrant having their own data type, **boolean**, and assembly language instructions. Typically, a data value is set to zero to represent FALSE and any nonzero value for TRUE. Boolean assembly language instructions can perform logical operations on these values. Unlike logical instructions, which generate one result per bit of the operands, boolean instructions generate only one result. To illustrate the difference, consider the case in which A = 0000 0010 and B = 0000 0001. The logical AND of these binary values produces the result 0000 0000. However, if they are boolean values, A and B are both TRUE, since they are both nonzero. Their boolean AND must produce a result of TRUE, represented by a nonzero value.

Computers must also deal with character data. The characters are stored as binary values encoded using **ASCII**, **EBCDIC**, **UNICODE**, or some other character encoding standard. Rather than arithmetically or logically manipulating characters, a computer may concatenate strings of characters, replace some characters with others, or otherwise manipulate character strings. Some assembly language instruction sets include instructions to directly manipulate character data. Others use routines constructed from other instructions to achieve the same result.

3.2.3 Addressing Modes

When a microprocessor accesses memory, to either read or write data, it must specify the memory address it needs to access. An assembly language instruction may use one of several **addressing modes** to generate this address. This subsection presents some of the more commonly used addressing modes. A microprocessor's instruction set may use some or all of these modes, depending on its design. In these examples, the LDAC instruction loads data from memory into the microprocessor's *AC* register. (This instruction is taken from the instruction set of the Relatively Simple CPU, which we describe in detail later in this chapter.)

3.2.3.1   Direct Mode

In this mode, the instruction includes a memory address; the CPU accesses that location in memory. For example, the instruction LDAC 5 reads the data from memory location 5 and stores the data in the CPU's accumulator. This mode is typically used to load operands and values of variables into the CPU.

3.2.3.2   Indirect Mode

Indirect mode starts off very much like direct mode, but then performs a second memory access. The address specified in the instruction is not the address of the operand; it is the address of a memory location that contains the address of the operand. For example, the LDAC 5 instruction in indirect mode, often denoted as LDAC @5 or LDAC (5), first retrieves the contents of location 5, say 10. Then the CPU goes to location 10, reads the contents of that location and loads the data into the CPU. This is used by compilers and operating systems with relocatable code and data.

3.2.3.3   Register Direct and Register Indirect Modes

Register modes work the same as direct and indirect modes, except they do not specify a memory address. Instead, they specify a register. If register R contains the value 5, the LDAC R instruction copies the value 5 from register R into the CPU's accumulator. The indirect instruction, LDAC (R) or LDAC @R, performs just as the direct mode instruction LDAC 5 did. Here the indirection comes from reading the address from the register instead of the first memory access.

3.2.3.4   Immediate Mode

In the immediate mode, the operand specified is not an address; it is the actual data to be used. The instruction LDAC #5 moves the data value 5 into the accumulator.

3.2.3.5   Implicit Mode

Implicit mode does not explicitly specify an operand; the instruction implicitly specifies the operand because it always applies to a specific register. This isn't usually used for load instructions. It is more commonly found in such instructions as CLAC, which clears the accumulator (sets its value to zero) in the Relatively Simple CPU. No operand is needed because this instruction always refers to the accumulator. This mode is used in CPUs that use a stack to store data. They do not have to specify an operand, since it is implicit that the operand must come from the stack.

3.2.3.6   Relative Mode

In this mode, the operand supplied is an offset, not the actual address. It is added to the contents of the CPU's program counter register to generate the required address. The program counter contains the address of the current instruction being executed, so the same relative instruction will produce different addresses at different locations in the program. (As discussed in Chapters 6 and 7, the program counter value is incremented during the instruction fetch cycle. The value used to calculate the correct address is actually the address of the *next* instruction.) If the relative mode instruction LDAC $5 is located at memory location 10, and it takes up two memory locations, the next instruction is at location 12. The instruction reads data from location (12 + 5 =) 17 and stores it in the accumulator. This mode is particularly useful for short jumps and relocatable code.

3.2.3.7 Index Mode and Base Address Mode

Index mode works like relative mode, except the address supplied by the instruction is added to the contents of an index register instead of the program counter. If the index register contains the value 10, the instruction LDAC 5(X) reads data from location (5 + 10 =) 15 and stores it in the accumulator.

Base address mode works exactly the same as index mode, except that the index register is replaced by a base address register. In theory, index mode instructions supply the base address and the index register supplies the offset to that base address. Base address mode instructions supply the offset to the base address stored in the base address register. In practice, only one of the two modes is used, usually index mode.

Figure 3.3 shows how the address is generated in each of these modes.

3.2.4 Instruction Formats

When an assembly language instruction is converted to its equivalent machine code, it is represented as a binary value called the **instruction code**. This value is in a specific format; different groups of bits represent different parts of the instruction. One group may represent the operation to be performed (the **opcode**), while other groups select the operands of the operation. A microprocessor may have one format for all instructions, or several different formats; each instruction has only one instruction code format.

Consider a simplified example for the operation $A = B + C$. This instruction has one operation, addition, two source operands, B and C, and one destination operand, A. If a microprocessor can perform 16 different operations, addition being one of them, then it needs four bits to specify one of the operations (because $2^4 = 16$). Here, we assume the bit pattern 1010 specifies addition. Also assume that there are only four possible operands for this operation, A, B, C, and D. The microprocessor needs two bits to specify each operand. For this example, 00 represents A, 01 represents B, 10 represents C, and 11 represents D.

A microprocessor may be designed to work with instructions that specify 3, 2, 1, or 0 operands. We will look at these instruction formats

FiguRE 3.3

Address generation using address modes: (a) direct, (b) indirect, (c) register direct, (d) register indirect, (e) immediate, (f) implicit, (g) relative, and (h) indexed

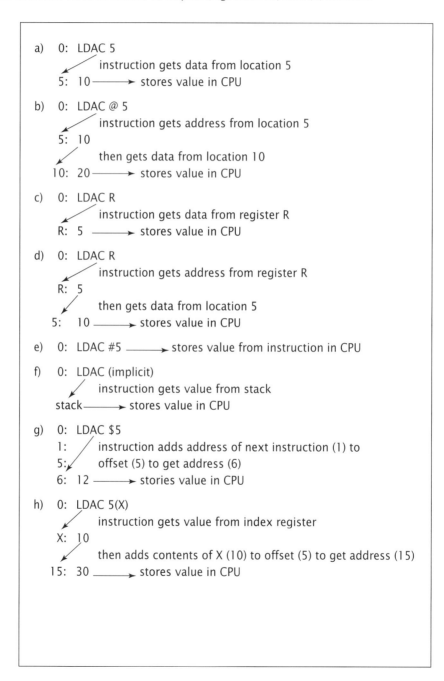

a) 0: LDAC 5
                   instruction gets data from location 5
    5: 10   → stores value in CPU

b) 0: LDAC @ 5
                   instruction gets address from location 5
    5: 10
              then gets data from location 10
   10: 20   → stores value in CPU

c) 0: LDAC R
                   instruction gets data from register R
    R: 5   → stores value in CPU

d) 0: LDAC R
                   instruction gets address from register R
    R: 5
              then gets data from location 5
    5: 10   → stores value in CPU

e) 0: LDAC #5   → stores value from instruction in CPU

f) 0: LDAC (implicit)
              instruction gets value from stack
  stack   → stores value in CPU

g) 0: LDAC $5
    1:    instruction adds address of next instruction (1) to
    5:    offset (5) to get address (6)
    6: 12   → stories value in CPU

h) 0: LDAC 5(X)
                   instruction gets value from index register
    X: 10
              then adds contents of X (10) to offset (5) to get address (15)
   15: 30   → stores value in CPU

for each case, and the instructions needed to perform the operation $A = B + C$.

If a microprocessor uses three-operand instructions, its instruction code must have bit fields for the opcode and the three operands. In this example, the instruction code requires four bits for the opcode and two bits for each of the three operands, for a total of ten bits. This format is shown in Figure 3.4(a).

FIGURE 3.4

Instruction code formats and assembly language programs and machine code to calculate $A = B + C$ for (a) three-operand, (b) two-operand, (c) one-operand, and (d) zero-operand instructions

4 bits	2 bits	2 bits	2 bits
opcode	operand #1	operand #2	operand #3

ADD A,B,C $(A=B+C)$ 1010 00 01 10

(a)

4 bits	2 bits	2 bits
opcode	operand #1	operand #2

MOVE A,B $(A=B)$ 1000 00 01
ADD A,C $(A=A+C)$ 1010 00 10

(b)

4 bits	2 bits
opcode	operand

LOAD B $(Acc=B)$ 0000 01
ADD C $(Acc=Acc+C)$ 1010 10
STORE A $(A=Acc)$ 0001 00

(c)

4 bits
opcode

PUSH B $(Stack=B)$ 0101
PUSH C $(Stack=C,B)$ 0110
ADD $(Stack=B+C)$ 1010
POP A $(A=stack)$ 1100

(d)

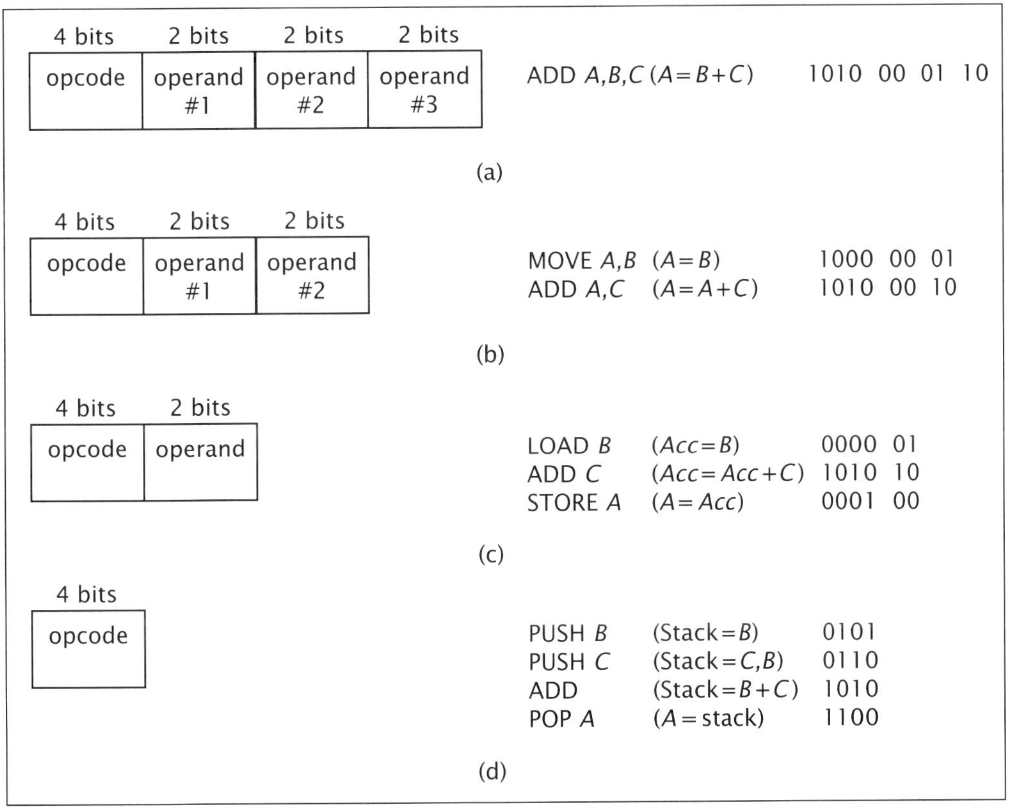

The assembly language program to perform the operation $A = B + C$ on this microprocessor is trivial; it consists of a single instruction. Figure 3.4(a) shows this assembly language program and its equivalent instruction code.

A microprocessor that uses two-operand instructions is more limited than a microprocessor that uses three-operand instructions, but its instruction codes use fewer bits. In two-operand instructions, the first operand is both the destination and one of the source operands. A single two-operand instruction cannot perform the operation $A = B + C$, but it can set $A = A + B$. As a result, it may require several instructions to perform an operation. Figure 3.4(b) shows the format of the two-operand instruction code for this example, along with the assembly language program and machine language code to perform the function $A = B + C$. (We define 1000 to be the opcode for the MOVE instruction.)

A one-operand instruction format becomes more difficult to use. For example, how do you add two values when you can only specify one operand? The trick to this is that an accumulator register is always the destination and one of the source registers. This is implicit and is not specified as part of the instruction code. Figure 3.4(c) shows the instruction code format and the assembly language and machine code needed to perform the operation $A = B + C$.

Finally, we consider the extreme, zero-operand case. In this case, all operands are drawn from a stack. A stack in a computer is sort of like a stack of trays in a cafeteria. You take (pop) a tray off the top of the stack. You enter the cafeteria, see what is being served, and lose your appetite. As you leave, you place (push) your tray back on to the top of the stack.

In computers, a stack works in a similar manner. You push data onto a stack and pop data off of the stack. Just as you deal with only the top of the stack of trays (unless you're one of those people who grabs a tray from the middle of the stack), you only interact with the top element of the stack. The computer only needs a pointer to that element to use the stack. A zero-operand computer pushes its operands onto the stack. An operation pops its operands off the top of the stack, performs its operation, and pushes its result back onto the stack. To store its result, a zero-operand computer pops the result off the stack into the appropriate destination. Figure 3.4(d) shows the instruction code format for zero-operand instructions and the assembly language and machine code to perform the operation $A = B + C$.

Looking at the code in Figure 3.4, we can see that fewer operands usually translates into more instructions to accomplish the same task. There isn't usually the perfect linear progression shown in this example, but the rule is valid. What isn't shown is that the hardware to implement the microprocessor becomes less complex as the number of operands decreases. In addition, microprocessors whose instructions specify fewer operands can usually execute instructions more quickly than those which specify more operands.

This example was simplified to illustrate the differences between three-, two-, one-, and zero-operand instructions. In practice, these instructions require many more bits than used in these examples. An operand field may specify an arbitrary memory address, rather than one of four registers. This could require 16, 32, or even more bits per operand. In addition, it may be necessary to include a few bits to specify one of the addressing modes for each operand.

3.3   Instruction Set Architecture Design

The design of an instruction set architecture is arguably the most important step in the design of a microprocessor. A poorly designed ISA, even if it is implemented well, leads to a bad microprocessor. A well-designed instruction set architecture, on the other hand, can result in a powerful microprocessor that can meet a variety of needs. This section examines some of the issues to be considered when designing an instruction set architecture.

There is no magic formula for designing instruction set architectures. The same requirements can lead to different ISA designs, each of which could be valid. As with many engineering designs, the designer must evaluate tradeoffs in performance and such constraining issues as size and cost when developing ISA specifications.

A good way to start designing an instruction set architecture is to decide what you want to have when you finish. Specifically, answer the question *What should the instruction set architecture and its processor be able to do*?

If the processor is to be used for general-purpose computing, such as in a personal computer, it will probably require quite a rich instruction set architecture. It will need a relatively large instruction set to perform the wide variety of tasks it must accomplish. It may also need many registers for some of these tasks. In contrast, consider a specialized processor, for example, one designed specifically to control a microwave oven. The tasks this processor must perform are known well in advance; these tasks are only those needed to control the oven. This is the issue of **completeness** of the instruction set architecture; that is, does the instruction set have all of the instructions a program needs to perform its required task?

At the other end of this argument is the issue of instruction **orthogonality**. Instructions are orthogonal if they do not overlap, or perform the same function. A good instruction set minimizes the overlap between instructions; this provides the programmer with the necessary functions in a minimum of instructions.

Consider an absurd example, a microprocessor with 10 different instructions that perform the exact same function, for example, a jump. A programmer needs only one of these jump instructions; the rest are redundant. However, each instruction adds extra hardware and complexity to the CPU, which must recognize and process all 10 instruction codes. The redundant instructions add to the cost of the CPU, but provide no benefit to the user. Eliminating the redundant instructions improves the orthogonality of the instruction set, while reducing the cost and complexity of the CPU.

Another area in which the designer can optimize the instruction set architecture is the register set. Registers have a large effect on the performance of a CPU. The CPU can store data in its internal registers instead of memory. The CPU can retrieve data from its registers much more quickly than from memory. For many program segments, such as program loops, having data in registers significantly speeds up program execution. Having too few registers causes a program to make more references to memory, thus reducing performance.

General-purpose CPUs have many registers, since they have to process different types of programs. Intel's Itanium microprocessor, for example, has 128 general-purpose registers for integer data and another 128 registers for floating-point data. For dedicated CPUs, this many registers would be overkill. (A microwave oven controller doesn't need this many registers; in fact, it doesn't need any floating-point registers at all.) Having too many registers adds unnecessary hardware to the CPU without providing any benefits.

In the next two sections we examine two instruction set architectures. We look at the issues of completeness, orthogonality, and register set design when we review these ISAs.

Some other design issues for instruction set architectures are raised by the following questions.

Does this processor have to be backward compatible with other microprocessors?
Backward compatibility could be an issue for special-purpose processors, but it is much more important for general-purpose microprocessors. Consider Intel's family of microprocessors used in personal computers. If the instruction set architecture of the Pentium II microprocessor were not backward compatible with the ISA of the Pentium microprocessor, it would not be able to run code written for the Pentium. This code includes Microsoft Windows, numerous word processors, spreadsheets, and other office productivity applications, as well as many programs written by companies for their own use. Without backward compatibility, users would have shunned the new processor rather than buy new programs and rewrite their own custom code; the new processor would have been a huge failure. In fact, Intel's Itanium processor contains hardware designed exclusively to maintain backward compatibility.

What types and sizes of data will the microprocessor deal with?
If a microprocessor will have to process floating-point data, for example, it is important to include instructions in the instruction set architecture that work on floating-point data. It is also necessary to incorporate registers to store floating-point values. (These registers may

be used exclusively for floating-point data, or they may be used for both floating-point and other data types. This is a decision to be made by the designers.) If, on the other hand, the processor does not use floating-point data, the microwave oven controller being one such processor, then these instructions introduce design costs without providing any benefit. They should be excluded from the ISA, as should any floating point registers that are not used for any other purpose.

Are interrupts needed?
Very few tasks absolutely require that a microprocessor have interrupts, but many tasks can be performed more efficiently if interrupts are incorporated into the microprocessor. The designers must examine the tasks to be performed when deciding whether or not to include interrupts in their design. If interrupts are included, the instruction set architecture must include the instructions and registers needed to process the interrupts.

Are conditional instructions needed?
As discussed in the previous section, a jump or branch instruction may be conditional; that is, some condition outside of the instruction determines whether or not the jump is taken. Microprocessors generally include **flags**, 1-bit registers that store the value of various conditions. Typical flags include the zero flag (set to 1 when an operation produces a result of zero), the carry flag (set to 1 when an arithmetic operation generates a carry out of 1), and the sign flag (set to 1 when an arithmetic operation on signed integers produces a negative result).

3.4   A Relatively Simple Instruction Set Architecture

This section describes the instruction set architecture of a Relatively Simple microprocessor, or central processing unit (CPU). This CPU was designed as an instructional aid and draws its features from several real microprocessors. This microprocessor is too limited to run anything as complex as a personal computer; however, it has about the right level of complexity to control a microwave oven or other consumer appliance. Here, we review the memory model, registers, and instruction set that comprise its instruction set architecture. In Chapters 4, 6, and 7, we examine its use in a computer system and the internal design of the microprocessor itself.

First let's take a look at the memory model. This microprocessor can access 64K ($= 2^{16}$) bytes of memory, with each byte having 8 bits, or 64K $\times$ 8 of memory. This does not mean that every computer constructed using this Relatively Simple CPU must have a full 64K of memory; a system based on this microprocessor can have less memory if it doesn't need the maximum 64K of memory.

In this processor, inputting data from and outputting data to external devices, such as the microwave oven's keypad and digital display, are treated as memory accesses. There are two types of input/output (I/O) interactions that you can design a CPU to perform. In isolated I/O, input and output devices are treated as being separate from memory. Different instructions access memory and I/O devices. Memory mapped I/O, on the other hand, treats I/O devices as memory locations; the CPU accesses these I/O devices using the same instructions that it uses to access memory. This is described in more detail in Chapter 4. For now, it is sufficient to know that no separate I/O instructions are needed in the instruction set of a microprocessor that uses memory mapped I/O, such as the Relatively Simple CPU described here.

There are three registers in the ISA of this processor. The first, the accumulator (*AC*), is an 8-bit register. As in many microprocessors, the accumulator of this CPU receives the result of any arithmetic or logical operation. It also provides one of the operands for arithmetic and logical instructions that use two operands. (This is similar to the one-operand instructions described earlier in this chapter.) Whenever data is loaded from memory, it is loaded in to the accumulator; data stored to memory also comes from *AC*.

Register *R* is an 8-bit general purpose register. It supplies the second operand of all two-operand arithmetic and logical instructions. It can also be used to store data that the accumulator will soon need to access.

Finally, there is a 1-bit zero flag, *Z*. There are no instructions that explicitly set *Z* to 0 or 1. (There is one exception to this, which really isn't an exception.) Instead, *Z* is set whenever an arithmetic or logical instruction is executed. If the result of the instruction is 0, then *Z* is set to 1 to indicate that a zero result was generated. Otherwise it is set to 0.

There are several other registers in this Relatively Simple CPU that cannot be directly accessed by the programmer. The processor uses them to access memory, to fetch instructions, and to store data temporarily as the CPU executes instructions. As such, these registers are a part of the CPU but are not a part of the instruction set architecture. We examine these additional registers and their functions when we design this CPU later in this text.

The final component of the instruction set architecture for this Relatively Simple CPU is its instruction set, shown in Table 3.1. The instruction set contains 16 instructions, each having an 8-bit instruction code. (Only 4 bits are needed to distinguish the 16 instructions; however, we will add more instructions to this instruction set later in this text. For now, it is sufficient to accept the instruction codes as presented.)

Table 3.1

Instruction set for a Relatively Simple CPU

Instruction	Instruction Code	Operation
NOP	0000 0000	No operation
LDAC	0000 0001 Γ	$AC = M[\Gamma]$
STAC	0000 0010 Γ	$M[\Gamma] = AC$
MVAC	0000 0011	$R = AC$
MOVR	0000 0100	$AC = R$
JUMP	0000 0101 Γ	GOTO Γ
JMPZ	0000 0110 Γ	IF (Z=1) THEN GOTO Γ
JPNZ	0000 0111 Γ	IF (Z=0) THEN GOTO Γ
ADD	0000 1000	$AC = AC + R$, If ($AC + R = 0$) Then $Z = 1$ Else $Z = 0$
SUB	0000 1001	$AC = AC - R$, If ($AC - R = 0$) Then $Z = 1$ Else $Z = 0$
INAC	0000 1010	$AC = AC + 1$, If ($AC + 1 = 0$) Then $Z = 1$ Else $Z = 0$
CLAC	0000 1011	$AC = 0$, $Z = 1$
AND	0000 1100	$AC = AC \wedge R$, If ($AC \wedge R = 0$) Then $Z = 1$ Else $Z = 0$
OR	0000 1101	$AC = AC \vee R$, If ($AC \vee R = 0$) Then $Z = 1$ Else $Z = 0$
XOR	0000 1110	$AC = AC \oplus R$, If ($AC \oplus R = 0$) Then $Z = 1$ Else $Z = 0$
NOT	0000 1111	$AC = AC'$, If ($AC' = 0$) Then $Z = 1$ Else $Z = 0$

The LDAC, STAC, JUMP, JMPZ, and JPNZ instructions all require a 16-bit memory address, represented here by Γ. Since each byte of memory is 8 bits wide, these instructions each require 3 bytes in memory. The first byte contains the opcode for the instruction and the last two bytes contain the address. Following the convention used by Intel's 8085 microprocessor, described in the next section, the second byte will contain the low-order 8 bits of the address and the third byte will contain the high-order 8 bits of the address. For example, consider the following instruction; the H in 1234H indicates that this is data in hexadecimal format.

25:    JUMP 1234H

The instruction would be stored in memory as

25:    0000 0101 (JUMP)
26:    0011 0100 (34H)
27:    0001 0010 (12H)

Figure 3.5 shows the instruction formats for the Relatively Simple CPU.

Instruction formats for the Relatively Simple CPU: (a) 3-byte and (b) 1-byte formats

byte 1	Instruction code
byte 2	Low-order 8 bits of Γ
byte 3	High-order 8 bits of Γ

(a)

byte 1	Instruction code

(b)

The instructions in this instruction set can be grouped into the categories of instruction types described earlier in this chapter. However, the NOP instruction, which performs no operation, doesn't fit easily into any category; for now, we'll throw it in with the data movement instructions.

The NOP, LDAC, STAC, MVAC, and MOVR instructions are data transfer instructions. The NOP performs no operation. The LDAC operation loads data from memory. It reads the data from memory location Γ, denoted M[Γ], and stores it in the accumulator register AC. The STAC operation does the opposite, copying data from AC to memory location Γ. The LDAC instruction uses the direct addressing mode. The MVAC instruction copies the data in AC to register R, and the MOVR instruction copies data from R to AC. The MOVR instruction uses the implicit addressing mode.

There are three program control instructions in this instruction set: JUMP, JMPZ, and JPNZ. The JUMP instruction is unconditional; it always jumps to location Γ. For example, the JUMP 1234H instruction always jumps to location 1234H. The JUMP instruction uses the immediate addressing mode, since the jump address is specified in the instruction. The other two program control instructions, JMPZ and JPNZ, are conditional. If their conditions are met, $Z = 1$ for JMPZ and $Z = 0$ for JPNZ, these instructions jump to address Γ; otherwise they continue on with the next instruction. Consider a JMPZ 1234H instruction stored at location 25 in memory:

25:     JMPZ 1234H

As with the JUMP instruction, this JMPZ instruction is stored at locations 25, 26, and 27. If $Z = 1$, the jump is taken and the processor next executes the instruction at address 1234H. However, if $Z = 0$, the jump is not taken. Instead, the CPU continues with the next instruction, which is found in memory location 28.

Finally there are the data operation instructions. The ADD, SUB, INAC, and CLAC instructions are arithmetic instructions. The ADD instruction adds the contents of AC and R, storing their sum back in AC. This instruction also sets the zero flag Z to 1 if the sum is 0, or to 0 if the sum is any nonzero value. The SUB instruction works in a similar manner, except it subtracts the value in R from the value in AC. The INAC instruction adds 1 to the value in AC and sets Z to its proper value.

The CLAC instruction appears to treat Z differently than the other data operation instructions, but it actually does not. As its primary operation, this instruction sets AC to 0. It also always sets Z to 1. In the other instructions, Z is set to 1 only if the result of the operation is 0; Z is set to 0 whenever the result is any nonzero value. You could think of this instruction as setting Z in this way. Since the result of the operation is always 0, though, Z would always be set to 1. For this instruction, always setting Z to 1 is equivalent to conditionally setting Z to 1 when the instruction sets AC to 0.

The last four data operation instructions are logical instructions. As their names imply, the AND, OR, and XOR instructions logically AND, OR, and XOR the values in AC and R, storing the result in AC. The NOT instruction sets AC to its bitwise complement. As with the arithmetic instruction, these logic instructions also set Z to 1 whenever the result of the operation is 0, and set Z to 0 otherwise. The AND and OR instructions use the implied addressing mode.

To illustrate the use of this instruction set architecture, we can examine a program to perform a simple task. The Relatively Simple CPU must be programmed to calculate the sum

$$1 + 2 + \cdots + n, \text{ or } \sum_{i=1}^{n} i$$

This could be written as a high-level language code snippet as follows.

$$total = 0;$$
$$\text{FOR } i = 1 \text{ TO } n \text{ DO } \{total = total + i\};$$

When implementing this using the Relatively Simple instruction set architecture, we store the value n in a memory location labeled n, and the result in a memory location labeled *total*. Memory location i is used to store the value of the sum counter. (The labels n, *total*, and i are absolute memory addresses. If it helps to visualize how the code works, consider them to have the values 1000H, 1001H, and 1002H.)

This already points out one of the obvious shortcomings of the Relatively Simple instruction set architecture, a lack of internal registers. Most ISAs include many general purpose registers for storing data. The code for this function spends a significant amount of time interacting with memory to load and store these values. Later in this chapter, we write the code to perform the same task using the 8085 microprocessor. Its larger register set reduces the size of the program needed to perform the same task.

Before writing the actual code, we must determine the steps needed to perform the required function. The following algorithm, used for this example, calculates the total properly.

> **1:** $total = 0, i = 0$
> **2:** $i = i + 1$
> **3:** $total = total + i$
> **4:** IF $i \neq n$ THEN GOTO **2**

The Relatively Simple CPU code to implement this algorithm is as follows. Comments indicate how the code corresponds to the statements in the algorithm.

```
          CLAC        ⎫
          STAC total  ⎬  total = 0, i = 0
          STAC i      ⎭
  Loop:   LDAC i      ⎫
          INAC        ⎬  i = i + 1
          STAC i      ⎭
          MVAC        ⎫
          LDAC total  ⎪
          ADD         ⎬  total = total + i
          STAC total  ⎭
          LDAC n      ⎫
          SUB         ⎬  IF i ≠ n THEN GOTO Loop
          JPNZ Loop   ⎭
```

The first block of statements sets *total* and *i* to 0 by clearing the accumulator and storing this value in these two memory locations. The next block, which sets $i = i + 1$, is self-explanatory. Note that this leaves the new value of *i* in the accumulator register, AC. The next four statements perform the operation $total = total + i$. First *i* is copied from AC to R; then *total* is loaded into AC. The two are added and the result is stored in memory. The last three instructions check for the end of the loop. The value n is loaded into AC and the value of *i*, still stored in register R, is subtracted from it. If they are equal, this will set AC to 0 and $Z = 1$; otherwise the Z flag will be set to 0. If Z is 0, the last instruction jumps back to the loop to perform another iteration. If $Z = 1$, however, $i = n$ and the algorithm terminates. The CPU continues by executing whatever instruction comes after the JPNZ *Loop* instruction. Table 3.2 shows a trace of the code for $n = 5$.

There are some limits to this algorithm. Since the result is stored in a single 8-bit memory location, it cannot have a value greater than

Table 3.2

Execution trace of the loop summation program

Instruction	1st Loop	2nd Loop	3rd Loop	4th Loop	5th Loop
CLAC	$AC = 0$				
STAC *total*	*total* = 0				
STAC *i*	$i = 0$				
LDAC *i*	$AC = 0$	$AC = 1$	$AC = 2$	$AC = 3$	$AC = 4$
INAC	$AC = 1$	$AC = 2$	$AC = 3$	$AC = 4$	$AC = 5$
STAC *i*	$i = 1$	$i = 2$	$i = 3$	$i = 4$	$i = 5$
MVAC	$R = 1$	$R = 2$	$R = 3$	$R = 4$	$R = 5$
LDAC *total*	$AC = 0$	$AC = 1$	$AC = 3$	$AC = 6$	$AC = 10$
ADD	$AC = 1$	$AC = 3$	$AC = 6$	$AC = 10$	$AC = 15$
STAC *total*	*total* = 1	*total* = 3	*total* = 6	*total* = 10	*total* = 15
LDAC *n*	$AC = 5$	$AC = 5$	$AC = 5$	$AC = 5$	$AC = 5$
SUB	$AC = 4$, $Z = 0$	$AC = 3$, $Z = 0$	$AC = 2$, $Z = 0$	$AC = 1$, $Z = 0$	$AC = 0$, $Z = 1$
JPNZ *Loop*	JUMP	JUMP	JUMP	JUMP	NO JUMP

255 (FFH). Therefore, n must be less than or equal to 22; any larger value generates a result greater than 255. Also, since i is incremented before it is compared to n, n cannot be 0. Thus, this program works only for $1 \le n \le 22$.

What do you think of this instruction set architecture? It does meet its goal of being an instructional aid. As we will see when we design this CPU in Chapters 6 and 7, it is complex enough to illustrate many CPU design principles without getting bogged down in its own complexity. However, as a practical CPU it leaves something to be desired.

First of all, is its instruction set complete? For simple applications, the answer may be yes. It has enough different instructions to perform many tasks. It would be nice to have some additional instructions—for example, to decrement the accumulator—but this is not absolutely essential. If the application uses floating point data, then this instruction set is not sufficiently complete without specific floating point instructions. For general purpose computers, such as personal computers, this instruction set is woefully inadequate.

This instruction set is fairly orthogonal. We could use DeMorgan's Law to implement a logical OR using the AND and NOT instructions, and delete the OR instruction from the instruction set. However, it is much quicker to logically OR two values with a single OR instruction.

Here, it is preferable to be a little less orthogonal; the improved performance of the CPU with the OR instruction justifies the extra hardware needed in the CPU. Sometimes a CPU's instruction set is better when it is not completely orthogonal.

The register set for this ISA is its weakest point. Looking back at the code to generate the sum $1 + 2 + \cdots + n$, we see that the loop counter i is stored in memory. Every time we increment the counter, we load it into the CPU from memory, increment it, and store it back into memory. We also store the sum, *total*, in memory. If this CPU had more general purpose registers, we could store both values within the CPU and remove most of the memory access instructions from the program. This would greatly speed up the program. The lack of registers in this ISA results in slower task execution and decreased performance.

3.5 Real World Example: The 8085 Microprocessor Instruction Set Architecture

This section examines the instruction set architecture of Intel's 8085 microprocessor. The Intel 8085 is more complex than the Relatively Simple CPU, but not so complex as to overwhelm the student with details. In spite of its simplicity and age (the 8085 was developed over 20 years ago), this processor still has practical applications, such as the Sojourner robot mentioned earlier in this chapter.

3.5.1 The 8085 Microprocessor Register Set

Register sets that are very limited, such as that of the Relatively Simple CPU, are easy to implement in hardware. However, you pay for this simplicity with larger programs. For example, much of the code for the program to calculate a sum read data from and wrote data to memory. If there were more registers within the CPU, we could have stored data in these registers instead. This would have simplified the code needed to add the numbers.

For this reason, the 8085 microprocessor contains several general purpose data registers. As in the Relatively Simple CPU, the 8085 has an accumulator register, *A*. This register always receives the result of an 8-bit arithmetic or logical instruction; it also provides one of the operands for all such instructions that use two operands.

The 8085 has six general purpose registers, named *B*, *C*, *D*, *E*, *H*, and *L*. Many instructions access these registers individually, although some access them in pairs. The pairs are not arbitrary; *B* and *C* are always a pair, as are *D* and *E*, and *H* and *L*. Register pair *HL* is often used to point to a memory location. This microprocessor uses a stack; it includes a 16-bit stack pointer register, *SP*, which contains the address of the top of the stack.

HISTORICAL PERSPECTIVE: Intel's Early Microprocessors

Today's microprocessors, running at clock frequencies of 1GHz (one billion cycles per second) or more, come from humble beginnings. Intel's first general purpose microprocessor, the 4004, was introduced in 1971. It processed 4-bit data values and had an instruction set with 45 instructions. It could address only 4Kb of memory and ran at a then-blazing speed of 740 KHz.

The following year, Intel expanded on this design to create the 8008, the first 8-bit general purpose microprocessor. Its memory limit was enhanced to 16 Kb, and its maximum clock frequency was raised to 800 KHz. Its instruction set was also increased to 48 instructions.

In 1974, Intel introduced its next 8-bit microprocessor, the 8080. This processor was backward compatible with the machine code of the 8008; it was Intel's first microprocessor to exhibit this feature. It had 72 instructions, addressed 64 Kb of memory, and had a clock frequency of 2 MHz.

The 8085 microprocessor debuted in 1977. It was backward compatible with the machine code of the 8080 (and hence with the 8008), and could also address 64 Kb of memory. It used the same instruction set as the 8080 microprocessor, except it added two instructions dealing with interrupts. It ran at 6.25 MHz.

In 1978, Intel introduced its 8086 microprocessor. Unlike Intel's previous microprocessors, and all Intel microprocessors that followed it, this one was not backward compatible with its predecessors. This microprocessor was used in the original IBM personal computer and started a succession of microprocessors that continues today.

The 8085 microprocessor has five flags, collectively referred to as the **flag register**: They are listed below.

- The **sign flag**, S, indicates the sign of a value calculated by an arithmetic or logical instruction. In two's complement notation, a value with a 1 as its most significant bit is negative; a leading 0 indicates a positive (or zero) value. An instruction that modifies S sets its value to the most significant bit of its result.
- The **zero flag**, Z, works the same as in the Relatively Simple CPU. It is set to 1 if an arithmetic or logical instruction produces a result of 0; it is set to 0 otherwise.
- The **parity flag**, P, is set to 1 if the result of an arithmetic or logical operation has an even number of 1's; otherwise it is set to 0.
- The **carry flag**, CY, is set when an arithmetic operation generates a carry out. For example, the addition 1111 0000 + 1000 0000

= 1 0111 0000 adds two 8-bit values but generates a 9-bit result. The left-most 1 is stored in *CY*; if the addition did not generate a carry out of 1, a 0 would be stored in *CY* instead.

- The **auxiliary carry flag**, *AC*, is similar to the carry flag. Instead of indicating a carry out, however, it denotes a carry from the lower half of the result to the upper half. Consider the addition 0000 1111 + 0000 1000 = 0001 0111. This addition generated a carry from the lower half (bit 3) to the upper half (bit 4) in the result. This is primarily used with binary coded decimal operations, discussed in Chapter 8.

One other register in the 8085 microprocessor that is part of its instruction set architecture is interrupt mask, *IM*, used to enable and disable interrupts, and to check for pending interrupts. The programmer can read and set the values in this register to process interrupts.

3.5.2 The 8085 Microprocessor Instruction Set

The 8085 instruction set contains a total of 74 instructions. Using the classification introduced earlier, we break the instruction set into three parts: data movement instructions, data operation instructions, and program control instructions. Note the following conventions used for all instructions.

- *r*, *r*1 and *r*2 indicate any 8-bit register *A, B, C, D, E, H,* or *L*.
- *M* indicates a memory location. When a location is represented as *M[HL]*, the address of the memory location is stored in register pair *HL*.
- *rp* indicates register pair *BC, DE, HL*, or the stack pointer *SP*. By convention, the register pairs are represented by the first register of the pair: *B* for *BC*, *D* for *DE*, and *H* for *HL*.
- Γ is a 16-bit address or data value. As in the Relatively Simple CPU, the low-order 8 bits of Γ are stored in the memory location directly following the opcode, and the high-order 8 bits are stored in the next location.
- *n* is an 8-bit address or data value stored in memory immediately after the opcode.
- *cond* is a condition for conditional instructions. It can have the following values.

NZ ($Z = 0$)	Z ($Z = 1$)
P ($S = 0$)	N ($S = 1$)
PO ($P = 0$)	PE ($P = 1$)
NC ($CY = 0$)	C ($CY = 1$)

What follows is a whirlwind tour of the 8085 instruction set. It introduces the basic functions of the instructions, but not their intricate details. The reader should refer to an 8085 reference manual for more details on this instruction set.

The data movement instructions are shown in Table 3.3, along with the operations they perform. None of these instructions, except for the POP PSW instruction, modify the values of the flags.

Table 3.3

Data movement instruction for the 8085 microprocessor

Instruction	Operation	Instruction	Operation
NOP	No operation	LDAX rp	$A = M[rp]$ $(rp = BC, DE)$
MOV $r1$, $r2$	$r1 = r2$	STAX rp	$M[rp] = A$ $(rp = BC, DE)$
MOV r, M	$r = M[HL]$	XCHG	$DE \leftrightarrow HL$
MOV M, r	$M[HL] = r$	PUSH rp	Stack $= rp$ $(rp \neq SP)$
MVI r, n	$r = n$	PUSH PSW	Stack $= A$, flag register
MVI M, n	$M[HL] = n$	POP rp	$rp =$ Stack $(rp \neq SP)$
LXI rp, Γ	$rp = \Gamma$	POP PSW	A, flag register $=$ Stack
LDA Γ	$A = M[\Gamma]$	XTHL	$HL \leftrightarrow$ Stack
STA Γ	$M[\Gamma] = A$	SPHL	$SP = HL$
LHLD Γ	$HL = M[\Gamma], M[\Gamma+1]$	IN n	$A =$ input port n
SHDL Γ	$M[\Gamma], M[\Gamma+1] = HL$	OUT n	output port $n = A$

The MOV instructions move data from one place to another, either between registers or between a register and memory. When MOV moves data to or from memory, it uses the 16-bit value in register pair HL as the memory address. The MVI instruction is an immediate mode instruction that moves the data specified in the instruction to the register or data location specified; again, HL contains the address of the memory location. For example, if $HL = 1234H$, the instruction MVI M, 56 moves the data value 56 to memory location 1234H. The LXI instruction is a 16-bit immediate move; it loads its data (Γ) into the register pair specified by the instruction.

LDA and STA are direct mode instructions similar to the LDAC and STAC instructions in the Relatively Simple CPU. They transfer data between the memory location at address Γ and the accumulator register A. The LHLD and SHLD instructions move data between register pair HL and memory. The LDAX and STAX instructions are similar to the MOV r, M and MOV M, r instructions, except they only move data to and from register A, and register pairs BC or DE supply the memory address instead of HL. The XCHG instruction swaps the contents of register pairs DE and HL.

The 8085 microprocessor can control a stack in memory. The PUSH rp operation pushes the contents of a register pair onto the stack. This is useful for saving values before executing a subroutine. To save the contents of the accumulator and the flags, collectively called the **processor status word** or **PSW**, the 8085 has the PUSH PSW instruction. The POP *rp* and POP PSW instructions are the opposite of the PUSH instructions; they read data off of the stack and write it into the appropriate registers. The XTHL instruction exchanges the top two elements of the stack with the contents of register pair *HL*, and the SPHL instruction copies the contents of register pair *HL* to the stack pointer *SP*.

The last two data movement instructions interact with external devices. Unlike the Relatively Simple CPU, the 8085 microprocessor uses isolated I/O. Separate instructions access memory and input/output devices; the IN and OUT instructions access I/O devices for this microprocessor. Unlike memory, which uses a 16-bit address, I/O ports on the 8085 microprocessor only have 8-bit addresses. Since it is unlikely that this CPU would ever have to interact with more than 256 different I/O devices, this limitation on I/O address size is quite reasonable.

Figure 3.6 shows the general instruction formats for these instructions. Some instructions have fields to specify registers, while others are fixed.

Table 3.4 shows the data operation instructions for the 8085 microprocessor. Most, though not all, instructions in this class affect the flags, as indicated in the table.

The ADD, ADI, SUB, and SUI instructions add and subtract data. As before, the memory address for the ADD *M* and SUB *M* instructions is stored in register pair *HL*; instructions that do this use an implied register indirect mode. The ADC, ACI, SBB, and SBI instructions do the same, except that they include the carry bit *CY* in their computations. This bit is added to the sum or subtracted from the difference generated by the instruction.

The INR and DCR instructions increment (add 1 to) or decrement (subtract 1 from) the contents of a register or memory. These instructions do not modify the carry flag, but they do affect the other flags. The INX and DCX instructions increment and decrement register pairs, treating them as a single 16-bit value. The DAD instruction adds the contents of the specified register pair to the contents of *HL*; this instruction affects only the carry flag. The DAA instruction adjusts data to a valid binary coded decimal format.

The ANA, ANI, ORA, ORI, XRA, and XRI instructions perform logical AND, OR, and XOR operations. The CMP and CPI instructions compare the contents of *A* and the specified value by performing the subtraction *A* − *value*. However, these instructions do not store the result of the subtraction; they only use the computation to set the values of the flags.

The RLC, RRC, RAL, and RAR instructions rotate data in the accumulator; they all set the carry flag. Finally, the CMA, CMC, and STC instructions complement the contents of the accumulator and carry flag, and set the carry flag to 1.

FIGURE 3.6

Instruction formats for the 8085 microprocessor: (a) one-byte, (b) two-byte, and
(c) three-byte formats

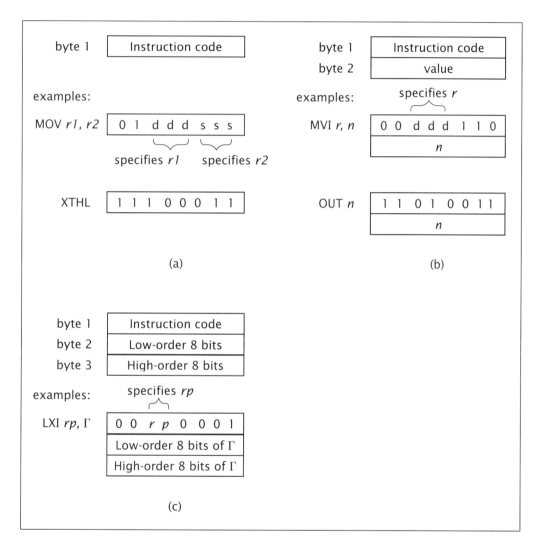

(a)

(b)

(c)

Table 3.5 shows the remaining 13 program control instructions.
DI, EI, RIM, and SIM are included here because they deal with interrupts, which ultimately affect program control. None of these instructions modify the flags.

The JUMP and J*cond* operations jump as in the Relatively Simple
CPU. If the condition is met (or always for the JUMP instruction), the
microprocessor jumps to address Γ. (If the condition is not met, the
microprocessor simply proceeds to the next instruction.) The PCHL instruction jumps to the address stored in register pair *HL*.

Table 3.4

Data operation instruction for the 8085 microprocessor

Instruction	Operation	Flags
ADD r	$A = A + r$	All
ADD M	$A = A + M[HL]$	All
ADI n	$A = A + n$	All
ADC r	$A = A + r + CY$	All
ADC M	$A = A + M[HL] + CY$	All
ACI n	$A = A + n + CY$	All
SUB r	$A = A - r$	All
SUB M	$A = A - M[HL]$	All
SUI n	$A = A - n$	All
SBB r	$A = A - r - CY$	All
SBB M	$A = A - M[HL] - CY$	All
SBI n	$A = A - n - CY$	All
INR r	$r = r + 1$	Not CY
INR M	$M[HL] = M[HL] + 1$	Not CY
DCR n	$r = r - 1$	Not CY
DCR M	$M[HL] = M[HL] - 1$	Not CY
INX rp	$rp = rp + 1$	None
DCX rp	$rp = rp - 1$	None
DAD rp	$HL = HL + rp$	CY
DAA	Decimal adjust	All

Instruction	Operation	Flags
ANA r	$A = A \wedge r$	All
ANA M	$A = A \wedge M[HL]$	All
ANI n	$A = A \wedge n$	All
ORA r	$A = A \vee r$	All
ORA M	$A = A \vee M[HL]$	All
ORI n	$A = A \vee n$	All
XRA r	$A = A \oplus r$	All
XRA M	$A = A \oplus M[HL]$	All
XRI n	$A = A \oplus n$	All
CMP r	Compare A and r	All
CMP M	Compare A and M[HL]	All
CPI n	Compare A and n	All
RLC	$CY = A_7, A = A_{6-0}, A_7$	CY
RRC	$CY = A_0, A = A_0, A_{7-1}$	CY
RAL	$CY, A = A, CY$	CY
RAR	$A, CY = CY, A$	CY
CMA	$A = A'$	None
CMC	$CY = CY'$	CY
STC	$CY = 1$	CY

The CALL and C*cond* instructions call a subroutine. To do this, they push the return address—the address of the next instruction—onto the stack and jump to address Γ. The RET and R*cond* instructions return from a subroutine by popping the return address off of the stack and jumping to that address. RSTn is the restart instruction. It is a software interrupt, and acts like a subroutine call. It pushes its return address onto the stack and goes to the appropriate location.

The RIM and SIM instructions move data between the interrupt mask, *IM*, and register *A*. While in *A*, the processor can set or reset individual mask bits. The DI and EI instructions disable and enable interrupts. Finally, the HLT instruction halts the operations of the microprocessor.

3.5.3 A Simple 8085 Program

As in the previous section, we examine a program that calculates the sum $1 + 2 + \cdots + n$ and stores it in memory location *total*. The value *n* is initially stored in a memory location labeled *n*.

Table 3.5

Program control instruction for the 8085 microprocessor

Instruction	Operation
JUMP Γ	GOTO Γ
J*cond* Γ	If condition is true then GOTO Γ
PCHL	GOTO address in *HL*
CALL Γ	Call subroutine at Γ
C*cond* Γ	If condition is true then call subroutine at Γ
RET	Return from subroutine
R*cond*	If condition is true then return from subroutine
RSTn	Call subroutine at 8*n (n = 5.5, 6.5, 7.5)
RIM	$A = IM$
SIM	$IM = A$
DI	Disable interrupts
EI	Enable interrupts
HLT	Halt the CPU

When developing this program, we calculate the sum as $n + (n - 1) + \cdots + 1$. As will be seen in the code, this generates the same result while simplifying the program. This program follows the algorithm

1: $i = n, sum = 0$
2: $sum = sum + i, i = i - 1$
3: IF $i \neq 0$ THEN GOTO **2**
4: $total = sum$

Unlike the program for the Relatively Simple CPU, the 8085 program stores its working values in CPU registers. Register B will hold the value i, and *sum* will be stored in register A. This reduces the number of memory accesses, resulting in a shorter, faster program. The 8085 code to perform this algorithm is

```
         LDA n     } i = n
         MOV B, A  }
         XRA A     } sum = A ⊕ A = 0
 Loop:   ADD B     } sum = sum + i
         DCR B     } i = i - 1
         JNZ Loop  } IF i ≠ 0 THEN GOTO Loop
         STA total } total = sum
```

This program requires only seven instructions, as opposed to 13 for the Relatively Simple CPU program. Its loop section, which is executed n times, has only three instructions; the same loop for the Relatively Simple CPU program has 10 instructions. Its trace for $n = 5$ is shown in Table 3.6.

Table 3.6

Execution trace of the 8085 loop summation program

Instruction	1st Loop	2nd Loop	3rd Loop	4th Loop	5th Loop
LDA n MOV B, A	$B = 5$				
XRA A	$A = 0$				
ADD B	$A = 5$	$A = 9$	$A = 12$	$A = 14$	$A = 15$
DCR B	$B = 4,$ $Z = 0$	$B = 3,$ $Z = 0$	$B = 2,$ $Z = 0$	$B = 1,$ $Z = 0$	$B = 0,$ $Z = 1$
JNZ $Loop$	JUMP	JUMP	JUMP	JUMP	NO JUMP
STA $total$					$total = 15$

Note that this program initially sets $i = n$ and decrements it once per iteration of the loop. This is done to avoid the final comparison with n. In the Relatively Simple CPU program, we incremented i during every iteration of the loop and then checked to see whether it was equal to n. In this program, we start at n and decrement once per loop iteration; we must check to see whether i has reached 0. The DCR instruction performs both tasks. It decrements the value i and sets the Z flag as part of the decrement operation. When $B = 0$, Z is set to 1 and the JNZ instruction does not jump, thus exiting the loop.

3.5.4 ANALYZING THE 8085 INSTRUCTION SET ARCHITECTURE

The 8085 microprocessor certainly has a larger ISA than the Relatively Simple CPU, but is it better? To answer this question, we examine the 8085 instruction set architecture for completeness, orthogonality, and register set design.

The 8085 microprocessor's instruction set is more complete than that of the Relatively Simple CPU and is suitable for such applications as the microwave oven controller. However, it is not sufficient for more complex applications, such as personal computers.

One clear advantage of the 8085's ISA as opposed to that of the Relatively Simple CPU is its ability to use subroutines. For many applications, subroutines reduce the amount of code needed; the Relatively Simple CPU has no mechanism for handling subroutines. The 8085 microprocessor also incorporates interrupts, and its instruction set has everything the programmer needs in order to process interrupts. However, like the Relatively Simple CPU, it cannot easily process floating point data.

The instruction set is also fairly orthogonal. For example, note that there is no clear accumulator instruction in the 8085's instruction set. The instruction XRA A exclusive ORs the accumulator with itself, which always sets *A* to 0. A separate clear accumulator instruction would have been redundant.

The register set for the 8085 is mostly sufficient. As shown in the simple program loop, it has enough registers to store a limited number of parameters during program execution, and thus avoid memory accesses which slow down task completion. The 8085 also has more flags than the Relatively Simple CPU. It would be nice to have a few extra registers, but the registers in this ISA are sufficient for most tasks.

3.6 SUMMARY

Specifying the instruction set architecture is the first, and arguably most important, step in the process of designing a microprocessor. The ISA specifies the microprocessor as seen from the outside. It includes the instruction set that the microprocessor can process, its user accessible registers, and how it interacts with memory. The instruction set architecture does not specify how the processor is designed, just what it must be able to do.

Programming languages vary in level and functionality. A high-level language, such as C++, must be compiled and linked to form a machine language program. An assembly language program is assembled to produce a machine language program. The microprocessor actually executes this machine language program, not the original high-level or assembly language program. Java applets follow a different path; they are compiled to bytecodes that are executed by a virtual machine. The virtual machine is a program that runs on a computer; it inputs the bytecode and performs the functions of its original Java program. The instruction set architecture is concerned only with the machine language (and thus assembly language) of a microprocessor.

When designing an ISA, an important goal is completeness, that is, ensuring that the ISA allows a designer to accomplish the desired goal. The instruction set should include the instructions needed to program all desired tasks. The instructions should be orthogonal, minimizing overlap, to reduce the digital logic within the microprocessor without reducing its capabilities. The processor should also include enough registers to minimize memory accesses, thus improving performance.

An ISA specifies not only an instruction set, but also the types of data these instructions process. The ISA also specifies the addressing modes each instruction can use, and the format for each instruction.

Problems

1 A microprocessor instruction set includes the following instructions. Classify each instruction as data movement, data operation, or program control.

    a) XTOY ($X = Y$)
    b) CLX ($X = 0$)
    c) JX Γ (IF $X = 1$ THEN GOTO Γ)
    d) XMLY ($X = X * Y$)
    e) XNEG ($X = X' + 1$)

2 Repeat problem 1 for the following instructions.

    a) ANTB ($A = A \wedge B'$)
    b) J55 (GOTO 55)
    c) XSTY (M[X] = Y)
    d) A2BC ($B = A$, $C = A$)
    e) INBC ($BC = BC + 1$)

3 What addressing mode is used by each of the following instructions for the Relatively Simple CPU?

    a) JPNZ Γ
    b) MVAC
    c) NOT

4 What addressing mode is used by each of the following instructions for the Relatively Simple CPU?

    a) MOVR
    b) JMPZ Γ
    c) SUB

5 What addressing mode is used by each of the following instructions for the Relatively Simple CPU?

    a) CLAC
    b) STAC Γ
    c) XOR

6 What addressing mode is used by each of the following instructions for the 8085 microprocessor?

    a) MOV $r1$, $r2$
    b) LXI rp, Γ
    c) SPHL
    d) ACI n
    e) JUMP Γ

7 What addressing mode is used by each of the following instructions for the 8085 microprocessor?

    a) R*cond*
    b) LDA Γ
    c) LHLD Γ
    d) LDAX *rp*
    e) ORA *r*

8 What addressing mode is used by each of the following instructions for the 8085 microprocessor?

    a) SUB *r*
    b) ORA *M*
    c) RAL
    d) CMC
    e) XRI *n*

9 Given $R = 10$, $PC = 20$, and index register $X = 30$, show the value of the accumulator for the following instructions. All memory locations Q contain the value $Q + 1$. Each instruction uses two memory locations.

    a) LDAC 10
    b) LDAC (10)
    c) LDAC *R*
    d) LDAC @*R*
    e) LDAC #10
    f) LDAC $10
    g) LDAC 10(X)

10 Repeat Problem 9 for $R = 30$, $PC = 10$, and $X = 20$.

11 Repeat Problem 9 for $R = 20$, $PC = 30$, and $X = 10$.

12 Show the code to perform the computation $X = A + (B * C) + D$ using microprocessors that use the following instruction formats. Do not modify the values of A, B, C, and D. If necessary, use temporary location T to store intermediate results.

    a) three-operand instructions
    b) two-operand instructions
    c) one-operand instructions
    d) zero-operand instructions

13 Repeat Problem 12 for the computation $X = A * B * C + D * (E + F)$. Do not modify the values of A, B, C, D, E, and F. If necessary, use temporary location T to store intermediate results.

14   Repeat Problem 12 for the computation $X = (A - (B * C)) * (D + E * F)$. Do not modify the values of $A, B, C, D, E,$ and F. If necessary, use temporary location T to store intermediate results.

15   If the code is to calculate $A = B + C$, given in Section 3.2, microprocessors require the following amounts of time to fetch, decode, and execute each instruction. Which microprocessor calculates A the fastest?

Microprocessor	Instruction Type	Time per instruction
Microprocessor 0	zero-operand instructions	35 ns
Microprocessor 1	one-operand instructions	50 ns
Microprocessor 2	two-operand instructions	70 ns
Microprocessor 3	three-operand instructions	100 ns

16   The code you wrote for Problem 12 is run on microprocessors with the instruction times given in Problem 15. Which processor calculates $X = A + (B * C) + D$ the fastest?

17   The code you wrote for Problem 13 is run on microprocessors with the instruction times given in Problem 15. Which processor calculates $X = A * B * C + D * (E + F)$ the fastest?

18   The code you wrote for Problem 14 is run on microprocessors with the instruction times given in Problem 15. Which processor calculates $X = (A - (B * C)) * (D + E * F)$ the fastest?

19   Write a program for the Relatively Simple CPU to add the ten values in memory locations 1001H through 100AH and store the result in memory location 1000H. Assume the result will always be less than 256.

20   Repeat Problem 19 for the 8085 microprocessor.

21   Write a program for the Relatively Simple CPU to calculate the Fibonacci value $f(n)$, where $f(0) = f(1) = 1$ and $f(n) = f(n - 1) + f(n - 2)$ for $n > 1$. Assume that $n > 1$ and that it is stored in memory location n, and that the result will always be less than 256.

22   Repeat Problem 21 for the 8085 microprocessor.

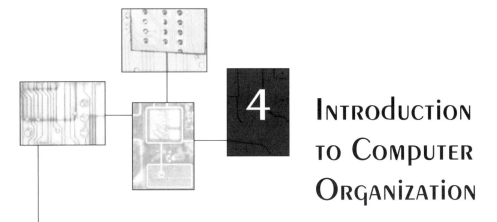

4 Introduction to Computer Organization

The instruction set architecture, described in Chapter 3, provides a good description of what a microprocessor can do, but it provides virtually no information on how to use the microprocessor. The ISA describes the instructions that the microprocessor can process, but says nothing about how the processor accesses these instructions. A system designer needs more information than the ISA provides in order to design a complete computer system.

In this chapter, we examine the organization of basic computer systems. A simple computer has three primary subsystems. The **central processing unit**, or **CPU**, performs many operations and controls the computer. A **microprocessor** usually serves as the computer's CPU. The **memory** subsystem is used to store programs being executed by the CPU, along with the program's data. The **input/output**, or **I/O**, subsystem allows the CPU to interact with input and output devices, such as the keyboard and monitor of a personal computer, or the keypad and digital display of a microwave oven.

This chapter begins with an overview of basic system organization, including the system buses used by the CPU, memory subsystem, and I/O subsystem to communicate with each other. Next, we examine the three system components in more detail. We describe the functionality and organization of each component, as well as its interface with the rest of the computer system. Finally we look at the organization of two computer systems, one based on the Relatively Simple CPU, introduced in Chapter 3, and another based on Intel's 8085 microprocessor. In later chapters, we examine the subsystems and system architecture in greater detail.

4.1 Basic Computer Organization

Most computer systems, from the embedded controllers found in automobiles and consumer appliances to personal computers and mainframes, have the same basic organization. This organization has three main components: the CPU, the memory subsystem, and the I/O subsystem. We discuss each of these components in more detail later in this chapter. The generic organization of these components is shown in Figure 4.1.

Figure 4.1

Generic computer organization

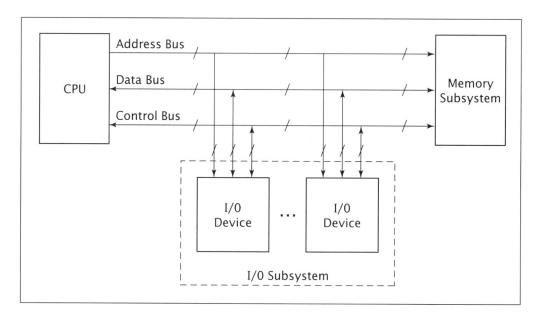

In this section, we first describe the system buses used to connect the components in the computer system. Then we examine the instruction cycle, the sequence of operations that occurs within the computer as it fetches, decodes, and executes an instruction.

4.1.1 System Buses

Physically, a **bus** is a set of wires. The components of the computer are connected to the buses. To send information from one component to another, the source component outputs data onto the bus. The destination component then inputs this data from the bus. As the complexity of a computer system increases, it becomes more efficient (in terms of minimizing connections) at using buses rather than direct connections between every pair of devices. Buses use less space on a circuit board and require less power than a large number of direct connections. They also require fewer pins on the chip or chips that comprise the CPU.

The system shown in Figure 4.1 has three buses. The uppermost bus in this figure is the **address bus**. When the CPU reads data or instructions from or writes data to memory, it must specify the address of the memory location it wishes to access. It outputs this address to the address bus; memory inputs this address from the address bus and uses it to access the proper memory location. Each I/O device, such as a keyboard, monitor, or disk drive, has a unique address as well. When accessing an I/O device, the CPU places the address of the device on the address bus. Each device can read the address off of the bus and determine whether it is the device being accessed by the CPU. Unlike the other buses, the address bus always receives data from the CPU; the CPU never reads the address bus.

Data is transferred via the **data bus**. When the CPU fetches data from memory, it first outputs the memory address on its address bus. Then memory outputs the data onto the data bus; the CPU can then read the data from the data bus. When writing data to memory, the CPU first outputs the address onto the address bus, then outputs the data onto the data bus. Memory then reads and stores the data at the proper location. The processes for reading data from and writing data to the I/O devices are similar.

The **control bus** is different from the other two buses. The address bus consists of n lines, which combine to transmit one n-bit address value. Similarly, the lines of the data bus work together to transmit a single, multibit value. In contrast, the control bus is a collection of individual control signals. These signals indicate whether data is to be read into or written out of the CPU, whether the CPU is accessing memory or an I/O device, and whether the I/O device or memory is ready to transfer data. Although this bus is shown as bidirectional in Figure 4.1, it is really a collection of (mostly) unidirectional signals. Most of these signals are output from the CPU to the memory and I/O subsystems, although a few are output by these subsystems to the CPU. We examine these signals in more detail when we look at the instruction cycle and the subsystem interface.

A system may have a hierarchy of buses. For example, it may use its address, data, and control buses to access memory, and an I/O controller. The I/O controller, in turn, may access all I/O devices using a second bus, often called an **I/O bus** or a **local bus**. The Practical Perspective describes the PCI bus, a local bus commonly used in personal computers.

4.1.2   Instruction Cycles

The **instruction cycle** is the procedure a microprocessor goes through to process an instruction. First the microprocessor **fetches**,

PRACTICAL PERSPECTIVE: THE PERIPHERAL COMPONENT INTERCONNECT BUS

Early IBM personal computers, starting with the PC-AT, used a single bus to interface with I/O devices. The **Industry Standard Architecture**, or **ISA**, bus was used to connect the CPU and I/O devices within the computer. The ISA bus incorporated the address, data, and control buses into a single standard. The ISA bus could transfer data at clock speeds up to 8 MHz (8 million cycles per second.)

As computer performance improved, this bus became a bottleneck in system performance. Designers developed faster local buses, separate from the main system bus, for interacting with I/O devices. Of these, the **Peripheral Component Interconnect**, or **PCI**, bus is the most commonly used in personal computers.

The PCI bus transfers data at speeds of up to 66 MHz and contains 100 signals. Thirty-two of these signals are for address bus information, and another 32 are multiplexed address/data lines. (Part of the time, these lines carry address bus information and the rest of the time they carry data bus information.) The remaining lines incorporate control bus signals and signals used for error checking and reporting, as well as signals to support cache memory and interrupts. See Chapters 9 and 10 for a discussion of cache memory and interrupts in computer systems.

or reads, the instruction from memory. Then it **decodes** the instruction, determining which instruction it has fetched. Finally, it performs the operations necessary to **execute** the instruction. (Some people also include an additional element in the instruction cycle to store results. Here, we include that operation as part of the execute function.) Each of these functions—fetch, decode, and execute—consists of a sequence of one or more operations.

Let's start where the computer starts, with the microprocessor fetching the instruction from memory. First, the microprocessor places the address of the instruction on to the address bus. The memory subsystem inputs this address and decodes it to access the desired memory location. (We look at how this decoding occurs when we examine the memory subsystem in more detail later in this chapter.)

After the microprocessor allows sufficient time for memory to decode the address and access the requested memory location, the microprocessor asserts a **READ** control signal. The *READ* signal is a signal on the control bus which the microprocessor asserts when it is ready to read data from memory or an I/O device. (Some processors have a different name for this signal, but all microprocessors have a signal to perform this function.) Depending on the microprocessor, the *READ* signal may be active high (asserted = 1) or active low (asserted = 0).

When the *READ* signal is asserted, the memory subsystem places the instruction code to be fetched onto the computer system's data bus. The microprocessor then inputs this data from the bus and stores it in one of its internal registers. At this point, the microprocessor has fetched the instruction.

Next, the microprocessor decodes the instruction. Each instruction may require a different sequence of operations to execute the instruction. When the microprocessor decodes the instruction, it determines which instruction it is in order to select the correct sequence of operations to perform. This is done entirely within the microprocessor; it does not use the system buses.

Finally, the microprocessor executes the instruction. The sequence of operations to execute the instruction varies from instruction to instruction. The execute routine may read data from memory, write data to memory, read data from or write data to an I/O device, perform only operations within the CPU, or perform some combination of these operations. We now look at how the computer performs these operations from a system perspective.

To read data from memory, the microprocessor performs the same sequence of operations it uses to fetch an instruction from memory. After all, fetching an instruction is simply reading it from memory. Figure 4.2(a) shows the timing of the operations to read data from memory.

FIGURE 4.2

Timing diagrams for (a) memory read and (b) memory write operations

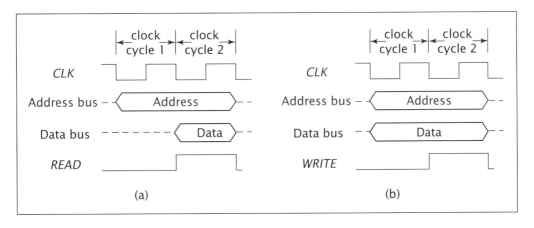

(a)   (b)

In Figure 4.2, notice the top symbol, *CLK*. This is the computer **system clock**; the microprocessor uses the system clock to synchronize its operations. The microprocessor places the address onto the bus at the beginning of a **clock cycle**, a 0/1 sequence of the system clock. One clock cycle later, to allow time for memory to decode the address and access its data, the microprocessor asserts the *READ* signal. This causes memory to place its data onto the system data bus. During this clock cycle, the microprocessor reads the data off the system bus and stores it in one of its registers. At the end of the clock cycle it removes the address from the address bus and deasserts the *READ* signal. Memory then removes the data from the data bus, completing the memory read operation.

The timing of the memory write operation is shown in Figure 4.2(b). The processor places the address and data onto the system buses during the first clock cycle. The microprocessor then asserts a **WRITE** control signal (or its equivalent) at the start of the second clock cycle. Just as the *READ* signal causes memory to read data, the *WRITE* signal triggers memory to store data. Some time during this cycle, memory writes the data on the data bus to the memory location whose address is on the address bus. At the end of this cycle, the processor completes the memory write operation by removing the address and data from the system buses and deasserting the *WRITE* signal.

The I/O read and write operations are similar to the memory read and write operations. Recall from Chapter 3 that a processor may use either **memory mapped I/O** or **isolated I/O**. If the processor supports memory mapped I/O, it follows the same sequences of operations to input or output data as to read data from or write data to memory, the sequences shown in Figure 4.2. (Remember, in memory mapped I/O, the processor treats an I/O port as a memory location, so it is reasonable to treat an I/O data access the same as a memory access.) Processors that use isolated I/O follow the same process but have a second control signal to distinguish between I/O and memory accesses. (CPUs that use isolated I/O can have a memory location and an I/O port with the same address, which makes this extra signal necessary.) For example, the 8085 microprocessor has a control signal called $IO/\overline{M}$. The processor sets $IO/\overline{M}$ to 0 for the entire length of a memory read or write operation. For I/O operations, the processor sets $IO/\overline{M}$ to 1 for the duration of the I/O read or write operation.

Finally, consider instructions that are executed entirely within the microprocessor. The INAC instruction of the Relatively Simple CPU, and the MOV $r1$, $r2$ instruction of the 8085 microprocessor, can be executed without accessing memory or I/O devices. As with instruction decoding, the execution of these instructions does not make use of the system buses.

4.2 CPU Organization

The CPU controls the computer. It fetches instructions from memory, supplying the address and control signals needed by memory to access its data. The CPU decodes the instruction and controls the execution procedure. It performs some operations internally, and supplies the address, data, and control signals needed by memory and I/O devices to execute the instruction. Nothing happens in the computer unless the CPU causes it to happen.

Internally, the CPU has three sections, as shown in Figure 4.3. The **register section**, as its name implies, includes a set of registers and a bus or other communication mechanism. The registers in a processor's instruction set architecture are found in this section of the CPU. The system address and data buses interact with this section of the CPU. The register section also contains other registers that are not directly accessible by the programmer. The Relatively Simple CPU includes registers to latch the address being accessed in memory and a temporary storage register, as well as other registers that are not a part of its instruction set architecture. (See Chapter 6.)

FIGURE 4.3

CPU internal organization

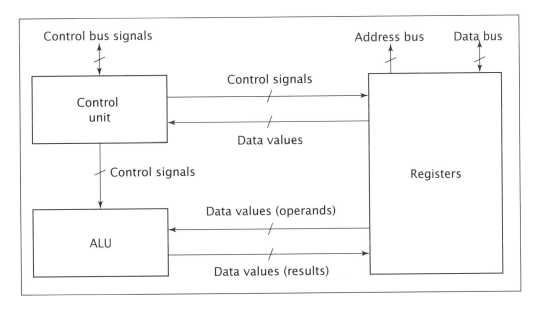

During the fetch portion of the instruction cycle, the processor first outputs the address of the instruction onto the address bus. The processor has a register called the **program counter**; the CPU keeps the address of the next instruction to be fetched in this register. Before the CPU outputs the address onto the system's address bus, it retrieves the address from the program counter register. At the end of the instruction fetch, the CPU reads the instruction code from the system data bus. It stores this value in an internal register, usually called the **instruction register** or something similar.

The **arithmetic/logic unit**, or **ALU**, performs most arithmetic and logical operations, such as adding or ANDing values. It receives its operands from the register section of the CPU and stores its results back in the register section. Since the ALU must complete its operations within a single clock cycle, it is constructed using only combinatorial logic. The ADD instructions in the Relatively Simple CPU and the 8085 microprocessor use the ALU during their executions.

Just as the CPU controls the computer (in addition to its other functions), the control unit controls the CPU. This unit generates the internal control signals that cause registers to load data, increment or clear their contents, and output their contents, as well as cause the ALU to perform the correct function. These signals are shown as control signals in Figure 4.3. The control unit receives some data values from the register unit, which it uses to generate the control signals. This data includes the instruction code and the values of some flag registers. The control unit also generates the signals for the system control bus, such as the *READ*, *WRITE*, and *IO/$\overline{M}$* signals. A microprocessor typically performs a sequence of operations to fetch, decode, and execute an instruction. By asserting these internal and external control signals in the proper sequence, the control unit causes the CPU and the rest of the computer to perform the operations needed to correctly process instructions.

This description of the CPU is incomplete. Current processors have more complex features that improve their performance. One such mechanism, the instruction pipeline, allows the CPU to fetch one instruction while simultaneously executing another instruction. Instruction pipelines are examined in Chapter 11.

In this section we have introduced the CPU from a system perspective, but we have not discussed its internal design. In Chapter 6 we introduce the internal architecture of several hardwired CPUs. We examine the registers, data paths, and control unit, all of which act together to cause the CPU to properly fetch, decode, and execute instructions. Microsequenced CPUs have the same registers, ALUs and data paths as hardwired CPUs, but completely different control units. They are examined in Chapter 7. The hardware to perform arithmetic functions, as in the ALU or a separate floating point unit, are described in Chapters 6 and 8.

4.3 Memory Subsystem Organization and Interfacing

In this section we examine the construction and functions of the memory subsystem of a computer. We review the different types of physical memory and the internal organization of their chips. We discuss the construction of the memory subsystem, as well as multibyte word organizations and advanced memory organizations.

4.3.1   Types of Memory

There are two types of memory chips: read only memory (ROM) and random access memory (RAM). **Read Only Memory** (**ROM**) chips are designed for applications in which data is only read. (This data can include program instructions.) These chips are programmed with data by an external programming unit before they are added to the computer system. Once this is done, the data usually does not change. A ROM chip always retains its data, even when power to the chip is turned off. As an example, an embedded controller for a microwave oven might continuously run one program that does not change. That program would be stored in a ROM.

Random Access Memory (**RAM**), also called read/write memory, can be used to store data that changes. This is the type of memory referred to as X MB of memory in ads for PCs. Unlike ROM, RAM chips lose their data once power is shut off. Many computer systems, including personal computers, include both ROM and RAM.

4.3.1.1   ROM Chips

There are several types of ROM chips, which are differentiated by how and how often they can be programmed. A **masked ROM**, or simply a ROM, is programmed with data as the chip is fabricated. The mask used to create the chip is designed with the required data hard-wired into it. These chips are useful for consumer appliances, where large numbers of units are produced, and, once installed, data will not be changed.

A **PROM** is a **programmable ROM**. Unlike the ROM, the PROM can be programmed by the user with any standard PROM programmer. Rather than being hard-wired, the PROM has a series of internal connections similar to fuses. Programming data into the PROM essentially blows the proper fuses so that each word of memory stores the correct value. Because these fuses cannot be restored once they are blown, PROMs can only be programmed once. These chips are well suited for prototyping, and for applications that could use a ROM but will not have a sufficient quantity of units manufactured to justify the cost of the ROM mask.

An **EPROM** is an **erasable PROM**. As its name implies, an EPROM can be programmed like a PROM, but its contents can be erased and the chip reprogrammed. Programming an EPROM is akin to charging capacitors. The charged and uncharged capacitors cause each word of memory to store the correct value. These chips have a small clear window on their faces. The chip is erased by being placed under ultraviolet light, which causes the capacitors to leak their charge, thus resetting the chip's contents. When in use, the window is usually covered with opaque tape to prevent any ultraviolet rays in room light or sunlight from inadvertently destroying the contents of the chip. Because they are erasable, but are used in applications where their data does not change, EPROMs are typically used in product development labs and in prototypes.

An **EEPROM**, sometimes denoted **E²PROM**, is an electrically erasable PROM. It works like an EPROM, except its contents are erased and reprogrammed electrically, rather than by using ultraviolet light. Unlike the EPROM, which must be entirely erased and then reprogrammed, it is possible to modify individual locations of the EEPROM while leaving other locations unchanged. Also, it takes only seconds to reprogram an EEPROM; it takes about 20 minutes to erase an EPROM. EEPROMs can be used in applications where the contents will be changed only rarely, as long as the programming hardware needed to reprogram the chip is included in the system circuitry. One common use for EEPROMs is the **basic input/output system**, or **BIOS**, of personal computers. This chip is usually not modified, except once or twice in the computer's lifetime when the BIOS is updated with a newer version of its software.

A special type of EEPROM called a **flash EEPROM** is electrically erasable in blocks of data, rather than individual locations. It is well suited for applications that write blocks of data and can be used as a solid state hard disk. It is also used for data storage in digital cameras. Flash EEPROM can only be rewritten with data a finite number of times, which currently limits its widespread use in computer systems.

Regardless of the type of ROM, the external configuration is (almost) the same. A chip with 2^n words, each having m bits, has n address inputs, A_{n-1} to A_0, and m data outputs, D_{m-1} to D_0. (The data pins serve as inputs when the chip is being programmed.) It also has a chip enable input (CE) and an output enable (OE), or equivalent enable inputs with different names. Both must receive high (logic 1) signals if the chip is to output data; otherwise its outputs are the high impedance Z. (Some chips have active low values CE' and/or OE'.) All ROMs except the masked ROM also have a programming control input (V_{pp}), which is used by the chip programmer to enter data into the chip.

4.3.1.2   RAM Chips

Unlike ROM chips, RAM chips are differentiated by how they maintain their data. **Dynamic RAM**, or **DRAM**, chips are like leaky capacitors. Initially data is stored in the DRAM chip, charging its memory cells to their maximum values. The charge slowly leaks out and would eventually go too low to represent valid data. Before this happens, however, **refresh** circuitry reads the contents of the DRAM and rewrites the data to its original locations, thus restoring the memory cells to their maximum charges. DRAM is used to construct the RAM in personal computers.

Static RAM, or **SRAM**, is more like a register than a leaky capacitor. Once data is written to SRAM, its contents stay valid; it does not have to be refreshed. Static RAM is faster than DRAM, but it is also much more expensive. The cache memory in personal computers is constructed from SRAM.

The external configuration of both types of RAM is identical. Each $2^n \times m$ chip has n address inputs and m bidirectional data pins, which are similar to those of the ROM chip except that the data pins can also input data under normal operating conditions. Like ROM chips, RAM chips have a chip enable (CE or CE'). In place of the output enable, RAM chips may have either one read enable input (RD or RD') and one write enable input (WR or WR'), or one combined signal, such as R/W'. The R/W' signal would be set to 1 for a memory read operation or 0 for a memory write. Unless CE is active, the chip's outputs are tri-stated, regardless of the value of R/W'.

4.3.2   Internal Chip Organization

The internal organizations of ROM and RAM chips are similar. To illustrate the simplest organization, a **linear organization**, consider an 8×2 ROM chip, as shown in Figure 4.4. For simplicity, programming components are not shown. This chip has three address inputs and two data outputs, and 16 bits of internal storage arranged as eight 2-bit locations.

The three address bits are decoded to select one of the eight locations, but only if the chip enable is active. If CE = 0, the decoder is disabled and no location is selected. The tri-state buffers for that location's cells are enabled, allowing data to pass to the output buffers. If both CE and OE are set to 1, these buffers are enabled and the data is output from the chip; otherwise the outputs are tri-stated.

As the number of locations increases, the size of the address decoder needed in a linear organization becomes prohibitively large. To remedy this problem, the memory chip can be designed using multiple dimensions of decoding. To illustrate this organization, consider the **two-dimensional organization** of the same 8×2 ROM chip shown in Figure 4.5. This configuration has four rows with four bits per row; each row holds two data values. For example, the first row of the ROM shown in Figure 4.5 contains the data at addresses 0 and 1. The two high-order address bits of the two locations in each row are the same. These two high-order address bits select one of the four rows, and the low-order address bit selects one of the two locations in the row. The chip enable and output enable work as in the linear organization of Figure 4.4.

In larger memory chips, this savings can be significant. Consider a 4096×1 chip. The linear organization will require a 12 to 4096 decoder, the size of which is proportional to the number of outputs. (The size of an n to 2^n decoder is thus said to be $O(2^n)$.) If the chip is organized as a 64×64 two-dimensional array instead, it will have two 6 to 64 decoders: one to select one of the 64 rows and the other to select one of the 64 cells within the row. The size of the decoders is proportional to 2×64, or $O(2 \times 2^{n/2}) = O(2^{n/2 + 1})$. For this chip, the two decoders together are about 3 percent of the size of the one larger decoder.

FIGURE 4.4

Internal linear organization of an 8 × 2 ROM chip

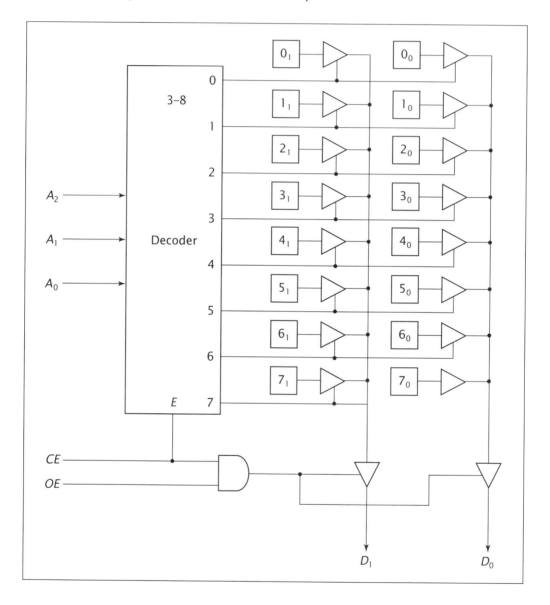

4.3.3 MEMORY SUBSYSTEM CONFIGURATION

It is very easy to set up a memory system that consists of a single chip. We simply connect the address, data, and control signals from their system buses and the job is done. However, most memory systems require more than one chip. Following are some methods for combining memory chips to form a memory subsystem.

FiGURE 4.5

Internal two-dimensional organization of an 8 × 2 ROM chip

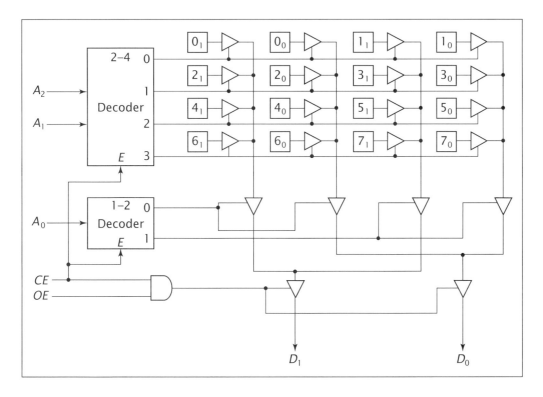

Two or more chips can be combined to create memory with more bits per location. This is done by connecting the corresponding address and control signals of the chips, and connecting their data pins to different bits of the data bus. For example, two 8 × 2 chips can be combined to create an 8 × 4 memory, as shown in Figure 4.6. Both chips receive the same three address inputs from the bus, as well as the same chip enable and output enable signals. (For now it is only important to know that the signals are the same for both chips; we show the logic to generate these signals shortly.) The data pins of the first chip are connected to bits 3 and 2 of the data bus, and those of the other chip are connected to bits 1 and 0.

When the CPU reads data, it places the address on the address bus. Both chips read in address bits A_2, A_1, and A_0 and perform their internal decoding. If the CE and OE signals are activated, the chips output their data onto the four bits of the data bus. Since the address and enable signals are the same for both chips, either both chips or neither chip is active at any given time. The computer never has only one of the two active. For this reason, they act just as a single 8 × 4 chip, at least as far as the CPU is concerned.

FIGURE 4.6

An 8 × 4 memory subsystem constructed from two 8 × 2 ROM chips

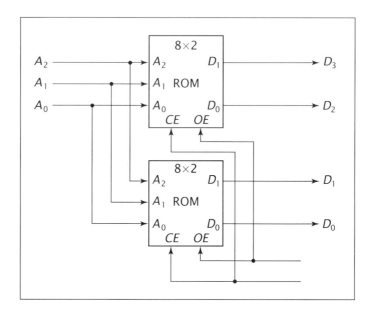

Instead of creating wider words, chips can be combined to create more words. The same two 8 × 2 chips could instead be configured as a 16 × 2 memory subsystem. This is illustrated in Figure 4.7(a). The upper chip is configured as memory locations 0 to 7 (0000 to 0111) and the lower chip as locations 8 to 15 (1000 to 1111). The upper chip always has $A_3 = 0$ and the lower chip has $A_3 = 1$. This difference is used to select one of the two chips. When $A_3 = 0$, the upper chip is enabled and the lower chip is disabled; when $A_3 = 1$, the opposite occurs. (As shown in the figure, other conditions must also occur or neither chip will be selected.) The output enables can be connected, since only the chip that is enabled will output data. Since both chips correspond to the same data bits, both are connected to D_1 and D_0 of the data bus.

This configuration uses **high-order interleaving**. All memory locations within a chip are contiguous within system memory. However, this does not have to be the case. Consider the configuration shown in Figure 4.7(b), which uses **low-order interleaving**. The upper chip is enabled when $A_0 = 0$, or by addresses XXX0, in this case 0, 2, 4, 6, 8, 10, 12, and 14. The lower chip is enabled when $A_0 = 1$, which is true for addresses 1, 3, 5, 7, 9, 11, 13, and 15. Both look the same to the CPU, but low-order interleaving can offer some speed advantages for pipelined memory access, discussed later in this text, and for CPUs that can read data from more than one memory location simultaneously.

Figure 4.7

A 16 × 2 memory subsystem constructed from two 8 × 2 ROM chips with (a) high-order interleaving and (b) low-order interleaving

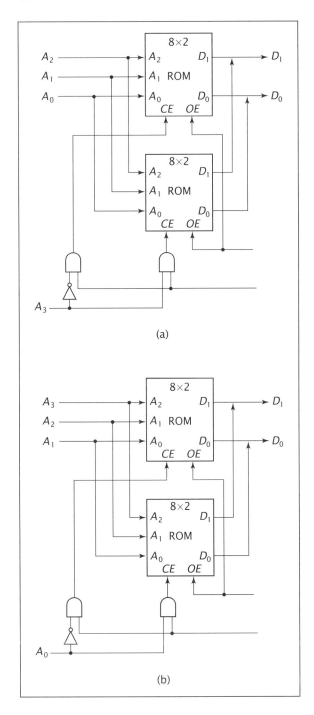

The next step in these designs is to develop the *CE* and *OE* input logic. Of these, the output enable is more straightforward. The CPU generally outputs a control signal called *RD* or *RD'*, or something similar, which it sets active when it wants to read data from memory. This signal is sufficient to drive *OE*; the logic to drive *CE* ensures that only the correct chip outputs data.

The chip enable signal makes use of the unused address bits. To illustrate, assume that the 8×4 memory of Figure 4.6 is used in a system with a 6-bit address bus. Furthermore, assume this chip corresponds to locations 0 to 7 (00 0000 to 00 0111). Address bits A_2, A_1, and A_0 select a location within the memory chips; bits A_5, A_4, and A_3 must be 000 for the chips to be active. The 8×4 memory, with control signals, is shown in Figure 4.8. This figure includes the $IO/\overline{M}$ signal that is supplied by processors that use isolated I/O.

The Historical Perspective describes two data allocation methods, the **von Neumann architecture** and the **Harvard architecture**.

FIGURE 4.8

An 8×4 memory subsystem constructed from two 8×2 ROM chips with control signals

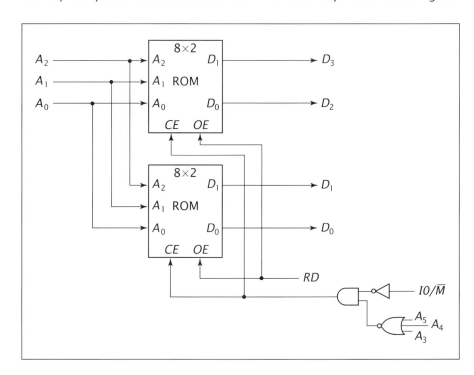

HISTORICAL PERSPECTIVE: The von Neumann and Harvard Architectures

The von Neumann and Harvard architectures can both be implemented using the computer organization shown in Figure 4.1. They differ in how data is arranged in memory. The von Neumann architecture allows instructions and data to be mixed and stored in the same memory module, while the Harvard architecture uses separate memory modules for instructions and data.

Modern computers predominantly follow the von Neumann architecture, but use some elements of the Harvard architecture. A personal computer with a Pentium microprocessor running Windows NT has a von Neumann architecture, for example, but the operating system assigns sections of memory to either instructions or data. Since any section of memory can be assigned to either instructions or data, this is not a Harvard architecture. The Harvard architecture requires that a memory module *always* be assigned to the same one of the two.

The same computer does use the Harvard architecture in its cache memory. The lowest level of cache memory in this personal computer contains 8K of instruction memory and 8K of data memory.

4.3.4   Multibyte Data Organization

Many data formats use more than one 8-bit byte to represent a value, whether it is an integer, floating point number, or character string. Most CPUs assign addresses to 8 bit memory locations, so these values must be stored in more than one location. It is necessary for every CPU to define the order it expects for the data in these locations.

There are two commonly used organizations for multibyte data: **big endian** and **little endian**. (*Gulliver's Travels* by Jonathan Swift is the source of these terms.) In big endian format, the most significant byte of a value is stored in location X, the following byte in location $X + 1$, and so on. For example, the hexadecimal value 0102 0304H (H for hexadecimal) would be stored, starting in location 100H, as shown in Table 4.1(a).

In little endian, the order is reversed. The least significant byte is stored in location X, the next byte in location $X + 1$, and so on. The same value, in little endian format, is shown in Table 4.1(b).

The same organizations can be used for bits within a byte. In big endian organization, bit 0 is the right-most bit of a byte; the left-most bit is bit 7. In little endian organization, the left-most bit is bit 0 and bit 7 is the right-most bit.

Which endian organization is used for bytes and words does not impact the performance of the CPU and computer system. As long as the

Table 4.1

Data organization in (a) big endian and (b) little endian formats

Memory Address	Data (in hex)	Memory Address	Data (in hex)
100	01	100	04
101	02	101	03
102	03	102	02
103	04	103	01

<table>
<tr><td>(a)</td><td>(b)</td></tr>
</table>

CPU is designed to handle a specific format, neither is better than the other. The main problem comes in transferring data between computers with different endian organizations. For example, if a computer with little endian organization transfers the value 0102 0304H to a computer with big endian organization without converting the data, the big endian computer will read the value as 0403 0201H. There are programs which can convert data files from one format to the other, and some microprocessors have special instructions to perform the conversion.

One other issue of concern for multibyte words is **alignment**. Modern microprocessors can read in more than one byte of data at a time. For example, the Motorola 68040 microprocessor can read in four bytes simultaneously. However, the four bytes must be in consecutive locations that have the same address except for the two least significant bits. This CPU could read locations 100, 101, 102, and 103 simultaneously, but not locations 101, 102, 103, and 104. This case would require two read operations, one for locations 100 (not needed), 101, 102, and 103, and the other for 104, 105 (not needed), 106 (not needed), and 107 (not needed).

Alignment simply means storing multibyte values in locations such that they begin at a location that also begins a multibyte read block. In this example, this means beginning multibyte values at memory locations that have addresses evenly divisible by four, thus guaranteeing that a four-byte value can be accessed by a single read operation.

Some CPUs, particularly RISC CPUs, require all data to be aligned. Other CPUs do not; they can usually align data internally. In general, nonaligned CPUs have more compact programs, because no locations are left unused by alignment. However, aligned CPUs can have better performance because they may need fewer memory read operations to fetch data and instructions.

4.3.5 Beyond the Basics

The memory subsystem described in this chapter is sufficient for small, embedded computers. Personal computers and mainframes, however, require more complex hierarchical configurations. These computers include small, high-speed **cache memory**. The computer loads data from the physical memory into the cache; the processor can access data in the cache more quickly than it can access the same data in physical memory. Many microprocessors include some cache memory right on the processor chip. A computer that includes cache memory must also have a **cache controller** to move data between the cache and physical memory.

At the other extreme, modern computers include **virtual memory**. This mechanism uses a hard disk as a part of the computer's memory, expanding the memory space of the computer while minimizing cost, since a byte of hard disk costs less than a byte of RAM. As with the cache, virtual memory needs a controller to move data between physical memory and the hard disk. Virtual and cache memory are covered in Chapter 9.

4.4   I/O Subsystem Organization and Interfacing

The CPU treats memory as homogeneous. From the CPU's perspective, each location is read from and written to in exactly the same way. Each memory location performs the same function—it stores a data value or an instruction for use by the CPU.

Input/output (I/O) devices, on the other hand, are very different. A personal computer's keyboard and hard disk perform vastly different functions, yet both are part of the I/O subsystem. Fortunately for the system designer, the interfaces between the CPU and the I/O devices are very similar.

As shown in Figure 4.1, each I/O device is connected to the computer system's address, data, and control buses. Each I/O device includes I/O interface circuitry; it is actually this circuitry that interacts with the buses. The circuitry also interacts with the actual I/O device to transfer data.

Figure 4.9(a) shows the generic interface circuitry for an input device, such as a keyboard. The data from the input device goes to the tri-state buffers. When the values on the address and control buses are correct, the buffers are enabled and data passes on to the data bus. The CPU can then read in this data. When the conditions are not right, the logic block does not enable the buffers; they are tri-stated and do not place data onto the bus.

The key to this design is the **enable logic**. Just as every memory location has a unique address, each I/O device also has a unique address. The enable logic must not enable the buffers unless it receives the correct address from the address bus. It must also get the correct control signals from the control bus. For an input device, an *RD* (or *RD'*) signal must be asserted (as well as the *IO/$\overline{M}$* signal, or equivalent,

Figure 4.9
An input device: (a) with its interface and (b) the enable logic for the tri-state buffers

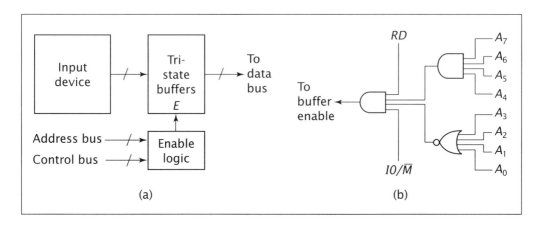

(a)   (b)

in systems with isolated I/O). Figure 4.9(b) shows the enable logic for an input device at address 1111 0000 on a computer system with an 8-bit address and control signals RD and $IO/\overline{M}$. Note that this uses only combinatorial logic. Since the enable signal must be generated within a single clock cycle, sequential components cannot be used in the design of its logic.

The design of the interface circuitry for an output device, such as a computer monitor, is somewhat different than that for the input device. As shown in Figure 4.10(a), the tri-state buffers are replaced by a register. The tri-state buffers are used in input device interfaces to make sure that no more than one device writes data to the bus at any time. Since the output devices read data from the bus, rather that write data to it, they don't need the buffers. The data can be made available to all output devices; only the device with the correct address will read it in.

The **load logic** plays the role of the enable logic in the input device interface. When this logic receives the correct address and control signals, it asserts the LD signal of the register, causing it to read data from the system's data bus. The output device can then read the data from the register at its leisure while the CPU performs other tasks. The logic to generate the load signal for an output device at address 1111 0000 is shown in Figure 4.10(b). It is identical to that for the input device shown in Figure 4.9(b), except the WR signal is used instead of the RD signal.

A variant of this design replaces the register with tri-state buffers. The same logic used to load the register is used to enable the tri-state buffers instead. Although this can work for some designs, the

Figure 4.10

An output device: (a) with its interface and (b) the load logic for the register

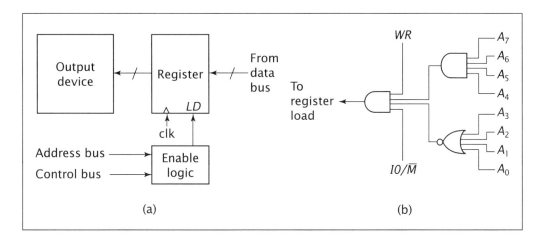

output device must read in data while the buffers are enabled. Once they are disabled, the outputs of the buffers are tri-stated and the data is no longer available to the output device.

Some devices are used for both input and output. A personal computer's hard disk drive falls into this category. Such a device requires a combined interface that is essentially two interfaces, one for input and the other for output. Some logic elements, such as the gates that check the address on the address bus, can be used to generate both the buffer enable and register load signals. Figure 4.11 shows a combined I/O interface for address 1111 0000.

Figure 4.11

A bidirectional input/output device with its interface and enable/load logic

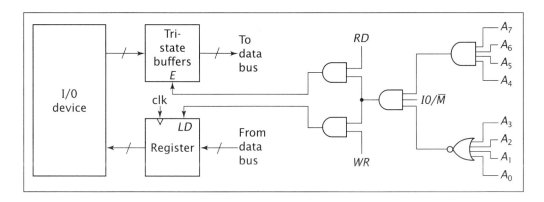

I/O devices are much slower than CPUs and memory. For this reason, they can have timing problems when interacting with the CPU. To illustrate this, consider what happens when a CPU wants to read data from a disk. It may take the disk drive several milliseconds to position its heads properly to read the desired value. In this time, the CPU could have read in invalid data and fetched, decoded, and executed thousands of instructions.

Most CPUs have a control input signal called **READY** (or something similar). Normally this input is high. When the CPU outputs the address of the I/O device and the correct control signals, enabling the tri-state buffers of the I/O device interface, the I/O device sets *READY* low. The CPU reads this signal and continues to output the same address and control signals, which cause the buffers to remain enabled. In the hard disk drive example, the drive rotates the disk and positions its read heads until it reads the desired data. Then it outputs the data through the buffers onto the data bus and sets *READY* high again. The CPU then reads the data from the bus and continues its normal operation. The extra clock cycles generated by having *READY* set low are called **wait states**. CPUs can also use the *READY* signal to synchronize data transfers with the memory subsystem.

These I/O interfaces are fine for small computers, such as the microwave oven controller, but they suffer from poor performance in larger computer systems. In all but the smallest systems, it is not acceptable for the CPU to have to wait thousands of clock cycles for data from an I/O device. Many systems use **interrupts** so they can perform useful work while waiting for the much slower I/O devices.

These I/O interfaces are also not suited to large data transfers. In the systems in this chapter, each byte of data transferred between an I/O device and memory must pass through the CPU. This is inefficient for many common operations, such as loading a program from disk into memory. **Direct memory access**, **DMA**, is a method used to bypass the CPU in these transfers, thus performing them much more quickly. We examine interrupts, DMA, and other I/O interfacing topics in detail in Chapter 10.

4.5 A Relatively Simple Computer

So far in this chapter we have described the overall system configuration for simple computers and their subsystems. Now, we need to put all of these pieces together in one system. In this section we design a computer that uses the Relatively Simple CPU, introduced in Chapter 3. This computer will have 8K of ROM starting at address 0, followed by 8K of RAM. It will also have a memory mapped, bidirectional I/O port at address 8000H.

ENQUIRIES

Pearson Education (Harlow)

P.O. Box 88

Edinburgh Gate

Harlow

Essex. CM20 2JE

United Kingdom

E-mail: enq.orders@pearsoned-ema.com

UK:	Tel	01279 623928
	Fax	01279 414130

Int'l	Tel	+44 (0)1279 623925
	Fax	+44 (0)1279 623627

Pearson Education (Amsterdam)

Concertgebouwplein 25

1071 LM Amsterdam

Netherlands

Tel	+31 (0)20 575 5800
Fax	+31 (0)20 664 5334

Dorling Kindersley

Penguin Books

Bath Road

Harmondsworth

West Drayton

Middlesex

UB7 0DA

Dorling Kindersley

UK:	Tel	020 8757 4400
	Fax	020 8757 4020

Int'l:	Tel	+44 (0)20 8757 4450
	Fax	+44 (0)20 8757 4297

1. **GENERAL**

(A) In these Conditions "The Company" means Pearson Education Limited or its authorised agent and where applicable any other company which is part of the Pearson Group or any third party for whom Pearson Education Limited provides a contracted service. "Goods" means the goods covered by The Company's invoice. "The Customer" means the person, firm or company placing an order with The Company or shown on the invoice as being liable to pay for Goods.

(B) All orders are accepted and Goods supplied subject to the following terms and conditions ("these Conditions") which shall govern the contract and cannot be altered by The Customer's Terms of Purchase. No addition to or variation from these Conditions shall be binding on The Company unless it is in writing and signed by a duly authorised representative of The Company.

(C) Goods must not be sold to the general public before their publication date, that is the date which is shown on the invoice or despatch documentation or which The Company otherwise indicates as the first day that any goods may be sold to the general public.

(D) All Goods are sold on a 'firm sale' basis and are subject to the condition that they shall not, without the prior written consent of The Company, be lent, re-sold, hired out, or otherwise circulated in any form of binding or cover other than that in which they are published and without similar conditions including this condition being imposed on any subsequent purchaser.

2. **ORDERS**

(A) No order submitted to The Company shall be deemed to be accepted by The Company unless and until confirmed in writing (either by invoice submitted with Goods delivered or otherwise) by The Company. Once despatched, Goods must be accepted and paid for by The Customer and notice of cancellation will not be accepted.

(B) The Company reserves the immediate right, at any time (without prejudice to any other remedy) to terminate the contract constituted by these Conditions or to cancel any uncompleted order or to suspend delivery in the event that any amounts payable by The Customer are overdue or there is any breach by The Customer of any of its obligations under these Conditions or for any other reason which, at the discretion of The Company, justifies such action.

(C) The price of Goods shall be the published price as shown on the invoice less such discount as may have been agreed between The Company and The Customer in writing as shown on the invoice. The price is exclusive of any applicable value added or other sales tax which The Customer shall be liable to pay. Prices are subject to change without prior notification (before or after Goods are invoiced, in the latter case only as a consequence of pricing or invoicing error).

(D) The Company reserves the right to charge any extra costs incurred by The Company in meeting The Customer's order requirements including, without limitation, with respect to orders below a minimum size and deliveries to an address other than The Customer's usual business address.

3. **DELIVERY AND RISK**

(A) Goods supplied in the UK and the Republic of Ireland will be delivered carriage paid to the delivery address shown on The Company's invoice or to The Customer's designated Shipper or Agent or, if none is shown, to the person to whom the invoice is addressed/despatched. The means of delivery shall be at The Company's discretion. Goods supplied outside the UK and the Republic of Ireland, including those supplied through UK based exporters, will be supplied exclusive of any costs of packaging, carriage and insurance, unless previously agreed otherwise in writing with The Company. Any delivery dates are given as estimates only and in no circumstances shall The Company be liable for any loss whatsoever suffered or caused through late delivery or non-delivery. Neither The Company nor its carriers are obliged to provide loading or unloading facilities on delivery.

(B) The risk of loss and/or damage (but not title) to Goods supplied by The Company shall pass to The Customer when they are delivered to The Customer or other person to whom The Company has been authorised by The Customer to deliver the Goods, whether expressly or by implication, and The Company shall not be liable for the safety of the Goods thereafter. (Accordingly, The Customer should insure the Goods thereafter against such risks as may be commercially prudent).

(C) Any damage to the goods in transit, or shortages in the Goods delivered, must be notified to the relevant carrier within 10 days of receipt (packing and contents to be held for inspection). On no account will claims be considered if notified outside this period.

(D) By accepting delivery of The Goods The Customer acknowledges receipt of and thereby agrees to be bound by these Conditions and further acknowledges that these Conditions comprise the only conditions upon which the Goods are supplied.

PEARSON EDUCATION LIMITED
STANDARD TERMS AND CONDITIONS OF SALE

4. **RETURNS**

(A) Returns will only be considered by The Company at its discretion within 12 months of supply. Returns permission must be requested from the publisher of the Goods in question. Credit will be subject to the returns conditions and policies imposed by the publisher concerned (copy can be obtained from customer Enquiry numbers listed) which are in addition to these Conditions. Authorisation by a publisher's representative does not confer automatic credit for returns if the returns conditions and policies are not adhered to.

RETURNS ADDRESS:

PEARSON EDUCATION LIMITED,
RETURNS DEPARTMENT,
MAGNA PARK,LUTTERWORTH
LEICESTERSHIRE, LE17 4XH.

(B) ISBN and full details of the books requested to be returned must be provided. The relevant invoice number must be quoted. If this is not possible, the minimum information required is the account number to which the goods were charged. Failure by The Customer to provide correct information will delay the processing procedure. The Company reserves the right to refuse to credit any Goods returned by The Customer where no evidence of purchase is provided.

(C) Subject to the provisions of this paragraph 4, old editions, or out of print editions, may be returned within 3 months of the publication of a new edition provided such returns are made within 12 months of original supply.

(D) Unauthorised returns, will, at The Company's discretion, be sent back to The Customer at The Customer's risk and expense, or be credited at a reduced rate or subject to the imposition of some other penalty.

(E) Goods returned from exhibitions must be listed and packed separately with the complete number of parcels stated. Invoice numbers must always be quoted for these returns.

(F) Defective and incorrect supplies should be returned immediately quoting the relevant invoice number and the reason for return.

(G) All parcels returned by The Customer should be clearly marked as returned Goods and should be enclosed with full details of the reason for the return. Only complete books may be returned and not title pages unless otherwise authorised in advance by The Company in writing.

(H) The Company will not accept books back for credit unless they are in resaleable condition. Credit will not be given for any goods received that are price stickered, security tagged, damaged or defaced in any way.

(I) All returns should be delivered by a carrier who can provide proof of delivery. The Company is not liable for any returns lost in transit. All returns should be securely packed using materials of sufficient strength and quality to ensure safe arrival. Returns remain the responsibility and property of The Customer until receipt in The Company's warehouse. The Customer is liable for any shortages or damages during transit. All returns are made at The Customer's expense and accordingly The Company will not accept any charges levied by shipping/transport agents.

(J) The Company will not give returns permission for software or books specially ordered from our USA offices or for special price deals.

(K) The Company's standard returns limit for UK trade customers is 10% (by value) of a customer's previous year's net purchases.

5. **TITLE**

(A) Notwithstanding any other provision of these Conditions, ownership of all Goods shall remain vested in The Company (which reserves the right to dispose of them) until The Company has received payment in full of all debts owing by The Customer to The Company.

(B) In the event that payment is overdue in whole or in part or upon the commencement of any act or proceedings in which The Customer's solvency is involved, The Company may, without prejudice to any of its other rights, recover or resell the Goods or any of them and may enter upon The Customer's premises by its servants or agents for that purpose. The Customer agrees to pay The Company all costs of repossession.

(C) Where The Customer sells the Goods or any of them prior to acquiring the ownership of them, all money received from such sale shall be held by The Customer as trustee for The Company until all sums due to The Company from The Customer have been duly paid.

6. **PAYMENT**

(A) Orders from Customers who do not have an agreed credit account will only be accepted against prepayment in full. Where such a credit account exists all Goods are supplied subject to the credit terms from time to time granted by The Company. Time is of the essence with respect to The Customer's payment obligations. Payment may not be withheld or delayed by The Customer for unauthorised returns or otherwise without the prior written agreement of The Company.

(B) The Company reserves the right to charge interest on overdue amounts accruing on a daily basis from the date payment is due until the date of the actual payment (both before and after any judgement). The rate of interest charged will be equal to 4% above HSBC Bank plc base rate from time to time in force.

7. **LIABILITY**

(A) The Company shall be liable for death or personal injury resulting from negligence of The Company, its servants or agents (but not independent contractors) while acting in the course of their employment by The Company.

(B) The Company does not make or give any warranty, representation or undertaking as to the quality of the Goods, their correspondence with description or fitness for purpose, that the Goods are not defamatory, injurious, obscene, unlawful or in breach of copyright or in any other manner whatsoever. So far as is permitted by law and except as provided in these Conditions, all implied warranties, conditions or other terms are hereby excluded.

(C) Save as and to the extent provided by these Conditions, The Company shall not in any circumstances be liable to The Customer or any successor or assignee of The Customer in respect of any loss of whatever nature occurring to The Customer arising from the supply of Goods or from non delivery, delayed delivery, damage to or loss of the Goods owing to any act or omission by The Company (including negligence) or any cause not within The Company's control including (without limitation) fire, flood, accident, strike, plant breakdown, shortage of supplies, riot, lock-out, trade dispute, industrial action, terrorism, nuclear accident, war, insurrection, act of restraint of Government.

(D) The Company shall not in any circumstances whatsoever and howsoever arising be liable for any indirect or consequential loss howsoever caused.

(E) The Customer shall notify The Company immediately in writing of any claim or infringement of any patent, copyright, design, trade mark or other industrial or intellectual property rights in the Goods of which The Customer becomes aware.

8. **TERMINATION AND GENERAL**

(A) The contract constituted by these Conditions shall terminate immediately if any order is made for the bankruptcy of, or an effective resolution is passed for the winding-up of, The Customer, or if The Customer being a company is unable to pay its debts within the meaning of Section 123 of the Insolvency Act 1986 or any statutory re-enactment or modification thereof, or makes a composition with creditors or if a supervisor, receiver, administrator, administrative receiver or other encumbrancer takes possession of or is appointed over the whole or any part of the assets of The Customer.

(B) If any agreement between The Company and a publisher expires or is terminated for any reason, The Company may terminate the contract constituted by these Conditions immediately or at any time afterwards in relation to the Goods supplied by that publisher.

(C) The termination of the contract constituted by these Conditions shall not affect any rights or obligations of the parties arising before such termination.

(D) These Conditions and all contracts under these Conditions are governed by and shall be construed in accordance with the laws of England and all disputes shall be submitted to the exclusive jurisdiction of the English courts.

(E) In the event of The Company notifying The Customer that a publication contains a libellous or serious erroneous statement and should therefore be withdrawn from sale, The Customer shall comply with the request immediately. In such circumstances, The Customer shall be entitled to return all unsold stock of that publication for credit and this shall be the limit of The Company's liability to The Customer.

First let's look at the CPU. Since it uses 16-bit addresses, it has 16 address pins, labeled A_{15} through A_0. It accesses the system data bus via pins D_7 through D_0. This CPU also has two control lines, *READ* and *WRITE*. Since it uses memory mapped I/O, it does not need a control signal such as $IO/\overline{M}$. Figure 4.12 shows the configuration of this computer so far. Only the details of the CPU are included; we develop the other parts as we progress through the design.

A Relatively Simple computer: CPU details only

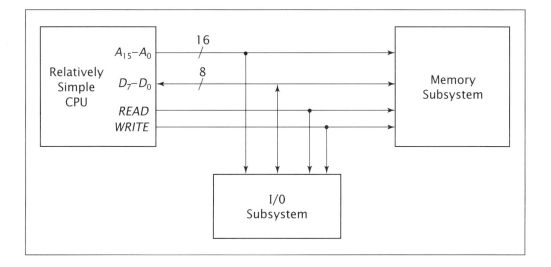

Now we develop the memory subsystem. The system specification calls for 8K of ROM starting at address 0. The ROM contains all addresses in the range 0 to 8K − 1, or 0000 0000 0000 0000 to 0001 1111 1111 1111 in binary. The 8K of RAM immediately follows the ROM and has addresses 8K to 16K − 1, or 0010 0000 0000 0000 to 0011 1111 1111 1111. To simplify the design, we will use one 8K ROM chip and one 8K RAM chip in this computer's memory subsystem.

To access a memory chip, the processor must supply an address used by the chip, as well as the proper control signals. An 8K memory chip has 2^{13} internal memory locations. It has a 13-bit address input to select one of these locations. In this system, the address input of each chip receives CPU address bits A_{12} to A_0 from the system address bus. The remaining three bits, A_{15}, A_{14}, and A_{13}, will be used to select one (or neither) of the memory chips.

Look again at the range of addresses for the ROM chip, or 0000 0000 0000 0000 to 0001 1111 1111 1111. The top three address bits

FIGURE 4.13

A Relatively Simple computer: memory subsystem details

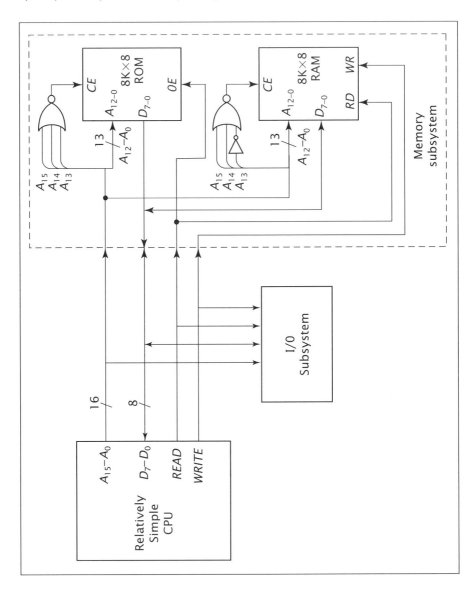

are 000 for all addresses in this range. The ROM chip should be enabled when $A_{15}A_{14}A_{13} = 000$. Similarly, the RAM chip is enabled when $A_{15}A_{14}A_{13} = 001$. We can use combinatorial logic to realize these functions and set the chip enable signals of the memory chips.

The ROM chip also has an output enable. We only need to connect the *READ* signal from the control bus to the ROM's output enable. The

FIGURE 4.14
A Relatively Simple computer: final design

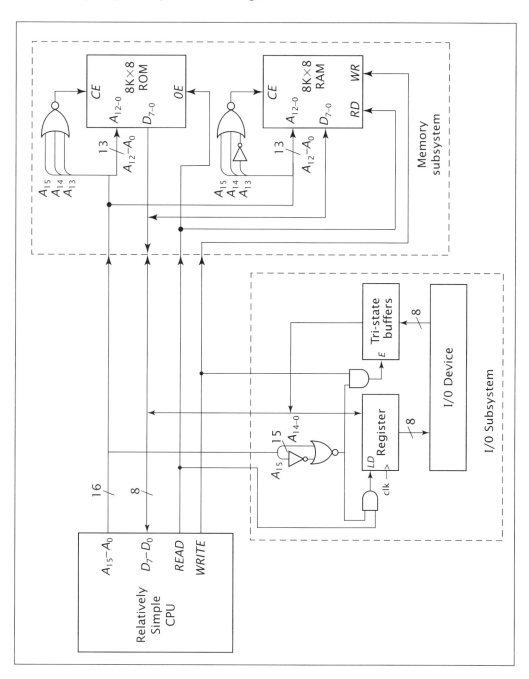

ROM chip will output data only when both its output enable and chip enable signals are asserted. If only one is asserted, the chip does not output data. The RAM has two control inputs, *RD* and *WR*. The *READ* and *WRITE* signals from the control bus can drive these two signals. (The CPU is designed to ensure that these two signals are never asserted at the same time.) These signals, in conjunction with the chip enable logic, guarantee that only one memory location, in only one memory chip, is accessed at any time. Figure 4.13 shows the design of this computer with the details of the memory subsystem shown.

Finally, we design the I/O subsystem. The system specifies one bidirectional I/O port at address 8000H, or 1000 0000 0000 0000 in binary. We use the address and the control signals to enable the input and output interface circuitry for this port.

The I/O subsystem for this computer is very similar to the design shown in Figure 4.11. We use a register to store data output to the device, and tri-state buffers to pass through data to be input from the device. There are only two changes we need to make in the design for our system. The first is easy; since the Relatively Simple CPU uses memory mapped I/O, we remove the $IO/\overline{M}$ signal from the circuit. The second is not difficult either. We must change the address logic so that it recognizes address 8000H instead of the address F0H that it recognizes now. This is fairly simple to do using combinatorial logic. Figure 4.14 shows the final design of this computer system, including the I/O subsystem.

4.6 Real World Example: An 8085-based Computer

The Relatively Simple CPU was designed as an instructional aid; this computer is not used in real engineering applications. The 8085-based computer designed by Intel engineers is. Intel published this design and made it widely available to encourage designers to use this microprocessor and other Intel components in their designs.

One feature of the 8085 microprocessor requires some explanation. Instead of having 16 address pins and 8 data pins, the 8085 has eight multiplexed pins for both the data bits and the low order eight bits of the address bus. These pins are labeled AD_7 through AD_0. During the first clock cycle of a memory access, these pins contain the low-order half of the address. For the rest of the memory access, they are used to transmit or receive data. This was done to minimize the number of pins on the microprocessor chip.

This won't work without additional circuitry. Memory needs to have the entire address available or it can't access its data. To correct this, the chip designers included an **address latch enable** signal, **ALE**. This signal is set to logic 1 during the first clock cycle of a memory or I/O access, and 0 for the duration of the access. It is used to load a register with the low order address bits so they will be available from the register even after they are removed from the *AD* pins. This is called **demultiplexing** the bus; a simple circuit to perform this operation is shown in Figure 4.15. During the first clock cycle, the 8085 outputs the low-order eight bits of the address, A_7 through A_0, on these pins. The *ALE* signal is high, causing this value to be loaded in to the latch. At the end of the first clock cycle, the *ALE* signal goes low, and the values of A_7 to A_0 are stored in the latch; the bus is now free to be used to transmit data bits D_7 through D_0. In the computer presented in this section, this function is performed inside the specialized chips, probably using something very similar to this circuit.

Figure 4.15

Demultiplexing the *AD* pins of the 8085 microprocessor

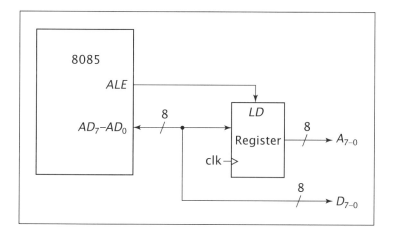

Figure 4.16 shows a minimal system configuration for a computer that uses the 8085 microprocessor. This system has only three chips. Intel engineers designed special chips for use with the 8085 microprocessor that combine several functions. This reduces the size of the circuit board needed by the computer and the wiring between the components, both of which reduce the cost of manufacturing the system.

This system has 2K of EPROM starting at location 0; its address range is 0 to 2K − 1, or 0000 0000 0000 0000 to 0000 0111 1111 1111 in binary. The system also has 256 bytes of RAM starting at address 4K; its range is 0001 0000 0000 0000 to 0001 0000 1111 1111. It has four 8-bit I/O ports at addresses 00H, 01H, 19H, and 1AH, and a 6-bit I/O port at address 1BH.

The **8755A** chip contains the 2K of EPROM and the two I/O ports at addresses 00H and 01H. (Since the 8085 uses isolated I/O, it is possible to have both a memory location and an I/O port with the same

Figure 4.16

A minimal 8085-based computer system (MCS 80/85™ Family User's Manual. Reprinted by permission of Intel Corporation, Copyright Intel Corporation 1979.)

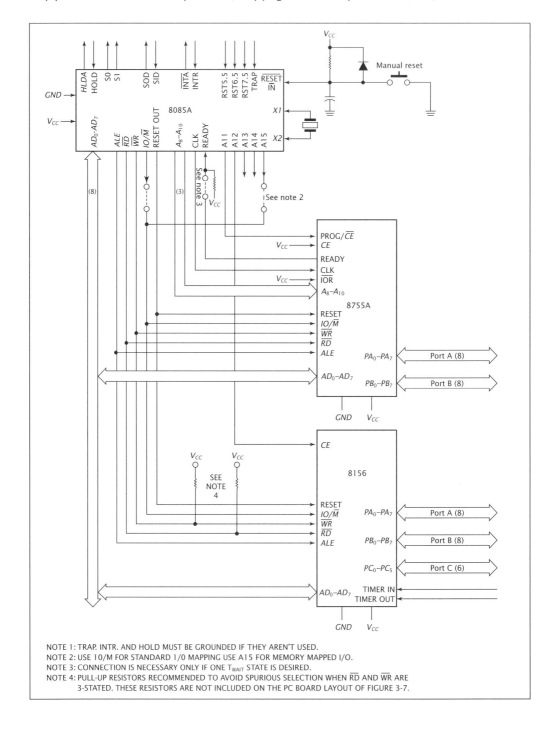

NOTE 1: TRAP. INTR. AND HOLD MUST BE GROUNDED IF THEY AREN'T USED.
NOTE 2: USE 10/M FOR STANDARD I/O MAPPING USE A15 FOR MEMORY MAPPED I/O.
NOTE 3: CONNECTION IS NECESSARY ONLY IF ONE T_{WAIT} STATE IS DESIRED.
NOTE 4: PULL-UP RESISTORS RECOMMENDED TO AVOID SPURIOUS SELECTION WHEN $\overline{RD}$ AND $\overline{WR}$ ARE
3-STATED. THESE RESISTORS ARE NOT INCLUDED ON THE PC BOARD LAYOUT OF FIGURE 3-7.

address, as this system does.) This chip has two enable signals. One, *CE*, is active high. The V_{CC} input to this enable is a logic 1, always high, so this enable input is always active. The second, *PROG/CE̅*, is active low. Address bit A_{11} drives this input; the chip is enabled whenever $A_{11} = 0$.

Looking at this circuit, we can see that addresses 0 to 2K − 1 do enable this chip. Other addresses that have $A_{11} = 0$, such as 1111 0000 0000 0000, also enable this chip. This can happen because A_{15} through A_{12} are not used to select this chip. This is called **foldback** and is a common design practice in smaller systems. It reduces the logic needed to generate the enable signal. However, the hardware designer must ensure that no other memory components use the foldback addresses. The programmer must also ensure that no instruction uses the other addresses.

The 8755A chip also shows two I/O ports. To explain how to access these ports, we first must describe how the 8085 implements I/O instructions. Recall that the 8085 uses 8-bit addresses for its IN and OUT instructions. When executing one of these instructions, it places the address on both A_{15} through A_8 and AD_7 through AD_0. Although the microprocessor removes the address from AD_7 through AD_0 after the first clock cycle of an I/O read or write, just as in the memory read or write, the address remains on A_{15} through A_8 for the entire I/O operation. Thus an I/O address with $A_{11} = 0$ (or $A_3 = 0$) enables the 8755A.

Although the 8755A has two visible I/O ports, it actually has four addressable ports. Ports *A* and *B* have $A_1 A_0 (=A_9 A_8) = 00$ and 01, respectively. Each port in the 8755A has a **data direction register**, **DDR**, which determines whether *A* and *B* are input or output ports. (The 8755A actually allows each bit of the ports to be set to input or output individually. Although it is possible to set some bits of a port to input and others to output, in practice the entire port is usually set to one or the other.) The CPU writes data to the DDRs to set the direction of the port. The DDRs for ports *A* and *B* have $A_1 A_0 = 10$ and 11, respectively.

As with the memory in the 8755A, the I/O ports also have foldback. Here we choose address 00H for port *A*, 01H for port *B*, 02H for port *A*'s DDR, and 03H for port *B*'s DDR.

The **8156** chip contains 256 bytes of RAM, two 8-bit I/O ports, and one 6-bit I/O port. The chip is enabled when $A_{12} = 1$; since this computer doesn't use most of the high-order address bits to enable this chip, it also has foldback. We select 4K, or 1000H, as the starting address.

As with the 8755A, the 8156 chip has more I/O ports than are shown in Figure 4.16. Instead of data direction registers for each port, the CPU outputs commands to a single command register; these commands set the direction of the I/O ports. The 8156 also contains a status register that the CPU can read to obtain configuration information about the ports. (This does not input data from the ports; that is done

---

HISTORICAL PERSPECTIVE: The Sojourner Rover

In 1996, the United States National Aeronautics and Space Administration (NASA) launched the Mars Pathfinder spacecraft. This spacecraft spent seven months traveling to and landing on the planet Mars. Once there, it released a robot rover, called Sojourner, which explored the surface near the Pathfinder and transmitted readings back to the spacecraft. Pathfinder then sent these readings back to Earth. Pathfinder successfully touched down on the Martian surface on July 4, 1997.

Sojourner uses a single 80C85 microprocessor to control its operation. Running at a clock speed of 2 MHz, this processor was not chosen for its speed. In fact, it was chosen because it was capable of performing the required functions and because this version of the 8085 microprocessor can function properly in the radiation-rich environment of space beyond the protection of Earth's atmosphere.

The Sojourner's computer uses much more than the 64K of memory addressable by the 8085 microprocessor. It has a 16K ROM that is accessed by the computer at startup. The programs in this ROM (actually a PROM) start the rover and initiate memory management. After starting up, this code disables the PROM and enables 64K or RAM, which serves as the system's main memory.

The rover's computer also includes 176K of ROM and 512K of RAM, which are used for storage. The ROM contains programs that the computer loads into its main memory and executes as needed. The ROM also stores some data tables used by the programs. The RAM is used for temporary data storage. Although they are constructed from memory chips, they are more akin to a hard disk in a personal computer in that they are used solely for storage. A hard disk, however, could not have withstood the radiation of space, nor the rigors of interplanetary travel.

---

by directly accessing the ports.) The three low-order bits of the address select among the I/O ports on this chip. $A_2A_1A_0 = 000$ selects the command register (for output from the CPU) or the status register (for input to the CPU). Setting $A_2A_1A_0 = 001$, 010, or 011 accesses ports A, B, or C, respectively. The chip also has a timer; setting $A_2A_1A_0 = 100$ or 101 accesses the timer.

The system design shown in Figure 4.16 is well suited for a number of applications. Consider, for example, a microwave oven with a keypad and digital display, several sensors (which indicate things such as whether or not the oven door is open), and subsystems that are controlled by the processor (such as the power level). This computer system could be used to control a microwave oven with no hardware modifications. We would use one port to read the keypad whenever a key is pressed, and another to read the remaining sensors. A third I/O port could drive the digital display, and a fourth port would control the power and other subsystems. The main control program would be stored in the EPROM of the 8755A chip. The RAM in the 8156 would be used for temporary data storage.

4.7   SUMMARY

A computer generally consists of three subsystems: the CPU, memory, and the input/output subsystem. These subsystems communicate with each other using buses. The processor sends out the address to be accessed in memory or the address of the I/O device via the address bus. The data bus carries data between the subsystems. Information sent on the control bus coordinates all data transfers.

To process an instruction, the processor goes through an instruction cycle. This, in turn, consists of cycles to fetch an instruction from memory, decode the instruction, and execute the instruction. All instructions are fetched and decoded in the same way, but the execute cycle is different for every instruction.

The CPU contains three sections. The register section is used for data storage. It contains the registers of the processor's ISA as well as other registers not directly accessible by the programmer. The arithmetic/logic unit performs computations on data with the CPU. Since it must complete its operations within a single clock cycle, it is constructed using only combinatorial logic. The control unit outputs signals to control the rest of the processor. By outputting the control signals in the correct order, it causes the processor to fetch, decode, and execute instructions.

There are several types of memory chips used in computer design. The data in read only memory chips, including ROM, PROM, EPROM, and EEPROM, is fixed; their data does not change, and remains valid when the computer is turned off. The computer can modify the contents of random access memory, SRAM, and DRAM; its contents are lost when power is turned off. Internally, all memory chips are organized as linear arrays or multi-dimensional arrays. Decoders select the memory location specified by the memory chip's address inputs. Memory chips can be combined to increase the number of bits at an address and/or the number of addresses in the memory subsystem.

A computer system can use one of two types of I/O access. Memory mapped I/O treats an I/O device as if it were a memory location. The same instructions are used to access both memory and I/O devices, but memory and the I/O device cannot both use the same address. Isolated I/O uses different instructions to access I/O devices and memory. It requires an additional control line to distinguish between the two, but this allows memory and I/O devices to both use the same address.

Problems

1 Show the internal linear configuration of a 32×2 memory chip.

2 Show the internal two-dimensional configuration of a 32×2 memory chip.

3 Show the internal organization of a 16×4 memory chip that minimizes the total size of the address decoders.

4 Show the internal organization of a 16×4 memory chip; make the array of memory cells as square as possible.

5 Design a 16×4 memory subsystem with high-order interleaving using 8×2 memory chips for a computer system with an 8-bit address bus.

6 Design a 32×8 memory subsystem with high-order interleaving using 16×2 memory chips for a computer system with an 8-bit address bus.

7 Design a 16×4 memory subsystem with low-order interleaving using 8×2 memory chips for a computer system with an 8-bit address bus.

8 Design a 32×8 memory subsystem with low-order interleaving using 16×2 memory chips for a computer system with an 8-bit address bus.

9 Design a 32×8 memory subsystem with split interleaving (one high-order bit and one low-order bit are interleaved) using 8×4 memory chips for a computer system with an 8-bit address bus.

10 Assume the memory subsystem of Figure 4.7 is connected to a CPU with an 8-bit address bus. Show the logic to generate the *CE* and *OE* signals if these chips correspond to memory addresses

    a) 0 to 15
    b) 16 to 31
    c) 240 to 255

11 Show how the following values are stored in memory in big endian and little endian formats. Each value starts at location 22H.

    a) 12345678H
    b) 0927H
    c) 5551212H

12 Show a valid alignment of the values in Problem 11 for a system which can access four bytes of data simultaneously.

13 Design an interface for an input device which has binary address 1010 1010. Its computer system uses isolated I/O.

14 Repeat Problem 13 for a computer system with memory mapped I/O.

15 Design an interface for an output device which has binary address 0011 1001. Its computer system uses isolated I/O.

16 Repeat Problem 15 for a computer system with memory mapped I/O.

17 Design an interface for a bidirectional input/output device that has binary address 1000 0001. Its computer system uses isolated I/O.

18 Repeat Problem 17 for a computer system with memory mapped I/O.

19 A computer system with an 8-bit address bus and an 8-bit data bus uses isolated I/O. It has 64 bytes of EEPROM starting at address 00H constructed using 64×4 chips; 128 bytes of RAM starting at address 40H constructed using 32×8 chips; an input device with a *READY* signal at address 40H; and an output device with no *READY* signal at address 80H. Show the design for this system. Include all enable and load logic.

20 A computer system with an 8-bit address bus and an 8-bit data bus uses memory mapped I/O. It has 32 bytes of ROM starting at address 00H constructed using a single 32×8 chip; 128 bytes of RAM starting at address 80H constructed using 64×4 chips; a bidirectional input/output device with no *READY* signal at address 40H; and an input device with no *READY* signal at address 60H. Show the design for this system. Include all enable and load logic.

21 A computer system with an 8-bit address bus and an 8-bit data bus uses isolated I/O. It has 128 bytes of EPROM starting at address 00H constructed using 128×2 chips; 32 bytes of RAM starting at address E0H constructed using 16×8 chips; an input device with a *READY* signal at address 00H; an output device with a *READY* signal at address FFH; and a bidirectional input/output device with no *READY* signal at address 80H. Show the design for this system. Include all enable and load logic.

22   A computer system with an 8-bit address bus and an 8-bit data bus uses memory mapped I/O. It has 128 bytes of PROM starting at address 00H constructed using 32×4 chips; 96 bytes of RAM starting at address 80H constructed using one 64×8 chip and several 32×2 chips; an input device with a *READY* signal at address F0H; an output device with a *READY* signal at address F1H; and a bidirectional input/output device with a *READY* signal at address F2H. Show the design for this system. Include all enable and load logic.

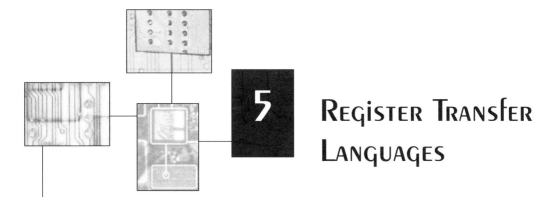

5 Register Transfer Languages

Micro-operations are the basis for most sequential digital systems. Unlike the operations specified by assembly language instructions, micro-operations are much simpler actions: the movement (actually copying) of data from one register, memory location, or I/O device to another; modify stored values, such as incrementing or clearing a register; perform arithmetic or logical functions, such as adding two values and storing the result in a register; and otherwise modify a stored value, such as overwriting the value in a register with another constant value.

Consider the process you would go through to buy a gallon of milk. First you get into your car and close the door. You put the car key in the ignition and start the car. Next, you drive to the store, park your car, and turn the car off. You enter the store, pick up a gallon of milk, pay for the milk, and leave the store. Then you get into your car, close the door, put the key in the ignition, start the car, drive home, park the car, turn the car off, go into your home, and put the milk in the refrigerator.

You can think of every individual operation in this sequence as a micro-operation. By performing these micro-operations in the correct order, you ultimately perform a larger task, buying a gallon of milk. A sequential digital system does the same thing. By performing a sequence of micro-operations that move and modify data, a sequential digital system performs a larger task. For example, a CPU performs a sequence of micro-operations to fetch, decode, and execute an instruction.

The data **transfer** performed by a micro-operation is only half the story. It is also necessary to specify the **conditions** under which each transfer occurs.

These conditions ensure that the micro-operations are executed in the correct order. Specifying the correct micro-operation transfers and conditions makes it possible to specify any sequential digital system.

For all but the simplest sequential digital systems, it is inefficient to design the system directly using digital logic. Instead, a designer uses a **hardware description language** (**HDL**) to specify the conditions and transfers of the micro-operations that correspond to the system's requirements. The HDL specification can be used to verify that the logic of the design is correct; it can also be translated into the final hardware design of the system.

The HDL specification of a system is much easier to understand than a schematic, especially for complex systems. The designer creates a design using HDL; the design looks something like a computer program written in a high-level language, such as C. Finding logical connections in the design is much simpler than tracing connections through a schematic. The text of the design is also more likely to convey the reason the connection is needed and under what conditions it is active. In addition, the design file can be input to a **circuit analysis and design** (**CAD**) program, which can simulate the behavior of the circuit under all conditions specified by the user. (Note that this definition of CAD is different from the traditional definition of CAD, computer-aided design or computer-aided drafting.) Simulating the system's behavior with a CAD program allows the user to debug the design before it is physically constructed. This saves time and money, and is a standard practice throughout the engineering industry.

In this chapter we first introduce micro-operations, including their translation into digital logic. Then we examine a simple HDL called Register Transfer Language, or RTL. RTL is more of a pseudolanguage, lacking the formal structure of traditional HDLs. It can be used to specify the logic of a system but does not translate directly to hardware without some ambiguity. First we look at how to specify a sequential system using RTL, then how to convert the RTL specification to a digital design. Finally, we study VHDL, a more rigorous HDL that is an accepted standard used by almost all CAD programs. Unlike RTL, VHDL can specify both the logic and implementation of a system.

5.1   Micro-Operations and Register Transfer Language

A micro-operation, or **μop**, specifies an operation whose result is stored, typically in a register or memory location. The operation can be as simple as copying data from one register to another, or more complex, such as adding the contents of two registers and storing the result in a third register. When designing a sequential digital system, the designer can specify the behavior of the system first, using micro-operations, and then design the hardware to match this specification.

To illustrate the format of a micro-operation, consider a digital system with two 1-bit registers, X and Y. The micro-operation that copies the contents of register Y to register X can be expressed as $X \leftarrow Y$. (Sometimes this is expressed as $Y \rightarrow X$; however, for consistency, we use the left arrow notation throughout this text.) The micro-operation does not indicate how data is copied from Y to X; it merely specifies the transfer to be made. The micro-operation may be implemented via a direct connection, as shown in Figure 5.1(a), or by way of a bus, as in Figure 5.1(b). Both are valid implementations of the micro-operation; it is the job of the system designer to choose the best implementation for the system under design.

FIGURE 5.1

Implementations of the micro-operation $X \leftarrow Y$ using (a) a direct connection and (b) a bus connection

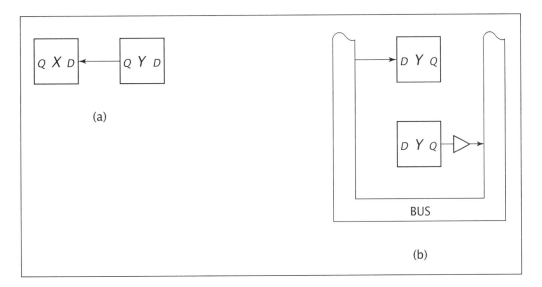

(a)

BUS

(b)

The set of micro-operations for a system is mostly sufficient for designing its data paths, the connections between components used for data transfers. However, this set does not indicate the conditions under which the transfers occur. In Figure 5.1, for example, both designs provide a path for data to flow from register Y to register X, but neither specifies when X should load this data.

Assume that the transfer should occur when control input α is high. The transfer could be written as

$$\text{IF } \alpha \text{ THEN } X \leftarrow Y$$

RTL and other hardware description languages often use a compact notation of the form

conditions: micro-operations

to represent the micro-operations and the conditions under which they occur. When all conditions to the left of the colon are asserted, the data transfers specified by the micro-operations (there can be more than one) are performed. The previous transfer could be written as

$$\alpha: X \leftarrow Y$$

In terms of the hardware used to implement this data transfer, the same data paths as shown in Figure 5.1 are still used. The conditions that cause a transfer to occur do not change the path taken by the data. Instead, the conditions are used to assert the control signals on the system hardware. As shown in Figure 5.2, α is used to load register X and, in the bus-based implementation, to enable the tri-state buffer so that the contents of register Y are placed on the bus.

FIGURE 5.2

Implementations of the data transfer $\alpha: X \leftarrow Y$ with control signals: (a) with direct path, and (b) using a bus

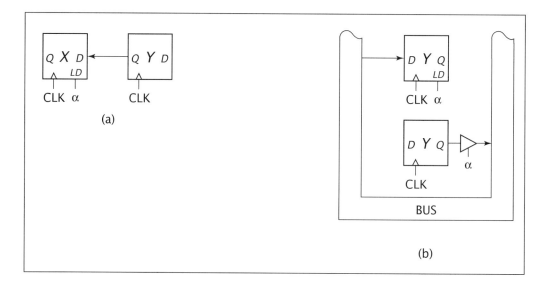

One way to improve system performance is to perform two or more micro-operations simultaneously. In this notation, the micro-operations are separated by commas; the order in which they are written is unimportant because they are performed concurrently. For

example, if a system is to perform the transfers $X \leftarrow Y$ and $Y \leftarrow Z$ whenever $\alpha = 1$, this can be expressed as either

$$\alpha: X \leftarrow Y, \; Y \leftarrow Z$$

or

$$\alpha: Y \leftarrow Z, \; X \leftarrow Y$$

(Recall that it is possible to both read from and write to a register simultaneously.) The value read from Y is the previous value, not the value loaded in from register Z. For example, if $X = 0$, $Y = 1$, and $Z = 0$ just before α becomes 1, these micro-operations set $X = 1$ (the original value of Y) and $Y = 0$. This is particularly useful for shift operations. Figure 5.3 shows the hardware to implement these micro-operations. Note that a single bus cannot be used here because a bus can hold only one value at a time. When $\alpha = 1$, both Y and Z must travel on the data paths simultaneously.

Implementation of the data transfer $\alpha: X \leftarrow Y, \; Y \leftarrow Z$

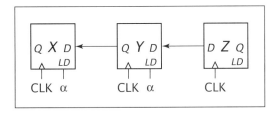

When a professor writes something on a blackboard, it is possible for many students to read the writing simultaneously. The same is true for registers in digital systems. It is possible to copy the same data to more than one destination simultaneously. Consider the transfers that occur in the following case when $\alpha = 1$.

$$\alpha: X \leftarrow Y, \; Z \leftarrow Y$$

Register Y can be read by many other registers simultaneously; both micro-operations can be performed concurrently. One implementation of this is shown in Figure 5.4.

On the other hand, it is not possible for many professors to write something on the same location of a blackboard simultaneously. The writing would become garbled and would make no sense. Similarly, a digital system cannot write two different values to the same register concurrently. For instance, the statement

$$\alpha: X \leftarrow Y, \; X \leftarrow Z$$

Figure 5.4

Implementation of the data transfer α: $X \leftarrow Y$, $Z \leftarrow Y$

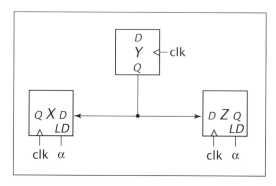

is not valid. When $\alpha = 1$, would register X end up with the contents of register Y or the contents of register Z, or some garbled combination of the two? A digital system design cannot include this type of ambiguity. Since the result to be stored in register X cannot be stated with any certainty, the statement should not be implemented.

Sometimes it is necessary to move a constant value into a register, rather than data from another register. The following are valid conditions and micro-operations in RTL that transfer constant data.

$$\alpha: X \leftarrow 0$$
$$\beta: X \leftarrow 1$$

Figure 5.5 shows three different ways to perform these two transfers. The first circuit sets X by loading data for both transfers. Either α or β can assert the register's load signal, and the multiplexer ensures that the proper data is made available. If $\alpha = 0$ and $\beta = 0$, the multiplexer still outputs data, 0 in this case, because it consists entirely of combinatorial logic. However, since its load signal is low, register X ignores this data and retains its value.

The second circuit loads data exactly the same as in the first circuit; however, its data is generated directly by signal β. When $\alpha = 1$ and $\beta = 0$, register X loads in the data value 0, the value of β. When $\beta = 1$ and $\alpha = 0$, it loads in the value 1. When both $\alpha = 0$ and $\beta = 0$, the input data value 0 is ignored by the register because its load signal is not asserted. In general, this type of design becomes too complex for all but the simplest data input values.

The final circuit makes use of the register's clear input to simplify the hardware. When $\alpha = 1$, register X is set to 0 by being cleared, rather than by being loaded with the data value 0. When $\beta = 1$, the register is loaded with the value 1 as before. Since this is the only value stored in X via a load operation, it is hard-wired to the data input of register X.

FIGURE 5.5

Three implementations of the data transfers α: $X \leftarrow 0$ and β: $X \leftarrow 1$: (a) using a multiplexer to select the data input, (b) using β as the data input, and (c) using the CLR signal

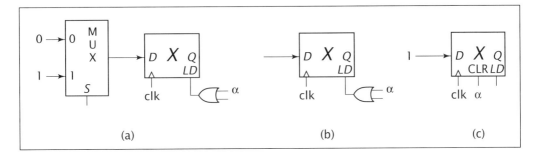

(a)   (b)   (c)

This scenario ignores the case when both $\alpha = 1$ and $\beta = 1$. When this happens, the register will try to clear its value and load in the value 1 simultaneously. This is not an acceptable situation. There are two ways the situation can be resolved. First, if the hardware that generates α and β can ensure that they are never both set to 1 simultaneously, the system can remain as is without any changes. If not, the conditions can be modified so that they are **mutually exclusive**. All of the following three options are valid. In the first, X is set to 1 when both α and β are 1. In the second, X is set to 0. In the third set, neither condition is met and the value of X is not changed.

$$\alpha\beta': X \leftarrow 0 \qquad \alpha: X \leftarrow 0 \qquad \alpha\beta': X \leftarrow 0$$
$$\beta: X \leftarrow 1 \qquad \alpha'\beta: X \leftarrow 1 \qquad \alpha'\beta: X \leftarrow 1$$

All of the operations so far have dealt with individual 1-bit registers. Real systems, however, use multibit registers to store larger data values. When transferring data between registers of the same size, and between corresponding bits, it is not necessary to specify each individual bit transfer. For example, consider the case when $\alpha = 1$ in which data is transferred from 4-bit register Y to 4-bit register X such that bit 3 of X (X_3) receives the contents of Y_3, or $X_3 \leftarrow Y_3$, and also $X_2 \leftarrow Y_2$, $X_1 \leftarrow Y_1$, and $X_0 \leftarrow Y_0$. Since this often happens in real systems, these transfers can be expressed using the notation

$$\alpha: X \leftarrow Y$$

Since X and Y are each four bits wide, it is implicit that this includes all four bit-to-bit transfers. The hardware to implement this is shown in Figure 5.6, which is the same as that of Figure 5.1, except the 4 indicates that each connection is four bits wide.

Sometimes it is necessary to access individual bits or groups of bits within a register. Individual bits can be referred to by subscripts,

FIGURE 5.6

Implementations of the 4-bit data transfer α: $X \leftarrow Y$: (a) using a direct connection, and (b) using a bus

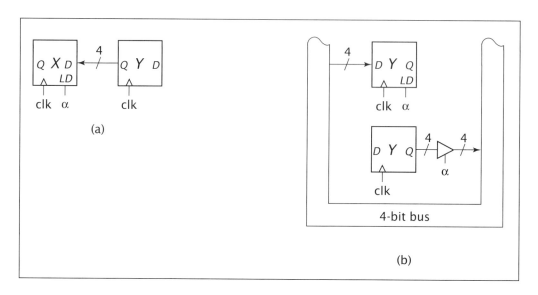

such as or X_3 or Y_2. Groups of bits can be referred to as **ranges** in RTL; they are enclosed in parentheses. For instance, X_3, X_2, and X_1 can be written as $X(3–1)$ or $X(3:1)$. The individual bits or bit ranges can then be used in micro-operations just as their entire registers are used. For instance, the following statements are all valid.

$$\alpha:\ X(3{-}1) \leftarrow Y(2{-}0)$$
$$\beta:\ X_3 \leftarrow X_2$$
$$\Gamma:\ X(3{-}0) \leftarrow X(2{-}0), X_3$$

Take particular note of the last statement. It is not possible to express bits X_2, X_1, X_0, and X_3 (in that order) as a contiguous range. Instead, they can be expressed as subranges separated by commas. They could have been expressed as subranges within the parentheses as an alternative, $X(2{-}0,3)$ in this case. Either form represents the transfers $X_3 \leftarrow X_2$, $X_2 \leftarrow X_1$, $X_1 \leftarrow X_0$, and $X_0 \leftarrow X_3$.

Every micro-operation shown in this chapter so far simply moves data from one register to another or loads a predetermined constant value into a register. There are also micro-operations that perform arithmetic, logical and shift operations on data. Table 5.1 shows some of the more commonly used arithmetic and logical micro-operations.

There are four basic types of shift micro-operations, each of which has two variants, one that shifts left and the other that shifts right. The **linear shift** is the simplest of the shift operations. Each bit

Table 5.1

Arithmetic and logical micro-operations

Operation	Example
Add	$X \leftarrow X + Y$
Subtract	$X \leftarrow X - Y$ or $X \leftarrow X + Y' + 1$
Increment	$X \leftarrow X + 1$
Decrement	$X \leftarrow X - 1$
AND	$X \leftarrow X \wedge Y$ or $X \leftarrow XY$
OR	$X \leftarrow X \vee Y$
XOR	$X \leftarrow X \oplus Y$
NOT	$X \leftarrow /X$ or $X \leftarrow X'$

value is shifted one position to the left (or right). The end bit is discarded, and a value of 0 is shifted into the vacated bit. For example, if $X = 1011$, the shift left operation on X discards the left-most 1, shifts 011 one position left, and loads a 0 in the right-most position, resulting in a value of 0110. A right shift, on the other hand, would have discarded the right-most 1, shifted 101 right, and inserted a leading 0, resulting in the value 0101.

The second type of shift operation is the **circular shift**. Circular shifts work just like linear shifts, except the bit that would be discarded in the linear shift is instead circulated back and loaded in place of the 0. For $X = 1011$, the left and right circular shifts yield the results 0111 and 1101, respectively.

The **arithmetic shift** was developed to work with numbers that have signed formats. In these formats, the left-most bit is the sign bit. The algorithms that work on this data require that the sign bit remain unchanged by the shift operations, which is the purpose of the arithmetic shifts. They work much like linear shifts, except the sign bit remains the same. For $X = 1011$, the arithmetic shift left yields the result 1110. Here, the value of the second left-most bit is lost. The arithmetic right shift would produce the result 1101. Even though the sign bit remains unchanged, it is still used as part of the right data shift. The reason for this will become clear as we study the arithmetic algorithms of Chapter 8.

When encoding decimal data, **Binary Coded Decimal** format, or **BCD**, is frequently used. In this notation, each decimal digit is represented by four bits. The **decimal shift** was developed specifically for BCD representation. It acts like a linear shift, except it shifts one digit, or four bits, instead of just one bit. For $X = 1001\ 0111$, the decimal shift left results in the value 0111 0000, and the decimal shift right produces the value 0000 1001.

Table 5.2 shows the shift operations and their representations. Note that a shift operation that stores its result in the same register from which it receives its data can be expressed as simply the shift micro-operation. For example, $X \leftarrow shl(X)$ and $shl(X)$ are equivalent. Of course, if the source and destination registers are different, as in $Y \leftarrow shl(X)$, then both registers must be specified.

Table 5.2

Shift micro-operations

Operation	Notation
Linear shift left	$shl(X)$
Linear shift right	$shr(X)$
Circular shift left	$cil(X)$
Circular shift right	$cir(X)$
Arithmetic shift left	$ashl(X)$
Arithmetic shift right	$ashr(X)$
Decimal shift left	$dshl(X)$
Decimal shift right	$dshr(X)$

One special type of transfer occurs between a register and memory, either reading from or writing to memory. It is necessary to specify not only memory, but also the address in memory to be accessed. It is possible to specify an absolute memory location. For example, the transfers $M[55] \leftarrow AC$ and $AC \leftarrow M[55]$ transfer data between register AC and memory location 55. However, this would require the address to be hard-wired in the circuitry. As more addresses are used, this becomes unnecessarily complex.

In general, it is preferable to store the address value in a register and have the register supply the address to memory. This register is usually referred to as an **address register** and labeled AR. In this configuration, the system would first perform the micro-operation $AR \leftarrow 55$, then either $M[AR] \leftarrow AC$ or $AC \leftarrow M[AR]$. This requires only one connection from the outputs of AR to the address inputs of memory. By convention, if only one address register is used, it does not have to be specified. The previous micro-operations could be expressed as $M \leftarrow AC$ and $AC \leftarrow M$.

5.2 Using RTL to Specify Digital Systems

Register transfer language can be used to specify the behavior of any sequential digital system, from the simplest to the most complex. In this section we examine the use of RTL to specify the function of digital components and simple systems. Hardware implementation of RTL code is also presented.

5.2.1 Specification of Digital Components

At the simple end of the design spectrum, consider the D flip-flop, shown in Figure 5.7(a). Its function can be expressed by the single RTL statement

$$LD: Q\leftarrow D$$

Whenever the LD input is high, the value on the D input is loaded and made available on the Q output. Note that this only happens on the rising edge, or 0 to 1 transition, of the clock. In this and all RTL code, it is implicit that the clock must have the correct transition or level in addition to the stated conditions in order for the micro-operation to occur.

FIGURE 5.7

D flip-flop: (a) without and (b) with clear input

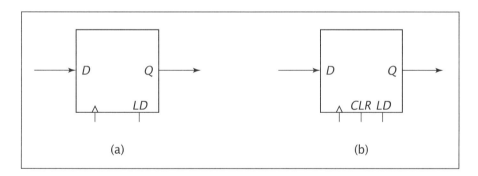

(a)   (b)

Figure 5.7(b) shows the D flip-flop, but this time with a synchronous clear input. When $CLR = 1$, the flip-flop should be set to 0. A first try at creating the RTL code for this component might yield

$$LD: Q\leftarrow D$$
$$CLR: Q\leftarrow 0$$

However, this system fails when D, LD, and CLR are all equal to 1. Since $LD = 1$, the first statement will set $Q\leftarrow 1$. Likewise, $CLR = 1$ causes the second statement to set $Q\leftarrow 0$. Both set Q simultaneously, which is clearly not possible.

As before, the solution is to modify the conditions so they are mutually exclusive. Either of the following is valid. The first gives precedence to the CLR input, while the latter gives LD priority.

$$CLR'LD: Q\leftarrow D \qquad LD: Q\leftarrow D$$
$$CLR: Q\leftarrow 0 \qquad LD'CLR: Q\leftarrow 0$$

In this RTL code, note the combined condition in the RTL statement $CLR'LD$: $Q \leftarrow D$. It is possible to require more than one condition to be met in order for a micro-operation to occur. Here, $Q \leftarrow D$ only if both $CLR = 0$ ($CLR' = 1$) and $LD = 1$.

As a second example, consider the JK flip-flop without a CLR input. Its behavior can be specified in RTL as follows.

$$J'K: Q \leftarrow 0$$
$$JK': Q \leftarrow 1$$
$$JK: Q \leftarrow Q'$$

When $J = K = 0$, no condition is met and the flip-flop retains its previous value. No RTL statement is included for this case because no transfer is needed.

One final example is the n-bit shift register. Bit Q_{n-1} is its most significant bit and Q_0 is its least significant bit. When its SHL signal is high, it shifts its data one position to the left. Input S_{in} is shifted into the least significant bit position. The SHL micro-operation cannot be used to specify the function of this register because that micro-operation always causes a 0 to be shifted into the right-most position. Here, S_{in} can be either 0 or 1. Instead, the shift register can be specified by the single RTL statement

$$SHL: Q \leftarrow Q(n-2:0), S_{in}$$

5.2.2 Specification and Implementation of Simple Systems

Specifying individual components in RTL isn't terribly useful. The behavior of individual components was already specified, usually as a truth table, before the component was designed. The RTL code doesn't provide any new information on the functions of a component.

The best use of RTL is to specify the behavior of an entire system, independent of the components used to implement the system. For example, consider a system (or subsystem of a larger system) with four 1-bit flip-flops. The transfers can be specified by the following RTL code. This code assumes that conditions j, o, h, and n are mutually exclusive.

$$j: M \leftarrow A$$
$$o: A \leftarrow Y$$
$$h: R \leftarrow M$$
$$n: Y \leftarrow R, M \leftarrow R$$

This RTL code can be implemented in several different ways. In this example, since most registers receive data from only one source, it is possible to transfer data using direct connections. The exception is register *M*, which can receive data from either register *A* or register *R*. A multiplexer can be used to select the correct input. Since input 1 (*R*) is passed through only under condition *n*, this condition is sufficient to drive the select input of the multiplexer. Figure 5.8 shows the data paths for this system.

FIGURE 5.8

Data paths of the system to implement the RTL code using direct connections

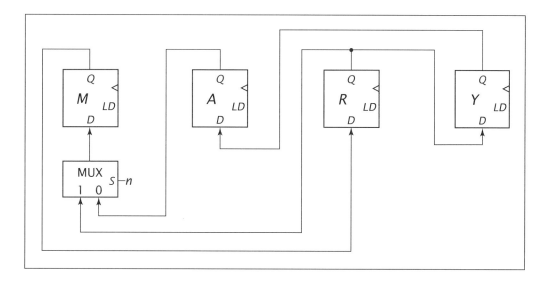

This routes the data to the correct flip-flop inputs, but it does not complete the transfer. No register has actually loaded any data yet. It is necessary to assert the *LD* signal of the flip-flops at the right times to load the data and complete the transfer. Flip-flop *M* is loaded whenever *j* = 1 (*M←A*) or *n* = 1 (*M←R*). Logically ORing these signals together produces the *LD* input for *M*. Flip-flops *A*, *R*, and *Y* are loaded under single conditions *o*, *h*, and *n*, respectively. These signals directly drive the load inputs of their respective flip-flops. The complete circuit, with the *LD* signals, is shown in Figure 5.9.

For more complex systems, direct connections become impractical. The number of connections becomes too large, and the connections eventually require much more hardware and space than the components that they connect. For such systems, a **bus** is a viable alternative. All components can send their data to the bus, although no more than one may do so at any given time. All components receive data from the bus. Several components can read data from the bus concurrently. The bus replaces all of the direct connections. As more

FIGURE 5.9

Complete design of the system to implement the RTL code using direct connections

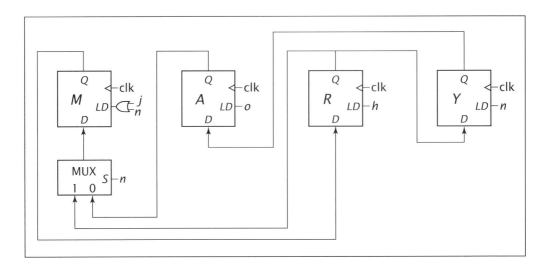

components are added to a system, they are simply connected to the bus; no additional data paths are required.

Buses can be implemented using either tri-state buffers or multiplexers. As shown in Figure 5.10, the output of each register must pass through a tri-state buffer before it is placed on to the bus. Only one buffer may be enabled at any time, or the data on the bus can become unpredictable. The buffer enable signals are set to ensure that the value to be transferred under a given condition is placed on the bus whenever that condition occurs. In this example, the system includes the RTL statement j: $M \leftarrow A$; therefore, j must enable the buffer that places the contents of register A on to the bus. The other buffer enables are set in a similar manner.

Note that the register load signals are the same as in the implementation with direct connections. This illustrates one of the advantages of bus-based systems; they can be partitioned and their sections designed separately. For example, consider the buffer for register M, which is enabled by control input h. The task of the buffer is not to pass the value of M on to the bus so that it can be read in by register R. Rather, its task is to place the contents of M on to the bus so that it can be read by whatever register should read it in. This is more than semantics; this argument highlights the fact that the buffer enables the flow of data but has no control over or information about which registers read the data. Similarly, the LD signal of register R does not

FIGURE 5.10

Complete design of the system to implement the RTL code using a bus and tri-state buffers

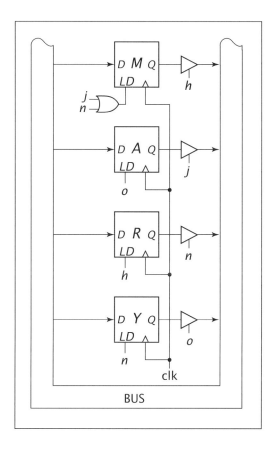

BUS

cause register R to read in the value on the bus that came from register M. It triggers register R to read in the data from the bus that was placed there by some buffer over which it has no control. Placing data onto and reading data off of the bus are controlled independently. By setting the control signals properly, the correct data is placed onto and read off of the bus to realize the desired micro-operations, and thus to implement the system correctly.

It is also possible to implement a system bus using a multiplexer. Figure 5.11 shows the same system implemented with multiplexers instead of tri-state buffers. The control inputs are configured so they place the same data onto the bus as the tri-state buffers did under identical conditions. The rest of the system is unchanged.

Complete design of the system to implement the RTL code using a bus and multiplexer

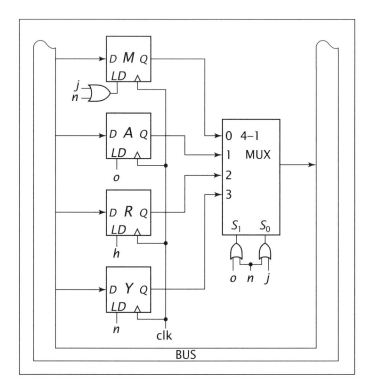

5.3 More Complex Digital Systems and RTL

Now that we've gone through the basics of using RTL to specify sequential digital systems, and implementing these systems using digital logic, let's look at a couple of more complex examples: a modulo 6 counter and a toll booth controller. (The reader may wish to refer to Chapter 2, in which we derived the designs for these systems in detail.)

5.3.1 Modulo 6 Counter

Our goal is to design a modulo 6 counter. First we specify the function of the counter using RTL, then we implement the RTL code using digital logic. The modulo 6 counter is a 3-bit counter that counts through the sequence

$$000\rightarrow001\rightarrow010\rightarrow011\rightarrow100\rightarrow101\rightarrow000\rightarrow... \ (0\rightarrow1\rightarrow2\rightarrow3\rightarrow4\rightarrow5\rightarrow0\rightarrow...)$$

Its input U controls the counter. When $U = 1$, the counter increments its value on the rising edge of the clock. When $U = 0$, it retains its current value regardless of the value of the clock. The value of the count is represented as the 3-bit output $V_2 V_1 V_0$. An additional output, C, is 1 when going from 5 to 0, and 0 otherwise. In this example, the C output remains at 1 until the counter goes from 0 to 1.

The finite state machine for this counter must have six states, arbitrarily labeled S_0, S_1, S_2, S_3, S_4, and S_5. State S_i corresponds to counter output i; the states follow the sequence

$$S_0 \rightarrow S_1 \rightarrow S_2 \rightarrow S_3 \rightarrow S_4 \rightarrow S_5 \rightarrow S_0 \rightarrow \dots$$

In addition, we include two more states, S_6 and S_7, to handle the case when the modulo 6 counter powers up in an invalid state. (In Chapter 2 we derived the state table and state diagram for this counter; refer to that chapter for the details of their derivation.) For the purposes of developing the RTL specification for this counter, we only need the state table and diagram; we no longer need the information used to develop them. The state table for this counter is shown in Table 5.3 and the state diagram is given in Figure 5.12.

State table for the modulo 6 counter

Present State	U	Next State	C	$V_2 V_1 V_0$
S_0	0	S_0	1	000
S_0	1	S_1	0	001
S_1	0	S_1	0	001
S_1	1	S_2	0	010
S_2	0	S_2	0	010
S_2	1	S_3	0	011
S_3	0	S_3	0	011
S_3	1	S_4	0	100
S_4	0	S_4	0	100
S_4	1	S_5	0	101
S_5	0	S_5	0	101
S_5	1	S_0	1	000
S_6	X	S_0	1	000
S_7	X	S_0	1	000

To specify this system in RTL, we first define conditions S_0 to S_7 to correspond to $V_2 V_1 V_0 = 000$ to 111, respectively. Then we consider each possible action of the modulo 6 counter. When the counter's value is 000 to 100 and its U (up) signal is asserted, the output of the counter is incremented. This corresponds to conditions $(S_0 + S_1 + S_2 + S_3 + S_4)U$. (On the left side of the colon, "+" indicates logical OR; to the right of the colon it indicates arithmetic add.) Under this condition, C is also set to 0. Using V to represent the value $V_2 V_1 V_0$, these two actions can be expressed as $V \leftarrow V + 1$, $C \leftarrow 0$. The resulting RTL statement is

Figure 5.12
State diagram for the modulo 6 counter

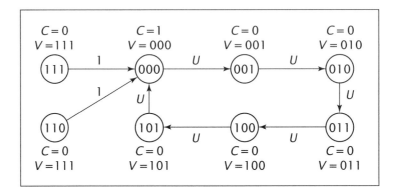

$$(S_0 + S_1 + S_2 + S_3 + S_4)U: V \leftarrow V + 1, C \leftarrow 0$$

Continuing, when the counter is in state S_5 ($V = 101$) and $U = 1$, the counter must be reset to 000 and C must be set to 1, or

$$S_5 U: V \leftarrow 0, C \leftarrow 1$$

The same happens during an invalid state, regardless of the value of U:

$$S_6 + S_7: V \leftarrow V + 1, C \leftarrow 0$$

This leaves only the condition $(S_0 + S_1 + S_2 + S_3 + S_4 + S_5)U'$ unaccounted for. This condition is true when the counter is in a valid state and $U = 0$. Under these conditions, the counter retains its current values for its output and C. Since no data transfer takes place, no RTL statement is needed for these conditions. In RTL, when no condition is met, no transfer occurs.

Since $S_5 U$ and $S_6 + S_7$ trigger the same micro-operations, they can be combined. Thus the behavior of the modulo 6 counter can be expressed by the following two RTL statements:

$$(S_0 + S_1 + S_2 + S_3 + S_4)U: V \leftarrow V + 1, C \leftarrow 0$$
$$S_5 U + S_6 + S_7: V \leftarrow 0, C \leftarrow 1$$

Figure 5.13 shows two implementations of this RTL code. The first uses a 3-bit parallel adder to generate $V + 1$ and sets C separately. Notice that the decoder converts $V_2 V_1 V_0$ to the state values S_0 to S_7. The second uses a 3-bit counter. C is set to 1 either when counting from 101 to 000 or when it is reset from an invalid state. Both are valid implementations of the RTL code, although the second design is much simpler.

5.3.2 Toll Booth Controller

Now consider a more complex design example, a toll booth controller. The toll booth controller has two external sensors. The first, C, indi-

FIGURE 5.13

Two implementations of the RTL code for the modulo 6 counter: (a) using a register, and (b) using a counter

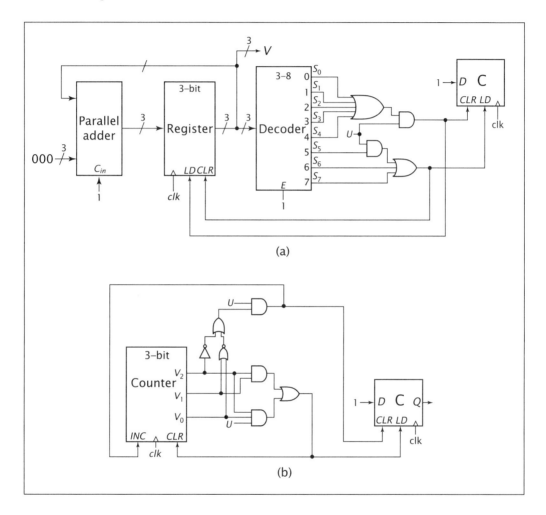

(a)

(b)

cates whether a car is at the toll booth; $C = 1$ when a car is present and $C = 0$ otherwise. The second sensor indicates whether a coin has been deposited in the toll booth's collection basket and the coin's value. This sensor sets $I_1 I_0 = 00$ if no coin has been deposited, $I_1 I_0 = 01$ if a nickel has been deposited, $I_1 I_0 = 10$ if a dime has been deposited, and $I_1 I_0 = 11$ if a quarter has been deposited.

The toll booth has two output lights and an output alarm. When a car pulls into the toll booth, a red light (R) is lit. It remains lit until the driver deposits at least 35 cents, at which point the red light goes off and the green light (G) is lit. The green light remains lit until the car leaves the toll booth; when this happens, the red light is lit again. If the car leaves the toll booth without paying the full toll, the red light remains lit and the alarm (*A*) is activated. The alarm remains active until another car enters the toll booth; then it is turned off.

This controller can be implemented as a finite state machine with ten states. These states and their outputs are shown in Table 5.4. Table 5.5 shows the state table for this controller and Figure 5.14

TABLE 5.4

States for the toll booth controller

State	Condition	R	G	A
S_{NOCAR}	No car in toll booth	1	0	0
S_0	Car in toll booth, 0 cents paid	1	0	0
S_5	Car in toll booth, 5 cents paid	1	0	0
S_{10}	Car in toll booth, 10 cents paid	1	0	0
S_{15}	Car in toll booth, 15 cents paid	1	0	0
S_{20}	Car in toll booth, 20 cents paid	1	0	0
S_{25}	Car in toll booth, 25 cents paid	1	0	0
S_{30}	Car in toll booth, 30 cents paid	1	0	0
S_{PAID}	Car in toll booth, full toll paid	0	1	0
S_{CHEAT}	Car left toll booth without paying full toll	1	0	1

TABLE 5.5

State table for the toll booth controller

Present State	C	$I_1 I_0$	Next State	R	G	A	Present State	C	$I_1 I_0$	Next State	R	G	A
S_{NOCAR}	1	XX	S_0	1	0	0	S_{15}	0	XX	S_{CHEAT}	1	0	1
S_{PAID}	0	XX	S_{NOCAR}	1	0	0	S_{15}	1	01	S_{20}	1	0	0
S_{CHEAT}	1	XX	S_0	1	0	0	S_{15}	1	10	S_{25}	1	0	0
S_0	0	XX	S_{CHEAT}	1	0	1	S_{15}	1	11	S_{PAID}	0	1	0
S_0	1	01	S_5	1	0	0	S_{20}	0	XX	S_{CHEAT}	1	0	1
S_0	1	10	S_{10}	1	0	0	S_{20}	1	01	S_{25}	1	0	0
S_0	1	11	S_{25}	1	0	0	S_{20}	1	10	S_{30}	1	0	0
S_5	0	XX	S_{CHEAT}	1	0	1	S_{20}	1	11	S_{PAID}	0	1	0
S_5	1	01	S_{10}	1	0	0	S_{25}	0	XX	S_{CHEAT}	1	0	1
S_5	1	10	S_{15}	1	0	0	S_{25}	1	01	S_{30}	1	0	0
S_5	1	11	S_{30}	1	0	0	S_{25}	1	10	S_{PAID}	0	1	0
S_{10}	0	XX	S_{CHEAT}	1	0	1	S_{25}	1	11	S_{PAID}	0	1	0
S_{10}	1	01	S_{15}	1	0	0	S_{30}	0	XX	S_{CHEAT}	1	0	1
S_{10}	1	10	S_{20}	1	0	0	S_{30}	1	01	S_{PAID}	0	1	0
S_{10}	1	11	S_{PAID}	0	1	0	S_{30}	1	10	S_{PAID}	0	1	0
							S_{30}	1	11	S_{PAID}	0	1	0

FIGURE 5.14
State diagram for the toll booth controller

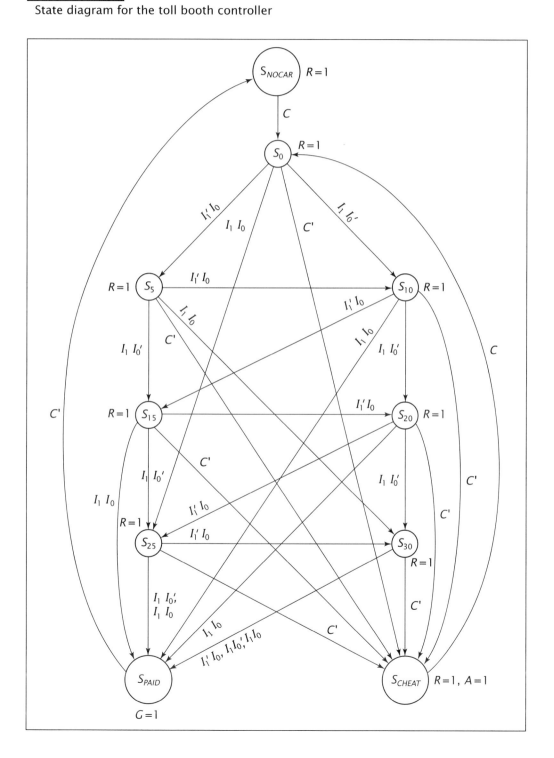

shows its state diagram. (See Chapter 2 for the derivation of the state table and state diagram.)

Since this state machine has ten states, we need a 4-bit value to encode the states. We use T to represent this value. The encoding is shown in Table 5.6.

Table 5.6

State value assignments for the toll booth controller

State	T	R	G	A
S_{NOCAR}	0000	1	0	0
S_0	0001	1	0	0
S_5	0010	1	0	0
S_{10}	0011	1	0	0
S_{15}	0100	1	0	0
S_{20}	0101	1	0	0
S_{25}	0110	1	0	0
S_{30}	0111	1	0	0
S_{PAID}	1000	0	1	0
S_{CHEAT}	1001	1	0	1
Unused	1010−1111	1	0	0

The next step is to convert the rows of the state table to RTL statements. Consider the first statement. When the controller is in state S_{NOCAR} and $C = 1$, it goes to state S_0, which has a state value of 0001. Assuming that the state value is stored in a 4-bit register labeled T, this can be expressed as

$$S_{NOCAR}C:\ T \leftarrow 0001$$

If we want to reset the outputs after every transition, this statement would also have to include micro-operations $R \leftarrow 1$, $G \leftarrow 0$, and $A \leftarrow 0$. In this example, we consider the outputs separately from the state transitions.

States S_{PAID} and S_{CHEAT} also have only one transition apiece. They can be expressed in RTL as

$$S_{PAID}C':\ T \leftarrow 0000$$
$$S_{CHEAT}C:\ T \leftarrow 0001$$

State S_0 has four possible transitions in the state table. Converting each individually produces the following RTL code.

$$S_0 C': T \leftarrow 1001$$
$$S_0 CI_1' I_0: T \leftarrow 0010$$
$$S_0 CI_1 I_0': T \leftarrow 0011$$
$$S_0 CI_1 I_0: T \leftarrow 0110$$

We derive the RTL code for the other states in the same manner. The code for the entire controller, excluding outputs, is shown in Table 5.7. The final entry corresponds to all unused states unconditionally going to state 0000.

Table 5.7

RTL code for the toll booth controller, excluding outputs

$S_{\text{NOCAR}} C: T \leftarrow 0001$	$S_{15} CI_1' I_0: T \leftarrow 0101$
$S_{\text{PAID}} C': T \leftarrow 0000$	$S_{15} CI_1 I_0': T \leftarrow 0110$
$S_{\text{CHEAT}} C: T \leftarrow 0001$	$S_{15} CI_1 I_0: T \leftarrow 1000$
$S_0 C': T \leftarrow 1001$	$S_{20} C': T \leftarrow 1001$
$S_0 CI_1' I_0: T \leftarrow 0010$	$S_{20} CI_1' I_0: T \leftarrow 0110$
$S_0 CI_1 I_0': T \leftarrow 0011$	$S_{20} CI_1 I_0': T \leftarrow 0111$
$S_0 CI_1 I_0: T \leftarrow 0110$	$S_{20} CI_1 I_0: T \leftarrow 1000$
$S_5 C': T \leftarrow 1001$	$S_{25} C': T \leftarrow 1001$
$S_5 CI_1' I_0: T \leftarrow 0011$	$S_{25} CI_1' I_0: T \leftarrow 0111$
$S_5 CI_1 I_0': T \leftarrow 0100$	$S_{25} CI_1 I_0': T \leftarrow 1000$
$S_5 CI_1 I_0: T \leftarrow 0111$	$S_{25} CI_1 I_0: T \leftarrow 1000$
$S_{10} C': T \leftarrow 1001$	$S_{30} C': T \leftarrow 1001$
$S_{10} CI_1' I_0: T \leftarrow 0100$	$S_{30} CI_1' I_0: T \leftarrow 1000$
$S_{10} CI_1 I_0': T \leftarrow 0101$	$S_{30} CI_1 I_0': T \leftarrow 1000$
$S_{10} CI_1 I_0: T \leftarrow 1000$	$S_{30} CI_1 I_0: T \leftarrow 1000$
$S_{15} C': T \leftarrow 1001$	$T_3(T_2 + T_1): T \leftarrow 0000$

Now we must develop RTL code to generate the outputs. As noted earlier, it is possible to reload the outputs during every transition. However, this adds a great deal of unnecessary hardware in this design, since most of the transitions do not modify the outputs. Instead, this design loads 1-bit registers R, G, and A only when they are changed. Output R changes from 1 to 0 only when entering state S_{PAID}, and changes from 0 to 1 only when leaving state S_{PAID}. Output G does exactly the opposite, becoming 1 when entering S_{PAID} and 0 when leaving it. Finally, output A becomes 1 whenever it enters S_{CHEAT} and 0 when it leaves S_{CHEAT}. After reviewing the state table, we find that the following transitions, shown in Table 5.8, set the outputs. Note that we reset all outputs when entering state S_0. This is done to handle the situation in which the controller powers up to a valid state but with incorrect output values.

Table 5.8

RTL code for the toll booth controller outputs

$$
\begin{aligned}
S_{PAID}C'&: \quad R \leftarrow 1, G \leftarrow 0 \\
S_{CHEAT}C&: \quad R \leftarrow 1, G \leftarrow 0, A \leftarrow 0 \\
S_{NOCAR}C&: \quad R \leftarrow 1, G \leftarrow 0, A \leftarrow 0 \\
S_0 C'&: \quad A \leftarrow 1 \\
S_5 C'&: \quad A \leftarrow 1 \\
S_{10}C'&: \quad A \leftarrow 1 \\
S_{10}CI_1 I_0&: \quad R \leftarrow 0, G \leftarrow 1 \\
S_{15}C'&: \quad A \leftarrow 1 \\
S_{15}CI_1 I_0&: \quad R \leftarrow 0, G \leftarrow 1 \\
S_{20}C'&: \quad A \leftarrow 1 \\
S_{20}CI_1 I_0&: \quad R \leftarrow 0, G \leftarrow 1 \\
S_{25}C'&: \quad A \leftarrow 1 \\
S_{25}CI_1 I_0'&: \quad R \leftarrow 0, G \leftarrow 1 \\
S_{25}CI_1 I_0&: \quad R \leftarrow 0, G \leftarrow 1 \\
S_{30}C'&: \quad A \leftarrow 1 \\
S_{30}CI_1' I_0&: \quad R \leftarrow 0, G \leftarrow 1 \\
S_{30}CI_1 I_0'&: \quad R \leftarrow 0, G \leftarrow 1 \\
S_{30}CI_1 I_0&: \quad R \leftarrow 0, G \leftarrow 1 \\
T_3(T_2 + T_1)&: \quad R \leftarrow 1, G \leftarrow 0, A \leftarrow 0
\end{aligned}
$$

Table 5.9 shows the complete RTL code for the toll booth controller. Several statements have been combined for simplicity; a few have not been optimized to improve readability. Note that more than one statement's conditions can be met simultaneously. As long as this does not cause two transitions to modify the same register simultaneously, this is acceptable. In fact, it can simplify the job of partitioning the design, making it easier to design the system hardware.

Table 5.9

Complete RTL code for the toll booth controller

$$(S_0 + S_5 + S_{10} + S_{15} + S_{20} + S_{25} + S_{30})C': T \leftarrow 1001$$
$$S_{\text{PAID}}C': T \leftarrow 0000$$
$$(S_{\text{NOCAR}} + S_{\text{CHEAT}})C: T \leftarrow 0001$$
$$S_0 CI_1'I_0: T \leftarrow 0010$$
$$S_0 CI_1 I_0': T \leftarrow 0011$$
$$S_0 CI_1 I_0: T \leftarrow 0110$$
$$S_5 CI_1'I_0: T \leftarrow 0011$$
$$S_5 CI_1 I_0': T \leftarrow 0100$$
$$S_5 CI_1 I_0: T \leftarrow 0111$$
$$S_{10} CI_1'I_0: T \leftarrow 0100$$
$$S_{10} CI_1 I_0': T \leftarrow 0101$$
$$S_{10} CI_1 I_0: T \leftarrow 1000$$
$$S_{15} CI_1'I_0: T \leftarrow 0101$$
$$S_{15} CI_1 I_0': T \leftarrow 0110$$
$$S_{15} CI_1 I_0: T \leftarrow 1000$$
$$S_{20} CI_1'I_0: T \leftarrow 0110$$
$$S_{20} CI_1 I_0': T \leftarrow 0111$$
$$S_{20} CI_1 I_0: T \leftarrow 1000$$
$$S_{25} CI_1'I_0: T \leftarrow 0111$$
$$S_{25} CI_1: T \leftarrow 1000$$
$$S_{30} C(I_1 + I_0): T \leftarrow 1000$$
$$T_3(T_2 + T_1): T \leftarrow 0000$$

$$S_{\text{PAID}}C': R \leftarrow 1, G \leftarrow 0$$
$$(S_{\text{NOCAR}} + S_{\text{CHEAT}})C: R \leftarrow 1, G \leftarrow 0, A \leftarrow 0$$
$$(S_0 + S_5 + S_{10} + S_{15} + S_{20} + S_{25} + S_{30})C': A \leftarrow 1$$
$$(S_{10} + S_{15} + S_{20} + S_{25} + S_{30})CI_1 I_0: R \leftarrow 0, G \leftarrow 1$$
$$(S_{25} + S_{30})CI_1 I_0': R \leftarrow 0, G \leftarrow 1$$
$$S_{30} CI_1'I_0: R \leftarrow 0, G \leftarrow 1$$
$$T_3(T_2 + T_1): R \leftarrow 1, G \leftarrow 0, A \leftarrow 0$$

5.4   Real World Example: VHDL-VHSIC Hardware Description Language

The RTL used so far in this chapter is a **pseudolanguage**. It does not have the rigor of a formal language; a specification written in RTL can be ambiguous. For example, consider the RTL code for the toll booth controller in the previous section, shown in Table 5.9. As the designers,

PRACTICAL PERSPECTIVE: Hardware Description Languages

There are two predominant hardware description languages used by designers, VHDL and Verilog. Both provide comparable capabilities, but they are not compatible. Unfortunately, they have pretty much split the market, which leads companies to standardize on one or the other (which reduces the pool of potential designers) or support both (which increases costs).

we know that R, G, and A are 1-bit values. However, that is never made clear anywhere in this controller's code. The micro-operation $R \leftarrow 0$ could set a 1-bit register R to 0, or it could set an 8-bit register R to 0.

This ambiguity can be tolerated by human designers. We can note, outside of the RTL code, such things as register sizes and include these parameters in our designs. However, we ultimately want to use computerized design tools to speed up the design process, and computerized tools cannot tolerate the ambiguities inherent to RTL code. In order to reap the benefits of such design tools, we need a more rigorous hardware description language.

In this section we introduce VHDL and provide an overview of its most common elements. This section gives enough information to demonstrate the capabilities of VHDL and to design some simple systems, but it is by no means a complete primer on VHDL. A full description of VHDL and its use would require an entire book of its own, and many such books are readily available. First we introduce the uses of VHDL and its syntax, then we use VHDL to design the modulo 6 counter described earlier in this chapter. We design the counter as a finite state machine, then redesign it as a digital circuit. Finally, we introduce a few of the more useful, advanced features of VHDL.

5.4.1 VHDL Syntax

Very high speed integrated circuit (VHSIC) hardware description language (VHDL) was developed to provide a standard for designing digital systems. Like a high-level computer language, such as C or C++, VHDL specifies a formal syntax. The designer creates a design file (or files) using that syntax just as a programmer writes a C program. The designer then synthesizes the design using any design package that can accept VHDL files. This is equivalent to the programmer compiling the C program: It checks for errors in syntax and declarations, but not in logic. Finally, the designer debugs the design using simulation tools.

VHDL was developed to meet the need for a standard hardware description language. Design systems use VHDL to design custom ICs and **application-specific ICs** (**ASICs**), as well as to fit designs onto existing **programmable logic devices** (**PLDs**).

VHDL offers the designer several advantages. One of its greatest benefits is its **portability**. Just as a valid C program can be compiled by any compliant C compiler, a VHDL design can be synthesized by any design system that supports VHDL. This does not tie the user to one design system or design system manufacturer. The VHDL file is **device independent**. The same file can be used to implement the design on a custom IC, an ASIC, or any PLD that is capable of containing the design.

VHDL designs can be **simulated** by the design system, allowing the designer to verify a design's performance before committing it to hardware. VHDL files also provide good documentation of a system's design. But perhaps the greatest benefit of VHDL is that it allows the user to specify the system at various levels. The designer can design the system using a high level of abstraction, such as a finite state machine, down to a low-level digital logic implementation.

There are some disadvantages to VHDL as well. VHDL source code often becomes long and difficult to follow, especially at a low level of abstraction. It is often less intuitive than a block diagram or RTL description of the same system. Also, different design tools may produce different valid designs for the same system. This usually happens with VHDL at the highest levels of abstraction, which specify the behavior of a system but provide no details about its implementation.

VHDL design code has three primary sections: **library declarations**, the **entity section**, and the **architecture section**. The first section is the simplest. It consists of statements that specify libraries to be accessed and modules of these libraries to be used. For those familiar with C programming, these statements are similar to "include" statements in C.

The most commonly used library is called IEEE, after the organization that formalized the VHDL standard. Of the modules in this library, the `std_logic_1164` library is used most often. This module specifies, among other things, input and output declarations for the designer to use, much like stdio.h in C. These two components would be written as follows.

```
library IEEE;
use IEEE.std_logic_1164.all;
```

More than one library and module may be used in a design. All libraries and modules used are listed in this portion of the VHDL design file.

In the second section, the entity section, the designer specifies the name of the design and its inputs and outputs. The designer does not specify the logic that uses and drives these signals here; that is done in the architecture section. The basic format for this section is as follows:

```
entity module_name is
    port(
        input1, input2,...inputp:     in std_logic;
        output1, output2,...outputo:  out std_logic;
        inout1, inout2,...inoutn:     inout std_logic;
        buffer1, buffer2, ...bufferm: buffer std_logic;
        invec1, invec2,...invecl:     in std_logic_vector(range);
        outvec1, outvec2,...outveck:  out std_logic_vector(range);
        iovec1, iovec2,...iovecj:     inout std_logic_vector(range);
        bufvec1, bufvec2, ...bufveci: buffer std_logic_vector(range)
    );
end module_name;
```

The first two lines specify the name of the module and initiate the declaration of its signals. The signals `input1, input2,...inputp` are of type `in std_logic`. This declares them as inputs to the design. If the design is to be synthesized as a chip (custom, ASIC, or PLD), these inputs will be assigned to pins on the chip during synthesis. Similarly, the signals of type `out std_logic` define outputs of the design. Type `inout std_logic` defines bidirectional signals, which can either input or output data. Finally, type `buffer std_logic` is used for internal signals within the design that are neither input nor output. Signals with this declaration may be used for internal storage or to generate intermediate results for use by the rest of the design.

The next four declarations perform the same functions as the first four, except that they declare vectors of values. This is similar to declaring an array in a high-level language. The **range** can be expressed as either *lowvalue* to *highvalue* or *highvalue* downto *lowvalue*. If a design has more than one vector of any type with different ranges, separate statements are used for each range size:

```
invector1:  in std_logic_vector(3 downto 0);
invector2:  in std_logic_vector(4 downto 2);
invector3:  in std_logic_vector(1 to 8);
```

The final section of the VHDL design file is the architecture section. This section specifies the behavior and/or internal logic of the system under design. Its basic format is as follows:

```
architecture arch_name of module_name is
type and additional signal declarations;

begin
    process1: process(signal list)
        begin
```

```
                    statements defining behavior/logic;
            end process process1;
     .
     .

     .
      processn: process(signal list)
            begin
                    statements defining behavior/logic;
            end process processn;
   end arch_name;
```

The first line specifies the name of the architecture and the entity to which it belongs. The next line is used to specify any new **types** (similar to enumerated types in C) and new signals local to this architecture.

The remainder of the architecture section consists of one or more **processes**. Each process defines the behavior and/or logical implementation of all or part of the architecture. The processes are not necessarily mutually exclusive. If desired, signals from one process can affect other processes. This is particularly useful for partitioning a design into modules, each of which can be implemented as a process. In addition, each process can be designed at a different level of abstraction. One process can describe the behavior of a module while another describes the digital hardware implementation of its module.

5.4.2   VHDL Design with a High Level of Abstraction

VHDL can be used to design sequential systems at various levels of abstraction. A **high level of abstraction** might be the finite state machine description of a system, while a digital logic design would be a **low level of abstraction**. To illustrate the use of VHDL to design a system using a high level of abstraction, we can design the modulo 6 counter as a finite state machine. This design is based solely on the state table of Table 5.3 and the state diagram of Figure 5.12. Later we redesign this counter at a low level of abstraction, specifying the boolean functions for the state values and system outputs.

To create the VHDL design for this counter, we begin with the library declarations and entity section. In the library declarations, we will only need the standard IEEE library and its `std_logic_1164` module. In the entity section, we declare the system's inputs and outputs. The modulo 6 counter has two inputs, U and the system clock, which we label *clk*. It has 1-bit output C, and 3-bit output V. We define V as a 3-bit vector with indices 2, 1, and 0. The library declarations and entity section of this design are as follows:

```
library IEEE;
use IEEE.std_logic_1164.all;

entity mod6 is
    port(
            U,clk: in std_logic;
                C: out std_logic;
                V: out std_logic_vector(2 downto 0)
        );
end mod6;
```

Now we must develop the architecture section of the modulo 6 counter. But before specifying the system's behavior, the architecture declares a new enumerated type, **states**. This type has eight possible values, S_0 to S_7, which correspond to the six valid and two invalid states of the counter. It declares two signals, *present_state,* and *next_state,* to be of this type. As you might guess from their names, *present_state,* will indicate which state, S_0 to S_7, the modulo 6 counter is presently in, and *next_state,* contains the state that the counter goes to next. This is done using the following VHDL code:

```
architecture amod6 of mod6 is
    type states is (S0, S1, S2, S3, S4, S5, S6, S7);
    signal present_state, next_state: states;
```

Beyond these declarations, we partition this design into two processes. The first looks at the present state of the counter and its input values, and generates the desired outputs and next state value. The second process makes the actual transition from the present state to the next state.

The first procedure is named state_mod6. It uses a **case** statement, which is similar to case statements in high-level programming languages, to handle each state separately. To better describe how this statement works, consider the VHDL code for the state_mod6 procedure:

```
  state_mod6: process(present_state,u)
       begin
            case present_state is
                when S0 => V<="000"; C<='1';
                        if (U='1') then next_state <= S1;
                            else next_state <= S0;
                        end if;
                when S1 => V<="001"; C<='0';
                        if (U='1') then next_state <= S2;
                            else next_state <= S1;
                        end if;
                when S2 => V<="010"; C<='0';
```

```
                              if (U='1') then next_state <= S3;
                                    else next_state <= S2;
                              end if;
                    when S3 => V<="011"; C<='0';
                              if (U='1') then next_state <= S4;
                                    else next_state <= S3;
                              end if;
                    when S4 => V<="100"; C<='0';
                              if (U='1') then next_state <= S5;
                                    else next_state <= S4;
                              end if;
                    when S5 => V<="101"; C<='0';
                              if (U='1') then next_state <= S0;
                                    else next_state <= S5;
                              end if;
                    when S6 => V<="111"; C<='0';
                              next_state <= S0;
                    when S7 => V<="111"; C<='0';
                              next_state <= S0;
              end case;
          end process state_mod6;
```

The case statement has eight possible outcomes, one for each possible value (S_0 to S_7) of present_state. To illustrate the function of the code for each value of the case statement, consider the condition when the *present_state* is S_0. The first line sets output V to 000 and output C to 1, the outputs associated with this state, as shown in Figure 5.12. The remaining lines generate the next state. If $U = 1$, the signal *next_state* is set to the next state in the state diagram. Otherwise it is set to the same value as the current state. States S_1 to S_5 operate in a similar manner. States S_6 and S_7 both output $V = 111$ and $C = 0$, the values used to indicate an invalid state. Both states unconditionally set the next state to S_0.

The second process is *state_transition*. On the rising edge of the clock it copies the *next_state* value generated by process *state_mod6* to *present_state*. Although *state_mod6* generates the next state value, the transition to this state occurs in process *state_transition*. Once the new value of *present_state* is set, it is used by *state_mod6* to select the next value for the case statement. The code for this module is

```
state_transition: process(clk)
    begin
          if rising_edge(clk) then present_state <= next_state;
          end if;
          end process state_transition;
```

Figure 5.15 shows the complete VHDL code for the modulo 6 counter designed using a high level of abstraction.

Figure 5.15

VHDL file to implement the modulo 6 counter using a high level of abstraction

```
library IEEE;
use IEEE.std_logic_1164.all;

entity mod6 is
     port(
          U,clk: in std_logic;
             C: out std_logic;
             V: out std_logic_vector(2 downto 0)
        );
end mod6;

architecture amod6 of mod6 is
     type states is (S0, S1, S2, S3, S4, S5, S6, S7);
     signal present_state, next_state: states;
begin
     state_mod6: process(present_state,u)
          begin
               case present_state is
                    when S0 => V<="000"; C<='1';
                         if (U='1') then next_state <= S1;
                              else next_state <= S0;
                         end if;
                    when S1 => V<="001"; C<='0';
                         if (U='1') then next_state <= S2;
                              else next_state <= S1;
                         end if;
                    when S2 => V<="010"; C<='0';
                         if (U='1') then next_state <= S3;
                              else next_state <= S2;
                         end if;
                    when S3 => V<="011"; C<='0';
                         if (U='1') then next_state <= S4;
                              else next_state <= S3;
                         end if;
                    when S4 => V<="100"; C<='0';
                         if (U='1') then next_state <= S5;
                              else next_state <= S4;
                         end if;
                    when S5 => V<="101"; C<='0';
                         if (U='1') then next_state <= S0;
                              else next_state <= S5;
```

```
                              end if;
                 when S6 => V<="111"; C<='0';
                     next_state <= S0;
                 when S7 => V<="111"; C<='0';
                     next_state <= S0;
              end case;
          end process state_mod6;
     state_transition: process(clk)
          begin
              if rising_edge(clk) then present_state <= next_state;
              end if;
          end process state_transition;
end amod6;
```

5.4.3 VHDL Design with a Low Level of Abstraction

A more circuit-oriented designer may prefer a logic design, using a low level of abstraction. VHDL supports this level of abstraction as well. To illustrate this, we can redesign the modulo 6 counter as a logic design. The digital logic design for the modulo 6 counter is shown in Figure 5.16. (See Chapter 2 for a description of how we developed this design, but note that this circuit includes logic to handle the unused states S_6 and S_7, which was not included in the Chapter 2 design.)

Figure 5.17 shows the complete VHDL code for this system. It uses the typical IEEE library and its *std_logic_1164* module. It has the same inputs (*U* and *clk*) as the state machine implementation of the counter. It also has the same outputs; V_2, V_1, and V_0 are shown separately, rather than as a vector, to illustrate another way to declare these outputs. There are three logic signals, q_2, q_1, and q_0, not used in the state machine design, which correspond to the 3-bit output of the register in Figure 5.16.

The architecture section uses a single process, cct_mod6. On the rising edge of the clock, q_2, q_1, and q_0 are loaded with new values. These values are taken directly from the digital logic used to generate the next state in Figure 5.16. The entire if statement is equivalent to loading the register with the next state of the counter. The remaining statements set the counter's outputs. As in Figure 5.16, the outputs depend only on the present state and not on the system clock.

Neither level of abstraction is better than the other insofar as both produce valid results. They are suited for designers with different design perspectives. The state machine design might have been designed by a systems engineer as well as a digital designer. By specifying the behavior of the system from a state machine perspective,

Figure 5.16

Logic design for the modulo 6 counter

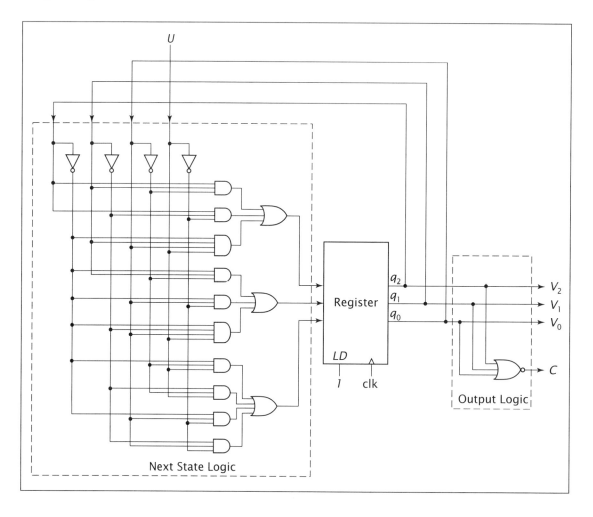

the VHDL file does not need to specify any details about the implementation. This design does not specify any explicit components, only the transfers that must occur for the system to function properly.

In contrast, the low-level file shows an implementation using digital logic. The values input to q_2, q_1, and q_0 are the inputs to the flip-flops. The outputs correspond to the output logic of the Moore machine implementation of the modulo 6 counter. Because the equations are derived by the designer, this type of design would typically be created by a logic designer.

FiGURE 5.17

VHDL file to implement the modulo 6 counter using a low level of abstraction

```
library IEEE;
use IEEE.std_logic_1164.all;

entity mod6 is
      port(
                  U,clk: in std_logic;
            q2,q1,q0: buffer std_logic;
          V2,V1,V0,C: out std_logic
      );
end mod6;

architecture amod6 of mod6 is
begin
      cct_mod6: process(q2,q1,q0,U,clk)
            begin
                  if rising_edge(clk) then
                        q2 <= (q2 and (not q1) and (not q0)) or
                              (q2 and (not q1) and (not U)) or
                              ((not q2) and q1 and q0 and U);
                        q1 <= ((not q2) and q1 and (not q0)) or
                              ((not q2) and q1 and (not U)) or
                              ((not q2) and (not q1) and q0 and U);
                        q0 <= ((not q2) and (not q0) and U) or
                              ((not q1) and (not q0) and U) or
                              ((not q2) and q0 and (not U)) or
                              ((not q1) and q0 and (not U));
                  end if;
                  V2 <= q2;
                  V1 <= q1;
                  V0 <= (q2 and q1) or q0;
                   C <= not(q2 or q1 or q0);
            end process cct_mod6;
end amod6;
```

5.5 SUMMARY

Micro-operations specify simple operations in which a value is copied from one location to another, or the result of an arithmetic or logical operation is stored in a register. Micro-operations form the basis for sequential digital systems. By performing a series of micro-operations in the correct sequence, a digital system can accomplish a larger task.

PRACTICAL PERSPECTIVE: SOME ADVANCED CAPABILITIES of VHDL

This section has introduced only the most rudimentary elements of VHDL, sufficient for simple designs like the modulo 6 counter, but VHDL has more advanced capabilities as well. For a more complete description of VHDL, please refer to one of the many books dedicated exclusively to VHDL.

Components

In VHDL, it is possible to define a component and then use that component in a larger design. For example, the modulo 6 counter could be used as a component in a digital clock to count the tens of seconds and tens of minutes.

   This feature makes it possible to build a toolbox of components that can be used in multiple designs, and to use components designed by others. This can improve designer productivity and system reliability. The rationale for using components is similar to that for using and reusing objects in object oriented programming languages such as C++.

Timing

The designs presented in this section are idealized; they do not account for any propagation delays within their architectures. VHDL allows the designer to specify a propagation delay using the `after` clause. This clause is appended to a standard assignment statement, as shown in the following example.

$$C <= not(q2 \ or \ q1 \ or \ q0) \ after \ 5ns;$$

In this case, the value is not stored until 5 ns have elapsed. This does not affect the logic of the design directly, but it is useful for simulation.

Simulation

One of the greatest advantages of VHDL is that it allows the designer to simulate the performance of a design before committing it to silicon or programming it into a PLD. This allows the designer to check for logic errors as well as timing errors and greatly reduces the time needed to debug a design. However, simulations are not perfect. Even after simulating a design, it is still necessary to test the programmed chip to verify that the design performs properly.

   Digital designers use hardware description languages to design digital circuits of varying complexity, from simple components to microprocessors. Using informal HDLs, such as RTL, a designer can specify the functions that must occur in a system and the conditions under which they occur. The designer can then design a circuit to meet this specification.

More formal HDLs, such as VHDL, are well suited for use by computer-aided design tools. Such tools allow the user to input an HDL specification for a system using various levels of abstraction, ranging from a high-level state machine specification to a low-level digital circuit specification. The design tool verifies the syntax of the design and creates the files needed to produce a hardware implementation of the design, either using a custom IC or a PLD. These tools typically allow the designer to simulate the design before implementing it in hardware.

Problems

1 Write valid RTL statements that realize the following transitions. All registers are 1-bit wide.

a) IF $\alpha = 1$ THEN copy X to W and copy Z to Y
b) IF $\alpha = 1$ THEN copy X to W; otherwise copy Z to Y
c) IF $\alpha = 0$ THEN copy X to W

2 Show the hardware to implement the RTL statements developed for Problem 1.

3 Write the RTL code for the following transitions. All registers are 1-bit wide. Signals α and β are never equal to 1 simultaneously.

a) IF $\alpha = 1$ THEN copy Y to X
   IF $\beta = 1$ THEN copy Y' to X
b) IF $\alpha = 1$ THEN set X to 0
   IF $\beta = 1$ THEN set X to X'

4 Show the hardware to implement the RTL statements developed for Problem 3.

5 Show the RTL and hardware to implement a shuffle operation on 8-bit register X when $\alpha = 1$. A shuffle of the sequence ABCDEFGH would produce the result AEBFCGDH.

6 Show the hardware to implement the following RTL code.

a) α: $X \leftarrow X + Y$
b) β: $X \leftarrow X + Y' + 1$
c) Γ: $X \leftarrow X \oplus Y$

7 Show the hardware to implement all three of the RTL statements of Problem 6 in one combined system. Control hardware ensures that no more than one of the control signals α, β, and Γ is active at any time.

8 For $X = 1001\ 1001\ 0000\ 0010$, show the result of the following operations.

    a) shl(X)
    b) shr(X)
    c) cil(X)
    d) cir(X)
    e) ashl(X)
    f) ashr(X)
    g) dshl(X)
    h) dshr(X)

9 Repeat Problem 8 for $X = 1000\ 0011\ 1001\ 0101$.

10 Repeat Problem 8 for $X = 0101\ 1001\ 0111\ 1000$.

11 Show the hardware to implement the following micro-operations. X consists of four D flip-flops. Each micro-operation occurs when $\alpha = 1$.

    a) shl(X)
    b) shr(X)
    c) cil(X)
    d) cir(X)

12 Show the hardware to implement the following micro-operations. X consists of 12 flip-flops. Each micro-operation occurs when $\alpha = 1$.

    a) ashl(X)
    b) ashr(X)
    c) dshl(X)
    d) dshr(X)

13 Show the RTL code to specify the following micro-operations. Each micro-operation occurs when $\alpha = 1$.

    a) shr(X)
    b) cil(X)
    c) cir(X)
    d) ashl(X)
    e) ashr(X)
    f) dshl(X)
    g) dshr(X)

14 Develop RTL code to implement the 4-state string checker from Chapter 2.

15 Design the hardware to implement the RTL code developed in Problem 14.

16 Develop RTL code to implement the 8-state string checker from Chapter 2.

17 Design the hardware to implement the RTL code developed in Problem 16.

18 Design the 4-state string checker introduced in Chapter 2 as a state machine using VHDL.

19 Design the 4-state string checker introduced in Chapter 2 as a digital circuit using VHDL.

20 Design the 8-state string checker introduced in Chapter 2 as a state machine using VHDL.

21 Design the 8-state string checker introduced in Chapter 2 as a digital circuit using VHDL.

22 Design the toll booth controller as a state machine using VHDL.

23 Design the toll booth controller as a digital circuit using VHDL.

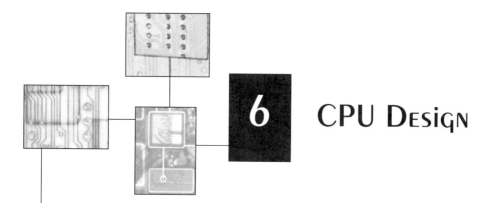

6 CPU Design

As we saw in Chapter 4, a CPU contains three main sections: the register section, the arithmetic/logic unit (ALU), and the control unit. These sections work together to perform the sequences of micro-operations needed to perform the fetch, decode, and execute cycles of every instruction in the CPU's instruction set. In this chapter we examine the process of designing a CPU in detail.

To demonstrate this design process, we present the designs of two CPUs, each implemented using **hardwired control**. (A different type of control, which uses a **microsequencer**, is examined in Chapter 7.) We start by analyzing the applications for the CPU. For instance, will it be used to control a microwave oven or a personal computer? Once we know its application, we can determine the types of programs it will run, and from there we can develop the instruction set architecture (ISA) for the CPU. Next, we determine the other registers we need to include within the CPU that are not a part of its ISA. We then design the state diagram for the CPU, along with the micro-operations needed to fetch, decode, and execute each instruction. Once this is done, we define the internal data paths and the necessary control signal. Finally, we design the control unit, the logic that generates the control signals and causes the operations to occur.

In this chapter we present the complete design of two simple CPUs, along with an analysis of their shortcomings. We also look at the internal architecture of the Intel 8085 microprocessor, whose instruction set architecture was introduced in Chapter 3.

6.1 Specifying a CPU

The first step in designing a CPU is to determine its applications. We don't need anything as complicated as an Itanium microprocessor to control a microwave oven; a simple 4-bit processor would be powerful enough to handle this job. However, the same 4-bit processor would be woefully inadequate to power a personal computer. The key is to match the capabilities of the CPU to the tasks it will perform.

Once we have determined the tasks a CPU will perform, we must design an instruction set architecture capable of handling these tasks. We select the instructions a programmer could use to write the application programs and the registers these instructions will use.

After this is done, we design the state diagram for the CPU. We show the micro-operations performed during each state and the conditions that cause the CPU to go from one state to another. A CPU is just a complex finite state machine. By specifying the states and their micro-operations, we specify the steps the CPU must perform in order to fetch, decode, and execute every instruction in its instruction set.

Figure 6.1

Generic CPU state diagram

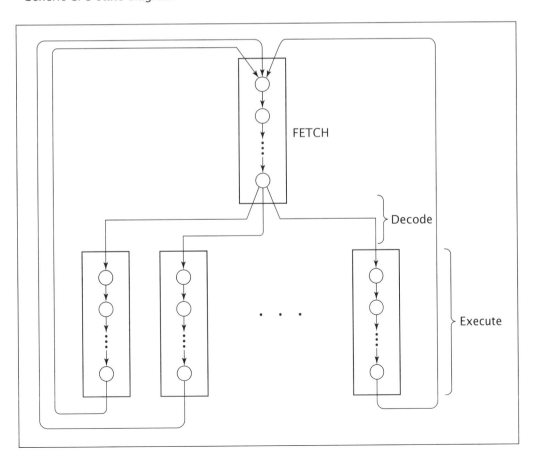

In general, a CPU performs the following sequence of operations:

- **Fetch cycle**: Fetch an instruction from memory, then go to the decode cycle.
- **Decode cycle**: Decode the instruction—that is, determine which instruction has been fetched—then go to the execute cycle for that instruction.
- **Execute cycle**: Execute the instruction, then go to the fetch cycle and fetch the next instruction.

A generic state diagram is shown in Figure 6.1 on page 215. Note that the decode cycle does not have any states. Rather, the decode cycle is actually the multiple branches from the end of the fetch routine to each individual execute routine.

6.2   Design and Implementation of a Very Simple CPU

In this section, we specify and design a Very Simple CPU, probably the simplest CPU you will ever encounter. This CPU isn't very practical, but it is not meant to be. The sole application of this CPU is to serve as an instructional aid, to illustrate the design process without burdening the reader with too many design details. In the next section, we design a more complex CPU, which builds on the design methods presented here.

6.2.1   Specifications for a Very Simple CPU

To illustrate the CPU design process, consider this small and somewhat impractical CPU. It can access 64 bytes of memory, each byte being 8 bits wide. The CPU does this by outputting a 6-bit address on its output pins A[5..0] and reading in the 8-bit value from memory on its inputs D[7..0].

This CPU will have only one programmer-accessible register, an 8-bit **accumulator** labeled *AC*. It has only four instructions in its instruction set, as shown in Table 6.1.

Table 6.1

Instruction set for the Very Simple CPU

Instruction	Instruction Code	Operation
ADD	00AAAAAA	AC←AC + M[AAAAAA]
AND	01AAAAAA	AC←AC ∧ M[AAAAAA]
JMP	10AAAAAA	GOTO AAAAAA
INC	11XXXXXX	AC←AC + 1

As noted earlier, this is a fairly impractical CPU for several reasons. For example, although it can perform some computations, it cannot output the results.

In addition to *AC*, this CPU needs several additional registers to perform the internal operations necessary to fetch, decode, and execute instructions. The registers in this CPU are fairly standard and are found in many CPUs; their sizes vary depending on the CPU in which they are used. This CPU contains the following registers:

- A 6-bit **address register**, *AR*, which supplies an address to memory via A[5..0]
- A 6-bit **program counter**, *PC*, which contains the address of the next instruction to be executed
- An 8-bit **data register**, *DR*, which receives instructions and data from memory via D[7..0]
- A 2-bit **instruction register**, *IR*, which stores the opcode portion of the instruction code fetched from memory

A CPU is just a complex finite state machine, and that dictates the approach we take in designing this CPU. First, we design the state diagram for the CPU. Then we design both the necessary data paths and the control logic to realize the finite state machine, thus implementing the CPU.

6.2.2   Fetching Instructions from Memory

Before the CPU can execute an instruction, it must fetch the instruction from memory. To do this, the CPU performs the following sequence of actions.

1. Send the address to memory by placing it on the address pins A[5..0].
2. After allowing memory enough time to perform its internal decoding and to retrieve the desired instruction, send a signal to memory so that it outputs the instruction on its output pins. These pins are connected to D[7..0] of the CPU. The CPU reads this data in from those pins.

The address of the instruction to be fetched is stored in the program counter. Since A[5..0] receive their values from the address register, the first step is accomplished by copying the contents of *PC* to *AR*. Thus the first state of the fetch cycle is

$$\text{FETCH1:} \quad AR \leftarrow PC$$

Next, the CPU must read the instruction from memory. The CPU must assert a **READ** signal, which is output from the CPU to memory, to cause memory to output the data to D[7..0]. At the same time, the CPU must read the data in and store it in *DR*, since this is the only register used to access memory. By waiting until one state after FETCH1, the CPU gives memory the time to access the requested data (which is an instruction in this case). The net result is, at first,

FETCH2: $DR \leftarrow M$

In fact, there is another operation that will be performed here. We must also increment the program counter, so FETCH2 should actually be as follows:

FETCH2: $DR \leftarrow M, PC \leftarrow PC + 1$

See Practical Perspective: Why a CPU Increments PC During the Fetch Cycle for the reasoning behind this.

Finally, there are two other things that the CPU will do as part of the fetch routine. First, it copies the two high-order bits of *DR* to *IR*. As shown in Table 6.1, these two bits indicate which instruction is to be executed. As we will see in the design of the control logic, it is necessary to save this value in a location other than *DR* so it will be available to the control unit. Also, the CPU copies the six low-order bits of *DR* to *AR* during the fetch routine. For the ADD and AND instructions, these bits contain the memory address of one of the operands for the instruction. Moving the address to *AR* here will result in one less state in the execute routines for these instructions. For the other two instructions, it will not cause a problem. They do not need to access memory again, so they just won't use the value loaded into *AR*. Once they return to the FETCH routine, FETCH1 will load *PC* into *AR*, over-

PRACTICAL PERSPECTIVE: Why a CPU Increments PC During the Fetch Cycle

To see why a CPU increments the program counter during FETCH2, consider what would happen if it did not increment *PC*. For example, assume that the CPU fetched an instruction from location 10. In FETCH1, it would perform the operation $AR \leftarrow PC$ (which has the value 10). In FETCH2, it would fetch the instruction from memory location 10 and store it in *DR*. Presumably the CPU would then decode the instruction and execute it, and then return to FETCH1 to fetch the next instruction. However, *PC* still contains the value 10, so the CPU would continuously fetch, decode, and execute the same instruction!

The next instruction to be executed is stored in the next location, 11. The CPU must increment the *PC* some time before it returns to the fetch routine. To make this happen, the designer has two options: have every instruction increment the *PC* as part of its execute routine, or increment the *PC* once during the fetch routine. The latter is much easier to implement, so CPUs take this approach.

writing the unused value. These two operations can be performed in one state as

FETCH3: $IR \leftarrow DR[7..6]$, $AR \leftarrow DR[5..0]$

The state diagram for the fetch cycle is shown in Figure 6.2.

FIGURE 6.2

Fetch cycle for the Very Simple CPU

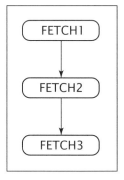

6.2.3   DECODING INSTRUCTIONS

After the CPU has fetched an instruction from memory, it must determine which instruction it has fetched so that it may invoke the correct execute routine. The state diagram represents this as a series of branches from the end of the fetch routine to the individual execute routines. For this CPU, there are four instructions and thus four execute routines. The value in *IR*, 00, 01, 10, or 11, determines which execute routine is invoked. The state diagram for the fetch and decode cycles is shown in Figure 6.3 on page 220.

6.2.4   EXECUTING INSTRUCTIONS

To complete the state diagram for this CPU, we must develop the state diagram for each execute routine. Now we design the portion of the state diagram for each execute routine and the overall design for the CPU. The state diagrams for the individual execute routines are fairly simple, so they are only included in the diagram of the finite state machine for the entire CPU.

6.2.4.1   ADD INSTRUCTION

In order to perform the ADD instruction, the CPU must do two things. First, it must fetch one operand from memory. Then it must add this operand to the current contents of the accumulator and store the result back into the accumulator.

FIGURE 6.3

Fetch and decode cycles for the Very Simple CPU

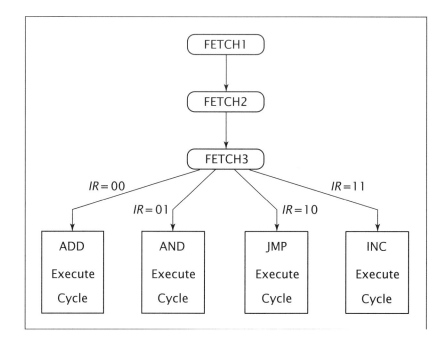

To fetch the operand from memory, the CPU must first make its address available via A[5..0], just as it did to fetch the instruction from memory. This is done by moving the address into *AR*. However, this was already done in FETCH3, so the CPU can simply read the value in immediately. (This is the time savings mentioned earlier.) Thus,

$$\text{ADD1:}\quad DR \leftarrow M$$

Now that both operands are within the CPU, it can perform the actual addition in one state.

$$\text{ADD2:}\quad AC \leftarrow AC + DR$$

These two operations comprise the entire execute cycle for the ADD instruction. At this point, the ADD execute cycle would branch back to the fetch cycle to begin fetching the next instruction.

6.2.4.2 AND INSTRUCTION

The execute cycle for the AND instruction is virtually the same as that for the ADD instruction. It must fetch an operand from memory, making use of the address copied to *AR* during FETCH3. However, instead of adding the two values, it must logically AND the two values. The states that comprise this execute cycle are

$$AND1: \quad DR \leftarrow M$$
$$AND2: \quad AC \leftarrow AC \wedge DR$$

6.2.4.3   JMP Instruction

Any JMP instruction is implemented in basically the same way. The address to which the CPU must jump is copied into the program counter. Then, when the CPU fetches the next instruction, it uses this new address, thus realizing the JMP.

The execute cycle for the JMP instruction for this CPU is quite trivial. Since the address is already stored in $DR[5..0]$, we simply copy that value into PC and go to the fetch routine. The single state which comprises this execute cycle is

$$JMP1: \quad PC \leftarrow DR[5..0]$$

In this case, we actually had a second choice. Since this value was copied into AR during FETCH3, we could have performed the operation $PC \leftarrow AR$ instead. Either is acceptable.

6.2.4.4   INC Instruction

The INC instruction can also be executed using a single state. The CPU simply adds 1 to the contents of AC and goes to the fetch routine. The state for this execute cycle is

$$INC1: \quad AC \leftarrow AC + 1$$

The state diagram for this CPU, including the fetch, decode, and execute cycles, is shown in Figure 6.4 on page 222.

6.2.5   Establishing Required Data Paths

The state diagram and register transfers specify what must be done in order to realize this CPU. Now we must design the CPU so that it actually does these things. First, we look at what data transfers can take place and design the internal data paths of the CPU so this can be done. The operations associated with each state for this CPU are

$$FETCH1: \quad AR \leftarrow PC$$
$$FETCH2: \quad DR \leftarrow M, PC \leftarrow PC + 1$$
$$FETCH3: \quad IR \leftarrow DR[7..6], AR \leftarrow DR[5..0]$$
$$ADD1: \quad DR \leftarrow M$$
$$ADD2: \quad AC \leftarrow AC + DR$$
$$AND1: \quad DR \leftarrow M$$
$$AND2: \quad AC \leftarrow AC \wedge DR$$
$$JMP1: \quad PC \leftarrow DR[5..0]$$
$$INC1: \quad AC \leftarrow AC + 1$$

Figure 6.4

Complete state diagram for the Very Simple CPU

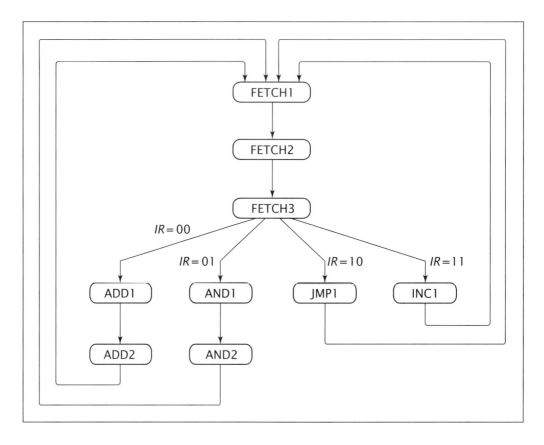

(If this looks like RTL code, you're headed in the right direction!) Note that memory supplies its data to the CPU via pins D[7..0]. Also recall that the address pins A[5..0] receive data from the address register, so the CPU must include a data path from the outputs of *AR* to A.

To design the data paths, we can take one of two approaches. The first is to create **direct paths** between each pair of components that transfer data. We can use multiplexers or buffers to select one of several possible data inputs for registers that can receive data from more than one source. For example, in this CPU, *AR* can receive data from *PC* or *DR*[5..0], so the CPU would need a mechanism to select which one is to supply data to *AR* at a given time. This approach could work for this CPU because it is so small. However, as CPU complexity increases, this becomes impractical. A more sensible approach is to create a **bus** within the CPU and route data between components via the bus.

To illustrate the bus concept, consider an interstate highway that is 200 miles long and has about as many exits. Assume that each exit connects to one town. When building roads, the states had two choices: They could build a separate pair of roads (one in each direction) between every pair of towns, resulting in almost 40,000 roads, or one major highway with entrance and exit ramps connecting the towns. The bus is like the interstate highway: It consolidates traffic and reduces the number of roads (data paths) needed.

We begin by reviewing the data transfers that can occur to determine the functions of each individual component. Specifically, we look at the operations that load data into each component. It is not necessary to look at operations in which a component supplies the data or one of the operands; that will be taken care of when we look at the component whose value is being changed. First we regroup the operations, without regard for the cycles in which they occur, by the register whose contents they modify. This results in the following:

AR: $AR \leftarrow PC$; $AR \leftarrow DR[5..0]$
PC: $PC \leftarrow PC + 1$; $PC \leftarrow DR[5..0]$
DR: $DR \leftarrow M$
IR: $IR \leftarrow DR[7..6]$
AC: $AC \leftarrow AC + DR$; $AC \leftarrow AC \wedge DR$; $AC \leftarrow AC + 1$

Now we examine the individual operations to determine which functions can be performed by each component. *AR*, *DR*, and *IR* always load data from some other component, made available by the bus, so they only need to be able to perform a parallel load. *PC* and *AC* can load data from external sources, but they both need to be able to increment their values. We could create separate hardware that would increment the current contents of each register and make it available for the register to load back in, but it is easier to design each register as a counter with parallel load capability. In that way, the increment operations can be performed solely within the register; the parallel load is used to implement the other operations.

Next, we connect every component to the system bus, as shown in Figure 6.5 on page 224. Notice that we have included tri-state buffers between the outputs of the registers and the system bus. If we did not do this, all the registers would place their data onto the bus at all times, making it impossible to transfer valid data within the CPU. Also, the outputs of *AR* are connected to pins A[5..0], as required in the CPU specification. At this point, the CPU does not include the control unit, nor the control signals; we will design those later. Right now our goal is to ensure that all data transfers can occur. Later we will design the control unit to make sure that they occur properly.

FIGURE 6.5

Preliminary register section for the Very Simple CPU

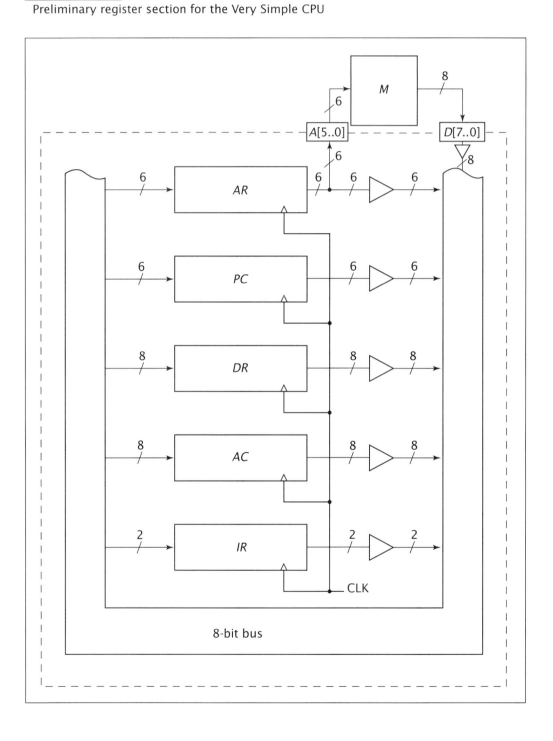

Now we look at the actual transfers that must take place and modify the design accordingly. After reviewing the list of possible operations, we note several things:

1. *AR* only supplies its data to memory, not to other components. It is not necessary to connect its outputs to the internal bus.
2. *IR* does not supply data to any other component via the internal bus, so its output connection can be removed. (The output of *IR* will be routed directly to the control unit, as shown later.)
3. *AC* does not supply its data to any component; its connection to the internal bus can also be removed.
4. The bus is 8 bits wide, but not all data transfers are 8 bits; some are only 6 bits and one is 2 bits. We must specify which registers send data to and receive data from which bits of the bus.
5. *AC* must be able to load the sum of *AC* and *DR*, and the logical AND of *AC* and *DR*. The CPU needs to include an ALU that can generate these results.

The first three changes are easy to make; we simply remove the unused connections. The fourth item is more of a bookkeeping matter than anything else. In most cases, we simply connect registers to the lowest order bits of the bus. For example, *AR* and *PC* are connected to bits 5..0 of the bus, since they are only 6-bit registers. The lone exception is *IR*. Since it receives data only from *DR*[7..6], it should be connected to the high-order 2 bits of the bus.

Now comes the tricky part. Since *AC* can load in one of two values, either $AC + DR$ or $AC \wedge DR$, the CPU must incorporate some arithmetic and logic circuitry to generate these values. (Most CPUs contain an arithmetic/logic unit to do just that.) In terms of the data paths, the ALU must receive *AC* and *DR* as inputs, and send its output to *AC*. There are a couple of ways to route the data to accomplish this. In this CPU we hardwire *AC* as an input to and output from the ALU, and route *DR* as an input to the ALU via the system bus.

At this point the CPU is capable of performing all of the required data transfers. Before proceeding, we must make sure transfers that are to occur during the same state can in fact occur simultaneously. For example, if two transfers that occur in the same state both require that data be placed on the internal bus, they could not be performed simultaneously, since only one piece of data may occupy the bus at a given time. (This is another reason for implementing $PC \leftarrow PC + 1$ by using a counter for *PC*; if that value was routed via the bus, both operations during FETCH2 would have required the bus.) As it is, no state of the state diagram for this CPU would require more than one value to be placed on the bus, so this design is OK in that respect.

The modified version of the internal organization of the CPU is shown in Figure 6.6. The control signals shown will be generated by the control unit.

FIGURE 6.6
Final register section for the Very Simple CPU

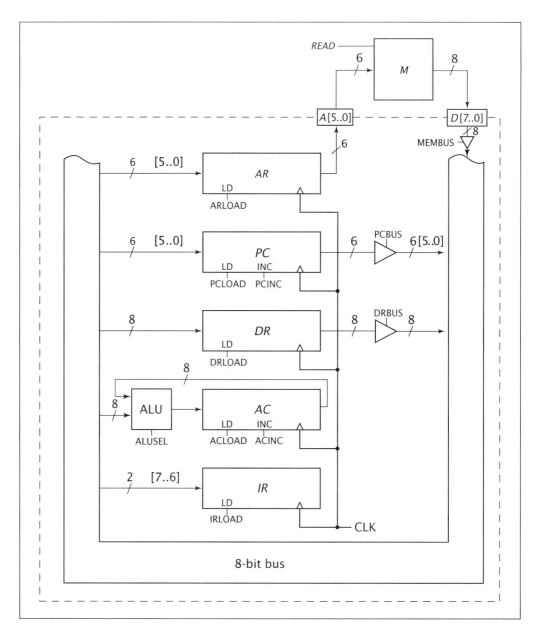

6.2.6 DESIGN OF A VERY SIMPLE ALU

The ALU for this CPU performs only two functions: adds its two inputs or logically ANDs its two inputs. The simplest way to design this ALU is to create separate hardware to perform each function and then use a multiplexer to output one of the two results. The addition is implemented using a standard 8-bit parallel adder. The logical AND operation is implemented using eight 2-input AND gates. The outputs of the parallel adder and the AND gates are input to an 8-bit 2 to 1 multiplexer. The control input of the MUX is called S (for select). The circuit diagram for the ALU is shown in Figure 6.7.

FIGURE 6.7

A Very Simple ALU

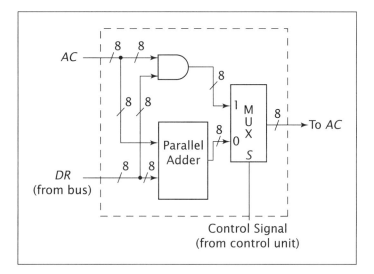

6.2.7   DESIGNING THE CONTROL UNIT USING HARDWIRED CONTROL

At this point it is possible for the CPU to perform every operation necessary to fetch, decode and execute the entire instruction set. The next task is to design the circuitry to generate the control signals to cause the operations to occur in the proper sequence. This is the **control unit** of the CPU.

There are two primary methodologies for designing control units. Hardwired control uses sequential and combinatorial logic to generate control signals, whereas microsequenced control uses a lookup memory to output the control signals. Each methodology has several design variants. This chapter focuses on hardwired control; microsequenced control is covered in Chapter 7.

This Very Simple CPU requires only a very simple control unit. The simplest control unit has three components: a counter, which contains the current state; a decoder, which takes the current state and generates individual signals for each state; and some combinatorial logic to take the individual state signals and generate the control signals for each component, as well as the signals to control the counter.

These signals cause the control unit to traverse the states in the proper order. A generic version of this type of hardwired control unit is shown in Figure 6.8.

Generic hardwired control unit

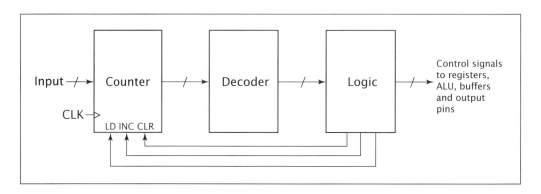

For this CPU, there are a total of 9 states. Therefore, a 4-bit counter and a 4-to-16-bit decoder are needed. Seven of the outputs of the decoder will not be used.

The first task is to determine how best to assign states to the outputs of the decoder, and thus values in the counter. The following guidelines may help.

1. *Assign FETCH1 to counter value 0 and use the CLR input of the counter to reach this state.* Looking at the state diagram for this CPU, we see that every state except FETCH1 can only be reached from one other state. FETCH1 is reached from four states, the last state of each execute routine. By allocating FETCH1 to counter value 0, these four branches can be realized by asserting the CLR signal of the counter, which minimizes the amount of digital logic needed to design the control unit.

2. *Assign sequential states to sequential counter values and use the INC input of the counter to traverse these states.* If this is done, the control unit can traverse these sequential states by asserting the INC signal of the counter, which also reduces the digital logic needed in the control unit. This CPU would assign FETCH2 to counter value 1 and FETCH3 to counter value 2. It would also assign ADD1 and ADD2 to consecutive counter values, as well as AND1 and AND2.

3. *Assign the first state of each execute routine based on the instruction opcodes and the maximum number of states in the execute routines. Use the opcodes to generate the data input to the counter and the LD input of the counter to reach the proper execute routine.* This point squarely addresses the implementation of in-

struction decoding. Essentially, it implements a mapping of the opcode to the execute routine for that instruction. It occurs exactly once in this and all CPUs, at the last state of the fetch cycle.

To load in the address of the proper execute routine, the control unit must do two things. First, it must place the address of the first state of the proper execute routine on the data inputs of the counter. Second, it must assert the LD signal of the counter. The LD signal is easy; it is directly driven by the last state of the fetch cycle, FETCH3 for this CPU. The difficulty comes in allocating counter values to the states.

Toward that end, consider the list of instructions, their first states, and the value in register IR for those instructions, as shown in Table 6.2. The input to the counter is a function of the value of IR. The goal is to make this function as simple as possible. Consider one possible mapping, $10IR[1..0]$. That is, if $IR = 00$, the input to the counter is 1000; for $IR = 01$, the input is 1001, and so on. This would result in the assignment shown in Table 6.3.

Table 6.2

Instructions, first states, and opcodes for the Very Simple CPU

Instruction	First State	*IR*
ADD	ADD1	00
AND	AND1	01
JMP	JMP1	10
INC	INC1	11

Table 6.3

Counter values for the proposed mapping function

IR[1..0]	Counter Value	State
00	1000 (8)	ADD1
01	1001 (9)	AND1
10	1010 (10)	JMP1
11	1011 (11)	INC1

Although this would get to the proper execute routine, it causes a problem. Since state ADD1 has a counter value of 8, and state AND1 has a counter value of 9, what value should we assign to ADD2 and how would it be accessed from ADD1? This could be done by incorporating additional logic, but this is not the best solution for the design.

Looking at the state diagram for this CPU, we see that no execute routine contains more than two states. As long as the first states of the execute routines have counter values at least two apart, it is possible to store the execute routines in sequential locations. This is accomplished by using the mapping function $1IR[1..0]0$, which results in counter values of 8, 10, 12, and 14 for ADD1, AND1, JMP1, and INC1, respectively. To assign the execute routines to consecutive values, we assign ADD2 to counter value 9 and AND2 to counter value 11.

Now that we have decided which decoder output is assigned to each state, we can use these signals to generate the **control signals** for the counter of the control unit and for the components of the rest of the CPU. For the counter, we must generate the INC, CLR, and LD signals. INC is asserted when the control unit is traversing sequential states, during FETCH1, FETCH2, ADD1, and AND1. CLR is asserted at the end of each execute cycle to return to the fetch cycle; this happens during ADD2, AND2, JMP1, and INC1. Finally, as noted earlier, LD is asserted at the end of the fetch cycle during state FETCH3. Note that each state of the CPU's state diagram drives exactly one of these three control signals. The circuit diagram for the control unit at this point is shown in Figure 6.9.

FIGURE 6.9

Hardwired control unit for the Very Simple CPU

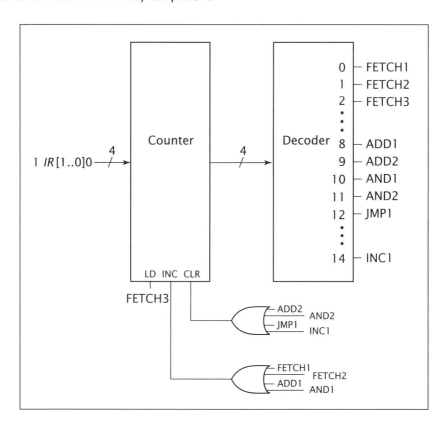

These state signals are also combined to create the control signals for *AR*, *PC*, *DR*, *IR*, *M*, the ALU, and the buffers. First consider register *AR*. It is loaded during states FETCH1 (*AR←PC*) and FETCH3 (*AR←DR[5..0]*). By logically ORing these two state signals together, the CPU generates the LD signal for *AR*. It doesn't matter which value is to be loaded into *AR*, at least as far as the LD signal is concerned. When the designers create the control signals for the buffers, they will ensure that the proper data is placed on the bus and made available to *AR*. Following this procedure, we create the following control signals for *PC*, *DR*, *AC*, and *IR*:

> PCLOAD = JMP1
> PCINC = FETCH2
> DRLOAD = FETCH1 ∨ ADD1 ∨ AND1
> ACLOAD = ADD2 ∨ AND2
> ACINC = INC1
> IRLOAD = FETCH3

The ALU has one control input, ALUSEL. When ALUSEL = 0, the output of the ALU is the arithmetic sum of its two inputs; if ALUSEL = 1, the output is the logical AND of its inputs. Setting ALUSEL = AND2 routes the correct data from the ALU to *AC* when the CPU is executing an ADD or AND instruction. At other times, during the fetch cycle and the other execute cycles, the ALU is still outputting a value to *AC*. However, since *AC* does not load this value, the value output by the ALU does not cause any problems.

Many of the operations use data from the internal system bus. The CPU must enable the buffers so the correct data is placed on the bus at the proper time. Again, looking at the operations that occur during each state, we can generate the enable signals for the buffers. For example, *DR* must be placed onto the bus during FETCH3 (*IR←DR[7..6]*, *AR←DR[5..0]*), ADD2 (*AC←AC + DR*), AND2 (*AC←AC ∧ DR*) and JMP1 (*PC←DR[5..0]*). (Recall that the ALU receives *DR* input via the internal bus.) Logically ORing these state values produces the DRBUS signal. This procedure is used to generate the enable signals for the other buffers as well:

> MEMBUS = FETCH2 ∨ ADD1 ∨ AND1
> PCBUS = FETCH1

Finally, the control unit must generate a READ signal, which is output from the CPU. This signal causes memory to output its data value. This occurs when memory is read during states FETCH2, ADD1, and AND1, so READ can be set as follows:

> READ = FETCH2 ∨ ADD1 ∨ AND1

The circuit diagram for the portion of the control unit that generates these signals is shown in Figure 6.10. This completes the design of the Very Simple CPU.

FIGURE 6.10
Control signal generation for the Very Simple CPU

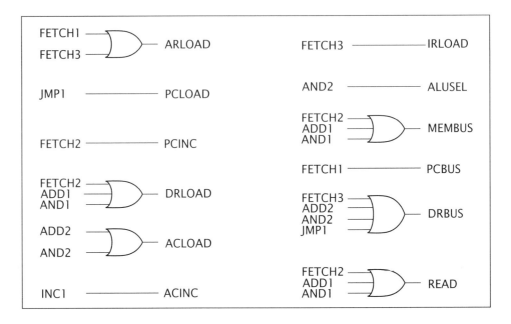

6.2.8 DESIGN VERIFICATION

Now that we have designed the CPU, we must verify that it works properly. To do so, we trace through the fetch, decode, and execute cycles of each instruction. Consider this segment of code, containing each instruction once:

$$
\begin{aligned}
&0: \quad \text{ADD4} \\
&1: \quad \text{AND5} \\
&2: \quad \text{INC} \\
&3: \quad \text{JMP 0} \\
&4: \quad \text{27H} \\
&5: \quad \text{39H}
\end{aligned}
$$

The CPU fetches, decodes, and executes each instruction following the appropriate state sequences from the state diagram:

ADD4:	FETCH1→FETCH2→FETCH3→ADD1→ADD2
AND5:	FETCH1→FETCH2→FETCH3→AND1→AND2
INC:	FETCH1→FETCH2→FETCH3→INC1
JMP 0:	FETCH1→FETCH2→FETCH3→JMP1

Table 6.4 shows the trace of the execution of one iteration of this program. We can see that the program processes every instruction correctly. Initially all registers contain the value 0.

Table 6.4

Execution trace

Instruction	State	Active Signals	Operations Performed	Next State
ADD 4	FETCH1	PCBUS, ARLOAD	$AR\leftarrow0$	FETCH2
	FETCH2	READ, MEMBUS, DRLOAD, PCINC	$DR\leftarrow04H$, $PC\leftarrow1$	FETCH3
	FETCH3	DRBUS, ARLOAD, IRLOAD	$IR\leftarrow00$, $AR\leftarrow04H$	ADD1
	ADD1	READ, MEMBUS, DRLOAD	$DR\leftarrow27H$	ADD2
	ADD2	DRBUS, ACLOAD	$AC\leftarrow0 + 27H = 27H$	FETCH1
AND 5	FETCH1	PCBUS, ARLOAD	$AR\leftarrow1$	FETCH2
	FETCH2	READ, MEMBUS, DRLOAD, PCINC	$DR\leftarrow45H$, $PC\leftarrow2$	FETCH3
	FETCH3	DRBUS, ARLOAD, IRLOAD	$IR\leftarrow01$, $AR\leftarrow05H$	AND1
	AND1	READ, MEMBUS, DRLOAD	$DR\leftarrow39H$	AND2
	AND2	DRBUS, ALUSEL, ACLOAD	$AC\leftarrow27H \wedge 39H = 31H$	FETCH1
INC	FETCH1	PCBUS, ARLOAD	$AR\leftarrow2$	FETCH2
	FETCH2	READ, MEMBUS, DRLOAD, PCINC	$DR\leftarrow C0H$, $PC\leftarrow3$	FETCH3
	FETCH3	DRBUS, ARLOAD, IRLOAD	$IR\leftarrow11$, $AR\leftarrow00H$	INC1
	INC1	ACINC	$AC\leftarrow21H + 1 = 22H$	FETCH1
JMP 0	FETCH1	PCBUS, ARLOAD	$AR\leftarrow3$	FETCH2
	FETCH2	READ, MEMBUS, DRLOAD, PCINC	$DR\leftarrow80H$, $PC\leftarrow4$	FETCH3
	FETCH3	DRBUS, ARLOAD, IRLOAD	$IR\leftarrow10$, $AR\leftarrow00H$	JMP1
	JMP1	DRBUS, PCLOAD	$PC\leftarrow0$	FETCH1

6.3   Design and Implementation of a Relatively Simple CPU

The CPU designed in the previous section is named appropriately: It is indeed very simple. It illustrated design methods that are too simple to handle the complexity of a larger CPU. This section presents the design of a more complex, but still relatively simple CPU. This CPU has a larger instruction set with more complex instructions. Its design follows the same general procedure used to design the Very Simple CPU.

6.3.1   Specifications for a Relatively Simple CPU

Chapter 3 introduced the instruction set architecture for the Relatively Simple CPU. This CPU can access 64K bytes of memory, each 8 bits wide, via address pins A[15..0] and bidirectional data pins D[7..0].

Three registers in the ISA of this processor can be directly controlled by the programmer. The 8-bit accumulator, *AC*, receives the result of any arithmetic or logical operation and provides one of the operands for arithmetic and logical instructions, which use two operands. Whenever data is loaded from memory, it is loaded into the accumulator; data stored to memory also comes from *AC*. Register *R* is an 8-bit general purpose register. It supplies the second operand of all two-operand arithmetic and logical instructions. It can also be used to temporarily store data that the accumulator will soon need to access. Finally, there is a 1-bit zero flag, *Z*, which is set whenever an arithmetic or logical instruction is executed.

The final component of the instruction set architecture for this Relatively Simple CPU is its instruction set, shown in Table 6.5.

Table 6.5

Instruction set for a Relatively Simple CPU

Instruction	Instruction Code	Operation
NOP	0000 0000	No operation
LDAC	0000 0001 Γ	$AC \leftarrow M[\Gamma]$
STAC	0000 0010 Γ	$M[\Gamma] \leftarrow AC$
MVAC	0000 0011	$R \leftarrow AC$
MOVR	0000 0100	$AC \leftarrow R$
JUMP	0000 0101 Γ	GOTO Γ
JMPZ	0000 0110 Γ	IF (Z=1) THEN GOTO Γ
JPNZ	0000 0111 Γ	IF (Z=0) THEN GOTO Γ
ADD	0000 1000	$AC \leftarrow AC + R$, IF ($AC + R = 0$) THEN $Z \leftarrow 1$ ELSE $Z \leftarrow 0$
SUB	0000 1001	$AC \leftarrow AC - R$, IF ($AC - R = 0$) THEN $Z \leftarrow 1$ ELSE $Z \leftarrow 0$
INAC	0000 1010	$AC \leftarrow AC + 1$, IF ($AC + 1 = 0$) THEN $Z \leftarrow 1$ ELSE $Z \leftarrow 0$
CLAC	0000 1011	$AC \leftarrow 0$, $Z \leftarrow 1$
AND	0000 1100	$AC \leftarrow AC \wedge R$, IF ($AC \wedge R = 0$) THEN $Z \leftarrow 1$ ELSE $Z \leftarrow 0$
OR	0000 1101	$AC \leftarrow AC \vee R$, IF ($AC \vee R = 0$) THEN $Z \leftarrow 1$ ELSE $Z \leftarrow 0$
XOR	0000 1110	$AC \leftarrow AC \oplus R$, IF ($AC \oplus R = 0$) THEN $Z \leftarrow 1$ ELSE $Z \leftarrow 0$
NOT	0000 1111	$AC \leftarrow AC'$, IF ($AC' = 0$) THEN $Z \leftarrow 1$ ELSE $Z \leftarrow 0$

As in the Very Simple CPU, this Relatively Simple CPU contains several registers in addition to those specified in its instruction set architecture. Differences between these registers and those of the Very Simple CPU are italicized:

- A *16-bit* address register, *AR*, which supplies an address to memory via A[*15..0*]
- A *16-bit* program counter, *PC*, which contains the address of the next instruction to be executed *or the address of the next required operand of the instruction*
- An 8-bit data register, *DR*, which receives instructions and data from memory *and transfers data to memory* via D[7..0]
- An *8-bit* instruction register, *IR*, which stores the opcode fetched from memory
- *An* 8-bit *temporary register,* TR, *which temporarily stores data during instruction execution*

Besides the differences in register size, there are several differences between the registers for this CPU and the Very Simple CPU. These changes are all necessary to accommodate the more complex instruction set.

First of all, notice that the program counter can hold not only the address of the next instruction, but also the address of the next operand. In the Very Simple CPU, the only operand is an address that is fetched along with the opcode. The Relatively Simple CPU uses 8-bit opcodes and 16-bit addresses. If the opcode and address were packed into one word, it would have to be 24 bits wide. For instructions that do not access memory, the 16-bit address portion of the instruction code would be wasted. To minimize unused bits, the CPU keeps each word/byte 8 bits wide, but uses multiple bytes to store the instruction and its address. Part of the time the *PC* will be pointing to the memory byte containing the opcode, but at other times it will be pointing to the memory bytes containing the address. This may seem a bit confusing, but it will become clearer during the design of this CPU.

The Very Simple CPU could not output data. The Relatively Simple CPU provides this capability, and it does so by making data available on the bidirectional pins D[7..0]. For this design, this data is provided solely from *DR*.

Most CPUs have more than one internal register for manipulating data. For this reason, the Relatively Simple CPU includes a general purpose register, *R*. Internal registers improve the performance of the CPU by reducing the number of times memory must be accessed. To illustrate this, consider the ADD instruction of the Very Simple CPU. After fetching and decoding the instruction, the CPU had to fetch the operand from memory before adding it to the accumulator. The Relatively Simple CPU adds the contents of register *R* to *AC*, eliminating the memory access and reducing the time needed to perform the addition.

Most CPUs have several general purpose registers; this CPU has only one to illustrate the use of general purpose registers while still keeping the design relatively simple.

Most CPUs contain internal data registers that cannot be accessed by the programmer. This CPU contains temporary register *TR*, which it uses to store data during the execution of instructions. As we will see, the CPU can use this register to save data while it fetches the address for memory reference instructions. Unlike the contents of *AC* or *R*, which are directly modified by the user, no instruction causes a permanent change in the contents of *TR*.

Finally, most CPUs contain **flag registers**, or **flags**, which show the result of a previous operation. Typical flags indicate whether or not an operation generated a carry, the sign of the result, or the parity of the result. The Relatively Simple CPU contains a zero flag, *Z*, which is set to 1 if the last arithmetic or logical operation produced a result equal to 0. Not every instruction changes the contents of *Z* in this and other CPUs. For example, an ADD instruction sets *Z*, but a MOVR (move data from *R* into *AC*) instruction does not. Most CPUs contain conditional instructions that perform different operations, depending on the value of a given flag. The JMPZ and JPNZ instructions for this CPU fall into this category.

6.3.2   Fetching and Decoding Instructions

This CPU fetches instructions from memory in exactly the same way as the Very Simple CPU does, except at the end of the fetch cycle. Here *IR* is 8 bits and receives the entire contents of *DR*. Also, $AR \leftarrow PC$, instead of $DR[5..0]$ because that is the next address it would need to access. The fetch cycle thus becomes

$$
\begin{aligned}
&\text{FETCH1:} &&AR \leftarrow PC \\
&\text{FETCH2:} &&DR \leftarrow M,\ PC \leftarrow PC + 1 \\
&\text{FETCH3:} &&IR \leftarrow DR,\ AR \leftarrow PC
\end{aligned}
$$

The state diagram for this fetch cycle is exactly the same as that of the Very Simple CPU shown in Figure 6.2.

We also follow the same process for decoding instructions that we used for the Very Simple CPU. Here, *IR* is 8 bits wide and there will be more possible branches. The state diagram for the fetch and decode cycles is shown in Figure 6.11.

There is one particularly unusual feature of the state diagram in Figure 6.11. Two of the instructions, JMPZ and JPNZ, have two different execute routines. These conditional instructions will be executed in one of two ways, depending on the value of *Z*. Either they will jump to address Γ or they will not. Each execute routine implements one of these two possibilities; the value of *Z* determines which is selected.

Figure 6.11

Fetch and decode cycles for the Relatively Simple CPU

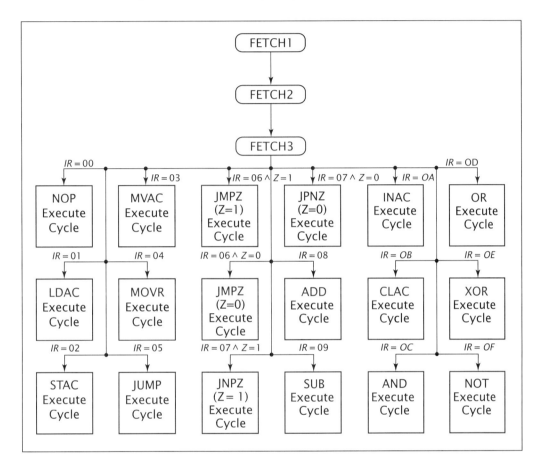

6.3.3   Executing Instructions

The final task in creating the state diagram for this CPU is to prepare the state diagrams for the execute routines. As before, we develop them individually and combine them into a final state diagram.

6.3.3.1   NOP Instruction

The NOP is the easiest instruction to implement. The CPU does nothing and then goes to the fetch routine to fetch the next instruction. This could be accomplished either by having the fetch routine branch back to its own beginning or by creating a single state that does nothing as the execute routine. In this CPU we use the latter approach. The state diagram for this execute routine contains the single state

NOP1:   (No operation)

6.3.3.2 LDAC Instruction

LDAC is the first of the multiword instructions in this CPU. It contains three words: the opcode, the low-order half of the address, and the high-order half of the address. The execute routine must get the address from memory, then get data from that memory location and load it into the accumulator.

Remember that, after the instruction has been fetched from memory, the program counter contains the next address in memory. If the instruction consisted of a single byte, the *PC* would contain the address of the next instruction. Here, however, it contains the address of the first operand, the low-order half of the address Γ. This CPU uses this value of *PC* to access the address.

First the CPU must get the address from memory. Since the address of the low-order half of address Γ was loaded into *AR* during FETCH3, this value can now be read in from memory. The CPU must also do two other things at this time: Because the CPU has read in the data whose address is stored in *PC*, it must increment *PC*, and because it will need to get the high-order half of the address from the next memory location, it must also increment *AR*. The CPU could simply increment *PC* now and then load it into *AR* during the next state, but incrementing *AR* now will reduce the number of states needed to execute the LDAC instruction. Thus the first state of this execute routine is

LDAC1: $DR \leftarrow M$, $PC \leftarrow PC + 1$, $AR \leftarrow AR + 1$

Having fetched the low-order half of the address, the CPU now must fetch the high-order half. It must also save the low-order half somewhere other than *DR*; otherwise it will be overwritten by the high-order half of address Γ. Here we make use of the temporary register *TR*. Again, the CPU must increment *PC* or it will not have the correct address for the next fetch routine. The second state is

LDAC2: $TR \leftarrow DR$, $DR \leftarrow M$, $PC \leftarrow PC + 1$

Now that the CPU contains the address, it can read the data from memory. To do this, the CPU first copies the address into *AR*, then reads data from memory into *DR*. Finally, it copies that data into the accumulator and branches back to the fetch routine. The states to perform these operations are

LDAC3: $AR \leftarrow DR, TR$
LDAC4: $DR \leftarrow M$
LDAC5: $AC \leftarrow DR$

6.3.3.3 STAC Instruction

Although the STAC instruction performs the opposite operation of LDAC, it duplicates several of its states. Specifically, it fetches the memory address in exactly the same way as LDAC; states STAC1, STAC2, and STAC3 are identical to LDAC1, LDAC2, and LDAC3, respectively.

Once AR contains the address, this routine must copy the data from AC to DR, then write it to memory. The states that comprise this execute routine are

$$\text{STAC1:}\quad DR{\leftarrow}M,\ PC{\leftarrow}PC + 1,\ AR{\leftarrow}AR + 1$$
$$\text{STAC2:}\quad TR{\leftarrow}DR,\ DR{\leftarrow}M,\ PC{\leftarrow}PC + 1$$
$$\text{STAC3:}\quad AR{\leftarrow}DR,TR$$
$$\text{STAC4:}\quad DR{\leftarrow}AC$$
$$\text{STAC5:}\quad M{\leftarrow}DR$$

At first glance, it may appear that STAC3 and STAC4 can be combined into a single state. However, when constructing the data paths later in the design process, we decided to route both transfers via an internal bus. Since both values cannot occupy the bus simultaneously, we chose to split the state in two rather than create a separate data path. This process is not uncommon, and the designer should not be concerned about needing to modify the state diagram because of data path conflicts. Consider it one of the tradeoffs inherent to engineering design.

6.3.3.4   MVAC and MOVR Instructions
The MVAC and MOVR instructions are both fairly straightforward. The CPU simply performs the necessary data transfer in one state and goes back to the fetch routine. The states that comprise these routines are

$$\text{MVAC1:}\quad R{\leftarrow}AC$$

and

$$\text{MOVR1:}\quad AC{\leftarrow}R$$

6.3.3.5   JUMP Instruction
To execute the JUMP instruction, the CPU fetches the address just as it did for the LDAC and STAC instructions, except it does not increment PC. Instead of loading the address into AR, it copies the address into PC, so any incremented value of PC would be overwritten anyway. This instruction can be implemented using three states.

$$\text{JUMP1:}\quad DR{\leftarrow}M,\ AR{\leftarrow}AR + 1$$
$$\text{JUMP2:}\quad TR{\leftarrow}DR,\ DR{\leftarrow}M$$
$$\text{JUMP3:}\quad PC{\leftarrow}DR,TR$$

6.3.3.6   JMPZ and JPNZ Instructions
The JMPZ and JPNZ instructions each have two possible outcomes, depending on the value of the Z flag. If the jump is to be taken, the CPU follows execution states exactly the same as those used by the JUMP

instruction. However, if the jump is not taken, the CPU cannot simply return to the fetch routine. After the fetch routine, the *PC* contains the address of the low-order half of the jump address. If the jump is not taken, the CPU must increment the *PC* twice so that it points to the next instruction in memory, not to either byte of Γ. The states to perform the JMPZ instruction are as follows. Note that the JMPZY states are executed if $Z = 1$ and the JMPZN states are executed if $Z = 0$.

JMPZY1: $DR \leftarrow M, AR \leftarrow AR + 1$
JMPZY2: $TR \leftarrow DR, DR \leftarrow M$
JMPZY3: $PC \leftarrow DR, TR$

JMPZN1: $PC \leftarrow PC + 1$
JMPZN2: $PC \leftarrow PC + 1$

The states for JPNZ are identical but are accessed under opposite conditions—that is, JPNZY states are executed when $Z = 0$ and JPNZN states are traversed when $Z = 1$.

JPNZY1: $DR \leftarrow M, AR \leftarrow AR + 1$
JPNZY2: $TR \leftarrow DR, DR \leftarrow M$
JPNZY3: $PC \leftarrow DR, TR$

JPNZN1: $PC \leftarrow PC + 1$
JPNZN2: $PC \leftarrow PC + 1$

6.3.3.7 THE REMAINING INSTRUCTIONS

The remaining instructions are each executed in a single state. For each state, two things happen: The correct value is generated and stored in *AC*, and the zero flag is set. If the result of the operation is 0, *Z* is set to 1; otherwise it is set to 0. Since this happens during a single state, the CPU cannot first store the result in *AC* and then set *Z*: It must perform both operations simultaneously. For now we simply specify the states and defer the implementation until later in the design process. The states for these execute routines are as follows.

ADD1: $AC \leftarrow AC + R$, IF $(AC + R = 0)$ THEN $Z \leftarrow 1$ ELSE $Z \leftarrow 0$
SUB1: $AC \leftarrow AC - R$, IF $(AC - R = 0)$ THEN $Z \leftarrow 1$ ELSE $Z \leftarrow 0$
INAC1: $AC \leftarrow AC + 1$, IF $(AC + 1 = 0)$ THEN $Z \leftarrow 1$ ELSE $Z \leftarrow 0$
CLAC1: $AC \leftarrow 0, Z \leftarrow 1$
AND1: $AC \leftarrow AC \wedge R$, IF $(AC \wedge R = 0)$ THEN $Z \leftarrow 1$ ELSE $Z \leftarrow 0$
OR1: $AC \leftarrow AC \vee R$, IF $(AC \vee R = 0)$ THEN $Z \leftarrow 1$ ELSE $Z \leftarrow 0$
XOR1: $AC \leftarrow AC \oplus R$, IF $(AC \oplus R = 0)$ THEN $Z \leftarrow 1$ ELSE $Z \leftarrow 0$
NOT1: $AC \leftarrow AC'$, IF $(AC' = 0)$ THEN $Z \leftarrow 1$ ELSE $Z \leftarrow 0$

The state diagram for this entire CPU is shown in Figure 6.12.

FIGURE 6.12

Complete state diagram for the Relatively Simple CPU

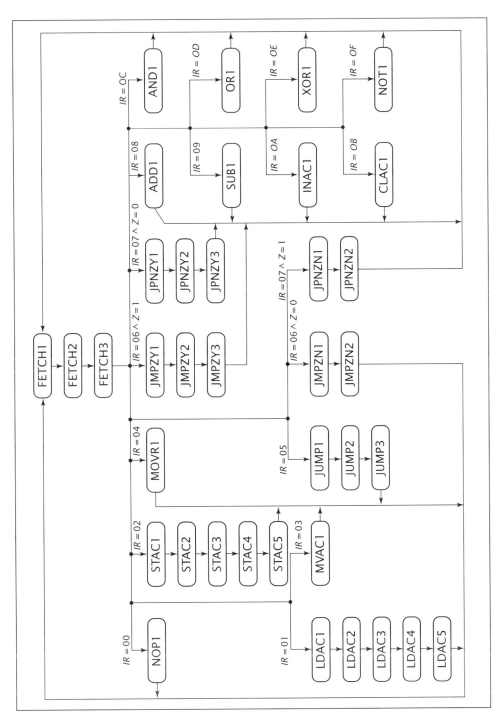

6.3.4 Establishing Data Paths

As with this Very Simple CPU, the Relatively Simple CPU uses an internal data bus to move data between components. First we regroup the data transfers by destination.

AR:	$AR \leftarrow PC$; $AR \leftarrow AR + 1$; $AR \leftarrow DR, TR$
PC:	$PC \leftarrow PC + 1$; $PC \leftarrow DR, TR$
DR:	$DR \leftarrow M$, $DR \leftarrow AC$
IR:	$IR \leftarrow DR$
R:	$R \leftarrow AC$
TR:	$TR \leftarrow DR$
AC:	$AC \leftarrow DR$; $AC \leftarrow R$; $AC \leftarrow AC + R$; $AC \leftarrow AC - R$;
	$AC \leftarrow AC + 1$; $AC \leftarrow 0$; $AC \leftarrow AC \wedge R$; $AC \leftarrow AC \vee R$;
	$AC \leftarrow AC \oplus R$; $AC \leftarrow AC'$
Z:	$Z \leftarrow 1$; $Z \leftarrow 0$ (both conditional)

From these operations, we select the functions of each component:

- *AR* and *PC* must be able to perform a parallel load and increment. Both registers receive their data from the internal bus.
- *DR*, *IR*, *R*, and *TR* must be able to load data in parallel. For now each register will receive its data from the internal bus. As we will see later in the design process, this will not work and more than one connection will have to be changed.
- *AC* will require a lot of work, as will *Z*. This CPU will utilize an ALU to perform all of these functions. The ALU will receive *AC* as one input and the value on the internal bus as the other input. *AC* will always receive its input from the ALU. The CPU will also use the output of the ALU to determine whether or not the result is 0 for the purpose of setting *Z*.

Although the CPU could use a register with parallel load, increment, and clear signals for *AC*, we will only use a register with parallel load and have the ALU create values *AC* + 1 and 0 when necessary. This is done to facilitate the proper setting of *Z*. The *Z* flag is implemented as a 1-bit register with "parallel" load.

Now we connect every component to the system bus, including tri-state buffers where necessary. We also connect output pins A[15..0] and bidirectional pins D[7..0]. The preliminary connections are shown in Figure 6.13.

Next we modify the design based on the following considerations.

1. As in the Very Simple CPU, *AR* and *IR* of the Relatively Simple CPU do not supply data to other components. We can remove their outputs to the internal bus.
2. Pins D[7..0] are bidirectional, but the current configuration does not allow data to be output from these pins.

FIGURE 6.13

Preliminary register section for the Relatively Simple CPU

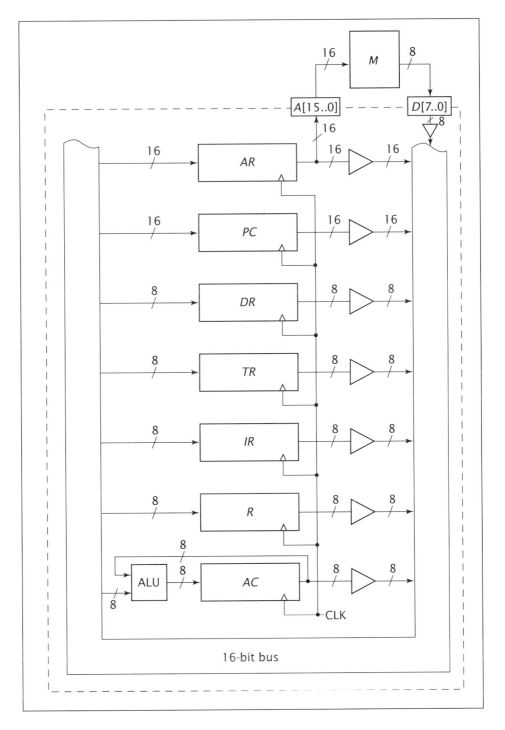

3. The 16-bit bus is not fully used by all registers. We must specify which bits of the data bus are connected to which bits of the registers.
4. Register *Z* is not connected to anything.

To address the first point, we simply remove the unused connections. The second point is also straightforward: A standard way to implement bidirectional pins is to use a pair of buffers, one in each direction. One buffer is used to input data from the pins and the other outputs data to the pins. The two buffers must never be enabled simultaneously. This configuration is shown in Figure 6.14.

Figure 6.14

Generic bidirectional data pin

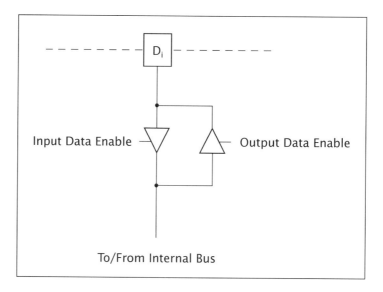

Unlike the Very Simple CPU, it is not a trivial matter to assign connections between the registers and the bits of the data bus in the Relatively Simple CPU. *AR* and *PC* are 16-bit registers connected to a 16-bit bus, so they present no problem. The remaining 8-bit registers can be connected to bits 7..0 of the bus. Although this configuration allows almost every individual transfer to take place, it causes problems for several states:

• During FETCH3, the CPU must transfer *IR←DR* and *AR←PC* simultaneously. As configured, both transfers would need to use bits 7..0 of the internal bus at the same time, which is not allowable. Since *IR* receives data only from *DR*, it is possible to establish a direct path from the output of *DR* to the input of *IR*, allowing *IR←DR* to occur without using the internal bus. This allows the CPU to perform both operations simultaneously. We can also disconnect the input of *IR* from the internal bus, since it no longer receives data from the bus.

- During LDAC2 and several other states, *TR←DR* and *DR←M* need to use the bus simultaneously. Fortunately, *TR* also receives data only from *DR*, so the CPU can include a direct path from the output of *DR* to the input of *TR*, just as we did for *IR*. The input of *TR* is also disconnected from the internal bus.

- During LDAC3 and several other states, *DR* and *TR* must be placed on the bus simultaneously, *DR* on bits 15..8 and *TR* on bits 7..0. However, *DR* is connected to bits 7..0 of the bus. One way to handle this is simply to connect the output of *DR* to bits 15..8 instead of bits 7..0, but that would cause a problem during LDAC5 and other states, which need *DR* on bits 7..0. Another solution, implemented here, is to route the output of *DR* to both bits 15..8 and bits 7..0. Separate buffers with different enable signals must be used because *DR* should not be active on both halves of the bus simultaneously.

Finally, we must connect register *Z*. Reviewing the states and their functions, we see that *Z* is only set when an ALU operation occurs. It is set to 1 if the value to be stored in *AC* (which is the output of the ALU) is 0; otherwise it is set to 0. To implement this, we NOR together the bits output from the ALU. The NOR will produce a value of 1 only if all bits are 0; thus the output of the NOR gate can serve as the input of *Z*. This is why we implemented the increment and clear operations via the ALU, rather than incorporating them directly into the *AC* register.

Figure 6.15 on page 246 shows the internal organization of the CPU after incorporating these changes.

6.3.5   Design of a Relatively Simple ALU

All data that is to be loaded into *AC* must pass through the ALU. To design the ALU, we first list all transfers that modify the contents of *AC*.

LDAC5: $AC←DR$
MOVR1: $AC←R$
ADD1: $AC←AC + R$
SUB1: $AC←AC - R$
INAC1: $AC←AC + 1$
CLAC1: $AC←0$
AND1: $AC←AC \wedge R$
OR1: $AC←AC \vee R$
XOR1: $AC←AC \oplus R$
NOT1: $AC←AC'$

FIGURE 6.15

Final register section for the Relatively Simple CPU

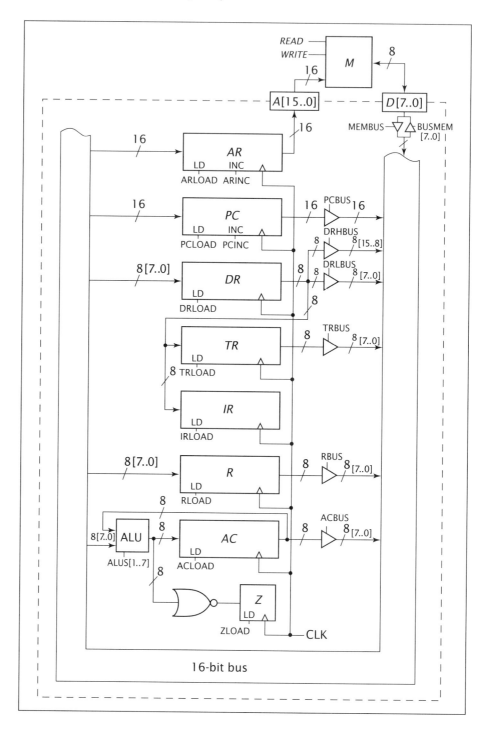

An arithmetic/logic unit (ALU) can be designed just as its name implies: We can design one section to perform the arithmetic instructions and another section to perform the logical instructions. A multiplexer selects data from the correct section for output to *AC*.

First we design the arithmetic section. To do this, we rewrite the arithmetic instructions to indicate the source of their operands:

$$LDAC5: \quad AC \leftarrow BUS$$
$$MOVR1: \quad AC \leftarrow BUS$$
$$ADD1: \quad AC \leftarrow AC + BUS$$
$$SUB1: \quad AC \leftarrow AC - BUS$$
$$INAC1: \quad AC \leftarrow AC + 1$$
$$CLAC1: \quad AC \leftarrow 0$$

Each of these instructions can be implemented by using a parallel adder with carry in by modifying the input values, rewriting each operation as the sum of two values and a carry:

$$LDAC5: \quad AC \leftarrow 0 + BUS + 0$$
$$MOVR1: \quad AC \leftarrow 0 + BUS + 0$$
$$ADD1: \quad AC \leftarrow AC + BUS + 0$$
$$SUB1: \quad AC \leftarrow AC + BUS' + 1$$
$$INAC1: \quad AC \leftarrow AC + 0 + 1$$
$$CLAC1: \quad AC \leftarrow 0 + 0 + 0$$

Note that subtraction is implemented via two's complement addition, as described in Chapter 1. For now we design the data paths; we implement the control logic later in the design process.

The first input to the parallel adder is either the contents of *AC* or 0. The ALU can use a multiplexer to select one of these two values and pass it to one input of the parallel adder. Similarly, the ALU uses a multiplexer to send *BUS*, *BUS'*, or 0 to the second input. The ALU could also use a multiplexer to supply the carry input, but that would be overkill. We simply use a control input to directly generate this value.

The logical operations are relatively straightforward. Since there are four logical operations, we use an 8-bit 4 to 1 multiplexer. The inputs to the MUX are $AC \wedge BUS$, $AC \vee BUS$, $AC \oplus BUS$, and AC'.

Finally, a multiplexer selects the output of either the parallel adder or the logic multiplexer to output to *AC*. The entire ALU design is shown in Figure 6.16 on page 248.

6.3.6 Designing the Control Unit Using Hardwired Control

The Relatively Simple CPU has a total of 37 states, making it too complex to implement efficiently using the same design as the Very Simple CPU's control unit. Instead of using one register to generate the state, this control unit uses two registers and combines their outputs to

FIGURE 6.16

A Relatively Simple ALU

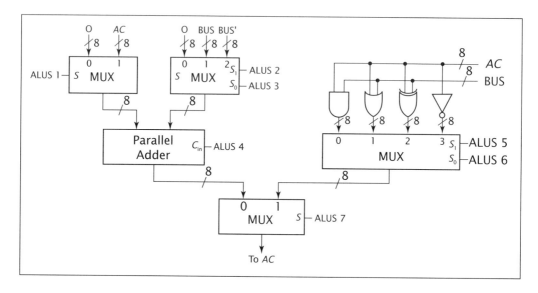

generate the state value. One value is the opcode of the instruction. The other is a counter to keep track of which state in the fetch or execute routine should be active.

The opcode value is relatively easy to design. The opcode is stored in *IR*, so the control unit can use that register's outputs as inputs to a decoder. Since the instruction codes are all of the form 0000 XXXX, we only need to decode the four low-order bits. We NOR together the four high-order bits to enable the decoder. Then the counter can be set up so that it only has to be incremented and cleared, and never loaded; this greatly simplifies the design. These components, and the labels assigned to their outputs, are shown in Figure 6.17.

The fetch routine is the only routine that does not use a value from the instruction decoder. Since the instruction is still being fetched during these states, this decoder could have any value during the instruction fetch. Just as with the Very Simple CPU, this control unit assigns T0 to FETCH1, since it can be reached by clearing the time counter. We assign T1 and T2 to FETCH2 and FETCH3, respectively.

The states of the execute routines depend on both the opcode and time counter values. T3 is the first time state of each execute routine, T4 is the second, and so on. The control unit logically ANDs the correct time value with the output of the instruction multiplexer corresponding to the proper instruction. For example, the states of the LDAC execute routine are

$$LDAC1 = ILDAC \land T3$$
$$LDAC2 = ILDAC \land T4$$

FIGURE 6.17

Hardwired control unit for the Relatively Simple CPU

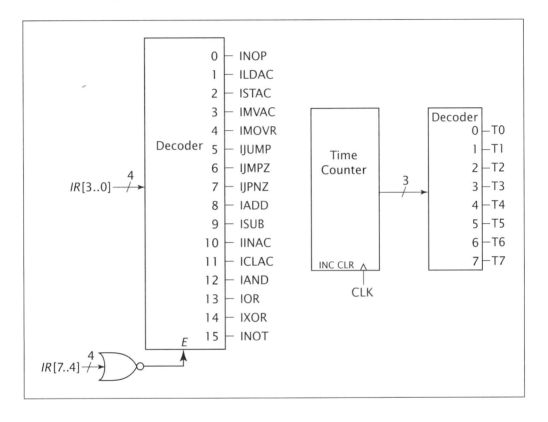

$$LDAC3 = ILDAC \wedge T5$$
$$LDAC4 = ILDAC \wedge T6$$
$$LDAC5 = ILDAC \wedge T7$$

The complete list of states is given in Table 6.6 on page 250.

Having generated the states, we must generate the signals to supply the CLR and INC inputs of the time counter. The counter is cleared only at the end of each execute routine. To do this, we logically OR the last state of each execute routine to generate the CLR input. The INC input should be asserted at all other times, so it can be implemented by logically ORing the remaining states together. As an alternative, the INC input can be the complement of the CLR input, since, if the control unit is not clearing the counter, it is incrementing the counter.

Following the same procedure we used for the Very Simple CPU, we generate the register and buffer control signals. Table 6.7 on page 251 shows the values for the buffers and *AR*. The remaining control signals are left as design problems for the reader.

Table 6.6

State generation for a Relatively Simple CPU

State	Function	State	Function
FETCH1	T0	JMPZY1	IJMPZ $\wedge$ Z $\wedge$ T3
FETCH2	T1	JMPZY2	IJMPZ $\wedge$ Z $\wedge$ T4
FETCH3	T2	JMPZY3	IJMPZ $\wedge$ Z $\wedge$ T5
NOP1	INOP $\wedge$ T3	JMPZN1	IJMPZ $\wedge$ Z' $\wedge$ T3
LDAC1	ILDAC $\wedge$ T3	JMPZN2	IJMPZ $\wedge$ Z' $\wedge$ T4
LDAC2	ILDAC $\wedge$ T4	JPNZY1	IJPNZ $\wedge$ Z $\wedge$ T3
LDAC3	ILDAC $\wedge$ T5	JPNZY2	IJPNZ $\wedge$ Z $\wedge$ T4
LDAC4	ILDAC $\wedge$ T6	JPNZY3	IJPNZ $\wedge$ Z $\wedge$ T5
LDAC5	ILDAC $\wedge$ T7	JPNZN1	IJPNZ $\wedge$ Z' $\wedge$ T3
STAC1	ISTAC $\wedge$ T3	JPNZN2	IJPNZ $\wedge$ Z' $\wedge$ T4
STAC2	ISTAC $\wedge$ T4	ADD1	IADD $\wedge$ T3
STAC3	ISTAC $\wedge$ T5	SUB1	ISUB $\wedge$ T3
STAC4	ISTAC $\wedge$ T6	INAC1	IINAC $\wedge$ T3
STAC5	ISTAC $\wedge$ T7	CLAC1	ICLAC $\wedge$ T3
MVAC1	IMVAC $\wedge$ T3	AND1	IAND $\wedge$ T3
MOVR1	IMOVR $\wedge$ T3	OR1	IOR $\wedge$ T3
JUMP1	IJUMP $\wedge$ T3	XOR1	IXOR $\wedge$ T3
JUMP2	IJUMP $\wedge$ T4	NOT1	INOT $\wedge$ T3
JUMP3	IJUMP $\wedge$ T5		

Finally, we generate the ALU control signals in the same manner. For example, ALUS1 = ADD1 $\vee$ SUB1 $\vee$ INAC1 and ALUS4 = SUB1 $\vee$ INAC1. The remaining control signals are left as exercises for the reader.

6.3.7 Design Verification

To verify the design of this CPU, the designer should prepare a trace of the execution, as was done for the Very Simple CPU. For the JMPZ and JPNZ instructions, the trace should show the execution under all possible circumstances, in this case $Z = 0$ and $Z = 1$. This is left as an exercise for the reader.

To perform the trace, students may use the RS-CPU simulator package. This package is a Java applet that can be run using any standard Web browser with Java enabled. Using this package, the reader can enter a program and step through the fetch, decode, and execution of the individual instructions. The package may be accessed at the textbook's companion Web site, along with its instructions.

Table 6.7

Control signal values for a Relatively Simple CPU

Signal	Value
PCBUS	FETCH1 ∨ FETCH3
DRHBUS	LDAC3 ∨ STAC3 ∨ JUMP3 ∨ JMPZY3 ∨ JPNZY3
DRLBUS	LDAC5 ∨ STAC5
TRBUS	LDAC3 ∨ STAC3 ∨ JUMP3 ∨ JMPZY3 ∨ JPNZY3
RBUS	MOVR1 ∨ ADD1 ∨ SUB1 ∨ AND1 ∨ OR1 ∨ XOR1
ACBUS	STAC4 ∨ MVAC1
MEMBUS	FETCH2 ∨ LDAC1 ∨ LDAC2 ∨ LDAC4 ∨ STAC1 ∨ STAC2 ∨ JUMP1 ∨ JUMP2 ∨ JMPZY1 ∨ JMPZY2 ∨ JPNZY1 ∨ JPNZY2
BUSMEM	STAC5
ARLOAD	FETCH1 ∨ FETCH3 ∨ LDAC3 ∨ STAC3
ARINC	LDAC1 ∨ STAC1 ∨ JUMP1 ∨ JMPZY1 ∨ JPNZY1

6.4   Shortcomings of the Simple CPUs

The CPUs presented in this chapter were designed as educational tools. Although they share many features with commonly used microprocessors, they are not representative of the current state of CPU design. Several common features were excluded from the Very Simple and Relatively Simple CPUs in an attempt to incorporate the essential features without overwhelming the reader. Consider the feature sets of these CPUs to be the result of an engineering education design tradeoff.

Following are some of the features found in many CPUs that are not present in either of the CPUs developed in this chapter.

6.4.1   More Internal Registers and Cache

One of the best ways to improve the performance of a microprocessor is to incorporate more storage within the CPU. Adding registers and cache makes it possible to replace some external memory accesses with much faster internal accesses.

To illustrate this, consider the ADD instructions for the Very Simple and Relatively Simple CPUs. The ADD instruction for the Very Simple CPU adds the contents of the accumulator to that of a memory location. It requires two states: one to read the value from memory (ADD1), and another to add the two values and store the result in the accumulator (ADD2). The Relatively Simple CPU, however, adds the contents of the accumulator and register R. Because the CPU does not access memory, it executes the ADD instruction in a single state

(ADD1). Removing memory accesses from other instructions by using internal registers reduces the time needed to execute the instructions in a similar manner.

Having more registers within the CPU also improves performance in programs that have subroutines. Consider a program for a CPU with no internal data registers, other than an accumulator. Assume this program invokes a subroutine, and this subroutine must receive six data values from the main program as passed parameters. The main program would have to write those six values to predetermined memory locations. The subroutine would have to read the values from memory and write its results back to memory. Finally, the main program would have to read the results from memory. If the CPU contained enough registers, the main program could store the parameters in its internal registers. The subroutine would not need to access memory because the CPU already contained the data in its registers. On completion, the main program would receive the results via the registers. Overall, a large number of memory accesses are thus avoided.

As processors have become more complex, designers have included more storage within the CPU, both in registers and internal cache memory. See Historical Perspective: Storage in Intel Microprocessors.

HISTORICAL PERSPECTIVE: Storage in Intel Microprocessors

Since the introduction of its first microprocessor in 1971, Intel has steadily increased the number of general purpose registers in its microprocessors. The 4004, Intel's first microprocessor, had no general purpose registers per se, although a complete 4-chip computer, consisting of the 4001, 4002, 4003, and 4004 chips, included 16 RAM locations that were used as registers. Its successors, the 8008, 8080, and 8085, incorporated six general purpose registers, as well as an accumulator, within the processor chip itself. The 8086 microprocessor has eight general purpose registers, as do the 80286, 80386, and 80486 microprocessors. The Pentium microprocessor also has 8 internal general purpose registers, but they are 32 bits wide, as opposed to the 16 bits of its predecessors. Intel's most recent microprocessor (as of this writing), the Itanium microprocessor, has 128 general purpose integer registers and an additional 128 general purpose floating point registers.

Intel first introduced cache memory into its Pentium microprocessor, starting with 16K of cache memory. It soon increased this to 32K, and further increased the amount in later processors. The Itanium microprocessor contains three levels of cache with over 4 MB of cache memory.

6.4.2   Multiple Buses Within the CPU

Buses are efficient media for routing data between components within a CPU. However, a bus may only contain one value at any given time. For that reason, most CPUs contain several buses. Multiple buses allow multiple data transfers to occur simultaneously, one via each bus. This reduces the time needed to fetch, decode, and execute instructions, thus improving system performance.

Consider the register section of the Relatively Simple CPU, shown in Figure 6.15. Most data transfers are routed via the 16-bit bus; every register except *IR* either outputs data to or inputs data from the bus. However, most of these components never need to communicate with each other. For example, it is possible to route data from *R* to *AR*, but it is never necessary to do so. If multiple buses were used, components that transfer data among themselves could be connected to more than one bus, or there could be connections established between buses. For the Relatively Simple CPU, one bus could be set up for address information and another for data. One possible configuration, which uses three buses, is shown in Figure 6.18 on page 254.

Another benefit of multiple buses is the elimination of direct connections between components. Recall that the Relatively Simple CPU included direct connections from *DR* to *TR* and *IR* so that multiple data transfers could occur simultaneously during FETCH3, LDAC2, STAC2, JUMP2, JMPZY2, and JPNZY2. As the number of registers within the CPU increases, this becomes increasingly important.

6.4.3   Pipelined Instruction Processing

In the CPUs developed in this chapter, one instruction is fetched, decoded, and executed before the next instruction is processed. In pipelining, instructions are processed like goods on an assembly line. While one instruction is being decoded, the next instruction is fetched, and while the first instruction is being executed, the second is decoded and a third instruction is fetched. Overlapping the fetch, decode, and execute of several instructions allows programs to be executed more quickly, even though each individual instruction requires the same amount of time.

Although this process has some problems, particularly with conditional and unconditional jump instructions, it offers significant increases in performance. Pipelining is discussed in detail in Chapter 11.

6.4.4   Larger Instruction Sets

Having a larger number of instructions in a processor's instruction set generally allows a program to perform a function using fewer instructions. For example, consider a CPU that can logically AND two values and complement one value, but cannot logically OR two values. To

FIGURE 6.18

Register section for the Relatively Simple CPU using multiple buses

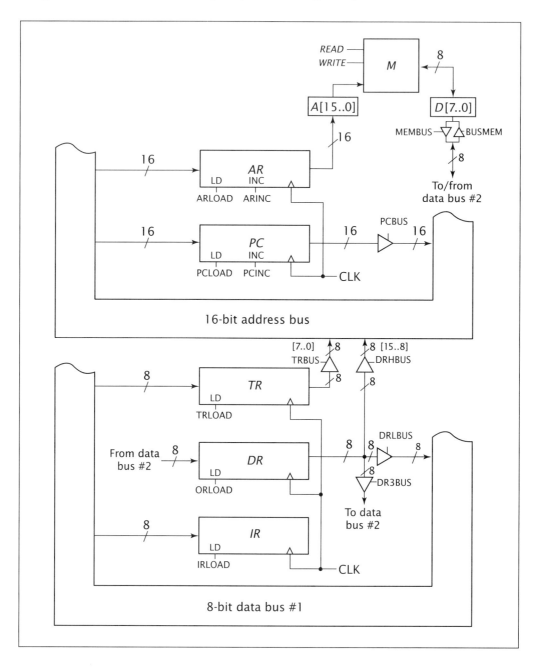

FIGURE 6.18

(continued)

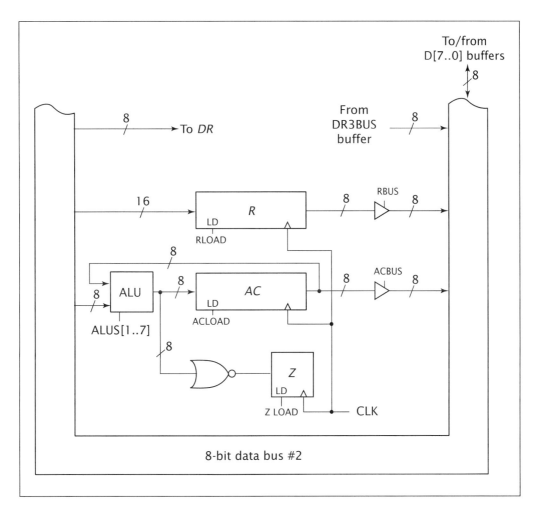

8-bit data bus #2

perform a logical OR of two values, A and B, it would perform the following instructions:

> Complement A
> Complement B
> AND A and B
> Complement the result

If this CPU contained an OR instruction, only one instruction would be needed instead of four.

There is considerable debate over how many instructions a CPU should have. As the number of instructions increases, so does the time needed to decode the instructions, which limits the clock speed of the

CPU. This is the basis of the complex versus reduced instruction set computing debate, which is examined more closely in Chapter 11.

6.4.5 Subroutines and Interrupts

Almost all CPUs have hardware to handle subroutines, typically a stack pointer, and instructions to call and return from the subroutine. Most CPUs also have interrupt inputs to allow external hardware to interrupt the current operations of the CPU. This is useful for such things as updating the computer's display, since it is preferable for the CPU to perform useful work and to be interrupted when the screen must be refreshed, rather than spending time polling the screen controller to determine whether it needs to be updated. Interrupts are described in more detail in Chapter 10.

6.5 Real World Example: Internal Architecture of the 8085 Microprocessor

In Chapters 3 and 4, we examined the instruction set architecture of the 8085 microprocessor and a computer based on this microprocessor. In this section, we look inside the 8085 and compare its organization to that of the Relatively Simple CPU.

The internal organization of Intel's 8085 microprocessor is shown in Figure 6.19. (Note that some elements of the design, such as internal control signals, are present but not shown in the figure.) As with the other CPUs described so far, the 8085 contains a register section, an ALU and a control unit. Note that the interrupt control and serial I/O control blocks are not exclusively a part of any one section. In fact, part of these blocks are components of the control unit and the rest of the blocks are parts of the register section. Let's look at these sections in some detail.

The easiest component to examine is the 8085's ALU. It performs all arithmetic, logic, and shift instructions, making its result available to the registers via the 8-bit internal data bus. Control signals from the control unit, not shown in Figure 6.19, select the function to be performed by the ALU.

The register section contains the user-accessible registers specified in the 8085's instruction set architecture: *A*, *B*, *C*, *D*, *E*, *H*, *L*, *SP*, and the flags. This section also contains the microprocessor's instruction register and program counter, a temporary register that it uses to input data to the ALU, and an address latch, which is equivalent to the *AR* register in the Relatively Simple CPU. Although not shown in Figure 6.19, two additional temporary registers are used by the microprocessor to store data during the execution of an instruction. They serve the same purpose as the *TR* register in the Relatively Simple CPU.

Although not registers, the address and data/address buffers are included in the register section. Under certain conditions, the 8085 does not access the system address and data buses. During these

Figure 6.19

Internal organization of the 8085 microprocessor (MCS 80/85™ Family User's Manual. Reprinted by permission of Intel Corporation, Copyright Intel Corporation 1979.)

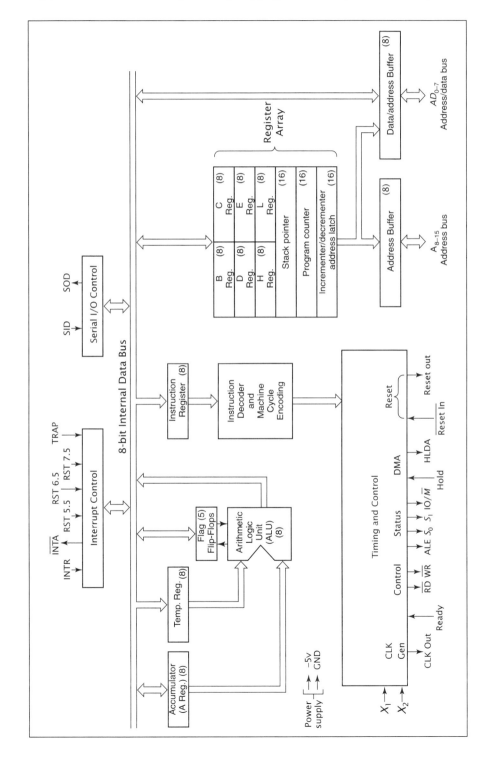

times, it must tri-state its connections to these buses; this is the function of these buffers. This happens when the computer is performing a DMA transfer, described in detail in Chapter 10. In addition, the data/address buffers determine whether data is input to or output from the CPU, just as was done with the Relatively Simple CPU.

The interrupt control block contains the interrupt mask register. The user can read the value from this register or store a value into that register, so it is included in the microprocessor's instruction set architecture and its register section. The serial I/O control block also contains a register to latch serial output data.

The registers communicate within the CPU via the 8-bit internal data bus. Although it is not very clear in Figure 6.19, the connection from the register array (the block containing registers B, C, D, E, H, L, SP, and PC) is wide enough for one register to place data onto the bus while another register reads the data from the bus, as when the instruction MOV B,C is executed. When data is read from memory, such as during an instruction fetch, or from an I/O device, the data is passed through the data/address buffer on to the internal data bus. From there, it is read in by the appropriate register.

The control section consists of several parts. The timing and control block is equivalent to almost the entire control unit of the Relatively Simple CPU. It sequences through the states of the microprocessor and generates external control signals, such as those used to read from and write to memory. Although not shown, it also generates all of the internal control signals used to load, increment and clear registers; to enable buffers; and to specify the function to be performed by the ALU.

The instruction decoder and machine cycle encoding block takes the current instruction (stored in the instruction register) as its input and generates state signals that are input to the timing and control block. This is similar to the function performed by the 4-to-16 decoder in the control unit of the Relatively Simple CPU, as shown in Figure 6.17. Essentially, it decodes the instruction. The decoded signals are then combined with the timing signals in the timing and control block to generate the internal control signals of the microprocessor.

Finally, the interrupt control and serial I/O control blocks are partially elements of the control unit. The interrupt control block accepts external interrupt requests, checks whether the requested interrupts are enabled, and passes valid requests to the rest of the control unit. (As with the internal control signals, the path followed by these requests is not shown in Figure 6.19 but it is present nonetheless.) The serial I/O control block contains logic to coordinate the serial transfer of data into and out of the microprocessor.

The 8085 microprocessor addresses several but not all of the shortcomings of the Relatively Simple CPU. First of all, it contains more general purpose registers than the Relatively Simple CPU. This allows the 8085 to use fewer memory accesses than the Relatively

Simple CPU to perform the same task. The 8085 microprocessor also has a larger instruction set, and has the ability to handle subroutines and interrupts. However, it still uses only one internal bus to transfer data, which limits the number of data transfers that can occur at any given time. The 8085 also does not use an instruction pipeline. Like the Relatively Simple CPU, it processes instructions sequentially—it fetches, decodes, and executes one instruction before fetching the next instruction.

6.6 SUMMARY

In previous chapters, we looked at the CPU from the point of view of the programmer (instruction set architecture) and the system designer (computer organization). In this chapter, we examined the CPU from the perspective of the computer architect.

To design a CPU, we first develop its instruction set architecture, including its instruction set and its internal registers. We then create a finite state machine model of the micro-operations needed to fetch, decode, and execute every instruction in its instruction set. Then we develop an RTL specification for this state machine.

A CPU contains three primary sections: the register section, consisting of the registers in the CPU's ISA as well as other registers not directly available to the programmer, the ALU, and the control unit. The micro-operations in its RTL code specify the functions to be performed by the register section and the ALU. These micro-operations are used to design the data paths within the register section, including direct connections and buses, and the functions of each register. The micro-operations also specify the functions of the ALU. Since the ALU must perform all of its calculations in a single clock cycle, it is constructed using only combinatorial logic.

The conditions under which each micro-operation occurs dictate the design of the control unit. The control unit generates the control signals that load, increment, and clear the registers in the register section. The control unit also enables the buffers used to control the CPU's internal buses. The function to be performed by the ALU is specified by the control unit. By outputting the control signals in the proper sequence, the control unit causes the CPU to properly fetch, decode, and execute every instruction in its instruction set.

PROBLEMS

1 A CPU with the same registers as the Very Simple CPU, connected as shown in Figure 6.6, has the following instruction set and state diagram. Show the RTL code for the execute cycles for each instruction. Assume the RTL code for the fetch routine is the same as that of the Very Simple CPU.

Instruction	Instruction Code	Operation
JMP1	00AAAAAA	$PC \leftarrow AAAAAA + 1$
INC2	01XXXXXX	$AC \leftarrow AC + 2$
ADD1	10AAAAAA	$AC \leftarrow AC + M[AAAAAA] + 1$
SKIP	11XXXXXX	$PC \leftarrow PC + 1$

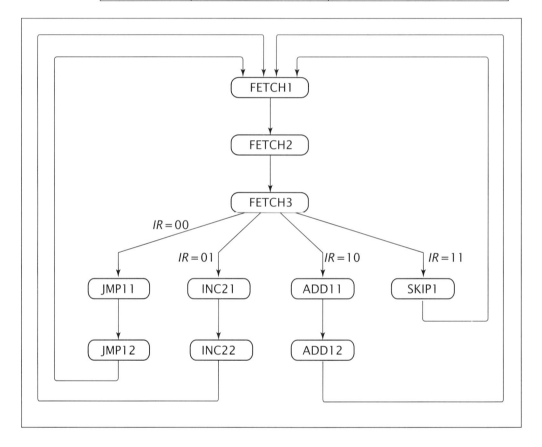

2   A CPU with the same registers as the Very Simple CPU, connected as shown in Figure 6.6, has the state diagram on the next page and following RTL code. Show the instruction set for this CPU.

FETCH1: $AR \leftarrow PC$
FETCH2: $DR \leftarrow M, PC \leftarrow PC + 1$
FETCH3: $IR \leftarrow DR[7..6], AR \leftarrow DR[5..0]$
001:        $DR \leftarrow M, AR \leftarrow AR + 1$
002:        $AC \leftarrow AC + DR$
003:        $DR \leftarrow M$

004:        $AC \leftarrow AC + DR$
011:        $DR \leftarrow M, PC \leftarrow PC + 1$
012:        $AC \leftarrow AC \wedge DR$
1X1: $AC \leftarrow AC + 1, DR \leftarrow M$
1X2: $AC \leftarrow AC \wedge DR$

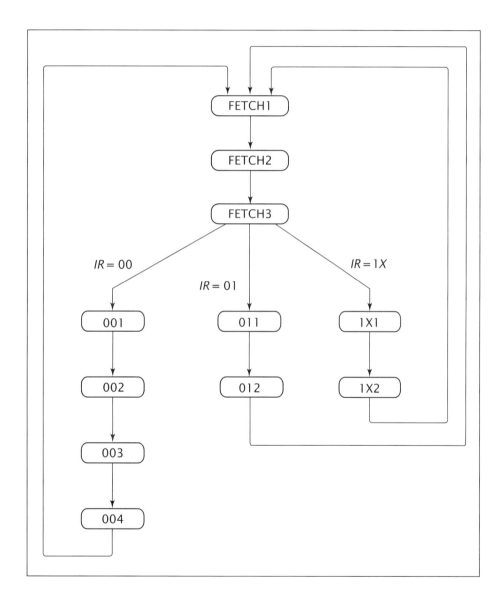

3 Develop a control unit for the state diagram in Problem 2.

4 The following control unit is supposed to realize the state diagram, also shown, but it does not. Show the state diagram it actually realizes.

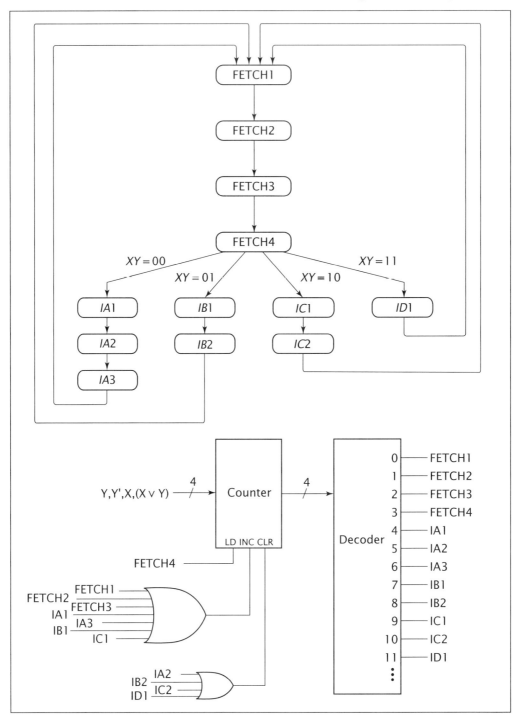

5 Modify the control unit of Problem 4 so that it realizes the state diagram properly.

6 We wish to modify the Very Simple CPU to incorporate a new instruction, CLEAR, which sets $AC \leftarrow 0$; the instruction code for CLEAR is 111X XXXX. The new instruction code for INC is 110X XXXX; all other instruction codes remain unchanged. Show the new state diagram and RTL code for this CPU.

7 For the CPU of Problem 6, show the modifications necessary for the register section.

8 For the CPU of Problem 6, show the modifications necessary for the control unit. Include the hardware needed to generate any new or modified control signals.

9 Verify the functioning of the CPU of Problems 6, 7, and 8 for the new instruction.

10 We wish to modify the Very Simple CPU to incorporate a new 8-bit register, R, and two new instructions. MVAC performs the transfer $R \leftarrow AC$ and has the instruction code 1110 XXXX; MOVR performs the operation $AC \leftarrow R$ and has the instruction code 1111 XXXX. The new instruction code for INC is 110X XXXX; all other instruction codes remain unchanged. Show the new state diagram and RTL code for this CPU.

11 For the CPU of Problem 10, show the modifications necessary for the register section.

12 For the CPU of Problem 10, show the modifications necessary for the control unit. Include the hardware needed to generate any new or modified control signals.

13 Verify the functioning of the CPU of Problems 10, 11, and 12 for the new instructions.

14 Enhance the Very Simple ALU to perform the following operations, in addition to those it currently performs.

$$\text{shl:} \quad AC \leftarrow AC + AC$$
$$\text{neg:} \quad AC \leftarrow AC' + 1$$
$$\text{ad1:} \quad AC \leftarrow AC + DR + 1$$

15 Show the logic needed to generate the control signals for registers PC, DR, TR, and IR of the Relatively Simple CPU.

16 Show the logic needed to generate the control signals for registers *R*, *AC*, and *Z* of the Relatively Simple CPU.

17 Show the logic needed to generate the control signals for the ALU of the Relatively Simple CPU.

18 Verify the functioning of the Relatively Simple CPU for all instructions, either manually or using the CPU simulator.

19 Modify the Relatively Simple CPU to include a new instruction, SETR, which performs the operation $R \leftarrow 1111\ 1111$. Its instruction code is 0001 0000. Show the modified state diagram and RTL code for this CPU. (*Hint:* One way to implement this is to clear *R* and then decrement it.)

20 For the CPU of Problem 19, show the modifications necessary for the register section.

21 For the CPU of Problem 19, show the modifications necessary for the control unit. Include the hardware needed to generate any new or modified control signals.

22 Verify the functioning of the CPU of Problems 19, 20, and 21 for the new instruction.

23 Modify the Relatively Simple CPU to include a new 8-bit register, *B*, and five new instructions as follows. Show the modified state diagram and RTL code for this CPU.

Instruction	Instruction Code	Operation
ADDB	0001 1000	$AC \leftarrow AC + B$
SUBB	0001 1001	$AC \leftarrow AC - B$
ANDB	0001 1100	$AC \leftarrow AC \wedge B$
ORB	0001 1101	$AC \leftarrow AC \vee B$
XORB	0001 1110	$AC \leftarrow AC \oplus B$

24 For the CPU of Problem 23, show the modifications necessary for the register section and the ALU.

25 For the CPU of Problem 23, show the modifications necessary for the control unit. Include the hardware needed to generate any new or modified control signals.

26 Verify the functioning of the CPU of Problems 23, 24, and 25 for the new instructions.

27 For the Relatively Simple CPU, assume the CLAC and INAC instructions are implemented via the CLR and INC signals of the AC register, instead of through the ALU. Modify the input and control signals of Z so it is set properly for all instructions.

28 Design a CPU that meets the following specifications.

- It can access 64 words of memory, each word being 8 bits wide. The CPU does this by outputting a 6-bit address on its output pins A[5..0] and reading in the 8-bit value from memory on its inputs D[7..0].
- The CPU contains a 6-bit address register (*AR*) and program counter (*PC*); an 8-bit accumulator (*AC*) and data register (*DR*); and a 2-bit instruction register (*IR*).
- The CPU must realize the following instruction set.

Instruction	Instruction Code	Operation
COM	00XXXXXX	$AC \leftarrow AC'$
JREL	01AAAAAA	$PC \leftarrow PC + 00AAAAAA$
OR	10AAAAAA	$AC \leftarrow AC \vee M[00AAAAAA]$
SUB1	11AAAAAA	$AC \leftarrow AC - M[00AAAAAA] - 1$

29 Design a CPU that meets the following specifications.

- It can access 256 words of memory, each word being 8 bits wide. The CPU does this by outputting an 8-bit address on its output pins A[7..0] and reading in the 8-bit value from memory on its inputs D[7..0].
- The CPU contains an 8-bit address register (*AR*), program counter (*PC*), accumulator (*AC*), and data register (*DR*), and a 3-bit instruction register (*IR*).
- The CPU must realize the following instruction set. Note that α is an 8-bit value stored in the location immediately following the instruction.

Instruction	Instruction Code	Operation
LDI	000XXXXX α	$AC \leftarrow \alpha$
STO	001XXXXX α	$M[\alpha] \leftarrow AC$
ADD	010XXXXX α	$AC \leftarrow AC + M[\alpha]$
OR	011XXXXX α	$AC \leftarrow AC \vee M[\alpha]$
JUMP	100XXXXX α	$PC \leftarrow \alpha$
JREL	101AAAAA	$PC \leftarrow PC + 000AAAAA$
SKIP	110XXXXX	$PC \leftarrow PC + 1$
RST	111XXXXX	$PC \leftarrow 0, AC \leftarrow 0$

30 Modify the Relatively Simple CPU so that it can use a stack. The changes required to do this are as follows.

- Include a 16-bit stack pointer (*SP*) register that holds the address of the top of the stack.
- The CPU must realize the following additional instructions. Note that operations separated by semicolons occur sequentially, and operations separated by commas occur simultaneously. Also note that the value of *PC* used by the CALL instruction is the value of *PC* after Γ has been fetched from memory.

Instruction	Instruction Code	Operation
LDSP	10000000 Γ	$SP \leftarrow \Gamma$
CALL	10000010 Γ	$SP \leftarrow SP - 1$; $M[SP] \leftarrow PC[15..8], SP \leftarrow SP - 1$; $M[SP] \leftarrow PC[7..0], PC \leftarrow \Gamma$
RET	10000011	$PC[7..0] \leftarrow M[SP], SP \leftarrow SP + 1$; $PC[15..8] \leftarrow M[SP], SP \leftarrow SP + 1$
PUSHAC	10000100	$SP \leftarrow SP - 1$; $M[SP] \leftarrow AC$
POPAC	10000101	$AC \leftarrow M[SP], SP \leftarrow SP + 1$
PUSHR	10000110	$SP \leftarrow SP - 1$; $M[SP] \leftarrow R$
POPR	10000111	$R \leftarrow M[SP], SP \leftarrow SP + 1$

7 MICROSEQUENCER CONTROL UNIT DESIGN

In Chapter 6 we went through the complete design process for two simple CPUs with hardwired control units. The control unit of each CPU uses combinatorial and sequential logic to generate the CPU's internal and external control signals. These control signals cause the CPU to perform the desired micro-operations in the correct order to fetch, decode, and execute the instructions in the processor's instruction set.

Hardwired control is one of the two most commonly used control methods. In this chapter we look at the other popular control method, **microsequencing**. Instead of generating the control signals using combinatorial and sequential logic, a **microsequencer** stores its control signals in a **lookup ROM**, the **microcode memory**. By accessing the locations of the ROM in the correct order, the lookup ROM asserts the control signals in the proper sequence to realize the instructions in the processor's instruction set.

We begin by examining the basic structure of a microsequencer, how it generates the control signals needed to perform micro-operations, and how it produces these signals in the correct sequence. We describe the three primary methods used to store control signal values in microcode memory. Then we design microcoded control units for the Very Simple CPU and Relatively Simple CPU; we do not have to redesign either the register section or the ALU of the processors when using a different control unit. Next, we examine ways to reduce the number of words in microcode without reducing the capabilities of the processor. We then discuss the advantages and disadvantages of microsequenced control as compared to hardwired control. Finally, we examine a (mostly) microcoded processor, Intel's Pentium microprocessor.

7.1 BASIC MICROSEQUENCER DESIGN

When we designed the Very Simple and Relatively Simple CPUs in Chapter 6, we developed the state diagram for each CPU, then designed a control unit to implement the state diagram. When we designed the control unit for each CPU, we designed a finite state machine. The hardwired control unit starts in one state and, based on its data inputs (which include the instruction code and flag values), goes to a new state. During each state the hardwired control unit generates outputs (the control signals for the registers, buffers, and ALU, and the signals that control memory and I/O devices). In this section we examine the structure of microsequencers, a different type of control unit.

7.1.1 MICROSEQUENCER OPERATIONS

A microsequencer is also designed as a finite state machine. Consider the generic microsequencer shown in Figure 7.1. The register stores a value that corresponds to one state in the CPU's state diagram. It serves as the address that is input to the microcode memory. This memory outputs a **microinstruction**, the contents of the memory location for that address. Collectively, all of the microinstructions comprise the **microcode**, or **microprogram**, for the CPU.

Generic microsequencer organization

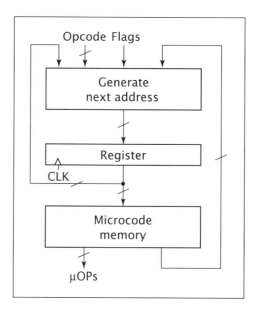

The microinstruction consists of several bit fields, which can be divided into two broad groups. The first group is the micro-operations (the *micro* part of the microsequencer). These signals are output from the microsequencer to the rest of the CPU. They are either input to combinatorial logic to generate the CPU's control signals, or they directly produce the control signals. (In a state diagram, these are the outputs associated with the state.)

The second group of bits of the microinstruction are used to generate the next address to be stored in the register (the *sequencer* part of the microsequencer). These bits, along with the instruction's opcode and flag values, are input to combinatorial logic that generates the address of the next microinstruction. This is equivalent to making a transition from one state to another in the state diagram. The microsequencer makes this transition based on its current state and the value of its inputs.

The microsequencer may follow any sequence of addresses the designer wishes to use, but there are only a few standard ways of generating these addresses. The *generate next address* block of the microsequencer typically generates all possible next addresses and then selects the correct next address to pass along to the register.

One possible value of the next address is the next address in microcode memory, the current address plus 1. A typical high-level language computer program has blocks of statements that are executed sequentially; programmers avoid "spaghetti code" which jumps around from place to place. Microcode routines also usually occupy sequential locations in microcode memory. This improves readability and makes debugging the microprogram easier. In many CPUs, the microinstructions that comprise the fetch routine and each individual execute routine are stored in consecutive locations. A microsequencer typically uses a parallel adder to generate the value of the current address plus 1 as a possible next address.

Another possible address is an absolute address supplied by microcode memory. Some jumps are inevitable in microcode. For instance, at the end of every execute routine, the microsequencer must jump back to the beginning of the fetch routine. Jumps can also be used to make more efficient use of microcode memory.

Every microsequencer must be able to access the correct execute routine. A microsequencer uses **mapping logic** to perform this function. The opcode of the fetched instruction is input to the mapping hardware, which converts, or maps, this opcode to the address of the first microinstruction of the instruction's execute routine. By loading this address into its register, the microsequencer branches to the correct execute routine. The mapping hardware is used only once in the CPU: at the end of the fetch cycle.

Like regular computer programs written in high-level or assembly language, a microsequencer can have subroutines. When several instructions must perform the same sequence of micro-operations as part of their execution, the sequence can be implemented as a **microsubroutine**. When a microsubroutine is called, the address is specified by the microcode memory as an absolute address, just as for a jump. The return address, the current address plus 1, is stored in a **microsubroutine register** or **hardware stack**. This address is used to return from the microsubroutine.

A microsequencer might have specialized hardware to generate other possible next addresses, but these four—the current address plus 1, an absolute address, a mapping function, and a microsubroutine return address—are the most common. A microsequencer does not have to use all of these possible next addresses; as covered in Section 7.2, the microsequencer for the Very Simple CPU uses only two of the four. However, every microsequencer uses the mapping address to go from the last state of the fetch routine to the correct execute routine.

7.1.2 MICROINSTRUCTION FORMATS

Each microsequencer can have its own format for its microinstructions. However, every microinstruction must follow this format, even if a particular microinstruction does not use the value of certain bits. Figure 7.2 shows a typical layout for a microinstruction; the order of the fields may vary from CPU to CPU. Let's look at each field separately.

FIGURE 7.2

Generic microinstruction format

SELECT	ADDR	MICRO-OPERATIONS

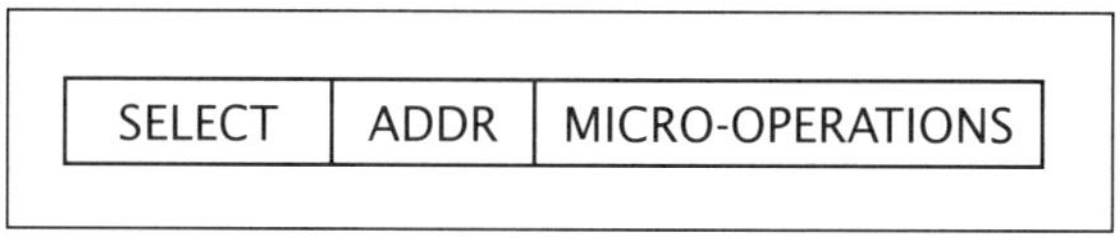

The **SELECT field** determines the source of the address of the next microinstruction. (Note that it does not specify the actual address, only the source of the address.) For instance, consider the final microinstruction of a fetch routine. Its select bits would instruct the next address generator to pass along the mapping address through to the microsequencer's register.

Some CPUs have conditional instructions, such as the JMPZ and JPNZ instructions of the Relatively Simple CPU. The execute routines for these instructions perform different functions for different values of a **condition flag**. For these CPUs, part of the SELECT field chooses a flag to be checked. The value of this flag is then combined with the remaining select bits to determine the source of the next address. An example of this occurs in the design of the microsequencer for the Relatively Simple CPU, later in this chapter.

Next is the **ADDR field**, which simply specifies an absolute address. The microsequencer uses this address when performing an absolute jump (such as from the end of an execute routine to the beginning of the fetch routine). Microinstructions that specify another source for the next address, such as the mapping address, do not use the bits of this field. Most microprogrammers set these unused bits to zero. The more rebellious microprogrammers use these bits to encode secret messages, the names of their dogs, or whatever happens to come to mind as they're writing that portion of microcode.

The final portion of the microcode is the **MICRO-OPERATIONS field** or fields. There are three primary methods used to specify micro-operations: **horizontal microcode**; **vertical microcode**; and **direct generation of control signals**. We describe each of these methods here. In the next section, we see how to use each method to implement a microsequencer for the Very Simple CPU.

To implement horizontal microcode, we first list every micro-operation performed by the CPU. (The designer usually assigns a mnemonic to each micro-operation.) Then we assign one bit in the micro-operations field of the microinstruction to each micro-operation. This can result in large microinstructions. For instance, if a CPU performs 50 different micro-operations, the micro-operation field uses 50 bits for every microinstruction.

Most microinstructions perform no more than a few micro-operations; many perform only one. In microsequencers that use horizontal microcode, most of the micro-operation bits are not active and perform no useful function. One way to reduce the number of bits in the micro-operations field is to use vertical microcode.

In vertical microcode, the micro-operations are grouped into fields. Each micro-operation is assigned a unique encoded value in this field. For example, 16 micro-operations could be encoded using four bits, with each micro-operation assigned a unique binary field value from 0000 to 1111. (We can actually encode only 15 micro-operations using four bits; we must reserve one value to indicate that no micro-operation in this field is to be performed by the microinstruction.) Vertical microinstructions require fewer bits than their equivalent horizontal microinstructions. However, microsequencers that use vertical microcode must incorporate a decoder for each micro-operation field to generate the actual micro-operation signals.

In both horizontal and vertical microcode, the CPU must convert the micro-operation signals to the control signals that load, clear, and increment registers, enable buffers, and select the function to be performed by the ALU. A third type of microcode dispenses with the micro-operations altogether. Instead, it stores the values of the control signals directly in the microinstruction. For instance, one bit might connect directly to the load signal of the CPU's address register, while another would drive the increment input of the program counter. This method does not require additional logic to convert the outputs of the microcode memory to control signals. However, this type of code is less readable and thus more difficult to debug.

7.2   Design and Implementation of a Very Simple Microsequencer

To illustrate the process of microsequencer design, consider the Very Simple CPU developed in Chapter 6. In this section, we redesign this CPU, this time using a microsequencer instead of hardwired control.

It is not necessary to redesign the CPU from scratch. The instruction set, finite state machine, data paths, and ALU are the same. There is no change in the flow of data within the CPU, only in the way the control signals are generated.

7.2.1   The Basic Layout

Figure 7.3 shows the basic layout of the Very Simple microsequencer. Notice that only two possible next addresses are used: the opcode mapping and an absolute jump. To understand why this can be done, consider the state diagram for this CPU, shown in Figure 6.4. The last state of the fetch cycle, FETCH3, goes to one of the four execute routines. This must be implemented via the mapping input. The remaining states must each go to one specific next state, which we implement using an absolute jump. Although we could have implemented some of these branches by adding 1 to the current address, we cannot perform the branches from the end of each execute routine to FETCH1 in this way. The CPU would still need the absolute jump address, so we use that absolute jump for all of these transitions and exclude the increment option (and its associated hardware).

Because there are two possible addresses, the microsequencer must select one or the other. To do this, we use a multiplexer. The select bit is generated by the microsequencer to choose the correct next address. For this CPU, the selection is unconditional. In every state, this CPU knows with absolute certainty the source of its next address, but this is not the case for all microsequencers.

We must determine several things for this CPU. For starters, how many bits wide is the absolute address output from the microcode memory? To determine this, we return to the state diagram for this CPU. It contains a total of nine states, each of which is represented by one microinstruction. The minimum number of bits needed to select among them is 4; this is the size of the absolute address. Since the mapping hardware also generates an address of the same size, its out-

Figure 7.3

Microsequencer for the Very Simple CPU

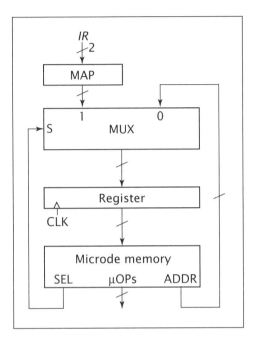

put is also 4 bits wide. That is the same size as the output of the multiplexer that is input to the register and the output of the register that is input to the address inputs of the microcode memory.

7.2.2   Generating the Correct Sequence and Designing the Mapping Logic

We now design the portion of the microcode that sequences through the states of the finite state machine. To do this, we first assign each state of the finite state machine to an address in microcode. Unlike with the hardwired control unit, it is not strictly necessary to assign states within the fetch or execute routines to consecutive addresses. In practice, however, this is usually done to improve microcode readability and to facilitate debugging. The primary consideration is the allocation of addresses for the first state of each execute routine, since this determines the logic to implement the mapping function. For this CPU, the microsequencer will use the same mapping function that was used for the hardwired control unit, namely 1IR[1..0]0. This produces addresses of 1000, 1010, 1100, and 1110 (8, 10, 12, and 14) for ADD1, AND1, JMP1, and INC1, respectively. The hardware to implement the mapping becomes a few wires, which is the simplest possible mapping logic. This is shown in Figure 7.4.

FIGURE 7.4

Mapping logic for the Very Simple Microsequencer

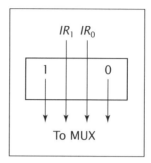

The addresses for the remaining states can be assigned somewhat arbitrarily. Here we assign consecutive states to consecutive locations in microcode memory. The resulting assignment is shown in Table 7.1.

TABLE 7.1

State addresses for the Very Simple Microsequencer

State	Address
FETCH1	0000 (0)
FETCH2	0001 (1)
FETCH3	0010 (2)
ADD1	1000 (8)
ADD2	1001 (9)
AND1	1010 (10)
AND2	1011 (11)
JMP1	1100 (12)
INC1	1110 (14)

Now we set up the microcode to sequence through these states properly. To go unconditionally to a specific state, the microsequencer supplies the address of that state via the ADDR field and selects it using the SEL field. For example, to go from FETCH1 to FETCH2, the microsequencer will specify SEL = 0 and ADDR = 0001 in location 0, the location corresponding to FETCH1. Setting SEL = 0 causes the microsequencer to get its next address from the ADDR field; setting the ADDR field to 0001 causes it to go to the location corresponding to state FETCH2. Except for FETCH3, we do this for every state in the state diagram. FETCH3 must map to the correct execute routine, so it requires SEL = 1 to select the mapping address. Since the contents of the ADDR field are not used in this microinstruction, it doesn't matter what value it has. This portion of the microcode for this CPU, everything except the micro-operations, is shown in Table 7.2. By tracing through the code, we can verify that it traverses the correct sequence of states for every instruction.

Table 7.2

Partial microcode for the Very Simple Microsequencer

State	Address	SEL	ADDR
FETCH1	0000 (0)	0	0001
FETCH2	0001 (1)	0	0010
FETCH3	0010 (2)	1	XXXX
ADD1	1000 (8)	0	1001
ADD2	1001 (9)	0	0000
AND1	1010 (10)	0	1011
AND2	1011 (11)	0	0000
JMP1	1100 (12)	0	0000
INC1	1110 (14)	0	0000

7.2.3   Generating the Micro-Operations Using Horizontal Microcode

As noted, a microsequencer has two tasks: to generate the correct micro-operations and to follow the correct sequence of states. We have taken care of generating the correct sequence; now our task is to generate the correct micro-operations and their associated control signals. This can be done using horizontal microcode, vertical microcode, and direct generation of the control signals.

In horizontal microcode, each micro-operation is represented by one bit in each microinstruction. The greater the number of micro-operations, the larger each word of microcode will be. We start by examining the RTL code for the CPU and listing every micro-operation that occurs; duplicate micro-operations are listed only once. We list the micro-operations to be performed in the Very Simple CPU and assign mnemonics to them. (Later, each mnemonic will become the name of a 1-bit field in the microinstructions; it is easier to work with the mnemonics when writing the microcode.) The micro-operations and their mnemonics are shown in Table 7.3.

Since there are nine micro-operations, each word of microcode requires 9 bits to represent them, 1 bit per micro-operation. A value of 1 means the micro-operation is to occur and a value of 0 means that it does not. To complete the microcode, we simply fill in the values for the micro-operations. The resultant microcode is shown in Table 7.4.

Table 7.3
Micro-operations and their mnemonics for the Very Simple CPU

Mnemonic	Micro-Operation
ARPC	$AR \leftarrow PC$
ARDR	$AR \leftarrow DR[5..0]$
PCIN	$PC \leftarrow PC + 1$
PCDR	$PC \leftarrow DR[5..0]$
DRM	$DR \leftarrow M$
IRDR	$IR \leftarrow DR[7..6]$
PLUS	$AC \leftarrow AC + DR$
AND	$AC \leftarrow AC \wedge DR$
ACIN	$AC \leftarrow AC + 1$

Note that the sequencing portion of this microcode is the same as shown in Table 7.2; adding the micro-operations does not change the order of the microinstructions that the CPU must follow.

Table 7.4
Preliminary horizontal microcode for the Very Simple Microsequencer

State	Address	SEL	ARPC	ARDR	PCIN	PCDR	DRM	IRDR	PLUS	AND	ACIN	ADDR
FETCH1	0000 (0)	0	1	0	0	0	0	0	0	0	0	0001
FETCH2	0001 (1)	0	0	0	1	0	1	0	0	0	0	0010
FETCH3	0010 (2)	1	0	1	0	0	0	1	0	0	0	XXXX
ADD1	1000 (8)	0	0	0	0	0	1	0	0	0	0	1001
ADD2	1001 (9)	0	0	0	0	0	0	0	1	0	0	0000
AND1	1010 (10)	0	0	0	0	0	1	0	0	0	0	1011
AND2	1011 (11)	0	0	0	0	0	0	0	0	1	0	0000
JMP1	1100 (12)	0	0	0	0	1	0	0	0	0	0	0000
INC1	1110 (14)	0	0	0	0	0	0	0	0	0	1	0000

Before generating the control signals, we review the microcode to see how it can be optimized. Notice that, for all states, ARDR and IRDR have the same value. We don't need two outputs to represent the same value; we can use one output to drive both micro-operations, AIDR, which combines both micro-operations $AR \leftarrow DR[5..0]$ and $IR \leftarrow DR[7..6]$. The revised microcode is shown in Table 7.5.

Table 7.5

Optimized horizontal microcode for the Very Simple Microsequencer

State	Address	S E L	A R P C	A I D R	P C I N	P C D R	D R M	P L U S	A N D	A C I N	ADDR
FETCH1	0000 (0)	0	1	0	0	0	0	0	0	0	0001
FETCH2	0001 (1)	0	0	0	1	0	1	0	0	0	0010
FETCH3	0010 (2)	1	0	1	0	0	0	0	0	0	XXXX
ADD1	1000 (8)	0	0	0	0	0	1	0	0	0	1001
ADD2	1001 (9)	0	0	0	0	0	0	1	0	0	0000
AND1	1010 (10)	0	0	0	0	0	1	0	0	0	1011
AND2	1011 (11)	0	0	0	0	0	0	0	1	0	0000
JMP1	1100 (12)	0	0	0	0	1	0	0	0	0	0000
INC1	1110 (14)	0	0	0	0	0	0	0	0	1	0000

Finally, we use these micro-operation signals to generate the control signals needed by the rest of the CPU. Here we are only concerned with the function performed by each micro-operation. It does not matter which microinstructions perform each micro-operation. For example, consider register *AR*. The ARLOAD signal must be active whenever either ARPC or AIDR is active, since both load *AR*. Simply ORing these signals together produces ARLOAD. The other control signals are generated the same way. The complete list of control signals is given in Table 7.6.

By comparing the logic in Table 7.6 with the circuits shown in Figure 6.10, we see that horizontal microcode can reduce the logic needed to generate the control signals. In this case, the savings is especially clear for DRLOAD and MEMBUS, which are directly generated here.

7.2.4   GENERATING THE MICRO-OPERATIONS USING VERTICAL MICROCODE

Horizontal microcode also has some disadvantages. For instance, the micro-operations section of the microcode of Table 7.5 consists mostly of zeroes; in fact, over 85 percent of the bits are inactive. Vertical microcode offers a way to reduce the number of bits in this section of the microcode.

Recall that, in vertical microcode, the micro-operations are grouped into fields such that no more than one micro-operation in a field is active during any state. Then a unique field value is assigned to each micro-operation in the field. For example, a field with eight different micro-operations would require 3 bits; each value from 000 to 111

Table 7.6

Control signal values for the Very Simple CPU

Signal	Value
ARLOAD	ARPC ∨ AIDR
PCLOAD	PCDR
PCINC	PCIN
DRLOAD	DRM
ACLOAD	PLUS ∨ AND
ACINC	ACIN
IRLOAD	AIDR
ALUSEL	AND
MEMBUS	DRM
PCBUS	ARPC
DRBUS	AIDR ∨ PCDR ∨ PLUS ∨ AND
READ	DRM

would be assigned to one of the eight micro-operations. The micro-operation field bits are output from the microcode memory to a decoder. The outputs of the decoder are the micro-operations directly generated under horizontal microcode. This is illustrated in Figure 7.5.

Figure 7.5

Generic generation of micro-operations from vertical microcode

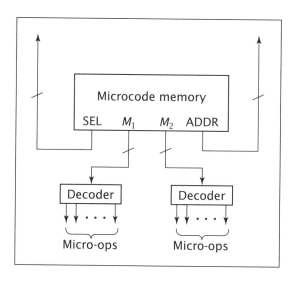

Now we look at how to design the microcoded control unit for the Very Simple CPU using vertical microcode. Just as before, we start with the instruction set, state diagram, data paths, and ALU that were developed for the hardwired version of this CPU; they don't need to be changed. Also, the sequencing hardware, mapping logic, and sequencing portion of the microcode (SEL and ADDR) are the same as for the horizontal microcode design. (Regardless of how the micro-operations are represented, the microsequencer must traverse the states in the same way.) We also use the same micro-operations as in the horizontally microcoded design, including the combined micro-operation AIDR.

From here, the task is to allocate the micro-operations to different fields. Following are guidelines to help you do this.

1. *Whenever two micro-operations occur during the same state, assign them to different fields.* Each field can output the value of only one micro-operation during a cycle. If two micro-operations are to occur simultaneously, they cannot be in the same field.

2. *Include a NOP in each field if necessary.* It is very likely that some states will not require that any micro-operations in a given field be active. As shown in Figure 7.5, some value must be output from the microcode memory, even when no micro-operation is active. Reserving one value as a NOP, and generating that value when no micro-operation is active, alleviates the problem of generating unneeded micro-operations.

3. *Distribute the remaining micro-operations to make best use of the micro-operation field bits.* The designer should try to make the best use of the field bits. For example, a field with five, six, seven, or eight micro-operations (including a NOP) requires 3 bits. Assigning eight micro-operations to this field produces the most efficient microcode. This correctly implies that your fields do not necessarily have to be the same size.

4. *Group together micro-operations that modify the same registers in the same fields.* Because two micro-operations cannot modify the same register simultaneously, it is possible to place them in the same micro-operation field. This is usually done unless it increases the size of the fields.

We can use these heuristics as we design the vertical microcode for this CPU. First, we examine the micro-operations for simultaneous operations; note that DRM and PCIN both occur during FETCH2 and must be assigned to different fields. This CPU requires (at least) two fields for its micro-operations, which we label *M1* and *M2*. Including a NOP in each field yields the following.

M1	*M2*
NOP	NOP
DRM	PCIN

Since PCIN and PCDR both modify PC, we add PCDR to *M2* for now. Next, we arbitrarily assign the remaining micro-operations to the fields, keeping micro-operations that change the same register in the same field. One possible scenario produces the following assignment.

M1	*M2*
NOP	NOP
DRM	PCIN
ACIN	PCDR
PLUS	ARPC
AND	AIDR

Each field has five micro-operations, thus requiring 3 bits per field for a total of 6 bits. By juggling the assignments around, we can reduce the total number of bits. Simply moving AIDR from *M2* to *M1* changes the number of micro-operations in *M1* and *M2* from 5 and 5, respectively, to 6 and 4, respectively. *M1* still requires 3 bits, but *M2* now requires only 2 bits. Every word of microcode would be one bit less wide.

We can take this to a greater extreme by moving ARPC and PCDR from *M2* to *M1*. *M2* now has eight micro-operations, each requiring 3 bits, and *M2* has two micro-operations, requiring a single bit. The total of 4 bits is the minimum possible for this configuration. The final values are shown in Table 7.7.

Table 7.7

Micro-operation field assignments and values

M1			**M2**	
Value	Micro-operation		Value	Micro-operation
000	NOP		0	NOP
001	DRM		1	PCIN
010	ARPC			
011	AIDR			
100	PCDR			
101	PLUS			
110	AND			
111	ACIN			

Using these values, we generate the final microcode for this CPU, shown in Table 7.8.

Note that the NOP in *M1* is never used. It is not strictly necessary to include a NOP here, but excluding it does not help in this case.

Now that the field bits are set, the microsequencer hardware must be enhanced to convert the bit values to the micro-operations

TABLE 7.8
Vertical microcode for the Very Simple Microsequencer

State	Address	SEL	*M1*	*M2*	ADDR
FETCH1	0000 (0)	0	010	0	0001
FETCH2	0001 (1)	0	001	1	0010
FETCH3	0010 (2)	1	011	0	XXXX
ADD1	1000 (8)	0	001	0	1001
ADD2	1001 (9)	0	101	0	0000
AND1	1010 (10)	0	001	0	1011
AND2	1011 (11)	0	110	0	0000
JMP1	1100 (12)	0	100	0	0000
INC1	1110 (14)	0	111	0	0000

they represent. For *M1*, we simply input this field to a 3-to-8 decoder, as shown in Figure 7.6. The outputs of the decoder correspond to the micro-operations shown in Table 7.7. For example, output 2 of the decoder is the micro-operation ARPC; the remaining outputs are assigned in the same way. Since output 0 represents the NOP, which does nothing, it is not connected. For *M2*, no decoder is needed, since it has only 1 bit. This bit drives PCIN directly.

FIGURE 7.6
Generating micro-operations from vertical microcode for the Very Simple CPU

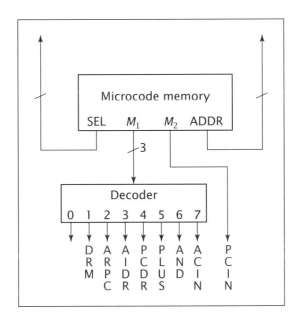

PRACTICAL PERSPECTIVE: Nanoinstructions

Instead of encoding individual micro-operations, it is possible to encode all micro-operations in a single field. This can be done when the same micro-operations occur together repeatedly in the microcode. The microcode memory outputs a value that points to a location in **nanomemory**, as shown in Figure 7.A. The nanomemory acts as a lookup table; it outputs **nanoinstructions**, the micro-operations for that microinstruction. Note that the bits used for sequencing, the SEL and ADDR fields, are not changed.

Figure 7.A
Generating micro-operations using nanomemory

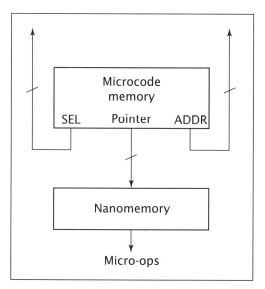

Using nanomemory can reduce the overall size of memory in a microsequencer. If 10 different microinstructions assert exactly the same micro-operations, all of these microinstructions can point to a single location in nanomemory.

Consider a microsequencer with 128 microinstructions and 32 different micro-operations. A horizontally microcoded microsequencer would require $128 \times 32 = 4,096$ bits of storage for its micro-operations. Now assume that only 16 unique combinations of micro-operations occur in these 128 microinstructions. We could store these 16 patterns in a 16×32 nanomemory. Each of the 128 microinstructions would require a 4-bit field to point to the correct pattern in nanomemory. This would require $16 \times 32 = 512$ bits for nanomemory and an additional $128 \times 4 = 512$ bits for pointers in microcode memory. The total of 1,024 bits is one-fourth the number of bits used by horizontal microcode to generate the same micro-operations.

At this point, we have exactly the same micro-operations as were generated by the horizontally microcoded design. Thus, the final control signals are generated using the same logic, shown in Table 7.6.

Comparing the horizontally and vertically microcoded systems, we see that each has some advantages. The control unit using vertical microcode uses a smaller microcode memory, that is, fewer bits per word. (Each uses the same number of words.) Encoding the micro-operations into fields results in words that are 9 bits wide for the vertical microcode, as opposed to 13 bits wide for the horizontal microcode. However, the vertically microcoded control unit requires additional hardware, specifically the decoder that converts *M1* to its micro-operations.

7.2.5   Directly Generating the Control Signals from the Microcode

Instead of outputting micro-operations from the microcode memory and then generating the control signals from these micro-operations, we could output the control signals directly. As before, the sequencing portion of the control unit design remains the same. This portion includes the mapping logic, next address multiplexer, register, and microcode memory, as well as the microcode fields SEL and ADDR.

In place of the micro-operations (in the horizontal microcode design) or *M1* and *M2* (in the vertical microcode design), the microsequencer can include 1 bit for each control signal. For each word of microcode memory, each control bit is set to 1 if the signal is to be active, and 0 otherwise.

To illustrate this, consider the micro-operations that occur during FETCH2, *DR←M* and *PC←PC* + 1. To implement *DR←M,* we must enable READ to output data from memory, MEMBUS to allow this data onto the internal system bus, and DRLOAD to load the data from the bus into *DR.* Also, we must enable PCINC to perform the second micro-operation. All other signals must be set to zero for this microinstruction so that no other micro-operation is triggered. Doing this for every microinstruction produces the microcode shown in Table 7.9.

In Table 7.9, note that DRLOAD, MEMBUS, and READ always have the same value. Just as with the micro-operations ARDR and IRDR in the horizontal microcode design, we can combine these signals because they always have the same value. One bit can be used instead of three; that one bit can drive all three signals. The revised microcode, with the one bit labeled *DMR,* is shown in Table 7.10.

Directly generating the control signals offers an advantage over the other two methods. It does not require additional logic to convert the outputs of the microcode memory to control signals. However, this type of code is less readable and thus more difficult to debug.

Table 7.9

Microcode to directly generate control signals for the Very Simple Microsequencer

State	Address	SEL	AR LOAD	PC LOAD	PC INC	DR LOAD	AC LOAD	AC INC	IR LOAD	ALU SEL	MEM BUS	PC BUS	DR BUS	READ	ADDR
FETCH1	0000 (0)	0	1	0	0	0	0	0	0	0	0	1	0	0	0001
FETCH2	0001 (1)	0	0	0	1	1	0	0	0	0	1	0	0	1	0010
FETCH3	0010 (2)	1	1	0	0	0	0	0	1	0	0	0	1	0	XXXX
ADD1	1000 (8)	0	0	0	0	1	0	0	0	0	1	0	0	1	1001
ADD2	1001 (9)	0	0	0	0	0	1	0	0	0	0	0	1	0	0000
AND1	1010 (10)	0	0	0	0	1	0	0	0	0	1	0	0	1	1011
AND2	1011 (11)	0	0	0	0	0	1	0	0	1	0	0	1	0	0000
JMP1	1100 (12)	0	0	1	0	0	0	0	0	0	0	0	1	0	0000
INC1	1110 (14)	0	0	0	0	0	0	1	0	0	0	0	0	0	0000

Table 7.10

Optimized microcode to directly generate control signals

State	Address	SEL	AR LOAD	PC LOAD	PC INC	DMR	AC LOAD	AC INC	IR LOAD	ALU SEL	PC BUS	DR BUS	ADDR
FETCH1	0000 (0)	0	1	0	0	0	0	0	0	0	1	0	0001
FETCH2	0001 (1)	0	0	0	1	1	0	0	0	0	0	0	0010
FETCH3	0010 (2)	1	1	0	0	0	0	0	1	0	0	1	XXXX
ADD1	1000 (8)	0	0	0	0	1	0	0	0	0	0	0	1001
ADD2	1001 (9)	0	0	0	0	0	1	0	0	0	0	1	0000
AND1	1010 (10)	0	0	0	0	1	0	0	0	0	0	0	1011
AND2	1011 (11)	0	0	0	0	0	1	0	0	1	0	1	0000
JMP1	1100 (12)	0	0	1	0	0	0	0	0	0	0	1	0000
INC1	1110 (14)	0	0	0	0	0	0	1	0	0	0	0	0000

7.3   Design and Implementation of a Relatively Simple Microsequencer

The microsequencer we developed in the previous section provided an introduction to microsequencer design, but it was not complex enough to illustrate all of the concepts of microsequencer design. This section builds on the basics and adds new concepts to design a microsequenced control unit for the Relatively Simple CPU. Just as with the Very Simple CPU, this design uses the same instruction set, data paths, and ALU as in the hardwired control design.

7.3.1   Modifying the State Diagram

Unlike the microsequencer design, this control unit requires a modified state diagram for its CPU. Look at the original state diagram shown in Figure 6.12: At the end of the fetch cycle, the state diagram maps directly to either state JMPZY1 or state JMPZN1 (or to state JPNZY1 or state JPNZN1) for the correct opcode, depending on the value of Z. In a microsequencer, the Z flag would have to be input to the mapping logic. In general, the mapping logic receives only the opcode as its input, and conditions are handled elsewhere in the microsequencer. To illustrate this standard design principle, we modify the state diagram to do this. Instead of having FETCH3 map to JMPZY1, JMPZN1, JPNZY1, and JPNZY2, we create two new states, JMPZ1 and JPNZ1, and have FETCH3 map to these instead. In turn, each of these states branches to its correct routine, depending on the value of Z. The modified portion of the state diagram for these two instructions is shown in Figure 7.7. The rest of the state diagram remains the same.

7.3.2   Designing the Sequencing Hardware and Microcode

Unlike the design of the Very Simple Microsequencer, unconditional branches and maps are not sufficient for this CPU. Specifically, the recently created states JMPZ1 and JPNZ1 can each branch to one of two possible states, depending on the value of Z. To do this, we include the capability to perform a conditional branch in the microsequencer. This conditional branch will go to one of two next addresses. If the condition is met, it will go to the address specified in the ADDR field; if not, it will go to the next location in microcode memory, the current address plus 1.

The basic layout for this microsequencer is shown in Figure 7.8; there are several differences between this microsequencer and the Very Simple Microsequencer of Figure 7.3. One obvious change is that now there are three possible next addresses instead of two. Since the conditional branch can go to either a location specified by ADDR or

FIGURE 7.7

Modified conditional jump execute routines

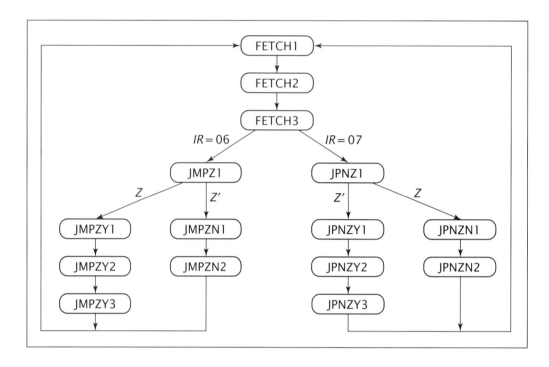

the current location plus 1, and this CPU can't know beforehand which next address it will use, they both must be made available. As always, the microsequencer must have a mapping input to access the correct execute routine. The box labeled "+1" is a hardware incrementer. It must consist only of combinatorial logic, because its result has to be available within a single clock cycle; a parallel adder is usually used to realize this function. Also, since there are now three possible next addresses, the microsequencer needs a larger multiplexer with two control inputs to select among them.

Before going into the rest of the hardware, we develop the mapping function and its associated mapping logic. Since the state diagram now has 39 states, the microsequencer needs a 6-bit address.

Remember that the mapping hardware does not actually output the address of the desired execute routine; rather, it outputs the address of the first state of the routine. The first state can easily branch to any other location, so it is not absolutely essential to keep all routines in consecutive locations; however, routines are usually stored in consecutive locations to improve readability.

FIGURE 7.8

Microsequencer for the Relatively Simple CPU

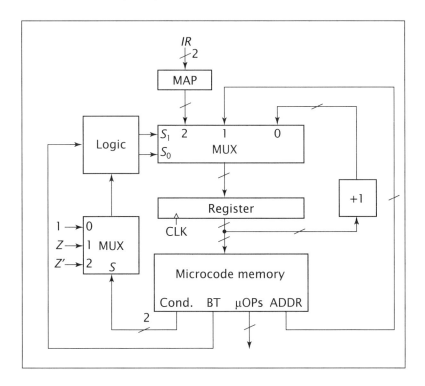

In this CPU we use the mapping function $IR[3..0]00$. This assigns NOP1 to location 0, LDAC1 to location 4, and so on. The fetch states are assigned to locations 1, 2, and 3, and the remaining states are allocated as shown in Table 7.11. Note that JMPZY1 immediately follows JMPZ1, and JPNZY1 immediately follows JPNZ1. This is very important later in the design process.

Since states JMPZ1 and JPNZ1 may each require one of two possible next addresses, the next address cannot be selected directly from the microcode, as was done with the SEL signal in the Very Simple Microsequencer. The microsequencer must incorporate this condition signal into the logic that determines the source of the next address.

This is done by breaking the process into two parts. First, we select the desired condition using a multiplexer. The inputs to the multiplexer are all of the possible conditions that may be considered when making a transition from one state to another. Here, Z and Z' may be used during JMPZ1 and JPNZ1. We also include a hardwired

Table 7.11

State assignments for the Relatively Simple Microsequencer

State	Location	State	Location	State	Location
FETCH1	1	STAC5	34	JPNZY1	29
FETCH2	2	MVAC1	12	JPNZY2	30
FETCH3	3	MOVR1	16	JPNZY3	31
NOP1	0	JUMP1	20	JPNZN1	45
LDAC1	4	JUMP2	21	JPNZN2	46
LDAC2	5	JUMP3	22	ADD1	32
LDAC3	6	JMPZ1	24	SUB1	36
LDAC4	7	JMPZY1	25	INAC1	40
LDAC5	33	JMPZY2	26	CLAC1	44
STAC1	8	JMPZY3	27	AND1	48
STAC2	9	JMPZN1	41	OR1	52
STAC3	10	JMPZN2	42	XOR1	56
STAC4	11	JPNZ1	28	NOT1	60

1 as an input for unconditional jumps. The multiplexer selects one of these values and outputs it as the condition value. The microcode memory supplies the condition select signals to choose which condition is used. (Even though the microsequencer may not know the value of a condition to test, it does know which condition must be checked during each state.) Table 7.12 shows the condition values.

Table 7.12

Condition values

Condition	Type	$S_1 S_0$
1	Unconditional	00
Z	$Z = 1$	01
Z'	$Z = 0$	10

Next, we use combinatorial logic to convert this condition value, along with a branch type supplied by the microsequencer, to the appropriate select signals to choose the correct source for the next address. These branch types will be of the form

```
IF (condition) THEN Next Address = SOURCE1
               ELSE Next Address = SOURCE2
```

or

```
REGARDLESS OF condition Next Address = SOURCE
```

To determine the exact branch types, we turn to the state diagram for the CPU. MAP and unconditional branches can be handled easily. Conditional jumps, however, depend on the layout of the microcode. In this CPU, JMPZ1 and JPNZ1 will branch to one of two locations. If both possible next states were at remote locations, the microsequencer would have to be able to specify both addresses directly. However, since each state has one of its two possible next states at the next address in microcode memory, it only has to supply one branch address and the current address plus 1. Therefore, one of the branch types must be

```
IF (condition) THEN Next Address = ADDR
ELSE Next Address = Current Address + 1
```

This branch type can also be used to perform unconditional branches by selecting the "1" input to the condition multiplexer, always generating a value of 1 for the condition. Table 7.13 shows the values of the branch types for this CPU.

Table 7.13

Branch types

Branch Type	BT	Branch Function
JUMP (J)	0	IF (condition)THEN Next Address = ADDR ELSE Next Address = Current Address + 1
MAP (M)	1	Next Address = MAP

Given the branch types and condition values, it is possible to design the logic to generate the select signals for the next address multiplexer. Table 7.14 shows the desired values, which result in S_1 = BT and S_0 = (condition value).

Table 7.14

Branch logic

BT	Condition	Next Address	$S_1 S_0$
0	0	Current address + 1	0 0
0	1	ADDR	0 1
1	X	MAP	1 0

Table 7.15

Partial microcode for the Relatively Simple Microsequencer

State	Address	Condition	BT	ADDR
FETCH1	1	1	JUMP	2
FETCH2	2	1	JUMP	3
FETCH3	3	X	MAP	X
NOP1	0	1	JUMP	1
LDAC1	4	1	JUMP	5
LDAC2	5	1	JUMP	6
LDAC3	6	1	JUMP	7
LDAC4	7	1	JUMP	33
LDAC5	33	1	JUMP	1
STAC1	8	1	JUMP	9
STAC2	9	1	JUMP	10
STAC3	10	1	JUMP	11
STAC4	11	1	JUMP	34
STAC5	34	1	JUMP	1
MVAC1	12	1	JUMP	1
MOVR1	16	1	JUMP	1
JUMP1	20	1	JUMP	21
JUMP2	21	1	JUMP	22
JUMP3	22	1	JUMP	1
JMPZ1	24	Z'	JUMP	41
JMPZY1	25	1	JUMP	26
JMPZY2	26	1	JUMP	27
JMPZY3	27	1	JUMP	1
JMPZN1	41	1	JUMP	42
JMPZN2	42	1	JUMP	1
JPNZ1	28	Z	JUMP	45
JPNZY1	29	1	JUMP	30
JPNZY2	30	1	JUMP	31
JPNZY3	31	1	JUMP	1
JPNZN1	45	1	JUMP	46
JPNZN2	46	1	JUMP	1
ADD1	32	1	JUMP	1
SUB1	36	1	JUMP	1
INAC1	40	1	JUMP	1
CLAC1	44	1	JUMP	1
AND1	48	1	JUMP	1
OR1	52	1	JUMP	1
XOR1	56	1	JUMP	1
NOT1	60	1	JUMP	1

At this point we can implement the sequencing portion of the microcode using the same process as we used for the Very Simple CPU's microsequencer. This portion of the microsequencer is shown in Table 7.15.

7.3.3 Completing the Design Using Horizontal Microcode

Before designing the micro-operations portion of the microcode, we create a list of all possible micro-operations. Just as with the Very Simple CPU, we examine each state, list the micro-operations (without duplicates), and assign mnemonics to them. The micro-operations for this CPU are shown in Table 7.16. We incorporate the 22 micro-operations as fields in the microcode and set the values as was done for the Very Simple CPU. The complete microcode is shown in Table 7.17.

Table 7.16

Micro-operations for the Relatively Simple Microsequencer

Mnemonic	Micro-Operation	Mnemonic	Micro-Operation
ARPC	$AR \leftarrow PC$	ACDR	$AC \leftarrow DR$
ARIN	$AR \leftarrow AR + 1$	ACR	$AC \leftarrow R$
ARDT	$AR \leftarrow DR, TR$	PLUS	$AC \leftarrow AC + R$
PCIN	$PC \leftarrow PC + 1$	MINU	$AC \leftarrow AC - R$
PCDT	$PC \leftarrow DR, TR$	ACIN	$AC \leftarrow AC + 1$
DRM	$DR \leftarrow M$	ACZO	$AC \leftarrow 0$
DRAC	$DR \leftarrow AC$	AND	$AC \leftarrow AC \wedge R$
IRDR	$IR \leftarrow DR$	OR	$AC \leftarrow AC \vee R$
RAC	$R \leftarrow AC$	XOR	$AC \leftarrow AC \oplus R$
ZALU	$Z \leftarrow$ data from ALU	NOT	$AC \leftarrow /AC'$
TRDR	$TR \leftarrow DR$	MDR	$M \leftarrow DR$

Finally, we combine these micro-operations to generate the CPU's control signals using the same procedure as before. A few of these signals are shown in Table 7.18. The remaining signals are left as exercises for the reader.

Table 7.17

Complete microcode for the Relatively Simple Microsequencer

State	Address	Condition	BT	ARPC	ARIN	ARDT	PCIN	PCDT	DRM	DRAC	IRDR	RAC	ZALU	TRDR	ACDR	ACR	PLUS	MINU	ACIN	ACZO	AND	OR	XOR	NOT	MDR	ADDR
FETCH1	1	1	J	1	0	0	0	0	0	0	0	0	0	0	0	0	0	0	0	0	0	0	0	0	0	2
FETCH2	2	1	J	0	0	0	1	0	1	0	0	0	0	0	0	0	0	0	0	0	0	0	0	0	0	3
FETCH3	3	X	M	1	0	0	0	0	0	0	1	0	0	0	0	0	0	0	0	0	0	0	0	0	0	X
NOP1	0	1	J	0	0	0	0	0	0	0	0	0	0	0	0	0	0	0	0	0	0	0	0	0	0	1
LDAC1	4	1	J	0	1	0	1	0	1	0	0	0	0	0	0	0	0	0	0	0	0	0	0	0	0	5
LDAC2	5	1	J	0	0	0	1	0	1	0	0	0	0	1	0	0	0	0	0	0	0	0	0	0	0	6
LDAC3	6	1	J	0	0	1	0	0	0	0	0	0	0	0	0	0	0	0	0	0	0	0	0	0	0	7
LDAC4	7	1	J	0	0	0	0	0	1	0	0	0	0	0	0	0	0	0	0	0	0	0	0	0	0	33
LDAC5	33	1	J	0	0	0	0	0	0	0	0	0	0	0	1	0	0	0	0	0	0	0	0	0	0	1
STAC1	8	1	J	0	1	0	1	0	1	0	0	0	0	0	0	0	0	0	0	0	0	0	0	0	0	9
STAC2	9	1	J	0	0	0	1	0	1	0	0	0	0	1	0	0	0	0	0	0	0	0	0	0	0	10
STAC3	10	1	J	0	0	1	0	0	0	0	0	0	0	0	0	0	0	0	0	0	0	0	0	0	0	11
STAC4	11	1	J	0	0	0	0	0	0	1	0	0	0	0	0	0	0	0	0	0	0	0	0	0	0	34
STAC5	34	1	J	0	0	0	0	0	0	0	0	0	0	0	0	0	0	0	0	0	0	0	0	0	1	1
MVAC1	12	1	J	0	0	0	0	0	0	0	0	1	0	0	0	0	0	0	0	0	0	0	0	0	0	1
MOVR1	16	1	J	0	0	0	0	0	0	0	0	0	0	0	0	0	1	0	0	0	0	0	0	0	0	1
JUMP1	20	1	J	0	1	0	0	0	1	0	0	0	0	0	0	0	0	0	0	0	0	0	0	0	0	21
JUMP2	21	1	J	0	0	0	0	0	1	0	0	0	0	1	0	0	0	0	0	0	0	0	0	0	0	22
JUMP3	22	1	J	0	0	0	0	1	0	0	0	0	0	0	0	0	0	0	0	0	0	0	0	0	0	1
JMPZ1	24	Z'	J	0	0	0	0	0	0	0	0	0	0	0	0	0	0	0	0	0	0	0	0	0	0	41
JMPZY1	25	1	J	0	1	0	0	0	1	0	0	0	0	0	0	0	0	0	0	0	0	0	0	0	0	26
JMPZY2	26	1	J	0	0	0	0	0	1	0	0	0	0	1	0	0	0	0	0	0	0	0	0	0	0	27
JMPZY3	27	1	J	0	0	0	0	1	0	0	0	0	0	0	0	0	0	0	0	0	0	0	0	0	0	1
JMPZN1	41	1	J	0	0	0	1	0	0	0	0	0	0	0	0	0	0	0	0	0	0	0	0	0	0	42
JMPZN2	42	1	J	0	0	0	1	0	0	0	0	0	0	0	0	0	0	0	0	0	0	0	0	0	0	1
JPNZ1	28	Z	J	0	0	0	0	0	0	0	0	0	0	0	0	0	0	0	0	0	0	0	0	0	0	45
JPNZY1	29	1	J	0	1	0	0	0	1	0	0	0	0	0	0	0	0	0	0	0	0	0	0	0	0	30
JPNZY2	30	1	J	0	0	0	0	0	1	0	0	0	0	1	0	0	0	0	0	0	0	0	0	0	0	31
JPNZY3	31	1	J	0	0	0	0	1	0	0	0	0	0	0	0	0	0	0	0	0	0	0	0	0	0	1

Table 7.17

(continued)

State	Address	Condition	BT	ARPC	ARIN	ARDT	PCIN	PCDT	DRM	DRAC	IRDR	RAC	ZALU	TRDR	ACDR	ACR	PLUS	MINU	ACIN	ACZO	AND	OR	XOR	NOT	MDR	ADDR
JPNZN1	45	1	J	0	0	0	1	0	0	0	0	0	0	0	0	0	0	0	0	0	0	0	0	0	0	46
JPNZN2	46	1	J	0	0	0	1	0	0	0	0	0	0	0	0	0	0	0	0	0	0	0	0	0	0	1
ADD1	32	1	J	0	0	0	0	0	0	0	0	0	1	0	0	0	1	0	0	0	0	0	0	0	0	1
SUB1	36	1	J	0	0	0	0	0	0	0	0	0	1	0	0	0	0	1	0	0	0	0	0	0	0	1
INAC1	40	1	J	0	0	0	0	0	0	0	0	0	1	0	0	0	0	0	1	0	0	0	0	0	0	1
CLAC1	44	1	J	0	0	0	0	0	0	0	0	0	1	0	0	0	0	0	0	1	0	0	0	0	0	1
AND1	48	1	J	0	0	0	0	0	0	0	0	0	1	0	0	0	0	0	0	0	1	0	0	0	0	1
OR1	52	1	J	0	0	0	0	0	0	0	0	0	1	0	0	0	0	0	0	0	0	1	0	0	0	1
XOR1	56	1	J	0	0	0	0	0	0	0	0	0	1	0	0	0	0	0	0	0	0	0	1	0	0	1
NOT1	60	1	J	0	0	0	0	0	0	0	0	0	1	0	0	0	0	0	0	0	0	0	0	1	0	1

Table 7.18

Some control signal values for the Relatively Simple CPU

Signal	Value
TRBUS	ARDT $\vee$ PCDT
ARLOAD	ARPC $\vee$ ARDT
ARINC	ARIN
PCINC	PCIN
DRLOAD	DRM $\vee$ DRAC
IRLOAD	IRDR
RLOAD	RAC
ZLOAD	ZALU

7.4   Reducing the Number of Microinstructions

In the Relatively Simple CPU, several states perform exactly the same micro-operations. For example, during both states LDAC1 and STAC1, the CPU performs the micro-operations $DR{\leftarrow}M$, $PC{\leftarrow}PC + 1$, $AR{\leftarrow}AR + 1$. In our current design for the Relatively Simple CPU's microsequenced control unit, each of these states uses a separate microinstruction.

In this section we examine two ways to take advantage of this redundancy to reduce the number of microinstructions needed by the control unit. The first method uses microsubroutines to combine repeated micro-operations into a single block of microinstructions, which are accessed by two or more execute routines. The other method uses microcode jumps to access microinstructions shared by two or more routines.

7.4.1   Microsubroutines

Just as high-level and assembly language code uses subroutines, a microsequencer can also use microsubroutines. As with high-level code, a microsequencer uses microsubroutines for sequences of actions that are performed in more than one routine in microcode. Having the code appear only once reduces the number of locations of microcode required. However, there is a tradeoff in using microsubroutines: The microsequencer hardware must be enhanced to implement the microsubroutine calls and returns.

Reviewing the micro-operations for the Relatively Simple CPU, we note that states LDAC1, LDAC2, and LDAC3 perform the same micro-operations as states STAC1, STAC2, and STAC3, respectively. In each case, the three states obtain a 16-bit address from memory and load it into AR. To illustrate how microsubroutines work, we modify the initial design to implement these states as a microsubroutine.

Although the microsubroutine occurs directly after FETCH3, it cannot be called from that state because FETCH3 must map to the correct execute routine. Also, the microsequencer could not generate the right return address. To resolve this, we create dummy states LDAC0 and STAC0. FETCH3 maps to one of these states when a LDAC or STAC instruction is decoded. These states perform no micro-operations and call the microsubroutine. On completion, the microsubroutine returns to the next location, which contains LDAC4 or STAC4. The modified portion of the state diagram for these instructions is shown in Figure 7.9. The new state assignments are listed in Table 7.19. Note that SUB1, SUB2, and SUB3 perform exactly the same micro-operations as LDAC1 (STAC1), LDAC2 (STAC2), and LDAC3 (STAC3), respectively.

Figure 7.9

Modified LDAC and STAC execute routines using microsubroutines

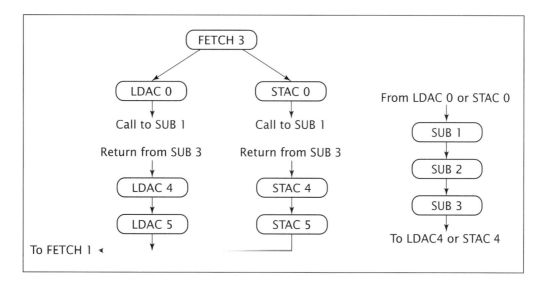

Table 7.19

Revised state assignments for the Relatively Simple CPU

State	Location
LDAC0	4
LDAC4	5
LDAC5	6
STAC0	8
STAC4	9
STAC5	10
SUB1	61
SUB2	62
SUB3	63

When a microsubroutine is called, the address of the routine is supplied by the ADDR output of the microcode memory. Since the microsequencer already does this for branches, it does not require any additional hardware. However, the microsequencer must store the return address so it can continue once the subroutine terminates. If a microinstruction at address X calls a microsubroutine, the routine must return to address $X + 1$. This requires the following modifications to the microsequencer.

1. The microsequencer must include a microsubroutine register to store the return address, which is the current address plus 1.
2. The designer must modify the next address generation hardware to include the microsubroutine register as a possible source for the next address.
3. The designer must also modify the next address multiplexer select logic to account for the possible selection of the return address. The logic must also generate a load signal for the microsubroutine register.
4. The list of branch types must be expanded to include microsubroutine call and return types.
5. The microcode must be modified to correctly access the microsubroutine.

The modified microsequencer hardware, excluding the details of the logic block, is shown in Figure 7.10. Notice that the same incrementer used to generate current address plus 1 for the next address

FIGURE 7.10

Microsequencer for the Relatively Simple CPU with microsubroutines

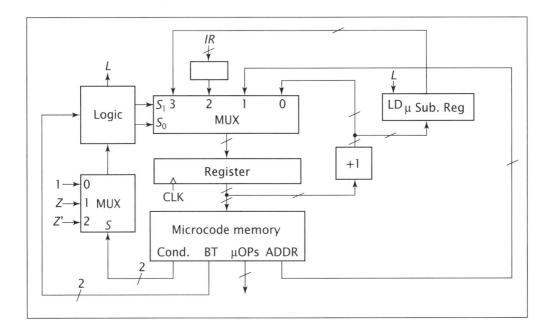

multiplexer is also used to generate the input to the microsubroutine register. Also note that much of the hardware, including the condition multiplexer, remains unchanged.

Before designing the revised next address logic, we must define the branch types. In addition to the conditional jump and unconditional map, unconditional microsubroutine call and return branch types are also required. Therefore, BT must be expanded to two bits to select among these four types. Table 7.20 shows the branch types.

Table 7.20

Revised branch types for the Relatively Simple Microsequencer

Branch Type	BT_1BT_0	Branch Function
JUMP	00	IF (condition) THEN Next Address = ADDR ELSE Next Address = Current Address + 1
MAP	01	Next Address = MAP
CALL	10	Next Address = ADDR, Microsubroutine Register = Current Address + 1
RET	11	Next Address = Microsubroutine Register

We create a table and generate the next address multiplexer control signals S_1 and S_0, just as before. This table is also used to generate L, the load signal for the microsubroutine register. The values shown in Table 7.21 lead to the following design for the logic component

Table 7.21

Revised branch logic

BT_1BT_0	Condition	Next Address	S_1S_0	L
0 0	0	Current Address + 1	0 0	0
0 0	1	ADDR	0 1	0
0 1	0	MAP	1 0	0
0 1	1	MAP	1 0	0
1 0	0	ADDR	0 1	1
1 0	1	ADDR	0 1	1
1 1	0	Microsubroutine register	1 1	0
1 1	1	Microsubroutine register	1 1	0

$$S_1 = BT_0$$
$$S_0 = BT_1 \vee (/BT_0' \wedge \text{condition value})$$
$$L = BT_1 \wedge /BT_0'$$

Now we modify the microcode for these execute routines. Since the micro-operations are defined, we proceed as before to generate the microcode, which is shown in Table 7.22.

Table 7.22

Revised microcode for the Relatively Simple Microsequencer

State	Address	Condition	BT	ARPC	ARINT	ARDINT	PCIDINT	PCIDT	DRM	DRAC	IRDR	RAC	ZALU	TRDR	ACCDR	ACLDR	PLUS	MINUS	ACINUN	ACIZNO	ANDD	ORR	XORT	NOTR	MDR	ADDR
LDAC0	4	1	C	0	1	0	1	0	1	0	0	0	0	0	0	0	0	0	0	0	0	0	0	0	0	61
LDAC4	5	1	J	0	0	0	0	0	1	0	0	0	0	0	0	0	0	0	0	0	0	0	0	0	0	6
LDAC5	6	1	J	0	0	0	0	0	0	0	0	0	0	0	1	0	0	0	0	0	0	0	0	0	0	1
STAC0	8	1	C	0	1	0	1	0	1	0	0	0	0	0	0	0	0	0	0	0	0	0	0	0	0	61
STAC4	9	1	J	0	0	0	0	0	0	1	0	0	0	0	0	0	0	0	0	0	0	0	0	0	0	10
STAC5	10	1	J	0	0	0	0	0	0	0	0	0	0	0	0	0	0	0	0	0	0	0	0	1	1
SUB1	61	1	J	0	1	0	1	0	1	0	0	0	0	0	0	0	0	0	0	0	0	0	0	0	0	62
SUB2	62	1	J	0	0	0	1	0	1	0	0	0	1	0	0	0	0	0	0	0	0	0	0	0	0	63
SUB3	63	1	R	0	0	1	0	0	0	0	0	0	0	0	0	0	0	0	0	0	0	0	0	0	0	X

Although not shown in this table, all other microinstructions in this CPU must be modified slightly. Since *BT* was expanded from one bit to two, every microinstruction must now use a 2-bit value for this field. Also, note that the address field of SUB3 is arbitrary. Since this microinstruction returns from a microsubroutine, the next address is received from the microsubroutine register; the contents of the ADDR field for this microinstruction are not used.

7.4.2 Microcode Jumps

Notice that the unconditional and conditional jump instructions have several states that perform the same micro-operations. This is to be expected since, if a jump is to be taken, it is processed in exactly the same way. This redundancy could be eliminated by creating a micro-subroutine. Instead, we can modify the state diagram so that these instructions access the same states directly. One set of states will perform a jump and another set will handle a conditional jump not taken. The routines will branch to the correct states.

The revised state diagram for the JUMP, JMPZ, and JPNZ instructions is shown in Figure 7.11. Since JUMP1, JUMP2, and JUMP3 are identical to JMPZY1, JMPZY2, and JMPZY3, and also to JPNZY1, JPNZY2, and JPNZY3, all but the JUMP states are eliminated. The states that previously branched to JMPZY1 and JPNZY1 now branch to JUMP1 instead. Since it is not possible to supply two arbitrary possible next addresses, JMPZN1 and JPNZN1 cannot be combined. However, it is still possible to combine JMPZN2 and JPNZN2.

FIGURE 7.11

Modified jump and conditional jump execute routines

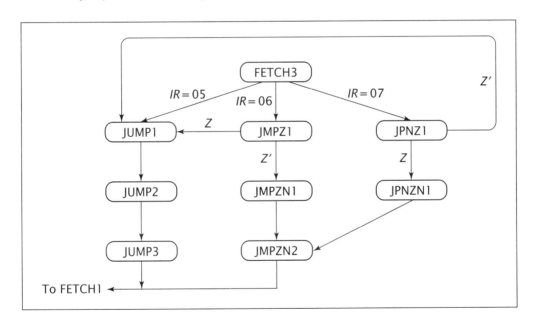

The revised microcode for these routines is shown in Table 7.23. Notice that the micro-operations remain the same, since the actual micro-operations to be performed are not changed. Only the sequencing information is modified.

Table 7.23

Further revised microcode for the Relatively Simple Microsequencer

State	Address	Condition	BT	ARPC	ARIN	ARDT	PCIN	PCDT	DRM	DRAC	IRDR	RAC	ZALU	TRDR	ACDR	ACR	PLUS	MINU	ACIN	ACZO	AND	OR	XOR	NOT	MDR	ADDR
JUMP1	20	1	J	0	1	0	0	0	1	0	0	0	0	0	0	0	0	0	0	0	0	0	0	0	0	21
JUMP2	21	1	J	0	0	0	0	0	1	0	0	0	0	1	0	0	0	0	0	0	0	0	0	0	0	22
JUMP3	22	1	J	0	0	0	0	1	0	0	0	0	0	0	0	0	0	0	0	0	0	0	0	0	0	1
JMPZ1	24	Z	J	0	0	0	0	0	0	0	0	0	0	0	0	0	0	0	0	0	0	0	0	0	0	20
JMPZN1	25	1	J	0	0	0	1	0	0	0	0	0	0	0	0	0	0	0	0	0	0	0	0	0	0	26
JMPZN2	26	1	J	0	0	0	1	0	0	0	0	0	0	0	0	0	0	0	0	0	0	0	0	0	0	1
JPNZ1	28	Z′	J	0	0	0	0	0	0	0	0	0	0	0	0	0	0	0	0	0	0	0	0	0	0	20
JPNZN1	45	1	J	0	0	0	1	0	0	0	0	0	0	0	0	0	0	0	0	0	0	0	0	0	0	26

7.5 Microprogrammed Control vs. Hardwired Control

When designing a CPU, the designer must use either a micropro-grammed control unit or a hardwired control unit. Each method has its strengths and weaknesses, and each is used in major microprocessors. Intel's Pentium-series processors use microcoded control, and Digital/Compaq's Alpha microprocessor uses hardwired control. Following are a few points for the designer to consider when deciding which to use.

7.5.1 Complexity of the Instruction Set

As the number of instructions increases, the complexity of the hardware needed to generate the control signals also increases. For example, having more instructions may lead to more micro-operations that assert the load signal of the accumulator, which increases the logic needed to generate the control signal. For hardwired control, there are also more states that assert these micro-operations, leading to increased combinatorial logic needed to generate the register load, increment and clear signals.

For horizontal microsequencer control, each micro-operation corresponds to one bit of microcode. Having a micro-operation asserted more often does not change the complexity of the combinatorial logic that generates the actual control signal, since the same bit is checked for every state. However, having more, different micro-operations that cause a register to be loaded will increase the complexity of the logic because more bits of microcode must be checked. However, this increase in complexity is less than that for hardwired control.

Vertical microsequencer control also increases the complexity of the control logic. As with horizontal microcode, the increased number of micro-operations that cause a register to be loaded translates to an increased number of bits of microcode that must be combined to generate the load signal. The greater number of micro-operations also requires either more or larger decoders to convert the micro-operation field bits to their corresponding micro-operations.

Microsequencers that directly generate their control signals do not need more hardware as a result of additional micro-operations. The control signals each correspond to one bit of microcode, no matter how many micro-operations assert the signal.

7.5.2   Ease of Modification

Ease of modification refers to the extendability of the CPU design to include more instructions and/or internal components in the future. A hardwired control unit requires hardware modifications to extend the CPU, while a microcoded control unit often needs only microprogram changes. In general (though not always), it is easier to modify microcode than to redesign hardware.

7.5.3   Clock Speed

Hardwired CPUs can generally run at higher clock speeds than their microcoded counterparts. The combinatorial logic used by hardwired CPUs to generate control signals is usually faster than the lookup time of the microcode ROM. The higher clock speed translates into less time required per state and faster instruction execution.

As with most engineering designs, the decision about which method to use depends on the requirements for the CPU.

7.6   Real World Example: A (Mostly) Microcoded CPU: The Pentium Microprocessor

As the complexity of a CPU increases, so does the complexity of its control unit. Hard-wired control units can increase in size to the point where it is no longer feasible to use this type of control unit. Microsequencers also increase in size, but at a much slower rate than hard-wired control units. For this reason, many current microprocessors use microcoded control units.

HISTORICAL PERSPECTIVE: How the Pentium Got Its Name

Prior to the Pentium, Intel gave its processors numeric names, such as 8085, 8086, 80286, 80386, and 80486. However, United States law did not allow them to trademark these numbers, so other companies could develop compatible microprocessors and name them using the same numbers. To distinguish their processors from those of their competitors, Intel broke with this scheme and decided to give their next processor a name that they could trademark. They solicited suggestions from their employees, finally selecting the name Pentium for its next microprocessor. Other manufacturers continued with the 80X86 designation or developed their own scheme for naming successor processors.

Intel's Pentium microprocessor uses (mostly) microcoded control. Its internal organization is shown in Figure 7.12. Comparing the internal organization of the Pentium to that of the 8085 microprocessor, introduced in Chapter 6, we can see that the Pentium is much more complex. This is to be expected, since the Pentium was developed more than 20 years after the 8085.

Now let's look at the Pentium's internal components, starting with its internal storage. Its internal register file contains eight integer registers. The **floating point unit**, or **FPU**, contains an additional eight registers which are used exclusively for floating point operations. The Pentium also contains 32K (or 16K in early models) of **cache memory**, which is used to speed up access to instructions and data. We look at the Pentium's cache memory in more detail in Chapter 9.

The Pentium contains one or two special-purpose functional units. The floating point unit processes all floating point instructions. It contains hardware designed specifically to handle floating point numbers; we look at floating point algorithms in detail in Chapter 8. Some Pentium microprocessors also include an **MMX** unit to handle instructions designed for use with multimedia applications.

The control unit consists of the blocks labeled *Control Unit, Instruction Decode*, and *Control ROM*. Although not shown in Figure 7.12, the control unit also receives data from the condition flags. The control unit sends control signals to the other components within the Pentium; for clarity, these signals are not shown in Figure 7.12.

The Pentium also includes two **instruction pipelines**. We discuss instruction pipelines in detail in Chapter 11. For now, think of an instruction pipeline as an assembly line. Each stage of the pipeline performs some part of the fetch-decode-execute sequence needed to process an instruction. By having different stages process different instructions simultaneously, the pipeline speeds up program execution.

Internal organization of the Pentium microprocessor (*Pentium Processor Family Develolper's Manual.* Reprinted by permission of Intel Corporation, Copyright Intel Corporation 1996, 1997.)

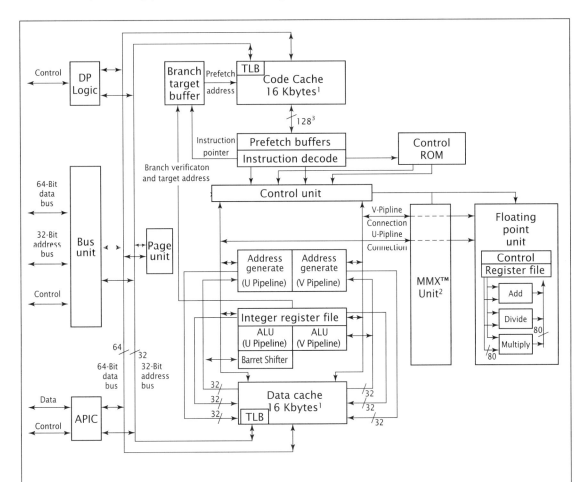

NOTES:

1. The Code and Data caches are each 8 Kbytes in size on the Pentium® processor (75/90/100/120/133/150/166/200).

2. The MMX Unit is present only on the Pentium processor with MMX™ technology.

3. The internal instruction bus is 256 bits wide on the Pentium processor (75/90/100/120/133/150/166/200).

The two pipelines in the Pentium microprocessor can perform two integer operations simultaneously. Because of the complexity of pipelines, they are usually controlled in part by special, hardwired control logic. This is the case with the Pentium microprocessor, which is why the control unit of the Pentium microprocessor is mostly, but not totally, microcoded.

7.7 SUMMARY

A microsequencer is one type of control unit used in microprocessors. Unlike the hardwired control units introduced in the previous chapter, which use logic gates to generate their control signals, a microsequencer stores its control signals in a lookup ROM. The control unit outputs the control signal values by reading data from the lookup ROM. Regardless of which type of control unit is used, the rest of the CPU is designed in exactly the same way as detailed in the previous chapter.

A microsequencer consists of three main parts: the microcode memory, the next address generator, and a register that contains the address of the current microinstruction. The microcode, or microprogram, is stored in microcode memory. It consists of the microinstructions to fetch, decode, and execute every instruction in the microprocessor's instruction set. The next address generator ensures that the microsequencer accesses the microinstructions in the order necessary to process each instruction in the instruction set properly. It uses mapping logic to access the correct execute routine for each instruction.

Each microinstruction contains several fields. Its select, condition, and address fields are used by the next address generator to select the correct address for the next microinstruction. Its micro-operation fields are used to generate the control signals for the rest of the CPU. The micro-operations may be encoded using horizontal microcode or vertical microcode, or they may directly generate the control signals.

Both hardwired and microsequencer control units are used in modern CPU design. Hardwired control units, found in RISC processors, are faster than microsequencers. Microsequencers, however, are easier to modify, and are used in many current microprocessors, including Intel's Pentium family.

Problems

1 The Very Simple Microsequencer is modified such that the states are assigned to the following addresses. Show the mapping logic needed for these assignments.

State	Address
FETCH1	0000
FETCH2	0001
FETCH3	0010
ADD1	0011
ADD2	0100
AND1	0101
AND2	0110
JMP1	0111
INC1	1000

2 Rewrite the optimized horizontal microcode for the Very Simple Microsequencer using the state assignments from Problem 1.

3 A CPU is specified by the following RTL code. Partition the micro-operations into fields such that the total number of bits is minimized. Each micro-operation OP**2 returns to FETCH1.

$$\begin{aligned}
\text{FETCH1:} &\quad AR \leftarrow PC \\
\text{FETCH2:} &\quad DR \leftarrow M,\ PC \leftarrow PC + 1 \\
\text{FETCH3:} &\quad IR, AR \leftarrow DR \\
\text{OP001:} &\quad DR \leftarrow M \\
\text{OP002:} &\quad AC \leftarrow AC \oplus DR \\
\text{OP011:} &\quad AC \leftarrow AC',\ PC \leftarrow PC + 1 \\
\text{OP012:} &\quad AC \leftarrow AC + 1 \\
\text{OP101:} &\quad DR \leftarrow M,\ AC \leftarrow AC + 1 \\
\text{OP102:} &\quad DR \leftarrow DR + 1 \\
\text{OP111:} &\quad DR \leftarrow M \\
\text{OP112:} &\quad PC \leftarrow PC + DR[5..0]
\end{aligned}$$

4 Verify the functioning of the Very Simple CPU using horizontal microcode.

5 Verify the functioning of the Very Simple CPU using vertical microcode.

6 Verify the functioning of the Very Simple CPU using direct generation of control signals.

7 We wish to modify the Very Simple CPU, as in Problem 6 in Chapter 6, to incorporate a new instruction, CLEAR, which sets $AC \leftarrow 0$; the instruction code for CLEAR is 111X XXXX. The new instruction code for

INC is 110X XXXX; all other instruction codes remain unchanged. Show the new state diagram and RTL code, the modifications necessary for the register section, and the changes needed for the microsequencer and its horizontal microcode. Verify the functioning of the new instruction.

8 Repeat Problem 7 for the microsequencer with vertical microcode. Show the new assignment of micro-operations to fields.

9 Repeat Problem 7 for the microsequencer that directly generates control signals.

10 We wish to modify the Very Simple CPU, as in Problem 10 in Chapter 6, to incorporate a new 8-bit register, R, and two new instructions. MVAC performs the transfer $R \leftarrow AC$ and has the instruction code 1110 XXXX; MOVR performs the operation $AC \leftarrow R$ and has the instruction code 1111 XXXX. The new instruction code for INC is 110X XXXX; all other instruction codes remain unchanged. Show the new state diagram and RTL code, the modifications necessary for the register section, and the changes needed for the microsequencer and its horizontal microcode. Verify the functioning of the new instruction.

11 Repeat Problem 10 for the microsequencer with vertical microcode. Show the new assignment of micro-operations to fields.

12 Repeat Problem 10 for the microsequencer that directly generates control signals.

13 Compare the work needed to add instructions to the Very Simple CPU using hardwired control with the work needed to add instructions using microsequenced control.

14 We wish to modify the Relatively Simple CPU, as in Problem 19 in Chapter 6, to include a new instruction, SETR, which performs the operation $R \leftarrow 1111\ 1111$. Its instruction code is 0001 0000. Show the new state diagram and RTL code, the modifications necessary for the register section, and the changes needed for the microsequencer and its horizontal microcode. Verify the functioning of the new instruction.

15 We wish to modify the Relatively Simple CPU, as in Problem 23 in Chapter 6, to include a new 8-bit register, B, and five new instructions as follows. Show the new state diagram and RTL code, the modifications necessary for the register section, and the changes needed for the microsequencer and its horizontal microcode. Verify the functioning of the new instructions.

Instruction	Instruction Code	Operation
ADDB	0001 1000	$AC \leftarrow AC + B$
SUBB	0001 1001	$AC \leftarrow AC - B$
ANDB	0001 1100	$AC \leftarrow AC \wedge B$
ORB	0001 1101	$AC \leftarrow AC \vee B$
XORB	0001 1110	$AC \leftarrow AC \oplus B$

16 Design the logic to generate the control signals for the Relatively Simple CPU using horizontal microcode *not* given in Table 7.18.

17 Consider the Relatively Simple CPU as modified to use microsubroutines. Assume that LDAC0 and STAC0, instead of performing no operations and calling the microsubroutine, each perform the microoperations DRM, PCIN, and ARIN, and call the microsubroutine. Modify the microsubroutine so the LDAC and STAC instructions perform the same functions as before.

18 Redesign the microsequencer control unit for the Relatively Simple CPU so it uses vertical microcode. Show the revised microcode and list the micro-operations in each field.

19 Redesign the microsequencer control unit for the Relatively Simple CPU so it directly generates the control signals. Show the revised microcode.

20 Verify the functioning of the Relatively Simple CPU using horizontal microcode. Show the execution trace for each instruction. Remember to trace the execution of all conditional instructions at least once under each possible condition.

21 Design the CPU of Problem 28 in Chapter 6 using a microsequencer that directly generates control signals.

22 Design the CPU of Problem 29 in Chapter 6 using a microsequencer with vertical microcode.

23 Modify the Relatively Simple CPU as in Problem 30 in Chapter 6 using the microsequencer with horizontal microcode.

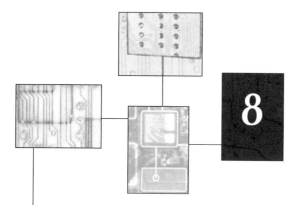

8   COMPUTER ARITHMETIC

When we examine the RTL code for the Very Simple and Relatively Simple CPUs, it is easy to see that the most frequently performed operation is copying data from one place to another. These operations copy data from one register to another, or between a register and a memory location; the value is not modified as it is copied. For example, in the fetch cycle for these CPUs, only the micro-operation $PC \leftarrow PC + 1$ changes a value; all other micro-operations copy a value to another location unchanged.

This does not mean that a CPU should only include micro-operations that move data. A CPU that only copies data, but does not modify it, ultimately cannot perform much useful work.

As an analogy, consider an automobile. I use my headlights much more frequently than my windshield wipers, but that doesn't mean that I shouldn't have both on my car. The headlights, useful though they are, cannot clear my windshield no matter how hard they try. One can think of arithmetic micro-operations as the wipers. Though used less frequently than data-copying micro-operations (the headlights), they perform functions that the data-copying micro-operations cannot. A CPU must be able to modify data to perform most desired functions. Instructions and micro-operations that perform arithmetic and logical functions are an important part of any CPU.

In this chapter we examine arithmetic algorithms and their hardware implementations for several commonly used number formats. We start with fixed-point notations. Technically, a **fixed-point notation** is any number in which the number of digits to the right of the decimal point (or radix point in bases other than base ten) does not change. For example, an amount of money in US dollars is typically expressed in the form $xxx.xx, always using two digits to the right of the decimal point to represent cents. In computers, fixed-point notations are almost always used to represent integers, with no bits or digits to the right of the radix point. This chapter examines unsigned and signed fixed-point notation, along with the procedures to add, subtract, multiply, and divide these numbers and the hardware used to implement these procedures. It also introduces **binary-coded decimal**, or **BCD**, notation and operations. BCD notation represents each individual digit of a decimal number as a group of binary bits; the other formats would convert an entire decimal value to its equivalent binary value.

Next, we describe some specialized hardware to improve the performance of arithmetic operations. Pipelining is a method that actually takes more time to produce a single result; however, it allows more than one operation to be performed simultaneously, which speeds up computations overall. Lookup tables can be used to replace arithmetic circuits. Operands are input to the table, which looks up the result of the operation for those operands and outputs the result. Wallace trees are combinatorial circuits used to speed up fixed-point multiplication.

Finally, this chapter covers floating-point notations and their arithmetic operations. Many applications must express numbers with varying numbers of digits or bits to the right of the radix point. By definition, in fixed-point notation the number of digits or bits to the right of the radix point cannot vary; floating-point notation was designed for just this task. This chapter examines floating-point notation, its characteristics, and the procedures and hardware used to add, subtract, multiply, and divide these numbers. It also describes the IEEE 754 floating-point standard, which defines (mostly) set ways of representing and processing these numbers. Virtually all modern CPUs that process floating-point numbers adhere to this standard.

8.1   Unsigned Notation

This section examines the basic algorithms for addition, subtraction, multiplication, and division of numbers in unsigned binary notation. We also present the hardware used to implement these algorithms. In addition to performing their operations on numbers in unsigned notation, these algorithms serve as the basis for arithmetic algorithms for signed, BCD, and floating-point representations. Note that numbers can be either positive or negative in some unsigned notation. The term *unsigned notation* only implies that the notation does not have a separate bit to represent the sign of the number.

There are two commonly used unsigned notations. The first, **non-negative notation**, treats every number as either zero or a positive value. An n-bit number can have a value ranging from 0 (all bits are zero) to $2^n - 1$ (all bits are 1).

Another approach is to consider the number to be in two's complement format. In this format, both positive and negative numbers can be represented; values for n-bit numbers range from -2^{n-1} to $2^{n-1} - 1$. Negative numbers have a 1 as the most significant bit and positive numbers (and zero) have 0 as the leading bit. A positive number (or zero) is represented exactly the same as in non-negative notation. A negative number, however, has no equivalent value in non-negative notation. A negative number is represented as the two's complement of its absolute value, which is calculated as the bitwise complement of its absolute value (the number's one's complement) + 1. For example, the 4-bit representation of -5 is derived by first complementing its absolute value, 5 (0101), which produces the one's complement value 1010; adding 1 to this value yields the two's complement of 1011. Table 8.1 shows the values represented by 8-bit numbers in both non-negative and two's complement unsigned notation.

Table 8.1

Numeric values in unsigned notation

Binary Representation	Unsigned Non-Negative	Unsigned Two's Complement
0000 0000	0	0
0000 0001	1	1
...	...	...
0111 1111	127	127
1000 0000	128	-128
1000 0001	129	-127
...	...	...
1111 1111	255	-1

8.1.1 Addition and Subtraction

For both the non-negative and two's complement notations, addition and subtraction are fairly straightforward. Addition is implemented as a straight binary addition. It is realized in hardware by using a parallel adder, as shown in Figure 8.1. Here, X and Y are 8-bit registers; the circuit performs the micro-operation ADD: $X \leftarrow X + Y$. As long as the result is within the normal range of values, 0 to $2^n - 1$ for non-negative numbers or -2^{n-1} to $2^{n-1} - 1$ for two's complement numbers, this circuit works as desired.

FIGURE 8.1

Implementation of the micro-operation $X \leftarrow X + Y$

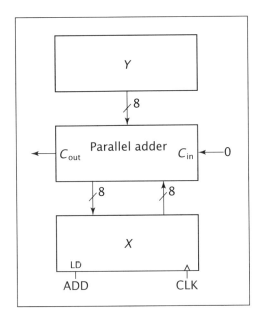

A problem arises, however, when the result cannot be represented as an 8-bit value. For the non-negative notation, consider the addition 255 + 1, 1111 1111 + 0000 0001. Straight binary addition yields the result 1 0000 0000, a 9-bit value, which cannot be stored in an 8-bit register. The extra bit generates a carry out from the parallel adder, which indicates an **arithmetic overflow**. In non-negative notation, this carry bit can set an **overflow flag**, signaling the rest of the system that an overflow has occurred, and that the result generated is not entirely correct. The rest of the system can either fix the result or handle the error appropriately.

In two's complement notation an overflow can occur at either end of the numeric range. At the positive end, adding 127 + 1, 0111 1111 + 0000 0001, yields a result of 1000 0000. However, in two's complement notation, this is −128, not the desired value of +128. Similarly, (−128) + (−1), 1000 0000 + 1111 1111, produces 0111 1111, which is +127 instead of −129. In this notation, the key to recognizing overflow is to check not only the carry out, but also the carry in to the most significant bit of the result. If the two carries are equal, then there is no overflow. To illustrate this, consider the additions shown in Figure 8.2. The additions produce carries in to and out of the most significant bit that are equal for (a) and (c); (b) and (d) produce overflows. Overflow can be handled in the same way as for non-negative numbers. Overflow only occurs when two numbers with the same sign are added. Adding two numbers with different signs always produces a valid result.

FIGURE 8.2

Overflow generation in unsigned two's complement addition

```
   126      0 1 1 1 1 1 1 0              127      0 1 1 1 1 1 1 1
   +1       0 0 0 0 0 0 0 1              +1       0 0 0 0 0 0 0 1
            0 1 1 1 1 1 1 1                       1 0 0 0 0 0 0 0
              0 0                                   0 1

              (a)                                   (b)


  -127      1 0 0 0 0 0 0 1             -128      1 0 0 0 0 0 0 0
  + (-1)    1 1 1 1 1 1 1 1             + (-1)    1 1 1 1 1 1 1 1
            1 0 0 0 0 0 0 0                       0 1 1 1 1 1 1 1
              1 1                                   1 0

              (c)                                   (d)
```

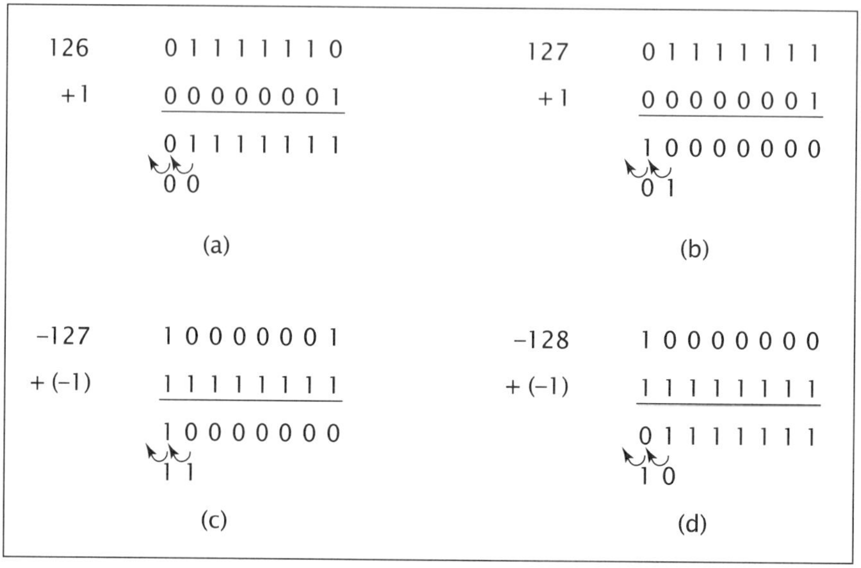

Subtraction can be converted to addition and performed in a similar manner. Essentially, $X - Y$ is implemented as $X + (-Y)$. First, Y is converted to $-Y$ by taking its two's complement, as described earlier. This value and X are then added together. Figure 8.3 shows one implementation of this procedure for the micro-operation SUB: $X \leftarrow X - Y$. Here, Y is complemented and the extra 1 is added as the carry in of the parallel adder.

For non-negative unsigned numbers, the result of this subtraction can never be greater than $2^n - 1$. The danger here is that the result could be less than zero. For example, $1 - 2$ would be implemented as 0000 0001 + 1111 1110 = 1111 1111, or 255, which is not a correct result. For these numbers, an overflow occurs if the subtraction (implemented via two's complement addition) produces a carry out of 0, rather than 1. Figure 8.4 shows this overflow generation for several data values. Computations (b) and (d) produce overflows; (a) and (c) do not.

Subtracting numbers in two's complement notation is also implemented as $X - Y = X + (-Y)$. Here an overflow occurs under the same conditions as in two's complement addition.

FIGURE 8.3
Implementation of the micro-operation $X \leftarrow X - Y$

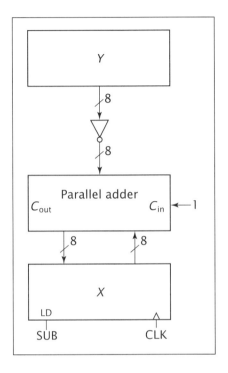

FIGURE 8.4
Overflow generation in unsigned two's complement subtraction

2	0 0 0 0 0 0 1 0		1	0 0 0 0 0 0 0 1
−1	1 1 1 1 1 1 1 1		−2	1 1 1 1 1 1 1 0
	1 0 0 0 0 0 0 0 1			0 1 1 1 1 1 1 1 1
	(a)			(b)
255	1 1 1 1 1 1 1 1		254	1 1 1 1 1 1 1 0
−254	0 0 0 0 0 0 1 0		−255	0 0 0 0 0 0 0 1
	1 0 0 0 0 0 0 0 1			0 1 1 1 1 1 1 1 1
	(c)			(d)

8.1.2 Multiplication

Multiplication can be envisioned as repeated additions. Multiplying a number by n gives the same result as adding n copies of the number together. This process leads to one implementation of multiplication, for $x \cdot y$, which is described as

$$z = 0;$$
$$\text{FOR } i = 1 \text{ TO } y \text{ DO } \{z = z + x\}$$

This process is undesirable for several reasons, primarily because it is very slow. It requires y additions; since y varies, so does the amount of time needed to calculate $x \cdot y$. Ideally, the calculation should take the same amount of time for all possible values.

Even so, that is not how people typically multiply numbers. Consider the calculation shown here:

$$
\begin{array}{r}
x = 27 \\
y = 253 \\
\hline
81 \\
135 \\
54 \\
\hline
6831
\end{array}
$$

First, 27 is multiplied by 3, the least significant digit of y. Then it is multiplied by the next least significant digit, 5. This result is placed one position to the left of the previous product because it is being multiplied by a value, 5, located one digit to the left of 3. Next, 27 is multiplied by 2; this result is moved one position further to the left. Finally, the values are added together.

This process is called **shift-add multiplication**. Each partial product is calculated and shifted to the left the proper number of places; then the **partial products** are added together. It is clearly faster than adding 27 to a running total 253 times. With some modifications to simplify the hardware implementation, this is the basic process used to multiply unsigned non-negative binary numbers.

The first of these modifications is that sums are calculated after every partial product is generated, rather than once at the end of the process. Adders with two inputs are fairly easy to construct, whereas adders with three or more inputs become much more complex. Thus the previous calculation becomes

$$
\begin{array}{rl}
x = 27 & \\
y = 253 & \\
\hline
81 & \\
135 & \\
\hline
1431 & \leftarrow \textit{sum calculated} \\
54 & \\
\hline
6831 & \leftarrow \textit{final sum calculated}
\end{array}
$$

No more than two values are added together at any time.

Examining this calculation reveals more opportunities to improve the implementation. Notice that each partial product aligns differently with the previous value, specifically, one additional position to the left. In terms of hardware, this would require the partial product to be routed to many different locations. The hardware would be much simpler if the result were always sent to the same place. Also notice that the sum of the running total and the partial product results in unnecessary work. The partial product contains no value in some of the rightmost positions, yet a result is generated for these places because the running total contains values in these locations. For example, the second sum generates 31 in the last two digits even though nothing needs to be added there.

Both of these can be improved by shifting the running total rather than the partial product. After each partial product is generated and added to the running total, the running total is shifted one position to the right. The calculation of $27 \cdot 253$ is thus implemented as follows.

$$
\begin{array}{rl}
x = & 27 \\
y = & \underline{253} \\
 & 81 \\
 & 81 \qquad \leftarrow \textit{shifted one position right} \\
 & \underline{135} \\
 & 1431 \qquad \leftarrow \textit{1 is carried down, not added} \\
 & 1431 \qquad \leftarrow \textit{shifted one position right} \\
 & \underline{54} \\
 & 6831 \qquad \leftarrow \textit{31 is carried down, not added} \\
 & 6831 \qquad \leftarrow \textit{one final shift}
\end{array}
$$

Notice that the same two columns of digits are added for each addition. Also note that digits already shifted to the right of these columns are simply carried down, not added. Before, these digits were part of the addition, but still generated the same result.

Using binary, rather than decimal, values produces one more significant benefit. In decimal multiplication, each partial product can have one of 10 possible values, depending on the digit of the multiplier. In binary, the multiplicand is multiplied by either 0 or 1, resulting in a partial product of zero ($X \cdot 0 = 0$) or the value of the multiplicand ($X \cdot 1 = X$). This can be implemented without actually multiplying two values; it is only necessary to select one of two.

The following algorithm implements shift-add multiplication of the contents of two n-bit registers, X and Y, storing the result in two n-bit registers, U and V. U contains the high-order half of the result and V contains the low-order half. C is a 1-bit register used to store the carry of an addition.

```
U = 0;
FOR i = 1 TO n DO
        {IF Y₀ = 1 THEN CU = U + X;
        linear shift right CUV;
        circular shift right Y}
```

Consider the multiplication $13 \cdot 11, 1101 \cdot 1011$. Table 8.2 shows the values in all registers for the execution of this algorithm; initially $X = 1101$ and $Y = 1011$. It can easily be verified that the algorithm produces the correct result.

Table 8.2

Trace of the shift-add algorithm

Function	i	C	U	V	Y	Comments
$U = 0$			0000	0000	1011	
if $Y_0 = 1$	1	0	1101			$Y_0 = 1$, add
shr (CUV)		0	0110	1000		
cir (Y)					1101	
if $Y_0 = 1$	2	1	0011			$Y_0 = 1$, add
shr (CUV)		0	1001	1100		
cir (Y)					1110	
if $Y_0 = 1$	3					$Y_0 = 0$
shr (CUV)		0	0100	1110		
cir (Y)					0111	
if $Y_0 = 1$	4	1	0001			$Y_0 = 1$, add
shr (CUV)			1000	1111		
cir (Y)					1011	Original value
DONE			1000	1111		Result = 143

The next task is to implement this algorithm in RTL code. X, Y, U, and V are n-bit values, and C is a 1-bit value. Mechanisms are also needed to initiate and terminate the algorithm, and to implement the loop counter i. A signal called $START$ will initiate the algorithm. On termination, the algorithm will set a 1-bit value, $FINISH$, to 1. The loop counter i has the minimum number of bits needed to store the value n. Instead of counting up to n, the loop counter starts with a value of n and counts down to 0; this simplifies the hardware design for this code.

The RTL code to realize this algorithm, with these changes, is as follows. Note that $Z = 1$ when $i = 0$, and **1**, **2**, and **3** are consecutive states, that is, the algorithm goes from **1** to **2** to **3**.

$$\begin{array}{rl}
\textbf{\textit{1}}: & U\leftarrow 0,\ i\leftarrow n\\
Y_0\textbf{\textit{2}}: & CU\leftarrow U + X\\
\textbf{\textit{2}}: & i\leftarrow i - 1\\
\textbf{\textit{3}}: & \text{shr}(CUV),\ \text{cir}(Y)\\
Z'\textbf{\textit{3}}: & \text{GOTO } \textbf{\textit{2}}\\
Z\ \textbf{\textit{3}}: & FINISH\leftarrow 1
\end{array}$$

Table 8.3 shows a trace of the RTL code for $13 \cdot 11$. Again, $X = 1101$ and $Y = 1011$. It is the same as the trace of Table 8.2, except it shows the conditions met and micro-operations performed during every cycle. As before, it produces the correct result.

Table 8.3

Trace of the RTL code for the shift-add algorithm

Conditions	Micro-operations	i	C	U	V	Y	Z	FINISH
START		x	x	xxxx	xxxx	1011		0
1	$U\leftarrow0,\ i\leftarrow4$	4		0000				0
Y_0**2,2**	$CU\leftarrow U + X,$ $i\leftarrow i - 1$	3	0	1101				0
3,Z′3	shr(CUV), cir(Y), GOTO **2**		0	0110	1xxx	1101		
Y_0**2,2**	$CU\leftarrow U + X,$ $i\leftarrow i - 1$	2	1	0011				0
3,Z′3	shr(CUV), cir(Y), GOTO **2**		0	1001	11xx	1110		
2	$i\leftarrow i - 1$	1						0
3,Z′3	shr(CUV), cir(Y), GOTO **2**		0	0100	111x	0111		
Y_0**2,2**	$CU\leftarrow U + X,$ $i\leftarrow i - 1$	0	1	0001			1	
3,Z3	shr(CUV), cir(Y), FINISH$\leftarrow1$		0	1000	1111	1011		1

The final step in design process is to develop hardware for this RTL code. As was the case with the CPUs designed in previous chapters, this hardware consists of two parts: a register section in which micro-operations are performed, and a control unit to generate the required control signals and state values. To simplify this design, we implement X as an n-bit register, and Y, U, and V as n-bit shift registers, which shift right when their SHR signals are asserted. Register i is a down counter with enough bits to hold the value n. C and FINISH are implemented as 1-bit registers. The data paths between these registers are all set up to realize the transfers required by the micro-operations of this RTL code. Also note that the bits of i are NORed together to generate Z; Z is 1 only when all bits of i are 0, or $i = 0$. This is simpler than comparing i to n and requires only one NOR gate, rather than an n-bit comparator; this is the reason i counts down from n to 0 instead of up from 0 to n. Figure 8.5 shows the logic to implement the shift-add multiplication algorithm.

Hardware implementation of the shift-add multiplication algorithm

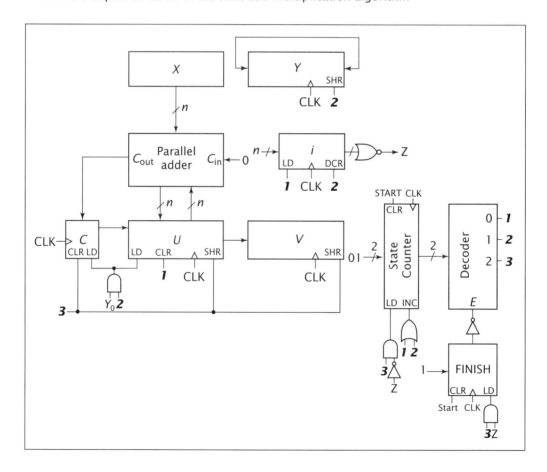

Now let's look at the control unit, also shown in Figure 8.5, to see how the RTL code is realized. When *START* is asserted, the state counter is cleared. *FINISH* is also cleared to 0, which enables the decoder. The decoder now asserts output *1*, which clears register U and loads the value n into register i. The state counter is then incremented to 01, which activates state output **2**. This always decrements register i, and, if the least significant bit of register Y (Y_0) is 1, it stores $U + X$ in register pair CU. If $Y_0 = 0$, it leaves C and U unchanged. The state counter is again incremented to 10, asserting state output **3**. At this time, the contents of registers C, U, and V are shifted one position to the right. (Since a 0 is shifted into C, it is simply cleared.) Also, one of two things happens in this state. If $Z = 0$, $i \neq 0$ and the algorithm is not yet done. The state counter is loaded with the value 01, causing the decoder to assert the output for state **2**; this implements the "GOTO **2**" operation. However, if $Z = 1$, then $i = 0$ and the algorithm is done. It sets *FINISH* to 1, which disables the decoder; no outputs, **1**, **2**, or **3**, are asserted. In this state, no control signals are asserted and the hardware halts its operations.

This algorithm can be optimized, and its hardware requirements reduced, if both operands do not need to be preserved. Specifically, if the value in Y can be sacrificed, its value can be stored in register V instead. The product now calculated is $UV \leftarrow X \cdot V$. The least significant bit of V is checked; if it is 1 then the addition takes place. During the shift, this bit is lost; it is no longer needed at that point. The revised RTL code is

	1:	$U \leftarrow 0$, $i \leftarrow n$
V_0	**2**:	$CU \leftarrow U + X$
	2:	$i \leftarrow i - 1$
	3:	shr(CUV)
Z'	**3**:	GOTO **2**
Z	**3**:	*FINISH* $\leftarrow 1$

The only differences are, first, that the condition for $CU \leftarrow U + X$ is now V_0**2** instead of Y_0**2**, and second that the cir(Y) operation is removed. The hardware for this RTL code is the same as in Figure 8.5, except the LD signals of C and U are driven by $V_0 \land$ **2**, and register Y is removed from the circuit.

Table 8.4 on page 320 shows a trace of this algorithm for the product $13 \cdot 11$. Other than the absence of register Y and the initial value in register V, it is identical to the trace in Table 8.3.

8.1.2.1 Booth's Algorithm

For unsigned two's complement numbers, the preceding algorithm does not always work. Specifically, it does not work properly if one or both operands are negative, since it was designed to handle only positive numbers. In the previous example, 1101 and 1011 would represent -3 and -5, respectively, in two's complement notation. Their product is $+15$, whereas the result produced by the algorithm, 1000 1111, would be -113. It is still possible to use this algorithm by employing the following procedure.

Table 8.4

Trace of the RTL code for the modified shift-add algorithm

Conditions	Micro-operations	i	C	U	V	Z	FINISH
START		x	x	xxxx	1011		0
1	$U \leftarrow 0$, $i \leftarrow 4$	4		0000		0	
$V_0$2,2	$CU \leftarrow U + X$, $i \leftarrow i - 1$	3	0	1101		0	
3,Z'3	shr(CUV), GOTO 2		0	0110	1101		
$V_0$2,2	$CU \leftarrow U + X$, $i \leftarrow i - 1$	2	1	0011		0	
3,Z'3	shr(CUV), GOTO 2		0	1001	1110		
2	$i \leftarrow i - 1$	1				0	
3,Z'3	shr(CUV), GOTO 2		0	0100	1111		
$V_0$2,2	$CU \leftarrow U + X$, $i \leftarrow i - 1$	0	1	0001		1	
3,Z3	shr(CUV), FINISH$\leftarrow$1		0	1000	1111		1

```
IF multiplicand < 0 THEN multiplicand ← −multiplicand;
IF multiplier < 0 THEN multiplier ← −multiplier;
multiply using non-negative multiplication;
restore multiplicand and multiplier to original values;
IF exactly one of multiplier and multiplicand is negative,
           AND the other is not zero, THEN result ← −result
```

A less cumbersome method is to use **Booth's algorithm**. This algorithm works directly on two's complement numbers, eliminating the conversions between positive and negative values. Like the previous algorithm, it checks each bit of the multiplier, shifting the result one bit to the right for each bit it checks. However, it does not add data for every 1 in the multiplier. Instead, it performs a subtraction for the first 1 in a string of 1's, and an addition for the last 1 in the string. The rationale for this is that the string of 1's is treated as the difference of two values. For example, this algorithm treats the product $1011 \cdot 0111$ as $1011 \cdot (1000 - 0001)$, both of which produce the same result.

The algorithm to form the product $UV \leftarrow X \cdot Y$, where each is an n-bit value, can be expressed as follows. Y_{-1} is a 1-bit value; its purpose will be explained shortly.

```
U = 0; Y_-1 = 0;
FOR i = 1 TO n DO
{IF start of a string of 1's in Y THEN U = U - X (= U + X' + 1);
 IF end of a string of 1's in Y THEN U = U + X;
 arithmetic shift right UV;
 circular shift right Y AND copy Y_0 to Y_-1}
```

The key to detecting a string of 1's is to recall the previous bit to the right. If the least significant bit of Y, Y_0, and the last bits shifted out are 10, the 1 starts a string of 1's. For the value 01, the 0 ends a string of 1's. Two bits, 11, are within a string of 1's and require no action. Similarly, the bit pattern 00 requires neither addition nor subtraction by the algorithm. To check this, a 1-bit register, Y_{-1}, is used to store the last bit shifted out. Initially it is set to 0 so that an initial string of 1's can be detected.

Table 8.5 shows the execution of this algorithm for $X = -3$ (1101) and $Y = -5$ (1011). As expected, the algorithm produces the correct value 0000 1111 (+15).

Take particular note of the last iteration in Table 8.5, with $i = 4$. The algorithm performed the subtraction associated with the start of a string of 1's, but the addition corresponding to the end of this string

Table 8.5

Trace of Booth's algorithm

Function	i	U	V	Y	Y_{-1}	Comments
$U = 0$, $Y_{-1} = 0$		0000	0000	1011	0	
if start of string	1	0011				Start of string
if end of string						
ashr(UV)		0001	1000			
cir(Y), $Y_{-1} \leftarrow Y_0$				1101	1	
if start of string	2					Still within string
if end of string						
ashr(UV)		0000	1100			
cir(Y), $Y_{-1} \leftarrow Y_0$				1110	1	
if start of string	3					
if end of string		1101				End of string
ashr(UV)		1110	1110			
cir(Y), $Y_{-1} \leftarrow Y_0$				0111	0	
if start of string	4	0001				Start of string
if end of string						
ashr(UV)		0000	1111			
cir(Y), $Y_{-1} \leftarrow Y_0$				1011	1	Original value
DONE		0000	1111			Result $= +15$

never occurs. This is correct; if the multiplier has a 1 in its most significant bit, then the last subtraction has no corresponding addition.

This algorithm can be converted to RTL code and its corresponding hardware. Using the *START* signal and 1-bit register *FINISH*, as in the shift-add algorithm, we can realize this algorithm with the following RTL code. Again, U, V, X, and Y are n-bit values and Y_{-1} is a 1-bit value. As before, i counts down from n to 0. Note that condition $Y_0 Y_{-1}'$ corresponds to the start of a string of 1's, triggering the initial subtraction. Similarly, $Y_0' Y_{-1}$ is true at the end of a string of 1's; under this condition, the required addition is performed:

$$
\begin{array}{rl}
\boldsymbol{1}: & U \leftarrow 0,\ Y_{-1} \leftarrow 0,\ i \leftarrow n \\
Y_0 Y_{-1}' \boldsymbol{2}: & U \leftarrow U + X' + 1 \\
Y_0' Y_{-1} \boldsymbol{2}: & U \leftarrow U + X \\
\boldsymbol{2}: & i \leftarrow i - 1 \\
\boldsymbol{3}: & \mathrm{ashr}(UV),\ \mathrm{cir}(Y),\ Y_{-1} \leftarrow Y_0 \\
Z' \boldsymbol{3}: & \mathrm{GOTO}\ \boldsymbol{2} \\
Z \boldsymbol{3}: & FINISH \leftarrow 1
\end{array}
$$

This algorithm can be expressed more succinctly by combining the addition and subtraction into a single operation. Specifically, both the addition and subtraction can be implemented by the following RTL statement.

$$(Y_0 \oplus Y_{-1})\ \boldsymbol{2}: \quad U \leftarrow U + (X \oplus Y_0) + Y_0$$

Here, $(X \oplus Y_0)$ means that every bit of X is individually exclusive-ORed with Y_0. For $Y_0 = 1$ and $Y_{-1} = 0$, this becomes $U \leftarrow U + (X \oplus 1) + 1$. Since any bit exclusive-ORed with 1 produces its complement, $X \oplus 1 - X'$ and the micro-operation becomes $U \leftarrow U + X' + 1$, which is a realization of $U \leftarrow U - X$. When $Y_0 = 0$ and $Y_{-1} = 1$, this micro-operation becomes $U \leftarrow U + (X \oplus 0) + 0$. Any value exclusive-ORed with 0 produces the original value, so $X \oplus 0 = X$ and the micro-operation results in $U \leftarrow U + X$.

The hardware corresponding to the modified RTL code is shown in Figure 8.6. Like the shift-add design, it includes a register section and a control unit. Table 8.6 on page 324 shows a trace of the RTL code for $(-3) \cdot (-5)$, the same multiplication shown in Table 8.5. As before, $X = 1101$ and $Y = 1011$.

As with the shift-add algorithm, this algorithm can be modified to eliminate register Y by storing the multiplier in V. The RTL code and hardware implementations of the algorithm with this change are left as an exercise for the reader.

8.1.3 Division

Just as multiplication can be envisioned as repeated additions, division can be viewed as repeated subtractions. For example, $z = x \div y$ could be implemented by the following algorithm. The remainder is left in x.

FIGURE 8.6

Hardware implementation of Booth's multiplication algorithm

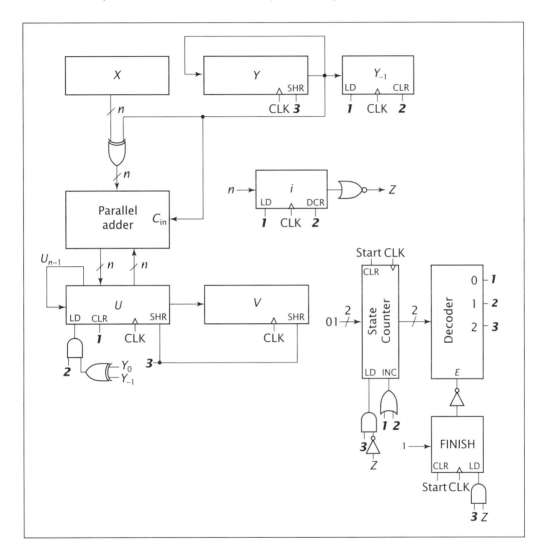

$$z = 0;$$
$$\text{WHILE } x \geq y \text{ DO } \{z = z + 1, x = x - y\}$$

As with the process that multiplies $x \cdot y$ via a series of y additions, this process is inefficient. It also requires a varying amount of time, depending on the final value of z.

Just as with multiplication, it is possible to employ a shifting algorithm to reduce the time needed to perform the division. Instead of shift-add, however, shift-subtract is needed. To illustrate this process, consider this calculation:

Table 8.6

Trace of the RTL code for Booth's algorithm

Conditions	Micro-operations	i	U	V	Y	Y_{-1}	Z	FINISH
START		x	xxxx	xxxx	1011	x		0
1	$U\leftarrow 0, Y_{-1}\leftarrow 0,$ $i\leftarrow 4$	4	0000			0	0	
$Y_0 Y_{-1}'\mathbf{2,2}$	$U\leftarrow U + X' + 1,$ $i\leftarrow i - 1$	3	0011				0	
$\mathbf{3},Z'\mathbf{3}$	ashr(UV), cir(Y), $Y_{-1}\leftarrow Y_0$, GOTO **2**		0001	1xxx	1101	1		
2	$i\leftarrow i - 1$	2					0	
$\mathbf{3},Z'\mathbf{3}$	ashr(UV), cir(Y), $Y_{-1}\leftarrow Y_0$, GOTO **2**		0000	11xx	1110	1		
$Y_0'Y_{-1}\mathbf{2,2}$	$U\leftarrow U + X,$ $i\leftarrow i - 1$	1	1101				0	
$\mathbf{3},Z'\mathbf{3}$	ashr(UV), cir(Y), $Y_{-1}\leftarrow Y_0$, GOTO **2**		1110	111x	0111	0		
$Y_0 Y_{-1}'\mathbf{2,2}$	$U\leftarrow U + X' + 1,$ $i\leftarrow i - 1$	0	0001				1	
$\mathbf{3},Z\mathbf{3}$	ashr(UV), cir(Y), $Y_{-1}\leftarrow Y_0$, FINISH$\leftarrow 1$		0000	1111	1011			1

$$
\begin{array}{r}
096 \\
71{\overline{\smash{)}6827}} \\
\underline{639} \\
437 \\
\underline{426} \\
11
\end{array}
$$

Although not explicitly shown, the first operation is to compare the divisor, 71, to the first two digits of the dividend, 68. Since 71 is greater than 68, it produces a result of 0 in the quotient. This is an important part of the division process in computers: It is used to detect overflow. Continuing, one more digit is brought into the portion to be checked. 71 divides 682 nine times, with a remainder of 43. Finally, the last digit is included, and 71 goes into 437 six times with a remainder of 11.

As with the shift-add multiplication procedure, a shift can be employed here so that the result of the subtraction is always routed to the same location. In this case, the dividend is shifted left, rather than right as in the shift-add multiplication algorithm. As the division progresses, the most significant digits are no longer needed. With this left shifting, the previous division is implemented as follows.

$$\begin{array}{r} 096 \\ 71\overline{\smash{)}6827} \end{array}$$

$$\underline{00}\quad \leftarrow 71 \text{ divides } 68 \text{ zero times}$$
$$682\quad \leftarrow bring\ down\ another\ digit$$
$$682\quad \leftarrow shift\ left\ one\ position$$
$$\underline{639}\quad \leftarrow 71 \text{ divides } 682 \text{ nine times}$$
$$437\quad \leftarrow bring\ down\ another\ digit$$
$$437\quad \leftarrow shift\ left\ one\ position$$
$$\underline{426}\quad \leftarrow 71 \text{ divides } 437 \text{ six times}$$
$$11\quad \leftarrow remainder$$

The first step, checking to see whether 71 divides 68, is an over-flow check that has no analogous operation in the shift-add multiplication algorithm. In a typical hardware implementation, the dividend (6827 in this example) is stored in a $2n$-bit register, or in two n-bit registers. The divisor (71) and the quotient (96) are stored in n-bit registers, and the remainder is left in one of the two dividend registers. If the upper half of the dividend is greater than or equal to the divisor, then the quotient will be too large to fit into its designated register. This is analogous to the decimal division $7827 \div 71$, where the dividend has four digits and the divisor has two. Because $78 \geq 71$, the quotient has at least three digits, one more than the storage size of its register. As an added benefit, attempting to divide by zero also generates an overflow.

Using binary data also simplifies this algorithm. The divisor can only divide the dividend 0 or 1 times, not any value from 0 to 9, as in decimal division. If the dividend is greater than or equal to the divisor, its corresponding bit in the quotient should be 1; otherwise it should be 0.

The following algorithm implements shift-subtract division of two binary values. The dividend is initially stored in UV, where U and V are each n bits wide. The divisor is stored in n-bit value X and the quotient in n-bit value Y. The remainder will be stored in U. C is a 1-bit value used to store the extra bit shifted out of U.

```
IF U ≥ X THEN exit with overflow;
Y = 0; C = 0;
FOR i = 1 TO n DO
        {linear shift left CUV;
        linear shift left Y;
        IF CU ≥ X THEN {Y₀ = 1, U = CU - X}}
```

Before we look at the operation of the entire algorithm, consider the circumstances under which the first step terminates the algorithm. For $112 \div 7$ with $n = 4$, $UV = 0111\ 0000$ and $X = 0111$. Since $U \geq X$, because both are 0111, the algorithm exits immediately. Had it proceeded, it should have produced a result of 16 (1 0000) and a remainder of zero. The value 1 0000 cannot be stored in a 4-bit register; this is the reason for the overflow. In practice, the algorithm would set an overflow flag to notify the CPU that it did not produce a valid result.

Table 8.7 shows the execution of this algorithm for $147 \div 13$. Initially, $U = 1001$, $V = 0011$, $X = 1101$, and $n = 4$.

Table 8.7

Trace of the shift-subtract division algorithm

Function	i	C	U	V	Y	Comments
initial		0	1001	0011	0000	
if $U \geq X$						$U < X$, no exit
shl(CUV)	1	1	0010	0110		
shl(Y)					0000	
if $CU \geq X$			0101		0001	$1\ 0010 \geq 1101$
shl(CUV)	2	0	1010	1100		
shl(Y)					0010	
if $CU \geq X$						$CU < X$
shl(CUV)	3	1	0101	1000		
shl(Y)					0100	
if $CU \geq X$			1000		0101	$1\ 0101 \geq 1101$
shl(CUV)	4	1	0001	0000		
shl(Y)					1010	
if $CU \geq X$			0100		1011	$1\ 0001 \geq 1101$

In the following RTL code for this algorithm, X, U, V, and Y are n-bit values, and C and *OVERFLOW* are 1-bit values. As before, $Z = 1$ when $i = 0$. For this algorithm, $G = 1$ if $U \geq X$. *FINISH* is the same as in the shift-add multiplication algorithm, and **1**, **2**, **3**, and **4** are a sequence of states.

$$
\begin{aligned}
G\textbf{1}: &\quad \textit{FINISH} \leftarrow 1, \textit{OVERFLOW} \leftarrow 1 \\
\textbf{2}: &\quad Y \leftarrow 0, C \leftarrow 0, \textit{OVERFLOW} \leftarrow 0, i \leftarrow n \\
\textbf{3}: &\quad \text{shl}(CUV), \text{shl}(Y), i \leftarrow i - 1 \\
(C + G)\textbf{4}: &\quad Y_0 \leftarrow 1, U \leftarrow U + X' + 1 \\
Z'\textbf{4}: &\quad \text{GOTO } \textbf{3} \\
Z\,\textbf{4}: &\quad \textit{FINISH} \leftarrow 1
\end{aligned}
$$

Most of the RTL code is a straightforward implementation of the algorithm, but the operations that occur under condition $(C + G)\textbf{4}$ require further explanation. Recall that the algorithm performs these operations if $CU \geq X$; that is, if X divides CU. G is active only if $U \geq X$. If $C = 0$, $CU = 0U = U$, and checking G is sufficient to determine whether

$CU \geq X$. However, if $C = 1$, then CU must be greater than X. In this case, CU is an $(n+1)$-bit value with a 1 in its most significant bit. Even if $U = 0$, this number is greater than any n-bit value. (For the 4-bit values used in the examples in this chapter, this simply says that 1 0000 must be greater than any 4-bit value. In the worst case, for $C = 1$, $U = 0000$, and $X = 1111$, and 1 0000 > 1111.) Thus, the condition $CU \geq X$ is equivalent to the conditions $U \geq X (G)$ or $C = 1(C)$, or $(C + G)$.

In this same RTL statement, notice the transfer $U \leftarrow U - X$. Since the result will be shifted left one position during the next cycle (**3**), it is not necessary to store the most significant bit of the subtraction in register C. The value of C will be shifted out during the next iteration of the loop, before it would be used. This can actually be implemented via two's complement addition as $U \leftarrow U + X' + 1$. Doing so makes it unnecessary to include C in the calculation.

Table 8.8 shows the trace of this RTL code for the operation $147 \div 13$. As before, $U = 1001$, $V = 0011$, $X = 1101$, and $n = 4$.

Table 8.8

Trace of the RTL code for the shift-subtract division algorithm

Conditions	Micro-operations	i	C	U	V	Y	Z	FINISH
START		x	x	1001	0011	xxxx		0
1	NONE							
2	$Y \leftarrow 0$, $C \leftarrow 0$, OVERFLOW $\leftarrow 0$, $i \leftarrow 4$	4	0			0000	0	
3	shl(CUV), shl(Y), $i \leftarrow i - 1$	3	1	0010	0110	0000	0	
$(C + G)$**4**,Z'**4**	$Y_0 \leftarrow 1$, $U \leftarrow U + X' + 1$, GOTO **3**			0101		0001		
3	shl(CUV), shl(Y), $i \leftarrow i - 1$	2	0	1010	1100	0010	0	
Z'**4**	GOTO **3**							
3	shl(CUV), shl(Y), $i \leftarrow i - 1$	1	1	0101	1000	0100	0	
$(C + G)$**4**,Z'**4**	$Y_0 \leftarrow 1$, $U \leftarrow U + X' + 1$, GOTO **3**			1000		0101		
3	shl(CUV), shl(Y), $i \leftarrow i - 1$	0	1	0001	0000	1010	1	
$(C + G)$**4**,Z**4**	$Y_0 \leftarrow 1$, $U \leftarrow U + X' + 1$, FINISH $\leftarrow 1$		0100		1011			1

The hardware to implement this algorithm is shown in Figure 8.7 on page 329. This is a **non-restoring division algorithm**. It does not perform the subtraction $U \leftarrow U - X$ unless $CU \geq X$. A second type of division is the **restoring division algorithm**. Instead of checking whether $CU \geq X$ before performing the subtraction, this algorithm first performs the subtraction and then checks whether or not CU was greater than or equal to X. If it was not, the algorithm adds X back to U, thus restoring its original value.

A restoring algorithm follows the same basic procedure as a non-restoring algorithm: It checks for overflow and, if no overflow occurs, it enters a shift-subtract loop. The main difference is the way in which comparisons are handled. In the non-restoring algorithm, CU is first compared to X; if $CU \geq X$, then it performs the subtraction $U = CU - X$. The restoring algorithm, on the other hand, performs the subtraction first. If it finds that CU was less than X, meaning that it should not have performed the subtraction, it performs the addition $U = U + X$ to restore U to its previous value.

The following algorithm implements a restoring shift-subtract division procedure. As before, the dividend is initially stored in UV, the divisor is stored in X, and the quotient is stored in Y. The remainder is left in U. These values are each n bits wide; C is a 1-bit value.

```
CU = U + X' + 1;
U = U + X, IF C = 1 THEN exit with overflow;
Y = 0;
FOR i = 1 TO n DO
        {linear shift left CUV;
        linear shift left Y;
        IF C = 1 THEN {U = U + X' + 1} ELSE {CU = U + X' + 1};
        IF C = 1 THEN {Y_0 = 1} ELSE {U = U + X}}
```

Before describing the algorithm, we must explain how the comparisons are performed. If the subtraction $CU = U - X$ is performed as the two's complement addition $CU = U + X' + 1$, this operation actually has two functions. The obvious function is that it performs the desired subtraction. Not so obvious, however, is that this also compares U to X. If $U \geq X$, this operation sets C to 1. It sets C to 0 only when $U < X$. Figure 8.8 illustrates this: In (a) and (b), C is set to 1, indicating that $U \geq X$; in (c), C is set to 0 because $U < X$.

Now let's examine the entire algorithm. In this algorithm, the first two statements check if $U \geq X$. If so, an overflow occurs; the first addition, $CU = U + X' + 1$, would set $C = 1$. However, if $U < X$, it sets C to 0. The next statement restores U to its previous value, since $(U + X' + 1) + X = (U - X) + X = U$. It also exits if an overflow occurred $(C = 1)$. If no overflow occurred, the algorithm initializes Y and enters the shift-subtract loop.

FIGURE 8.7

Hardware implementation of the shift-subtract division algorithm

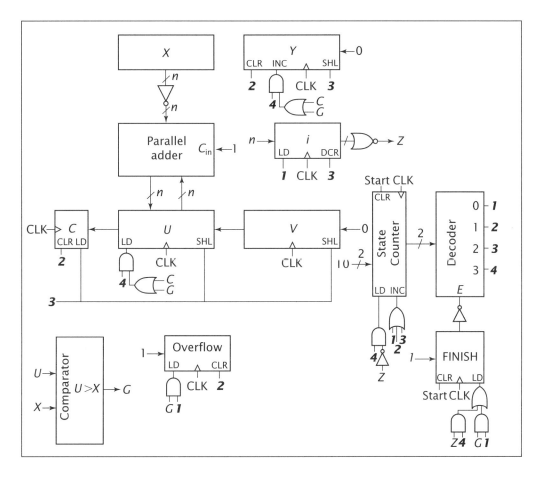

The shift-subtract loop starts by shifting CUV and Y, just as in the non-restoring algorithm. The next statement performs the subtraction and comparison of CU and X, setting $C = 1$ if $CU \geq X$. It performs this subtraction in one of two ways. If $C = 1$ before the subtraction, then CU must be greater than X. (Recall the non-restoring algorithm's worst case example, 1 0000 > 1111.) The algorithm performs the two's complement subtraction $U = U + X' + 1$, leaving C set to 1 to denote that $CU \geq X$. If C is 0, it performs the operation $CU = U + X' + 1$. This performs the subtraction and sets $C = 1$ only if $CU \geq X$. The net result is that, regardless of which subtraction is performed, $U = U - X$ and $C = 1$ if $CU \geq X$, and 0 otherwise.

The next step performs one of two operations. If $C = 1$, CU was greater than or equal to X. The subtraction was valid and does not

FIGURE 8.8

Calculating $CU = U + X' + 1$ also compares U and X: (a) positive result, (b) zero result, and (c) negative result

$U = 1001, X = 0101, X' + 1 = 1011$ $\qquad\qquad\qquad$ $U = 1001, X = 1001, X' + 1 = 0111$

$$
\begin{array}{rr}
U & 1001 \\
+X'+1 & 1011 \\
\hline
CU & 1\ 0100
\end{array}
\qquad\qquad\qquad\qquad
\begin{array}{rr}
U & 1001 \\
+X'+1 & 0111 \\
\hline
CU & 1\ 0000
\end{array}
$$

$\qquad\qquad$ (a) $\qquad\qquad\qquad\qquad\qquad\qquad\qquad\qquad$ (b)

$U = 1001, X = 1101, X' + 1 = 0011$

$$
\begin{array}{rr}
U & 1001 \\
+X'+1 & 0011 \\
\hline
CU & 0\ 1100
\end{array}
$$

$\qquad\qquad\qquad$ (c)

need to be restored. It is only necessary to set the appropriate bit of the quotient, Y_0, to 1. However, if $C = 0$, CU was less than X. The addition restores U to its original value.

A couple of examples may help to clarify this algorithm. First, consider the operation $225 \div 13$; its trace is shown in Table 8.9(a). Initially, $X = 1101$ and $n = 4$. The initial subtraction sets $C = 1$, indicating that an overflow will occur. (This is indeed the case, since $225 \div 13 = 17$ with a remainder of 4. The value 17 is 1 0001 in binary, which cannot be stored in a 4-bit register.) The next step restores U to its original value and exits with overflow.

An example without overflow is shown in Table 8.9(b). Just to be different, we divide 147 by 13. The first few steps check for overflow and initialize Y. Each group of three steps after that represents one iteration of the loop. Each iteration performs the appropriate shifts and subtraction/comparison. The last step in each iteration either updates the quotient (stored in Y) or restores the dividend (stored in U) to its proper value. As shown in Table 8.9, the algorithm correctly calculates $147 \div 13$ as 11 with a remainder of 4.

The RTL code to implement the restoring division algorithm, using the same values as in the non-restoring version, is as follows. It parallels the algorithm very closely, with the following exceptions.

Table 8.9

Trace of the restoring shift-subtract division algorithm (a) with overflow and (b) without overflow

Function	i	C	U	V	Y	Comments
initial			1110	0001		
$CU = U + X' + 1$		1	0001			
$U = U + X$		1	1110			Overflow, exit

(a)

Function	i	C	U	V	Y	Comments
initial			1001	0011		
$CU = U + X' + 1$		0	1100			
$U = U + X$			1001			No overflow
$Y = 0$					0000	
shl(CUV), shl(Y)	1	1	0010	0110	0000	
$U = U + X' + 1$			0101			$C = 1$
$Y_0 = 1$					0001	
shl(CUV), shl(Y)	2	0	1010	1100	0010	
$CU = U + X' + 1$		0	1101			$C = 0$
$U = U + X$			1010			
shl(CUV), shl(Y)	3	1	0101	1000	0100	
$U = U + X' + 1$			1000			$C = 1$
$Y_0 = 1$					0101	
shl(CUV), shl(Y)	4	1	0001	0000	1010	
$U = U + X' + 1$			0100			$C = 1$
$Y_0 = 1$					1011	done

(b)

- A 1-bit value, OVERFLOW, is set to 1 if overflow occurs; otherwise it is set to 0.
- A 1-bit value, *FINISH*, is set to 1 when the algorithm terminates, either by normal termination of the i loop or by overflow. This is the same as in the RTL specifications for the other algorithms in this chapter.
- Also as in the other algorithms, i counts down from n to 0. Again, $Z = 1$ whenever $i = 0$.
- The states normally progress from $\mathbf{1}_1$ to $\mathbf{1}_2$ to $\mathbf{2}$ to $\mathbf{3}$ to $\mathbf{4}_1$ to $\mathbf{4}_2$, unless a GOTO operation is encountered. States $\mathbf{1}_1$ and $\mathbf{1}_2$ are equivalent to state $\mathbf{1}$ in the non-restoring algorithm, and states $\mathbf{4}_1$ and $\mathbf{4}_2$ perform the same function as state $\mathbf{4}$ in the non-restoring algorithm.

$$\mathbf{1}_1\!: \quad CU \leftarrow U + X' + 1$$
$$\mathbf{1}_2\!: \quad U \leftarrow U + X$$
$$C\mathbf{1}_2\!: \quad FINISH \leftarrow 1, \ OVERFLOW \leftarrow 1$$
$$\mathbf{2}\!: \quad Y \leftarrow 0, \ OVERFLOW \leftarrow 0, \ i \leftarrow n$$
$$\mathbf{3}\!: \quad \text{shl}(CUV), \ \text{shl}(Y), \ i \leftarrow i - 1$$
$$C\mathbf{4}_1\!: \quad U \leftarrow U + X' + 1$$
$$C'\mathbf{4}_1\!: \quad CU \leftarrow U + X' + 1$$
$$C\mathbf{4}_2\!: \quad Y_0 \leftarrow 1$$
$$C'\mathbf{4}_2\!: \quad U \leftarrow U + X$$
$$Z\,\mathbf{4}_2\!: \quad FINISH \leftarrow 1$$
$$Z'\mathbf{4}_2\!: \quad \text{GOTO } \mathbf{3}$$

Table 8.10 shows a trace of this RTL code for the operation $147 \div 13$. It follows the same pattern as Table 8.9(b) and also produces the correct result.

TABLE 8.10

Trace of the RTL code for the restoring shift-subtract division algorithm

Conditions	Micro-operations	i	C	U	V	Y	Z	FINISH
START		x	x	1001	0011	xxxx		0
$\mathbf{1}_1$	$CU \leftarrow U + X' + 1$		0	1100				
$\mathbf{1}_2$	$U \leftarrow U + X$			1001				
2	$Y \leftarrow 0$, $OVERFLOW \leftarrow 0$, $i \leftarrow 4$	4				0000	0	
3	shl(CUV), shl(Y), $i \leftarrow i - 1$	3	1	0010	0110	0000	0	
$C\mathbf{4}_1$	$U \leftarrow U + X' + 1$			0101				
$C\mathbf{4}_2, Z'\mathbf{4}_2$	$Y_0 \leftarrow 1$, GOTO **3**					0001		
3	shl(CUV), shl(Y), $i \leftarrow i - 1$	2	0	1010	1100	0010	0	
$C'\mathbf{4}_1$	$CU \leftarrow U + X' + 1$		0	1101				
$C'\mathbf{4}_2, Z'\mathbf{4}_2$	$U \leftarrow U + X$, GOTO **3**			1010				
3	shl(CUV), shl(Y), $i \leftarrow i - 1$	1	1	0101	1000	0100	0	
$C\mathbf{4}_1$	$U \leftarrow U + X' + 1$			1000				
$C\mathbf{4}_2, Z'\mathbf{4}_2$	$Y_0 \leftarrow 1$, GOTO **3**					0101		
3	shl(CUV), shl(Y), $i \leftarrow i - 1$	0	1	0001	0000	1010	1	
$C\mathbf{4}_1$	$U \leftarrow U + X' + 1$			0100				
$C\mathbf{4}_2, Z\mathbf{4}_2$	$Y_0 \leftarrow 1$, $FINISH \leftarrow 1$					1011		1

The hardware for this algorithm is shown in Figure 8.9. Notice that we no longer need the comparator used to generate G in the nonrestoring algorithm. However, the inputs to the parallel adder are more complex, since it must now generate either $U + X$ or $U - X$. Also, since there are six states instead of four, the state counter and its decoder are slightly larger.

Unlike multiplication, there is no universally used division algorithm for unsigned notation in two's complement format. The following procedure can be used to divide these numbers using either of these division algorithms.

FIGURE 8.9

Hardware implementation of the restoring shift-subtract division algorithm

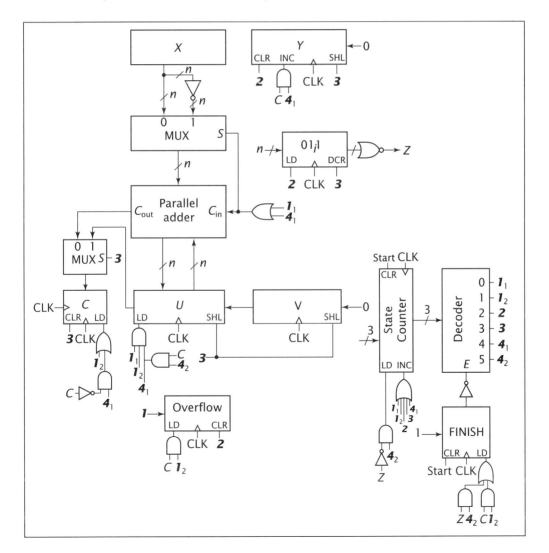

- IF dividend < 0 THEN dividend$\leftarrow$ $-$dividend.
- IF divisor < 0 THEN divisor$\leftarrow$ $-$divisor.
- Divide using either the non-restoring or restoring hardware.
- IF exactly one of dividend and divisor was negative, THEN quotient $\leftarrow$ $-$quotient.

The implementation is left as an exercise for the reader.

8.2 Signed Notations

The unsigned notations, non-negative and two's complement, are the basis for **signed-magnitude** and **signed-two's complement** notation. Similarly, the arithmetic algorithms for the two unsigned notations described earlier serve as the basis for the arithmetic operations on these two signed notations, often with very little modification. In this section we examine signed notations and their arithmetic operations.

8.2.1 Signed-Magnitude Notation

As its name implies, signed-magnitude notation has two parts. The *signed* part is a 1-bit value that is 0 for positive numbers (and for zero) and 1 for negative numbers. The *magnitude* is an n-bit value that holds the absolute value of the number in the same format as unsigned non-negative numbers. This is very much like the notations we use every day for decimal numbers. For example, $+3$ and -3 have the same magnitude representation, 3; only their signs differ. In binary, $+3$ would be represented as 0 (sign) 0011, and -3 would be represented as 1 (sign) 0011. Throughout this section, signed-magnitude notation takes form X_sX, where X_s is the 1-bit sign and X is the n-bit magnitude.

8.2.1.1 Addition and Subtraction

Adding and subtracting signed-magnitude numbers is more complex in signed-magnitude notation than in unsigned non-negative notation. Since these numbers can be positive or negative, their signs and relative magnitudes determine how the operation should be handled.

For the operation $U_sU \leftarrow X_sX \pm Y_sY$, we define AS as a flag indicating the operation to be performed; $AS = 0$ for addition and $AS = 1$ for subtraction. We also define $PM = X_s \oplus AS \oplus Y_s$. There are eight possible combinations of values of X_s, Y_s, and AS. Table 8.11 shows these combinations, the value of PM for each, and the result for $X = 3$ and $Y = 5$, and for $X = 5$ and $Y = 3$.

The operation to be performed depends on two things: the value of PM and the relative magnitudes of X and Y—that is, whether $X > Y$, $X = Y$, or $X < Y$. (Remember, in this notation X and Y are the magnitudes, not the entire number.) To simplify the process of implementing addition and subtraction, we divide it into two cases, $PM = 0$ and $PM = 1$.

The first case is the simpler of the two. As we can see in Table 8.11, whenever $PM = 0$, magnitudes X and Y are added together. Furthermore, the sign of the result is always the same as the sign of the first value, X_s. This can be realized by the micro-operations $U_s \leftarrow X_s$, $U \leftarrow X + Y$.

Unfortunately, this does not work, at least not for all values. It does not account for the overflow that can occur when X and Y are added. In Table 8.11, if X, Y, and U are each 3-bit values, there will be an overflow. The result, 1000, cannot be stored in a 3-bit register. However, this can be corrected fairly easily. As in the unsigned non-negative

Table 8.11

Addition and subtraction of signed-magnitude numbers

Operation	X_s	Y_s	AS	PM	X = 3, Y = 5	X = 5, Y = 3
$(+X) + (+Y)$	0	0	0	0	$(+3) + (+5) = +8$	$(+5) + (+3) = +8$
$(+X) - (+Y)$	0	0	1	1	$(+3) - (+5) = -2$	$(+5) - (+3) = +2$
$(+X) + (-Y)$	0	1	0	1	$(+3) + (-5) = -2$	$(+5) + (-3) = +2$
$(+X) - (-Y)$	0	1	1	0	$(+3) - (-5) = +8$	$(+5) - (-3) = +8$
$(-X) + (+Y)$	1	0	0	1	$(-3) + (+5) = +2$	$(-5) + (+3) = -2$
$(-X) - (+Y)$	1	0	1	0	$(-3) - (+5) = -8$	$(-5) - (+3) = -8$
$(-X) + (-Y)$	1	1	0	0	$(-3) + (-5) = -8$	$(-5) + (-3) = -8$
$(-X) - (-Y)$	1	1	1	1	$(-3) - (-5) = +2$	$(-5) - (-3) = -2$

notation, a carry out is generated whenever an overflow occurs. Instead of setting $U \leftarrow X + Y$, we can set $CU \leftarrow X + Y$. Then we copy the value in C to an overflow flag. The addition and subtraction of signed-magnitude numbers with $PM = 0$ can be expressed by the following RTL code:

$$PM'\mathbf{1}:\quad U_s \leftarrow X_s,\ CU \leftarrow X + Y$$
$$PM'\mathbf{2}:\quad OVERFLOW \leftarrow C$$

For $PM = 1$, the procedure becomes more complex. Depending on their relative magnitudes, the magnitude of the result may be $X - Y$ or $Y - X$. The algorithm must account for both cases. In addition, values that produce a result of 0 introduce a unique problem, which the algorithm must correct. However, one part of the procedure is simpler than when $PM = 0$. As with subtraction of unsigned numbers, this case can never produce an overflow.

Consider the relative magnitude problem. If $X > Y$, then U should get the value $X - Y$, or $X + Y' + 1$. However, if $X < Y$, $X - Y$ produces the negative of the desired value, $Y - X$, and this value must be negated; this can be done by taking its two's complement, or $(X - Y)' + 1$. Fortunately, the subtraction and comparison can be performed simultaneously. As with unsigned numbers, the operation $CU \leftarrow X + Y' + 1$ sets $C = 0$ if $X < Y$ and $C = 1$ if $X \geq Y$. It is possible to perform the subtraction and to determine whether or not it is necessary to negate the result in one operation.

The other problem is the 0 result problem. Since $X = Y$ in this case, $X + Y' + 1$ will always produce a 0 result (and $C = 1$). However, 0 must always be stored with its sign equal to zero. A person can easily recognize that $+0 = -0 = 0$, but computers usually require this value to be stored as $+0$; otherwise it will cause a problem when the value is used next. If a 0 is generated, the sign of the result must be set explicitly to zero.

It is also necessary to set the sign bit, U_s, when $X \neq Y$. As shown in Table 8.11, if $X > Y$, U_s should get the same value as X_s. When $X < Y$, U_s should get the complement of the value as X_s.

The following RTL code implements the addition and subtraction for values for which $PM = 1$. Note that, for $X > Y$, $C = 1$ and $Z = 0$; $C = 1$ and $Z = 1$ when $X = Y$; and $C = 0$ when $X < Y$. Also note that $OVERFLOW$ is set to 0, since this case cannot produce an overflow.

$$
\begin{array}{ll}
PM\mathbf{1}: & CU \leftarrow X + Y' + 1, \; OVERFLOW \leftarrow 0 \\
CZ'PM\mathbf{2}: & U_s \leftarrow X_s \\
CZPM\mathbf{2}: & U_s \leftarrow 0 \\
C'PM\mathbf{2}: & U_s \leftarrow X_s', \; U \leftarrow U' + 1
\end{array}
$$

When condition CZ' is true ($C = 1$ and $Z = 0$, or $X > Y$), the result $X - Y$ was properly stored in U. It is only necessary to set the sign of the result to that of X. The case CZ ($C = 1$ and $Z = 1$, or $X = Y$) also sets U to its proper value, 0. It is only necessary to set its sign to 0 so the value is stored as $+0$. In the last case, C' ($C = 0$, or $X < Y$), the value stored in U must be negated, and its sign must be the opposite of that of X.

The full RTL code for this algorithm, for both $PM = 0$ and $PM = 1$, follows. It includes a 1-bit value $FINISH$; as in the previous algorithms in this chapter, setting $FINISH$ to 1 terminates the algorithm.

$$
\begin{array}{ll}
PM'\mathbf{1}: & U_s \leftarrow X_s, \; CU \leftarrow X + Y \\
PM\mathbf{1}: & CU \leftarrow X + Y' + 1, \; OVERFLOW \leftarrow 0 \\
PM'\mathbf{2}: & OVERFLOW \leftarrow C \\
CZ'PM\mathbf{2}: & U_s \leftarrow X_s \\
CZPM\mathbf{2}: & U_s \leftarrow 0 \\
C'PM\mathbf{2}: & U_s \leftarrow X_s', \; U \leftarrow U' + 1 \\
\mathbf{2}: & FINISH \leftarrow 1
\end{array}
$$

To illustrate this algorithm, Table 8.12 shows the trace of this RTL code for several different values of $X_s X$ and $Y_s Y$. They include the four possible nonoverflow cases—$PM = 0$; $PM = 1$ and $X > Y$; $PM = 1$ and $X = Y$; and $PM = 1$ and $X < Y$—as well as two cases that generate overflow.

Table 8.12

Examples of addition and subtraction of signed-magnitude numbers

$U_sU = X_sX + Y_sY$ $X_sX = +3 = 0\ 0011$ $Y_sY = +5 = 0\ 0101$ *PM'1*: $U_s\leftarrow0$, $CU\leftarrow0\ 1000$ *PM'2*: $OVERFLOW\leftarrow0$ Result: $U_sU = 0\ 1000 = +8$ (a)	$U_sU = X_sX + Y_sY$ $X_sX = +5 = 0\ 0101$ $Y_sY = -3 = 1\ 0011$ *PM1*: $CU\leftarrow1\ 0010$, $OVERFLOW\leftarrow0$ *CZ'PM2*: $U_s\leftarrow0$ Result: $U_sU = 0\ 0010 = +2$ (b)
$U_sU = X_sX - Y_sY$ $X_sX = +5 = 0\ 0101$ $Y_sY = +5 = 0\ 0101$ *PM1*: $CU\leftarrow1\ 0000$, $OVERFLOW\leftarrow0$ *CZPM2*: $U_s\leftarrow0$ Result: $U_sU = 0\ 0000 = +0$ (c)	$U_sU = X_sX - Y_sY$ $X_sX = +3 = 0\ 0011$ $Y_sY = +5 = 0\ 0101$ *PM1*: $CU\leftarrow0\ 1110$, $OVERFLOW\leftarrow0$ *C'PM2*: $U_s\leftarrow1$, $U\leftarrow0010$ Result: $U_sU = 1\ 0010 = -2$ (d)
$U_sU = X_sX + Y_sY$ $X_sX = +13 = 0\ 1101$ $Y_sY = +5 = 0\ 0101$ *PM'1*: $U_s\leftarrow0$, $CU\leftarrow1\ 0010$ *PM'2*: $OVERFLOW\leftarrow1$ Result: $OVERFLOW$ (e)	$U_sU = X_sX - Y_sY$ $X_sX = -7 = 1\ 0111$ $Y_sY = +13 = 0\ 1101$ *PM'1*: $U_s\leftarrow1$, $CU\leftarrow1\ 0100$ *PM'2*: $OVERFLOW\leftarrow1$ Result: $OVERFLOW$ (f)

The hardware for this RTL code is shown in Figure 8.10. It shares many of the characteristics of the shift-subtract hardware shown in Figure 8.9 on page 333.

8.2.1.2 Multiplication and Division

The algorithms to multiply and divide signed-magnitude numbers are almost identical to their counterparts for unsigned non-negative numbers. The only exception is that the sign of the result must be set. In both cases, the sign of the result is 1 if and only if one of the operands is negative and the other operand is positive (not zero). If the result of the operation is zero, the sign of the result must be set to zero so the result is represented as $+0$.

Implementing these modifications to the shift-add multiplication algorithm, which calculates $UV\leftarrow X \cdot Y$, we developed the following RTL code, which multiplies signed-magnitude values X_sX and Y_sY. By convention, the sign of each register that stores the result is set. $T = 1$ if $UV = 0$; otherwise $T = 0$. As before, $Z = 1$ when $i = 0$.

Figure 8.10

Hardware implementation of signed-magnitude addition and subtraction

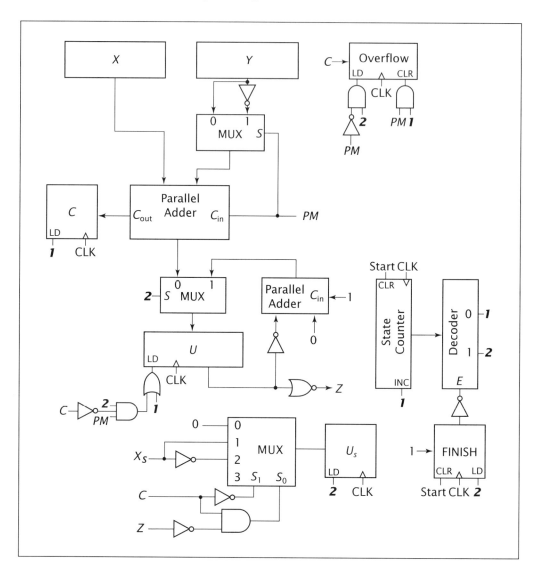

1: $U_s \leftarrow X_s \oplus Y_s$, $V_s \leftarrow X_s \oplus Y_s$, $U \leftarrow 0$, $i \leftarrow n$

Y_0**2**: $CU \leftarrow U + X$

2: $i \leftarrow i - 1$

3:   shr(CUV), cir(Y)

Z'**3**:   GOTO **2**

ZT**3**: $U_s \leftarrow 0$, $V_s \leftarrow 0$

Z**3**:   FINISH$\leftarrow 1$

Table 8.13 shows the trace of this RTL code for $(-13) \cdot (+11)$. It is virtually identical to the trace of the multiplication of unsigned non-negative values 13 and 11 shown in Table 8.3; the only difference is the operation that sets the sign bits U_s and V_s.

The design of the hardware to implement this RTL code is left as an exercise for the reader.

Division can be implemented using either the restoring or non-restoring algorithm for unsigned non-negative numbers. The same modifications used for the multiplication algorithm are also used for the division algorithm. The modifications to the RTL code are left as an exercise for the reader.

8.2.2   Signed-Two's Complement Notation

As with signed-magnitude numbers, signed-two's complement numbers have a 1-bit sign and an n-bit magnitude; they can also be represented in the form $X_s X$. However, unlike signed-magnitude numbers, the magnitude of a negative number is stored in two's complement format. For example, $+5$ and -3 are represented as 0 (sign) 0101 and

Table 8.13

Trace of the RTL code for the signed-magnitude shift-add algorithm

Conditions	Micro-operations	i	C	U	V	Y	Z	FINISH
START		x	x	xxxx	xxxx	1011		0
1	$U_s \leftarrow 1$, $V_s \leftarrow 1$, $U \leftarrow 0$, $i \leftarrow 4$	4		0000			0	
$Y_0 2,2$	$CU \leftarrow U + X$, $i \leftarrow i - 1$	3	0	1101			0	
$3, Z' 3$	shr(CUV), cir(Y), GOTO 2		0	0110	1xxx	1101		
$Y_0 2,2$	$CU \leftarrow U + X$, $i \leftarrow i - 1$	2	1	0011			0	
$3, Z' 3$	shr(CUV), cir(Y), GOTO 2		0	1001	11xx	1110		
2	$i \leftarrow i - 1$	1					0	
$3, Z' 3$	shr(CUV), cir(Y), GOTO 2		0	0100	111x	0111		
$Y_0 2,2$	$CU \leftarrow U + X$, $i \leftarrow i - 1$	0	1	0001			1	
$3, Z 3$	shr(CUV), cir(Y), FINISH$\leftarrow 1$		0	1000	1111	1011		1

1(sign) 1101, respectively. Just as the magnitude portion of a signed-magnitude number is equivalent to a non-negative unsigned number, the magnitude portion of a signed-two's complement number is equivalent to a two's complement unsigned number. Notice that positive numbers (and zero) are represented the same in either signed-magnitude or signed-two's complement notation. Only negative numbers are represented differently.

To add or subtract two signed-two's complement values, we simply treat the sign bit as the most significant bit of the magnitude. For instance, instead of treating $+5$ as 0 (sign) 0101, we simply treat it as the 5-bit value 00101. Similarly, -3 could be considered to be 11101. These representations are identical to the 5-bit unsigned two's complement representations of these numbers. This is true for all possible values: Concatenating the sign bit of a signed-two's complement number (as the most significant bit) with its n-bit magnitude produces the $(n + 1)$-bit unsigned two's complement representation of that number.

Once we do this, we can use the same procedures for adding and subtracting these numbers as we used for signed-two's complement numbers. Instead of dealing with n-bit numbers, they will use $(n + 1)$-bit numbers. As a byproduct of treating the sign as the most significant bit of the magnitude, the addition or subtraction implicitly sets the sign of the result. It does not have to be set explicitly, as was the case with signed-magnitude numbers. As with unsigned two's complement numbers, an overflow occurs when the carries in to and out of the most significant bit are different; in this case, that bit is the sign bit.

Multiplication can be implemented in a similar manner. Once the sign bits are taken to be the most significant bits of their corresponding magnitudes, we can multiply the numbers using Booth's algorithm. Again, each value is $(n + 1)$ bits, not n bits as in the version of Booth's algorithm introduced earlier in this chapter. Division could be implemented following the process to modify the unsigned two's complement procedure.

8.3 Binary Coded Decimal

The signed representations introduced in the previous section use binary bits to represent binary data. This is the most efficient storage scheme; every bit pattern represents a unique, valid value. In some applications, however, it may not be desirable to work with binary data. For example, consider a digital clock. Its output must always be displayed in decimal, but its internal components could keep track of the time in binary. The binary value must be converted to decimal before it can be displayed.

In applications such as a digital clock, it is sometimes preferable to store the value as a series of decimal digits, where each digit is separately represented as its binary equivalent. Although this is less efficient than standard binary notation in terms of storage, it is not necessary to convert this notation into decimal form. For applications, such as this, the savings (in terms of improved performance) achieved by not having to convert values to decimal may more than offset any loss in performance due to not using binary values.

The most common format used to represent decimal data is called **binary coded decimal**, or **BCD**. This section examines BCD data. First we describe the format itself. Then we modify algorithms for addition, subtraction, multiplication, and division from the previous section for this data format, along with their associated hardware.

8.3.1   BCD Numeric Format

In BCD notation, every four bits represent one decimal digit. For example, 0000 represents 0 and 1001 represents 9. For values from 0 to 9, their representations are the same as in binary. However, 4-bit values above 9 are not used in BCD, since they do not correspond to any decimal digit; 1010 to 1111 are not used. The loss of those values is the penalty for using BCD notation.

Multidigit decimal numbers are stored as multiple groups of 4 bits per digit. For instance, 27 is stored as 0010 0111 in BCD. (In binary, it would have been stored as 0001 1011.) This notation can be extended for any number of digits.

BCD is a signed notation. Its values can be positive or negative (or zero). It is similar to the signed-magnitude notation in that its magnitude is stored as the absolute value, and one bit is used to indicate the sign. BCD does not store negative numbers in two's complement (nor in its decimal equivalent, ten's complement, described shortly). In BCD, +27 and −27 are represented as 0(sign) 0010 0111 and 1(sign) 0010 0111, respectively.

8.3.2   Addition and Subtraction

Just as BCD and signed-magnitude notations are similar, so are the algorithms they employ to add and subtract numbers. In fact, with a couple of modifications to accommodate the BCD representation, the algorithm can be used with only two changes.

First, we adjust the hardware that adds numbers to account for the BCD representation. As long as the sum of two digits is no more than 9, a standard binary adder will produce the correct result. However, this is not always the case, and a BCD adder must produce the correct result for all values. There are two situations in which an error occurs. The first is when the result is not a valid BCD digit. For example, $5 + 6 = 0101 + 0110 = 1011$, which is not a valid BCD digit. The second occurs when the result is a valid BCD digit, but not the correct result. For example, $8 + 9 = 1(\text{carry})\ 0001$.

In either case, adding 6 to the result generated by a binary adder produces the correct result. (Six is the number of bit patterns from 1010 to 1111 that are not used in BCD. Adding 6 to the result has the effect of skipping over these unused values.) Figure 8.11 shows the hardware to add two BCD digits and produce the correct BCD result and carry. In this figure, notice that the two digits, X and Y, are first added together. Then this result is added to either 0 (0000) or 6 (0110) to produce the correct BCD sum. If the result, $S_3 S_2 S_1 S_0$, is not a valid BCD digit, then either $S_3 \wedge S_2 = 1$ or $S_3 \wedge S_1 = 1$. (We can easily verify that the six invalid bit patterns 1010 through 1111 meet one or both of these conditions, and that the 10 valid BCD values 0000 through 1001 do not.) In this case, the multiplexer control bit is set to 1, which causes 6 to be added to the result, correcting its decimal representation. The multiplexer select bit is also set to 1 if the addition of X and Y generates a carry out, as when $X = 8$ and $Y = 9$. This also causes the circuit to add 6 to the original sum,

FIGURE 8.11

A BCD adder

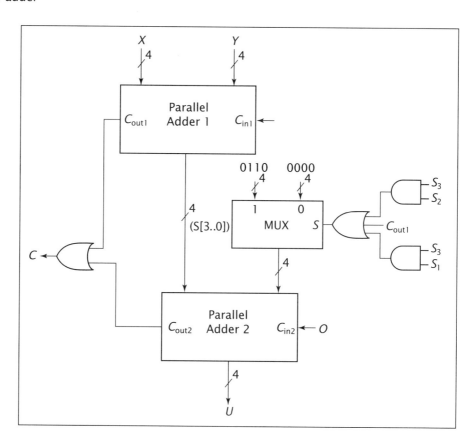

again producing the correct value. If either parallel adder generates a carry out of 1, the carry out of the BCD adder should also be 1. Just as with binary adders, multiple copies of this hardware can be cascaded by connecting their carry out/carry in signals to form a multidigit BCD adder.

The second change has to do with complements. During *PM**1*** and *C'PM**2*** of the signed-magnitude algorithm, a register's complemented value is used as an operand, either for subtraction or negation. For binary values, this is a one's complement; every bit is inverted. The same result can be achieved by subtracting the value to be complemented from another value that has all 1's as its bits. For example, if $U = 1010$, then $U' = 1111 - 1010 = 0101$. In addition, each of the computations adds 1 to the one's complement to produce the two's complement of the number.

The BCD equivalent of the one's complement is the **nine's complement**, generated by subtracting the value to be complemented from another value that has all 9s as its digits. Adding one to this value produces the ten's complement, the negative of the original value and BCD equivalent of the two's complement. For example, the nine's complement of 631 is $999 - 631 = 368$; adding one to this value produces the ten's complement of 369. Just as the two's complement is used in subtraction and negation for binary numbers, the ten's complement plays the same role for BCD numbers.

Figure 8.12 shows hardware to generate the nine's complement of a single BCD digit. Multiple copies of this hardware can be used to generate the nine's complement of a multidigit value. Unlike the BCD adder, there is no carry to cascade between stages, since subtracting any decimal digit from 9 cannot generate a borrow.

With these two changes, the algorithm for adding and subtracting signed-magnitude binary numbers can be used, exactly as written, for BCD numbers. For convenience, the algorithm is repeated here:

$$
\begin{aligned}
PM'\textbf{1}:\quad & U_s \leftarrow X_s,\ CU \leftarrow X + Y \\
PM\textbf{1}:\quad & CU \leftarrow X + Y' + 1,\ OVERFLOW \leftarrow 0 \\
PM'\textbf{2}:\quad & OVERFLOW \leftarrow C \\
CZ'PM\textbf{2}:\quad & U_s \leftarrow X_s \\
CZPM\textbf{2}:\quad & U_s \leftarrow 0 \\
C'PM\textbf{2}:\quad & U_s \leftarrow X_s',\ U \leftarrow U' + 1 \\
\textbf{2}:\quad & FINISH \leftarrow 1
\end{aligned}
$$

Using a BCD adder instead of a binary parallel adder produces the correct BCD result for the addition operations. Using a nine's complement generator to produce Y' (in *PM**1***) and U' (in *C'PM**2***) also yields the correct BCD result. Since X_s is still a 1-bit value, in *C'PM**2*** it is complemented using an inverter rather than via nine's complement.

FIGURE 8.12

Nine's complement generation hardware

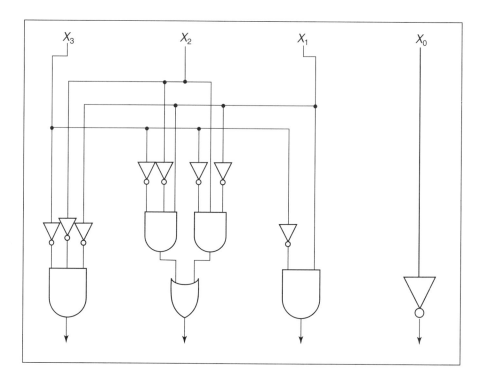

Table 8.14 shows a trace of this algorithm for several additions and subtractions. As in previous examples for other numeric notations, it covers all values of *PM*, $X > Y$, $X = Y$, and $X < Y$. It also shows two examples that generate an overflow.

The hardware for BCD addition and subtraction is shown in Figure 8.13 on page 346.

8.3.3 MULTIPLICATION AND DIVISION

Although very similar to their signed-magnitude counterparts, BCD multiplication and division require more extensive modifications than did the addition and subtraction algorithm. The changes in the hardware for the BCD adder and nine's complement circuitry, introduced in the previous algorithm, are also used for these algorithms.

In the binary shift-add algorithm, each bit of the multiplier is either 0 or 1. This means the multiplicand is added either 0 or 1 times during each iteration of the loop. In BCD, however, each digit of the multiplicand may have any value from 0 to 9; each iteration of the loop may have to perform up to nine additions. For this reason, we

Table 8.14

Examples of addition and subtraction of BCD numbers

$U_sU = X_sX + Y_sY$ $X_sX = +33 = 0\ 0011\ 0011$ $Y_sY = +25 = 0\ 0010\ 0101$ *PM'**1***: $U_s\leftarrow0$, $CU\leftarrow0\ 0101\ 1000$ *PM'**2***: $OVERFLOW\leftarrow0$ Result: $U_sU = 0\ 0101\ 1000 = +58$ (a)	$U_sU = X_sX + Y_sY$ $X_sX = +27 = 0\ 0010\ 0111$ $Y_sY = -13 = 1\ 0001\ 0011$ *PM**1***: $CU\leftarrow1\ 0001\ 0100$, $OVERFLOW\leftarrow0$ *CZ'PM**2***: $U_s\leftarrow0$ Result: $U_sU = 0\ 0001\ 0100 = +14$ (b)
$U_sU = X_sX - Y_sY$ $X_sX = +27 = 0\ 0010\ 0111$ $Y_sY = +27 = 0\ 0010\ 0111$ *PM**1***: $CU\leftarrow1\ 0000\ 0000$, $OVERFLOW\leftarrow0$ *CZPM**2***: $U_s\leftarrow0$ Result: $U_sU = 0\ 0000\ 0000 = +0$ (c)	$U_sU = X_sX - Y_sY$ $X_sX = +27 = 0\ 0010\ 0111$ $Y_sY = +33 = 1\ 0011\ 0011$ *PM**1***: $CU\leftarrow0\ 1001\ 0100$, $OVERFLOW\leftarrow0$ *C'PM**2***: $U_s\leftarrow1$, $U\leftarrow0000\ 0110$ Result: $U_sU = 1\ 0000\ 0110 = -6$ (d)
$U_sU = X_sX + Y_sY$ $X_sX = +81 = 0\ 1000\ 0001$ $Y_sY = +27 = 0\ 0010\ 0111$ *PM'**1***: $U_s\leftarrow0$, $CU\leftarrow1\ 0000\ 1000$ *PM'**2***: $OVERFLOW\leftarrow1$ Result: $OVERFLOW$ (e)	$U_sU = X_sX - Y_sY$ $X_sX = -21 = 1\ 0010\ 0001$ $Y_sY = +97 = 0\ 1001\ 0111$ *PM'**1***: $U_s\leftarrow1$, $CU\leftarrow1\ 0001\ 1000$ *PM'**2***: $OVERFLOW\leftarrow1$ Result: $OVERFLOW$ (f)

must incorporate an inner loop in the algorithm for these multiple additions.

The other changes account for the BCD notation. Instead of using binary shifts, which shift one bit at a time, the BCD algorithms use decimal shifts, which shift one BCD digit, or four bits at a time. The decimal shift right operation is denoted as **dshr**. Also, an entire BCD carry digit, C_d, is used instead of a 1-bit carry, since the multiple additions described in the previous paragraph can produce a carry that is greater than 1.

By incorporating these changes into the binary signed-magnitude shift-add multiplication algorithm, we produce the equivalent BCD multiplication algorithm. The RTL code to perform the multiplication $U_sUV\leftarrow X_sX \cdot Y_sY$ is as follows. In this algorithm, n is the number of decimal digits, not binary bits, in Y. Y_{d0} is the least significant BCD digit, or four low-order bits, of Y; it is used for the new inner loop. Also, $Z_{Y0} = 1$ when $Y_{d0} = 0$. As in the previous algorithms, $Z = 1$ when $i = 0$.

FIGURE 8.13

Hardware to implement BCD addition and subtraction

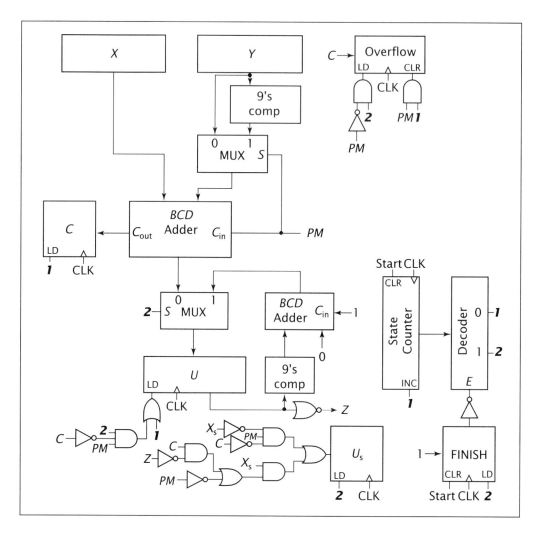

$$1: \quad U_s \leftarrow X_s \oplus Y_s, \; V_s \leftarrow X_s \oplus Y_s, \; U \leftarrow 0, \; i \leftarrow n, \; C_d \leftarrow 0$$

$$Z_{Y0}'2: \quad C_d U \leftarrow C_d U + X, \; Y_{d0} \leftarrow Y_{d0} - 1, \; \text{GOTO } 2$$

$$Z_{Y0}2: \quad i \leftarrow i - 1$$

$$3: \quad \text{dshr}(C_d UV), \; \text{dshr}(Y)$$

$$Z'3: \quad \text{GOTO } 2$$

$$ZT3: \quad U_s \leftarrow 0, \; V_s \leftarrow 0$$

$$Z3: \quad \textit{FINISH} \leftarrow 1$$

There are a few points to note in this algorithm. First, we see that C_d is set to 0 during state **1**. In the shift-add signed-magnitude algorithm, the operation during state **2** is $CU \leftarrow U + X$; C is not added, only set. Since multiple additions can occur, the carry must be included in the addition during Z_{Y0}**2**. Hence, C_d must be initialized. State **2** implements the multiple additions: The algorithm adds the multiplicand to the running total and decrements the least significant digit of the multiplier. The algorithm loops back to this state until the least significant digit of the multiplier is 0. This sets $Z_{Y0} = 1$, which exits the loop and decrements i. Unlike the signed-magnitude multiplication algorithm,

Table 8.15

Trace of the RTL code for the BCD shift-add algorithm

Conditions	Micro-operations	i	C_d	U	V	Y	Z_{Y0}	Z	FINISH
START		x	x	xx	xx	23	0		0
1	$U_s \leftarrow 0$, $V_s \leftarrow 0$, $U \leftarrow 00$, $i \leftarrow 2$, $C_d \leftarrow 0$	2	0	00				0	
Z_{Y0}'**2**	$C_dU \leftarrow C_dU + X$, $Y_{d0} \leftarrow Y_{d0} - 1$, GOTO **2**		0	71		22	0		
Z_{Y0}'**2**	$C_dU \leftarrow C_dU + X$, $Y_{d0} \leftarrow Y_{d0} - 1$, GOTO **2**		1	42		21	0		
Z_{Y0}'**2**	$C_dU \leftarrow C_dU + X$, $Y_{d0} \leftarrow Y_{d0} - 1$, GOTO **2**		2	13		20	1		
Z_{Y0}**2**	$i \leftarrow i - 1$	1						0	
3,Z'**3**	dshr(C_dUV), dshr(Y), GOTO **2**		0	21	3x	02	0		
Z_{Y0}'**2**	$C_dU \leftarrow C_dU + X$, $Y_{d0} \leftarrow Y_{d0} - 1$, GOTO **2**		0	92		01	0		
Z_{Y0}'**2**	$C_dU \leftarrow C_dU + X$, $Y_{d0} \leftarrow Y_{d0} - 1$, GOTO **2**		1	63		00	1		
Z_{Y0}**2**	$i \leftarrow i - 1$	0						1	
3,Z**3**	dshr(C_dUV), dshr(Y), FINISH $\leftarrow 1$			16	33	00	1		1

the BCD algorithm destroys the multiplier via this subtraction. For that reason, we use a decimal linear shift during state *3* instead of a circular shift.

Table 8.15 on page 347 shows a trace of the BCD multiplication algorithm for the operation 71 · 23. The design of the hardware to implement this RTL code is left as an exercise for the reader.

Division can be implemented using either a restoring or a nonrestoring algorithm. An inner loop to perform multiple subtractions must be incorporated into the algorithm. The modified RTL code and hardware designs are left as exercises for the reader.

8.4 Specialized Arithmetic Hardware

Over the years, designers have devised many ways to speed up arithmetic computations. In this section we review three of these innovations: pipelining, lookup tables, and Wallace tree multipliers. In addition, the Historical Perspective describes **coprocessors**, which were formerly used to speed up computations.

HISTORICAL PERSPECTIVE: Coprocessors

The earliest microprocessors could only perform simple arithmetic operations; they had no instructions nor digital logic for performing multiplication and division. The programmer had to write assembly language routines to perform these operations; the programs were similar to the algorithms presented earlier in this chapter. Intel's early microprocessors, up to the 8085, had this characteristic.

Starting with the 8086 microprocessor, Intel incorporated more advanced arithmetic instructions into its processors' instruction sets. These instructions could multiply and divide data, but they were relatively slow. Intel engineers also designed the microprocessors so that they could interact with a separate coprocessor chip. The coprocessor chip had specialized hardware that performed arithmetic calculations much more quickly than the microprocessor.

The coprocessor monitored instructions on the system's data bus. When the microprocessor fetched an instruction that the coprocessor could execute, the coprocessor sent a signal to the microprocessor indicating that it would perform the computation. The coprocessor then calculated the result and sent it to the microprocessor. If the coprocessor was not present, the microprocessor executed the instruction using its own, slower procedure.

As technology improved, it became possible to include more functions on the microprocessor chip. The functions of the coprocessor are now included in all current microprocessor chips.

8.4.1 Pipelining

An **arithmetic pipeline** is similar to an assembly line in a factory. Data enters a stage of the pipeline, which performs some arithmetic operation on the data. The results are then passed to the next stage, which performs its operations, and so on until the final computation has been performed. Each stage performs only its specific function; it does not have to be capable of performing the tasks of any other stage. For an arithmetic pipeline, an individual stage might be an adder or a multiplier, or the hardware to perform some other arithmetic function. It would not need to be capable of performing all of these operations.

A pipeline does not speed up an individual computation. As will be seen shortly, it introduces some overhead that actually slows down each computation. It improves performance by overlapping computations; each stage can operate on different data simultaneously. For example, in a three-stage pipeline, the first stage might process data set #1 while the second stage processes data set #2, and the last stage processes data set #3. The net effect is that results are output more quickly than in a non-pipelined arithmetic unit. This increases the **throughput**, the number of results generated per time unit.

Consider the following snippet of code:

$$\text{FOR } i = 1 \text{ TO } 100 \text{ DO } \{A[i] \leftarrow (B[i] \cdot C[i]) + D[i]\}$$

Assume that each operation, multiplication and addition, requires 10 ns to complete. A non-pipelined uniprocessor takes 20 ns to calculate $A[i]$, and 2,000 ns to execute the code (excluding the time needed to fetch the operands). A pipelined unit could break this computation into two stages, as shown in Figure 8.14. The first stage performs the multiplication and the second performs the addition. Notice that latches store the output of each stage in the pipeline.

Ignore the time delay of the latches for the moment. During the first 10 ns, the first stage calculates $B[1] \cdot C[1]$. In the next 10 ns, stage 2 adds this value to $D[1]$ and stores the result in $A[1]$. At the same time, stage 1 multiplies $B[2]$ and $C[2]$. During the following 10 ns, stage 1 forms $B[3] \cdot C[3]$ and stage 2 calculates the final value $A[2]$. Instead of 2,000 ns, this pipeline executes the code in 1,010 ns.

The most popular metrics used to measure the performance of a pipeline are throughput, just described, and **speedup**. A pipeline's speedup, S_n, is the amount of time needed to process n pieces of data using a non-pipelined arithmetic unit, divided by the time needed to process the same data using a k-stage pipeline.

Before expressing this as an equation, we define T_1 to be the amount of time needed to process one piece of data using a non-pipelined arithmetic unit, which is the clock period of this unit. We also define T_k to be the clock period of the k-stage pipeline. (Think of the non-pipelined unit as a one-stage pipeline, hence the notation T_1

FIGURE 8.14

A two-stage pipeline to implement the program loop

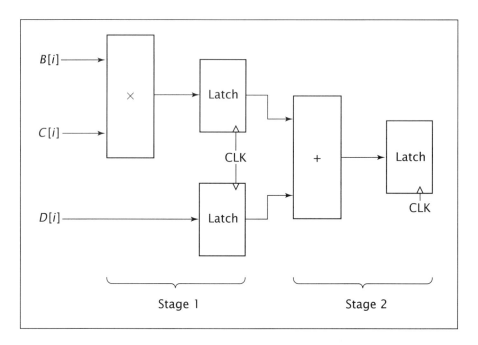

for its clock period.) If the stages have different minimum clock periods, or stage delays, T_k is the largest of these periods. In our example pipeline, $T_1 = 20$ ns and $T_k = 10$ ns.

The speedup of a pipeline can then be expressed as follows:

$$S_n = \frac{nT_1}{(k + n - 1)T_k}$$

Since the non-pipelined unit requires T_1 time to calculate one result, it requires $n \cdot T_1$ time to calculate n results. The pipelined unit requires k time units, each of duration T_k, to move the first piece of data through the pipeline. Because additional data enters the pipeline during every cycle, it will output the remaining $n - 1$ results during the next $n - 1$ cycles, one per cycle. Thus, the pipelined unit requires $(k + n - 1)$ cycles, each of T_k time, to calculate the same n results. For the previous example, the speedup can be calculated as follows:

$$S_{100} = \frac{nT_1}{(k + n - 1)T_k} = \frac{100 \cdot 20 \text{ ns}}{(2 + 100 - 1) \cdot 10 \text{ ns}} = 1.98$$

The steady-state speedup is the upper limit of the speedup that a pipeline can achieve. As n approaches infinity, $\dfrac{n}{k + n - 1}$ approaches 1, yielding the following value for steady-state speedup:

$$S_\infty = \frac{T_1}{T_k}$$

The maximum speedup occurs when each stage has the same delay. In this case, each of the k stages has a delay of $\frac{T_1}{k}$, and $T_k = \frac{T_1}{k}$. Thus the maximum speedup of a k-stage pipeline is calculated as follows:

$$S_\infty = \frac{T_1}{T_k} = \frac{T_1}{(T_1/k)} = k$$

If the stages have unequal delays, then some stages will have delays less than $\frac{T_1}{k}$, while one or more will have a delay greater than $\frac{T_1}{k}$. Since T_k is the maximum of these stage delays, this would set $T_k > \frac{T_1}{k}$ and reduce the speedup. For this reason, making the stage delays as close to each other as possible maximizes the speedup of the pipeline.

In reality, the latches require some amount of time to store their values. This is part of the overhead introduced by pipelines. If each latch needs 2 ns to load data, then each stage requires 12 ns, 10 to calculate its value and 2 to store its result. The pipeline would now require 1,212 ns to calculate A[1..100], which is still faster than the non-pipelined case. The actual speedup is

$$S_{100} = \frac{nT_1}{(k + n - 1)T_k} = \frac{100 \cdot 20 \text{ ns}}{(2 + 100 - 1) \cdot 12 \text{ ns}} = 1.65$$

However, if only one value, A[1], is calculated, the speedup is less than one:

$$S_1 = \frac{1 \cdot 20 \text{ ns}}{(2 + 1 - 1) \cdot 12 \text{ ns}} = 0.83$$

The pipeline is actually slower than the non-pipelined arithmetic unit, due to the delays of the latches at the end of each stage.

This is basic pipelining. As we will see in Chapter 11, pipelining is also used to speed up the fetching, decoding, and execution of instructions in CPUs.

8.4.2   Lookup Tables

Theoretically, any combinatorial circuit can be implemented by a ROM configured as a **lookup table**. The inputs to the combinatorial circuit serve as the address inputs of the ROM. The data outputs of the ROM correspond to the outputs of the combinatorial circuit. The ROM is programmed with data such that the correct values are output for any possible input values. This is the same rationale for generating control signals using a microcode memory in microsequencer control units.

For example, consider a 4×1 ROM programmed to mimic a two-input AND gate. Figure 8.15 shows this AND gate and its lookup ROM equivalent. The inputs to the AND gate serve as the address inputs to the ROM, and the output of the ROM corresponds to the AND gate output. By programming the ROM with the data shown, it outputs the same values as the AND gate for all possible values of X and Y.

FIGURE 8.15

(a) An AND gate and (b) its lookup ROM equivalent

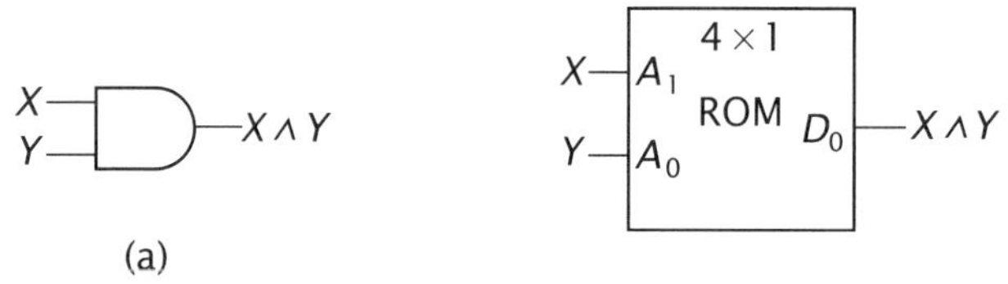

Address		Data
0	0	0
0	1	0
1	0	0
1	1	1

(a)

(b)

Recall the shift-add multiplication algorithm for unsigned non-negative numbers. The examples presented earlier in this chapter formed the product $UV \leftarrow X \cdot Y$, where U, V, X, and Y are 4-bit registers. An alternate implementation, using a lookup ROM, is shown in Figure 8.16. Registers X and Y supply the address inputs to the lookup ROM; its outputs are the product of X and Y, and are routed to registers U and V. Each of the 256 locations must contain the 8-bit product of X and Y. For example, location 1011 1101 contains the data 1000 1111, 143, the product of 1011 (11) and 1101 (13).

It is possible to implement many algorithms using this method, which offers some advantages over the other implementations pre-

---

HISTORICAL PERSPECTIVE: The Pentium Floating Point Bug

Lookup tables are used in modern CPUs; in fact, one was responsible for the famous Pentium floating point bug. While programming a lookup table in its Pentium microprocessor, Intel engineers accidentally left out two values. The data following the missing values were stored two locations ahead of their proper locations, resulting in slightly incorrect results for certain arithmetic operations. The resulting chip recall cost Intel hundreds of millions of dollars.

FIGURE 8.16

A multiplier implemented using a lookup ROM

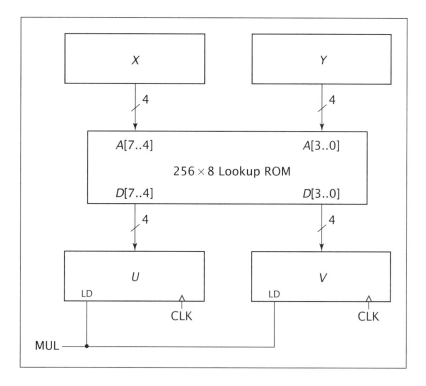

sented in this chapter. For example, the hardware shown in Figure 8.16 may be less complex than that of the original shift-add implementation shown in Figure 8.5. It can also multiply numbers more quickly than the shift-add hardware. However, the size of the lookup ROM grows rapidly as the size of the operands increases. Although the 4-bit multiplier requires a ROM of size 256×8, an equivalent 8-bit multiplier would use a 64K $\times$ 16 ROM.

8.4.3 WALLACE TREES

A **Wallace tree** is a combinatorial circuit used to multiply two numbers. Although it requires more hardware than shift-add multipliers, it produces a product in far less time. Instead of performing additions using standard parallel adders, Wallace trees use carry-save adders and only one parallel adder.

A carry-save adder can add three values simultaneously, instead of just two. However, it does not output a single result. Instead, it outputs both a sum and a set of carry bits. To illustrate this, consider the carry-save adder shown in Figure 8.17. Each bit S_i is the binary sum of bits X_i, Y_i, and Z_i. Carry bit C_{i+1} is the carry generated by this sum. To

FIGURE 8.17

A carry-save adder

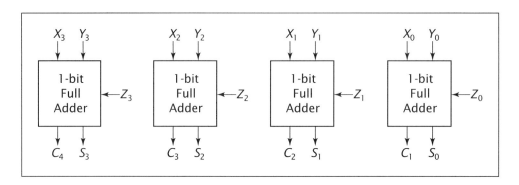

FIGURE 8.18

Generating partial products for multiplication using Wallace trees

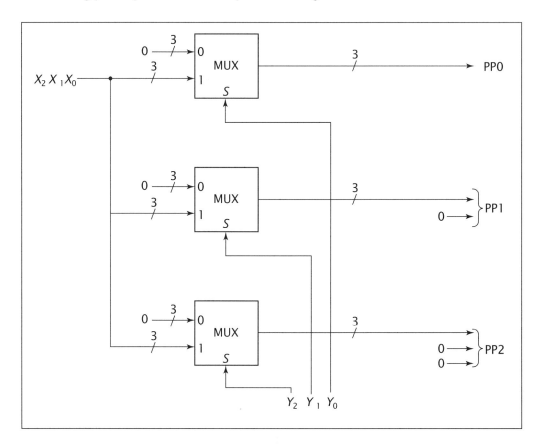

form a final sum, C and S must be added together. Because carry bits do not propagate through the adder, it is faster than a parallel adder. In a parallel adder, adding 1111 and 0001 generates a carry that propagates from the least significant bit, through each bit of the sum, to the output carry. Unlike the parallel adder, though, the carry-save adder does not produce a final sum.

Consider a numeric example. For $X = 0111$, $Y = 1011$, and $Z = 0010$, this carry-save adder would output $S = 1110$ and $C = 00110$. Note that C appears to be shifted one position to the left of S since the adder that generates S_i also generates C_{i+1}. Adding S and C using a parallel adder produces the result 10100 (20), which is 0111 (7) + 1011 (11) + 0010 (2).

To use a carry-save adder to perform multiplication, we first calculate the partial products of the multiplication, then input them to the carry-save adder. For example,

$$
\begin{array}{rl}
x = & 111 \\
y = & \underline{110} \\
& 000 \quad \leftarrow PP0 \\
& 111 \quad\;\; \leftarrow PP1 \\
& \underline{111} \qquad \leftarrow PP2 \\
& 101010 \quad \leftarrow \text{Final sum calculated}
\end{array}
$$

A 3 × 3 multiplier constructed using a carry-save adder

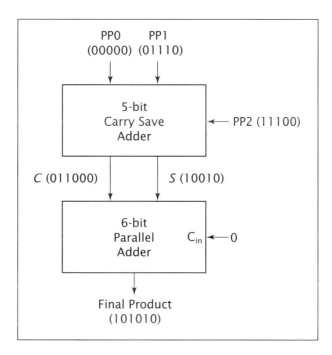

The partial products can be calculated by using the bits of y to select either the value x or 0, shifting the result to the left to properly align the partial products. In this example, $PP2$ is actually 11100, the 111 value of x shifted two positions to the left. It is shifted two places because bit y_2 was used to generate this partial product. Similarly, $PP1$ was set by y_1, so it is only shifted one position to the left. Figure 8.18 on page 354 shows one way to generate the partial products for this example.

We can use a 5-bit carry save adder to add the partial products $PP0$, $PP1$, and $PP2$. We then add its S and C outputs using a parallel adder to produce the final product. The hardware to perform this multiplication is shown in Figure 8.19 on page 355. Note that we incorporate the leading and trailing zeroes into the partial products to align the numbers properly.

Although this is technically a minimal Wallace tree, it does not fully explain the design principle. Figure 8.20 shows a Wallace tree for multiplying two 4-bit numbers. The first carry-save adder adds the first three partial products. The second carry-save adder adds the fourth partial product to the S and C outputs of the first adder. Finally, a parallel adder generates the product.

FIGURE 8.20

A 4 × 4 Wallace tree multiplier

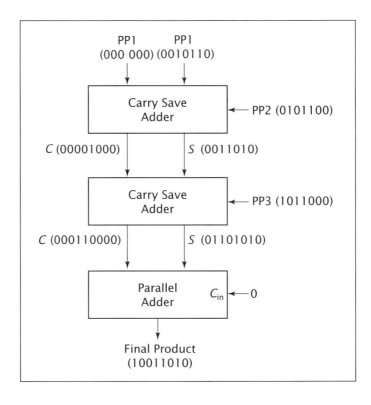

FIGURE 8.21

An 8 × 8 Wallace tree multiplier

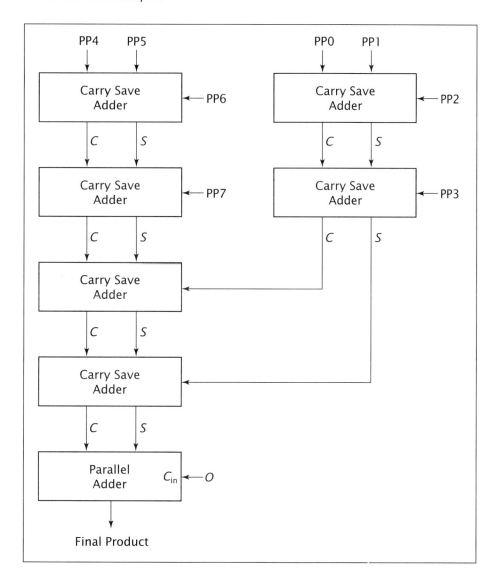

Consider the multiplication 1011 · 1110, which has partial products $PP0 = 000\ 0000$, $PP1 = 001\ 0110$, $PP2 = 010\ 1100$, and $PP3 = 101\ 1000$. The outputs of the first carry-save adder are $S = 011\ 1010$ and $C = 0000\ 1000$. The second carry-save adder generates $S = 0110\ 1010$ and $C = 0\ 0011\ 0000$, and the parallel adder outputs the final product 1001 1010.

The Wallace tree makes use of parallel operations for larger numbers of partial products, which occur when multiplying numbers with more bits. Figure 8.21 shows a Wallace tree for multiplying two 8-bit numbers.

8.5 Floating Point Numbers

All of the numeric formats presented in this chapter so far are fixed-point formats. In practice, they only represent integers, not fractions. However, a general purpose computer must be able to work with fractions with varying numbers of bits, or it will not be very useful. Clearly, it is desirable to allow a computer to use fractions for certain applications. This is the purpose of **floating point numbers**.

In this section we examine floating point numbers. We review their formats and how special numbers, such as 0, are handled. Characteristics of floating point numbers, such as precision and range, are studied. Finally, we present arithmetic algorithms for this numeric format.

8.5.1 Numeric Format

Floating point format is very similar to scientific notation. Recall that a number expressed in scientific notation has a sign, a fraction or *significand* (often erroneously called a *mantissa*), and an exponent. For example, the number -1234.5678 could be expressed as -1.2345678×10^3, where the sign is negative, the significand is 1.2345678, and the exponent is 3. This example uses base 10, but any base can be used to represent floating point numbers. In this section, all algorithms use base two because computers generally use base two to represent floating point numbers.

One disadvantage of scientific notation is that most numbers can be expressed in many different ways. For example, $-1234.5678 = -1.2345678 \times 10^3 = -1234567.8 \times 10^{-3}$, as well as several other representations. Computers are more efficient, and have much simpler hardware, if each number can have only one unique representation.

For this reason, floating point numbers must be **normalized**—that is, each number's significand is a fraction with no leading zeroes. Thus the only valid floating point representation for -1234.5678 is $-.12345678 \times 10^4$. (There is one exception to this rule; see the description of the IEEE 754 floating point standard in Section 8.6.)

This normalized representation works well for every possible number except zero. Since the number zero has only zeroes in its significand, it cannot be normalized. For this reason, a special value is assigned to zero; arithmetic algorithms must explicitly check for zero values and treat them as special cases. Positive and negative infinity also have special representations and require special treatment.

Another value that requires a special representation is **Not a Number**, or **NaN**. This value represents the result of illegal operations, such as $\infty \div \infty$ or taking the square root of a negative number. Also, compilers may assign the value NaN to uninitialized variables.

As with zero and infinity, NaN requires special treatment in floating point arithmetic algorithms.

A computer stores floating point numbers in a predefined format. Each number requires a 1-bit sign, a significand of some predetermined length, and an exponent of a given length. In this section, we define a floating point number to be of the form $X = X_S X_F X_E$, where X_S is the sign of X, X_F is its significand, and X_E is its exponent. Since each number is stored in normal form, it is implicit that the radix point is located to the left of the most significant bit of the significand and hence does not have to be explicitly stored. The value $X = -1234.5678$ ($= -.12345678 \times 10^4$) would be stored as $X_S = 1$, $X_F = 12345678$, and $X_E = 4$.

Notice that there is no sign bit for the exponent. This raises the question of how to represent negative exponents. Although one possibility is to use two's complement values, the prevalent practice is to use **biasing**. To illustrate this principle, assume that X_E has four bits, and should be able to represent all exponents from -8 to $+7$, inclusive. To do so, a set bias value is added to the actual exponent; the result is then stored in X_E. For this example, the bias should be set to 8. The smallest possible exponent, -8, is represented as $-8 + $ bias $= -8 + 8 = 0$, or 0000 in binary. The largest possible exponent, $+7$, is represented as $+7 + $ bias $= +7 + 8 = 15 = 1111$ in binary. The arithmetic algorithms must account for the bias when generating their results.

There is one optimization that can be used for binary floating point numbers. Since every normalized number (excluding 0, $\pm\infty$, and NaN) has a 1 as its most significant bit, this bit does not have to be explicitly stored in the significand register. However, the CPU hardware must account for this leading 1 when processing data.

8.5.2 NUMERIC CHARACTERISTICS

There are several characteristics inherent to floating point numbers. **Precision**, as its name implies, characterizes how precise a floating point value can be. It is defined as the number of bits in the significand; a computer that uses 8 bits for its significand has 8-bit precision. The greater the number of bits in the significand, the greater is the CPU's precision and the more precise is its value. Many CPUs have two representations for floating point numbers. One is usually called *single precision;* the other, having twice as many bits, is called *double precision.*

The **gap** is the difference between two adjacent values. Its value depends on the value of the exponent. For example, consider a floating point number with an 8-bit significand and the value $.1011\ 1010 \times 2^3$. Its adjacent values are $.1011\ 1001 \times 2^3$ and $.1011\ 1011 \times 2^3$, each of which produces a gap of $.0000\ 0001 \times 2^3 = 2^{-5}$. In general, the gap for floating point value X can be expressed as $2^{(X_E - \text{precision})}$.

The **range** of a floating point representation is bounded by its smallest and largest possible values. For example, a floating point number with an 8-bit significand (assuming the leading 1 is explicitly stored in the significand register) and a 4-bit exponent (which ranges from -8 to $+7$) has a range of $-.1111\ 1111 \times 2^7$ to $+.1111\ 1111 \times 2^7$, or -127.5 to $+127.5$.

To illustrate these characteristics, consider a floating point representation that has a 1-bit sign, an 8-bit exponent with a bias of 128, and a 23-bit significand. (This is a slightly modified version of the IEEE 754 single precision format described in the next section.) This format, as presented here, has a precision of 23 bits. Its range is $-.111\ 1111\ 1111\ 1111\ 1111\ 1111 \times 2^{127}$ to $+.111\ 1111\ 1111\ 1111$ $1111\ 1111 \times 2^{127}$, or approximately -1.7×10^{38} to $+1.7 \times 10^{38}$. Its gap depends on the actual value represented. For $.1 \times 2^{127}$, it is $2^{(127-23)} = 2^{104}$; for $.1 \times 2^{-128}$, the gap is $2^{(-128-23)}$, or 2^{-151}.

Overflow occurs when an operation produces a result that cannot be stored in a computer's floating point registers. In the example with the 8-bit significand and the 4-bit exponent with a bias of 8, multiplying $(.1 \times 2^6) \times (.1 \times 2^5)$ would produce a result of $.01 \times 2^{11} = .1 \times 2^{10}$. The exponent is greater than the maximum allowable exponent, 7 in this case. Overflow can be positive or negative, depending on the sign of the overflowed value. An overflowed value can be treated as $\pm\infty$, or NaN, or a flag can be set as in the fixed point algorithms.

Underflow occurs when an operation produces a result between zero and either the positive or negative smallest possible value. In the previous example, multiplying $(.1 \times 2^{-6}) \times (.1 \times 2^{-5})$ produces a result of $.1 \times 2^{-12}$, which lies between 0 and $.1 \times 2^{-8}$, the smallest representable value. As with overflow, underflow can be positive or negative. An underflowed value can be treated as zero, or an underflow flag can be set.

No matter how many bits a significand has, it cannot exactly represent every possible number. Furthermore, some operations produce results with significands that are too large for the CPU registers. Going back to the example format with 8-bit significands and 4-bit exponents, an operation that multiplies two values could produce a result with a 16-bit significand. This value must be transformed to fit into an 8-bit significand register. This process is called **rounding**.

The goal of rounding is usually to find a representation that is as close as possible to the actual desired value. For example, rounding the value $.1011\ 1010$ to 4 bits yields the value $.1100$. This is referred to as **rounding to nearest** or **unbiased rounding**; it has a maximum error of $\pm\frac{1}{2}$ LSB, one-half of the value of the least significant bit of the rounded result.

Although this is the most common method of rounding, there are several other methods for rounding numbers:

1. *Round toward 0*: The extra bits are simply truncated. This has a very simple hardware implementation, but it can produce results up to 1 LSB off. For example, the value $.1011\ 1111$ would be rounded to $.1011$.

2. *Round toward* $+\infty$: This is the ceiling function for fractions. All values are rounded up to the next possible value. This results in negative values being truncated and positive values being rounded up to the next valid value. If all unsaved bits are 0, the value remains unchanged. For example, $-.1011\ 1111$, $.1011\ 0000$, and $.1011\ 0001$ are rounded to the values $-.1011$, $.1011$, and $.1100$, respectively.

3. *Round toward* $-\infty$: This is a floor function for fractions. Negative values are rounded down and positive values are truncated. In this method, $-.1011\ 0001$, $.1011\ 0000$, and $.1011\ 1111$ are rounded to the values $-.1100$, $.1011$, and $.1011$, respectively.

Table 8.16 gives a few examples to illustrate how numbers are rounded to different values by the different rounding methods. Each 8-bit value is rounded to four bits.

Table 8.16

Rounded values using various rounding methods

Value	Round to Closest	Round Toward 0	Round Toward $+\infty$	Round Toward $-\infty$
.0110 1001	.0111	.0110	.0111	.0110
−.0110 1001	−.0111	−.0110	−.0110	−.0111
.1000 0111	.1000	.1000	.1001	.1000
−.1000 0111	−.1000	−.1000	−.1000	−.1001
.1000 0000	.1000	.1000	.1000	.1000

All of these rounding operations, except round toward 0, require additional bits beyond those in the final representation. One or two bits are usually sufficient. The most significant of these bits is the **round bit**, followed by the **guard bit**. As we will see in the algorithms for floating point operations, these bits are extensions of the result. A third bit, often used by shift-add algorithms, is called the **sticky bit**. It is usually initialized to 0 and is set to 1 if a bit value of 1 is shifted right out of the guard bit. Unlike the round and guard bits, the sticky bit keeps its value of 1 regardless of future shifts. This bit may replace the guard bit in some implementations. It is also used in the implementations of the floating point algorithms.

8.5.3 Addition and Subtraction

The process of adding and subtracting floating point numbers is similar to the processes for signed-magnitude numbers, with two important differences. Since a few values have special representations, the algorithm must explicitly check whether either operand is 0, $\pm\infty$, or

NaN, and whether the result is 0 or $\pm\infty$. Also, since the operands may have different exponents, their significands must be aligned. For example, in the operation $(.1011 \times 2^3) - (.1100 \times 2^2)$, the significands are stored as 1011 and 1100, respectively. Simply subtracting these two values will not yield the correct result. Since the second operand's exponent is less than that of the first operand, its significand must be shifted to the right. Essentially, this changes the representation of $.1100 \times 2^2$ to $.0110 \times 2^3$. Once the exponents are the same, we can subtract the significands.

This shift/align/subtract (or add) procedure is sufficient to handle most floating point addition and subtraction. However, it only works for numbers in standard floating point format. If either or both operands are 0, $\pm\infty$, or NaN, this procedure will not work. These numbers have special representations and must be handled differently.

Table 8.17 shows the possible values of the two operands X and Y, and the result of the operation $U \leftarrow X \pm Y$. In this table, $AS = 0$ if X and Y are added, or 1 if they are subtracted. (The X's in the table are the value of X, not don't cares.)

Table 8.17

Results of operations for special format floating point numbers

$X \backslash Y$	0	$\pm\infty$	NaN	Normalized
0	X	$(AS \oplus Y_S)Y$	Y	$(AS \oplus Y_S)Y$
$\pm\infty$	X	X	Y	X
NaN	X	X	X	X
Normalized	X	$(AS \oplus Y_S)Y$	Y	Calculate value

The rules for determining these values are as follows.

1. If $Y = 0$, then $U \leftarrow X \pm 0 = X$, so $U \leftarrow X$, else
2. If $X = 0$ and $Y \neq$ NaN, then $U \leftarrow 0 \pm Y$. If $AS = 0$ then $U \leftarrow Y$, otherwise $U \leftarrow -Y$, else
3. If $X =$ NaN then $U \leftarrow X (=$ NaN$)$, else
4. If $Y =$ NaN then $U \leftarrow Y (=$ NaN$)$, else
5. If $X = \pm\infty$ then $U \leftarrow X$, else
6. If $Y = \pm\infty$ then, $U \leftarrow Y$ if $AS = 0$, otherwise $U \leftarrow -Y$, else
7. Calculate U using the regular addition/subtraction procedure

Note that, unlike ∞, NaN does not have a sign; there is no $+$NaN nor $-$NaN, just plain NaN. This is the reason that statement 2 specifically requires $Y \neq$ NaN. Also notice what happens when one of the operands is $\pm\infty$ and the other is NaN. In this case, the result is set to NaN; NaN has precedence over $\pm\infty$ in floating point operations.

The following algorithm produces $U \leftarrow X \pm Y$. It shares many of the elements of the signed-magnitude addition/subtraction procedure. Each value has three registers, a 1-bit sign (U_s for register U), an n-bit significand (U_F), and an m-bit exponent (U_E). As with the signed-magnitude algorithm, $AS = 0$ for addition and $AS = 1$ for subtraction, and $PM = X_s \oplus AS \oplus Y_s$. We also define $N_{REG} = 1$ if the value in REG is NaN (where REG is either X or Y), $Z_{REG} = 1$ if $REG = 0$, and $I_{REG} = 1$ if $REG = \pm\infty$. Finally, we define $E_{XY} = 1$ if $X_E > Y_E$ and $E_{YX} = 1$ if $Y_E > X_E$.

$$
\begin{array}{rl}
(I_X N_Y' + N_X + Z_Y)\mathbf{1}: & U \leftarrow X,\ FINISH \leftarrow 1 \\
(N_Y' Z_X Z_Y' + I_X' I_Y N_X')\mathbf{1}: & U \leftarrow (Y_S \oplus AS)Y_F Y_E,\ FINISH \leftarrow 1 \\
(I_Y N_X + N_X' N_Y)\mathbf{1}: & U \leftarrow Y,\ FINISH \leftarrow 1 \\
E_{XY}\mathbf{2}: & \mathrm{shr}(Y_F),\ Y_E \leftarrow Y_E + 1,\ \text{GOTO } \mathbf{2} \\
E_{YX}\mathbf{2}: & \mathrm{shr}(X_F),\ X_E \leftarrow X_E + 1,\ \text{GOTO } \mathbf{2} \\
PM'\mathbf{3}: & CU_F \leftarrow X_F + Y_F \\
PM\mathbf{3}: & CU_F \leftarrow X_F + Y_F' + 1 \\
\mathbf{3}: & U_S \leftarrow X_S,\ U_E \leftarrow X_E,\ C_E \leftarrow 0 \\
CPM'\mathbf{4}: & \mathrm{shr}(CU_F),\ C_E U_E \leftarrow U_E + 1 \\
C_E PM'\mathbf{5}: & U \leftarrow U_S \infty \\
PM'\mathbf{5}: & FINISH \leftarrow 1 \\
C'PM\mathbf{4}: & U_S \leftarrow U_S',\ U_F \leftarrow U_F' + 1 \\
Z_U' C_E' U_{F(n-1)}'PM\mathbf{5}: & \mathrm{shl}(U_F),\ C_E U_E \leftarrow U_E - 1,\ \text{GOTO } \mathbf{5} \\
(Z_U + C_E)PM\ \mathbf{5}: & U \leftarrow 0,\ FINISH \leftarrow 1 \\
C_E' U_{F(n-1)}PM\ \mathbf{5}: & FINISH \leftarrow 1
\end{array}
$$

State $\mathbf{1}$ performs the operations encompassed in Table 8.17. If X and/or Y are 0, $\pm\infty$, or NaN, this step sets the result to the correct value and exits (by our standard method of setting $FINISH$ to 1).

State $\mathbf{2}$ aligns the significands. Whichever operand has the smaller exponent is shifted to the right, and its exponent incremented, until the exponents are equal. For example, if $X = .1101 \times 2^5$ and $Y = .1000 \times 2^3$, Y_F is shifted right, and its exponent is incremented, twice. This results in $Y_F = 0010$ and $Y_E = 5$, which is $.0010 \times 2^5$. State $\mathbf{3}$ performs the addition or subtraction and sets the sign of the result.

At this point the algorithm divides into two cases. If $PM = 0$, the two values were added. If the addition set $C = 1$, it produced a result of the form 1.xxxx. It is normalized by shifting the significand one position to the right and incrementing the exponent. If this results in an overflow of the exponent (using biased notation), the final result is set to $\pm\infty$; otherwise it is correct.

Table 8.18 illustrates this case ($PM = 0$) for the operation $(.1101 \times 2^3) + (.1110 \times 2^2)$. State $\mathbf{1}$ checks for special values. Since both X and Y are normalized, nothing happens in this state. Entering state $\mathbf{2}$,

$X_E > Y_E$, so $E_{XY} = 1$. The significand of Y, Y_F, is shifted one position to the right and its exponent is incremented; it loops back to state **2**. This process would be repeated until the two exponents, X_E and Y_E, are equal. In this example, this happens after the first iteration. At this point, the algorithm has branched back to state **2**. Since $X_E = Y_E$, E_{XY} and E_{YX} are both 0. No operations are performed and the algorithm goes on to state **3**.

Table 8.18

Trace of the RTL code for $(X = .1101 \times 2^3) + (Y = .1110 \times 2^2)$

Conditions	Micro-operations	C	U_S	U_F	U_E	Y_S	Y_F	Y_E	C_E	FINISH
1	None					0	1110	2		
E_{XY} **2**	shr(Y_F), $Y_E \leftarrow Y_E + 1$, GOTO **2**						0111	3		
2	None									
PM'**3, 3**	$CU_F \leftarrow X_F + Y_F$, $U_S \leftarrow X_S$, $U_E \leftarrow X_E$, $C_E \leftarrow 0$	1	0	0100	3				0	
CPM'**4**	shr(CU_F), $C_E U_E \leftarrow U_E + 1$	0		1010	4				0	
PM'**5**	FINISH$\leftarrow$1									1

Since $PM = 0$, the two magnitudes are added together in state **3**; a carry bit C holds any overflow. Also in this state, the sign and exponent of the result are set, and C_E is initialized.

State **4** checks for and normalizes a result of the form 1.xxxx. That did happen in this example; C was set to 1 during state **3**. The significand is shifted one bit to the right and the exponent of the result is incremented to 4.

During this operation, it is possible to generate an overflow. For example, if the 4-bit exponent of the result was 1111, this operation would have set it to $1111 + 1 = 1\ 0000$. The 1 would be stored in C_E, an exponent carry flag. If this happens, the result must be set to $\pm\infty$, but this doesn't occur in this example. Instead, the algorithm simply terminates in state **5**. It is easy to verify that the algorithm produces the correct result, $(.1101 \times 2^3) + (.1110 \times 2^2) = (.1010 \times 2^4)$, or $6.5 + 3.5 = 10$.

If $PM = 1$, the two values were subtracted. If this subtraction sets $C = 0$, then the magnitude must be negated and the sign inverted, just as in the signed-magnitude algorithm. This is done in state **4**. At the end of this state, the result is either of the form .0xxx or .1xxx. If its significand has a leading 0 ($U_{F(n-1)}'$), the significand is shifted one position to the left and its exponent is decremented. This process is repeated until $U_{F(n-1)} = 1$, $U_F = 0$, or the exponent goes below its minimum value ($C_E = 1$). In the former case, the number is in normal form and the algorithm terminates. If the magnitude is 0, or the exponent underflows, the result is forcibly set to 0.

Table 8.19 shows an example of this case of the algorithm for the operation $(.1101 \times 2^3) - (.1110 \times 2^2)$. As in the previous example, states **1** and **2** check for special values and align the significands. In state **3**, the significands are subtracted and the sign and exponent of the result are set.

Table 8.19

Trace of the RTL code for $(X = .1101 \times 2^3) - (Y = .1110 \times 2^2)$

Conditions	Micro-operations	C	U_S	U_F	U_E	Y_S	Y_F	Y_E	C_E	FINISH
1	None					0	1110	2		
E_{XY}**2**	shr(Y_F), $Y_E \leftarrow Y_E + 1$, GOTO **2**						0111	3		
2	None									
PM**3**, **3**	$CU_F \leftarrow X_F + Y_F' + 1$, $U_S \leftarrow X_S$, $U_E \leftarrow X_E$, $C_E \leftarrow 0$	1	0	0110	3				0	
4	None									
$Z_U'C_E'U_{F(n-1)}'$PM**5**	shl(U_F), $C_E U_E \leftarrow U_E - 1$, GOTO **5**			1100	2				0	
$C_E'U_{F(n-1)}$PM**5**	FINISH$\leftarrow$1									1

During state **4**, the result would be negated, if necessary. In this example, the result is correct, so no operations occur during this state.

In state **5**, the value is normalized. There is only one leading 0 in the significand, so only one left shift is performed. When the algorithm loops back to state **5**, the significand is normalized, and the exponent did not underflow, so the algorithm is finished. As might be expected, it correctly calculates $(.1101 \times 2^3) - (.1110 \times 2^2) = (.1100 \times 2^2)$, or $6.5 - 3.5 = 3$.

The design of the hardware uses many elements of that for the signed-magnitude adder/subtractor. It is left as an exercise for the reader.

8.5.4 Multiplication and Division

As with signed-magnitude numbers, floating point multiplication is implemented using a shift-add process, with a few modifications. As was the case for addition and subtraction, this algorithm must first check for operands that are 0, NaN, or $\pm\infty$. It then performs the multiplication by multiplying the significands and adding the exponents. It also checks for overflow and underflow. The product of the significands will either be of the form .1xxx or .01xx. (In the worst case, the result will be .1000 $\times$ .1000 = .0100. No product of two normalized numbers can produce a result with a significand less than .01.) If the significand has a leading zero, it must be normalized and rechecked for underflow.

As with addition and subtraction, a floating point multiplication algorithm must first check for special values. If either operand is 0, the result is set to 0; if not, and either or both operands are NaN, the result is NaN. If neither of these cases occurs, and at least one of the operands is $\pm\infty$, the result is set to ∞ with the proper sign. In any of these cases, the algorithm terminates. If neither operand is 0, $\pm\infty$, or NaN, the algorithm sets the sign and exponent of the result.

The exponent should be set to the sum of the exponents of the two operands. When setting the exponent, recall that each operand includes the bias value. Simply adding the exponents includes the bias twice. It is necessary to subtract the bias once to return the exponent to its properly biased representation. For example, consider the multiplication $(.1101 \times 2^3) \times (.1110 \times 2^2)$. If a bias of 8 is used, these two exponents are stored as 11 and 10, respectively. Adding them yields the value 21, which corresponds to 2^{13} when using a bias of 8. Clearly this product will be nowhere near 2^{13}. In reality, the bias was included twice, once in 11 and once in 10. Subtracting the extra bias yields an exponent of 13, which corresponds to the desired value of 2^5 in this notation.

Once this is done, the algorithm checks this exponent for overflow and underflow. If overflow occurs, the result is set to $\pm\infty$, depending on the sign calculated in state **1**. If the exponent is below the minimum representable value, the algorithm sets the result to 0. In either case, the algorithm terminates.

Next, the algorithm multiplies the significands. It uses the same shift-add procedure as was used for signed-magnitude numbers. It is not necessary to check for a zero result since the values that were multiplied were in normal form.

Finally, the algorithm normalizes and rounds the result. Since this could cause an underflow, the algorithm must again check for underflow, setting the result to 0 if underflow occurs.

The following RTL code implements this algorithm. U_R, U_G, and U_T are the round, guard, and sticky bits of register U. Also, $M_E = 1$ if $U_E < 0$, and $Z_i = 1$ if $i = 0$.

$$(Z_X + Z_Y)\mathbf{1}: \quad U \leftarrow 0,\ FINISH \leftarrow 1$$
$$(N_X + N_Y)Z_X'Z_Y'\mathbf{1}: \quad U \leftarrow NaN,\ FINISH \leftarrow 1$$
$$N_X'N_Y'Z_X'Z_Y'(I_X + I_Y)\mathbf{1}: \quad U \leftarrow (X_s \oplus Y_s)\infty,\ FINISH \leftarrow 1$$
$$N_X'N_Y'Z_X'Z_Y'I_X'I_Y'\mathbf{1}: \quad C_E U_E \leftarrow X_E + Y_E - bias,\ U_s \leftarrow X_s \oplus Y_s$$
$$C_E\mathbf{2}: \quad U \leftarrow U_s\infty,\ FINISH \leftarrow 1$$
$$M_E\mathbf{2}: \quad U \leftarrow 0,\ FINISH \leftarrow 1$$
$$\mathbf{3}: \quad U_F \leftarrow 0,\ i \leftarrow n$$
$$Y_{F(0)}\mathbf{4}: \quad CU_F \leftarrow U_F + X_F$$
$$\mathbf{4}: \quad i \leftarrow i - 1$$
$$\mathbf{5}: \quad shr(CU_FU_RU_G),\ U_T \leftarrow U_G \wedge U_T,\ shr(Y_F)$$
$$Z_i'\mathbf{5}: \quad GOTO\ \mathbf{4}$$
$$U_{F(n-1)}\mathbf{6}: \quad U_F \leftarrow U_F + ((U_R \wedge (U_G \vee U_T)) \vee (U_{F(0)} \wedge U_R)),$$
$$FINISH \leftarrow 1$$
$$U_{F(n-1)}'\mathbf{6}: \quad shl\ (U_FU_RU_GU_T),\ U_E \leftarrow U_E - 1$$
$$M_E\mathbf{7}: \quad U \leftarrow 0,\ FINISH \leftarrow 1$$
$$M_E'\mathbf{7}: \quad U_F \leftarrow U_F + ((U_R \wedge U_G) \vee (U_{F(0)} \wedge U_R)),\ FINISH \leftarrow 1$$

State **1** handles the special cases when X and/or Y is 0, $\pm\infty$, or NaN, according to the rules summarized in Table 8.17. It also sets the sign and exponent of the result. State **2** checks for overflow and underflow. The next three states, **3**, **4**, and **5**, implement the shift-add multiplication of the significands.

If the result is in normal form ($U_{F(n-1)} = 1$), the algorithm rounds the significand during state **6** and terminates. It rounds up if either the extra bits are 11x or 101, or if the least significant bit of the significand is 1 and the round bit is 1. For example, if $U_F = .1011\ 0011$, $U_R = 1$, $U_G = 1$, and $U_T = 0$, the value is treated as $.1011\ 1011\ 110$, which is rounded up to $.1011\ 1100$. If U_G and U_T are 0, the value would be treated as $.1011\ 1101\ 100$. By convention, when the round bit is 1 but the guard and sticky bits are zero, the value is rounded up only if its least significant bit is 1.

If the result is not normalized, its magnitude must be in the form $.01xx$. It is shifted left once in state **6** and its exponent is decremented. If this causes an underflow, the result is set to 0. Otherwise, it is rounded as before, except the sticky bit is not checked. (Since the value was just shifted left, the sticky bit was set to 0.)

To illustrate this algorithm, consider the multiplication $(.1101 \times 2^3) \times (.1110 \times 2^2)$, or 6.5×3.5. Assuming bias $= 0$, the algorithm starts with $X_s = 0$, $X_F = 1101$, $X_E = 0011$, $Y_s = 0$, $Y_F = 1110$, and $Y_E = 0010$. The trace of this algorithm for these values is shown in Table 8.20.

Since neither value is 0, $\pm\infty$, or NaN, state **1** only sets the exponent and sign of the result. The exponent has a valid value, so no operations occur during state **2**, and the magnitude and loop counter are

Table 8.20

Trace of the RTL code for $(X = .1101 \times 2^3) \times (Y = .1110 \times 2^2)$

Conditions	Micro-operations	i	C	U_F	U_R	U_G	U_T	Y_F	C_E	U_E	U_S	FINISH
$N_X'N_Y'Z_X'Z_Y'I_X'I_Y'\mathbf{1}$	$C_E U_E \leftarrow X_E + Y_E$ $- \text{bias}, U_S \leftarrow X_S \oplus Y_S$							1110	0	0101	0	
2	None											
3	$U_F \leftarrow 0, i \leftarrow n$	4		0000	0	0	0					
4	$i \leftarrow i - 1$	3										
$Z_i'\mathbf{5,5}$	$\text{shr}(CU_F U_R U_G),$ $U_T \leftarrow U_G \vee U_T,$ $\text{shr}(Y_F), \text{GOTO } \mathbf{4}$		0	0000	0	0	0	0111				
$Y_{F(0)}\mathbf{4,4}$	$CU_F \leftarrow U_F + X_F,$ $i \leftarrow i - 1$	2	0	1101								
$Z_i'\mathbf{5,5}$	$\text{shr}(CU_F U_R U_G),$ $U_T \leftarrow U_G \vee U_T,$ $\text{shr}(Y_F), \text{GOTO } \mathbf{4}$		0	0110	1	0	0	0011				
$Y_{F(0)}\mathbf{4,4}$	$CU_F \leftarrow U_F + X_F,$ $i \leftarrow i - 1$	1	1	0011								
$Z_i'\mathbf{5,5}$	$\text{shr}(CU_F U_R U_G),$ $U_T \leftarrow U_G \vee U_T,$ $\text{shr}(Y_F), \text{GOTO } \mathbf{4}$		0	1001	1	1	0	0001				
$Y_{F(0)}\mathbf{4,4}$	$CU_F \leftarrow U_F + X_F,$ $i \leftarrow i - 1$	0	1	0110								
5	$\text{shr}(CU_F U_R U_G),$ $U_T \leftarrow U_G \vee U_T,$ $\text{shr}(Y_F)$		0	1011	0	1	1	0000				
$U_{F(n-1)}\mathbf{6}$	$U_F \leftarrow U_F + ((U_R \wedge$ $(U_G \vee U_T)) \vee$ $(U_{F(0)} \wedge U_R)),$ $FINISH \leftarrow 1$			1011								1

initialized during state **3**. The loop consisting of states **4** and **5** is then executed four times to multiply magnitudes X_F and Y_F using a shift-add procedure. We check the result during state **6**; since it is already normalized, we round the result and exit the algorithm. The final result, $.1011 \times 2^5 = 22$, is the closest possible 4-bit representation of the actual result, 22.75.

Division is also similar to its shift-subtract counterpart. A floating point division algorithm would first check for 0, NaN, and $\pm\infty$ values, as did the floating point multiplication algorithm. Unlike in its signed-magnitude counterpart, however, overflow does not occur if $X_F > Y_F$. In this case, we shift X_F right one position and we decrement

X_E. Then we set the exponent of the result and division proceeds as in signed-magnitude division. Overflow and underflow are checked as in the floating point multiplication algorithm. The result is then normalized, possibly by more than one place.

8.6   Real World Example: The IEEE 754 Floating Point Standard

By the late 1970s, computer manufacturers were implementing floating point operations in many computers, but in incompatible ways. The effect of this was that the same program might generate different results on different computers, which was clearly unacceptable.

For this reason, IEEE developed the IEEE 754 floating point standard. This standard defines set formats and operation modes. All computers conforming to this standard would (almost) always calculate the same result for the same computation. However, this standard does not specify arithmetic procedures and hardware to be used to perform computations. For example, a CPU can meet the standard whether it uses shift-add hardware or a Wallace tree to multiply two significands.

Today the IEEE 754 standard is used in virtually all CPUs that have floating point capability. This section briefly describes this format. It also introduces denormalized numbers, a concept allowed in this standard that has not yet been examined in this chapter.

8.6.1   Formats

The IEEE 754 standard specifies two precisions for floating point numbers. Single precision numbers have 32 bits: 1 for the sign; 8 for the exponent; and 23 for the significand. The significand also includes an implied 1 to the left of its radix point (except for special values and denormalized numbers, discussed in the next subsection). Unlike the floating point format described earlier, normalized significands in this format fall in the range $1 \leq significand < 2$. The exponent uses a bias of 127, having a range of -126 to $+127$. The exponent values 0000 0000 (= -127) and 1111 1111 (= $+128$) are used for special numbers.

Table 8.21(a) shows the representation of $+19.5$ (=10011.1 or 1.00111×2^4 in binary) in single precision format. Note that the leading 1 is not included in the significand; its presence is implicit in this standard. Also, the exponent 4 is represented as 1000 0011, or 131, due to the addition of the bias of 127.

Double precision numbers use 64 bits: 1 for the sign; 11 for the exponent; and 52 for the significand. As in single precision, the significand has an implied leading 1 for most values. The exponent has a bias of 1023 and a range from -1022 to $+1023$. Again, the smallest and largest exponent values, -1023 and $+1024$, are reserved for

TABLE 8.21

Single (a) and double (b) precision representations in the IEEE 754 standard format

Value	Sign	Significand	Exponent
+19.5	0	001 1100 0000 0000 0000 0000	1000 0011
0	0	000 0000 0000 0000 0000 0000	0000 0000
$\pm\infty$	0 or 1	000 0000 0000 0000 0000 0000	1111 1111
NaN	0 or 1	Any nonzero value	1111 1111
Denormalized	0 or 1	Any nonzero value	0000 0000

(a)

Value	Sign	Significand	Exponent
+19.5	0	0011 1000 0000 0000 0000 0000 0000 0000 0000 0000 0000 0000 0000	100 0000 0011
0	0	0000 0000 0000 0000 0000 0000 0000 0000 0000 0000 0000 0000 0000	000 0000 0000
$\pm\infty$	0 or 1	0000 0000 0000 0000 0000 0000 0000 0000 0000 0000 0000 0000 0000	111 1111 1111
NaN	0 or 1	Any nonzero value	111 1111 1111
Denormalized	0 or 1	Any nonzero value	000 0000 0000

(b)

special numbers. Table 8.21(b) shows the representation of +19.5 in double precision format. Again, the exponent is stored as 4 + bias, or 4 + 1023 = 1027, for this value.

Zero, $\pm\infty$, and NaN have predefined representations in both single and double precision formats. The value 0 has a significand equal to 0 and an exponent with all bits set to 0. Infinity also has a significand equal to 0, but its exponent has every bit set to 1; the sign bit indicates whether the value is $+\infty$ or $-\infty$. An exponent of all 1's and any nonzero significand indicate a value of NaN.

We introduced four types of rounding in Section 8.5: round toward the nearest; round toward 0; round toward $+\infty$; and round toward $-\infty$. The IEEE 754 standard requires that *round toward nearest* be the default rounding method, and that the others be available for the user to select. Thus, two processors that meet the IEEE 754 specification could produce slightly different results for the same computation if they were set to use different rounding methods.

8.6.2 DENORMALIZED VALUES

In the IEEE 754 standard, most values are normalized; that is, they have an implicit leading 1 in their significands. In addition to the special values described previously, however, there is one more class of values that does not use this implied 1, the **denormalized** values. In this standard, a denormalized number has an exponent of all zeroes and a nonzero significand, as shown in Table 8.21.

To illustrate the purpose of denormalized numbers, consider the single precision format. The smallest positive number among normalized values has an exponent of 0000 0001 (= -126) and a significand of 000 0000 0000 0000 0000 0000 (1.0 with the implied 1), or a value of 1.0×2^{-126}. The denormalized representation allows the computer to use even smaller nonzero values. The denormalized format has an exponent of 0000 0000, which is treated as -126. However, the implicit leading 1 is not used here; the 23 bits of the significand represent the entire value. For example, a significand of 100 0000 0000 0000 0000 0000 would represent $0.1 \times 2^{-126} = 2^{-127}$. The smallest positive representation for a single precision denormalized number is .000 0000 0000 0000 0000 0001 $\times$ $2^{-126} = 2^{-149}$. For double precision, the smallest positive representation yields a value of 2^{-1074}.

8.7 SUMMARY

A microprocessor must be capable of processing numeric data in one or more formats if it is to be useful. Unsigned numbers can be stored in non-negative or two's complement format. Algorithms, such as Booth's algorithm, have been developed to add, subtract, multiply, and divide numbers in these formats. The algorithms have been coded in RTL and implemented using digital logic.

Signed numeric formats use a separate bit to denote the sign of a number. The signed-magnitude and signed-two's complement formats are the two most commonly used signed numeric formats. The algorithms and hardware used to perform arithmetic operations on numbers in these formats are based on the algorithms and hardware for unsigned numeric formats.

The binary coded decimal format stores each digit of a decimal number separately. Although this representation requires more bits than traditional binary formats, it is useful for some functions that operate solely on decimal data. BCD is a signed format, and its arithmetic algorithms and hardware are based on those used for the signed-magnitude numeric format.

Digital designers have developed several ways to speed up arithmetic computations, and thus improve system performance. Arithmetic pipelines overlap computations, processing several operations simultaneously. Lookup tables store the results of operations in a lookup ROM, allowing a computer to read, rather than calculate, a result. Wallace trees speed up multiplication by calculating and adding partial products in parallel.

Floating point numbers are used to represent numbers with fractions having a varying number of bits. A floating point number consists of a sign bit, a significand, and an exponent. The significand and exponent determine the precision and gap of a floating point value and, with the sign bit, determine its range. The number of values that can be expressed by a floating point notation can be extended by using denormalized values. Algorithms and hardware used to add, subtract, multiply, and divide these numbers are based on those for the signed numeric formats.

Problems

1 Give the two's complements of the following values. Each number is represented as an 8-bit value.

   a) 64
   b) 33
   c) −1

2 Show the representation of the following values in unsigned non-negative notation and unsigned two's complement notation. Each number is 8 bits.

   a) 29
   b) −128
   c) 199

3 Show the representation of the following values in signed-magnitude notation and signed-two's complement notation. Including the sign bit, each number has a total of 8 bits.

   a) −63
   b) 147
   c) 85

4 What is the result of the following operations on unsigned non-negative numbers?

   a) 1011 0100 − 0111 0111
   b) 0011 1000 + 1100 1101
   c) 1000 1011 + 0111 0100
   d) 0111 0100 − 1000 1011

5 What is the result of the following operations on unsigned two's complement numbers?

a) 1011 0100 − 0111 0111
b) 0011 1000 + 1100 1101
c) 1000 1011 + 0111 0100
d) 0111 0100 − 1000 1011

6 For numbers in unsigned two's complement notation, show that adding two numbers with different signs always produces a valid result.

7 Show the trace of the RTL code for the shift-add multiplication $UV \leftarrow X \cdot Y$ for $X = 9$ and $Y = 14$.

8 Verify that the RTL code for the multiplication $UV \leftarrow X \cdot V$ correctly multiplies 9 and 14.

9 Show the trace of the RTL code for Booth's algorithm for $X = 0110$ and $Y = 1011$.

10 Modify the RTL code for Booth's algorithm to perform the operation $UV \leftarrow X \cdot V$. Show the hardware for the modified algorithm.

11 Show the trace of the RTL code for the restoring division algorithm for $UV = 0110\ 1011$ and $X = 1010$.

12 Show the trace of the RTL code for the non-restoring division algorithm for $UV = 0110\ 1011$ and $X = 1010$.

13 In the shift-subtract division algorithm, combine $G1$ and **2** into one state **1**. Show the modified RTL code and hardware.

14 Modify the restoring shift-subtract division algorithm so $OVERFLOW$ is set only during state 1_2, and not during state **2**.

15 Modify the RTL code for the non-restoring division algorithm for use with unsigned two's complement numbers.

16 Modify the RTL code for the restoring division algorithm for use with unsigned two's complement numbers.

17 Show the trace of the signed-magnitude addition/subtraction algorithm for the following data. All magnitudes are four bits.

a) $X (= +7) + Y (= -9)$
b) $X (= +7) - Y (= -9)$
c) $X (= -7) + Y (= +9)$
d) $X (= -7) - Y (= +9)$

18 Modify the signed-magnitude addition/subtraction algorithm so *OVERFLOW* is set in only one micro-operation. Show the modified RTL code and hardware.

19 Show the trace of the signed-magnitude multiplication algorithm for the following data. All magnitudes are 4 bits.

   a) $X = +7, Y = -9$
   b) $X = -13, Y = +0$
   c) $X = +15, + Y = +15$

20 Design the hardware to implement the RTL code for multiplication of signed-magnitude numbers.

21 Modify the non-restoring division algorithm for unsigned non-negative numbers so that it can be used for signed-magnitude numbers.

22 Modify the restoring division algorithm for unsigned non-negative numbers so that it can be used for signed-magnitude numbers.

23 Show the trace of the BCD addition/subtraction algorithm for the following data. All magnitudes are two digits.

   a) $X (= +7) + Y (= -9)$
   b) $X (= +13) - Y (= +49)$
   c) $X (= +15) + Y (= +15)$

24 Show the trace of the BCD multiplication algorithm for the following values of X and Y. All registers are two digits wide.

   a) $X = +17, Y = +23$
   b) $X = +71, Y = -32$
   c) $X = -39, Y = -10$

25 Design the hardware to implement the RTL code for the BCD multiplication algorithm.

26 Develop the RTL code to implement a non-restoring division algorithm for BCD numbers.

27 Develop the RTL code to implement a restoring division algorithm for BCD numbers.

28 A three-stage pipeline is used to execute the code segment

$$\text{FOR } i = 1 \text{ TO } n \text{ DO } \{X[i] \leftarrow ((A[i] \cdot B[i]) + C[i]) \cdot D[i]\}$$

The first stage multiplies $A[i]$ and $B[i]$ in 20 ns, 15 ns for the multiplication and 5 ns to latch the result. The second stage adds this product to $C[i]$ in 15 ns, which includes the time for the output latch. The last stage performs the final multiplication and also requires 20 ns.

a) What is the clock period for this pipeline?
b) What is the steady-state speedup for this pipeline?
c) For what values of n does the pipeline produce results more quickly than a non-pipelined unit?
d) For what value of n is the speedup exactly 1.5?

29   Show the contents of a lookup ROM that implements a 3-bit $\times$ 3-bit multiplier.

30   Show the Wallace tree to perform 6×6 multiplication.

31   Show the hardware to generate the partial products for the 4×4 Wallace tree of Figure 8.20.

32   Show the outputs of each adder of the Wallace tree of Figure 8.21 for the product 1101 0110 $\times$ 1010 0001.

33   Design the hardware to implement the RTL code for the floating point addition/subtraction algorithm.

9 MEMORY ORGANIZATION

In Chapter 4 we looked at two simple computers consisting of a CPU, an input/output subsystem, and a memory subsystem. The memory subsystem of these computers was comprised solely of ROM and RAM. This is fine for simple computers that perform specific tasks, such as controling a microwave oven. For more complex computers, however, a memory subsystem consisting only of such physical memory would be relatively slow and somewhat limited.

Computer designers utilize several methods to design a memory system hierarchy that maximizes overall system performance at an acceptable cost. One important component of the memory hierarchy is cache memory. This is a high speed memory that reduces the amount of time the CPU needs in order to access data. Another component of the hierarchy is virtual memory, which expands the amount of memory the CPU can access while minimizing cost.

In this chapter, we examine the memory subsystem in detail. We first review the memory hierarchy of computer systems, which was developed to meet the goal of maximizing overall system performance at an acceptable cost. We review two important components of this hierarchy, cache memory and virtual memory, in detail. Then we review some extensions of these principles in real-world applications. Finally, we examine the memory hierarchy in a real world scenario, a Pentium-based personal computer running Microsoft Windows NT.

9.1 Hierarchical Memory Systems

A computer system usually is not constructed using a single type of memory. In fact, several types are used; they comprise the hierarchical memory system of the computer. A typical memory hierarchy is shown in Figure 9.1. The most well known element of the memory subsystem is the **physical memory**, which is constructed using dynamic random access memory (DRAM) chips. When a company advertises a personal computer for sale with 128 MB (or some other amount) of RAM, they are referring to physical memory.

FIGURE 9.1

Generic memory hierarchy

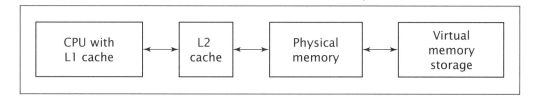

As processor speeds increase, physical memory becomes a bottleneck in system performance. A fast microprocessor may have a clock frequency of over 500 MHz, resulting in a clock period of less than 2 ns; fast DRAM has access times of about 30 times that value. A computer system with only physical memory would spend most of its time waiting for data. This is the motivation behind the use of **cache memory**.

Cache memory is constructed using static RAM (SRAM) chips. It is much faster than DRAM, with access times on the order of 10 ns. It is also much more expensive than the DRAM used to construct the physical memory, which is why computers usually aren't built using only SRAM. In the memory hierarchy, cache memory is situated closest to the microprocessor, since it is preferable to fetch instructions and data from this faster memory. A **cache controller** copies data from physical memory to cache memory before or when the CPU needs it.

Cache memory itself can be arranged hierarchically, usually with two levels. The first level, the **level 1 cache** or **L1 cache**, is incorporated directly into the microprocessor. The external **level 2 cache**, or **L2 cache**, is usually outside of the microprocessor.

On the other end of the hierarchy is **virtual memory**. Consider a processor that supplies a 32-bit address. This processor can directly access 4 GB of memory, but having this much memory raises the cost of a computer system considerably. Virtual memory resolves this problem by swapping data between physical memory and a storage device, usually a hard disk. When, or before, the processor needs the data, the virtual memory management hardware moves the data into physical memory. The virtual memory management hardware also keeps track of which virtual addresses are stored in which physical locations so the processor can access the data properly.

In general, the closer a component is to the processor, the faster it is and the more expensive it is. For the latter reason, memory system components tend to increase in size as they move further from the CPU.

9.2 Cache Memory

As noted earlier, the goal of cache memory is to minimize the processor's memory access time at a reasonable cost. Rather than construct the entire computer system using cache memory, most computers include a relatively small amount of cache memory between the CPU and physical memory. The main design problem with cache memory is with moving instructions and data into cache before the microprocessor tries to access them. If this is done, the processor retrieves the data from the relatively fast cache rather than the relatively slow physical memory, thus improving system performance.

In addition to the cache levels noted earlier, each level may contain two separate caches, one for instructions and the other for data; this is the principle behind the **Harvard architecture** for computers. Instead of having separate caches for instructions and data, it may have one unified cache for both.

There are several types of cache memory, as well as associative memory, a special type of RAM whose data is accessed by its contents, rather than by an address; this memory is used in some cache memory systems and in many virtual memory management systems.

9.2.1 Associative Memory

Cache memory can be constructed using either static RAM or **associative memory** (sometimes called **content addressable memory**), depending on the mapping scheme used. Static RAM is accessed just like most other types of memory: It receives an address and accesses the data at that address. Associative memory is accessed differently, and in this respect is unlike most other types of memory. To access data in associative memory, a portion of the data is specified. The associative memory searches all of its locations in parallel and marks the locations that match the specified data input. The matching data values are then read out sequentially.

To illustrate this, consider a simple associative memory consisting of eight words, each with 16 bits, as shown in Figure 9.2. First note that, in addition to the data bits, each word has one additional bit labeled V. This is the **valid bit**; a 1 in this position indicates that the word contains valid data and a 0 shows that the data is not valid. (Each bit of memory always contains a value, either 0 or 1, whether or not it represents valid data. For that reason, it is necessary to have a flag that explicitly marks the data as valid or invalid. This is important in determining data matches.)

To read a value from associative memory, the CPU must specify the data value to be matched and the bits of this data value that are to be checked. The first value is the **argument**, or data; the second is the **mask**, or **key**. For example, assume that the CPU wishes to access data in the associative memory of Figure 9.2 that has 1010 as its four high-

FIGURE 9.2

The internal organization of associative memory

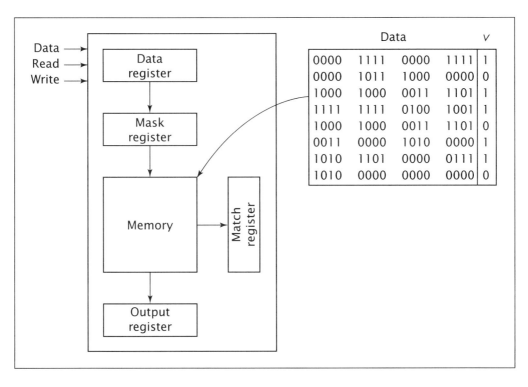

order bits. The CPU would load the value 1111 0000 0000 0000 into the **mask register**. Each bit that is to be checked, regardless of the value it should have, is set to 1; the other bits are set to zero. The CPU also loads the value 1010 XXXX XXXX XXXX into the **data register**. The four leading bits are the value to be matched, and the remaining 12 bits can have any value, since they will not be checked.

At this point, the associative memory checks each location in parallel. A match occurs if (1) for every bit position that has a value of 1 in the mask register, a location's bits are the same as those in the data register, and (2) the location's valid bit is set to 1. Consider location i, whose data bits are $M_{i,j}$ ($15 \geq j \geq 0$ in this example), and whose valid bit is V_i. For mask register bits K_j ($15 \geq j \geq 0$), and data register bits D_j ($15 \geq j \geq 0$), a match occurs if

$$\left(\prod_{j=0}^{15} (K'_j \vee (D_j \oplus M_{i,j})') \right) \wedge V_i = 1$$

This is true when, for every bit in memory location i, either the mask bit is 0 or the memory location bit is the same as the corresponding bit in the data register, and the memory location contains valid data.

Each memory location in the associative memory contains hardware to perform this operation. The associative memory contains a **match register**, which has one bit for each location in the associative memory. If a location generates a match, its bit in the match register is set to 1; otherwise it is set to 0.

In this example, the last two locations match the data in the data register, but only the next-to-last location has its valid bit set. The other location doesn't contain valid data, only a meaningless random bit pattern than by chance happens to match the desired data. As a result of this query, all locations would set their corresponding bits in the match register to 0, except for the next-to-last location, which sets its match bit to 1. Circuitry within the associative memory would then copy this data to its output register, making it available to the CPU. (If more than one match occurs, the data can be read out sequentially. However, for the applications of associative memory in cache and virtual memory systems, at most one match will occur.)

Writing data to associative memory is straightforward. The CPU supplies data to the data register and asserts the write signal. The associative memory checks for a location whose valid bit is 0; if it finds one, it stores the data in that location and sets its valid bit to 1. If no location is found, it must clear a location in order to store the data. How this location is chosen depends on the replacement algorithm employed by the memory.

9.2.2 Cache Memory with Associative Mapping

Associative memory can be used to construct a cache with **associative mapping**, or an **associative cache**. Consider the Relatively Simple CPU of Chapters 6 and 7, which can access 64K of 8-bit memory. An associative cache for this system could be constructed from associative memory that is 24 bits wide. As shown in Figure 9.3, the first 16 bits of each location would consist of a memory address and the last 8 bits would hold the data stored at that address in physical memory. The processor would output the address it wishes to access to the data register of the associative memory and the value 1111 1111 1111 1111 0000 0000 to its mask register. (In practice, the mask register needs to be set only once, not for every memory access, since its contents do not change.) If the data is in the cache, a match is recorded and the data is placed in the output register. If not, it is accessed from physical memory and also copied into the cache.

An alternate configuration uses a much wider memory and acts on **lines**, or **blocks** of data, rather than individual locations. For the same CPU, consider the associative cache shown in Figure 9.4. This memory stores four bytes of data in each location, each of which has the same address in physical memory except for the two low-order bits. In Figure 9.4, the bottom location contains the data for physical

Figure 9.3

Associative cache for the Relatively Simple CPU

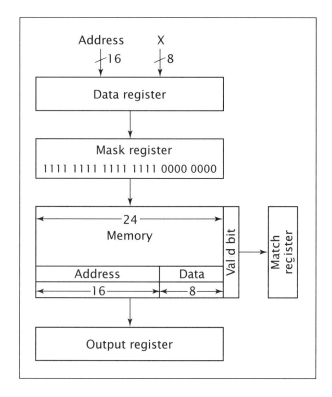

memory addresses 0000H to 0003H. Only the upper 14 bits are used to generate a match, since all data in an associative memory location have physical addresses for which these bits are the same. Once a match is generated, the two low-order bits are used to select the correct byte of data to output to the CPU.

Although the associative memory required for this configuration is much wider than the previous example (46 bits vs. 24 bits), it offers a significant benefit: It takes advantage of **locality of reference**. When an instruction at memory location X is accessed, it is very likely that the next instruction to be executed will be the instruction at location $X + 1$. Assume that, for associative memory with and without data blocks, the CPU must execute the instruction at location 0, which is not in the cache. In the configuration without blocks, the instruction is read from physical memory and copied into the cache. After this instruction has been executed, the CPU requests the instruction at location 1, which also is not in the cache. That instruction is also fetched from physical memory and copied into the cache. The same happens for the instructions at locations 2 and 3.

FIGURE 9.4

Associative cache with a line size of 4 bytes for the Relatively Simple CPU

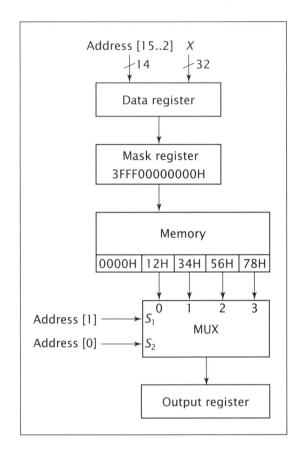

Now consider the same instructions executed using the cache with data blocks. When address 0 is requested, its value is read into the CPU from physical memory. However, the entire block at physical locations 0, 1, 2, and 3 is read into the cache simultaneously. When the CPU next executes the instructions at locations 1, 2, and 3, they are already in the cache and can be fetched from there, rather than from the slower physical memory. For this common pattern of instruction accesses, the cache with data blocks significantly outperforms the cache with single data values.

Data structures also make use of locality of reference. Compilers generally allocate elements of an array to contiguous memory locations. Since programs often access array elements in consecutive order, loading several data values into the cache simultaneously produces the same advantages as loading several consecutive instruction codes simultaneously.

9.2.3   Cache Memory with Direct Mapping

Associative memory is much more expensive than standard SRAM. A cache mapping scheme that can use standard SRAM can be much larger than an associative cache and still cost less. One such mapping scheme is **direct mapping**.

To illustrate direct mapping method, consider a 1K cache for the Relatively Simple CPU, as shown in Figure 9.5. This CPU accesses 64K 8-bit bytes of data using 16 address bits. Since the cache is 1K in size (and $1K = 2^{10}$), the 10 low-order address bits, the **index**, select one specific location in the cache. This location contains three fields. As in the associative cache, each location contains a valid bit to denote whether or not the location has valid data. In addition, a **tag** field contains the high-order bits of the original address that were not a part of the index. In this case, the six high-order bits are stored in the tag field. Finally, the cached data value is stored as the value.

Figure 9.5

Direct-mapped cache for the Relatively Simple CPU

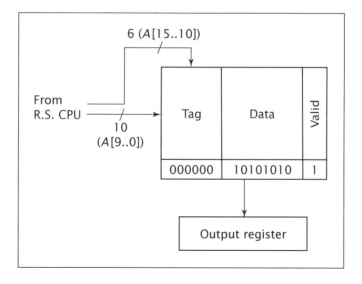

For example, consider location 0000 0011 1111 1111 of physical memory, which contains data 1010 1010. This data can be stored in only one location in cache, the location that has the same 10 low-order address bits as the original address, or 11 1111 1111. However, any address of the form XXXX XX11 1111 1111 would map to this same cache location. This is the purpose of the tag field. In Figure 9.5, the tag value for this location is 00 0000. This means that the data stored at location 11 1111 1111 is actually the data from physical memory location 0000 0011 1111 1111, in this case 1010 1010. Note that if the valid bit was 0, none of this would be considered because the data in the location is not valid.

As with associative cache, direct-mapped cache allows for lines of data. Consider the same size cache using 4-byte lines, as shown in Figure 9.6. Since the cache is still 1K in size, there are 256 lines of 4 bytes each. As in the direct-mapped cache without lines, a 6-bit tag is needed to show which line from main memory is stored in the cache. As is done in the associative cache with lines, the index bits are further partitioned. Of the 10 bits of the index, the eight high-order bits select the line and the two low-order bits select one byte from among the four in the line. This organization takes advantage of locality of reference for both data and program instructions in exactly the same way as does the associative cache with data blocks.

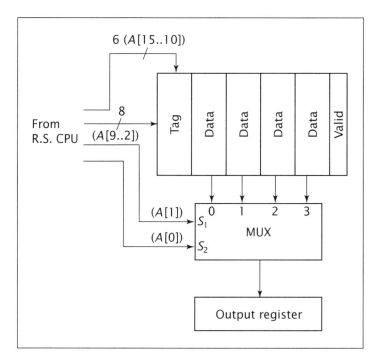

FIGURE 9.6

Direct-mapped cache with a line size of 4 bytes for the Relatively Simple CPU

The direct-mapped cache is much less expensive than the associative cache, but also much less flexible. In associative cache any word of physical memory can occupy any word of cache, but in direct-mapped cache each word of physical memory can be mapped to only one specific location. This can cause problems in certain programs.

For example, consider the following absurd code segment for the Relatively Simple CPU.

> 0000 0000 0000 0000 (0000H):   JUMP 1000H
>
> 0001 0000 0000 0000 (1000H):   JUMP 0000H

The first instruction is fetched and loaded into the cache. Based on its 10 low-order address bits, it is mapped to location 00 0000 0000 of the cache. Its tag value is set to the six high-order address bits, 00 0000. Now it is executed and the CPU fetches the instruction at location 1000H. Its 10 low-order bits are also 00 0000 0000, so it is fetched and loaded into the cache, along with a tag value of 00 0100, overwriting the previous value. This JUMP in turn goes to location 0000H, and the two instructions constantly overwrite each other, even though the remaining locations in cache are available.

A good compiler will allocate the code so this does not happen. However, it does illustrate a problem that can occur due to the inflexibility of direct mapping. Set-associative mapping seeks to alleviate this problem while taking advantage of the strengths of direct-cache mapping method.

9.2.4   Cache Memory with Set-Associative Mapping

A **set-associative cache** makes use of relatively low-cost SRAM (as opposed to associative memory) while trying to alleviate the problems of overwriting data inherent to direct mapping. It is organized like the direct mapped cache, except each address in cache can contain more than one data value. A cache in which each location can contain n bytes or words of data is called an **n-way set-associative cache**.

Consider the 1K, two-way set-associative cache for the Relatively Simple CPU, shown in Figure 9.7. Each location contains two groups of fields, one for each way of the cache. The tag field is the same as in the direct mapped cache, except it is 1 bit longer. Since the cache holds 1K data entries, and each location holds two data values, there are 512 locations in the cache. Nine address bits select the cache location and the remaining 7 bits specify the tag value. As before, the data field contains the data from the physical memory location. The count/valid field serves two purposes: One bit of this field is a valid bit, just as in the other cache mapping schemes; the other is the count value, used to keep track of when data was accessed. This information determines which piece of data will be replaced when a new value is loaded into the cache.

In the code example shown in section 9.2.3, this cache would not overwrite either instruction. The JUMP 1000H instruction would be fetched and stored in one way of cache location 0. Then the JUMP 0000H instruction would be fetched and stored in the other way of the same location. From there, the instructions would be fetched from cache and executed continuously.

Two-way set-associative cache for the Relatively Simple CPU

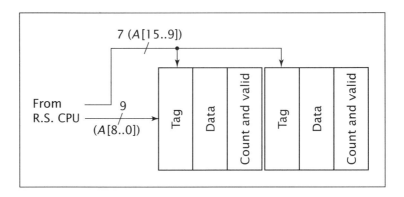

Two-way set-associative cache with a line size of 4 bytes for the Relatively Simple CPU

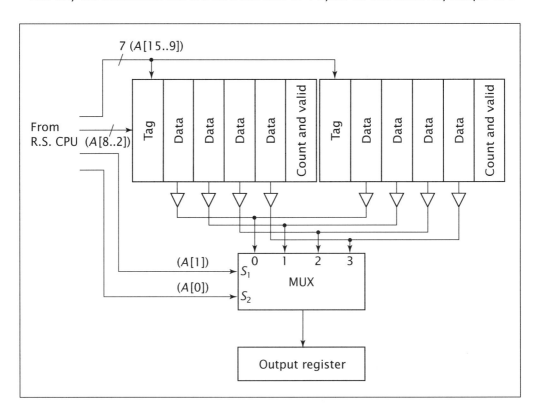

A set-associative cache can make use of data lines, just as a direct-mapped cache can. Of the address bits that select the data, the higher-order bits select a location and the lower-order bits select a data value. A two-way set-associative cache with 4 bytes of data per line is shown in Figure 9.8.

PRACTICAL PERSPECTIVE: Mapping Strategies in Current CPUs

Several trends in cache memory design have become evident over the past few years. Consider the cache configurations for several processors shown in Table 9.A. One obvious trend is that on-chip Level 1 caches are getting larger. As fabrication technologies allow designers to incorporate more components on the CPU chip, designers have added more cache memory.

Table 9.A

Level 1 cache configurations for current CPUs

Processor	L1 cache	Mapping
MIPS R5000 MIPS R10000	32K instruction + 32K data	Two-way set-associative
MIPS R20K	32K instruction + 32K data	Four-way set-associative
Alpha 21164	8K instruction + 8K data	Direct
Alpha 21264	64K instruction + 64K data	Two-way set-associative
Power 603e	16K instruction + 16K data	Two-way set-associative
Power 604e	32K instruction + 32K data	Four-way set-associative
Power 740 Power 750	32K instruction + 32K data	Eight-way set-associative
HP PA-8500 HP PA-8600	512K instruction + 1,024K data	Four-way set-associative
HP PA-8700	768K instruction + 1,536K data	Four-way set-associative

Another trend is in mapping strategies. Current CPUs have moved away from direct mapping in favor of set-associative mapping. Also, designers have been increasing the number of ways in set-associative caches. (If you think of direct mapping as one-way set-associative, these are both the same trend.)

A third trend, not shown in this table, is the inclusion of the Level 2 cache within the CPU. Earlier designs used the cache hierarchy shown in Figure 9.1, with the Level 1 cache inside the CPU and the Level 2 cache outside the CPU. Designers have begun to incorporate the Level 2 cache within the CPU as well, in order to increase overall CPU performance.

9.2.5 Replacing Data in the Cache

When a computer is powered up, it performs several functions necessary to ensure its proper operation. Among other tasks, it must initialize its cache. It does this by setting the valid bits to 0, much like asserting a register's clear input. This assures that no invalid data is improperly marked valid and indicates that the cache is empty.

The computer then (presumably) begins to execute a program. As it fetches instructions and data from memory, it loads these values into the cache. When the cache is empty or sparsely populated, this works well. Ultimately, however, the computer will need to move data into cache locations that are already occupied. The problem becomes deciding which data to move out of the cache and how to preserve that data in physical memory. Note that this applies only to data that is not already in the cache. If the CPU needs to access data that is already in the cache, it simply reads it from the cache; it does not write it into a second location within the cache.

Of the three mapping strategies, direct mapping offers the easiest solution to this problem. Since each address in physical memory maps to one specific location in cache, there is no choice to be made about which value will be replaced. In the 1K direct mapped cache for the Relatively Simple CPU shown in Figure 9.5, the cache currently stores the contents of physical memory location 0000 0011 1111 1111, which is 1010 1010, in cache location 11 1111 1111. If the CPU fetches an instruction from location 0000 0111 1111 1111, it must store the instruction in the same location in cache. The value currently in that location must be written back into its location in physical memory before the new tag and data values are loaded into the cache. If the cache uses lines of data, the entire line is stored back into physical memory and the entire new line is read into the cache.

The associative cache allows any location in physical memory to be mapped to any location in cache. It does not have to move data out of cache and back into physical memory unless it has no location without valid data. There are a number of replacement policies to select the location to be used. A few of the more popular ones are as follows.

1. *FIFO: First In First Out.* The FIFO replacement strategy fills the associative memory from its top location to its bottom location. When it copies data to its last location, the cache is full. It then goes back to the top location, replacing its data with the next value to be stored. (As part of this replacement, it may store the previous value back into physical memory before overwriting it.) It continues this process, working its way down to the bottom location and looping back to the top. This mechanism always replaces the data that was loaded into the cache first among all the data in the cache at that time.

This method requires nothing other than a register to hold a pointer to the next location to be replaced. Its performance is generally good.

2. *LRU: Least Recently Used.* The LRU strategy keeps track of the relative order in which each location is accessed and replaces the least recently used value with the new data. This requires a counter for each location in cache and generally is not used with associative caches. However, it is used frequently with set-associative cache memory.

3. *Random.* As its name implies, the random strategy randomly selects a location to use for the new data. In spite of the lack of logic to its selection of location, this replacement method produces good performance, near to that of the FIFO strategy.

The set-associative cache has restrictions not placed on the associative cache. Each location in physical memory is mapped to one specific location of cache; however, a replacement strategy is needed to determine which way within the location to use. A FIFO replacement policy can be used; this will simply loop through the ways of the location as before. A random policy can also be used. Many set-associative caches are designed using an LRU replacement strategy.

Figure 9.9 shows one location of a four-way set-associative cache. Initially (Figure 9.9(a)) there are three values stored in this location; note that the valid bit of the right-most set is 0. The count value for each data value indicates the relative order of access. The most recently accessed value has a count of 0, the next most recently accessed a count of 1, and so on. In this example, A was most recently accessed, then B; C was the least recently used.

Next, the CPU accesses location D, which also maps to this location in cache. Since there is an unused way in this location, D is written to it; no data is moved out of the cache (Figure 9.9(b)). However, each way's count value must be incremented to reflect the new order of access, D being most recently used, then A, B, and C, respectively.

Now assume the processor accesses location E, which must map to this cache location. The cache location is full, so there is no free ride this time; something has to be moved out of cache to make room for E. Since C was least recently used, indicated by the highest count value, it is removed from the cache (and written back into physical memory), and E is stored in that way. The counters are updated to show the new order of access (Figure 9.9(c)).

Finally, assume that A is accessed next. Since A is already in the cache, nothing needs to be replaced. However, the counters must be updated to reflect the new data access. This requires two actions. First, every set within the location whose count is less than that of the accessed value must be incremented by one. Also, the count of the accessed data must be set to 0, since it is now the most recently

FIGURE 9.9
Contents of one location of a four-way set-associative cache

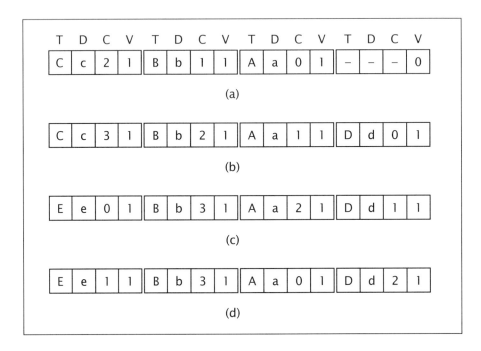

accessed. Sets whose count values were greater than that of the accessed data remain unchanged. In this example, Figure 9.9(d), the counts of E and D are incremented, the count of A is set to 0, and the count of B is unchanged. Ordering the data by count value, this changes the order of accesses (from most recent to least recent) from EDAB to AEDB.

9.2.6 WRITING DATA TO THE CACHE

As a microprocessor executes a program, it may have to write data into memory. If the location to which it writes is currently loaded in the cache, it must update the cached value, and possibly the value in physical memory as well. If the location is not in the cache at the time of the write operation, how it is handled depends on whether or not the cache controller will load it into the cache.

Two methodologies can be used to write data to the cache. In **write-through**, every time a value is written from the CPU into a location in the cache, it is also written to the corresponding location in physical memory. This guarantees that physical memory always contains the correct value, but it requires additional time for the writes to physical memory. In **write-back**, the value written to cache is not always written to physical memory. The value is written to physical memory only once, when the data is removed from the cache. This saves time used by write-through caches to copy their data to physical memory, but also introduces a time frame during which physical memory holds invalid data.

Consider a simple program loop:

```
for i = 1 to 1000 do
        x = x + i;
```

Assume that x is stored in the cache. (In practice, any decent compiler would load it into a CPU register before executing this loop, but ignore that for now.) During the execution of this loop, the CPU would write a value to x 1,000 times. Using a write-back policy would result in only one write to physical memory, while a write-through policy would produce 1,000 writes to physical memory. In this case, write-back offers a significant time savings. In particular, the CPU created a lot of temporary results that aren't needed outside of the loop, the values of x for $1 \le i \le 999$.

Performance, however, is not the only consideration. Sometimes the currency of data takes precedence. This is particularly true in multiprocessor systems, where one processor may need a value already stored in a second processor's cache. Since the first processor can only load the data into its cache from physical memory, and not from another processor's cache, physical memory should have the most current value.

Another situation that must be addressed is how to write data to locations not currently loaded into the cache, a **write miss**. One possibility is to load the location into cache and then write the new value to cache using either write-back or write-through. This is a **write-allocate policy**. A **write–no allocate policy** updates the value in physical memory without loading it into the cache. Caches that employ a write-back policy generally use write-allocate, while write-through caches usually employ a write–no allocate policy.

9.2.7   CACHE PERFORMANCE

The primary reason for including cache memory in a computer is to improve system performance by reducing the time needed to access memory. But claiming to improve performance isn't enough; we must verify and quantify this improvement.

The primary components of cache performance are **cache hits** and **cache misses**. Every time the CPU accesses memory, it checks the cache. If the requested data is in the cache, the CPU accesses the data in the cache, rather than physical memory; this is a cache hit. If the data is not in the cache, the CPU accesses the data from main memory (and usually writes the data into the cache as well). This is a cache miss.

The **hit ratio** is the percentage of memory accesses that are served from the cache, rather than from physical memory. The higher the hit ratio, the more times the CPU accesses the relatively fast cache memory and the better the system performance. The hit ratio can be determined via system simulation or by physically monitoring the computer system hardware while it executes code. Hit ratios of over 90 percent can be achieved under favorable conditions.

The **average memory access time**, T_M, is the weighted average of the cache access time, T_C, plus the access time for physical memory, T_P. The weighting factor is the hit ratio h. T_M can be expressed as

$$T_M = h \, T_C + (1 - h) \, T_P$$

Since T_C is much less than T_P, increasing the hit ratio reduces the average memory access time. Table 9.1 shows this for $T_C = 10$ ns, $T_P = 60$ ns, and various values of h.

Table 9.1

Hit ratios and average memory access times

h	T_M
0.0	60 ns
0.1	55 ns
0.2	50 ns
0.3	45 ns
0.4	40 ns
0.5	35 ns
0.6	30 ns
0.7	25 ns
0.8	20 ns
0.9	15 ns
1.0	10 ns

Now consider how this would work for the mapping strategies discussed earlier. Assume that a computer system has an associative cache, a direct-mapped cache, or a two-way set-associative cache of 8 bytes. (Real caches are much larger; this example is only meant to illustrate the concept.) The CPU accesses the following locations in the order shown. The subscript for each value is the low-order 3 bits of its address in physical memory.

$$A_0 \; B_0 \; C_2 \; A_0 \; D_1 \; B_0 \; E_4 \; F_5 \; A_0 \; C_2 \; D_1 \; B_0 \; G_3 \; C_2 \; H_7 \; I_6 \; A_0 \; B_0$$

Now we determine the hit ratio and average memory access times for this access pattern for each of the three cache configurations, assuming again that $T_C = 10$ ns and $T_P = 60$ ns.

First consider the associative cache. It is initially empty and uses a FIFO replacement policy. Table 9.2 shows the contents of the cache as each value is accessed. Seven out of the 18 accesses are hits, yielding a hit ratio of $h = 0.389$ and an average memory access time of $T_M = 40.56$ ns.

Table 9.2

Cache activity using associative cache

Data	A	B	C	A	D	B	E	F	A	C	D	B	G	C	H	I	A	B
	A	A	A	A	A	A	A	A	A	A	A	A	A	A	A	I	I	I
C		B	B	B	B	B	B	B	B	B	B	B	B	B	B	B	A	A
A			C	C	C	C	C	C	C	C	C	C	C	C	C	C	C	B
C					D	D	D	D	D	D	D	D	D	D	D	D	D	D
H							E	E	E	E	E	E	E	E	E	E	E	E
E								F	F	F	F	F	F	F	F	F	F	F
													G	G	G	G	G	G
															H	H	H	H
Hit?				✓		✓			✓	✓	✓	✓		✓				

The results for the direct-mapped cache are shown in Table 9.3. Its hit ratio is $h = 0.167$ and its average memory access time is $T_M = 50.67$ ns.

Finally, the results using the two-way set-associative cache are shown in Table 9.4. The cache uses an LRU replacement policy; count values are also shown in the table. Note that, because the cache is two-way, only four cache addresses, each with two ways, are used. This

Table 9.3

Cache activity using direct mapped cache

Data	A	B	C	A	D	B	E	F	A	C	D	B	G	C	H	I	A	B
0	A	B	B	A	A	B	B	B	A	A	A	B	B	B	B	B	A	B
C 1					D	D	D	D	D	D	D	D	D	D	D	D	D	D
A 2			C	C	C	C	C	C	C	C	C	C	C	C	C	C	C	C
C 3													G	G	G	G	G	G
H 4							E	E	E	E	E	E	E	E	E	E	E	E
E 5								F	F	F	F	F	F	F	F	F	F	F
6																I	I	I
7															H	H	H	H
Hit?										✓	✓			✓				

Table 9.4

Cache activity using two-way set-associative cache

Data	A	B	C	A	D	B	E	F	A	C	D	B	G	C	H	I	A	B
0	A-0	A-1	A-1	A-0	A-0	A-1	E-0	E-0	E-1	E-1	E-1	B-0	B-0	B-0	B-0	B-0	B-1	B-0
C 0		B-0	B-0	B-1	B-1	B-0	B-1	B-1	A-0	A-0	A-0	A-1	A-1	A-1	A-1	A-1	A-0	A-1
A 1					D-0	D-0	D-0	D-1	D-1	D-1	D-0	D-0	D-0	D-0	D-0	D-0	D-0	D-0
C 1								F-0	F-0	F-0	F-1	F-1	F-1	F-1	F-1	F-1	F-1	F-1
H 2			C-0	C-0	C-0	C-0	C-0	C-0	C-0	C-0	C-0	C-0	C-0	C-0	C-0	C-1	C-1	C-1
E 2																I-0	I-0	I-0
3													G-0	G-0	G-1	G-1	G-1	G-1
3															H-0	H-0	H-0	H-0
Hit?				✓		✓			✓	✓				✓			✓	✓

cache has a hit ratio of $h = 0.389$ and an average memory access time of $T_M = 40.56$ ns.

Now consider the same system, this time with data lines of 2 bytes. The data pairs that comprise the pertinent lines are A and J; B and D; C and G; E and F; and I and H. Using the same replacement policies (FIFO for the associative cache and LRU for the set-associative cache), and the same access times ($T_C = 10$ ns and $T_P = 60$ ns), we measure the performance for each cache again. The associative cache and the two-way set-associative cache each have a hit ratio of $h = 0.611$ and an average memory access time of $T_M = 29.44$ ns. The direct-mapped cache has $h = 0.389$ and $T_M = 40.56$ ns. The traces for the associative, direct, and two-way set-associative caches are shown in Tables 9.5, 9.6, and 9.7, respectively.

Table 9.5

Cache activity using associative cache with a line size of 2 bytes

Data	A	B	C	A	D	B	E	F	A	C	D	B	G	C	H	I	A	B
	A	A	A	A	A	A	A	A	A	A	A	A	A	A	I	I	I	I
C	J	J	J	J	J	J	J	J	J	J	J	J	J	J	H	H	H	H
A		B	B	B	B	B	B	B	B	B	B	B	B	B	B	B	A	A
C		D	D	D	D	D	D	D	D	D	D	D	D	D	D	D	J	J
H			C	C	C	C	C	C	C	C	C	C	C	C	C	C	C	B
E			G	G	G	G	G	G	G	G	G	G	G	G	G	G	G	D
							E	E	E	E	E	E	E	E	E	E	E	E
							F	F	F	F	F	F	F	F	F	F	F	F
Hit?				✓	✓	✓		✓	✓	✓	✓	✓	✓	✓		✓		

TABLE 9.6

Cache activity using direct-mapped cache with a line size of 2 bytes

Data	A	B	C	A	D	B	E	F	A	C	D	B	G	C	H	I	A	B
0	A	B	B	A	B	B	B	B	A	A	B	B	B	B	B	B	A	B
C 1	J	D	D	J	D	D	D	D	J	J	D	D	D	D	D	D	J	D
A 2			C	C	C	C	C	C	C	C	C	C	C	C	C	C	C	C
C 3			G	G	G	G	G	G	G	G	G	G	G	G	G	G	G	G
H 4							E	E	E	E	E	E	E	E	E	E	E	E
E 5							F	F	F	F	F	F	F	F	F	F	F	F
6																I	I	I	I
7															H	H	H	H
Hit?						✓		✓		✓		✓	✓	✓		✓		

TABLE 9.7

Cache activity using two-way set-associative cache with a line size of 2 bytes

Data	A	B	C	A	D	B	E	F	A	C	D	B	G	C	H	I	A	B
0	A-0	A-1	A-1	A-0	A-1	A-1	E-0	E-0	E-1	E-1	B-0	B-0	B-0	B-0	B-0	B-0	B-1	B-0
C 1	J-0	J-1	J-1	J-0	J-1	J-1	F-0	F-0	F-1	F-1	D-0	D-0	D-0	D-0	D-0	D-0	D-1	D-0
A 0		B-0	B-0	B-1	B-0	B-0	B-1	B-1	A-0	A-0	A-1	A-1	A-1	A-1	A-1	A-1	A-0	A-1
C 1		D-0	D-0	D-1	D-0	D-0	D-1	D-1	J-0	J-0	J-1	J-1	J-1	J-1	J-1	J-1	J-0	J-1
H 2			C-0	C-0	C-0	C-0	C-0	C-0	C-0	C-0	C-0	C-0	C-0	C-0	C-1	C-1	C-1	C-1
E 3			G-0	G-0	G-0	G-0	G-0	G-0	G-0	G-0	G-0	G-0	G-0	G-0	G-1	G-1	G-1	G-1
2															I-0	I-0	I-0	I-0
3															H-0	H-0	H-0	H-0
Hit?				✓	✓	✓		✓		✓		✓	✓	✓		✓	✓	✓

This analysis is not strictly accurate, since the time needed to transfer lines of 2 bytes should be greater than the time to load a single data value. It will not require twice the time since there can be some overlap between the two data accesses.

For all of these examples, several early misses occur as the caches are initially filled. As the number of data accesses increases, this initial filling becomes a smaller part of the overall cache performance, its effect being amortized over a larger number of accesses. Thus we should expect the overall hit ratio to increase and the average memory access time to decrease as more data is fetched.

9.3   VIRTUAL MEMORY

Most advanced CPUs can address more memory locations than physically exist in their computers. For example, a computer whose CPU issues 32-bit addresses can directly access 4 GB of memory, much more memory than most computers have. We resolve this problem by using **virtual memory**, which swaps data in and out of physical memory. Virtual memory makes it appear to the CPU that there is more physical memory than is actually present.

To understand how virtual memory works, compare it to cache memory. A cache memory works by moving data to and from physical memory. When the CPU requests data that is stored in cache, it receives this data faster than if it had to retrieve the data from physical memory, thus improving system performance. Some mechanism performs address translation from the physical memory address to the cache memory address so the data can be accessed. Another mechanism moves data from physical memory to the cache and, when necessary, from the cache back to physical memory.

Virtual memory works in a similar manner, but at one level up in the memory hierarchy. A **memory management unit** (**MMU**) moves data between physical memory and some slower storage device, usually a disk. This storage area may be referred to as a **swap disk** or **swap file**, depending on its implementation. Retrieving data from physical memory is much, much faster than accessing data from the swap disk. As with cache memory, it is necessary to translate the CPU address, the **logical address**, to its corresponding **physical memory address**. We also need a mechanism that moves data from the swap disk to physical memory and, if required, from physical memory back to the swap disk. Using virtual memory does not preclude the use of cache memory. Most modern systems use both.

There are two primary methods for implementing virtual memory: paging and segmentation.

9.3.1   PAGING

In paging, the entire range of logical addresses, those addresses that can be output by the CPU, is divided into contiguous blocks called **pages**. Each page is the same size, and each logical address resides in exactly one page. Compilers generally create code such that a page will contain either program instructions or data, but not both. Physical memory is divided into nonoverlapping **frames**; the size of each frame is the same as the size of one page. Figure 9.10 shows one such configuration for the Relatively Simple CPU, which has a logical address space with 64K locations. In this system, there is 16K of physical memory and the page size is 4K.

Paging moves pages from the swap disk to frames of the physical memory so data can be accessed by the processor. Any page can oc-

FIGURE 9.10
One possible memory configuration for the Relatively Simple CPU

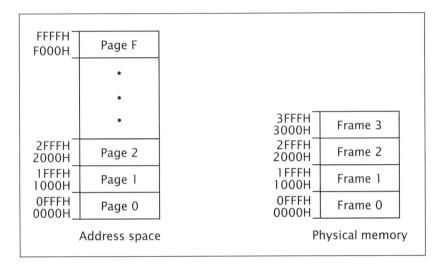

cupy any frame. This leads to several issues that must be resolved by a paging system:

1. When should a page be moved into physical memory?
2. How does the CPU find data in physical memory, especially if its logical address is not the same as its physical address?
3. What happens when all the frames have pages and the CPU needs to access data from a page not currently stored in physical memory?

All of these issues are handled by the memory management unit (MMU). As shown in Figure 9.11, the logical address is output from the CPU to the MMU. The MMU converts this address to a physical address, which it supplies to the cache and physical memory. If the data is not located in physical memory, it generates a **page fault** and moves the page from the swap disk to a frame, removing another page if necessary.

Throughout this process, the CPU has no information as to the actual physical location it is accessing. For example, the Relatively Simple CPU instruction LDAC 4234H is not interpreted as "load the data from logical memory location 4234H, which is actually stored in physical memory location 3234H, into the accumulator." Rather, it is more akin to "load the data from logical memory location 4234H into the accumulator," and it doesn't matter which physical memory location it currently occupies because the MMU will take care of that. Similarly, physical memory doesn't know which logical addresses are mapped to specific physical memory locations. In this example, the memory access is not interpreted as "output the data from location

FIGURE 9.11

MMU configuration within the memory hierarchy

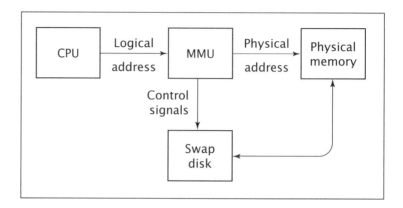

3234H, which corresponds to logical address 4234H." Instead, it is more like "output the data from location 3234H because that is where the MMU says the CPU's logical address is mapped to," and it isn't necessary to know what that logical address really is. Neither the CPU nor memory needs to know the other's memory address because the MMU handles the translation for them.

The MMU uses a **page table** to keep track of which pages are stored in which frames. Consider a page table for the Relatively Simple CPU system described earlier, with 16K of physical memory and 4K page size, as shown in Figure 9.12. The page table contains 16 locations, one for each page in the logical address space. Each location contains a 2-bit field, which denotes the frame in which that page is stored. Since each location must contain some value, whether or not the value represents valid data, each location must also contain a **valid bit** (sometimes called a **presence bit** or a **use bit**). This serves the same purpose as the valid bit in cache memory. There may also be other bits, shown here as the count bits and the dirty bit, which are used when moving pages out of physical memory; their purposes will be explained later in this section. In this example, page 0, corresponding to logical addresses 0000H-0FFFH, is stored in frame 1, physical addresses 1000H-1FFFH. Page 4 (4000H-4FFFH) is stored in frame 3 (3000H-3FFFH) and page 15 (F000H-FFFFH) is stored in frame 0 (0000H-0FFFH). Frame 2 is unoccupied.

The MMU uses the page table to calculate the required physical addresses. To do so, the MMU treats the logical address as two parts, a page number and an offset. Consider the LDAC 4234H instruction being executed on a system whose page table is shown in Figure 9.12. As seen in Figure 9.13, the four high-order bits of the logical address specify the page number and the remaining 12 bits are the **offset**. (The

Figure 9.12

(a) Page table and (b) corresponding physical memory

	Frame	Valid	Count	Dirty
0	0 1	1	1 0	0
1	0 0	0	0 0	0
2	0 0	0	0 0	0
3	0 0	0	0 0	0
4	1 1	1	0 1	1
5	0 0	0	0 0	0
6	0 0	0	0 0	0
7	0 0	0	0 0	0
8	0 0	0	0 0	0
9	0 0	0	0 0	0
A	0 0	0	0 0	0
B	0 0	0	0 0	0
C	0 0	0	0 0	0
D	0 0	0	0 0	0
E	0 0	0	0 0	0
F	0 0	1	0 0	0

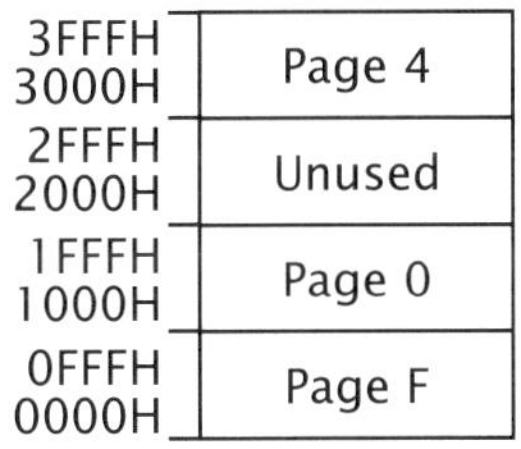 3FFFH 3000H	Page 4
2FFFH 2000H	Unused
1FFFH 1000H	Page 0
0FFFH 0000H	Page F

(a)   (b)

sizes are determined by the page size. Since each page is 4K in size, 12 bits are required to select a location within the page; the remaining bits select the page.) Here, the four high-order bits are 0100. This value is input to the page table as an address, and its contents are output. Since the valid bit is 1, this page resides in physical memory; the frame value 11 indicates that this page is mapped to frame 3 (11 in binary). The frame value is then concatenated with the 12-bit offset to produce the physical address 11 0010 0011 0100, or 3234H. Note that the process is the same for a memory read as for a memory write.

This mapping process works when the page resides in physical memory, but what happens when the page is not currently located in physical memory? For example, what would have happened if the

FIGURE 9.13

Conversion of logical address to physical address using the page table

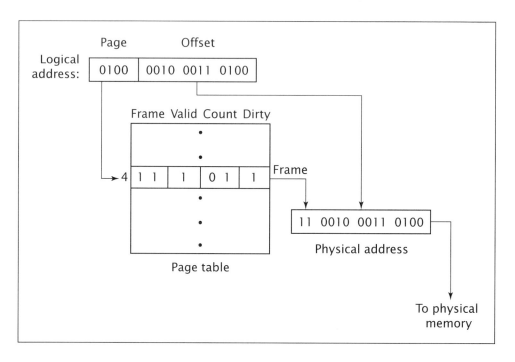

instruction to be executed was LDAC 5234H? In that case, the page number 0101 would have accessed page table location 5, which has a frame value of 00 and a valid bit of 0. The concatenation process will not produce a valid address because this page is not located in physical memory, as denoted by the 0 in its valid bit. This is referred to as a **page fault**.

In a page fault, the MMU would cause the page to be copied from the swap disk to a frame in physical memory. Since frame 2 is unused, it could be placed there. The MMU would then update its page table accordingly, setting the contents of location 5 to frame = 2, valid = 1, count = 0, and dirty = 0, and process the memory read request.

But what happens if all frames in physical memory already contained pages? In this case, the computer system could read the data directly from disk, but overall system performance would plummet. The solution is to clear a page out of physical memory and to move the newly requested page into the vacated frame. This practice of **demand paging** is used by virtually all MMUs.

The problem of deciding which page to replace is similar to that of replacing data in a cache. Its solutions are also similar. The MMU can implement a random, FIFO, or LRU replacement policy in the same way that these policies are used to replace data in an associative cache. If an LRU policy is used, the count bits in the page table keep track of the relative order of page accesses. When a page must be replaced, the page with the highest count value yields its frame to the new page. If a random or FIFO policy is used, the count bits are not needed and are not included in the page table.

When a page is removed from physical memory, one of two things happens to its data. If its contents were not changed, if for example it was read from but never written to, it is simply discarded, since it is the same as the copy on the swap disk. However, if its contents were modified, the new contents must be copied back to the swap disk so the page will produce the correct data when next accessed. This is similar to the write-back approach for cache memory. Because of the great time penalty in writing to the swap disk, MMUs use this method, rather than write-through, to update pages.

Denoting which process should be followed is the role of the **dirty bit**. When a page is loaded into a frame, its dirty bit entry in the page table is set to 0. A memory write operation causes the MMU to set its dirty bit to 1; memory reads do not change the value of the dirty bit. The dirty bit is only checked when the page is to be removed from physical memory. Since many pages are never modified, especially pages containing instructions, this mechanism improves system performance by reducing the number of writes to the swap disk; it introduces relatively little overhead, much less than the savings realized by not writing back unmodified pages.

Just as with caches, which use data blocks, paging takes advantage of locality of reference. Assume an instruction fetch from, say, logical address 0, generates a page fault and causes its page to be moved into physical memory. It is likely that the next instruction to be executed will be located at logical address 1. Because the entire page was moved into memory, this instruction is already in physical memory and does not generate a page fault. The same argument holds for data, as was described in the section on cache memory.

The MMU shown in Figure 9.13 does not optimally translate addresses. There is a time delay associated with reading the frame number from the page table, and this system may read the same value hundreds or thousands of times consecutively as it fetches contiguous instructions. For this reason, MMUs usually contain a **translation lookaside buffer**, or **TLB**, in addition to the page table. It performs the same function as the page table, generating the frame value, but it is faster and thus improves system performance.

A TLB can be constructed using an associative memory, as shown in Figure 9.14. When the CPU outputs a logical address, the MMU forwards it to both its page table and its TLB simultaneously. If the entry is stored in the TLB, it will output the frame number, concatenate it with the offset, and send this address to the cache and physical memory. If there is no match, the address translation proceeds as before. By speeding up the address translation process for recently accessed pages, the TLB takes advantage of locality of reference to improve system performance.

FIGURE 9.14

Conversion of logical address to physical address using the TLB

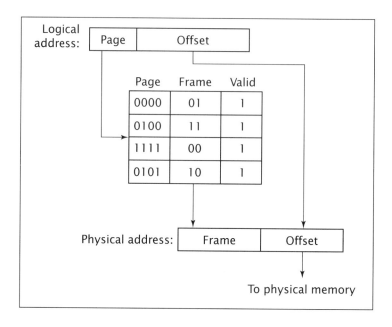

Note that the TLB does not necessarily contain count nor dirty bits, since this information is still held in the page table. Every entry in the TLB is also included in the page table, but the reverse is not necessarily true. In this simple example, the TLB contains one location for each frame, but this is not the case in larger systems.

To illustrate the functioning of the MMU, consider the same memory configuration for a computer that uses the Relatively Simple CPU. It must fetch, decode, and execute the following program.

0000H:	LDAC 4234H
0003H:	STAC 4235H
0006H:	JUMP 1000H
1000H–1063H:	(100 register instructions)
1064H:	JUMP 2000H
2000H–2031H:	(50 register instructions)
2032H:	JUMP 0100H
0100H–01C7H:	(200 register instructions)
01C8H:	JUMP 3000H
3000H–3063H:	(100 register instructions)
3064H:	JUMP 0000H
4234H:	27H (data value)

Table 9.8 shows the contents of the affected locations of the page table and the TLB for this code, using an LRU replacement policy. Each entry in the page table contains entries for the frame (F), valid bit (V), count (C), and dirty bit (D). The TLB entries contain the page (P), its frame (F), and a valid bit (V). The first instruction causes two pages to be loaded into memory: Page 0 contains the instruction and page 4 contains the data to be loaded into the accumulator. Because the instruction is fetched before the data, page 4 has the lower count value.

Table 9.8

Partial page table and TLB values using an LRU replacement policy

Page Table							
Address	**0000H**	**0003H**	**0006H**	**1000H–1064H**	**2000H–2032H**	**0100H–01C8H**	**3000H–3064H**	**0000H**
Page	F V C D	F V C D	F V C D	FV CD	F V C D	F V C D	F V C D	F V C D
0	0 1 1 0	0 1 1 0	0 1 0 0	0 1 1 0	0 1 2 0	0 1 0 0	0 1 1 0	0 1 1 0
1				2 1 0 0	2 1 1 0	2 1 2 0	2 1 3 0	- 0 - -
2					3 1 0 0	3 1 1 0	3 1 2 0	3 1 3 0
3							1 1 0 0	1 1 2 0
4	1 1 0 0	1 1 0 1	1 1 1 1	1 1 2 1	1 1 3 1	1 1 3 1	- 0 - -	2 1 0 0

TLB							
P F V	**P F V**	**P F V**	**P F V**	**P F V**	**P F V**	**P F V**	**P F V**
0 0 1	0 0 1	0 0 1	0 0 1	0 0 1	0 0 1	0 0 1	0 0 1
4 1 1	4 1 1	4 1 1	4 1 1	4 1 1	4 1 1	3 1 1	3 1 1
- -- 0	- -- 0	- -- 0	1 2 1	1 2 1	1 2 1	1 2 1	4 2 1
- -- 0	- -- 0	- -- 0	- -- 0	2 3 1	2 3 1	2 3 1	2 3 1

The next two instructions access the same pages and adjust the counters. The STAC instruction writes data to a memory location in page 4, so the dirty bit for that page entry is set to 1. Also note that the JUMP 1000H instruction does not access location 1000H; it merely sets the program counter to 1000H. This location will not be accessed, and its page will not be loaded into a frame, until the next instruction is fetched.

Next, the instructions in page 1 are executed; the MMU updates the page table and TLB to reflect this. These instructions are register instructions; other than the instruction fetch, they do not access memory. The CPU then executes the instructions at addresses 2000H through 2064H. The MMU adds page 2 to the TLB and its page table. At this point, every frame in physical memory is occupied.

Now the program jumps to location 100H and executes the next block of instructions. Since these instructions are located in page 0, which is already in physical memory, the TLB is not changed. Only the count bits of the page table are modified.

When the program tries to fetch the instruction at location 3000H, it generates a page fault. This time, however, all frames are occupied, so one page must be removed from physical memory to make room for the new page. Page 4, located in frame 1, has the highest count value, so it is the page that must go. Since its dirty bit is 1, caused by the STAC instruction at logical address 3, its contents are written back to the swap disk, and its entries in the page table and TLB are updated by setting its valid bit to 0. Page 3 is then loaded into frame 1 and the values in the page table and the TLB are updated.

After executing the instructions at locations 3000H through 3064H, the program jumps to address 0000H. The page for this instruction is already located in memory, so its page does not have to be reloaded. However, the LDAC instruction must access data at location 4234H, located on page 4, which is no longer in physical memory. This time page 1, in frame 2, has the highest count value, so it is cleared from physical memory. Since its dirty bit is 0 (because the program never wrote data to this page), it is not necessary to write the page back to the swap disk. From here the program would continue in its long, infinite loop.

Now consider the same program run on the same computer system, except this time the MMU uses a FIFO replacement policy instead of LRU. Table 9.9 shows the pertinent section of the page table and the TLB. First notice that the page table has no count bits. Since an FIFO replacement algorithm does not consider the order of page access when selecting the page to replace, they are not needed for this replacement policy. A single counter in the MMU keeps track of the next page to be replaced.

The program proceeds as before, and the MMU moves pages to physical memory frames and updates its page table and TLB. At address 3000H, the MMU selects page 0 to be removed from physical memory, even though it was the source of the previous instruction! Continuing on, the CPU eventually jumps to location 0000H. Since this page was just removed from memory, it must be reloaded. Unfortunately, the next page to be removed is page 4. This page is written back to the swap disk, since its dirty bit is 1, and page 0 is loaded into frame 1. Now the first instruction is executed and page 4 must be loaded back again, even though it was just removed. Since it was moved out before page 0 was loaded, there was no way of knowing it would be needed so soon. Even if it had known this, the FIFO replacement policy would not have taken that into account.

There is one particular facet of this example that isn't true in modern computer systems. In this example, the TLB contained one entry for each frame, and this works well for a system with only four

Table 9.9

Partial page table and TLB values using an FIFO replacement policy

Page Table							
Address	**0000H**	**0003H–0006H**	**1000H–1064H**	**2000H–2032H**	**0100H–01C8H**	**3000H–3064H**	**0000H**
Page	F V D	F V D	F V D	FVD	F V D	F V D	F V D
0	0 1 0	0 1 0	0 1 0	0 1 0	0 1 0	- - 0 -	1 1 0
1			2 1 0	2 1 0	2 1 0	2 1 0	- - 0 -
2				3 1 0	3 1 0	3 1 0	3 1 0
3						0 1 0	0 1 0
4	1 1 0	1 1 1	1 1 1	1 1 1	1 1 1	1 1 1	2 1 0

TLB						
P F V	**P F V**	**P F V**	**P F V**	**P F V**	**P F V**	**P F V**
0 0 1	0 0 1	0 0 1	0 0 1	0 0 1	3 0 1	3 0 1
4 1 1	4 1 1	4 1 1	4 1 1	4 1 1	4 1 1	0 1 1
- - - 0	- - - 0	1 2 1	1 2 1	1 2 1	1 2 1	4 2 1
- - - 0	- - - 0	- - - 0	2 3 1	2 3 1	2 3 1	2 3 1

frames. Real computer systems have thousands of frames; having a TLB with that many entries would be costly. In most computer systems, the TLB contains a relatively small number of entries as compared to the total number of frames. Unlike this example, it is possible to have a page in memory with an entry in the page table but not in the TLB. In this case, entries in the TLB would be updated using a FIFO or LRU replacement policy.

9.3.2 SEGMENTATION

Segmentation is another method of allocating memory that can be used instead of or in conjunction with paging. In its purest form, a program is divided into several **segments**, each of which is a self-contained unit, such as a subroutine or data structure.

Unlike pages, segments can vary in size. This requires the MMU to manage segmented memory somewhat differently than it would manage paged memory. A segmented MMU includes a segment table to keep track of the segments resident in memory. Since a segment can start at one of many addresses and can be of any size, each segment table entry must include the start address and segment size. Some systems allow a segment to start at any address, while others limit the start address. One such limit is found in the Intel X86 architecture, which requires a segment to start at an address that has 0000 as its four low-order bits. A system with this limitation would not need to store these four bits in its segment table, since their value is implicit. (In reality, the X86 architecture has so few segments, no more than six, that it uses individual segment registers rather than a segment table. However, the address translation process is basically the same.)

Figure 9.15 shows a simplified address translation scheme for segmented memory. The logical address is partitioned into a segment number and an offset. The segment number is input to the segment table, which, if the segment is located in memory, outputs the address of the start of the segment and the segment size. (If the segment is not in physical memory, it generates a segment fault, which causes the MMU to load the segment into memory.) The offset is compared to the segment size. If the offset is greater than or equal to the segment size, indicating that the location is not a part of the segment, an error is generated. If the offset has a valid value, it is added to the start of the segment address to generate the correct physical memory address. As

FiGURE 9.15

Conversion of logical address to physical address using segmentation

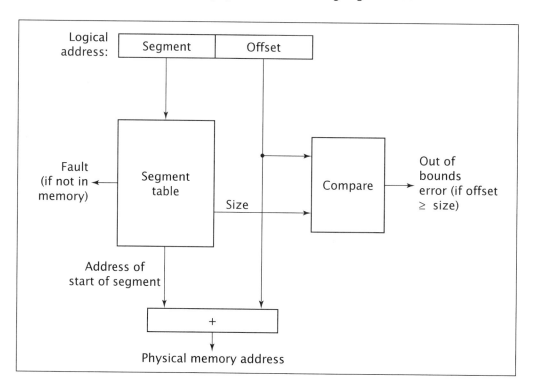

with paging, a segmented MMU can also have a TLB to speed up the generation of segment start addresses and sizes.

Figure 9.15 highlights a serious drawback of segmentation. In paging, the page number is sent to the page table (and TLB) to produce a frame number. This value is concatenated with the offset to produce the physical address. In segmentation, the start address generated by the segment table or TLB is *added* to the offset, a process much more time consuming than concatenation. Furthermore, the MMU must do this for every single memory access.

Because segments can have different sizes, this method has both advantages and disadvantages as compared to paging. Consider the paging example for the Relatively Simple CPU. In the paged memory implementation, each page is of size 4K. A program of size 4K + 1 would require the MMU to allocate two pages of memory, even though the second page would use only one of its 4K locations. This is referred to as **internal fragmentation**. If segmentation is used, a segment of exactly size 4K + 1 can be allocated, thus avoiding this problem.

Segmentation, however, has a problem called **external fragmentation**. Consider the situation shown in Figure 9.16. There are three segments resident in memory and 8K of free space. However, the free space is partitioned such that no segment greater than 3K can be loaded into memory without moving or removing one of the currently loaded segments. Although this can be done, it introduces overhead by moving data back to the swap disk or relocating it in memory, either of which reduces system performance.

Some segments do not have a set length, such as a segment that contains a stack or a data structure with dynamic allocation. For these segments, it is usually not practical to change the size of the segment

FIGURE 9.16

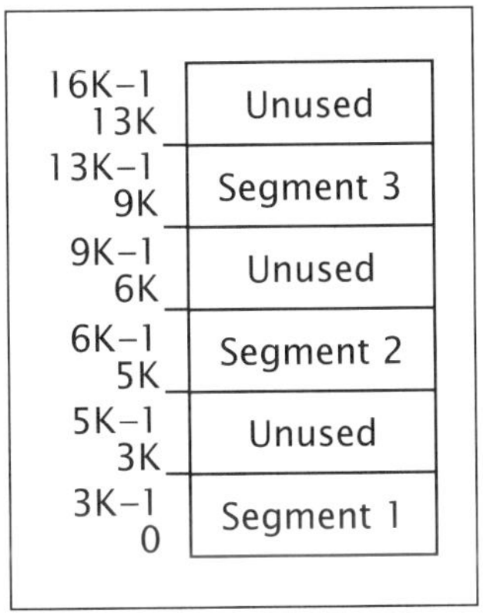

External fragmentation in physical memory caused by segmentation

as its contents change. Eventually the segment would collide with another segment in memory. For that reason, these segments are sized to some maximum size beyond which we would not expect the stack or data structure to grow. Although this does result in some internal fragmentation, it alleviates the problem of resizing and reallocating the segment.

It is possible to combine segmentation and paging by constructing a segment from pages, rather than as one contiguous block of memory. In this scenario, a logical address is broken into three parts: the segment number, the page number, and the offset. As shown in Figure 9.17, the segment number is input to the segment table, just as with nonpaged segmentation. However, instead of outputting a start address, the segment table outputs a pointer to one of several page tables, one for each segment, or an address for one large unified table. (If the segment is not resident in physical memory, it generates a fault.) The page table then outputs the corresponding frame number in physical memory, or issues a fault if the page is not resident in memory. The frame number is concatenated with the offset to produce the physical memory address.

Compared to pure segmentation, using segmentation with paging offers both advantages and disadvantages. The allocation of segments to physical memory is simpler since it is no longer necessary to find one contiguous block large enough to hold the entire segment. The pages that comprise the segment can be located anywhere in physical memory. The tradeoff for this simpler page allocation is that, although external fragmentation is eliminated, internal fragmentation is reintroduced. In addition, it is no longer necessary to explicitly store the size of the segment in the segment table. The valid bits of the page table entries provide the same information by indicating which (and thus how many) pages contain valid data. Finally, when the frame number is generated explicitly, it is no longer necessary to add the offset to a generated value; the quicker concatenation is used instead. However, this comes at the cost of a second level of table lookup, which at least partially mitigates this time savings.

9.3.3 MEMORY PROTECTION

A multitasking operating system may have several different programs, or parts of programs, resident in memory simultaneously. These program components may belong to one user or to different users. The operating system may also have components resident in memory. Some mechanism is needed to ensure that one component does not overwrite another, and that no component can read data from another that it should not be able to access. In addition, a component can be protected from its owner by restricting its mode of access. All of these fall under **memory protection**.

FIGURE 9.17

Conversion of logical address to physical address using segmentation with paging

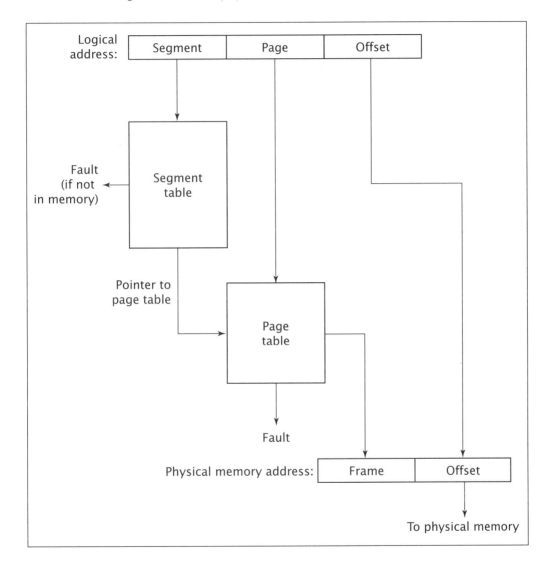

Although it could be possible to protect individual memory locations, if the appropriate mechanisms were incorporated into the computer system, it is impractical to do so. The overhead associated with protecting every memory location would be prohibitive. Even if this were feasible, it would not be necessary. Contiguous memory locations generally hold consecutive instructions of a program or consecutive data values of a data structure. In either case, the adjacent locations would require exactly the same protections.

A preferable option is to protect the segment or page, rather than individual locations. This produces the desired memory protection at an acceptable cost in terms of overhead. To accomplish this, **protection bits** are added to each entry in the segment or page table. (If segmentation with pages is used, it is only necessary to include protection bits in the segment table and not in the page tables.) These bits might signify that a segment or page is read only, read/write, or execute, and that it is a user segment or page or is owned by the operating system. This is also referred to as **supervisor** or **kernel mode**. Also, it is necessary to keep track of which segments or pages are associated with which users (or the kernel) so that one user cannot improperly read or overwrite another's data.

A multitasking operating system may allow more than one user or process to access a segment. Shared resources, such as the dynamic link libraries (DLLs) in Microsoft Windows, fall into this category. So do shared data structures. For example, a shared database should allow more than one user to read, and possibly write, data. In these cases, the operating system must set the appropriate memory protection for each user. It must also make sure that it does not remove the pertinent segment or page from memory until all users are finished with it.

9.4   Beyond the Basics of Cache and Virtual Memory

So far this chapter has presented the fundamental principles and simplified implementations of the cache memory and virtual memory components of a hierarchical memory system. In practice, more complex structures are needed as the size of memory increases.

9.4.1   Beyond the Basics of Cache Memory

The primary difference between cache memory as presented in this chapter and as implemented in the real world is that two levels of cache are usually used in most computers. As the manufacture of microprocessors grows more sophisticated, incorporating more cache directly within the microprocessor becomes possible. Including the Level 1 cache within the CPU improves the performance of the computer system; including the Level 2 cache within the CPU improves performance even more.

Another difference between our examples and the real world is the use of **split caches**. Instead of having a unified Level 1 cache that holds both instructions and data, an L1 cache is usually designed as two parallel caches: an instruction cache that stores only program

PRACTICAL PERSPECTIVE: Cache Hierarchy in the Itanium Microprocessor

Intel's Itanium microprocessor takes multiple levels of cache memory to the extreme. Its on-chip Level 1 cache is a split cache; both the instruction cache and data cache are four-way set-associative. Its Level 2 cache is also on-chip, but it is a unified, six-way set-associative cache.

The Itanium is manufactured as multiple components on a single die; the microprocessor itself is a single component. One of these components is the Level 3 cache. The Level 3 cache cannot supply data as quickly as the other two caches because it is not on-chip, but it is faster than external caches since it is on-die. In addition to these three caches, the Itanium also supports an external, Level 4 cache.

instructions and a data cache that stores only data. The compiler usually assigns instructions and data to different pages or segments, which simplifies the assignment of values to the caches. Also, if self-modifying code is not used, it is not necessary to include a write-back nor write-through capability in the instruction cache, since its data is always read, and never written by the CPU. (As a rule, self-modifying code should never be used; there is always a way to program a task without resorting to self-modifying code. Any efficiencies gained are more than mitigated by increased difficulties in debugging.)

9.4.2   Beyond the Basics of Virtual Memory

For the small computer systems shown in this chapter, the paging and segmentation schemes for managing virtual memory work well. However, their sizes become prohibitively large as the size of the virtual memory address space increases. For example, a CPU with a 32-bit address size, capable of accessing 4 GB of memory, and a 16K page size, would require 256K ($2^{18} = 262,144$) entries in its page table.

One way to resolve this problem is to implement the page table as a multilevel hierarchy. A primary table contains pointers to secondary tables (or portions of a unified secondary table). Figure 9.18 shows one way this could be implemented. The primary table would always be stored in memory in a page owned by the operating system. Secondary tables, or portions of the secondary table, could be moved in and out of physical memory as needed, just like any other page. This can be extended to multiple levels; the Alpha microprocessor can support up to four levels of page tables.

FIGURE 9.18
Multilevel page table hierarchy

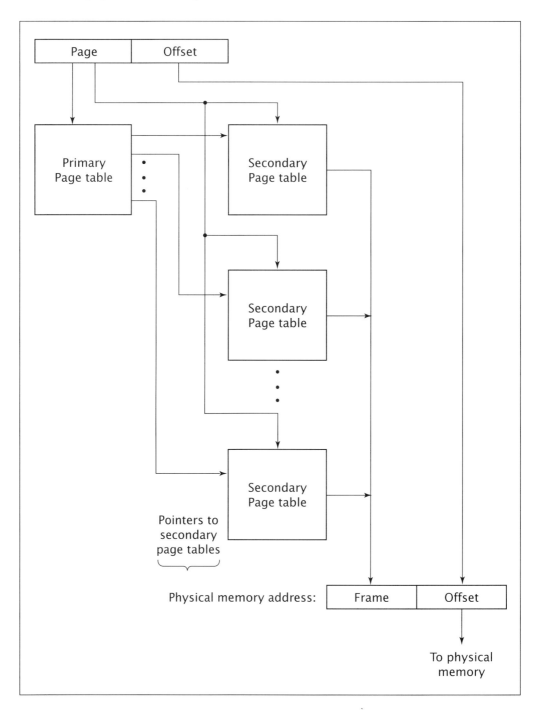

9.5   REAL WORLD EXAMPLE: MEMORY MANAGEMENT IN A PENTIUM/WINDOWS PERSONAL COMPUTER

To see how cache and virtual memory are used in real computers, consider a personal computer that has an Intel (original) Pentium microprocessor and runs Microsoft Windows NT. First we look at the system's cache memory, and then we examine its virtual memory manager. The memory hierarchy for this system is shown in Figure 9.19.

FIGURE 9.19

Memory hierarchy for a Pentium/Windows NT computer

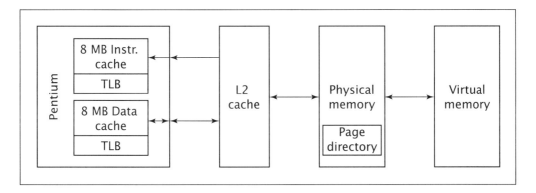

The system shown in Figure 9.19 has 16K of L1 cache within the Pentium microprocessor. The cache is divided evenly, with 8K for instructions (code) and 8K for data. The code cache is two-way set-associative with a line size of 32 bytes. Each line has a 20-bit tag. The entries in this cache are write protected. The CPU cannot write data to the cache; data can only be loaded from physical memory. The code cache also has its own 32-entry translation lookaside buffer, a cache within the cache, to translate the virtual addresses supplied by the microprocessor to the corresponding physical addresses used by physical memory. The TLB is constructed using associative memory. (This essentially implements virtual address mapping; the MMU uses these TLBs as well.) The code cache uses a pseudo-LRU replacement policy.

The data cache is also two-way set-associative with a line size of 32 bytes. It also has a TLB, but its TLB is larger than the TLB of the code cache. The data cache TLB has 64 entries for page of size 4 KB and eight entries for pages of size 4 MB. (The MMU also uses the TLB of the data cache to perform page translation.) It also uses a pseudo-LRU replacement policy.

Unlike the code cache, the CPU can write data to the data cache. Each individual line can be set for either write-back or write-through.

Different lines with different write policies can occupy the cache simultaneously. To support systems with multiple caches, particularly multiprocessor systems, the data cache supports the MESI protocol to maintain cache coherence. (See Chapter 12 for a discussion of cache coherence and this protocol.)

The personal computer also has an external L2 cache. The cache is constructed using SRAM and has a memory access time of approximately 10 ns. It is four-way set-associative and has a size of 256 KB. Unlike the L1 caches within the microprocessor, the L2 cache is a unified cache. It holds both instructions and data.

Unlike cache memory, which is managed exclusively by the microprocessor, virtual memory is handled by both the Pentium and Windows NT. Together, they support a 4-GB address space for each process. The low-order 2 GB of the address space is allocated to the individual processes, and the upper 2 GB are reserved for operating system components. This scheme allows different processes to use the same physical memory for operating system services while maintaining separate memory areas for their own applications.

The Pentium microprocessor can use either segmentation or paging, but the Windows NT virtual memory manager uses paging. The 10 high-order bits of the 32-bit virtual address select an entry in the **page directory**, which is stored in physical memory. This entry specifies the base address of a page table, as well as other bits that specify attributes of the page table, such as whether the table has been accessed, whether write-back or write-through is to be used, and whether or not the table is writable. The next 10 bits of the virtual address specify an offset, which is added to the base address of the page table. This sum generates an address within the page table that contains the address of the frame in physical memory and other information, such as a dirty bit. The frame address is concatenated with the 12 low-order bits of the virtual address to produce the physical address of the data to be accessed.

In addition to this page translation mechanism, the Pentium uses TLBs to speed up address translation. It uses the TLBs within the code and data caches for this purpose, rather than having separate TLBs that would basically contain the same information.

9.6   SUMMARY

The memory hierarchy of most computer systems includes not only physical memory, but also cache and virtual memory. Cache memory is a high-speed memory situated between the CPU and physical memory; one level of cache is often located within the CPU chip. Cache memory may be unified or split into separate instruction and data caches. The performance of cache memory is largely determined by its hit ratio and average memory access time.

Cache memory may employ one of three mapping strategies. Associative mapping is the most flexible, but it requires a relatively expensive associative memory rather than standard static RAM. Direct mapping is less flexible, but also less expensive. Set-associative mapping offers the advantages of direct mapping as well as some of the flexibility of associative mapping. Caches with set-associative memory employ FIFO, LRU, or Random replacement policies.

Virtual memory uses auxiliary storage, such as a disk, to expand the memory space available to the processor. It is much less costly than adding physical memory to a system and does not significantly degrade system performance. A memory management unit maps the logical addresses issued by the processor to their corresponding physical addresses.

A virtual memory system may use paging or segmentation. A paging system moves frames of fixed size between physical memory and virtual memory. The MMU uses page tables and translation lookaside buffers to keep track of which frame corresponds to each page. A system using segmentation manages segments of varying size. This reduces internal fragmentation but can introduce external fragmentation. It is possible to combine these two methods in a system that uses variable-sized segments constructed using a variable number of fixed-size pages.

Problems

1 For the 16×8 associative memory whose contents appear in the following table, what values should be stored in the data and mask registers to select the last location? Assume the first 8 bits are a tag and the rest are data.

Data	Valid
0000 1001 0010 0111	0
1011 0110 0011 0001	1
0101 1111 1100 0000	1
1101 0110 0111 1000	1
0000 0000 0000 0000	1
1111 0000 0111 1111	0
0110 1111 1000 0000	1
1111 0000 1111 0000	1

2 Which value(s) of the associative memory of Problem 1 are accessed under the following conditions?

a) Mask = 1111 0000 0000 0000, Data = 0000 1001 0010 0111
b) Mask = 0000 0000 0000 1111, Data = 1111 1111 1111 0000
c) Mask = 1111 0000 0000 1111, Data = 1111 0000 0000 1111

3 Show the layout of a cache for a CPU that can address 1M × 16 of memory; the cache holds 8K × 16 of data and has the following mapping strategies. Give the number of bits per location and the total number of locations.

a) Fully associative
b) Direct mapped
c) Two-way set-associative
d) Four-way set-associative

4 Repeat Problem 3 for a CPU that can access 256K × 8 of data and a 16K × 8 cache.

5 A computer system using the Relatively Simple CPU is to include a 1K associative cache with a line size of 2 bytes.

a) How many bits are in each location of the cache?
b) What mask value is needed for the associative memory?

6 For the computer system of Problem 5, show the contents of the cache after each instruction of the following Relatively Simple CPU code has been executed. (All values are given in hexadecimal.)

```
   0:  LDAC 4234
   3:  CLAC
   4:  JMPZ 000A
   7:  JUMP 0000
   A:  INAC
   B:  MVAC
   C:  ADD
   D:  STAC 0927
  10:  JUMP 0000
4234:  55
4235:  29
```

7 Repeat Problem 6 for a system with a 16-word direct-mapped cache.

8 Repeat Problem 6 for a system with a 16-word direct-mapped cache with a line size of 4 bytes.

9 Repeat Problem 6 for a system with a 32-word two-way set-associative cache.

10 Repeat Problem 6 for a system with a 32-word two-way set-associative cache with a line size of 2 bytes.

11 Repeat Problem 6 for a system with a 32-word two-way set-associative cache with a line size of 4 bytes.

12 A computer based on the Relatively Simple CPU contains a 16-word associative cache with an FIFO replacement policy. Show the contents of the cache during and after the execution of the following code. Also give the hit ratio for this program on this system.

```
   0:  LDAC 4234
   3:  STAC 4235
   6:  MVAC
   7:  INAC
   8:  ADD
   9:  JPNZ 0020
   C:  JUMP 0010
   F:  NOP
  10:  CLAC
  11:  JUMP 0020
  20:  LDAC 4235
  23:  JUMP 0029
  26:  JUMP 0000
  29:  AND
4235:  55
```

13 Repeat Problem 12 for a system with a 16-word associative cache with a line size of 2 bytes.

14 Repeat Problem 12 for a system with a 16-word direct-mapped cache.

15 Repeat Problem 12 for a system with a 16-word direct-mapped cache with a line size of 2 bytes.

16 Repeat Problem 12 for a system with a 16-word four-way set-associative cache with an LRU replacement policy.

17 Repeat Problem 12 for a system with a 16-word two-way set-associative cache with a line size of 2 bytes and an LRU replacement strategy.

18 A computer system has a cache with $T_C = 8$ ns and physical memory with $T_P = 65$ ns. If the hit ratio is 75 percent, what is the average memory access time?

19 A computer system with a cache has a physical memory with $T_P = 75$ ns, a hit ratio of 65 percent, and an average memory access time of $T_M = 39.9$ ns. What is the access time for the cache?

20 A computer system has a cache with $T_C = 10$ ns, a hit ratio of 80 percent, and an average memory access time of $T_M = 24$ ns. What is the access time for physical memory?

21 A computer system has a cache with $T_C = 10$ ns, physical memory with $T_P = 55$ ns, and physical memory with access time $T_M = 40$ ns. What is the hit ratio?

22 The following program is run on a computer system with the Relatively Simple CPU, which includes a 1K four-way set-associative cache. What is the hit ratio for this program on this system?

$$
\begin{array}{rl}
0: & \text{JUMP } 1000 \\
1000: & \text{JUMP } 2000 \\
2000: & \text{JUMP } 3000 \\
3000: & \text{JUMP } 4000 \\
4000: & \text{JUMP } 0000 \\
\end{array}
$$

23 A computer system using the Relatively Simple CPU has 4K of physical memory and uses 1K pages. Show the contents of the page table as the computer executes the following code. The MMU uses a FIFO replacement strategy.

$$
\begin{array}{rl}
0: & \text{LDAC } 4234 \\
3: & \text{JUMP } 1000 \\
10: & \text{JUMP } 3000 \\
100: & \text{JUMP } 1100 \\
1000: & \text{STAC } 4235 \\
1003: & \text{JUMP } 2000 \\
2000: & \text{JUMP } 0010 \\
3000: & \text{JUMP } 0100 \\
\end{array}
$$

24 Assume the computer of problem 23 has a two-entry TLB in its MMU. Show the contents of the TLB during the execution of the same code. Assume the TLB uses a FIFO replacement strategy.

25 Repeat Problem 24 using an LRU replacement strategy.

26 A computer system using the Relatively Simple CPU has 16K of physical memory and a segmented MMU. Given the following segment table, indicate the physical memory location corresponding to the following logical addresses.

    a) 554H

    b) 2100H

    c) 7501H

Address	Start	Size	Valid
0	1000	928	1
1	1800	100	0
2	1F00	231	1
3	1000	136	0
4	2C00	420	1
5	0000	A00	0
6	2222	555	0
7	3500	458	1
8	3000	55	0
9	3000	433	0
A	1157	321	0
B	0343	17	0
C	0100	525	0
D	0100	58	0
E	1F00	37	0
F	0400	237	1

27 For the same computer and segment table in Problem 26, what logical addresses correspond to the following physical addresses?

    a) 0631H

    b) 0140H

    c) 3001H

28 A computer system using the Relatively Simple CPU has 8K of physical memory and a segmented MMU with paging. The page size is 1K and a unified page table is used. For the following segment and page tables, give the physical memory locations corresponding to the following logical addresses.

    a) 0435H

    b) C238H

    c) CB21H

Segment table				**Page table**		
Address	**Page**	**Valid**		**Address**	**Frame**	**Valid**
0	05H	1		3FH	X	0
1	X	0		...	X	0
2	X	0		3BH	4	1
3	X	0		3AH	1	1
4	02H	1		39H	2	1
5	X	0		...	X	0
6	X	0		1CH	3	1
7	X	0		1BH	0	1
8	1BH	1		...	X	0
9	X	0		07H	0	0
A	X	0		06H	7	1
B	X	0		05H	5	1
C	39H	1		...	X	0
D	X	0		02H	6	1
E	X	0		01H	X	0
F	X	0		00H	X	0

29 For the same computer and tables of Problem 28, what logical addresses correspond to the following physical addresses?

    a) 543H

    b) 677H

    c) 1401H

30 A computer system using the Relatively Simple CPU has 16K of physical memory and a two-level paged MMU; the page size is 1K. For the following segment table and page tables, what physical addresses correspond to the following logical addresses?

    a) 0000H

    b) 4961H

    c) FFFFH

SEGMENT TABLE		
Ad	**Pg**	**V**
0	1	1
1	3	1
2	2	1
3	0	1

PAGE TABLE 0		
Ad	**Fr**	**V**
F	F	1
...	X	0
8	7	1
...	X	0
0	X	0

PAGE TABLE 1		
Ad	**Fr**	**V**
F	X	0
...	X	0
D	D	1
...	X	0
0	8	1

PAGE TABLE 2		
Ad	**Fr**	**V**
F	X	0
...	X	0
5	2	1
...	X	0
0	X	0

PAGE TABLE 3		
Ad	**Fr**	**V**
F	X	0
...	X	0
2	3	1
...	X	0
0	X	0

31 For the computer system and tables of Problem 30, what logical addresses correspond to the following physical addresses?

    a) 0912H

    b) 3456H

    c) 1FEDH

32 Given the following logical addresses and the physical addresses to which they are mapped, show the page table entries for the computer system of Problem 30. The values in the segment table are the same as shown in Problem 30.

    a) Logical address: 1534H; physical address: 3134H

    b) Logical address: 2492H; physical address: 1892H

    c) Logical address: BA07H; physical address: 2A07H

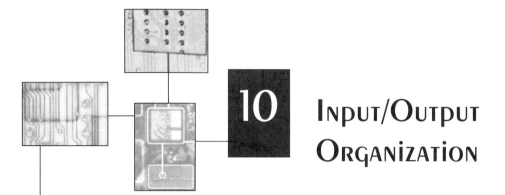

10 Input/Output Organization

In order to perform a useful function, computers must be capable of interacting with the outside world and devices other than memory. A personal computer, for example, must be able to accept user input via a keyboard and mouse, and to output results to a monitor or printer. It should be able to read data from and write data to hard and floppy disks. It may also be configured to access the outside world via a modem or network interface. Even small, embedded computers, such as those found in microwave ovens and other consumer appliances, input data from sensors and output signals to control the function of the appliance.

All of these are grouped into the category of input/output, or I/O, devices. Some, such as the keyboard, are input only; others are output only, such as the monitor. Still others, including the hard disk and modem, can both input and output data. Although their functions are very different, their interfaces with the CPU are largely the same. (See Section 4.4 for a basic description of these interfaces.)

In this chapter we examine input/output devices and their interfaces in greater detail. We also review programmed I/O and its implications for the CPU. Next, we introduce several methods for improving I/O performance, and thus system performance. These include interrupts, direct memory access, and I/O processors. Serial communication is then studied. Finally, we examine two popular serial communication standards, the RS-232-C serial interface and the universal serial bus (USB).

10.1 Asynchronous Data Transfers

Recall from Chapter 4 that an input/output device and CPU are connected by the system's address bus, data bus, and control bus. As shown in Figure 10.1, the address bus is output from the CPU and read in by the I/O device interface. The data bus may be bidirectional, as shown in the figure, or data may flow in only one direction if the device is input only or output only. The control bus may have some signals that go from the CPU to the device and others that travel in the opposite direction, but there should not be any individual control signals which are bidirectional.

Figure 10.1

Connections between a CPU and an I/O device

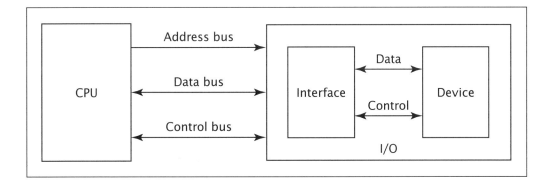

This type of interface is used for **synchronous data transfers**. Synchronous transfers usually occur when peripherals are located within the same computer as the CPU because their close proximity allows them to share a common clock and because data does not have to travel very far physically, which becomes a concern at higher clock frequencies.

When synchronous transfers are not viable, a computer can make use of **asynchronous data transfers**. Asynchronous transfers use control signals and their associated hardware to coordinate the movement of data. These data transfers do not require that the source and destination use the same system clock. There are four types of asynchronous data transfers, distinguished by whether the source or destination initiates the transfer, and by whether or not handshaking is used.

10.1.1 Source-Initiated Data Transfer

One of the simplest asynchronous transfers is the **source-initiated data transfer without handshaking**. In this mode, the **source** outputs its data, then strobes a control signal for a set amount of time; the **destination** device reads in the data during this time. The source device next deasserts the strobe and stops outputting data. Figure 10.2(a) shows the timing sequence for this type of transfer. The destination device never sends any information back to the source, so the source cannot know for sure whether the data was received. This

FIGURE 10.2

Source-initiated data transfer without handshaking: (a) timing and (b) implementation

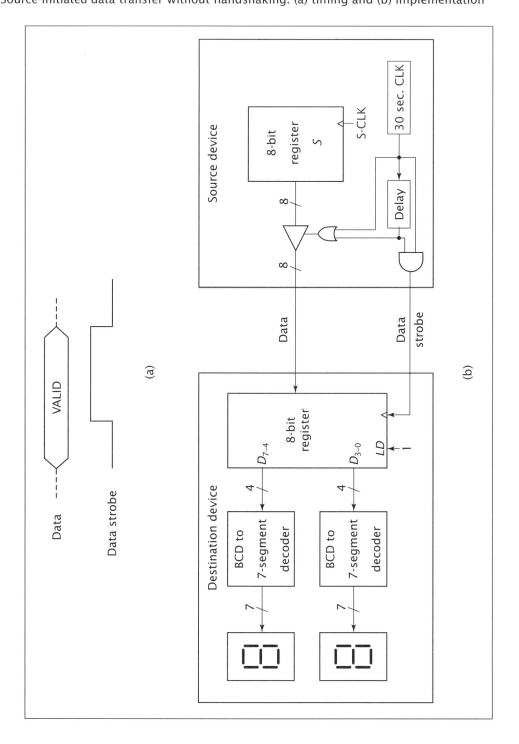

limits the usefulness of this type of transfer to certain applications. To understand this, imagine a classroom situation in which the professor writes on the blackboard and the students stare at the blackboard, giving no indication of whether or not they understand what was written. The professor has implemented a source initiated data transfer without handshaking. The professor is the source, the student is the destination, and the information written on the blackboard is the data.

Figure 10.2 shows an output device consisting of two seven-segment LEDs. Every 30 seconds, the source device sends an updated value to the output device. The output device loads this value into an 8-bit register; the register's outputs are converted to the appropriate signals to show the two digits on the LEDs.

The source is usually not the CPU but specialized interface chips designed to perform asynchronous transfers. These chips also interface with the CPU via synchronous interfaces. The LED example in Figure 10.2 is modeled as an 8-bit register, S, which is loaded with the new display value by the CPU. The synchronous interface with the CPU is not shown.

A circuit to realize this transfer is shown in Figure 10.2(b). A clock with a period of 30 seconds enables the tri-state buffers, which causes valid data to be made available to the output module. After a set delay, to account for the propagation delay of the tri-state buffers and to allow data to become stable, the **data strobe** signal is set high. (Even at the speed of electrons, nothing is instantaneous.) This rising edge causes the output device register to load in the new value, which in turn is passed through the decoders and is displayed on the seven-segment LEDs. When the 30-second clock goes low, the data strobe is set to 0 and, after a delay, the tri-state buffers are disabled and valid data is no longer available to the destination device. At this point, however, the output device has already read in this data, so it is no longer necessary for the source to output the data.

10.1.2 Destination-Initiated Data Transfer

In some cases, the destination device, rather than the source, initiates the data transfer. In **destination-initiated data transfer without handshaking**, the destination device transmits a data strobe signal to the source device which, after a brief delay, makes data available. After a set delay to ensure that valid data is ready, the destination device reads in this data and deasserts the data strobe. This in turn causes the source to stop transmitting valid data. This is analogous to the classroom situation in which a student (the destination) asks the professor (the source) a question. The professor gives the answer (the data) and then continues lecturing, not waiting for confirmation that the answer was heard by the student. The timing for this is shown in Figure 10.3(a).

FIGURE 10.3

Destination-initiated data transfer without handshaking: (a) timing and (b) implementation

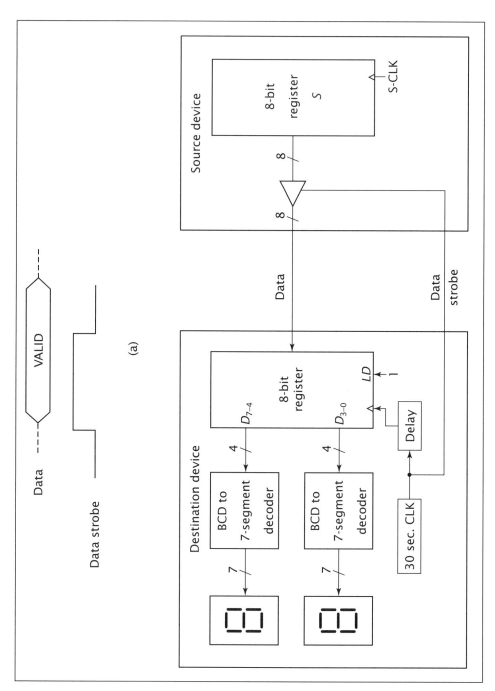

One possible hardware configuration to update the two-digit LED using destination-initiated transfer is shown in Figure 10.3(b). The 30-second clock goes high, setting the data strobe signal to 1. This enables the tri-state buffers and causes the source to transmit valid data. After a set delay to ensure that data is ready, the destination register reads the data. Next, the clock goes low, deasserting the data strobe and removing valid data.

10.1.3   Handshaking

The types of data transfers just described are useful with lower-cost peripherals, which do not have to confirm receipt of data. They are appropriate for transfers that always occur within a set amount of time. But some devices, particularly electromechanical devices, do not require the same amount of time for every transfer. These devices can use **handshaking** to coordinate their transfers.

Handshaking uses an additional control signal to indicate that data is ready or has been read in. In real-world applications, the source or destination device performs necessary operations before signaling that it is ready for data transfer.

The timing for a **source-initiated data transfer with handshaking** is shown in Figure 10.4(a). The source sets the data request signal high and then makes valid data available to the destination device. After the requisite delay to allow the data to stabilize, the destination device reads in the data. (In practice this is a minimum delay; the actual delay depends on how quickly the destination becomes ready to accept data.) Once the destination device has read the data, it sends a **data acknowledge** signal to the source. This tells the source that the destination has read in and no longer needs this data. The source sets its data request line low and stops sending data. The destination then resets its data acknowledge signal. In our classroom example, the professor (source) says she will write something on the blackboard that the students (destination) should know for the upcoming test, and that they should copy it into their notes. She then writes the information (data) on the blackboard, and leaves it there until the students say they have written it down (data acknowledge). She then erases the blackboard and continues her lecture.

One possible hardware configuration to update a seven-segment display using source-initiated data transfer with handshaking is shown in Figure 10.4(b). When the 30-second clock goes high, the data request flip-flop is set to 1; this sets the data request signal to 1. This in turn enables the tri-state buffers and makes valid data available to the destination. After the usual delay, the destination reads in the data and sends a data acknowledge signal to the source device. This clears the data request flip-flop, sets the data request signal low, and invalidates the data. (Note that this flip-flop has an asynchronous clear

FIGURE 10.4

FIGURE 10.4

Source-initiated data transfer with handshaking: (a) timing and (b) implementation

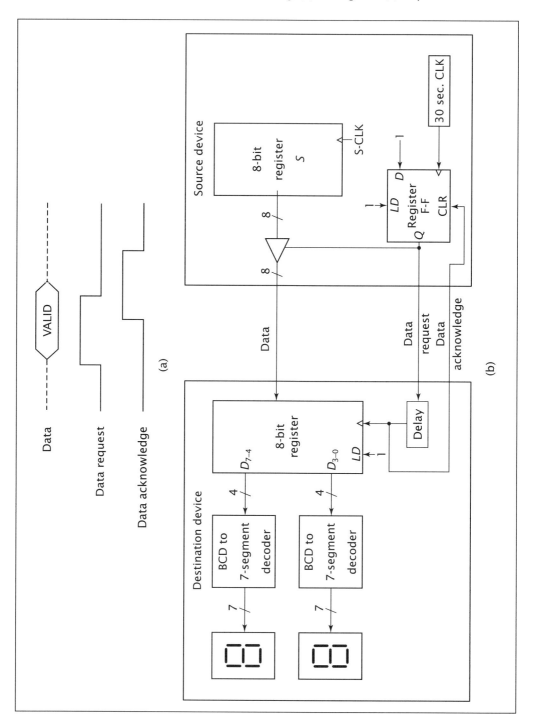

Figure 10.5
Destination-initiated data transfer with handshaking: (a) timing and (b) implementation

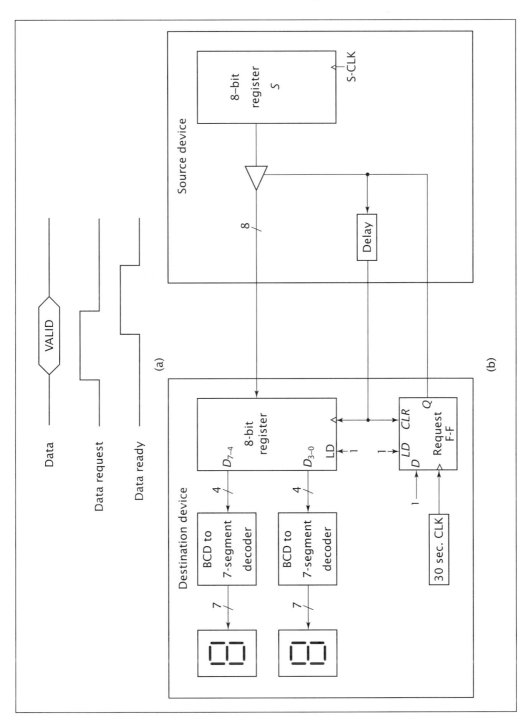

input, which sets the flip-flop to 0 regardless of the value of the clock.) Finally, the data acknowledge signal is set low.

The final type of asynchronous data transfer is **destination-initiated data transfer with handshaking**. Its timing diagram, shown in Figure 10.5(a), is similar to that of the source-initiated data transfer using handshaking, except that the data-acknowledge signal is replaced by a data-ready signal. Its hardware implementation for the seven-segment display is shown in Figure 10.5(b). In the last class-room analogy, the students ask the professor a question; she writes an answer on the blackboard and the students copy it down. After the students tell the professor that they are done, she erases the board and continues her lecture.

10.2 Programmed I/O

The function of **programmed I/O** is exactly what its name implies: A program instruction causes the CPU to input or output data. For example, consider a thermostat that controls both the heating and cooling systems of a home. It might perform the following sequence of operations.

1. Read temperature from external sensor.
2. If (temperature ≥ thermostat setting +2°) then turn on air conditioner.
3. If (temperature ≤ thermostat setting and air conditioner is on) then turn off air conditioner.
4. If (temperature ≤ thermostat setting −2°) then turn on heat.
5. If (temperature ≥ thermostat setting and heat is on) then turn off heat.
6. Go to start of sequence.

In this sequence, the first statement would be performed using pro-grammed I/O. The temperature sensor would be designed to generate a digital value corresponding to the actual temperature. The CPU would read this value via a synchronous input port as described in Chapter 4. The next four statements must read in the current thermo-stat setting via an input port. The portions of these statements that turn the air conditioner or heat on or off are also performed using pro-grammed I/O. The CPU would output these control signal values to a synchronous output port. The output port would send the signals to the air conditioning and heating units, turning them on or off as desired.

Recall from Chapter 4 that programmed I/O can be either isolated or memory mapped. Isolated I/O uses separate instructions to access I/O ports, while memory-mapped I/O treats I/O ports as memory loca-tions and accesses them using memory access instructions, such as LOAD and STORE. The Relatively Simple CPU, introduced in Chapters

6 and 7, cannot use isolated I/O as currently configured, but it can make use of memory-mapped I/O. Its LDAC and STAC instructions can be used to input and output data, respectively.

To illustrate this, consider an input port for the Relatively Simple CPU at address FFFFH. Whenever the instruction LDAC FFFF is executed, the CPU reads data from this port and stores it in its accumulator register.

To implement this I/O port, we must design the hardware for the input port so that it makes data available to the CPU when the CPU would read the data from the data bus. This occurs during state LDAC4, when the address bus contains the value FFFF and control signal READ is set to 1. (Internal CPU control signals MEMBUS and DR-LOAD are also set to 1, but they are of no direct concern to the input port. Even so, they are not accessible outside of the CPU, so the input port could not make use of their values anyway.)

Figure 10.6 shows one possible configuration for this input port. The tri-state buffers are only enabled when the address bus contains the value FFFFH and control bus signal READ = 1, exactly as needed for our memory-mapped I/O port. When this condition occurs, data from the input port passes on to the data bus of the computer and is read in by the CPU and stored in its data register. During the next state, the CPU moves this data from its data register into its accumulator.

Input port at address FFFFH

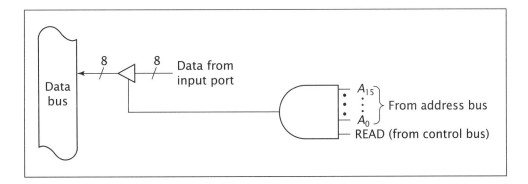

The software programmer is responsible for ensuring that the CPU never attempts to access memory location FFFFH; because the input port has been assigned to this address, it cannot be used by a memory location. For example, if the program counter contains the value FFFF as the CPU performs an instruction fetch (during state FETCH2), the CPU will input data from the input port and treat it as an instruction code, decoding and then executing the "instruction." In reality, this is not an instruction, but there is no way for the CPU to know that. This is one of the limitations of memory-mapped I/O, but the designer can usually overcome this problem with little difficulty.

Now consider the design of the thermostat using the Relatively Simple CPU. The CPU reads in the current temperature from the memory-mapped input port at address FFFFH and the thermostat setting from the port at address FFFE. The CPU controls the heating and air conditioning systems, writing one of the following four values to the output port at address FFFD.

> 01 = turn on air conditioning
> 02 = turn off air conditioning
> 03 = turn on heat
> 04 = turn off heat

The current status is stored in memory location 1000H. It has the following possible values. (This assumes that the heat and air conditioning are never both on at the same time.)

> 00 = heat and air conditioning are both off
> FF = heat is on
> FE = air conditioning is on

An algorithm for the control program for this system is shown in Figure 10.7. This algorithm is not optimal. For instance, the statements with labels HEATON, AIRON, and ALLOFF all read the current setting and temperature. An efficient program would combine these three into one code segment. Here, however, they are broken out to correspond to the final code, which replicates the operations because of the very limited storage within the CPU.

The Relatively Simple CPU assembly language code to implement the control algorithm shown in Figure 10.7 is as follows. This code assumes that the heat and air conditioning are never on simultaneously; that the temperature starts within 2° of the thermostat setting; and that the temperature never changes by more than 1° between loop iterations of the program. The hardware for this system is left as a design exercise for the reader.

```
START:    LDAC 1000
          INAC           (Sets Z = 1 if status = FF)
          JMPZ HEATON    (Heat is currently on)
          INAC           (Sets Z = 1 if status = FE)
          JMPZ AIRON     (Air conditioning is currently on)
ALLOFF:   LDAC FFFF
          MVAC           (R←current temperature)
          LDAC FFFE      (AC←current setting)
          SUB            (AC←setting - temperature)
          MVAC
          INAC
```

FIGURE 10.7

Thermostat control algorithm

```
START: Read current status
HEATON:    IF heat is on THEN{
           Read current setting and temperature;
           IF setting = temperature THEN{
                Turn off heat;
                Update status };
           GOTO START };
AIRON: IF air conditioning is on THEN{
           Read current setting and temperature;
           IF setting = temperature THEN{
                Turn off air conditioning;
                Update status };
           GOTO START };
ALLOFF:    ELSE (neither heat nor air conditioning is on){
           Read current setting and temperature;
           IF setting = temperature + 2 THEN{
                Turn on heat;
                Update status;
                GOTO START };
           IF setting = temperature - 2 THEN{
                Turn on air conditioning;
                Update status;
                GOTO START };
           GOTO START }; (when neither condition is met)
```

```
           INAC          (Sets Z = 1 if setting = temperature - 2)
           JMPZ TOAIR    (Turn on air conditioning)
           MOVR          (AC←setting - temperature)
           NOT
           INAC          (AC←temperature - setting)
           INAC
           INAC          (Sets Z = 1 if temperature = setting - 2)
           JMPZ TOHEAT   (Turn on heat)
           JUMP START    (No change, loop back)
TOAIR:     INAC          (AC was 0, this sets it to 1)
           STAC FFFD     (Turn on air conditioning)
           NOT           (AC←FE)
           STAC 1000     (Update status: air conditioning is on)
           JUMP START    (Loop back)
TOHEAT:    INAC
           INAC
```

```
            INAC             (AC←03)
            STAC  FFFD       (Turn on heat)
            CLAC
            NOT              (AC←FF)
            STAC  1000       (Update status: heat is on)
            JUMP  START      (Loop back)

HEATON:     LDAC  FFFF
            MOVR
            LDAC  FFFE
            SUB              (AC←setting - temperature)
            JPNZ  START      (setting ≠ temperature, leave heat on, loop back)
            INAC
            INAC
            INAC
            INAC             (AC←04)
            STAC  FFFD       (Turn off heat)
            CLAC
            STAC  1000       (Update status: heat and air conditioning off)
            JUMP  START      (Loop back)

AIRON:      LDAC  FFFF
            MOVR
            LDAC  FFFE
            SUB              (AC←setting - temperature)
            JPNZ  START      (setting ≠ temperature, leave air on, loop back)
            INAC
            INAC             (AC←02)
            STAC  FFFD       (Turn off air conditioning)
            CLAC
            STAC  1000       (Update status: heat and air conditioning off)
            JUMP  START      (Loop back)
```

To modify the Relatively Simple CPU to support isolated I/O we must add input and output instructions to the CPU's instruction set; create any necessary new control signals; add new states to the state diagram and develop the RTL code for the new states; modify the register section, ALU, and control unit hardware to support the new instructions; and ensure that these changes do not cause problems for any of the other instructions. In the remainder of this section, we present the new instructions and the design for the input instruction. The modifications needed to incorporate the output instruction are left as exercises for the reader.

10.2.1 New Instructions

For this design, we add two new instructions to the instruction set, one to input data and the other to output data. These instructions are

Table 10.1

Isolated I/O instructions for the Relatively Simple CPU

Instruction	Instruction Code	Operation
INPT	0010 0000 Γ	$AC \leftarrow$ Input port Γ
OTPT	0010 0001 Γ	Output port $\Gamma \leftarrow AC$

shown in Table 10.1. Unlike the IN and OUT instructions of the 8085 microprocessor, these instructions use 16-bit I/O addresses, allowing up to 64K I/O ports in a system.

10.2.2   New Control Signals

When using isolated I/O, we need a signal to distinguish between memory references and I/O references, such as the $IO/\overline{M}$ signal of the 8085 microprocessor. Without this signal, it is not possible to tell whether an address refers to a memory location or to an I/O port. In this design, we create a new signal called IO. $IO = 1$ for input/output operations and $IO = 0$ for memory reference operations.

10.2.3   New States and RTL Code

The INPT instruction works almost exactly like the LDAC instruction. The only difference is that, in state LDAC4, the LDAC instruction reads data from memory. During the corresponding state of the INPT instruction's execute routine, it must read data from an input port. The modification to the state diagram for this CPU is shown in Figure 10.8 and its RTL code is as follows:

$$\text{INPT 1:}\quad DR \leftarrow M,\ PC \leftarrow PC + 1,\ AR \leftarrow AR + 1$$
$$\text{INPT 2:}\quad TR \leftarrow DR,\ DR \leftarrow M,\ PC \leftarrow PC + 1$$
$$\text{INPT 3:}\quad AR \leftarrow DR, TR$$
$$\text{INPT 4:}\quad DR \leftarrow \text{Input port}$$
$$\text{INPT 5:}\quad AC \leftarrow DR$$

10.2.4   Modify the CPU Hardware for the New Instruction

Modifying the hardware for the new instruction can be broken into three tasks: (1) modify the register section; (2) modify the ALU; and (3) modify the control unit. (For this example, we use the hardwired control unit.) Reviewing the RTL code, we see that only one new micro-operation, $DR \leftarrow$ Input port, is used. Every other micro-operation is used in the LDAC execute routine and elsewhere. This new micro-operation can use the same data path as the micro-operation $DR \leftarrow M$, since both memory and I/O ports send data to the CPU via the system's data bus. Also, the new micro-operation does not use the ALU.

Figure 10.8

States to implement the INPT execute routine

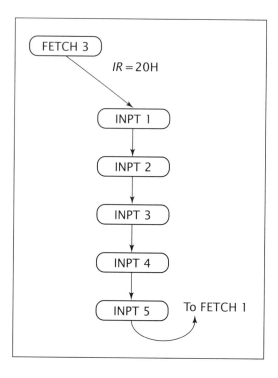

Hence, no modifications are necessary for the register section of the ALU. Only the control unit must be revised.

The first revision needed for the control unit is to enable it to recognize the new opcode and to properly sequence through the states of its execute routine. Figure 10.9 shows a circuit to generate signals for those five states. (The decoder is not optimal, but it will simplify the task of incorporating the OTPT instruction later.)

To ensure that these states are traversed in the proper sequence, we must incorporate them into the logic that drives the control inputs of the time counter. Each state requires the time counter to be incremented to reach the correct next state except for INPT5. This state must clear the counter to reach FETCH1. To achieve this, the counter control signals are modified as follows:

$$INC = (\text{old value of INC}) \vee INPT1 \vee INPT2 \vee INPT3 \vee INPT4$$
$$CLR = (\text{old value of CLR}) \vee INPT5$$

Next, the CPU's control signals must incorporate these state values to perform the transfers required during these states. Following

Figure 10.9

Hardware to generate the state signals for the INPT execute routine

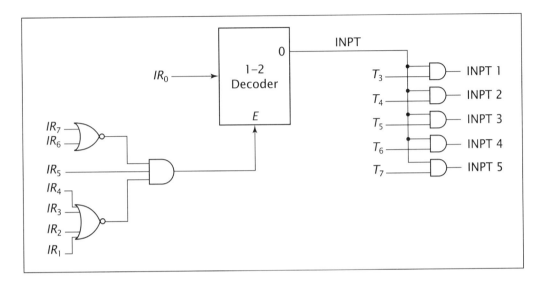

are the changes needed to incorporate state INPT1. The rest are left as exercises for the reader.

$$DRLOAD = (\text{old value of DRLOAD}) \lor INPT1$$
$$MEMBUS = (\text{old value of MEMBUS}) \lor INPT1$$
$$PCINC = (\text{old value of PCINC}) \lor INPT1$$
$$ARINC = (\text{old value of ARINC}) \lor INPT1$$

Finally, we must create the logic to generate the new control signal IO. This signal is set to 1 only when reading data from an input port or writing data to an output port. This only occurs during state INPT4, so IO can be configured as $IO = $ INPT4.

10.2.5   Make Sure Other Instructions Still Work

Within the CPU, the modifications made to incorporate the INPT instruction do not cause any problems for the other instructions. However, there is a problem outside of the CPU. Specifically, the memory module, as shown in Figure 6.18, does not incorporate IO into its READ control signal. This could cause memory to place data onto the system's data bus when the CPU is trying to read data from an input port, as during state INPT4. To remedy this, the READ input to the memory module can be modified as follows.

$$\text{Memory Read} = \text{READ} \land IO'$$

10.3 INTERRUPTS

As noted earlier, input/output devices are slower than memory, and the amount of time they require may vary. The uncertainty of when the device will be ready complicates the task of accessing I/O devices. In this section we examine **interrupts**, a mechanism for alleviating the delay caused by this uncertainty and for maximizing system performance.

10.3.1 Transferring Data Between the CPU and I/O Devices

One method used in smaller systems to alleviate the problem of I/O devices with variable delays is called **polling**. In polling, the CPU sends a request to transfer data to an I/O device. The I/O device processes the request and sets a device-ready signal when it is ready to transfer data. The CPU reads in this signal via another I/O address and checks the value. If the signal is set, it performs the data transfer. If not, it loops back, continually reading and testing the value of the device ready signal.

To illustrate this method, consider an input device in a computer system that uses the Relatively Simple CPU with the INPT ($AC \leftarrow$ Input port Γ) and OTPT (Output port $\Gamma \leftarrow AC$) instructions introduced in Table 10.1. The CPU initiates a request by outputting the value 01H to I/O address 1001H. It then polls input port 1002H until its least significant bit is 1; then it reads in data from input port 1000H. Figure 10.10 shows the hardware to accomplish this task. The device is set up as three I/O ports, two input and one output.

The software to implement the data transfer is as follows. Note that the first three instructions load the value 01H into register R. We do this to check the value of the device-ready signal.

FIGURE 10.10

Hardware to implement an I/O port that uses polling

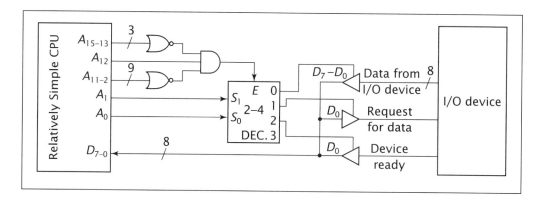

```
       CLAC
       INAC      (AC←1)
       MOVR      (R←1)
       OTPT 1001H (Output the value 01H to the I/O port at address 1001H)
LOOP:  INPT 1002H (Check whether the device is ready)
       AND       (AC = 1 and Z = 0 if device is ready)
       JMPZ LOOP  (If device not ready, AC = 0 and Z = 1, loop back)
       INPT 1000H (Device is ready, input data)
```

Polling is relatively straightforward in design and programming, and is often used when the CPU is not fully loaded. However, it is not appropriate for systems in which CPU time is at a premium. A slow device causes the CPU to remain in the polling loop for quite a long time. During this time, the CPU is merely waiting; it performs no useful work.

One way to resolve this is to use **wait states**. When wait states are used, the processor requests data from (or permission to send data to) an I/O device, which then asserts a wait signal that is sent to the CPU via the control bus. As long as the signal is asserted, the CPU stays in a wait state, still outputting the address of the I/O device and the values of the control signals needed to access the device, but not doing anything else. The I/O device continues to assert this wait signal until it is ready to send or receive data. (For example, a disk drive might assert the wait signal until it has positioned its read/write heads at the correct location on the disk.) Once it is ready, the I/O device deasserts its wait signal and the CPU completes the data transfer.

This method simplifies the job of the programmer. Unlike polling, we need no additional code to accommodate the variability of the timing of the I/O device; like polling, the CPU does not perform any useful work while waiting for the I/O device to become ready to transfer data.

To make use of this wasted CPU time, interrupts were developed. When interrupts are used with I/O devices, the CPU may output a request to the I/O device and, instead of polling the device or entering a wait state, the CPU then continues executing instructions, performing useful work. When the device is ready to transfer data, it sends an **interrupt request** signal to the CPU; this is done via a dedicated signal on the control bus. The CPU then acknowledges the interrupt, typically by asserting an **interrupt acknowledge** signal, and completes the data transfer. (This assumes that the instructions executed after the I/O request is issued and before the interrupt is asserted do not use the data to be transferred. If they do use the data, the CPU must wait until the transfer is completed before executing these instructions, or the instructions will use erroneous data.) Unlike polling or wait states, interrupts do not waste time waiting for the I/O device to become ready. However, the hardware requirements for interrupts are greater, especially within the CPU.

The rest of this section covers various facets of interrupts. In addition to external interrupts, CPUs also may use interrupts for internal events and software instructions.

10.3.2 Types of Interrupts

There are three types of interrupts, each with several different uses. Although each type serves a different purpose, the procedures for processing all types of interrupts are almost identical.

10.3.2.1 External Interrupts

External interrupts are used by the CPU to interact with input/output devices. The example in which the CPU requests a data transfer and the input device asserts an interrupt when it is ready, is a popular way to use interrupts. External interrupts improve system performance by allowing the CPU to execute instructions, instead of just waiting for the I/O device, while still performing the required data transfers.

External interrupts can also be used to initiate transfers, rather than to signal event completion. For example, consider the digital display in the examples of section 10.1. A 30-second clock triggers a circuit to update the digital display twice per minute. The 30-second clock used to start a transfer could be used instead to generate an interrupt to the CPU. In response to this interrupt, the CPU would output the new value to the display.

10.3.2.2 Internal Interrupts

Internal interrupts occur entirely within the CPU; no input/output devices play any role in these interrupts. Some interrupts in this class are purposely introduced as part of the system's function. For example, a timer built into the CPU (many CPUs have this feature) may generate an interrupt at a predetermined interval, such as every 0.1 seconds. This interrupt could be used to allocate CPU time to different tasks in a multitasking operating system. This would ensure that each task gets its appropriate time slices while relieving the software of the job of tracking time; the timer and internal interrupt take care of this.

Internal interrupts can also be used to handle exceptions that occur during the execution of valid instructions. As an example, a CPU might contain a perfectly valid divide instruction that generates an exception when its divisor is 0. (Recall that, in Chapter 8, we modeled this by setting a flag within the arithmetic unit.) In addition to the divide by zero exception, other exceptions include arithmetic overflow and page faults. Besides these exceptions, which may or may not occur, depending on the value of the operands, invalid instruction codes are also handled by internal interrupts.

10.3.2.3 Software Interrupts

Software interrupts are generated by specific interrupt instructions in the CPU's instruction set. They act like subroutine call statements, except they always go to a specific address; therefore, they do not explicitly specify the address of the handler routines. These routines, and how the CPU accesses them, are examined next.

10.3.3 Processing Interrupts

An interrupt triggers a sequence of events to occur within the computer system. These events acknowledge the interrupt and perform the actions necessary to service the interrupt. These events only occur if the interrupt is **enabled**; enabling and disabling interrupts are described later in this section.

The software to service the interrupt, which is written by the user, is called the **handler**. A handler is essentially a subroutine. There may be one handler routine for each interrupt or one unified handler routine for all interrupts. Once the handler routine has been executed, the CPU returns to where it left off in the main program, just as it would when returning from a subroutine.

Regardless of the configuration of the handler routine or routines, each interrupt is serviced by the following sequence of events.

10.3.3.1 Do Nothing (Until the Current Instruction Has Been Executed)

Examining the RTL code for the Relatively Simple CPU, we see that many execute routines consist of several steps. If such an execute routine is interrupted part way through, we would have to save the contents of many of the internal registers of the CPU, as well as the state information within the control unit. If we did not do this, it would not be possible to correctly complete the execution of that instruction.

In contrast, it is not necessary to save this information if the execute routine has been completed. Most of that information was saved to ensure that the execution of the interrupted instruction could be completed. If the instruction has been executed, this information is no longer needed and thus does not have to be saved.

To illustrate, consider this execute routine for the LDAC instruction for the Relatively Simple CPU:

$$LDAC1: \quad DR \leftarrow M, PC \leftarrow PC + 1, AR \leftarrow AR + 1$$
$$LDAC2: \quad TR \leftarrow DR, DR \leftarrow M, PC \leftarrow PC + 1$$
$$LDAC3: \quad AR \leftarrow DR, TR$$
$$LDAC4: \quad DR \leftarrow M$$
$$LDAC5: \quad AC \leftarrow DR$$

If this execute routine is interrupted after state LDAC1, the values of several registers must be saved in order for the rest of the routine to function properly after the handler routine is executed. In LDAC2, the value in *DR* is needed for the transfer *TR←DR*, and the previous value of *PC* is needed for *PC←PC* + 1. Less obvious, the transfer *DR←M* must use the value of *AR* calculated during LDAC1 so that it accesses the correct memory location. The values of *TR* and *AC* are overwritten later in the execute routine before they are read again, so they do not need to be saved. In addition to these registers, the contents of register *IR* and the time counter of the control unit must be saved in order to generate control signals LDAC2 to LDAC5. By contrast, if the interrupt is serviced after the execute routine is completed, only the contents of *PC* need to be saved. This is done to ensure that the handler routine returns to the correct location in the main program.

10.3.3.2 GET THE ADDRESS OF THE HANDLER ROUTINE (VECTORED INTERRUPTS ONLY)

Before beginning to describe this process, it is necessary to distinguish between **vectored interrupts** and **nonvectored interrupts**. Simply put, vectored interrupts supply the CPU with information, the **interrupt vector**, which is used to generate the address of the handler routine for that interrupt. It is possible for the interrupt to supply the entire address, or only a partial address. In contrast, a nonvectored interrupt uses a handler routine at a known address. Since this address is fixed, the CPU does not need any additional information to generate this address and access its handler routine.

Vectored interrupts are useful for CPUs that receive interrupt requests from several devices via the same control line. After a device sends an interrupt request, and the CPU finishes executing its current instruction, the CPU sends an acknowledge signal to the device, which places its vector on the system's data bus. The CPU reads the vector and, if necessary, generates the address of the handler routine.

10.3.3.3 INVOKE THE HANDLER ROUTINE

The handler routine is very much like a subroutine. When the CPU accesses the handler routine, it pushes the current value of the program counter onto the stack and loads the address of the handler routine into the program counter. (Loading the address into the program counter is also the method used to implement the JUMP instruction in the Relatively Simple CPU.) The handler routine then performs its tasks. When it is finished, it returns to the correct location by popping the value of the program counter off of the stack.

Handler routines serve different purposes, depending on the hardware or internal cause of their associated interrupts. For instance, a routine to handle a divide-by-zero error might simply set the result to $\pm\infty$ and return, or it might output an error message to the user. In contrast, external interrupts are usually associated with I/O data transfers. Each I/O device may have its own handler routine to access its hardware and input or output data. The handler routine would also process incoming data as required.

Regardless of the purpose of the handler routine, there are some things any handler routine may do. One is to disable any further interrupts. Depending on the function of a handler routine, it may be necessary to ensure that the handler routine is not itself interrupted. This will vary, depending on the interrupts and their priority.

A handler routine may clear the current interrupt. This is done to avoid having one interrupt request trigger more than one interrupt. Although this can be done within the handler routine, it is more likely to be performed by the CPU while the interrupt is being acknowledged and the handler routine is being accessed.

Finally, the handler routine should ensure that it leaves all pertinent registers with their initial values before returning to the main program. Since the interrupt can occur at any time, it cannot know which data values are being used by the main program. As a general rule, the handler routine should push the values of any data registers, whose contents it will modify, onto the stack at the beginning of the routine. Just before returning to the main program, it should pop these values back in to their registers. In this way, the values in the data registers remain consistent as the main program is executed. In the Relatively Simple CPU, a handler routine would save the contents of registers AC and R on the stack (if the handler routine uses these registers). The program counter was already pushed on to the stack as the handler routine was invoked. The contents of registers DR and IR are modified during the instruction fetch and do not need to be saved. The Z flag also must be saved if the handler routine includes any instructions that could modify its value.

10.3.4   Interrupt Hardware and Priority

Having examined what happens when an interrupt is requested, it is useful to study how the interrupt is requested. The simplest case is a system that has only one device capable of issuing a nonvectored interrupt request. This might be used in a simple embedded controller. A generic configuration for such a system is shown in Figure 10.11(a).

An external device sends an interrupt to the CPU by asserting its interrupt request (IRQ) signal. When the CPU is ready to process the interrupt request, it asserts its interrupt acknowledge signal (IACK), thus informing the I/O device that it is ready to proceed. Because its request has been acknowledged, the device sets IRQ low, which causes the CPU to set IACK low. As the handler routine proceeds, it transfers data between the CPU and the interrupting device. The timing of the IRQ and IACK signals is similar to that of the data-request and data-ready signals in the asynchronous destination-initiated data transfer with handshaking, shown in Figure 10.5. Unlike that transfer mode,

FIGURE 10.11

(a) Hardware and (b) timing for a nonvectored interrupt for a single device

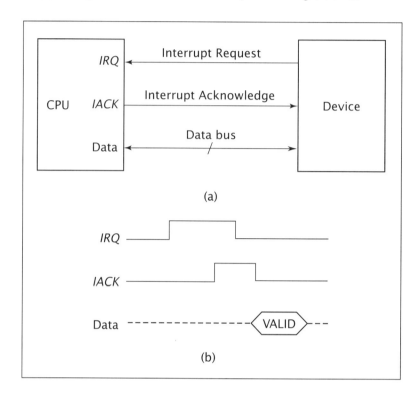

however, in a nonvectored interrupt, data is transferred later via a synchronous transfer.

A vectored interrupt is more complex. After acknowledging the interrupt, the CPU must input an interrupt vector from the device and call an **interrupt service routine** (handler); the address of this routine is a function of this vector. Figure 10.12 shows a hardware block diagram and timing diagram for this system.

A number or questions are raised by these configurations. For instance, what happens if a device deasserts IRQ before it is acknowledged? CPUs usually have an internal flip-flop that is set to 1 on the rising edge of IRQ. Even if IRQ is reset to 0, the flip-flop is still set, indicating that an interrupt request has occurred. The CPU would proceed to acknowledge and process the interrupt based on the value of this flip-flop rather than its IRQ input. If such a flip-flop is not present, the interrupt request might not be processed. This is alleviated by having the device continue to assert IRQ until IACK is asserted by the CPU.

What happens if, immediately after a device sets IRQ low, it issues another interrupt request? This can happen in real systems and

Figure 10.12

(a) Hardware and (b) timing for a vectored interrupt for a single device

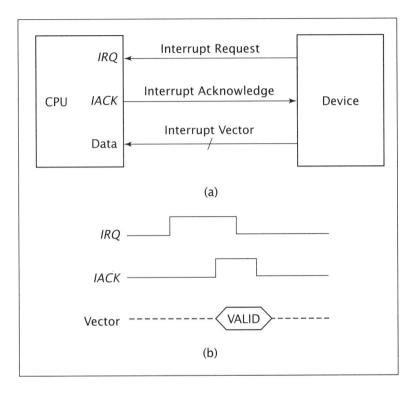

we must account for this in our design. Consider a CPU with an interrupt flip-flop: The initial interrupt sets this flip-flop to 1. When the CPU acknowledges the interrupt, setting IACK to 1, it also resets this flip-flop. Immediately after this, the second interrupt again sets this flip-flop to 1.

In this scenario, the CPU is processing the first interrupt request when it receives a second request. In general, a CPU will disable all interrupt requests from being processed while invoking the handler routine. The second interrupt request is latched into the interrupt request flip-flop, but the CPU does not yet act on it. Once the handler routine is invoked, it is up to the programmer to decide when to process any incoming interrupts. If the programmer wants the system to finish processing the first interrupt completely, the handler routine simply leaves interrupts disabled until the very end of the routine. In some applications, however, it may be desirable to let a second request interrupt the processing of the first. In this case, the handler routine would re-enable interrupts at or near its inception.

This scenario usually occurs when a computer system has more than one device generating interrupts. One method of handling multiple interrupts is to extend the nonvectored interrupt hardware shown in Figure 10.11(a) for multiple devices. Each device has its own IRQ and IACK signals, as shown in Figure 10.13. The priority is predetermined; usually IRQn has the highest priority and IRQ0 has the lowest. If more than one device requests an interrupt, the CPU acknowledges and serves the interrupt with the highest priority first.

FIGURE 10.13

Hardware for multiple nonvectored interrupts

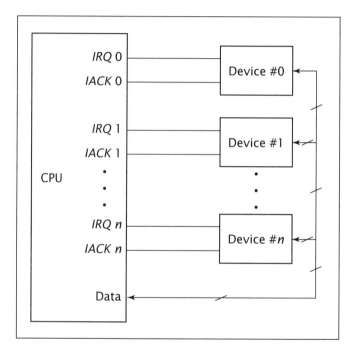

The question of how to handle a second incoming interrupt while a first interrupt is being processed is not as straightforward as in a system with only one interrupting device. In addition to enabling and disabling interrupts, we must also consider the priority of the interrupts. In general, the second interrupt is processed if its priority is higher than that of the interrupt currently being processed. If not, it remains pending until the current handler routine is complete. For example, assume the device connected to IRQ5 asserts an interrupt request; the CPU first acknowledges this request and then begins executing its handler routine. While the handler routine is being executed, IRQ7 is asserted. Since IRQ7 has a higher priority than the interrupt currently being processed, IRQ5, the CPU would interrupt the handler routine for IRQ5, acknowledge IRQ7, and execute its handler routine. On completion, the CPU would return and finish executing the handler routine for IRQ5. If IRQ2 was asserted instead of IRQ7, the CPU would finish executing the handler routine for IRQ5, since its priority is higher than that of IRQ2, and then service the interrupt for IRQ2.

This method works well when there are only a few IRQ/IACK pairs. However, as the number of interrupts increases, the number of pins needed by the CPU to accommodate these signals becomes prohibitive. For this reason, many CPUs use vectored interrupts.

One method used for prioritizing multiple interrupts is called **daisy chaining**. As shown in Figure 10.14, the interrupt request signals from the devices are wire-ORed together. (Logically, this is equivalent to having each interrupt request signal input to an OR gate, but

Figure 10.14

Daisy chaining

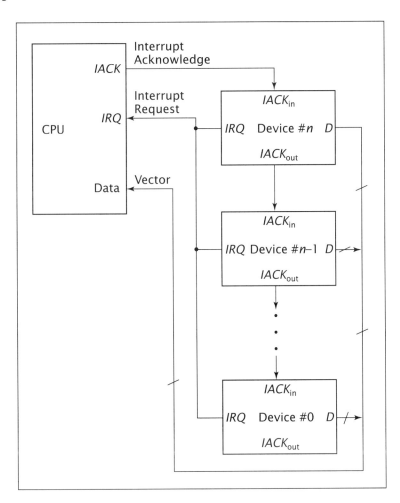

it is simpler to implement and to expand.) When the CPU receives an active IRQ input, it cannot know which device generated the interrupt request. It sends out an acknowledge signal and leaves it to the devices to work that out among themselves.

In this configuration, device #n receives the IACK signal directly from the CPU. If IACK is asserted, usually equal to 1, and this device requested an interrupt, it sets its $IACK_{out}$ signal to 0 and places its vector on to the data bus. The CPU reads in the vector and invokes the handler routine for this device. Since the CPU has only one IRQ input, the interrupt must be vectored in daisy chaining.

If this device did not request the interrupt, it sets its $IACK_{out}$ signal to 1, thus passing it along to device #$n - 1$. This device would proceed just as did the first device. This process would continue down the line until some device accepts the interrupt acknowledge, setting its $IACK_{out}$ signal to 0. All devices of lower priority would have $IACK_{in}$ = 0 and would set $IACK_{out}$ to 0, which indicates that they are blocked by an interrupt of higher priority.

Summarizing, each device can be in one of the states shown in Table 10.2. The invalid state ($IACK_{in}$ = 0 and $IACK_{out}$ = 1) is shown to account for all possible values of $IACK_{in}$ and $IACK_{out}$, but a device should never be in this state.

Table 10.2

Possible values of $IACK_{in}$ and $IACK_{out}$ and their states

$IACK_{in}$	$IACK_{out}$	State
1	1	Device has priority to interrupt but does not.
1	0	Device interrupts CPU.
0	1	Invalid state.
0	0	Device is blocked from interrupting by a device with higher priority (device may or may not be issuing an interrupt request).

Daisy chaining is straightforward and easy to implement. If we wish to add a new device to the system, we simply insert the device into the chain at the correct location for its priority, make its connections, and add its handler routine to the system's memory. However, because this configuration is sequential, it can introduce hardware delays, especially as the chain becomes longer. The small computer system interface (SCSI) used by many personal computers is an example of a daisy chain configuration.

We can also implement vectored interrupts using **parallel priority** by using a priority encoder, as shown in Figure 10.15. The IRQ input to the CPU is generated as in the daisy chain configuration, using a wired-OR of the IRQ signals from the devices. Note that buffers are needed to prevent the signals from corrupting the values input to the priority encoder. Unlike daisy chaining, however, the IACK signal simply enables a priority encoder. The output of this encoder is the value of the highest priority device requesting an interrupt. This value is placed on the data bus as the interrupt vector and is read in by the CPU, which then proceeds as before.

Implementing priority interrupts in parallel

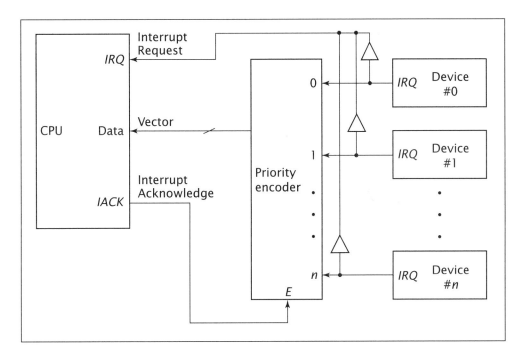

Unlike daisy chaining, in parallel priority the priority of the device does not determine the time needed to acknowledge the interrupt. Because all interrupt requests are processed in parallel, they all require the same amount of time. However, this system is much more difficult to expand than the daisy chain configuration.

10.3.5   Implementing Interrupts Inside the CPU

Having considered the effects of interrupts in the computer system, we now turn inward and look at how interrupts are processed inside the CPU. To illustrate how this is done, we add a vectored interrupt to the Relatively Simple CPU. From the perspective of the CPU, it is not necessary to know whether the devices are daisy chained or use a priority encoder to generate the interrupt vector. It is sufficient to know that they somehow generate this 8-bit vector.

The modified CPU has one IRQ input and propagates an acknowledge signal on its IACK output. It reads in the interrupt vector on its data pins, $D[7..0]$, and invokes the handler routine at address 1111 (vector) 0000.

In order to invoke the handler routine, the CPU must be able to call subroutines and must have a subroutine register. This example assumes that the Relatively Simple CPU has been enhanced to include a 16-bit stack pointer register, SP, and new instructions LDSP, PUSHAC, PUSHR, POPAC, POPR, CALL, and RET. These instructions are used to initialize SP, to call and return from a subroutine, and to save to and load data from the stack. Their functions are shown in Table 10.3. The CPU also has an interrupt pending flip-flop, IP, which is set to 1 on the rising edge of IRQ. The instruction IPRST clears this flip-flop. In addition, this CPU has an interrupt enable flip-flop, IE, which is set to 1 when interrupts are enabled and 0 when they are disabled. New instructions IESET and IERST control this flip-flop. Their functions, along with that of IPRST, are also shown in Table 10.3.

Table 10.3

New instructions for the Relatively Simple CPU

Instruction	Instruction Code	Operation
LDSP	10000000 Γ	$SP \leftarrow \Gamma$
CALL	10000010 Γ	$SP \leftarrow SP - 1$; $M[SP] \leftarrow PC[15..8]$, $SP \leftarrow SP - 1$; $M[SP] \leftarrow PC[7..0]$, $PC \leftarrow \Gamma$
RET	10000011	$PC[7..0] \leftarrow M[SP]$, $SP \leftarrow SP + 1$; $PC[15..8] \leftarrow M[SP]$, $SP \leftarrow SP + 1$
PUSHAC	10000100	$SP \leftarrow SP - 1$; $M[SP] \leftarrow AC$
POPAC	10000101	$AC \leftarrow M[SP]$, $SP \leftarrow SP + 1$
PUSHR	10000110	$SP \leftarrow SP - 1$; $M[SP] \leftarrow R$
POPR	10000111	$R \leftarrow M[SP]$, $SP \leftarrow SP + 1$
IESET	0100 0000	$IE \leftarrow 1$
IERST	0100 0001	$IE \leftarrow 0$
IPRST	0100 0010	$IP \leftarrow 0$

Perhaps the most difficult part of handling the interrupt is recognizing it and accessing the states to process the interrupt. This is done at the end of every execute cycle, and could be done in one of two ways. In the first method, shown in Figure 10.16(a), the branches that go to state FETCH1 are broken into two branches. If interrupts are enabled ($IE = 1$) and an interrupt is pending ($IP = 1$), these states branch to the beginning of the interrupt handler routine, state INT1, rather than to FETCH1. If either IE or IP is 0, no interrupt is processed and the CPU proceeds to FETCH1 to continue processing instructions.

Figure 10.16

Two methods to access the interrupt handler: (a) using separate FETCH1 and INT1 states, and (b) modifying FETCH1 to support interrupts

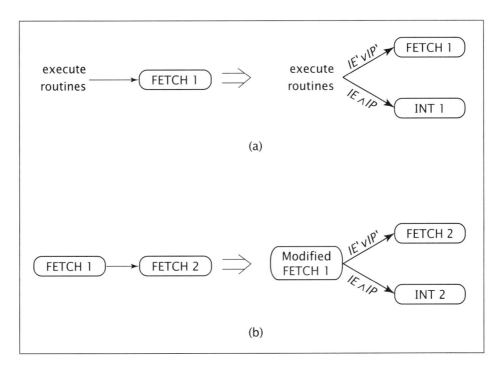

As an alternative, the branches going to state FETCH1 can remain the same, but the micro-operations associated with the state can be modified. In this method, state FETCH1 would consist of two sets of micro-operations of the following form.

```
(IE' ∨ IP') ∧ FETCH1:  (Micro-operations of FETCH1, performed when not servicing an interrupt)
    IE ∧ IP ∧ FETCH1:  (Micro-operations of INT1, performed when servicing an interrupt)
```

Upon completion, the CPU would branch to either FETCH2 or INT2, as shown in Figure 10.16(b). In this example we use the first option.

Now we must define how to access the interrupt handler. The CPU must first push the return address on to the stack, then read in the interrupt vector, and finally jump to the address corresponding to this vector, 1111 (vector) 0000.

The RTL code to perform this process is as follows. The first five states store the return address on the stack. During INT6, the vectored address is read into *DR*; this requires the CPU to set IACK to 1. Finally, the CPU generates the address corresponding to this vector and loads into *PC* during INT7. This state also clears the pending interrupt, since it has been serviced.

INT1:	$AR \leftarrow SP$
INT2:	$DR \leftarrow PC[15..8]$, $SP \leftarrow SP - 1$
INT3:	$M \leftarrow DR$, $AR \leftarrow AR - 1$, $SP \leftarrow SP - 1$
INT4:	$DR \leftarrow PC[7..0]$
INT5:	$M \leftarrow DR$
INT6:	$DR \leftarrow$ (vector from data bus)
INT7:	$PC \leftarrow 1111, DR, 0000$, $IP \leftarrow 0$

The implementation of this interrupt design is left as an exercise for the reader.

10.4 DIRECT MEMORY ACCESS

Another aspect of computer system performance that can be improved is the transfer of data between memory and I/O devices. This is a common operation in computer systems. Loading programs or data files from disk into memory, saving files on disk, and accessing virtual memory pages on any secondary storage medium all fall into this category of operations.

Consider a typical system consisting of a CPU, memory, and one or more input/output devices, such as that shown in Figure 4.1. Assume one of the I/O devices is a disk drive and that the computer must load a program from this drive into memory. The CPU would read the first byte of the program and then write that byte to memory. Then it would do the same for the second byte and each succeeding byte, until it had loaded the entire program into memory.

This is, at best, inefficient. Loading data into, and then writing data out of, the CPU significantly slows down the transfer. The CPU does not modify the data at all, so it only serves as an additional stop for data on the way to its final destination. The process would be much quicker if we could bypass the CPU and transfer data directly from the I/O device to memory. **Direct Memory Access**, or **DMA**, does exactly that.

10.4.1 INCORPORATING DIRECT MEMORY ACCESS (DMA) INTO A COMPUTER SYSTEM

A **DMA controller** implements direct memory access in a computer system. As shown in Figure 10.17, it connects directly to the I/O device at one end and to the system buses at the other end. It also interacts with the CPU, both via the system buses and two new direct connections. In this configuration, the DMA controller is sometimes referred to as a **channel**. In an alternate configuration, the DMA controller may be incorporated directly into the I/O device.

Figure 10.17

A computer system with DMA

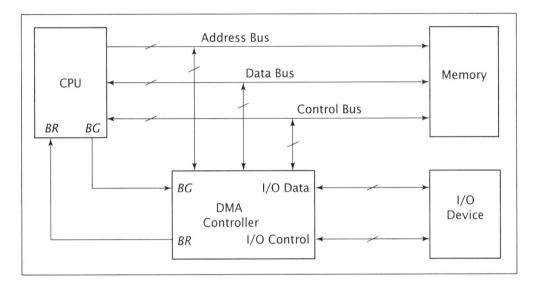

To transfer data from an I/O device to memory, the DMA controller first sends a **bus request** to the CPU by setting *BR* to 1. When it is ready to grant this request, the CPU sets its **bus grant** signal, *BG*, to 1. The CPU also tri-states its address, data, and control lines, thus truly granting control of the system buses to the DMA controller. The CPU will continue to tri-state its outputs as long as *BR* is asserted.

Now that the DMA controller has control of the system buses, it can perform the desired data transfers. To load data from an I/O device into memory, it asserts the appropriate I/O control signals and loads data from the I/O device into its internal DMA data register. Next, it writes this data to memory. To do this, it outputs the memory address onto the system's address bus and the data onto the data bus. (Exactly how the DMA controller obtains this address and the number of bytes of data to transfer will be explained shortly.) The DMA controller also asserts the appropriate signals on the system's control bus to cause memory to read the data. The DMA controller then writes the second data value to the following memory location, continuing until it has transferred the entire block of data.

Once this is done, the DMA controller no longer needs to use the system buses. It relinquishes its request by setting *BR* to 0. The CPU then sets *BG* to 0 and re-enables its address, data, and control lines, resuming its normal operation.

To understand how the DMA controller performs this transfer, we must examine its internal architecture. As shown in Figure 10.18, the DMA controller includes several registers. The **DMA address register** contains the memory address to be used in the data transfer. The CPU treats this register as one or more output ports. The **DMA count register**, sometimes called the **word count register**, contains the number of bytes of data to be transferred. Like the DMA address register, it too is treated as an output port (with a different address) by the CPU. The **DMA control register** accepts commands from the CPU. It is also treated as an output port by the CPU. Although not shown in this figure, most DMA controllers also have a **status register**. This register supplies information to the CPU, which accesses it as an input port. DMA controllers also usually include circuitry to abort the transfer if the I/O device is not ready in some predetermined amount of time. This is called **timeout**.

To initiate a DMA transfer, the CPU loads the address of the first memory location of the memory block (to be read to or written from) into the DMA address register. It does this via an I/O output instruc-

---

Figure 10.18

Internal configuration of a DMA controller. All buffer enable signals (not shown) are supplied by the DMA control unit and all register load signals (not shown) are derived from the system address and control buses.

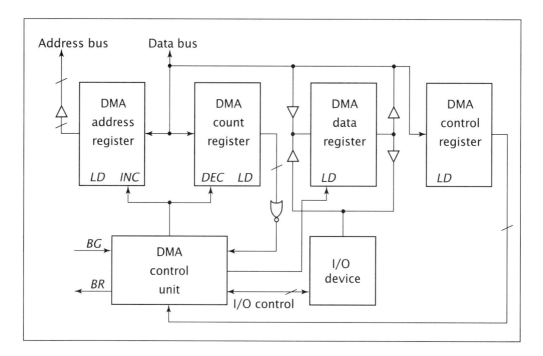

tion, such as the OTPT instruction for the Relatively Simple CPU. It then writes the number of bytes to be transferred into the DMA count register in the same manner. Finally, it writes one or more commands to the DMA control register. These commands may specify transfer options, such as the DMA transfer mode, but should always specify the direction of the transfer, either from I/O to memory or from memory to I/O. The last command must cause the DMA controller to initiate the transfer. The controller then sets *BR* to 1 and, once *BG* becomes 1, seizes control of the system buses.

To see how this works, assume that the DMA controller must move 4 bytes of data from its attached I/O device to memory starting at location 1000H. The CPU writes the value 1000H to the DMA address register and 4 to the DMA count register. It then outputs a value to the DMA control register, which causes it to initiate a transfer from the I/O device to memory. The DMA controller then sets *BR* to 1. The CPU soon sets *BG* to 1 and tri-states its pins, ceding control of the system buses to the DMA controller.

From here, the DMA controller takes over. It reads the first data value from the I/O device into its DMA data register and decrements the value in its count register, from 4 to 3 in this example. Then it outputs its address (1000H) onto the system's address bus and its data value from the DMA data register onto the system's data bus. It also asserts the appropriate values on the system's control bus to cause memory to store this value in location 1000H. Next, it increments the value in the DMA address register to 1001H and checks whether the DMA count register is 0. Since it is not, it repeats this process, reading data values from the I/O device and storing them in memory locations 1001H, 1002H, and 1003H.

After the last transfer, the value in the DMA count register is 0, indicating that the transfer is complete. The DMA controller sets *BR* to 0, which causes the CPU to set *BG* to 0. The DMA controller also tri-states its outputs to the system buses, returning control of the buses to the CPU.

10.4.2   DMA Transfer Modes

There are three different modes of DMA data transfer. They vary by how the DMA controller determines when to transfer data, but the actual data transfer process is the same for all three modes.

10.4.2.1   Burst Mode

Sometimes called **block transfer mode**, **burst mode** was illustrated in section 10.4.1. In burst mode, an entire block of data is transferred in one contiguous sequence. Once the DMA controller is granted access to the system buses by the CPU, it transfer all bytes of data in the data block before relinquishing control of the system buses back to the CPU. This mode is useful for loading programs or data files into memory, but it does render the CPU inactive for relatively long periods of time.

10.4.2.2 Cycle Stealing Mode

For systems in which the CPU should not be disabled for the length of time needed for burst transfer modes, **cycle stealing** is a viable alternative. In cycle stealing mode, the DMA controller obtains access to the system buses as in burst mode, using the *BR* and *BG* signals. However, it transfers one byte of data and then deasserts *BR*, returning control of the system buses to the CPU. It continually issues requests via *BR*, transferring one byte of data per request, until it has transferred its entire block of data.

By continually obtaining and releasing control of the system buses, the DMA controller essentially interleaves instructions and data transfers. The CPU processes an instruction, then the DMA controller transfers a data value, then the CPU processes another instruction, then the DMA controller transfers another data value, and so on. The data block is not transferred as quickly as in burst mode, but the CPU is not idled for as long as in that mode. A controller that must monitor data in real time or near real time may not be able to tolerate the delays associated with burst mode transfers, but it might have no problems with cycle stealing mode transfers.

10.4.2.3 Transparent Mode

Transparent mode requires the most time to transfer a block of data, yet it is also the most efficient in terms of overall system performance. In transparent mode, the DMA controller only transfers data when the CPU is performing operations that do not use the system buses. For example, the Relatively Simple CPU has several states that move or process data solely within the CPU:

NOP1:	(No operation)
LDAC5:	$AC \leftarrow DR$
JUMP3:	$PC \leftarrow DR, TR$
CLAC1:	$AC \leftarrow 0, Z \leftarrow 1$

The primary advantage of transparent mode is that the CPU never stops executing its programs. The DMA transfer is free in terms of time. However, the hardware needed to determine when the CPU is not using the system buses can be quite complex and relatively expensive. In addition, more advanced CPUs overlap their internal operations and use the system bus almost every cycle. For these reasons, this mode is generally not used in spite of its performance advantages.

10.4.3 Modifying the CPU to Work with DMA

In order for a CPU to be able to work with a DMA controller, it must have several features not shown in CPUs so far in this text.

One obvious change is the addition of control input *BR* and control output *BG*, along with the logic to generate *BG*. This logic depends on when the designer wants the CPU to be able to grant control of the system buses to the DMA controller. Most CPUs allow this to occur after some, but not all states. Typically, these CPUs allow DMA requests to be granted after the instruction has been fetched; after it has been decoded; after its operands have been fetched; after the instruction has been executed; and after its results have been stored. The CPU generally does not allow any of these processes to be suspended for a DMA request. To simplify the design, this example modifies the Relatively Simple CPU so that it serves DMA requests only at the beginning of the fetch cycle, immediately after the instruction has been executed.

When input BR is asserted and the Relatively Simple CPU reaches state FETCH1, it will grant access to the bus to the DMA controller, tristate its outputs, and suspend external operations. First consider how the CPU can set BG to 1. We can do this using combinatorial logic, setting and resetting BG asynchronously, or it can be implemented using a flip-flop. In this example we use the latter approach.

Because BG is latched, its operations can be expressed using RTL code. As the CPU enters FETCH1, if $BR = 1$, it sets BG to 1; it remains in state FETCH1 until BR is 0. If $BR = 0$, it sets BG to 0 and performs the other micro-operations associated with state FETCH1. Its RTL code is as follows; the branch back to FETCH1 is not shown.

$$BR \wedge \text{FETCH1:} \quad BG \leftarrow 1$$
$$BR' \wedge \text{FETCH1:} \quad BG \leftarrow 0, \text{(micro-operations of FETCH1)}$$

The two micro-operations that load BG could be combined into a single micro-operations, yielding the RTL code

$$\text{FETCH1:} \quad BG \leftarrow BR$$
$$BR' \wedge \text{FETCH1:} \quad \text{(micro-operations of FETCH1)}$$

Figure 10.19 shows the hardware to implement BG.

Figure 10.19
Hardware implementation of BG

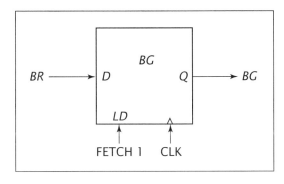

We must modify the control unit to implement the loop from FETCH1 back to itself while *BR* is 1. Figure 10.20 shows the modification needed for the state diagram. The modification of the hardwired control unit is left as an exercise for the reader.

FIGURE 10.20

Modified state diagram to accommodate *BR* and *BG*

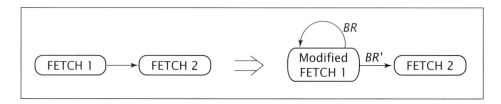

Finally, the CPU must tri-state its outputs whenever the DMA controller has access to the bus. Tri-state buffers must be added to address outputs *A*[15..0] and all control outputs. The data input/output signals already have tri-state buffers. The address and control outputs should be enabled at all times, except when the DMA controller has access to the system buses. This only occurs when *BG* = 1, so *BG'* can be used to enable the address and control bus buffers.

One task did not have to be performed as part of this process: We do not have to save any internal information. Unlike interrupts, which perform tasks that might disrupt the main program, DMA transfers suspend CPU operations; they do not modify internal values other than *BR* and *BG*. Because no values change, no values needed to be saved and then restored.

In many computers, DMA channels can be combined with other components on a single chip. See Practical Perspective: The i960 I/O Processor with Built-In DMA.

10.5 I/O PROCESSORS

The DMA controller introduced in the previous section can improve system performance by speeding up data transfers between memory and I/O devices. However, it still leaves some of the work for the CPU. Moreover, multiple transfers require separate DMA transfers, along with the necessary setup for each transfer. In some cases, data must be manipulated once it is read from the I/O device; the DMA controller can only transfer data. Each of these shortcomings is addressed by **I/O processors**.

I/O processors, sometimes called **I/O controllers**, **channel controllers**, or **peripheral processing units** (**PPUs**), perform the functions of DMA controllers and much more. In fact, they usually incorporate several DMA controllers within their circuitry.

As shown in Figure 10.21, the I/O processor is situated between the I/O devices and the rest of the system, very much like the DMA controller in Figure 10.17. Unlike the DMA controller however, the I/O processor connects to more than one I/O device. The I/O devices are grouped together on an I/O bus, as opposed to the regular system bus. Thus, one I/O processor can coordinate transfers from several different I/O devices.

FIGURE 10.21

System configuration incorporating an I/O processor

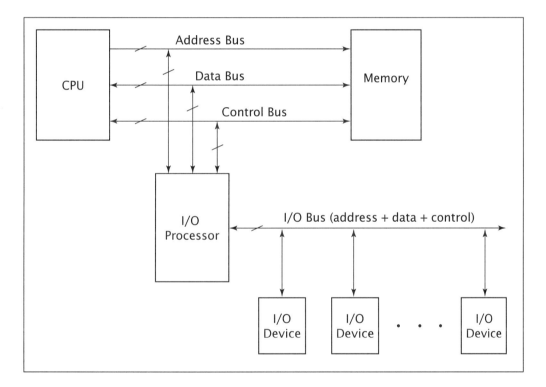

Generally speaking, I/O processors handle all of the interactions between the I/O devices and the CPU. The CPU's only direct I/O interaction is with the I/O processor itself. If the CPU must read in data from an I/O device or initiate a block transfer between an I/O device and memory, the CPU instructs the I/O processor to perform this task. The I/O processor coordinates the actual data transfer. The only exception is that the CPU coordinates the transfer of data between itself and the I/O processor.

Instead of loading values into registers, as with DMA, the CPU issues a series of I/O instructions to the I/O processor. The CPU typically stores these instructions in memory and sends a pointer to the instructions to the I/O processor. These instructions, often called *commands* to distinguish them from CPU instructions, fall into three categories. The first are the **block transfer commands**. Block transfer commands move blocks of data, just like DMA transfers, and they include the necessary parameters. A block transfer command might tell the I/O processor to read 32 bytes of data from the I/O device with port address 220H and write the data to memory starting at location 1000H. These instructions can be used to swap pages in and out of physical memory, and to load programs from disk to memory.

A second type of command performs arithmetic, logic, and branch operations. The arithmetic and logic instructions are useful for manipulating data so that it can be used by the CPU. For example, consider a CPU that has a 32-bit data bus and operates on 32-bit data values. If the CPU must read in data from an 8-bit input port, it would have to read four separate values and concatenate them into a single 32-bit value. Instead, the CPU can instruct the I/O processor to read the four values and, using arithmetic and logic commands, pack the data before sending it to the CPU. The branch operations can be used to jump to different locations within the command program, much as jump instructions branch to different locations in CPU programs.

The third type of command is **control commands**. These are usually hardware dependent and critical to the proper functioning of the computer system. Typical commands in this class could rewind the tape on a tape drive, cause a disk drive to seek a particular location, or instruct a printer to print a page.

An I/O processor sequence of commands can perform several sequential I/O transfers. Consider the following tasks:

1. Move 247 bytes of data from the disk drive at port address 9000H to memory, starting at address 1000H.
2. Read 1 byte of data from the input port at address 9001H into the accumulator of the CPU.
3. Write the contents of memory locations 2000H through 207FH to the printer at I/O address 9002H.

A system with a DMA controller but no I/O processor would first have to load data into the registers of the DMA controller for the disk drive, initiate the transfer, and wait for it to complete. Then it would input a byte of data from the I/O port at address 9001H. Finally, it would initiate a second DMA transfer to print the data block. In contrast, the CPU in a system with an I/O processor would write the commands needed to perform all three tasks into a contiguous block of memory and pass a pointer to this block to the I/O processor. This reduces the overhead associated with setting up the transfers.

While the I/O processor is performing its tasks, the CPU can continue to perform useful work. In systems such as those shown in this chapter, its work could be suspended while the I/O processor performs the block data transfers, just as with DMA transfers. (The CPU would continue to function while the I/O processor inputs the 1 byte of data in the second task.) However, advanced systems typically have memory partitioned into distinct modules. They have more than one set of system address, data, and control buses. Their operating systems can allow the CPU to access one module during a given time while granting access to a different module exclusively to the I/O processor during that time. By using different sets of buses, both the CPU and the I/O processor can perform their tasks simultaneously.

There is one question left unanswered in this sequence of I/O transfers: After the I/O processor read in the value from the input port at address 9001H, how did the CPU read it in to its accumulator? As part of its connections, the I/O processor should be able to issue an interrupt to the CPU. This interrupt would cause the CPU to read this value, either directly from the I/O processor or from a predetermined memory location in which the I/O processor stored the value. As an alternative, the I/O processor could set a value in a memory location signifying that its data is ready. This **semaphore** is similar in function to the device-ready input port of the circuit shown in Figure 10.10. As in polling, interrupts generally yield better performance because the CPU does not spend time checking to see whether the result is ready. These methods can also be used by the I/O processor to indicate that it has finished processing its commands.

PRACTICAL PERSPECTIVE: The i960 I/O Processor with Built-In DMA

In recent years, the increased need for computer communications bandwidth, particularly for Internet access, has outstripped the need for increased processing power. I/O processors help meet that need, particularly for Web servers and file servers.

Intel's i960 I/O processors perform the functions associated with IOPs and include other functional units to reduce a system's chip count. The i960 VH IOP runs at 100 MHz and has a 16K internal instruction cache for its I/O commands. It contains a PCI bus interface to interact with the system bus, and a separate local bus connection for communicating with I/O devices.

To increase performance, the i960 VH include a DMA controller with two channels. They can transfer 132 MB per second between the PCI bus and the local bus, or over 1Gb per second.

10.6 SERIAL COMMUNICATION

The input/output devices, DMA controllers, and I/O processors presented in this chapter all use parallel communication. They transmit more than one bit of data at a time. Some devices cannot handle more than one bit of data at any given time by design; they utilize **serial communication**. This may be done to reduce cost or to facilitate communication with devices outside of the computer system.

It is important to note that, almost always, the CPU does not communicate serially with such devices. Instead, the CPU interacts with the device using parallel communications; an interface or the device itself converts the data between serial and parallel forms.

There are several modes of serial communication. **Asynchronous serial communication** is used to interact with devices outside of the computer, such as when connecting to another computer via modem. The connected devices do not share a common clock and must synchronize their data transfers. They transmit individual bytes of data, rather than large blocks.

Synchronous serial transmission is more efficient. It transmits blocks of data in **frames**, which consist of leading transmission information, the data, and trailing transmission information. In spite of the word *synchronous* in the name, the two systems communicating generally do not share a clock. Instead, information is included as part of the transmission that allows the devices to synchronize their clocks.

10.6.1 SERIAL COMMUNICATION BASICS

When two devices communicate using asynchronous serial transmission, they do not share a common clock. They must have some means of synchronizing the flow of data. In order to do this, they must agree beforehand on several transmission parameters. One of these parameters is the speed, the number of **bits per second**, or **bps**. (formerly referred to as the **baud rate**.) Not agreeing on transmission parameters will cause data to be lost or corrupted. For example, if data is being transmitted at 28,800 bps but the receiver is reading the data at 14,400 bps, half the bits are being lost, including control bits, which will ultimately lead to corruption of the received data. In addition, the two devices must agree on the number of data bits per data transmission, whether or not a **parity bit** is transmitted along with the data (and, if so, whether odd or even parity checking is used), and the number of **stop bits** at the end of the transmission.

In asynchronous serial communication, each byte of data is transmitted as a separate entity. The main problems to be overcome in this transmission mode are for the receiving device to recognize when a transmission is occurring; when to read a bit of data; when the transmission is ending; and when the transmission line is idle, that is, no data is being transmitted.

When the transmission line is idle, its value is logic 1. To signal the start of transmission, the transmitting device outputs a single **start bit** of 0 onto the line. The line is set to 0 for one **bit time**, which is 1 divided by the number of bits per second. (For example, a system that transmits data at 28,800 bps has a bit time of $1 \div 28{,}800 = 34.72\mu s$.) The receiver notes the 1 to 0 transition on the line, waits ½ bit time (so that it samples data in the middle of the bit transmission to increase reliability), and resamples the value on the transmission line. If it is still 0, the receiver confirms that the initial 1 to 0 transition was a start bit, and not a glitch on the line. It then waits 1 bit time and reads a data bit off of the line, repeating this process for however many data bits are in the transmission. (The two devices agreed on the number of data bits before beginning the transmission.) The least significant bit of data is transmitted first, then the remaining bits are transmitted in order; the most significant bit is transmitted last. If there is a parity bit, the receiver waits the requisite 1-bit time and reads that bit in as well. Whether or not a parity bit is used, the receiver then reads in the stop bit or bits, which must be logic 1. Usually, 1, 1½, or 2 stop bits are used; the number of stop bits indicates the number of bit times for which the transmission line is set to 1, not the number of 1's placed on the line. For a system transmitting data at 28,800 bps that uses 1½ stop bits, the transmitting device sets the line to 1 for $1\tfrac{1}{2} \cdot 34.72\mu s = 52.08\mu s$. Any time after this, the transmitter may begin sending another piece of data. Figure 10.22 shows the value of a transmission line for the transmission of 2 bytes of data with a gap between their transmission. This system uses the N81 setting typical for many modem transmissions: no parity bit; 8 data bits; and 1 stop bit.

Transmitting numeric data this way is pretty straightforward, but character data requires a bit of work. We must encode each character as a unique binary value that both the sender and receiver recognize. Several standards exist for encoding characters. The most commonly

Figure 10.22

Sample transmission of 2 bytes of data

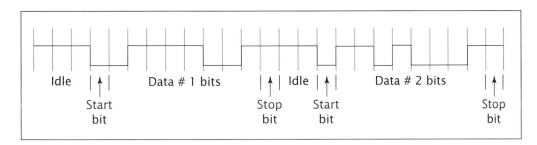

used is **ASCII**, the **American Standard Code for Information Interchange**. The ASCII standard specifies 128 characters, as shown in Table 10.4. The first 32 characters are **control codes**, or **nonprinting characters**. They specify characters used in printer and screen control (such as the carriage return), serial transmission (such as the acknowledge), or other device controls. The remaining characters are printable letters, numbers, and symbols.

Table 10.4

ASCII codes

ASCII Binary Code	----000	----001	----010	----011	----100	----101	----110	----111
0000---	NUL	SOH	STX	ETX	EOT	ENQ	ACK	BEL
0001---	BS	HT	LF	VT	FF	CR	SO	SI
0010---	DLE	DC1	DC2	DC3	DC4	NAK	SYN	ETB
0011---	CAN	EM	SUB	ESC	FS	GS	RS	US
0100---	Space	!	"	#	$	%	&	'
0101---	(	)	*	+	,	-	.	/
0110---	0	1	2	3	4	5	6	7
0111---	8	9	:	;	<	=	>	?
1000---	@	A	B	C	D	E	F	G
1001---	H	I	J	K	L	M	N	O
1010---	P	Q	R	S	T	U	V	W
1011---	X	Y	Z	[	\	]	^	—
1100---	`	a	b	c	d	e	f	g
1101---	h	i	j	k	l	m	n	o
1110---	p	q	r	s	t	u	v	w
1111---	x	y	z	{			}	~	DEL

Since most transmissions use eight data bits and ASCII codes require only seven bits, designers have developed extended ASCII implementations that add 128 more characters to the basic ASCII character set. There are several varieties of extended ASCII characters, which usually include special symbols and characters used in languages other than English.

In addition to ASCII, there are other standards for representing characters, such as **Unicode**, which is used by the Java programming language. Unicode uses 16-bit characters and includes characters from many different languages. As with most non-ASCII standards, its first 128 characters are identical to those in ASCII.

This system introduces a fairly large amount of overhead into the transmission. In the N81 example just given, every 8-bit data chunk requires the transmission of 10 bits: one start bit, the eight data bits, and one stop bit. The start and stop bits account for 20 percent of the total transmission, yet convey no data in and of themselves. They merely synchronize the devices so they can successfully transmit the other eight bits.

Synchronous transmission seeks to improve transmission performance by reducing this overhead. Instead of sending a start and stop bit for each data value, it concatenates several data values into a single data block. It appends appropriate information in front of and behind the data block to create a frame. This additional information represents overhead but normally at a lower percentage than the overhead associated with asynchronous serial transmission.

A common synchronous serial transmission standard, the **High-level Data Link Control**, or **HDLC**, is shown in Figure 10.23. The leading and trailing flags are used to synchronize and delimit the frames. The address and control fields specify the address of the destination and the function of the frame. The **cyclic redundancy check** (**CRC**) is used to catch errors in transmission, just as parity can be used in asynchronous transmissions.

Frame format for High-level Data Link Control

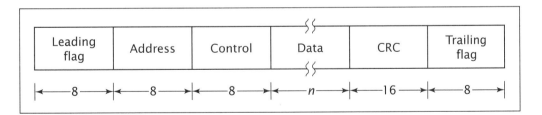

To determine the efficiency of the transmission, we calculate its overhead. If a frame contains 256 data bits, and the other fields contain 48 bits which are treated as overhead, 15.79 percent of the total 304 (256 + 48) bits are overhead. Larger data fields generally require the same overhead as smaller data fields, so they have lower overhead rates. If the frame contained 256 bytes of data, instead of 256 bits, its overhead would comprise only 2.3 percent of the total bits transmitted.

10.6.2 Universal Asynchronous Receiver/Transmitters (UARTs)

Asynchronous serial communication is a common function in computer systems. As with many popular functions, manufacturers have designed special chips to perform these functions and relieve the CPU of this task. For asynchronous serial communication, these specialized chips are called **universal asynchronous receiver/transmitters**, or **UARTs**.

As shown in Figure 10.24, the CPU sees the UART as just another parallel I/O device and interfaces with it accordingly. On its back end, the UART inputs and outputs (receives and transmits) data serially. It can interact with any device that can access serial data. In Figure 10.24, the UART exchanges data with a modem. To transmit data, the UART outputs sequential data to the modem, which modulates (the "MO" in *mo*dem) the data, combining it with a carrier frequency and transmitting it. To receive data, the modem accepts a signal at a different carrier frequency and demodulates (the "DEM" in mo*dem*) it, extracts the data, and transmits it serially to the UART.

Figure 10.24

A computer system incorporating a UART

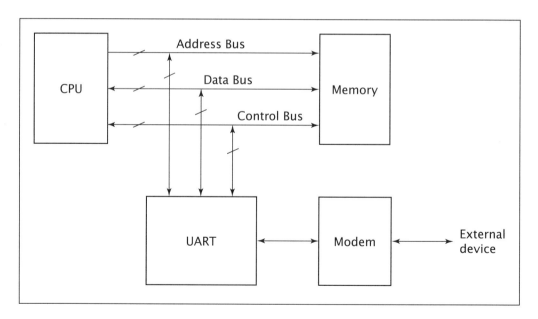

As shown in Figure 10.25, the UART has several internal registers, just as in the DMA controller. Like the DMA controller, the CPU treats these registers as individual I/O ports. A typical UART contains registers to hold transmitted and received data, a control register, and a status register, all of which are accessible to the CPU. It also contains shift registers, which convert data from parallel to serial (for data transmission) and from serial to parallel (for data reception). The UART's control unit also coordinates the insertion and removal of start, parity, and stop bits. A command sent from the CPU to the control register of the UART sets the number of data bits, parity, and the number of stop bits to be used in the transmission.

Figure 10.25

Internal configuration of a UART

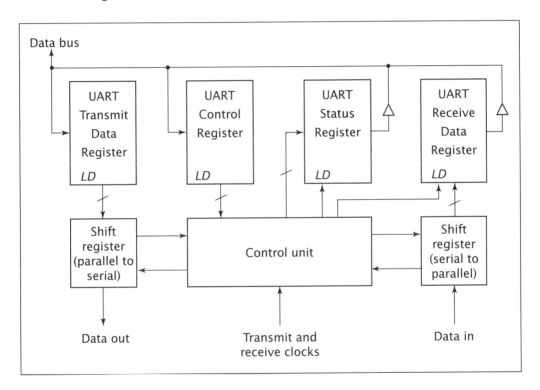

10.7   Real World Example: Serial Communication Standards

The standards for two serial connections typically found on IBM compatible personal computers are RS-232-C and the universal serial bus standard. The RS-232-C standard has been used by the serial ports of personal computers since their inception in 1981. This standard was originally defined in 1969 and was intended for connecting mainframe computers and terminals. More recently, personal computers have incorporated universal serial bus ports, which connect to up to 127 devices on a single port.

10.7.1   The RS-232-C Standard

The standard serial port of an IBM-compatible personal computer follows the **RS-232-C standard**. (Apple Macintosh computers follow a different standard.) The RS-232-C standard specifies nine signals, as follows. The serial port of most personal computers can transmit data at up to 115,200 bps.

- Request to Send
- Clear to Send
- Transmission Data
- Data Terminal Ready
- Data Set Ready
- Received Data
- Data Carrier Detect
- Ring Indicator
- Ground

The first two signals, Request to Send and Clear to Send, are used to specify whether the computer and the device it is communicating with, such as its modem, are powered on. When the computer is powered on, it sets the Data Set Ready signal to logic 1. The modem (or other serial device) sets the Data Terminal Ready signal to logic 1 when its power is on. Nothing else happens between these two devices unless both signals are asserted.

The Ring Indicator signal is used by the modem to inform the computer that it detects a ringing on its telephone line. This is used by modems that are set to answer incoming calls, but is not needed when the computer dials out to connect to an Internet service provider (ISP) or another computer.

When a modem connects to another computer, it negotiates a connection with the other computer's modem. This includes setting the bit rate of the transmission. (When you dial into an ISP, you may see a message saying "Connected at xxxxx bps;" this is the bit rate negotiated by the two modems.) Once the connection is set, the modem on your computer asserts the Data Carrier Detect signal, which remains asserted as long as the two modems are connected.

Once the modems have established communications, they can transmit data. The computer asserts the Request to Send signal, which tells the modem that it is ready to transmit and receive data. The modem asserts the Clear to Send signal, indicating that it is ready. No transmission occurs unless both signals are asserted.

From here, the computers and modem can transfer data using asynchronous data transfer. The computer sends data to the modem on the Transmission Data line. The modem receives this data, modulates it, and sends it out to the other computer. If the computer trans-

PRACTICAL PERSPECTIVE: The RS-422 Serial Standard

Unlike IBM-compatible personal computers, which use the RS-232-C standard, Apple's Macintosh computers follow the **RS-422 standard** for their serial ports. The signals for this standard are shown in Table 10.A.

Table 10.A

RS-422 signals

Symbol	Signal name
HSKo	Output Handshake
HSKi/Clock	Input Handshake or External Clock
TxD+	Transmission Data (plus)
TxD−	Transmission Data (minus)
RxD+	Receive Data (plus)
RxD−	Receive Data (minus)
GPIn	General Purpose Input
Ground	Signal Ground

The HSKo and HSKi/Clock signals are used to implement handshaking. Their functions are similar to the Request to Send, Data Terminal Ready, and Clear to Send signals of the RS-232-C standard. The General Purpose Input signal is often used like the RS-232-C Data Carrier Detect signal.

Unlike the RS-232-C standard, the RS-422 standard uses **differential voltage** to send data. In this form, transmitted data occupies two signals in each direction. The transmitted value depends on the difference in the voltage on the two signal lines. This improves the quality of the signal, making it more immune to electrical noise, and allows communication over longer distances.

mits data too quickly, the modem deasserts the Clear to Send signal, causing the computer to stop sending data. Once the modem has caught up, it reasserts the Clear to Send signal, enabling the computer to send more data. The modem sends data to the computer via the Received Data signal. Here, the computer deasserts the Request to Send signal if it falls behind in accepting data.

10.7.2 The Universal Serial Bus Standard

The RS-232-C bus does not supply address information to its connected device. Typically, only one device is connected to a single RS-232-C port, so no address is needed. In contrast, the **universal serial bus** (**USB**), available on many newer computers, can connect to several devices. The universal serial bus transmits data in packets, similar to the frames described in the previous section. This packet can specify an address, allowing several devices to be connected to one USB port.

The USB port is much faster than the RS-232-C port. The USB specification, version 1.1, allows transmission speeds up to 1.5 Mb/s. The new version 2.0 standard allows for speeds up to 480 Mb/s.

The USB standard specifies four types of packets, which are used to communicate between a computer and its USB peripherals. The **token packets** specify addresses and end points for a transfer, or a frame marker. **Data packets**, as their name implies, contain data transferred to or from a device. The **handshake packets** transfer information used to coordinate data transfers, such as the ACK (acknowledge) packet. Finally, there are **special packets** with several different functions.

Figure 10.26 shows the format for three packets used to transfer data. The **token packet** is used to initiate data transfers. It specifies the address (ADDR) of the device to send or receive data, and the direction of data flow; the direction is specified in the **packet identifier** (**PID**). The other two fields indicate the **end of packet** (**ENDP**) and a **cyclic redundancy check (CRC)**.

After sending a token packet to initiate transfers, the computer sends a data packet. Each data packet contains a PID, a data field, and a 16-bit CRC field. The data field can contain up to 8192 bits of data. This greatly reduces the overhead, which is normally much less than the 20 percent (or more) overhead for RS-232-C devices. Notice that this packet does not contain an address. The address was specified in the token packet sent before data was transmitted.

After receiving this data, the receiving device sends a handshake packet. This packet contains only an 8-bit PID. If the packet was received without any errors, the receiving device acknowledges successful receipt of the data. If there was an error in the packet, this PID indicates a negative acknowledge. (This happens when the CRC for the transmitted data, as calculated by the receiving device, does not match the CRC transmitted in the data packet.)

Because the USB can support multiple devices, a system that would require several RS-232-C ports might require only one USB. In that respect, it is very hardware efficient. However, there are significantly greater software requirements for USB as opposed to RS-232, since it must distinguish among its connected devices.

FIGURE 10.26

USB packet formats: (a) token packet, (b) data packet, and (c) handshake packet

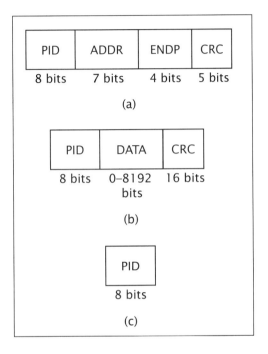

10.8 SUMMARY

A computer must be able to interact with the outside world or it cannot perform useful work. A computer may use asynchronous data transfer to perform this interaction, with either the source or destination initiating the data transfer, with or without handshaking. The computer may also use programmed I/O, either memory mapped or isolated, to interact with I/O devices. In any of these forms, the CPU must include the logic needed to access I/O devices and to process any I/O instructions in its instruction set.

Interrupts are an efficient method used by computers to interact with I/O devices. Instead of spending time polling I/O devices, the device issues an interrupt when it is ready to transfer data, allowing the CPU to perform other useful work while waiting for the I/O device. When processing an interrupt, the CPU first finishes executing its current instruction, then saves its current state, and finally invokes the interrupt's handler routine. A system can have more than one interrupt; multiple interrupts can be prioritized using daisy chaining or parallel priority hardware. In addition to external interrupts, a CPU may also support internal interrupts and software interrupts.

Direct memory access is used to speed up data transfers between memory and I/O devices. The CPU first sends information to a DMA controller, including the number of bytes to be transferred, the starting address in memory, and the direction of the data transfer, and then sends a start signal. The DMA controller obtains control of the system buses from the CPU and coordinates the transfer of data directly between memory and the I/O device. Bypassing the CPU greatly speeds up the data transfer. DMA controllers may transfer data in burst mode, cycle stealing mode, or transparent mode. I/O processors often use DMA to speed up their data transfers.

Serial communication is used to transmit data between a computer and an external device one bit at a time. Asynchronous devices, such as modems, often use UARTs to coordinate the parallel data transfer within the computer and the serial data transfers with the outside world. Synchronous serial communications can reduce the overhead associated with asynchronous communication. Standards have been developed for both asynchronous and synchronous communcations, including RS-232-C and USB.

Problems

1 Design the interface between register S and the CPU for the asynchronous interfaces in Section 10.1. (One interface should work for all four transfer modes.) The CPU has a 16-bit address bus and an 8-bit data bus, and accesses the register as a memory-mapped I/O port at address 0000H. Control signal $MEMW'$ is set to 0 when the CPU is writing data to the port.

2 Design the hardware to implement the thermostat controller of Section 10.2 using the Relatively Simple CPU.

3 Show the state diagram and RTL code to implement the OTPT instruction of Section 10.2.

4 Modify the hardware of Figure 10.9 to generate the signals for the states of the OTPT instruction.

5 Develop the modifications to the rest of the control signals needed to implement the INPT instruction of Section 10.2.

6 Modify the hardwired control unit of the Relatively Simple CPU to sequence properly and generate the correct control signals to realize the OTPT instruction. Ensure that all other instructions are still processed properly.

7 Modify the microsequenced control unit of the Relatively Simple CPU to incorporate the INPT instruction.

8 Modify the microsequenced control unit of the Relatively Simple CPU to incorporate the OTPT instruction.

9 Given the following sequence of events, show which routines the CPU is executing for times 0 to 100 ns. Each handler routine (with its interrupt request) takes 20 ns to complete.

Time	Action
0 ns	Start of main program
10 ns	IRQ1
20 ns	IRQ2
45 ns	IRQ3
60 ns	IRQ4

10 Repeat Problem 9 for the following sequence of events.

Time	Action
0 ns	Start of main program
10 ns	IRQ6
20 ns	IRQ5
45 ns	IRQ4
60 ns	IRQ3

11 Repeat Problem 9 for the following sequence of events.

Time	Action
0 ns	Start of main program
10 ns	IRQ4
20 ns	IRQ6
45 ns	IRQ1
60 ns	IRQ3

12 Why is daisy chaining simpler to implement than a system with multiple IRQ/IACK pairs of signals?

13 Design the hardware to input $IACK_{in}$ and IRQ from its device and correctly generate $IACK_{out}$.

14 Show the values of $IACK_{in}$ and $IACK_{out}$ for the sequence of interrupts in Problem 11.

15 Show the values of the signals in the parallel interrupt system of Figure 10.15 for the sequence of interrupts in Problem 11.

16 Design the hardware to implement flip-flop IE and the IESET and IERST instructions.

17 Design the hardware to implement flip-flop IP and the IPRST instruction.

18 Modify the hardware of the Relatively Simple CPU hardwired control unit to generate states INT1 to INT7, introduced in Section 10.3.5.

19 Modify the state diagram of the Relatively Simple CPU to incorporate interrupts as described in Section 10.3.5.

20 Modify the RTL code for the interrupt routine of Section 10.3.5 to implement interrupts via the method shown in Figure 10.16(b).

21 Modify the control signals of the Relatively Simple CPU to incorporate the RTL code to handle interrupts, as shown in Section 10.3.5. Include the hardware needed to generate IACK.

22 Design the logic for the *LD* signals for the DMA address, count, and control registers. They are located at addresses 8000H, 8001H, and 8002H, respectively.

23 Write a program using the assembly language of the Relatively Simple CPU (including the OTPT instruction) to implement a transfer using the DMA controller of Problem 22. The system must transfer 64 bytes of data from the I/O device to memory starting at location 1000H. In this system, the DMA address register is loaded with the most significant 8 bits of the address; the low-order 8 bits are always 0. The DMA count and control registers are 8 bits each. The value that must be written into the control register to initiate the DMA transfer is 02H. Memory locations 2000H, 2001H, and 2002H contain the values 10H, 40H, and 02H, respectively.

24 Modify the hardwired control unit of the Relatively Simple CPU to include the modified states shown in Figure 10.20.

25 Show any modifications to CPU internal control signals MEMBUS and BUSMEM needed to accommodate the DMA function for the Relatively Simple CPU, as described in Section 10.4.

26 An I/O processor can accept the following commands. M_1, M_2, C_1, C_2, I_1, and I_2 are all 8-bit values.

Instruction	Instruction Code	Operation
XFTM	1100 0000 M_1 M_2 C_1 C_2 I_1 I_2	Move (C_1C_2) bytes of data from I/O port (I_1I_2) to memory starting at location (M_1M_2).
XFFM	1100 0001 M_1 M_2 C_1 C_2 I_1 I_2	Move (C_1C_2) bytes of data from memory starting at location (M_1M_2), to I/O port (I_1I_2).

Show the contents of the memory locations that contain commands to perform the following sequence of transfers. First, move 32 bytes of data from I/O port 9900H to memory starting at location 1000H. Then move data from memory locations 1100H through 1927H to I/O port 9901H. Finally, move one byte of data from I/O port 9902H to memory location 1080H.

27 Determine the overhead percentage for asynchronous data transfers with the following parameters.

   a) No parity, 8 data bits, 1½ stop bits
   b) Parity, 7 data bits, 2 stop bits
   c) Parity, 5 data bits, 1 stop bit

28 Which of the following systems has less overhead?

   a) An asynchronous system with no parity, 6 data bits, and 1 stop bit, or a synchronous HDLC system with 96 data bits?
   b) An asynchronous system with no parity, 7 data bits, and 1½ stop bits, or a synchronous HDLC system with 168 data bits?
   c) An asynchronous system with no parity, 8 data bits, and 1 stop bit, or a synchronous HDLC system with 192 data bits?

29 Write a program for the Relatively Simple CPU to transmit the value in memory location 1111H using a UART. The data register of the UART is accessed at address 9800H. The command to initiate the transfer is located in memory location 1112H, and the address of the UARTs command register is 9801H.

30 A computer sends 1.5 KB (6,144 bits) of data to one of its USB peripherals.

a) Show the packets sent by the computer to perform this transfer. What is the total number of bits transferred?

b) What percentage of the bits transmitted is overhead?

c) How many bits would be required to send the same data using an RS-232-C serial port with no parity, 8 data bits, and 1 stop bit?

3

Advanced Topics

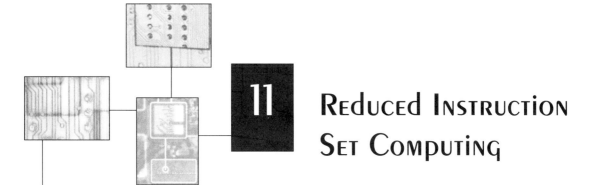

11 REDUCED INSTRUCTION SET COMPUTING

The world of microprocessors and CPUs can be divided into two parts: **complex instruction set computers** using **CISC** processors and **reduced instruction set computers** with **RISC** processors. Both seek to improve system performance, though paradoxically using directly opposite approaches.

As their names imply, CISC and RISC differ in the complexities of their instruction sets. CISC processors have larger instruction sets that often include some particularly complex instructions. These instructions usually correspond to specific statements in high-level languages. Intel's Pentium-class microprocessors fall into this category. In contrast, RISC processors exclude these instructions, opting for a smaller instruction set with simpler instructions. Processors such as MIPS and SPARC are RISC processors. There are a number of other differences, which we discuss in this chapter, but this is the most obvious difference between CISC and RISC. Each approach offers some advantages.

In this chapter we present the rationale for RISC processors, along with their most prevalent features. Then we describe their instruction sets and addressing modes. Next, we examine implementation issues and hazards. We also compare RISC and CISC methodologies in greater detail. Finally, we examine Intel's Itanium microprocessor, which incorporates several characteristics of RISC processors.

11.1 RISC Rationale

The first microprocessors ever developed were very simple processors with very simple instruction sets. As microprocessors became more complex, more instructions were incorporated into their instruction sets. Current CISC microprocessor instruction sets may include over 300 instructions. Some of these instructions, such as register moves, are used frequently; others are very specialized and are used only rarely.

In general, the greater the number of instructions in an instruction set, the larger the propagation delay is within the CPU. To illustrate this, consider the hardwired control unit for the Relatively Simple CPU, shown in Figure 6.17. We used a 4-to-16 decoder to generate outputs corresponding to the 16 instructions in the instruction set. If the CPU had 32 instructions, a 5-to-32 decoder would have been needed. This decoder would require more time to generate its outputs than the smaller 4-to-16 decoder would, which would reduce the maximum clock rate of the CPU. (Although two 4-to-16 decoders could be used instead of the 5-to-32 decoder, they would require external logic to generate the enable signals needed to select one of the two decoders. This would not reduce the propagation delay; in practice, it would actually increase the delay.)

This led some designers to consider eliminating some rarely used instructions from the instruction sets of CPUs. They reasoned that reducing the propagation delay within the CPU would allow the CPU to run at a higher frequency, thus performing each instruction more quickly.

However, as in most engineering designs, there is a tradeoff. The eliminated instructions generally correspond to specific statements in higher-level languages. Eliminating these instructions from the microprocessor's instruction set would force the CPU to use several instructions instead of one to perform the same function; this would invariably require more time. Depending on how frequently the eliminated instructions were needed, and the number of instructions needed to perform their functions, this approach might or might not improve system performance.

Consider a CPU that has a clock period of 20 ns. It is possible to remove some instructions from its instruction set and reduce its clock period to 18 ns. These instructions comprise 2 percent of all code in a typical program and would have to be replaced by three of the remaining instructions in an assembly language program. Assume that every instruction requires the same number of clock cycles, c, to be fetched, decoded, and executed.

If the instructions were not removed from the CPU's instruction set, 100 percent of the instructions would require $(20 \cdot c)$ ns to be processed. If they were removed, 98 percent of program code would require $(18 \cdot c)$ ns, since the CPU would have a lower clock period. The remaining 2 percent of the code would require three times as many instructions, or $(18 \cdot c \cdot 3)$ ns = $(54 \cdot c)$ ns. Comparing the two yields the following result.

$$100\%(20c) \text{ vs. } 98\%(18c) + 2\%(54c)$$
$$20c \text{ vs. } 17.64c + 1.08c$$
$$20 > 18.72$$

On average, the CPU with fewer instructions yields better performance in this case. However, if the removed instructions constitute 10 percent of the typical program, removing these instructions would actually reduce the overall performance of the CPU.

Having a reduced instruction set size, and less complex instructions, is just one characteristic of RISC processors. Many other features distinguish RISC processors from their CISC counterparts. The most common are as follows.

11.1.1 Fixed-Length Instructions

In RISC processors, every instruction has the same size. This does not mean that all instructions must have the same format, just that they must have the same number of bits. For instance, an immediate mode instruction might include an 8-bit operand. Other instructions might use these 8 bits for opcodes or address information.

11.1.2 Limited Loading and Storing Instructions Access Memory

All processors can load data from and store data to memory, but CISC processors often include other capabilities, such as logically ANDing the contents of the accumulator with a value from memory. RISC processors limit interaction with memory to loading and storing data. If a value from memory is to be ANDed with the accumulator, the CPU first loads the value into a register and then performs the AND operation.

11.1.3 Fewer Addressing Modes

In Chapter 4 we listed several common addressing modes. Some, such as indirect mode, require several memory accesses, which degrades system performance. RISC processors typically allow only a few addressing modes that can be processed quickly, such as register indirect and relative modes. As an example, consider the PowerPC 750 CPU, described in the Practical Perspective on page 480.

11.1.4 Instruction Pipeline

A pipeline is like an assembly line in which many products are being worked on simultaneously, each at a different station. This is the same rationale as for arithmetic pipelines, as discussed in Chapter 8. In RISC processors, one instruction is executed while the next is being decoded and its operands are being loaded, while the following instruction is being fetched. By overlapping these operations, the CPU executes one instruction per clock cycle, even though each instruction requires three cycles to be fetched, decoded, and executed. We examine instruction pipelines in more detail later in this chapter.

PRACTICAL PERSPECTIVE: Addressing Modes in the PowerPC 750 RISC CPU

The PowerPC 750 RISC processor supports only two addressing modes for its integer load and store instructions, but these two modes can be manipulated to implement additional addressing modes. The effective addresses calculated by the *register indirect with immediate index* mode and the *register indirect with index* mode are as follows; *rA* and *rB* are each one of the processor's 32 general purpose registers; *offset* is a 16-bit binary value; and *rA* ≠ 0.

Register indirect with immediate index mode: (*rA*) + *offset*
Register indirect with index mode: (*rA*) + *rB*

By setting *offset* to 0, the register indirect with immediate index mode generates an effective address of (*rA*) + *offset* = (*rA*) + 0 = (*rA*), which is the address associated with the register indirect addressing mode. The programmer can also load a predetermined value into *rA,* say *x*, before performing a load instruction using the register indirect with index mode. The effective address for this instruction becomes *x* + *rB*; this is an indexed address mode that uses *rB* as its index register.

11.1.5 Large Number of Registers

Having a large number of registers allows the CPU to store many operands internally. When the operands are needed, the CPU fetches them from the registers, rather than from memory. This reduces the access time significantly. The registers can also be used to pass parameters to subroutines in an efficient manner; this is accomplished using register windowing, described later in this chapter. CISC processors use more of their chip space for control logic than their RISC counterparts; RISC CPUs typically use this space for additional registers.

11.1.6 Hardwired Control Unit

Combinatorial logic generally has a lower propagation delay than a lookup ROM. For this reason, a hardwired control unit can run at a higher clock frequency than its corresponding microcoded control unit. For RISC processors, the benefit of a higher clock rate outweighs the advantages offered by microcoded control units, such as ease of modification. The control units for CISC processors are generally too complex to implement efficiently using hardwired control.

11.1.7 Delayed Loads and Branches

RISC processors use **delayed loads** and **delayed branches** to avoid wasting time. The RISC instruction pipeline can encounter hazards during branch instructions or consecutive instructions that use a common operand. Using delayed loads can avoid these hazards, or at least allow the CPU to perform useful work during what would otherwise be wasted time.

11.1.8   Speculative Execution of Instructions

Some instructions in programs may not be executed, depending on the circumstances. For example, a conditional jump may or may not be taken. If it is, the instruction to which it jumps should be executed; otherwise it should not. In **speculative execution**, the CPU executes the instruction but does not store its result. If the instruction is to be executed, the result is stored. If not, the result is discarded. The Itanium processor handles conditional jumps without any time loss at all.

11.1.9   Optimizing Compiler

Some of the features described so far can be easily implemented directly in hardware. Others benefit greatly from assignments made by an **optimizing compiler**. An optimizing compiler can arrange instructions to facilitate delayed loads and branches, as well as to optimally assign operands to registers. Fewer instructions make it much simpler to design an optimizing compiler for a RISC processor than for a CISC processor.

11.1.10   Separate Instruction and Data Streams

The instruction pipeline may need to access instructions and operands from memory simultaneously. Separating the instruction and data streams helps to avoid memory access conflicts.

11.2   RISC Instruction Sets

As their name implies, the instruction sets of RISC processors are reduced, or smaller in size than those of CISC processors. Whereas a CISC processor might have over 300 instructions in its instruction set, RISC CPUs typically have fewer than 100. These instructions perform a wide variety of functions, sufficient to handle any required tasks. Each instruction should be capable of being executed in a single clock cycle.

When developing a RISC instruction set, it is important not to reduce the set too much. Consider, for example, the instruction set of the Relatively Simple CPU (which is not a RISC CPU). This instruction set includes AND, OR, XOR, and NOT instructions. Using DeMorgan's Law (see Chapter 1), an OR operation can be implemented using only AND and NOT operations as follows.

$$A \text{ OR } B = \text{NOT}((\text{NOT } A) \text{ AND } (\text{NOT } B))$$

Similarly, an XOR operation can be realized using same operations:

$$A \text{ XOR } B = (A \text{ AND } (\text{NOT } B)) \text{ OR } ((\text{NOT } A) \text{ AND } B)$$
$$= \text{NOT}((\text{NOT}(A \text{ AND } (\text{NOT } B))) \text{ AND } (\text{NOT}((\text{NOT } A) \text{ AND } B)))$$

We can exclude the OR and XOR instructions from the instruction set and still allow the CPU to perform the same functions using DeMorgan's Law. However, just because we can exclude them does not mean that we should. The OR and XOR instructions are commonly used instructions; they appear often in typical code. Also, the number of instructions needed to replace them is high, especially for the XOR function. Removing these instructions would most likely decrease, rather than increase, system performance.

Because an RISC CPU must be capable of performing all functions required by a task, all basic types of instructions must be represented in a RISC instruction set. These types of instructions always include data move (load, store, and register move), ALU (arithmetic, logic, and shift), and branch instructions. Some RISC processors include additional classes of instructions. For example, the MIPS 4000 CPU includes a coprocessor and has 11 instructions in its instruction set to interact with it. This CPU also has 12 instructions for dealing with exceptions. Table 11.1 shows the complete list of types of instructions in the MIPS 4000 instruction set and the number of instructions for each type.

Table 11.1

Instruction breakdown for the MIPS 4000 CPU

Instruction Type	Number of Instructions
Data move	15
ALU	16
Multiply/Divide	8
Branch	25
Coprocessor	11
Exception	12
Special	2

RISC CPUs usually operate on only one or two data types directly, generally integer and possibly floating point. They may operate on different precisions or numbers of bits within a given data type. They do not include instructions to manipulate character strings or other data types directly. However, they can be programmed to deal with these data types using the existing instructions in their instruction sets. Although these operations may take longer without dedicated string instructions, overall system performance is improved by excluding them from the instruction set.

RISC processors may utilize different instruction formats, but every instruction must have the same number of bits regardless of which format is used. Furthermore, the CPU must be able to access each instruction code in a single memory-read operation. This is necessary to facilitate pipelining, described in the next section. As an example, Figure 11.1 shows the six formats used by the 32-bit SPARC CPU. Different types of instructions require different operands. For instance, the 30-bit displacement needed by the CALL instruction would be of no use to an ALU instruction. Multiple instruction formats are essential in order to allow a RISC CPU to process instructions of different types.

Instruction formats for the SPARC CPU

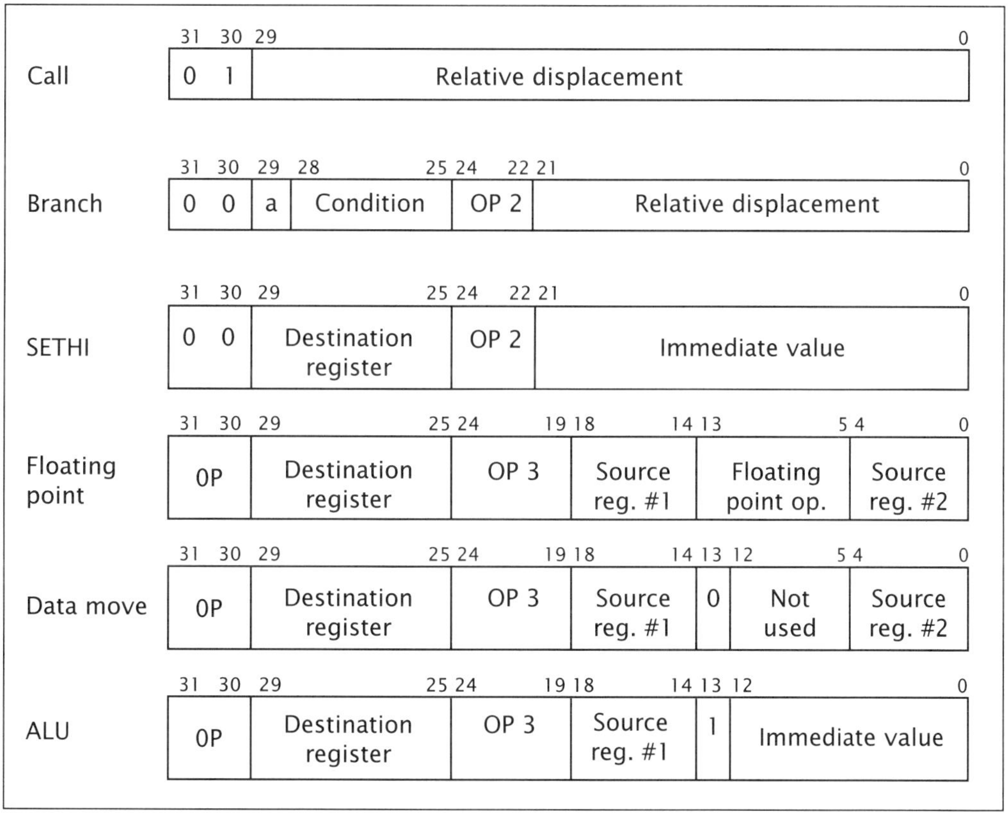

All these requirements explain why the Relatively Simple CPU is not a RISC processor, in spite of its small instruction set size. Its LDAC, STAC, JUMP, JMPZ, and JPNZ instructions require three 8-bit bytes, one for the opcode and two for address Γ. All other instructions use a single byte. These five instructions require a different number of bits and more memory references than the rest, violating a key rule of RISC methodology.

The instruction set of a RISC processor can only access memory using load and store instructions, but there may be several different load and store instructions in the instruction set. Recall from Table 11.1 that the MIPS 4000 microprocessor has 15 data move instructions. Of these, eight load data, but in different ways. The LB instruction loads a byte (8 bits) of data; the LH instruction loads a 16-bit halfword; and the LW instruction loads a 32-bit word of data. Other load instructions deal with unsigned data and the alignment of data.

RISC processors have fewer addressing modes than their CISC counterparts. However, all addressing modes have one characteristic in common. Their effective addresses can be computed in a single clock cycle. (This precludes the use of indirect addressing mode, which must make two sequential memory accesses.) Without this feature, it would be necessary to redesign the pipeline used to process instructions.

The RISC II processor has three primary memory addressing modes. It is possible to supply a relative address as part of the instruction code. (Since this CPU has 32 address and 32 data bits, only the low-order portion of the relative address is specified. The high-order bits are sign-extended from the most significant bit of this value.) This CPU also supports indexed and register indirect address modes.

The RISC II includes an interesting feature that allows it to extend its addressing modes. It includes a pseudoregister, $R0$, which always contains the value 0. This allows the programmer to use indexed mode to specify an absolute address. Indexed mode calculates its address by taking the address specified by the user and adding it to the contents of a register, which is also specified by the user. If the user specifies register $R0$, which always has a value of 0, the effective address will be the absolute address specified by the user in the instruction code.

11.3 INSTRUCTION PIPELINES AND REGISTER WINDOWS

The reduced number and complexity of the instructions in the instruction sets of RISC processors are the basis for the improved performance these CPUs can provide. It is the implementation of a RISC CPU, however, which actually produces this benefit. For instance, the smaller instruction set allows the designer to implement a hardwired control unit, which runs at a higher clock rate than its equivalent microsequenced control unit.

In this section we examine two implementation techniques commonly used in RISC processors to improve performance. As mentioned earlier, RISC CPUs use pipelined instruction units to break down the fetch-decode-execute procedure and to process several instructions in parallel. The instruction pipeline allows RISC processors to execute one instruction per clock cycle. The other technique is the incorporation of large numbers of registers within the CPU. This allows more variables to be stored in registers, rather than memory, which reduces the time needed to access data. The large number of registers also speeds up the passing of parameters to and results from subroutines.

11.3.1 Instruction Pipelines

An **instruction pipeline** is very similar to a manufacturing assembly line. Imagine an assembly line partitioned into four stages: The first stage receives some parts, performs its assembly task, and passes the results to the second stage; the second stage takes the partially assembled product from the first stage, performs its task, and passes its work to the third stage; the third stage does its work, passing the results to the last stage, which completes the task and outputs its results. As the first piece moves from the first stage to the second stage, a new set of parts for a new piece enters the first stage. Ultimately, every stage processes a piece simultaneously. This is how time is saved. Each product requires the same amount of time to be processed (actually slightly more, to account for the transfers between stages), but products are manufactured more quickly because several are being created at the same time.

An instruction pipeline processes an instruction the way the assembly line processes a product. The first stage fetches the instruction from memory. The second stage decodes the instruction and fetches any required operands. The third stage executes the instruction, and the fourth stage stores the result. As with the assembly line, each stage processes instructions simultaneously (after an initial **latency**, or delay, to fill the pipeline). This allows the CPU to execute one instruction per clock cycle.

This is one possible configuration of an RISC pipeline, the pipeline implemented in the SPARC MB86900 CPU. The IBM 801, the first RISC computer, also uses a four-stage instruction pipeline. Other processors, such as the RISC II, use only three stages; they combine the execute and store result operations in to a single stage. The MIPS processor uses a five-stage pipeline; it decodes the instruction and selects the operand registers in separate stages. These three configurations are shown in Figure 11.2. Note that each stage has a register that latches its data at the end of the stage to synchronize data flow between stages. The flow of instructions through each pipeline is shown in Figure 11.3. One instruction enters the pipeline per clock cycle. After the initial latency needed to fill the pipeline, one result is generated every clock cycle.

FIGURE 11.2
(a) Three-, (b) four-, and (c) five-stage RISC pipelines

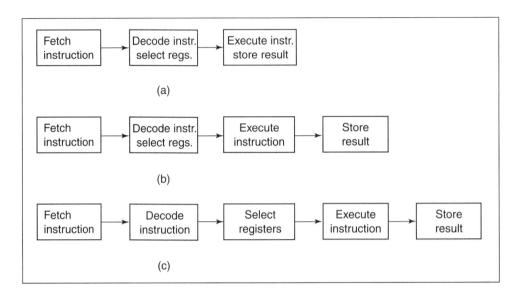

FIGURE 11.3

Data flow through (a) three-, (b) four-, and (c) five-stage RISC pipelines

Although we could employ several complete control units to process instructions, a single pipelined control unit offers several advantages. The primary advantage is the reduced hardware requirements of the pipeline. Since each stage performs only a portion of the fetch-decode-execute process, no stage needs to incorporate the hardware of a complete control unit; each stage only needs the hardware associated with its task. For example, the instruction-fetch stage only needs to read an instruction from memory. This stage does not need the hardware used to decode or execute instructions. Similarly, a stage that decodes instructions does not access memory; the instruction-fetch stage has already loaded the instruction from memory into an instruction register for the decode stage to use.

A second advantage of instruction pipelines is the reduced complexity of the memory interface. If each stage had a complete control unit, all stages could access memory. This would cause memory access conflicts, which would have to be resolved by the CPU. In practice, RISC CPUs generally partition their memory into instruction and data modules, much like the cache memory in Chapter 9. The instruction-fetch stage reads data only from the instruction memory module. The execute-instruction stage only accesses memory when it is reading data from the data memory module; at all other times it is dealing with data in registers. The store-result stage writes data to the data memory module. Specially designed memory can be configured to allow simultaneous read and write access to different locations, avoiding a memory access conflict by the execute-instruction and store-results stages of the pipeline.

As with the arithmetic pipelines of Chapter 8, the clock rate of the pipeline, and thus the CPU, is limited to that of its slowest stage. For instance, if a pipeline has four stages with delays of 20 ns, 20 ns, 100 ns, and 40 ns, the clock period must be at least 100 ns to account for the delay of the third stage. This results in a maximum clock rate of 10 MHz. In general, the pipeline achieves its maximum performance when all stages have the same delay.

This is why CPU designers have used different numbers of stages in their instruction pipelines. In some CPUs, the execute stage is divided into two sequential stages. In the previous example, assume that the 100 ns execute-instruction stage could be partitioned into two sequential stages, each with a propagation delay of 50 ns. (In practice, the delay would be slightly higher due to the latches at the end of each stage, but we will ignore this for now.) The pipeline would now have five stages with delays of 20 ns, 20 ns, 50 ns, 50 ns, and 40 ns. The clock period would be reduced to 50 ns and the clock frequency doubled to 20 MHz.

Sometimes we can use this same reasoning to reduce the number of stages in a pipeline. In the five-stage pipeline, we can combine stages 1 and 2 into a single stage with a propagation delay of 40 ns. (In practice, removing one of the two end-of-stage latches makes the delay slightly less than this.) Now the pipeline has four stages with propagation delays of 40 ns, 50 ns, 50 ns, and 40 ns, which is nearly optimal. Combining the first two stages slightly reduces their hardware complexity without reducing the clock frequency. In addition, having one fewer stage allows the pipeline to fill and produce results starting one clock cycle earlier.

The pipeline offers significant performance improvement over the non-pipelined CPU. As with arithmetic pipelines, the **speedup** is the ratio of the time needed to process n instructions using a non-pipelined control unit to the time needed using a pipelined control unit. Mathematically, this is expressed by the following formula.

$$S_n = \frac{nT_1}{(n + k - 1)T_k}$$

Here, T_1 is the time needed to process one instruction using a non-pipelined control unit, 180 ns in this example. The number of stages in the pipeline is k, and T_k is the clock period of the pipeline. In our example, $k = 4$ and $T_k = 50$ ns. The speedup for this pipeline becomes

$$S_n = \frac{n \cdot 180}{(n + 4 - 1) \cdot 50}$$

For steady state, $(n \to \infty)$, the maximum speedup is $S_n = 180/50 = 3.6$. In reality, the speedup would be slightly less than this for two reasons. First, this does not account for the first few cycles needed to fill the pipeline. In addition, the 180 ns includes time needed for latches at the end of each stage. In a non-pipelined CPU, these latches and their associated delays do not exist, and the actual time needed to process an instruction would be slightly less than 180 ns.

Pipelines do cause and encounter problems. One such problem is memory access. A pipeline must fetch an instruction from memory in a single clock cycle, but main memory usually is not fast enough to supply data this quickly. RISC processors must include cache memory, which is at least as fast as the pipeline. If a RISC CPU cannot fetch one instruction per clock cycle, it cannot execute one instruction per clock cycle. As we noted previously, the cache must separate instructions and data to avoid memory conflicts from the different stages of the pipeline.

Another problem is caused by branch statements. When a branch statement is executed, the instructions already in the pipeline should not be there. They are the instructions located sequentially after the branch statement, not the instructions to which the branch statement jumps. There is not much that the pipeline can do about this. Instead, an optimizing compiler is needed to reorder the instructions to avoid this problem. We cover this in greater detail in Section 11.4.

11.3.2   Register Windowing and Renaming

The reduced hardware requirements of RISC processors leave additional space available on the chip for the system designer. RISC CPUs generally use this space to include a large number of registers, sometimes more than 100. The CPU can access data in registers more quickly than data in memory, so having more registers makes more data available faster. Having more registers also helps reduce the number of memory references, particularly when calling and returning from subroutines.

Although a RISC processor has many registers, it may not be able to access all of them at any given time. Most RISC CPUs have some **global registers**, which are always accessible. The remaining registers are **windowed** so that only a subset of the registers are accessible at any specific time.

To understand how **register windows** work, consider the windowing scheme used by the SPARC processors, shown in Figure 11.4. (One piece of information is missing from this figure; we will discuss it shortly.) This processor can access any of 32 different registers at a given time. (Recall that the instruction formats for the SPARC in Figure 11.1 always use 5 bits to select a source or destination register, which can take on any of 32 different values.) Of these 32 registers, eight are global registers that are always accessible. The remaining 24 registers are contained in the register window.

As shown in Figure 11.4, the register windows overlap. In the SPARC processor, the overlap consists of eight registers. For example, the last eight registers of window 1 are also the first eight registers of window 2. Similarly, the last eight registers of window 2 are also the first eight registers of window 3. The middle eight registers of window 2 are local; they are not shared with any other window.

The RISC CPU must keep track of which window is active and which windows contain valid data. A **window pointer register** contains the value of the window that is currently active. A **window mask register** contains 1 bit per window and denotes which windows contain valid data.

Register windows provide their greatest benefit when the CPU calls a subroutine. During the calling process, the register window is moved down one window position. In the SPARC example, if window 1 is active and the CPU calls a subroutine, the processor activates window 2 by updating the window pointer and window mask registers. The CPU can pass parameters to the subroutine via the registers that overlap both windows, instead of through memory; this saves a significant amount of time in accessing data. The CPU can use the same registers to return results to the calling routine.

To illustrate how this works, consider a CPU with 48 registers. The CPU has four windows with 16 registers each, and an overlap of

FIGURE 11.4

Register windowing in the SPARC processor

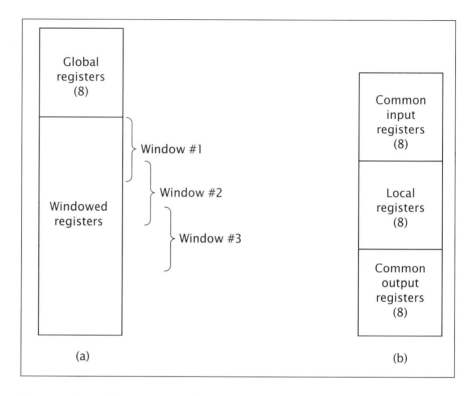

four registers between windows. Initially, the CPU is running a program using its first register window, as shown in Figure 11.5(a). It must call a subroutine and pass three parameters to the subroutine. The CPU stores these parameters in three of the four overlapping registers and calls the subroutine. Figure 11.5(b) shows the state of the CPU while the subroutine is active. The subroutine can directly access the parameters. Now the subroutine calculates a result to be returned to the main program. It stores this value in one of the overlapping registers and returns to the main program. This deactivates the second window; the CPU now works with the first window, as shown in Figure 11.5(c), and can directly access the result.

Most RISC processors that use register windowing have about eight windows. For the vast majority of programs, this is sufficient to handle subroutine calls. Other than for recursive subroutines, it is very unusual for a program to go beyond eight levels of calls. However, it is possible for the level of calls to exceed the number of windows, and the CPU must be able to handle this situation.

The windowing configuration shown in Figure 11.4 leaves out one important piece of information. The organization of the windowed registers is not linear, but circular. The last window overlaps

FIGURE 11.5

Register windowing in a CPU: (a) during execution of the main routine, (b) executing a subroutine, and (c) after returning from the subroutine

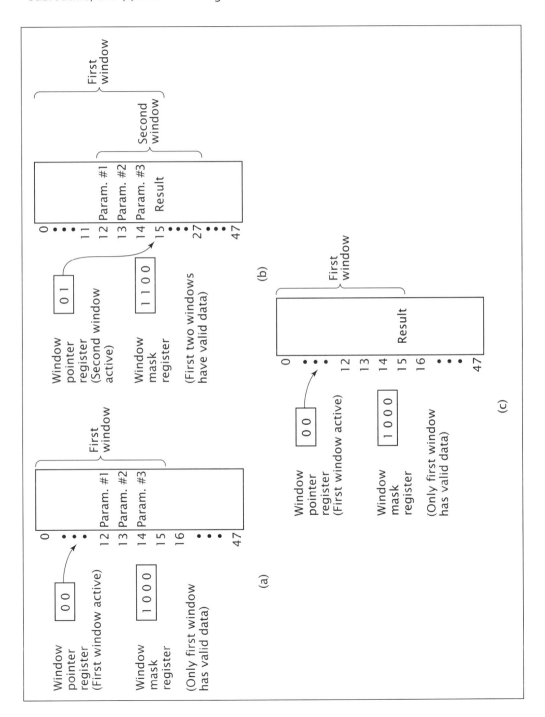

PRACTICAL PERSPECTIVE:
Register Windowing and Register Renaming in Real-World CPUs

Both register windowing and register renaming are used in modern processors. In addition to SPARC processors, the RISC II processor uses register windowing. The RISC II processor has 138 registers; 10 are global and the rest are windowed. Each of its eight windows contains 22 registers: six common input, ten local, and six common output. The UltraSPARC IIi processor also uses register windowing. The MIPS R10000, on the other hand, uses register renaming.

Intel's Itanium processor takes a unique approach. It has 128 integer registers, 32 of which are global. The remaining 96 registers are windowed, but the size of the window is not fixed; their size can be varied depending on the needs of the program under execution.

window 1; its common output registers are also the common input registers of the first window. If the program being executed causes the CPU to wrap around to a window already in use (as denoted by the window mask register), the processor saves the contents of the window's registers in memory as part of the subroutine call. It restores the values to the registers when the CPU returns from the subroutine.

More recent processors may use **register renaming** to add flexibility to the idea of register windowing. A processor that uses register renaming can select any registers to comprise its working register "window." The CPU uses pointers to keep track of which registers are active and which physical register corresponds to each logical register. Unlike register windowing, in which only specific groups of physical registers are active at any given time, register renaming allows any group of physical registers to be active.

The Practical Perspective looks at register windowing and register renaming in real-world CPUs.

11.4 Instruction Pipeline Conflicts

Although RISC instruction pipelines improve overall processor performance, they are far from perfect. In fact, they introduce problems not found in non-pipelined control units. Nevertheless, their benefits outweigh the conflicts caused by these problems, and all high-performance RISC processors incorporate instruction pipelines in their designs.

The conflicts caused by these pipelines fall into two categories. **Data conflicts** occur when the pipeline causes an incorrect data value to be used. **Branch conflicts** occur when a branch statement results in incorrect instructions being executed.

11.4.1 Data Conflicts

A data conflict occurs within a RISC pipeline when one instruction stores a result in a register and another instruction uses that value as an operand. Under certain conditions, the second instruction will read the old value before the first instruction has stored the new value. The second instruction uses the incorrect value of the operand in its calculations.

To illustrate this conflict, consider the following consecutive program statements. Initially, registers $R1$, $R2$, $R3$, $R4$, $R5$, and $R6$ contain the values 1, 2, 3, 4, 5, and 6, respectively.

$$1: R1 \leftarrow R2 + R3$$
$$2: R4 \leftarrow R1 + R3$$
$$3: R5 \leftarrow R6 + R3$$

If this code is executed on a RISC CPU that uses the three-stage pipeline shown in Figure 11.2(a), the following sequence of events will occur. During the first clock cycle, the first stage fetches the first instruction from memory. In the next clock cycle, the second stage decodes this instruction and fetches the data from registers $R2$ (2) and $R3$ (3). At the same time, the first stage fetches the second instruction from memory. During the third clock cycle, the first instruction is executed and the result (2 + 3 = 5) is stored in register $R1$. Also, the first stage fetches the third instruction from memory. Simultaneously, the second stage decodes the second instruction and fetches the contents of $R1$ and $R3$. The value of $R1$ loaded by this stage is the value at the beginning of this clock cycle, not the values stored by the third stage. It loads the values 1 for $R1$ and 3 for $R3$. This will ultimately set $R4$ to the incorrect value of 4 (= 1 + 3) instead of the correct value of 8 (= 5 + 3).

This simple example illustrates the data conflict problem encountered by RISC instruction pipelines. This problem occurs when one instruction stores a result in a register and a subsequent instruction reads the contents of that register before the first instruction has stored its result. Note that two instructions that read the same value do not cause a data conflict, since the value is not modified. In this example, all three instructions read the value of $R3$. Since no instruction changes its contents, no data conflict occurs.

There are several solutions to this data conflict problem. Some are handled in software, while others are resolved using additional hardware in the pipeline. Of these, the simplest is to have the compiler detect data conflicts and insert no-ops to avoid the conflict. For the previous code block, the compiler could rewrite the code as follows.

$$1: R1 \leftarrow R2 + R3$$
$$N: \textit{no-op}$$
$$2: R4 \leftarrow R1 + R3$$
$$3: R5 \leftarrow R6 + R3$$

Figure 11.6 shows the execution trace, the flow of data through the three-stage pipeline, for both blocks of code. The no-op statement in the second block delays the fetching of operands for the second instruction by one clock cycle. This delay allows the last stage of the pipeline to store the new value of $R1$ before it is loaded for use in executing the second instruction, thus avoiding the data conflict.

FIGURE 11.6

Execution trace of the code block: (a) without and (b) with no-op insertion

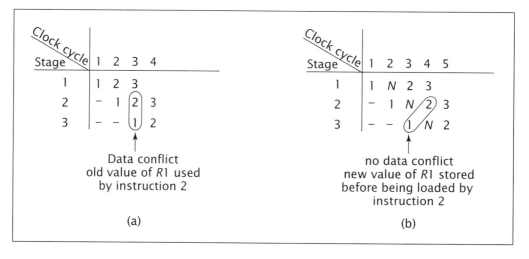

(a)   (b)

Although **no-op insertion** solves the data conflict problem, it reduces overall system performance. The no-op instruction does not perform useful work and require an extra clock cycle. It is a valid solution to the data conflict problem, but it is not optimal.

Another compiler-based solution can resolve this problem and yield better performance than no-op insertion. For some programs, the compiler can reorder some of the instructions to remove the data conflict. Of course, this can be done only if it does not change the results calculated by the program. For example, the code segment (without the no-op) could be reordered by swapping the second and third instructions, yielding the following:

$$1: R1 \leftarrow R2 + R3$$
$$3: R5 \leftarrow R6 + R3$$
$$2: R4 \leftarrow R1 + R3$$

Figure 11.7 shows the execution trace of the reordered code through a three-stage pipeline. Comparing this to the execution traces shown in Figure 11.6, we can see that this solution resolves the data conflict but does not waste the clock cycle used by the no-op. As with no-op insertion, **instruction reordering** resolves the data conflict by introducing a delay between the conflicting instructions. Unlike no-op insertion, however, instruction reordering performs useful work during this time.

FIGURE 11.7

Execution trace of the reordered code block

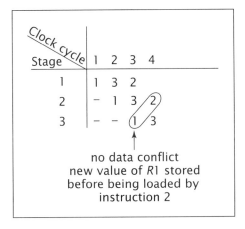

It is not always possible to reorder the instructions of a program to avoid data conflicts. For example, the following code segment cannot be reordered successfully:

$$1: R1 \leftarrow R1 + R2$$
$$2: R1 \leftarrow R1 + R3$$
$$3: R1 \leftarrow R1 + R4$$

In a case such as this, the compiler would have to resort to inserting no-ops to resolve the data conflicts.

No-op insertion and instruction reordering resolve data conflicts using only the compiler. Other solutions to this problem use additional hardware in the RISC instruction pipeline. One such method is **stall insertion**. In this method, the additional hardware detects data conflicts between instructions in the pipeline and inserts stalls, or introduces delays, to resolve the data conflicts. This is similar to no-op insertion, except it is handled by hardware, while the program is executing, rather than by the compiler while the program is being compiled. Figure 11.8 shows the execution trace of the same code block used throughout this section on a RISC processor that uses instruction stalls.

FIGURE 11.8

Execution trace of the code block with instruction stalls

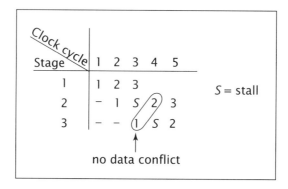

As with no-op insertion, stall insertion resolves the data conflict problem but reduces system performance. No useful work is performed during the stall, just as no useful work was performed while the no-op instruction executed.

A second hardware solution to the data conflict problem is **data forwarding**. After the instruction is executed, its result is stored, just as before, but the result is also forwarded directly to the stage that selects registers (retrieves operands). That stage gets the new value of the operand directly from the execute instruction stage of the pipeline before (or at the same time as) it is stored in the appropriate register. Figure 11.9 shows the data paths of the three-stage pipeline modified to implement data forwarding, along with the execution trace of the same three-instruction code block used throughout this section. Although it might appear that a data conflict still exists, the data forwarding hardware successfully resolves the conflict. The value of $R1$ for instruction 1 is calculated during clock cycle 3; as it is calculated, it is also forwarded back to stage two of the pipeline. Thus, stage two successfully fetches all of its operands by the end of the third clock cycle.

11.4.2   BRANCH CONFLICTS

Branch or jump statements can also cause conflicts within a RISC instruction pipeline. Unlike data conflicts, though, branch conflicts do not cause incorrect data values to be used. Instead, branch conflicts cause the CPU to execute instructions at times when they should not be executed.

The following code segment illustrates the branch conflict problem.

$$1: R1 \leftarrow R2 + R3$$
$$2: R4 \leftarrow R5 + R6$$
$$3: \text{JUMP } 10$$

4: $R7 \leftarrow R8 + R9$

5: $R10 \leftarrow R11 + R12$

⋮

10: $R13 \leftarrow R14 + R15$

The execution trace of this code, run using the three-stage pipeline shown in Figure 11.2(a), appears in Figure 11.10. One instruction enters the pipeline per clock cycle. After instruction 3 is executed, the CPU should branch to instruction 10; however, instructions 4 and 5 are already in the pipeline before instruction 3 is executed.

As with the data conflict problem, some solutions to this problem use only software (the compiler), some only hardware, and some both.

Figure 11.9

Data forwarding: (a) modified three-stage pipeline and (b) execution trace of the code block

(a)

Stage \ Clock cycle	1	2	3	4
1	1	2	3	
2	–	1	(2)	3
3	–	–	(1)	2

no data conflict due to data forwarding

(b)

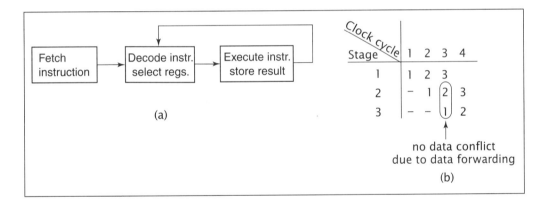

Figure 11.10

Execution trace of the code block illustrating a branch conflict

Stage \ Clock cycle	1	2	3	4	5	6
1	1	2	3	4	5	10
2	–	1	2	3	4	5	10
3	–	–	1	2	3	(4 5)

these instructions should not be executed

This problem is more complex than data conflict, though, because of conditional branch instructions, which may or may not branch during a given execution.

First we consider the simpler case of unconditional branch instructions, as in the previous code segment. Just as with data conflicts, it is possible to resolve a branch conflict by using no-op insertion. In this case, the compiler could insert two no-ops immediately after the jump statement:

$$
\begin{array}{ll}
1: & R1 \leftarrow R2 + R3 \\
2: & R4 \leftarrow R5 + R6 \\
3: & \text{JUMP 10} \\
N1: & \textit{no-op} \\
N2: & \textit{no-op} \\
4: & R7 \leftarrow R8 + R9 \\
5: & R10 \leftarrow R11 + R12 \\
& \vdots \\
10: & R13 \leftarrow R14 + R15
\end{array}
$$

The execution trace for this code is shown in Figure 11.11(a). The no-ops introduce a delay sufficient to ensure that instructions 4 and 5 are never introduced into the pipeline. However, just as in the data conflict problem, no useful work is performed during these cycles, thus reducing system performance.

FIGURE 11.11

Execution traces of the code block using: (a) no-op insertion, and (b) instruction reordering

Clock cycle Stage	1	2	3	4	5	6
1	1	2	3	N1	N2	10
2	–	1	2	3	N1	N2 10
3	–	–	1	2	3	N1

(a)

Clock cycle Stage	1	2	3	4	5
1	3	1	2	10	
2	–	3	1		
3	–	–	3		

(b)

Also as with data conflicts, it is often possible to use instruction reordering to resolve branch conflicts. For this code block, we can reorder the instructions as follows:

$$3: \text{JUMP } 10$$
$$1: R1 \leftarrow R2 + R3$$
$$2: R4 \leftarrow R5 + R6$$
$$4: R7 \leftarrow R8 + R9$$
$$5: R10 \leftarrow R11 + R12$$
$$\vdots$$
$$10: R13 \leftarrow R14 + R15$$

The execution trace for this code segment is shown in Figure 11.11(b). It offers improved system performance over no-op insertion because it performs useful work during every cycle. However, just as in data conflicts, it is not always possible to successfully reorder instructions. In these cases, the compiler would have to resort to inserting no-ops.

Stall insertion can also be used to handle branch conflicts. As with data conflicts, the pipeline would be modified to incorporate additional hardware that would recognize branch instructions. When the pipeline recognized a branch instruction, it would insert stalls into the pipeline to delay the fetching of the next instruction until after the branch instruction had been completed. This requires only one instruction to be checked, as opposed to two for data conflicts. The decode instruction stage would insert any necessary stalls to prevent incorrect instructions from entering the pipeline. However, just as with data conflicts, stalls degrade system performance.

Conditional branches present a much more difficult problem. Depending on their conditions during program execution, they may or may not be taken. The conditional JUMP instruction at the end of a program loop may be executed several times with different results. To illustrate this, consider the following code segment:

$$1: R10 \leftarrow 10$$
$$2: R1 \leftarrow R1 + R3$$
$$3: R2 \leftarrow R2 + R3$$
$$4: R10 \leftarrow R10 - 1$$
$$5: \text{IF } (R10 \neq 0) \text{ THEN GOTO } 2$$

In this program segment, the conditional GOTO statement (5) is accessed at the end of the loop. The first nine times it is called, its condition is met and it branches back. The tenth time, however, $R10$ is equal to 0 and the jump is not taken. The CPU must handle both cases successfully.

The three methods used for unconditional jumps, no-op insertion, instruction reordering, and stall insertion can also be used for conditional jumps. We can modify the code block using no-op insertion as follows. Note that we have also included a no-op instruction between statements 4 and 5; we did this to alleviate the data conflict on register $R10$. The two no-ops after statement 5 resolve the branch conflict.

        1:   $R10\leftarrow 10$
        2:   $R1\leftarrow R1 + R3$
        3:   $R2\leftarrow R2 + R3$
        4:   $R10\leftarrow R10 - 1$
        N1: *no-op*
        5:   IF $(R10 \neq 0)$ THEN GOTO 2
        N2: *no-op*
        N3: *no-op*

If instruction reordering is used instead, the no-ops may be replaced with useful instructions. Ignoring the data conflict for just a moment, this code could be reordered as follows:

        1: $R10\leftarrow 10$
        4: $R10\leftarrow R10 - 1$
        5: IF $(R10 \neq 0)$ THEN GOTO 4
        2: $R1\leftarrow R1 + R3$
        3: $R2\leftarrow R2 + R3$

Note that both statements 4 and 5 were moved to the front of the loop. Since statement 4 modifies the register tested by the conditional jump instruction, it must still be executed before the conditional jump. An execution trace can verify that this reordering resolves the branch conflict.

In this code segment, the data conflict on register $R10$ still exists. We can resolve this conflict using no-op insertion, stall insertion, or data forwarding. It can also be resolved by a particularly clever compiler. If we incorporate the first decrement of $R10$ into the statement that initially loads the register, we can reorder the remaining instructions without including no-ops. One possible reordering is

        1:   $R10\leftarrow 9 (= 10 - 1)$
        2:   $R1\leftarrow R1 + R3$
        5:   IF $(R10 \neq 0)$ THEN GOTO 2
        3:   $R2\leftarrow R2 + R3$
        4:   $R10\leftarrow R10 - 1$
        N: *no-op*
        5A: $R10\leftarrow R10 + 1$

Notice the last statement, 5A. Because we set $R10$ to 9 instead of 10, and because statement 4 is executed once per loop iteration, $R10$ is decremented to -1 instead of 0. Statement 5A restores $R10$ to its correct value, nullifying the extra subtraction. This is similar in concept to the restoring division algorithm in Chapter 8. However, care must be taken when doing something like this to ensure that no flags are changed to incorrect values.

Another method, which is somewhat similar to this, is **annulling**. In annulling, the instructions proceed through the pipeline as they normally would. If an instruction should not have been executed, because a previous instruction branched away from it, its results are not stored. Even though it might have been executed, as long as no results are stored it is as if the instruction was never processed. (Any flag values that would be modified by the instruction are not changed either.) To illustrate this, consider the original program loop, along with the instructions immediately after the loop:

$$1: R10 \leftarrow 10$$
$$2: R1 \leftarrow R1 + R3$$
$$3: R2 \leftarrow R2 + R3$$
$$4: R10 \leftarrow R10 - 1$$
$$5: \text{IF } (R10 \neq 0) \text{ THEN GOTO } 2$$
$$6: R4 \leftarrow R5 + R6$$
$$7: R7 \leftarrow R8 + R9$$

Figure 11.12 shows the execution trace for this code on a three-stage pipeline with data forwarding. Notice that statements 5, 6, and 7 are all in the pipeline during clock cycle 7, even though statement 5 should be followed by statement 2. The execution of statements 6 and 7 are annulled by the pipeline hardware, which knows that the branch in statement 5 is taken. During clock cycle 61, the branch is not taken and the loop terminates. This time, the execution of statements 6 and 7 during the following two clock cycles are not annulled and their results are stored.

FIGURE 11.12

Execution trace of the code block using annulling

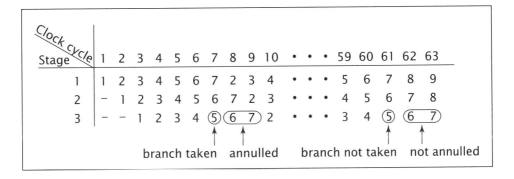

As with no-op insertion and stall insertion, this method degrades system performance. The annulled instructions might just as well have been no-ops from a performance perspective. The only time saving occurs after the last iteration of the loop. The execution of statements 6 and 7 during clock cycles 62 and 63 represents the only performance improvement over no-op instructions.

The performance of the pipeline could be improved by using **branch prediction**. Consider the same block of code being run on the same pipeline. Branch prediction allows the compiler or pipeline hardware to make an assumption as to whether or not the conditional branch will be taken. The CPU enters the most likely next instruction into the pipeline immediately after the conditional branch instruction. If its guess is right, the correct next instruction occurs immediately after the conditional branch instruction and is executed during the next clock cycle; no delay is introduced. If the guess is wrong, the results are annulled as before.

Figure 11.13 shows the execution trace of the previous code block using branch prediction. Since program loops usually execute more than once, the conditional branch is assumed always to occur. (This will be correct for every iteration except the last.) As shown in Figure 11.13, the loop and instructions 6 and 7 now require 47 clock cycles instead of 63, a time savings of over 25 percent.

FIGURE 11.13

Execution trace of the code block using branch prediction

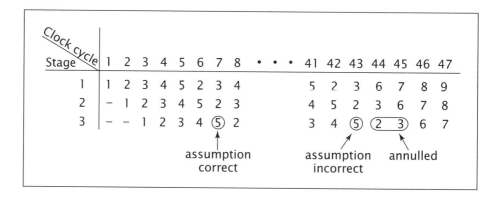

11.5 RISC vs. CISC

Given the differences between RISC and CISC, which is better? The answer to this question is that there is no one right answer to this question. Each has some features that are better than the other.

RISC processors have fewer and simpler instructions than CISC processors. As a result, their control units are less complex and easier to design. This allows them to run at higher clock frequencies than CISC processors and reduces the amount of space needed on the processor chip, so designers can use the extra space for additional registers and other components. Simpler control units can also lead to reduced development costs. With a simpler design, it is easier to incorporate parallelism into the control unit of a RISC CPU.

With fewer instructions in their instruction sets, the compilers for RISC processors are less complex than those for CISC processors. As a general guideline, CISC processors were originally designed for assembly language programming, whereas RISC processors are geared toward compiled, high-level language programs. However, the same compiled high-level program will require more instructions for a RISC CPU than for a CISC CPU.

The CISC methodology offers some advantages as well. Although CISC processors are more complex, this complexity does not necessarily increase development costs. Current CISC processors are often the most recent addition to an entire family of processors, such as Intel's Pentium family. As such, they may incorporate portions of the designs of previous processors in their families. This reduces the cost of design and can improve reliability, since the previous design has (presumably) been proved to work.

CISC processors also provide backward compatibility with other processors in their families. If they are pin compatible, it may be possible simply to replace a previous generation processor with the newest model without changing the rest of the computer's design. This same backward compatibility, whether pin compatible or not, allows the CISC CPU to run the same software as used by the predecessors in its family. For instance, a program that runs successfully on a Pentium II should also run successfully on a Pentium III. This can translate into significant savings for the user and can determine the success or failure of a microprocessor.

The fate of the Neanderthals is a topic hotly debated by anthropologists. On one side are those who believe that Homo sapiens and Neanderthals intermingled, eventually becoming a single species. Opposing this view are those who believe that Homo sapiens out-competed Neanderthals, ultimately driving them to extinction. No one can say with certainty which view is correct. Likewise no one can say who is right: Researchers who believe that RISC processors will replace CISC processors or those who believe the two will coexist, if not intermingle. Some see the RISC processor as the Homo sapiens, out-competing its Neanderthal CISC counterpart. This topic has been strongly debated, rebutted, and counter-rebutted for the past several years.

However one assigns RISC and CISC to this analogy, intermingling is currently underway. CISC designs generally incorporate instruction pipelines, which has improved performance dramatically in RISC processors. As technology allows more devices to be incorporated into a single microprocessor chip, CISC CPUs are adding more registers to their designs, again to achieve the performance improvements they provide to RISC processors. Newer processor families, such as PowerPC microprocessors, draw some features from RISC methodology and others from CISC, making them a hybrid of RISC and CISC.

11.6 Real World Example: The Itanium Microprocessor

Intel's Itanium microprocessor, though not an RISC CPU, borrows many features from RISC processors. It also introduces solutions to some of the problems that RISC processors face.

The Intel microprocessors that preceded Itanium were based on IA-32 instruction set architecture. For the Itanium microprocessor (and its successors), Hewlett-Packard and Intel collaborated to develop the **IA-64** instruction set architecture, a 64-bit architecture designed to promote the parallel execution of instructions.

Each instruction in the IA-64, and Itanium, architecture is 40 bits wide. The Itanium processor fetches 128-bit words, each of which have three instructions and an 8-bit template with information about dependencies between the instructions. The Itanium CPU has several internal function units that can execute the three instructions in parallel. The compiler, not the CPU, explicitly orders the instructions to maximize parallelism. In this respect, this CPU follows the **explicitly parallel instruction computing** (**EPIC**) design philosophy. The Itanium processor includes several integer and floating point units to execute instructions simultaneously.

The internal organization of the Itanium CPU is shown in Figure 11.14. By relegating the ordering of instructions to the compiler, the Itanium designers freed up quite a bit of space on the chip that would otherwise be needed to recognize and resolve data dependencies. The Itanium uses this free space for additional registers. It has 128 integer registers and 128 floating point registers. The Itanium processor also includes both Level 1 and Level 2 caches on the CPU chip itself. The Level 1 cache is split into separate data and instruction caches, each four-way set associative with its own TLB. The Level 2 cache is six-way set associative; it is a unified cache. The Level 3 cache shown in Figure 11.14 is outside of the CPU. An Itanium-based computer may also have an external Level 4 cache.

To ensure the commercial success of the Itanium processor, Intel had to make it able to run the code of its predecessors, Intel's Pentium line of microprocessors. The Itanium includes a separate control unit, the IA-32 decode and control section, to handle these instructions.

The Itanium processor uses **predication** to avoid the problem of conditional branches. Each instruction is assigned a 1-bit tag, its **predicate**, which can be set during program execution. If the predicate is true, the instruction is executed normally. If the predicate is

Figure 11.14

Internal organization of the Itanium microprocessor (courtesy Intel Corp.)

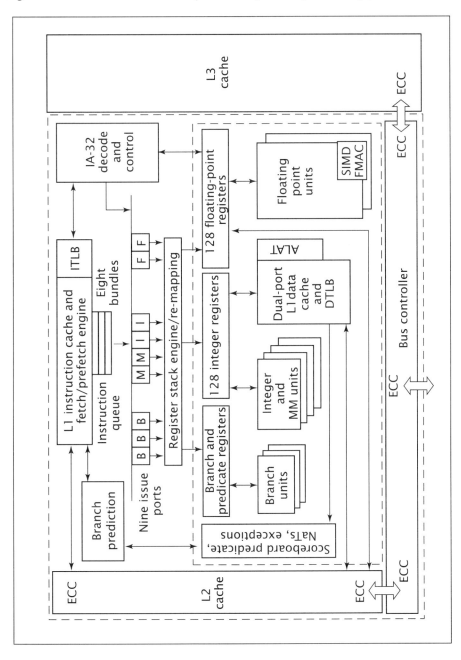

false, the instruction is still executed, but its results are not stored. This is similar to annulling. The tag is stored in one of the 64 1-bit predicate registers; each instruction is assigned one predicate register during program execution.

To understand how predication works, consider a high-level language example of a conditional instruction:

$$\text{IF } x = 0 \text{ THEN } y{\leftarrow}y + 1$$

We could rewrite this instruction in predicate form as follows:

$$y{\leftarrow}y + 1 \text{ IF } x = 0$$

Here, $x = 0$ is the predicate; we only perform the operation $y{\leftarrow}y + 1$ if this predicate is true. In the Itanium microprocessor, the instruction to perform this operation would check whether $x = 0$ while simultaneously calculating the value $y + 1$. When the predicate ($x = 0$) is true, it stores the result in y; otherwise it discards the result, leaving y unchanged.

The Itanium processor also uses **speculative execution** to execute register load instructions before it can be sure that the load instruction should be executed. It does this to reduce delays associated with fetching data from memory. Predication and normal instruction reordering by the compiler resolve most data dependency problems.

To illustrate how this works, consider the following high-level language code snippet:

```
 1: x←x + 1
 2: IF x > y THEN GOTO 10
 3: GOTO 20
        ⋮
10: w←z
```

In speculative execution, these instructions would be reordered as follows.

```
 1: x←x + 1
10: w←z
 2: IF x > y THEN GOTO 10
 3: GOTO 20
```

The $w{\leftarrow}z$ operation is scheduled before the conditional branch statement, even though the conditional branch instruction determines whether this operation should even occur. If the CPU should not have performed the operation $w{\leftarrow}z$ (because $x \le y$), it marks the register holding the result as invalid. Since only register load operations are executed speculatively, we do not have to worry about restoring invalid values in memory. We only need to retain the previous value of w in case it is needed, or generate an exception when it is next accessed.

11.7 Summary

RISC processors seek to improve system performance by taking a "less is more" approach. They reduce the number of instructions in their instruction sets to minimize the time needed to process each instruction. Toward this end, they use fixed length instructions, fewer addressing modes, and only load and store instructions to access memory. They also have hardwired control units, and separate instruction and data streams.

RISC processors use instruction pipelines to overlap instruction processing. Instruction pipelines improve overall system performance, but also introduce problems caused by data dependencies and branch conflicts. Processors resolve these problems using no-op insertion, instruction reordering, stalling, data forwarding, annulling, and branch prediction.

Most RISC processors include a large number of registers to reduce memory accesses, thus improving system performance. Processors generally have access to only a subset of these registers at any given time. They use register windowing or register renaming to coordinate access to the registers. Overlapping register windows provide an efficient method for transferring parameters and results between a program and its subroutines.

Problems

1 A CPU has a clock period of 25 ns. Some instructions can be removed from its instruction set to form a second CPU with a clock period to 24 ns. These instructions comprise 1 percent of typical code and must be replaced by four instructions each.

    a) Which CPU has the better performance?
    b) What percentage of typical code would the removed instructions have to comprise in order for the two CPUs to have the same performance?
    c) How many instructions would have to be needed to replace each of the removed instructions for the two CPUs to have the same performance?
    d) For what value of the clock period of the original CPU would the two CPUs have the same performance?
    e) For what value of the clock period of the second CPU would the two CPUs have the same performance?

2 Repeat Problem 1 for a CPU with a clock period of 15 ns and a reduced CPU with a clock period of 12 ns. The instructions removed from the instruction set of the first CPU comprise 2 percent of typical code and must be replaced by six instructions each.

3   Repeat Problem 1 for a CPU with a clock period of 18 ns and a reduced CPU with a clock period of 16 ns. The instructions removed from the instruction set of the first CPU comprise 4 percent of typical code and must be replaced by five instructions each.

4   A RISC instruction pipeline has three stages with propagation delays of 40 ns, 80 ns, and 50 ns, respectively.

> a) What are the clock period and steady-state speedup of the pipeline?
> b) If a non-pipelined CPU can process an instruction in 160 ns, what is the actual steady-state speedup of the pipeline?

5   A RISC instruction pipeline has four stages with propagation delays of 30 ns, 25 ns, 60 ns, and 40 ns, respectively.

> a) What are the clock period and steady-state speedup of the pipeline?
> b) If a non-pipelined CPU can process an instruction in 150 ns, what is the actual steady-state speedup of the pipeline?

6   A RISC instruction pipeline has five stages with propagation delays of 20 ns, 25 ns, 20 ns, 70 ns, and 40 ns, respectively.

> a) What are the clock period and steady-state speedup of the pipeline?
> b) If a non-pipelined CPU can process an instruction in 160 ns, what is the actual steady-state speedup of the pipeline?

7   It is possible to split the second stage of the pipeline of Problem 4 into two sequential stages with propagation delays of 45 ns and 35 ns, respectively.

> a) What are the clock period and steady-state speedup of the pipeline?
> b) If a non-pipelined CPU can process an instruction in 160 ns, what is the actual steady-state speedup of the pipeline?

8   It is possible to split the third stage of the pipeline of Problem 5 into two sequential stages with propagation delays of 20 ns and 40 ns, respectively.

> a) What are the clock period and steady-state speedup of the pipeline?
> b) If a non-pipelined CPU can process an instruction in 150 ns, what is the actual steady-state speedup of the pipeline?

9   It is possible to split the third stage of the pipeline of Problem 6 into two sequential stages with propagation delays of 25 ns and 45 ns, respectively.

> a) What are the clock period and steady-state speedup of the pipeline?
> b) If a non-pipelined CPU can process an instruction in 160 ns, what is the actual steady-state speedup of the pipeline?
> c) How can this pipeline be optimized further?

10 A RISC processor has 10 global registers and eight register windows, each having four common input registers, 10 local registers, and four common output registers. How many registers are in this CPU?

11 A RISC processor with 160 total registers has 16 global registers. Each register window has eight common input registers, 16 local registers, and eight common output registers. How many register windows are in this CPU?

12 A RISC processor with 192 total registers has 12 global registers. Each of its 10 register windows has six common input registers and six common output registers. How many local registers are in each register window?

13 A RISC processor with 188 total registers has 20 global registers. Each of its 12 register windows has 10 local registers. How many common input and common output registers are in each register window?

14 For the original code block in Section 11.4.1, how many no-ops must be inserted if the following pipelines are used?

   a) A four-stage pipeline
   b) A five-stage pipeline

15 The following code segment is to be executed on a RISC processor with the three-stage instruction pipeline shown in Figure 11.2(a).

$$1: R1 \leftarrow R2 + R3$$
$$2: R4 \leftarrow R1 + R2$$
$$3: R3 \leftarrow R1 + R4$$
$$4: R5 \leftarrow R2 + R6$$
$$5: R6 \leftarrow R1 + R2$$
$$6: R7 \leftarrow R5 + R6$$

Show the final code and execution trace if data conflicts are resolved by

   a) no-op insertion
   b) instruction reordering
   c) stall insertion
   d) data forwarding (The pipeline is modified to include the necessary connection from the execute instruction stage to the select registers stage for this method.)

16 Repeat Problem 15 for a RISC processor that uses the four-stage pipeline of Figure 11.2(b).

17 Repeat Problem 15 for a RISC processor that uses the five-stage pipeline of Figure 11.2(c).

18 The following code segment is to be executed on a RISC processor with the three-stage instruction pipeline shown in Figure 11.2(a).

$$1: R1 \leftarrow R2 + R3$$
$$2: R1 \leftarrow R1 + R2$$
$$3: R2 \leftarrow R3 + R4$$
$$4: R5 \leftarrow R6 + R7$$
$$5: R5 \leftarrow R5 + R7$$
$$6: R6 \leftarrow R1 + R2$$

Show the final code and execution trace if data conflicts are resolved by

a) no-op insertion
b) instruction reordering
c) stall insertion
d) data forwarding (The pipeline is modified to include the necessary connection from the execute instruction stage to the select registers stage for this method.)

19 Repeat Problem 18 for a RISC processor that uses the four-stage pipeline of Figure 11.2(b).

20 Repeat Problem 18 for a RISC processor that uses the five-stage pipeline of Figure 11.2(c).

21 Show the execution trace of the first code block in Section 11.4.2 using a three-stage pipeline that implements stall insertion.

22 Show the execution trace of the first two iterations of the loop in the code block in Section 11.4.2 that uses no-op insertion using a three-stage pipeline.

23 Show the execution trace of the first two iterations of the loop in the code block in Section 11.4.2 that uses instruction reordering (ignoring the data conflict) using a three-stage pipeline.

24 The following code segment is to be executed on a RISC processor with the three-stage instruction pipeline shown in Figure 11.2(a).

$$1: R1 \leftarrow R1 + R2$$
$$2: R3 \leftarrow R3 + R4$$
$$3: R5 \leftarrow R1 + R5$$

4: JUMP 9
5: $R6 \leftarrow R6 + R7$
6: $R7 \leftarrow R7 + R8$
$\vdots$
9: $R2 \leftarrow R1 + R3$

Show the final code and execution trace if branch conflicts are resolved by

a) no-op insertion
b) instruction reordering
c) stall insertion

25 Repeat Problem 24 for a RISC processor that uses the four-stage pipeline of Figure 11.2(b).

26 The following code segment is to be executed on a RISC processor with the three-stage instruction pipeline shown in Figure 11.2(a).

1: $R1 \leftarrow 3$
2: $R2 \leftarrow R2 + R3$
3: $R3 \leftarrow R3 + R4$
4: $R4 \leftarrow R1 + R2$
5: $R1 \leftarrow R1 - 1$
6: IF $(R1 \neq 0)$ THEN GOTO 2
7: $R5 \leftarrow R6 + R7$
8: $R6 \leftarrow R7 + R8$

Show the final code and execution trace if branch conflicts are resolved by

a) no-op insertion
b) instruction reordering
c) stall insertion

27 Repeat Problem 26 for a RISC processor that uses annulling without branch prediction.

28 Repeat Problem 26 for a RISC processor that uses annulling with branch prediction under the following circumstances.

a) The branch is assumed always to occur.
b) The branch is assumed never to occur.

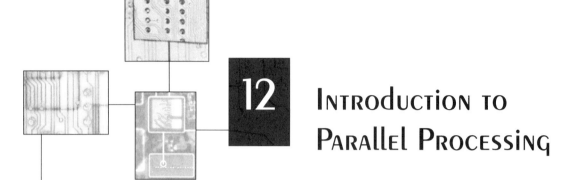

12 Introduction to Parallel Processing

The primary objective of any computer design is to create a computer that functions properly. It must correctly fetch, decode, and execute every instruction in its instruction set, producing correct results under all conditions. A computer that does not do this can serve no useful purpose.

Beyond this goal, computer architects may seek to maximize system performance. Within the CPU, the designer may incorporate an instruction pipeline to increase the number of instructions processed per clock cycle. A larger number of registers may be included in the CPU to reduce the number of memory accesses. The memory subsystem may include cache memory to reduce the time needed to load and store data. The computer may include virtual memory to increase the available address space at an acceptable cost. Direct memory access may be incorporated into the design to speed up transfers between memory and I/O devices. A processor may be designed to accept interrupts so that it does not need to waste time checking the status of I/O devices. A system may include an I/O processor to relieve the CPU of (almost) all I/O tasks.

Parallel processing is another method used to improve performance in a computer system. Simply put, parallelism is two or more things that happen at the same time. A uniprocessor (one CPU) system can achieve parallelism, both within the CPU and within the computer system as a whole. Most parallel processing systems, however, are multiprocessor (more than one CPU) systems. They achieve parallelism by having more than one processor performing tasks simultaneously.

The design of **multiprocessor systems** is not a straightforward extension of uniprocessor system design. From data conflicts and coordinating memory accesses by separate processors, to data communications, a host of issues must be addressed in multiprocessor system design.

In this chapter we introduce parallel processing designs and techniques. First, we examine parallelism in uniprocessor systems, both within and outside of the CPU. We introduce multiprocessor systems and their different organizations and taxonomies. We describe the communications mechanisms used to transfer data within the computer system. We examine the memory organizations within different architectures. Attributes of multiprocessor operating systems and parallel high-level languages are also covered. We introduce some parallel algorithms and how they are mapped onto different architectures. Finally, we present some alternative multiprocessor architectures.

12.1 PARALLELISM IN UNIPROCESSOR SYSTEMS

A computer system achieves parallelism when it performs two or more tasks simultaneously. In computer design, this is generally understood to mean that the tasks are not related to each other. A system that processes two different instructions simultaneously could be considered to perform parallel processing, whereas a system that performs different operations on the same instruction usually would not. For example, the Relatively Simple CPU includes the following RTL statement as part of its instruction FETCH routine.

$$\text{FETCH2:} \quad DR{\leftarrow}M,\ PC{\leftarrow}PC + 1$$

Although two micro-operations occur during this state, both are used to process the same instruction. This is not considered parallel processing. The Itanium microprocessor, introduced in Chapter 11, can execute several instructions simultaneously; in fact, it fetches three instructions in every 128-bit word. This would normally be considered parallel processing.

Some instances of parallelism in uniprocessor systems have already been covered in this text. One obvious example is the instruction pipeline introduced in Chapter 11. By overlapping the fetching, decoding, and execution of instructions, a RISC or CISC processor with an instruction pipeline exhibits parallelism. The arithmetic pipeline, introduced in Chapter 8, is another example of uniprocessor parallelism. The I/O processor, introduced in Chapter 10, is another example: It performs I/O data transfers while the CPU executes instructions—two distinct functions. A system with a DMA controller may also exhibit parallelism, but only if it operates in transparent mode. If the DMA controller uses burst mode or cycle stealing mode, the CPU suspends operation while the DMA controller is active; the two never operate in parallel.

A fixed arithmetic pipeline is not very useful in a CPU. Unless the exact function performed by the pipeline is required, the CPU cannot use the fixed pipeline. Instead, a **reconfigurable arithmetic pipeline** is better suited for general purpose computing. In a reconfigurable arithmetic pipeline, each stage has a multiplexer at its input. The multiplexer may pass input data, or the data output from other stages, to the stage inputs. The control unit of the CPU sets the select signals of the multiplexer to control the flow of data, thus configuring the pipeline. Figure 12.1 shows a simple, reconfigurable pipeline set to realize the function $A[i] \leftarrow B[i] \cdot C[i] + D[i]$. During the first clock cycle, the first stage receives the data inputs and calculates $B[i] \cdot C[i]$. Then in the second clock cycle, this value, along with the value of $D[i]$, is sent to stage 3, which performs the addition, generating the desired result.

Although arithmetic pipelines can perform many iterations of the same operation in parallel, they cannot perform different operations simultaneously. For example, there is no data dependency that would prohibit the following operations from being performed in parallel; however, a pipeline would not be suitable for this task.

$$A \leftarrow B + C$$
$$D \leftarrow E - F$$

Instead, a CPU may include a **vectored arithmetic unit** to perform different arithmetic operations in parallel. As shown in Figure 12.2, a vectored arithmetic unit contains multiple functional units. Some perform addition, others subtraction, and others perform different functions. To add two numbers, the control unit routes these values to an adder unit. In the code segment, the CPU would route B and C to an adder and send E and F to a subtracter, thus allowing the CPU to execute both instructions simultaneously.

As shown in Figure 12.2, input and output switches are needed to route the proper data to the correct arithmetic unit and to send the correct outputs to their proper destinations. The switches are set by the control unit; the logic needed by the control unit to set the switches can be complex, especially as the number of vectored arithmetic units increases. In addition, the added propagation delay of the switches partially offsets the gains achieved by processing more than one computation in parallel.

A problem not yet addressed is how to get all that data to the vectored arithmetic unit. It could be sent sequentially over existing connections, but that defeats the purpose of having a vectored arithmetic unit in the first place. In practice, a CPU may use multiple buses or very wide data buses that can transfer several data values simultaneously.

A system can improve performance by allowing multiple, simultaneous memory accesses. On a system level, this requires multiple address, data, and control buses, one set for each simultaneous memory

Figure 12.1

A reconfigurable pipeline with data flow for the computation $B[i] \cdot C[i] + D[i]$

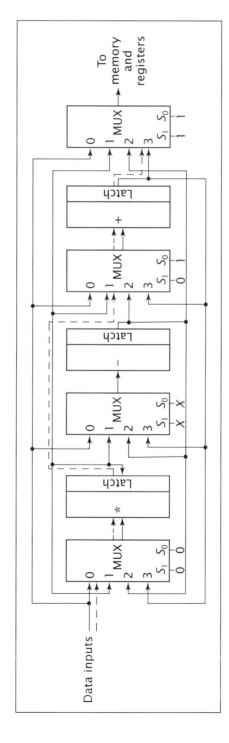

FiGURE 12.2

A vectored arithmetic unit

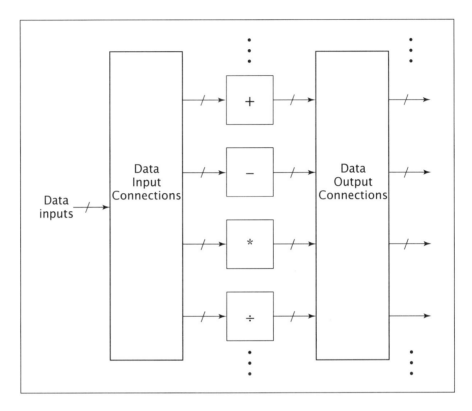

access. Within memory itself, the memory chips would have to be able to handle multiple transfers simultaneously.

Multiport memory is designed just for this purpose. A multiport memory chip usually has two sets of address, data, and control pins to allow two simultaneous data transfers to occur. Thus the CPU and DMA controller can transfer data concurrently, or a system with more than one CPU could handle simultaneous requests from two different processors.

This works well, as long as both requests are not to the same memory location. Although multiport memory can handle two requests to read data from the same location at the same time, it cannot process two simultaneous requests to write data to the same memory location, or simultaneous requests to read from and write to the same memory location. The data conflict could cause unpredictable results. The multiport memory will usually block one or both of the concurrent requests under these circumstances.

12.2 ORGANIZATION OF MULTIPROCESSOR SYSTEMS

Although it is possible to incorporate parallelism within uniprocessor systems, parallel processing systems generally incorporate more than one processor. There are many different ways to organize the processors and memory within a multiprocessor system, and different ways to classify these systems, including **Flynn's classification**, a commonly accepted taxonomy of computer organization based on the flow of instructions and data within the computer.

12.2.1 Flynn's Classification

As computer designs became more complex, they also diverged, becoming very different from one another. Several attempts have been made to categorize different designs based on various design parameters. Of these, the classification proposed by researcher Michael J. Flynn is the most commonly used, and possibly the only one in any common use.

Flynn's classification is based on instruction and data processing. A computer is classified by whether it processes a single instruction at a time or multiple instructions simultaneously, and whether it operates on one or multiple data sets. Its four categories are as follows:

1. *SISD:* Single instruction single data
2. *SIMD:* Single instruction multiple data
3. *MISD:* Multiple instruction single data
4. *MIMD:* Multiple instruction multiple data

Of these four classifications, SISD and MISD are the most straightforward. An SISD machine consists of a single CPU executing individual instructions on individual data values. This is the classic von Neumann architecture studied throughout this text and shown in Figure 4.1. Even if the processor incorporates internal parallelism, such as an instruction pipeline, the computer would still be classified as SISD.

The MISD classification is not practical to implement. Arguably, no significant MISD computers have ever been built. It is included in the taxonomy solely for completeness.

SIMD machines have been built and can serve a practical purpose. As its name implies, an SIMD machine executes a single instruction on multiple data values simultaneously using many processors. Since only one instruction is processed at any given time, it is not necessary for each processor to fetch and decode the instruction. Instead, a single control unit handles this task for all processors within the SIMD computer. This allows the processors to be less complex than traditional CPUs. Figure 12.3 shows a generic organization of an SIMD computer. In this organization, each processor receives control signals from a master control unit. Each processor may have a local memory, but this is not mandatory. There is also a communication network that the processors use to communicate with each other. Depending on the system, these connections can be fixed links between processors or they can be reconfigurable, allowing the connections to be changed during program execution. **Array processors** fall into this category of multiprocessors.

A generic SIMD organization

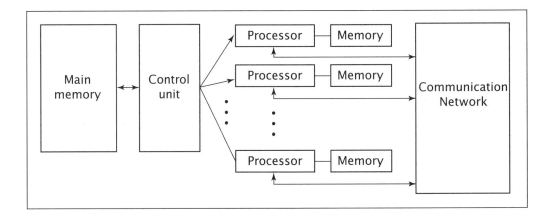

Although every processor receives the same control signals, they do not necessarily all execute the instruction. For some algorithms, it is necessary for some processors not to execute an instruction. An SIMD machine generally includes the capability to **mask**, or disable, individual processors. The processors that are enabled execute the current instruction. Those that are masked do not execute any instruction at all. (Under no circumstances can these processors execute a different instruction.)

SIMD machines are particularly useful for certain applications. Any application that uses matrix multiplication, for example, can be performed efficiently by SIMD computers. (We give an example of this later in this chapter.) Finite element analysis, which is used to model everything from the weather to nuclear weapons, is also a good candidate for SIMD computation.

Systems referred to as **multiprocessors** or **multicomputers** are usually MIMD machines. Unlike SIMD machines, the processors may execute different (i.e., multiple) instructions simultaneously. Therefore, each processor must include its own control unit. MIMD machines are well suited for general purpose use. The processors can be assigned to parts of the same task or to completely separate tasks.

Different MIMD computers may be better suited to specific tasks, depending on their topology and architecture, which affect interprocessor communication and interaction with memory.

12.2.2 System Topologies

The **topology** of a multiprocessor system refers to the pattern of connections between its processors. Various factors, typically involving a cost-performance tradeoff, determine which topology a computer designer will select for a multiprocessor system.

Although topologies differ greatly, standard metrics—diameter and bandwidth—are used to quantify them. The **diameter** is the maximum distance between two processors in the computer system. This is the maximum number of processors a message must pass through to reach its final destination (including the destination processor). The system's total **bandwidth** is the capacity of a communications link multiplied by the number of such links in the system. This is the bandwidth achieved if every link is active simultaneously, a best-case scenario which almost never occurs.

The **bisection bandwidth** is closer to a worst-case scenario. To determine the bisection bandwidth, we divide the network into two halves, each having the same number of processors (or within one if the total number of processors is odd). It is possible to partition the processors in many different ways. To calculate the bisection bandwidth, we split the processors so the number of links between the two halves is minimized; this represents the bottleneck of the multiprocessor system's communication links. The bisection bandwidth is the total bandwidth of the links connecting the two halves. It represents the maximum data transfer that could occur at the bottleneck in the topology.

The simplest topology is the **shared bus**, shown in Figure 12.4(a). In this topology, processors communicate with each other exclusively via this bus. However, the bus can handle only one data transmission at a time. In most shared bus systems, processors directly communicate with their own local memory, as shown in Figure 12.4, to limit traffic on the bus. Shared bus systems are easy to expand: Simply connect additional processors to the shared bus, along with the necessary bus arbitration circuitry. However, as more processors are added to the system, demand for the shared bus increases, resulting in delays while processors wait for the bus to become available. Its diameter is 1 and its total bandwidth is $1 \cdot l$, where l is the bandwidth of the bus. Its bisection bandwidth is also $1 \cdot l$.

The **ring** topology, shown in Figure 12.4(b), uses direct dedicated connections between processors instead of a shared bus. This allows all communication links to be active simultaneously. However, a piece of data may have to travel through several processors to reach its

FIGURE 12.4

MIMD system topologies: (a) shared bus, (b) ring, (c) tree, (d) mesh, (e) hypercube, and (f) completely connected

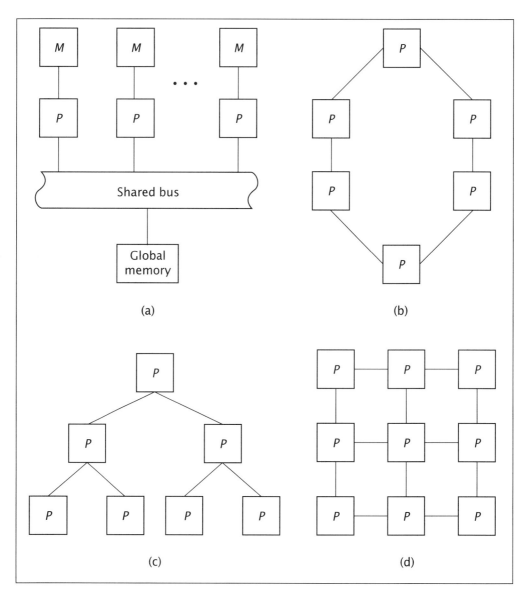

final destination. All processors must have two communication links, as opposed to the one used in a shared bus system. A ring with n processors has a diameter of $\lfloor n/2 \rfloor$, the floor, or largest integer less than or equal to $n/2$. Its total bandwidth is $n \cdot l$ and its bisection bandwidth is $2 \cdot l$.

FIGURE 12.4
(continued)

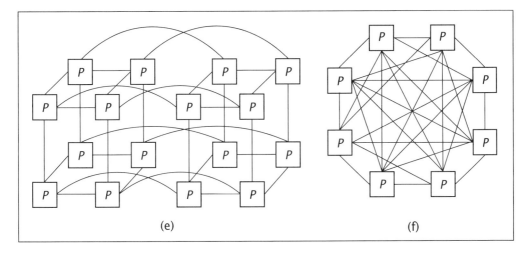

Figure 12.4(c) shows the **tree topology**. Like the ring, it uses direct connections between processors; each processor has three connections. Its primary advantage is its relatively low diameter of $2 \cdot \lfloor \lg n \rfloor$, where $\lg n$ is the base 2 logarithm of the number of processors. Its total bandwidth is $(n - 1) \cdot l$, but its bisection bandwidth is only $1 \cdot l$, indicating that this topology is subject to bottlenecks. Tracing through this topology, we can see that there is only one unique path between any pair of processors. The DADO computer uses this topology.

In the **mesh topology**, every processor connects to the processors above and below it, and to its right and left. Figure 12.4(d) shows a 3×3 mesh; left to right and top to bottom wraparound connections may or may not be present. Without wraparound connections, its diameter is $2\sqrt{n}$, its total bandwidth is $(2n - 2\sqrt{n}) \cdot l$ and its bisection bandwidth is $2\lceil \sqrt{n}/2 \rceil \cdot l$, where $\lceil \sqrt{n}/2 \rceil$ is the ceiling, or smallest integer greater than or equal to $\sqrt{n}/2$. With wraparound connections it has a diameter of $\sqrt{n}$, a total bandwidth of $2n \cdot l$ and a bisection bandwidth of $2\sqrt{n} \cdot l$. The Illiac IV was one of the first multiprocessors to employ this topology.

The **hypercube** is a multidimensional mesh. It has n processors, each with $\lg n$ connections. To illustrate its connectivity, assign each of the n processors a unique binary value from 0 to $n - 1$. Each processor connects to all other processors whose binary values differ by only one bit. For example, in the hypercube of Figure 12.4(e), processor 0 (0000) connects to processors 1 (0001), 2 (0010), 4 (0100), and 8 (1000). It has a relatively low diameter of $\lg n$, a total bandwidth of $(n/2) \cdot \lg n \cdot l$ and a bisection bandwidth of $(n/2) \cdot l$. Intel's early nCUBE system used a hypercube topology.

In the most extreme connection scheme, the processors are **completely connected**. As shown in Figure 12.4(f), every processor has $n - 1$ connections, one to each of the other processors. This increases the complexity of the processors as the system grows, but offers maximum communication capabilities. Its diameter is 1, since every processor communicates directly with every other processor. Its total bandwidth is $(n/2) \cdot (n - 1) \cdot l$ and its bisection bandwidth is $(\lfloor n/2 \rfloor \cdot \lceil n/2 \rceil) \cdot l$.

12.2.3 MIMD System Architectures

The architecture of an MIMD system, as opposed to its topology, refers to its connections with respect to system memory. The same topologies used to connect processors in Figure 12.4 could be used to connect processors to memory modules instead.

A **symmetric multiprocessor**, or **SMP**, is a computer system that has two or more processors with comparable capabilities. The processors do not have to be identical, although in practice they almost always are. All processors must be capable of performing the same functions; this is the symmetry of SMPs. The processors all have access to the same I/O devices and memory modules. An integrated operating system controls the entire computer system.

One type of SMP is the **uniform memory access** (**UMA**), architecture. Shown in Figure 12.5, UMA gives all CPUs equal (uniform) access to all locations in shared memory. They interact with shared memory via some communication mechanism, which may be as simple as a shared bus or as complex as a multistage interconnection network. Although not shown in Figure 10.5, each processor may have its own cache memory, not directly accessible by the other processors.

In contrast to UMA architectures, **nonuniform memory access** (**NUMA**), architectures do not allow uniform access to all shared memory locations. As shown in Figure 12.6, this architecture still allows all processors to access all shared memory locations. However, each processor can access the memory module closest to it, its local shared memory, more quickly than the other modules; hence, the memory access times are nonuniform. (Early multiprocessor designs referred to this as the *home memory*.) Each memory module has a different address range, so any memory address refers to a specific location within a specific module. Unlike UMA machines, NUMA computers may not be SMP. In general, NUMA machines are more scalable and can yield better performance than UMA computers. The Cray T3E supercomputer is a NUMA machine.

The **cache coherent NUMA** architecture, **CC-NUMA**, is similar to the NUMA architecture of Figure 12.6, except each processor includes cache memory. The cache can buffer data from memory modules that are not local to the processor, thus reducing the access time of the most lengthy memory transfers. However, this introduces a

Figure 12.5
Uniform memory access (UMA) architecture

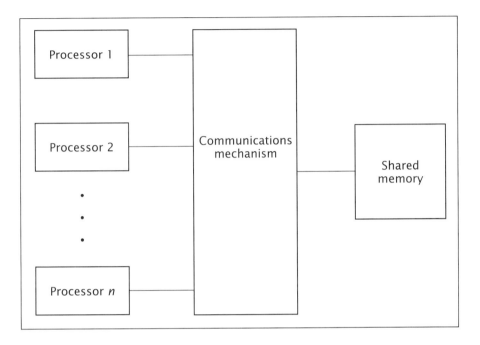

Figure 12.6
Nonuniform memory access (NUMA) architecture

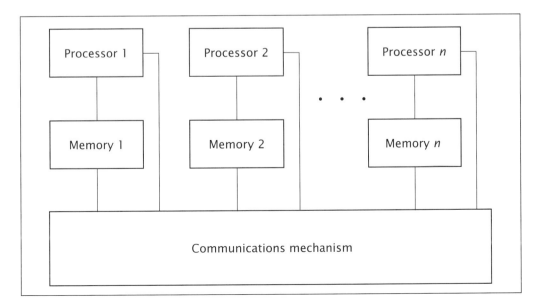

problem when two or more caches hold the same piece of data. When one processor changes the value of this data, the other caches' values are invalid. There are several methods to maintain consistency, or **coherence**, among these values; we examine this problem later in this chapter. Silicon Graphics' SGI Origin is one example of a CC-NUMA machine.

A somewhat extreme solution to this problem is **cache only memory access** (**COMA**) architecture. In this architecture, each processor's local memory is treated as a cache. As with the cache memory described in Chapter 9, when the processor requests data that is not in its cache (local memory), the system loads that data into local memory as part of the memory operation. If a data value is in more than one local memory at the same time, one copy is denoted as the **master copy**, which must be kept current and which supersedes all other copies. Only a few COMA systems, including Kendall Square Research's KSR1 and KSR2, and the Swedish Institute of Computer Science's Data Diffusion Machine (DDM), have ever been built.

In contrast to multiprocessors, a **multicomputer** is an MIMD machine in which all processors are not under the control of one operating system. Each processor or group of processors is under the control of a different operating system, or a different instantiation of the same operating system. However, there is generally one centralized scheduler that allocates processors to tasks and tasks to processors.

A **network of workstations** (**NOW**), or **cluster of workstations** (**COW**), is a good example of a multicomputer. NOWs and COWs

PRACTICAL PERSPECTIVE: The World's Largest Multicomputer?

The SETI@Home project is an extreme example of a network of workstations. A centralized server receives data from radio telescopes, which scan the skies in search of signals generated by extraterrestrial intelligent beings. A data processing program (and screen saver) are made available for interested persons to download from the SETI@Home Web site. The user installs this program on a personal computer or workstation. When run on a user's computer, the program contacts the SETI@Home server via the Internet, notifying the server that it is available to process data. The server selects an unprocessed data set and transmits it to the user's computer. The program then processes this data set on the user's computer without further interaction from the server. When it is finished, the user's computer notifies the server, sends it the final results, and requests another data set. Although the point is debatable, some argue that this system, consisting of the server, over one million personal computers and workstations, and the Internet as its communications mechanism, is the world's largest multicomputer.

PRACTICAL PERSPECTIVE: The Blue Gene Computer

IBM's forthcoming Blue Gene computer will be the most powerful computer ever developed. It will contain over 32,000 processing nodes arranged in a three-dimensional mesh. Each node will contain approximately 32 microprocessors—over one million microprocessors all told. The processors have a small instruction set containing only 57 instructions, much fewer than found in typical RISC CPUs. Each processor also includes some dynamic RAM and a 64K, eight-way set-associative instruction cache. This computer is designed to achieve a processing rate of 1 petaflop (one quadrillion, or 10^{15}, operations per second). Its first application will be to model proteins at the atomic level to determine how a protein folds, which determines its function in a biological system.

When built, Blue Gene will replace IBM's ASCI White as the world's fastest computer. ASCI White, developed under the U.S. Department of Energy's Accelerated Strategic Computing Initiative, consists of "only" 8,192 microprocessors, 6 TB (terabytes, or trillions of bytes) of memory, and 160 TB of disk storage. It performs 12.3 teraflop, or 12.3 trillion operations per second, and is used to simulate nuclear reactions.

are more than a group of workstations on a local area network; they have a master scheduler, which matches tasks and processors together. Once a task has been scheduled, the processors handle it without further intervention from the scheduler. They interact among themselves and notify the scheduler when the task is complete. One system, which may be the world's largest, is described in the Practical Perspective: The World's Largest Multicomputer?

One final architecture that requires some explanation is the **massively parallel processor** (**MPP**) architecture. This term originally described tightly coupled SIMD multiprocessor systems such as the Connection Machine and Goodyear's MPP. These computers used simple processing elements, typically at the level of an ALU, to process massive amounts of data in parallel. Usually the processors were connected in a two-dimensional grid and had their own local memory. In contrast, computers we call MPPs today generally consist of many self-contained nodes, each having a processor, memory, and hardware for implementing internal communications. The processors communicate with each other using shared memory. Current MPPs include those in Cray's T3 line (which are both MPP and CC-NUMA). IBM's Blue Gene computer, described in Practical Perspective: The Blue Gene Computer, will be the world's largest MPP and the most powerful multiprocessor of any type.

12.3 COMMUNICATION IN MULTIPROCESSOR SYSTEMS

Communication in multiprocessor systems, between processors and memory, I/O devices, and other processors, is a key factor in determining overall system performance. The fastest processors cannot achieve high levels of efficiency if they spend too much of their time waiting to send and receive data. For this reason, multiprocessor systems use hardwired connections, rather than the data packets described in Chapter 10, for communicating within the computer.

A multiprocessor system may have fixed connections for communications, or reconfigurable connections that can be changed during task execution or between tasks. In this section we examine both models, including multistage interconnection networks (MINs), a switching methodology used to maximize performance while minimizing cost. The routing algorithms used by MINs are also discussed.

12.3.1 Fixed Connections

Fixed connections are invariant; once they are set, they never change. Although this is inflexible, it is sufficient for many systems and is less costly than reconfigurable communications mechanisms. A system that incorporates a shared bus, as described in Section 12.2, is one example of a fixed connection communications mechanism. The other topologies shown in Figure 12.4 also use fixed connections.

One fixed connection topology not discussed so far is **clustering**. Figure 12.7 shows a 16-processor multiprocessor system that is divided into four clusters, each with four processors. The processors in each cluster are connected via their own shared bus, called the **cluster bus**. Two processors in the same cluster communicate via their cluster bus, leaving the intercluster communication mechanism and other cluster buses free for other communication. In theory, and in practice, all cluster buses could transmit data within their clusters simultaneously, thus maximizing data flow and minimizing processor delay.

The scheduler normally assigns processors within the same cluster to a task so that interprocessor communication is restricted to the cluster bus. Some tasks, however, may utilize processors in more than one cluster. For example, if the system of Figure 12.7 has a task that requires eight processors, it must use processors in at least two clusters. Thus, it is necessary to provide a mechanism for communication between processors in different clusters.

Each cluster includes an **intercluster gateway**, which handles data transfers between clusters. These gateways are connected by an intercluster communications mechanism, which may be a reconfigurable switching network (to be described shortly), or a fixed topology, such as the shared bus, ring, and other topologies shown in Figure 12.4. If a processor in one cluster must send data to a processor

FIGURE 12.7
A 16-processor multiprocessor that uses clustering

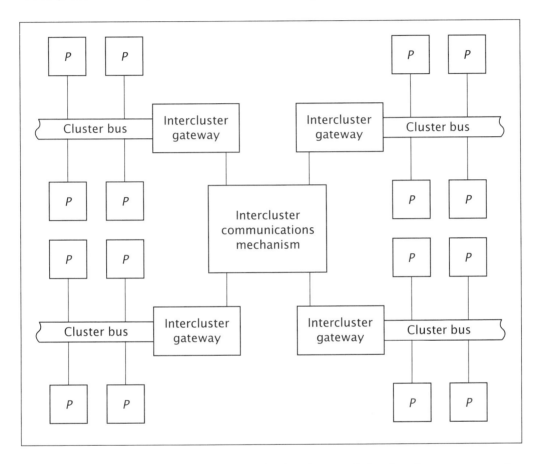

in a different cluster, it sends the data and destination processor information to its intercluster gateway. The gateway examines the destination processor information to determine its cluster. It then sends the data and destination, through the intercluster communications mechanism, to the intercluster gateway of the destination processor's cluster. The gateway of the destination cluster then sends the data to the destination processor. Note that the processors do not communicate directly with each other. Rather, they communicate only with their intercluster gateways. The gateways perform the intercluster communication among themselves.

12.3.2   RECONFIGURABLE CONNECTIONS

Not all tasks require the same processing resources. For some tasks, two processors may be sufficient; for others, 16 processors may not be enough. For a general purpose multiprocessor, the ability to reconfigure connections between processors and memory, I/O devices, and other processors can allow it to meet the needs of individual tasks and thus maximize system performance.

One mechanism used in reconfigurable communications mechanisms is the **crossbar switch**. As shown in Figure 12.8, a crossbar switch has n inputs and m outputs, and is said to be of size $n \times m$; in practice, n and m usually have the same value. (The terms *input* and *output* are arbitrary; data can flow in either direction through the network.) Each **crosspoint** within the switch is a connection point that can be closed to connect the input and output, or open to break the connection. There is one crosspoint for every possible input-output combination; a crossbar switch can realize all possible connections. In a multiprocessor system, the inputs (by convention) are connected to the processors, and the outputs are connected to the memory modules or the I/O devices, or back to the processors for interprocessor communication.

FIGURE 12.8

An $n \times m$ crossbar switch

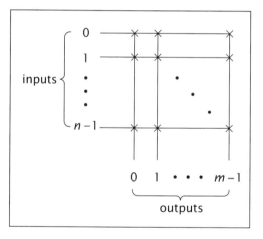

The greatest drawback of crossbar switches is their size. As the numbers of inputs and outputs increases, the size and hardware complexity of the crossbar switches increase rapidly. A crossbar with n inputs and n outputs has a hardware complexity of $O(n^2)$. Doubling the number of inputs and outputs increases the size of the crossbar switch by a factor of four.

To alleviate this problem, **multistage interconnection networks** (**MINs**) have been developed. These networks use smaller crossbar switches, often 2×2, connected by fixed links. The 2×2 switch, with its two possible settings for **permutation networks** (which connect their inputs to their outputs in a 1 to 1 manner only), is shown in Figure 12.9. By setting the switches to the correct states, the MIN realizes the desired connections between inputs and outputs. The procedure used for setting the switches of a MIN is called a **routing algorithm**.

FIGURE 12.9

A 2 × 2 crossbar switch and its settings

Straight   Exchange

We can classify multistage interconnection networks by their ability to connect inputs and outputs. Most MINs are designed to realize permutations, one-to-one connections between their inputs and outputs. A **nonblocking network** can realize any of the $n!$ connection patterns of its n inputs and n outputs. If the network can modify one connection without changing any others, it is called **strictly nonblocking**. If it can realize a new connection, but may have to reroute the path used to realize an existing connection in order to do so, it is called **rearrangeably nonblocking**. In contrast, a **blocking network** cannot realize every permutation of its inputs onto its outputs. Most blocking MINs can realize every possible input-output connection, but certain connections cannot be realized simultaneously.

Of the nonblocking MINs, the **Clos network** is the most widely known. It was originally developed for telephone switching systems, and was later adapted for use in multiprocessor systems and networking switches. A generic Clos network is shown in Figure 12.10. It has $N = n \cdot k$ inputs and outputs and three stages of switches. The first stage consists of k switches of size $n \times m$, that is, having n inputs and m outputs. The center stage has m switches of size $k \times k$. Each center stage switch receives one input from each first stage switch. The last stage incorporates k $m \times n$ switches which each receive one input from each second stage switch. If $m \geq n$, the network is rearrangeably nonblocking; if $m \geq 2n - 1$, it is strictly nonblocking.

We can modify the design parameters n, m, and k to produce different variants of the Clos network. The hardware complexity can vary from $O(n \lg n)$ to $O(n^2)$, depending on the values of the parameters. In practice, the individual switches of the network can be recursively replaced by smaller Clos networks.

The **Beneš network** was derived from the Clos network by setting $n = m = 2$ and $k = N/2$, and recursively decomposing the two $(N/2) \times (N/2)$ switches. For example, to create an 8 × 8 Beneš network,

Figure 12.10

Clos network

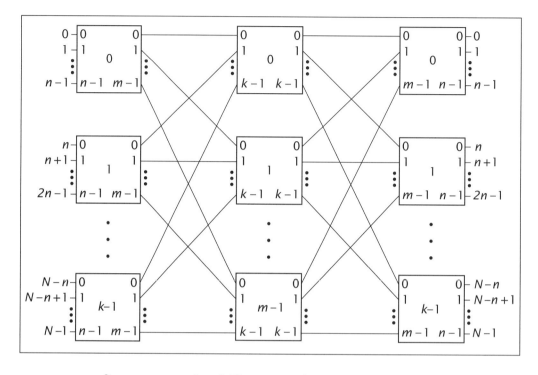

we first create an 8×8 Clos network consisting of four 2×2 switches in the first and last stages, and two 4×4 switches in the center stage. As in any Clos network, we connect one output of each first stage switch to an input of each center stage switch, and one input of each last stage switch to an output of each center stage switch. Then we convert the 4×4 center stage switches to 4×4 Beneš networks. Figure 12.11 shows the 8×8 Beneš network; dashed lines enclose the 4×4 switches, which were further decomposed into their own Beneš networks. This network is rearrangeably nonblocking and has a hardware complexity of $O(n \lg n)$.

It is not always necessary for an MIN used in a multiprocessor system to be nonblocking. A multiprocessor generally will not need to use every possible permutation realizable by its MIN. A blocking network that can realize the desired mappings can be a viable, and less costly, alternative. The routing process for these blocking networks can be much faster than that for nonblocking networks.

Figure 12.12(a) shows the 8×8 **Omega network**, a well-known blocking network which has a hardware complexity of $O(n \lg n)$. It is easy to see that this network is blocking when one considers the following argument. For eight possible inputs, there are a total of $8! = 40,320$ different possible permutations, or one-to-one mappings

FIGURE 12.11

An 8 × 8 Beneš network

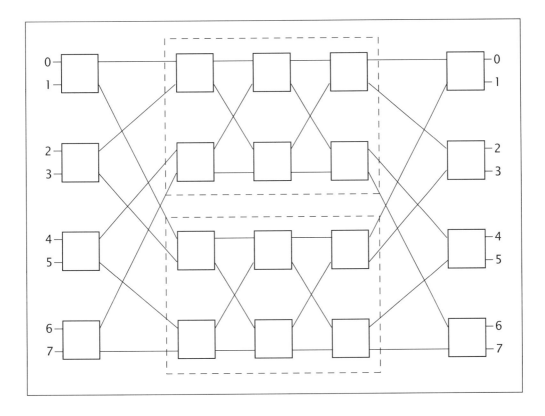

of the inputs onto the outputs. However, there are only 12 switches, each of which can be in one of the two possible states shown in Figure 12.9. Therefore, all the switches together can have $2^{12} = 4,096$ different settings, just over 10 percent of those needed to realize all possible permutations; the network cannot be nonblocking.

As drawn in this figure, the fixed links between every pair of stages are the same. They form a **perfect shuffle**, interleaving the first and second half of the outputs of the previous stage. The name shuffle is drawn from the action of shuffling a deck of cards. Assume that a pile of eight cards, numbered 0 to 7 in that order, is to be shuffled. First, the cards are cut into two piles, one containing cards 0, 1, 2, and 3, and the other containing 4, 5, 6, and 7. A perfect shuffle interleaves the cards into a pile ordered 0, 4, 1, 5, 2, 6, 3, 7. If the first stage switches of the Omega network are all set to straight, this is exactly the order of the original network inputs as they are routed to the second stage switch inputs, from top to bottom.

Other blocking MINs have been developed, many of which are isomorphic to each other. Consider the 8 × 8 **Baseline network**

FIGURE 12.12

An 8 × 8 (a) Omega network and (b) Baseline network

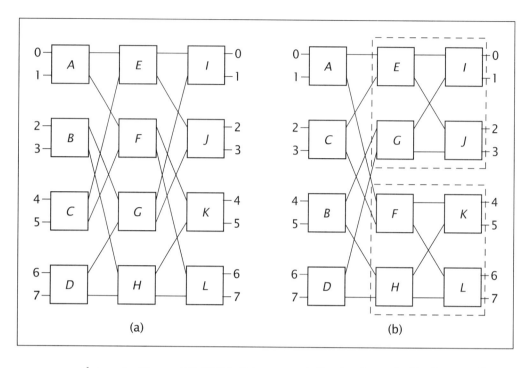

(a)   (b)

shown in Figure 12.12(b). It is essentially the front half of a Beneš network. To construct an $n \times n$ Baseline network, we start with one stage of $n/2$ 2 × 2 switches and two $(n/2) \times (n/2)$ switches. One output from each 2 × 2 switch is connected to an input of each $(n/2) \times (n/2)$ switch; then we replace the $(n/2) \times (n/2)$ switches with $(n/2) \times (n/2)$ baseline networks constructed in the same manner. In Figure 12.12(b), the two subnetworks enclosed by dashed lines are 4 × 4 baseline networks.

If we reposition the switches labeled B and C, and F and G, as in the Omega network, keeping the links with the switches as they are moved, we can see that the baseline network transforms into the Omega network. These two networks are **isomorphic**.

12.3.3 ROUTING ON MULTISTAGE INTERCONNECTION NETWORKS

The routing algorithm, or procedure used to set the switches, plays a critical role in the performance of a MIN. A slow routing algorithm will significantly reduce the overall performance of its multiprocessor system. A MIN may have several different algorithms which it can use. Since their run times are usually deterministic—known beforehand—one is chosen and incorporated into the system during its design.

Before examining routing algorithms for MINs, we must understand a bit about permutations—how they are represented and how they are combined. A permutation is often represented as a two-row matrix bounded by parentheses. The top row is the list of sources; under each entry is its destination. For example, the straight permutation of Figure 12.9 would be represented as $\begin{pmatrix} 0 & 1 \\ 0 & 1 \end{pmatrix}$. The switch's input 0 is routed to its output 0, and input 1 is routed to output 1. The exchange permutation would be represented as $\begin{pmatrix} 0 & 1 \\ 1 & 0 \end{pmatrix}$. The group of settings realizable by this switch is $\left\{ \begin{pmatrix} 0 & 1 \\ 0 & 1 \end{pmatrix}, \begin{pmatrix} 0 & 1 \\ 1 & 0 \end{pmatrix} \right\}$.

We can concatenate the settings of individual switches within a stage to form the settings for entire stages. In the Beneš network of Figure 12.11, assume that the switches in the first stage are set to realize the permutations $\begin{pmatrix} 0 & 1 \\ 0 & 1 \end{pmatrix}$, $\begin{pmatrix} 2 & 3 \\ 3 & 2 \end{pmatrix}$, $\begin{pmatrix} 4 & 5 \\ 5 & 4 \end{pmatrix}$, and $\begin{pmatrix} 6 & 7 \\ 6 & 7 \end{pmatrix}$. The setting for the entire stage is the concatenation of these settings, $\begin{pmatrix} 0 & 1 & 2 & 3 & 4 & 5 & 6 & 7 \\ 0 & 1 & 3 & 2 & 5 & 4 & 6 & 7 \end{pmatrix}$. The group of all possible settings is the cross product of the groups of settings of the individual switches in the stage. Thus the group of permutations realizable by stage 1 of this network, $P(S_1)$, can be expressed as follows.

$$P(S_1) = \left\{ \begin{pmatrix} 0 & 1 \\ 0 & 1 \end{pmatrix}, \begin{pmatrix} 0 & 1 \\ 1 & 0 \end{pmatrix} \right\} \times \left\{ \begin{pmatrix} 2 & 3 \\ 2 & 3 \end{pmatrix}, \begin{pmatrix} 2 & 3 \\ 3 & 2 \end{pmatrix} \right\} \times \left\{ \begin{pmatrix} 4 & 5 \\ 4 & 5 \end{pmatrix}, \begin{pmatrix} 4 & 5 \\ 5 & 4 \end{pmatrix} \right\} \times \left\{ \begin{pmatrix} 6 & 7 \\ 6 & 7 \end{pmatrix}, \begin{pmatrix} 6 & 7 \\ 7 & 6 \end{pmatrix} \right\}$$

To express the mapping realized by sequential permutations, we combine their permutations. Instead of concatenating them, we first feed the outputs into the second permutation. For example, consider the first stage of the 8×8 Beneš network and its output links. Assume that the first stage switches are set to realize the permutation $p(S_1) = \begin{pmatrix} 0 & 1 & 2 & 3 & 4 & 5 & 6 & 7 \\ 0 & 1 & 3 & 2 & 5 & 4 & 6 & 7 \end{pmatrix}$. (Note that $p(S_1)$ is a single permutation, while $P(S_1)$ is the set of all possible permutations of this stage.) The links are fixed and always realize the mapping $\begin{pmatrix} 0 & 1 & 2 & 3 & 4 & 5 & 6 & 7 \\ 0 & 4 & 1 & 5 & 2 & 6 & 3 & 7 \end{pmatrix}$. To combine their permutations, we trace each input to the first stage through that stage to its position in the output of the link field. For example, input 2 to the first stage is routed to output 3 of that stage. That is also input 3 of the link field, which is always routed to its output 5. Therefore, the first stage and first link field route input 2 to their output 5. Repeating this for every input yields the net result as $p(S_1) \times L_1 = \begin{pmatrix} 0 & 1 & 2 & 3 & 4 & 5 & 6 & 7 \\ 0 & 4 & 5 & 1 & 6 & 2 & 3 & 7 \end{pmatrix}$.

We can extend this procedure to the entire i-stage network to determine the permutation realized by the network. The permutation realized by the network can be expressed as the product of the stage and link permutations:

$$p = \left(\prod_{j=1}^{i-1} (p(S_j) \times L_j) \right) \times p(S_i)$$

Similarly, the set of all permutations realizable by the network is calculated as

$$P = \left(\prod_{j=1}^{i-1} (P(S_j) \times L_j) \right) \times P(S_i)$$

The **Looping Algorithm** is a recursive method used to set the switches of a Beneš network. Remember that the Beneš network is recursive in structure, consisting of two outer stages of switches enclosing two half-size Beneš networks. The looping algorithm makes use of this recursion as it sets the switches of the network. It takes the initial permutation, sets the switches in the outer stages, and generates the permutations to be realized by the two subnetworks. These permutations are processed recursively until the entire network is set. Its run time is $O(n \lg n)$.

To illustrate how the Looping Algorithm works, consider the 8×8 Beneš network that must realize the permutation $\begin{pmatrix} 0\,1\,2\,3\,4\,5\,6\,7 \\ 1\,2\,3\,4\,5\,6\,7\,0 \end{pmatrix}$. The Looping Algorithm begins by arbitrarily setting any one switch in an outer stage. For this example, we set the uppermost switch in the first stage to straight, realizing the permutation $\begin{pmatrix} 0\,1 \\ 0\,1 \end{pmatrix}$. This sends network input 0 to the upper subnetwork.

Each switch in the last stage receives one input from the upper subnetwork and one from the lower subnetwork. Since input 0 is routed to the upper subnetwork, and this input must be routed to network output 1, its switch must connect output 1 to the upper subnetwork. The uppermost switch in the last stage must be set to exchange.

This in turn causes output 0 to receive its data from the lower subnetwork. Its source is input 7, whose switch is set to straight to route it to the lower subnetwork. This causes input 6 to be routed to the upper subnetwork. The algorithm follows the same procedure, looping back and forth between inputs and outputs, until the original switch is reached. If any switches in the outer stages are not set, the algorithm sets another switch arbitrarily and begins again. The number of random choices needed depends only on the permutation to be routed; it is independent of the random choices made for switch settings.

At the end of the first pass of the Looping Algorithm, the outer stage switches are set as shown in Figure 12.13(a). The permutation to be realized by the upper and lower subnetworks are $\begin{pmatrix} 0\,2\,4\,6 \\ 1\,3\,5\,7 \end{pmatrix}$ and

$\begin{pmatrix} 1\ 3\ 5\ 7 \\ 2\ 4\ 6\ 0 \end{pmatrix}$ respectively. In this figure, we relabeled the inputs and outputs of the subnetworks to denote the positions of the network inputs and outputs. This is equivalent to forming $p(S_1) \times L_1$ and $L_4 \times p(S_5)$. Repeating the algorithm on the subnetworks yields the switch settings shown in Figure 12.13(b).

Unlike the Beneš network, which uses a centralized algorithm to set all of its switches, the Omega network uses a distributed, self-routing procedure. The switches examine the destinations of their input data and set themselves. No central routing hardware is needed. Because of this, the switches in each stage can be set in parallel, and the network can be set up in $O(\lg n)$ time, a significant improvement over the $O(n \lg n)$ time needed by the Looping Algorithm.

To understand the routing procedure, consider the first stage of the Omega network of Figure 12.12(a). All four switches send their upper outputs to switches E and G, and their lower outputs to switches F and H. Switches E and G both send their outputs to switches I and J; their data can only reach the outputs of these two switches, 0, 1, 2, and 3. Similarly, data from switches F and H can only reach outputs 4, 5, 6, and 7. Each first stage switch must be set so that its upper output has a destination with binary value 000, 001, 010, or 011, or has a 0 as the most significant bit of its destination. Similarly, the lower output of each switch must have a 1 as the most significant bit of its destination to reach output 100, 101, 110, or 111. A 0 in this bit position of a destination requires that the input be routed to the upper output; a 1 requires it to be sent to the lower output of the switch. If two inputs to a first stage switch have the same value in this bit position, the Omega network cannot realize this permutation.

Following the same logic, each second stage switch sends its upper output to switches I or K, which connect to outputs 0, 1, 4, and 5, or 000, 001, 100, and 101 in binary. The lower outputs can reach switches J or L, which can access outputs 2, 3, 6, and 7 (010, 011, 110, and 111). For this stage, the second bit of the destination determines the setting of the switch. Similarly, the least significant bit of the destination determines the setting of the switches in the third stage. Since its outputs are the outputs of the network, the last stage cannot block a permutation that has been routed successfully by the previous stages.

Figure 12.14(a) shows the successful routing of the permutation $\begin{pmatrix} 0\ 1\ 2\ 3\ 4\ 5\ 6\ 7 \\ 7\ 3\ 1\ 6\ 0\ 5\ 2\ 4 \end{pmatrix}$ on the 8×8 Omega network. We show the destination tags with the data as it passes through the network. Figure 12.14(b) shows the routing of the permutation $\left(\dfrac{0\ 1\ 2\ 3\ 4\ 5\ 6\ 7}{4\ 0\ 5\ 3\ 7\ 1\ 2\ 6}\right)$, which is blocked in the center stage.

Figure 12.13

Results of the Looping Algorithm (a) after one iteration and (b) final results

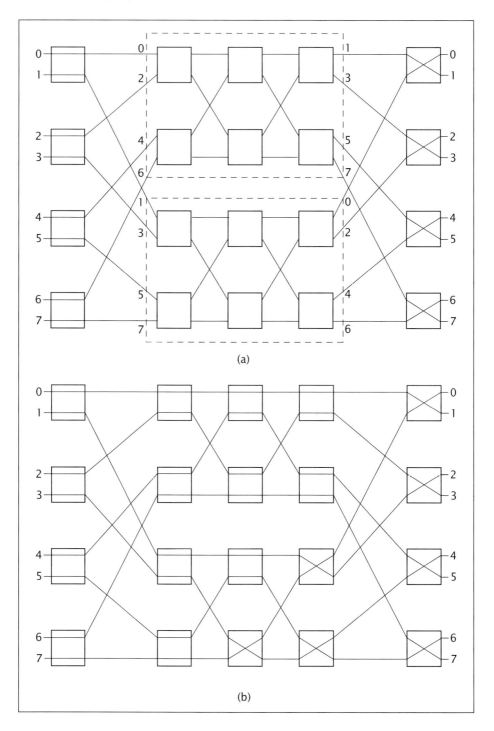

(a)

(b)

FIGURE 12.14

(a) Successful and (b) unsuccessful routing on the Omega network

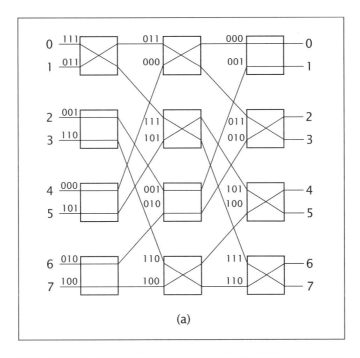

(a)

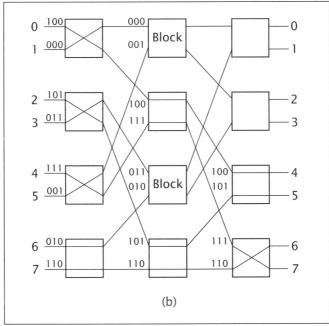

(b)

12.4 MEMORY ORGANIZATION IN MULTIPROCESSOR SYSTEMS

The descriptions of multiprocessor system architectures earlier in this chapter presented the different organizations of memory in these systems. We now examine the structure and function of shared memory, and memory problems introduced by the multiprocessor architectures and their solutions. First, we examine shared memory, both in its structure and in its use for message passing between processors. Then we describe the most significant problem in multiprocessor memory system design, cache coherence. Potential solutions, both hardware and software oriented, are discussed.

12.4.1 SHARED MEMORY

The UMA and NUMA architectures shown in Figures 12.5 and 12.6 both use **shared memory**. Through shared memory, the processors can access shared programs and data. They can also use the shared memory to communicate with each other via **message passing**.

In **direct message passing**, without the use of shared memory, one processor sends a message directly to another processor, usually in a data packet. This requires some synchronization between the two processors, or some sort of buffer between the two. Instead of a separate buffer, a multiprocessor system can use shared memory. The first processor writes its message to the shared memory and signals the second processor that it has a waiting message. When the second processor is ready, it reads the message from shared memory, possibly returning an acknowledge signal to the sender. The location of the message in shared memory is either known beforehand or sent with the message waiting signal.

In addition to message passing, the operating system uses shared memory to store information about its current state. **Semaphores** and other information stored in shared memory by the operating system can be accessed by any processor that needs the information. Information on the protection and availability of different portions of memory fall into this category.

In the UMA architecture of Figure 12.5, it might at first appear that all processors must try to access a single shared memory module, and that only one can be successful at any given time. In practice, the shared memory is partitioned into several modules, all of which can be accessed simultaneously. A four-processor UMA architecture with its shared memory partitioned into four modules, and a Beneš network to connect the processors to memory, is shown in Figure 12.15.

The process used to divide the shared address space among the memory modules is called **interleaving**. It is similar in concept to the methods used to combine memory chips, introduced in Chapter 4. In **high-order interleaving**, the shared address space is divided into

Figure 12.15
UMA system with shared memory

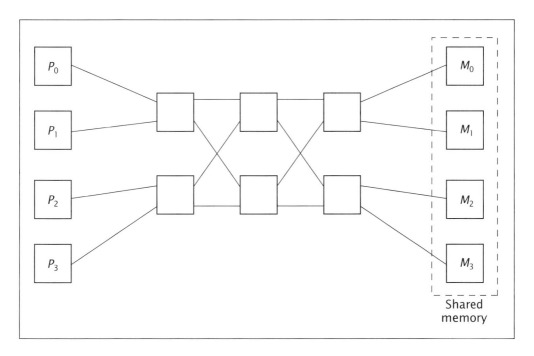

contiguous blocks of equal size. For example, if the system of Figure 12.15 contains 64 Mb of shared memory, the four modules would contain locations as shown in Table 12.1. The two high-order bits of an address determine the module in which its location resides; this is how high-order interleaving gets its name.

Table 12.1

Address ranges using high-order interleaving

Module	Address Range	Addresses
M_0	0 to 16M − 1	00 XXXX XXXX XXXX XXXX XXXX XXXX
M_1	16M to 32M − 1	01 XXXX XXXX XXXX XXXX XXXX XXXX
M_2	32M to 48M − 1	10 XXXX XXXX XXXX XXXX XXXX XXXX
M_3	48M to 64M − 1	11 XXXX XXXX XXXX XXXX XXXX XXXX

A less commonly used method of interleaving is called **low-order interleaving**. In this method, the low-order bits of a memory address determine its module. In the system of Figure 12.15, using low-order interleaving, module M_0 contains locations 0, 4, 8, ... 64M − 4, all of the addresses with 00 as the two low-order bits. Memory locations are assigned to the other memory modules in a similar manner. Table 12.2 shows the assignment of memory locations to modules in this system.

Table 12.2

Address ranges using low-order interleaving

Module	Address Range	Addresses
M_0	$i \bmod 4 = 0$ $(0 \le i \le 64M - 1)$	XX XXXX XXXX XXXX XXXX XXXX XX00
M_1	$i \bmod 4 = 1$ $(0 \le i \le 64M - 1)$	XX XXXX XXXX XXXX XXXX XXXX XX01
M_2	$i \bmod 4 = 2$ $(0 \le i \le 64M - 1)$	XX XXXX XXXX XXXX XXXX XXXX XX10
M_3	$i \bmod 4 = 3$ $(0 \le i \le 64M - 1)$	XX XXXX XXXX XXXX XXXX XXXX XX11

In a system with low-order interleaving, consecutive memory locations reside in different memory modules. Thus, a processor executing a program stored in a contiguous block of memory would need to access all four memory modules. Although it would be possible for all four processors to access different modules simultaneously, it would be very difficult to avoid memory conflicts. In contrast, this can be accomplished quite easily if high-order interleaving is used. If each processor is to execute a different program, the programs are simply stored in separate memory modules. The interconnection network is set to connect each processor to its proper memory module.

Low-order interleaving was originally used to reduce the delay in accessing memory. A CPU could output an address and read request to one memory module; while that memory module was decoding and accessing its data, the CPU could output another request to a different memory module, essentially pipelining its memory requests. Cache memory has greatly reduced the problem of memory delays, so low-order interleaving is not used very much in modern computers.

12.4.2 Cache Coherence

Just as in uniprocessor systems, cache memory can produce an improvement in the performance of multiprocessors by reducing the time needed to access data from memory. Unlike uniprocessor systems, however, multiprocessors have individual caches for each processor. This can lead to problems when two or more caches hold the value of the same memory location simultaneously. As one processor stores a value to that location in its cache, the other cache will have an invalid value in its location. Using a write-through cache will not resolve this problem, since it would update main memory but not the other caches. In addition, the extra writes to main memory would decrease system performance. This is the **cache coherence** problem.

To illustrate this cache coherence problem, consider a multi-processor system with four processors, each of which has a write-back cache. Assume that all four caches have loaded the contents of shared memory location 1234H, which is 56H. Then one of the processors, processor 0, writes the value 78H to this location in its cache. At this point, the caches do not all have the same value for this location; in fact, caches 1, 2, and 3 do not have the correct value. If one of the other processors reads the contents of location 1234H, it will read the old, incorrect value 56H instead of the correct value, 78H. Table 12.3 shows the cache values throughout this sequence of events.

Table 12.3

Cache values illustrating the cache coherence problem

Action	Cache 0	Cache 1	Cache 2	Cache 3
Initial	1234: 56	1234: 56	1234: 56	1234: 56
Processor 0 updates 1234H	1234: 78	1234: 56	1234: 56	1234: 56
Processor 3 reads 1234H				Reads 56H instead of 78H

It is possible to resolve the cache coherence problem during program compilation. The compiler can mark all shared data as **non-cacheable**, thus forcing all accesses to this data to be from shared memory. Although this resolves the problem, it lowers the cache hit ratio and reduces overall system performance. To reduce these effects and improve the hit ratio, a compiler may mark data as noncacheable only at specified, critical parts of the code.

Hardware solutions to the cache coherence problem are used much more than software, compile time solutions. One such scheme uses a **cache directory**. A directory controller is integrated with the main memory controller; it maintains a cache directory in main memory, which contains information on the contents of local caches. All cache writes are also sent to the directory controller so that it can update the cache directory. When a processor writes data to its cache, the directory controller checks to see which other caches also have that data. It invalidates that data in those caches by marking its locations as empty.

One popular solution to the cache coherence problem is called **snooping**. In snooping, each cache (sometimes called a *snoopy cache*) monitors memory activity on the system bus. Whenever it encounters a memory access (by another processor) to a location that it currently holds, it takes appropriate action. If the request is a memory read, and the contents in its cache are the same as those in main memory, it simply notes that another cache also contains this data. If the request is a memory read and the contents in its cache are different than those in main memory, the processor must have written data to the cache that has not yet been written back to main memory. The cache intercepts the memory read request, sending its data to both main memory and the cache which requested the data. If the request is a memory write, it simply marks its own data as invalid, essentially removing it from the cache. Note that this system requires a shared bus so that all caches can monitor all memory references. A system that uses an interconnection network, such as the system shown in Figure 12.15, cannot use snooping.

There are various protocols for marking and manipulating data within multiple caches. Of these, the **MESI** protocol is the most commonly used. In MESI each cache entry (block, sometimes called *line*) can be in one of the following four states.

1. *Modified:* The cache contains the memory value, but it is not the same as the value in shared memory. (A new value has been written to the cache by its processor, but not yet written back to shared memory.) No other cache holds this memory location.
2. *Exclusive:* The cache contains the memory value, which is the same as the value in shared memory. No other cache holds this memory location.
3. *Shared:* The cache contains the memory value, which is the same as the value in shared memory. Other caches may hold this memory location.
4. *Invalid:* The cache does not contain this memory location.

To illustrate how this protocol works, consider the four possible memory access scenarios: a read hit; a read miss; a write hit; and a write miss. Of these, the read hit is the most straightforward. The processor simply reads the data; the state of the data does not change. A read miss is more complicated. Since the data is not in its cache, the processor sends its read request to shared memory via the system bus. From here, several things can happen.

- If no cache contains the data, the memory management unit loads the data from main memory into the processor's cache and marks it as E (exclusive), since it is the only cache to contain the data.
- If one cache contains the data, marked as E, it loads the data into its cache and marks it as S (shared). The other cache changes its state for this data from E to S. (Since it is in state E, the other cache must have the same value for the data as main memory; otherwise it would have been in state M.)

- If more than one cache contains the data, they must have it marked as S. The processor loads the data into its cache and marks it as S. Since the other caches already have this data in state S, they do not have to change their states.
- If one cache contains the data marked as M (modified), main memory does not contain the correct value. The cache with the modified data temporarily blocks the memory read request and updates main memory. The read request then continues, and the data is marked as S. The cache which originally contained this data changes its state from M to S.

A write hit is relatively straightforward. Depending on the state of the data, one of the following occurs.

- If the cache contains the data in state M or E, it is the only cache currently holding the data. The processor writes the data to the cache. If the cache data was in state E, it is changed to state M. If it was already in state M, it retains this state.
- If the cache contains the data in state S, it writes the data and marks it as M. All other caches must mark this data as I (invalid), essentially removing it from their caches.

A write miss acts like a read miss followed by a write hit, optimized to avoid unnecessary work. It begins by issuing a **read with intent to modify** (**RWITM**) request to main memory. Then one of the following occurs.

- If no cache holds this data, one other cache holds the data marked as E, or one or more caches hold the data marked as S, the data is loaded from main memory into the cache and marked as M. The processor then writes the new data to the cache. Any other caches holding this data change their states from E or S to I.
- If one other cache holds this data as M, that cache temporarily blocks the request and writes its value back to main memory. It also marks its data as I. The original cache then loads the data and marks it as M, and its processor writes the new value to the cache. Although the write back to main memory is not necessary, since the value will soon become invalid, it simplifies the hardware implementation of the protocol.

Consider a four-processor system that uses cache snooping and the MESI protocol. Initially, no cache contains the contents of location 1234H. Then the following sequence of events occurs.

1. *Processor 0 reads this value.* Since this is a read miss, and no other cache contains this data, it loads the data from shared memory and marks it as E.

2. *Processor 1 reads this value.* This is also a read miss; it reads the data from shared memory and marks it as S. Cache 0 changes the state of this data from E to S.
3. *Processor 0 reads this value.* Since this is a read hit, it reads the data directly from cache. No states are changed.
4. *Processor 2 reads this value.* This is a read miss, so it reads the data from shared memory. Since other caches hold this data, this cache marks the data as S.
5. *Processor 0 writes new data to this location.* This is a write hit. It writes this data to the cache and marks it as M. Caches 1 and 2 mark this data as I.
6. *Processor 0 writes new data to this location.* Since this location is already marked as M, the processor simply writes the data to cache without changing its state.
7. *Processor 3 reads this value.* This is a read miss, so it issues a read request. Since cache 0 holds this data in state M, it temporarily blocks the request and writes the data to shared memory. It also sets its state to S. The data is then read in to cache 3 and marked as S.
8. *Processor 1 writes new data to this location.* This is a write miss, so cache 1 loads the data block and the processor writes the data to the cache, marking it as M. Caches 0 and 3 mark their copies of this data as I.
9. *Processor 2 writes new data to this location.* This is a write miss, so processor 2 issues a RWITM memory request. Cache 1 temporarily blocks this request, writes back its value to main memory and marks its copy of the data as I. Cache 2 then loads the value and marks it as M. Processor 2 then writes the new value to its cache.

Table 12.4 shows the status of the caches for this example.

Table 12.4

Cache values illustrating the cache coherence problem

Action	Result	Cache 0	Cache 1	Cache 2	Cache 3	Shared
P0 read	Read miss	1234:56 E				1234:56
P1 read	Read miss	1234:56 S	1234:56 S			1234:56
P0 read	Read hit	1234:56 S	1234:56 S			1234:56
P2 read	Read miss	1234:56 S	1234:56 S	1234:56 S		1234:56
P0 write	Write miss	1234:57 M	1234:XX I	1234:XX I		1234:56
P0 write	Write hit	1234:58 M				1234:56
P3 read	Read miss	1234:58 S			1234:58 S	1234:58
P1 write	Write miss	1234:XX I	1234:59 M		1234:XX I	1234:58
P2 write	Write miss		1234:XX I	1234:60 M		1234:59

12.5   Multiprocessor Operating Systems and Software

Regardless of the organization and architecture employed by a multiprocessor, the system cannot function well without proper software support. A **multiprocessor operating system** must coordinate tasks within the system. Parallel programming languages are needed so that applications can best make use of the parallel processors within the system.

A multiprocessor operating system must perform all of the tasks of a uniprocessor operating system, such as task swapping and memory management, as well as tasks that are unique to multiprocessor systems. For example, two tasks can **deadlock** if each holds exclusive access to a memory page or table, and each is waiting for the other to yield access to its page. A multiprocessor operating system must prevent this from happening.

Some pages of memory may be shared by more than one task. The operating system must allow this and ensure that the termination of one task does not remove the page from memory while other tasks are still using it. Since multiprocessor systems can use multiport memory, the operating system must coordinate connections between processors and memory by tracking and assigning memory ports to individual processors. To achieve optimum performance, it must implement **load balancing**, distributing tasks among processors to maximize processor utilization.

The operating system must schedule tasks and allocate processors to tasks. It must avoid conflicts to maximize performance. It must also enforce proper event ordering to ensure that correct results are generated. In the event of a processor failure, the operating system should ensure that the system continues to function, exhibiting a **graceful degradation of performance** rather than undergoing catastrophic failure.

A multiprocessor operating system can achieve parallelism by assigning different tasks to different processors. However, it cannot arbitrarily split individual tasks among several processors. Parallel programming languages can generate signals for the operating system to use in partitioning tasks.

There are several methods that a programming language can use to incorporate parallelism. The most widely used adds new parallel constructs to existing languages. The **fork** construct, used to spawn a separate process, and the **join** construct, used to synchronize processes, fall into this category. Parallel loop execution is another entry in this category. For example, consider the following code loop.

```
FOR i = 1 TO 1000 DO
    {A[i]←B[i] + C[i]}
```

The iterations of this loop are independent; no one iteration depends on any other. This loop could be parallelized, so that some or all of the loop iterations could be executed in parallel:

```
PARFOR i = 1 TO 1000 DO
    {A[i]←B[i] + C[i]}
```

When compiled, the program would include signals to the operating system that this loop can be unfolded and executed on several processors. The operating system would allocate one or more processors to the loop, depending on its load and the availability of processors. The program specifies what code *can* be executed in parallel, but the operating system decides what portion of this code *will* be executed in parallel.

It is also possible to achieve parallelism without using special constructs. A sequential programming language may include libraries that specify parallel operations. The programmer would write the program as if it were to be run on a sequential uniprocessor, and the compiler would insert parallel code. However, this yields a very limited amount of parallelism as compared to including explicit parallel constructs.

There are several deterrents to parallelism in programs. Just as conditional branch statements cause problems with instruction pipelines, they also inhibit parallelism in multiprocessor systems. Since the computer cannot know whether a conditional branch will be taken until it is executed, the compiler cannot know whether or not to schedule subsequent instructions in parallel with it.

Another factor inhibiting parallelism is data dependency. In Chapter 11 we examined one form of data dependency inherent to instruction pipelines, but there are others as well. Consider the following code segment.

$$1: A \leftarrow B + C$$
$$2: D \leftarrow A + E$$
$$3: A \leftarrow F + G$$

There is a data dependency between statements 1 and 2, because the value of A calculated in statement 1 is needed for statement 2. There is a different type of dependency between statements 2 and 3: The value of A used in statement 2 must be fetched before statement 3 stores a new value for A, otherwise the value calculated for D will be incorrect. (It is not necessary for D to be calculated before A, only for the old value of A to be fetched before the new value is stored.) This is sometimes referred to as **data anti-dependency**. If code is executed sequentially, this problem will never occur. It is only possible to have this type of dependency when instructions can be executed in parallel.

A third type of dependency exists between statements 1 and 3, sometimes called **data output dependency**. It requires that the value of A calculated in statement 1 be stored before the value calculated in statement 3. This ensures that subsequent statements will access the correct value of A. For example, if the next statement in this code segment is $H \leftarrow A + I$, the instruction clearly needs the value of A calculated in statement 3, not the value calculated in statement 1.

12.6 Parallel Algorithms

Parallel algorithms have been developed for many otherwise sequential functions. Some algorithms simply parallelize loops whose iterations are disjoint, such as the parallelized loop example in the previous section. Other algorithms totally restructure the flow of data to achieve parallelism. Regardless of the method used, these algorithms produce performance improvements and reduce the time needed to realize their functions.

A parallel algorithm may yield different performance when executed on multiprocessors with different topologies. For instance, an algorithm that yields good performance when run on a multiprocessor with a two-dimensional mesh organization may not do so well when run on a system with a tree organization. The mapping of a parallel algorithm onto a system is just as important in determining performance as the algorithm itself.

Two typical parallel algorithms are the bubble sort, one of the slower sequential sorting algorithms with parallel implementation that produces a significant improvement in performance; and matrix multiplication, which can also realize substantial performance improvement when executed in parallel.

12.6.1 Parallel Bubble Sort

The **bubble sort** is a well known, though inefficient, sequential sorting algorithm. The following code segment implements the bubble sort on the n elements of array A; A_1 receives the smallest element of the array and A_n receives the largest value.

```
FOR i = n - 1 DOWNTO 1 DO
    {FOR j = 1 TO i DO
        {IF A_j > A_{j+1} THEN A_j↔A_{j+1}}}
```

The operation $A_j \leftrightarrow A_{j+1}$ indicates that the two values are swapped. It is equivalent to the following code.

```
TEMP←A_j;
A_j←A_{j+1};
A_{j+1}←TEMP;
```

In its sequential form, the algorithm sets the $(i+1)th$ value during each iteration of the outer loop. After the last iteration, since all other values have been set correctly, A_1 is also set to its proper value. Its run time is $O(n^2)$.

It is possible to parallelize this algorithm, but we will have to change the order of operations. It is not possible to simply parallelize the inner FOR loop, since different iterations may modify the same values. For example, assume $A_1 = 3$, $A_2 = 2$, and $A_3 = 1$, and the inner loop is parallelized. For $j = 1$, $A_1 > A_2$ and these values should be swapped. Concurrently, for $j = 2$, $A_2 > A_3$, and these values should be swapped as well. It is not possible to swap A_2 in both operations simultaneously.

Instead of using the PARFOR construct on the algorithm as shown in its sequential form, we modify it to avoid having two simultaneous accesses to any data value. The parallel algorithm is

```
FOR i = n DOWNTO 1 DO
      {PARFOR j = ((i MOD 2) +1) TO n - 1 STEP 2 DO
          {IF A_j > A_{j+1} THEN A_j↔A_{j+1}}}
```

There are several things in this algorithm which we must explain. First, notice that the j loop is now a parallel loop with a step size of 2 instead of the default step of 1. The PARFOR statement allows multiple pairs of data to be compared and swapped at the same time. The STEP 2 avoids the data conflicts. For example, if $i = n = 8$, this loop has index values of $j = \{1,3,5,7\}$. It compares A_1 and A_2, A_3 and A_4, A_5 and A_6, and A_7 and A_8 in parallel. When $i = 7$ (or any odd value), it compares A_2 and A_3, A_4 and A_5, and A_6 and A_7 simultaneously. It alternates between these two patterns of compare operations to sort the data. Note that the outer loop of this algorithm requires n iterations, as opposed to $n - 1$ for the sequential algorithm. Nevertheless, its run time of $O(n)$ is a significant improvement over that of the sequential algorithm.

Table 12.5(a) shows the trace of the sequential version of this algorithm for $n = 8$ and $A_{1..8} = 8,7,6,5,4,3,2,1$. For clarity, we show the results after every iteration of the outer loop only. Each row of this

Table 12.5

Trace of the (a) sequential and (b) parallel bubble sort algorithms

i	j	$A_{1..8}$
—	—	8 7 6 5 4 3 2 1
7	1..7	7 6 5 4 3 2 1 8
6	1..6	6 5 4 3 2 1 7 8
5	1..5	5 4 3 2 1 6 7 8
4	1..4	4 3 2 1 5 6 7 8
3	1..3	3 2 1 4 5 6 7 8
2	1..2	2 1 3 4 5 6 7 8
1	1	1 2 3 4 5 6 7 8

i	j	$A_{1..8}$
—	—	8 7 6 5 4 3 2 1
8	1,3,5,7	7 8 5 6 3 4 1 2
7	2,4,6	7 5 8 3 6 1 4 2
6	1,3,5,7	5 7 3 8 1 6 2 4
5	2,4,6	5 3 7 1 8 2 6 4
4	1,3,5,7	3 5 1 7 2 8 4 6
3	2,4,6	3 1 5 2 7 4 8 6
2	1,3,5,7	1 3 2 5 4 7 6 8
1	2,4,6	1 2 3 4 5 6 7 8

(a)   (b)

trace incorporates up to $n - 1$ sequential iterations of the inner loop. Table 12.5(b) shows the trace of the parallel algorithm. Each row of this trace includes the $n/2$ or $n/2 - 1$ parallel iterations of the inner loop, which take constant, $O(1)$ time.

The parallel algorithm works well in this example, but it must be mapped to a multiprocessor correctly to work in practice. A linear array of n processors, each holding one value, works well for this algorithm, since each value is only compared to its nearest neighbor. A hypercube can also be used for this algorithm, as long as adjacent values of array A are stored in processors that directly communicate with each other. Multiprocessors with a shared bus or tree organization cannot adequately support the communication needs of this algorithm. Since all processors perform the same operations, but on different data, we can use an SIMD machine with inactive processors disabled at the appropriate times.

12.6.2   Parallel Matrix Multiplication

Matrix multiplication is a function used frequently in a wide variety of applications. One example is computer graphics, where matrix multiplication is used to move, rotate, and scale images. Other applications range from communication systems to financial modeling.

Two matrices can be multiplied only if the number of columns in the first matrix is equal to the number of rows in the second matrix. (Unlike scalar multiplication, the order of the two matrices being multiplied does affect the result.) To compute the matrix product $C = A \cdot B$, where A is of size $m \times n$, B is $n \times p$, and C must be $m \times p$, the individual elements of C are generated as follows:

$$C_{i,j} = \sum_{k=1}^{n} A_{i,k} \cdot B_{k,j} \, (1 \le i \le m, 1 \le j \le p)$$

In nonequation form, element $C_{i,j}$ is the dot product of row i of the first matrix and column j of the second matrix.

The following code segment performs this matrix multiplication.

```
FOR i = 1 TO m DO
      {FOR j = 1 TO p DO
            {C_{i,j} = 0;
             FOR k = 1 to n DO
                  {C_{i,j}←C_{i,j} + A_{i,k} · B_{k,j}}}}
```

In this routine, the outer loop sequences through the rows of the matrix and the j loop goes through the individual elements of the row. The innermost loop sums the products to generate one term of the product matrix C. Its run time is $O(mnp)$; for square matrices of size $n \times n$, this is $O(n^3)$.

It is not possible to parallelize all three loops in this algorithm. The innermost loop sets $C_{i,j}←C_{i,j} + A_{i,k} \cdot B_{k,j}$. This statement requires the value of $C_{i,j}$ calculated in the previous iteration of the loop and therefore must remain sequential. However, the other two loops merely select an element to be calculated. Since the computation of any one element of the product matrix is independent of the computation of any other element, these two loops can be parallelized. The parallel code for this algorithm is

```
PARFOR i = 1 TO m DO
    {PARFOR j = 1 TO p DO
        {C_{i,j} = 0;

        FOR k = 1 to n DO
            {C_{i,j}←C_{i,j} + A_{i,k} · B_{k,j}}}}
```

Unlike the sequential algorithm, which calculates one entry in its entirety before proceeding to the next entry, this version calculates partial results for every entry simultaneously. The run time for this algorithm is $O(p)$, or $O(n)$ when $n \times n$ square matrices are used.

Table 12.6 shows the traces of the sequential and parallel algorithms to generate the product

$$C = \begin{bmatrix} 1 & 0 & 1 \\ 1 & 2 & 1 \\ 2 & 2 & 0 \end{bmatrix} \cdot \begin{bmatrix} 2 & 1 & 2 \\ 1 & 2 & 0 \\ 2 & 0 & 1 \end{bmatrix} = \begin{bmatrix} 4 & 1 & 3 \\ 6 & 5 & 3 \\ 6 & 6 & 4 \end{bmatrix}$$

Each entry in the sequential trace corresponds to three iterations of the innermost loop, whereas each row of the parallel trace represents one iteration of this loop.

This algorithm can be executed on any multiprocessor, regardless of its connection topology. To do so, each processor must have a copy of the row of A and the column of B it uses to calculate its portion of matrix C stored in its local memory. This results in n copies of matrices A and B being stored in the local memories of the processors, since n processors use each row of A and each column of B. All of the processors storing the same row of A use the same element, $A_{i,k}$ simultaneously; similarly, all n processors use the same value $B_{k,j}$ at the same time.

It is possible to modify the algorithm so no two processors use the same element of A or B concurrently. Each element of each matrix is stored in only one processor. After each computation, these values are passed to the next processors to use them. The modified algorithm changes the index used to calculate the product terms of the sum. The algorithm still adds the same terms, but in different orders in some cases:

```
PARFOR i = 1 TO m DO
    {PARFOR j = 1 TO p DO
        {C_{i,j} = 0;
        FOR k = 1 to n DO
            {C_{i,j}←C_{i,j} + A_{i,x} · B_{x,j}}}} (x = ((i + j + k) MOD p) + 1)
```

Table 12.6

Trace of the (a) sequential and (b) parallel matrix multiplication algorithms

i	j	k	C
1	1	1..3	$\begin{bmatrix} 2+0+2 & - & - \\ - & - & - \\ - & - & - \end{bmatrix}$
1	2	1..3	$\begin{bmatrix} 4 & 1+0+0 & - \\ - & - & - \\ - & - & - \end{bmatrix}$
1	3	1..3	$\begin{bmatrix} 4 & 1 & 2+0+1 \\ - & - & - \\ - & - & - \end{bmatrix}$
2	1	1..3	$\begin{bmatrix} 4 & 1 & 3 \\ 2+2+2 & - & - \\ - & - & - \end{bmatrix}$
2	2	1..3	$\begin{bmatrix} 4 & 1 & 3 \\ 6 & 1+4+0 & - \\ - & - & - \end{bmatrix}$
2	3	1..3	$\begin{bmatrix} 4 & 1 & 3 \\ 6 & 5 & 2+0+1 \\ - & - & - \end{bmatrix}$
3	1	1..3	$\begin{bmatrix} 4 & 1 & 3 \\ 6 & 5 & 3 \\ 4+2+0 & - & - \end{bmatrix}$
3	2	1..3	$\begin{bmatrix} 4 & 1 & 3 \\ 6 & 5 & 3 \\ 6 & 2+4+0 & - \end{bmatrix}$
3	3	1..3	$\begin{bmatrix} 4 & 1 & 3 \\ 6 & 5 & 3 \\ 6 & 6 & 4+0+0 \end{bmatrix}$
—	—	—	$\begin{bmatrix} 4 & 1 & 3 \\ 6 & 5 & 3 \\ 6 & 6 & 4 \end{bmatrix}$

(a)

i	j	k	C
1..3	1..3	1	$\begin{bmatrix} 2 & 1 & 2 \\ 2 & 1 & 2 \\ 4 & 2 & 4 \end{bmatrix}$
1..3	1..3	2	$\begin{bmatrix} 2+0 & 1+0 & 2+0 \\ 2+2 & 1+4 & 2+0 \\ 4+2 & 2+4 & 4+0 \end{bmatrix}$
1..3	1..3	3	$\begin{bmatrix} 2+2 & 1+0 & 2+1 \\ 4+2 & 5+0 & 2+1 \\ 6+0 & 6+0 & 4+0 \end{bmatrix}$
—	—	—	$\begin{bmatrix} 4 & 1 & 3 \\ 6 & 5 & 3 \\ 6 & 6 & 4 \end{bmatrix}$

(b)

This modified algorithm works very well when run on an $m \times n$ mesh of processors with wraparound connections. As with the parallel bubble sort, this algorithm can be executed using an SIMD computer. Figure 12.16 shows the 3×3 mesh connected multiprocessor. Each processor shows the value of C that it calculates, and the initial values of matrices A and B that it stores. As shown in Figure 12.16, the values in the A matrix are routed one processor to the left after every iteration of the innermost loop. At the same time, the B matrix values are sent one processor up the column. The trace of this algorithm is left as an exercise for the reader.

Figure 12.16

A 3 × 3 mesh-connected multiprocessor and its initial values for the modified parallel matrix multiplication algorithm

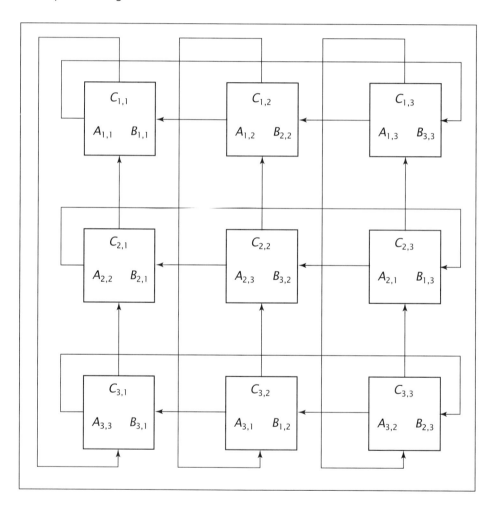

12.7 Alternative Parallel Architectures

The parallel architectures presented so far in this chapter are extensions of the classic von Neumann model. Beyond these systems, there are designs based on completely different models, such as dataflow computers, systolic arrays, and neural networks.

12.7.1 Dataflow Computing

In a typical von Neumann computer, whether a uniprocessor or multi-processor system, the execution of instructions is driven by the control structure of the program. Instructions are executed in the order that they occur in the program. One exception to this is the reordering of instructions based on data dependency.

Unlike these architectures, **dataflow computers** execute instructions based solely on the availability of their operands. This is an extension of the reordering based on data dependency. The dataflow computer performs the dependency checking during program execution, rather than during program compilation.

To understand how data flow computers work, it is first necessary to understand **dataflow graphs**. As a computer program is compiled, it is converted into its equivalent dataflow graph, which shows the data dependencies between statements and is used by the dataflow computer to generate the structures it needs to execute the program. Figure 12.17 shows a sample code segment and its dataflow graph.

FIGURE 12.17

A code segment and its dataflow graph

$$1. \ A \leftarrow B + C$$
$$2. \ D \leftarrow E + F$$
$$3. \ G \leftarrow A + H$$
$$4. \ I \leftarrow D + G$$
$$5. \ J \leftarrow I + K$$

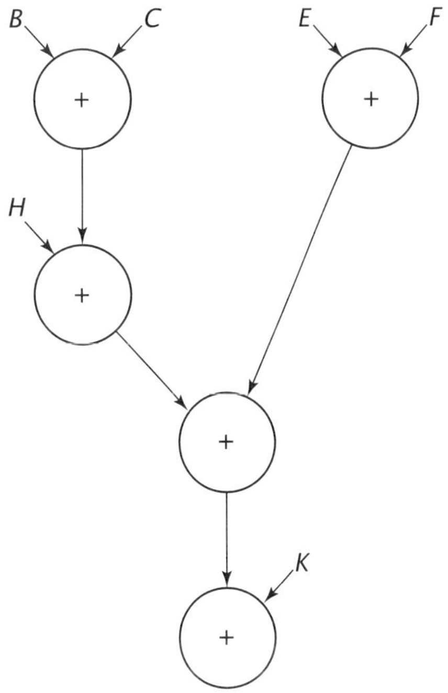

As shown in Figure 12.17, each vertex of the graph corresponds to the operation performed by one of the instructions. To simplify this system, only unary and binary operations are generally used; statements such as $A \leftarrow B + C + D$ are divided into multiple statements. The directed edges going to a vertex correspond to the operands of the function performed by the vertex, and the directed edge leaving the vertex represents the result generated by the function. (Note that only declarative vertices are shown here. There are also vertex types for conditional statements and other types of statements, not covered here.)

Dataflow computers avoid many data dependencies by using the **single assignment rule**. Simply put, this rule requires that no two statements write data to the same variable. Also, an operand of one equation cannot be written to by any later equation. For example, in the code block of Figure 12.17, no statement after statement 1 could write to B or to C. Enforcing this rule ensures that no data antidependencies or data output dependencies occur in any dataflow program. This means that we do not need to include hardware in the system to check for these types of dependencies.

To illustrate how the single assignment rule works, consider the following code segment.

$$1: A \leftarrow B + C$$
$$2: B \leftarrow A + D$$
$$3: C \leftarrow A + B$$
$$4: D \leftarrow C + B$$
$$5: A \leftarrow A + C$$

This code segment has four violations of the single assignment rule, starting with statement 2. The value stored by this statement, B, was used as an operand in statement 1, so it must be renamed. We arbitrarily rename it $B1$, and change all references to it later in this code. Similarly, values C and D, set by statements 3 and 4, are also used as operands in prior statements and must be renamed. Finally, statement 5 stores its result in A, the same variable used to store the result in statement 1. We must also change this variable's name. Note that statements 2, 3, and 5 all use A as an operand: This is not a violation of the single assignment rule. An operand can be used many times; it can only be written to once, before it is used in another operation. Figure 12.18 shows the revised code segment and dataflow graph for this code.

The dataflow graph describes the dependencies between statements and how data will flow between statements. An edge, however, does not show when data flows from one statement to another. The data that traverses an edge is called a **token**. When a token is available, it is represented as a dot on the edge, as shown in Figure 12.19. A vertex is ready to **fire**, or execute its instruction, when all edges have tokens, or the instruction's operands are all available.

FIGURE 12.18

The revised code segment and its dataflow graph

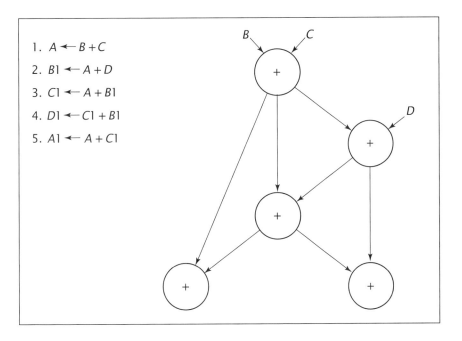

1. $A \leftarrow B + C$

2. $B1 \leftarrow A + D$

3. $C1 \leftarrow A + B1$

4. $D1 \leftarrow C1 + B1$

5. $A1 \leftarrow A + C1$

FIGURE 12.19

Dataflow graph for the code segment after statement 1 has been executed. Statement 2 is ready to fire and statements 3 and 5 each have one operand available.

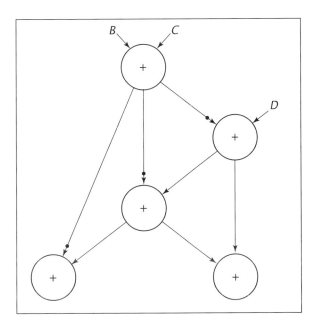

Within the computer system, dataflow vertices are usually stored as **I-structures**. A typical I-structure is shown in Figure 12.20(a). Each I-structure includes the operation to be performed, its operands (or space to store the operand when it is ready), and a list of destinations for its result. The empty parentheses in this figure denote a reserved space for an operand to be supplied by another I-structure. The destination 2/1 indicates that the result of this operation also serves as the first operand of statement 2. Since the order of operands is important for operations such as subtraction and division, the I-structure must specify the order of the operands. Figure 12.20(b) shows the dataflow graph of Figure 12.19, redrawn with I-structures in place of the vertices they represent, with $B = 2$, $C = 3$, and $D = 4$.

(a) An I-structure and (b) the dataflow graph of Figure 12.19 with I-structures

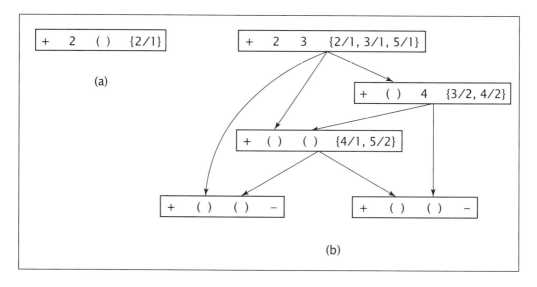

The architectures of dataflow systems fall into two categories. **Static architectures** allow only one token to reside on an edge at any given time, as would be the case in the examples shown so far. **Dynamic architectures**, on the other hand, allow multiple, tagged tokens to reside on an edge simultaneously. This is useful for allowing re-entrant code, as might be found in the operating system; the tag that accompanies a token denotes the instantiation of the code associated with the token.

Figure 12.21 shows the organization of the static dataflow computer. The I-store unit has two sections. The memory section stores the I-structures of the dataflow program. The update/ready section monitors completed instructions. When an instruction has executed, this section updates the I-structures that use its result. If any I-structures that use this operand become ready to fire, that is, have all their operands, they are sent to the **firing queue**. When they reach the front of the queue, they are sent to the next available processor and executed.

Figure 12.21
Static dataflow computer organization

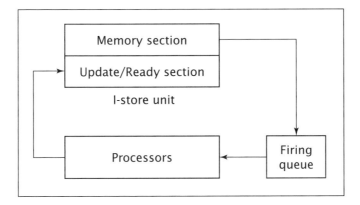

The organization of the dynamic dataflow computer is similar to that of the static system. The primary difference lies within the update/ready section. Since the tokens in dynamic systems are tagged, this unit must reconcile data destinations with their instantiations. For this reason, the update/ready unit of a dynamic dataflow computer is quite a bit more complex than its counterpart in the static organization.

Dataflow systems offer some advantages over conventional, von Neumann architectures. By executing instructions as their operands are available, they can achieve the maximum possible degree of parallelism. However, they also have their drawbacks, including the lack of commonly used high-level languages, the lack of hierarchical memory, and the overhead associated with firing instructions.

12.7.2   Systolic Arrays

A **systolic array** incorporates several processing elements into a regular structure, such as a linear array or mesh. Each processing element performs a single, fixed function (this function may be different for different processing elements), and communicates only with its neighboring processing elements. Data enters the systolic array via processing elements at the edges of the array, and the processing elements calculate their results based on these inputs.

In a systolic array, the timing for entering data into the array is crucial. No control signals are input to the array (only the system clock is input), so varying when data is entered is the only way to control the array.

To illustrate this concept, consider a simple 2×2 systolic array, which will be used to multiply two 2×2 matrices, A and B, forming the product $C = A \times B$. The systolic array is shown in Figure 12.22. Each element of the array has two inputs, denoted L (left) and U (up), and two outputs, R (right) and D (down). Each element of the array reads its L and U inputs, multiplies them, and adds the product to an internal register, which holds the running total. This running total is initially equal to 0. At the end of the clock cycle, it outputs the value on input L to its output R, and the value on input U to output D, making them available to its neighboring processing elements during the next clock cycle.

FIGURE 12.22

A 2×2 systolic array to multiply two matrices

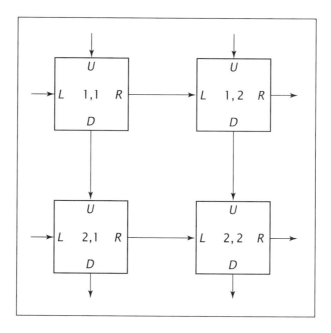

Each processing element of the systolic array, i,j, will calculate one term of the product, $C_{i,j}$. The first element, $C_{1,1}$, must be set to $A_{1,1}B_{1,1} + A_{1,2}B_{2,1}$; during the first clock cycle we input $A_{1,1}$ to input L and $B_{1,1}$ to input U of processing element 1,1. This processing element calculates $A_{1,1}B_{1,1}$ and adds it to its running total. All other processing elements generate no new results during this time; their running totals remain 0. The first clock cycle for this operation is shown in Figure 12.23(a).

FIGURE 12.23

Trace of the four clock cycles of the multiplication algorithm on the systolic array

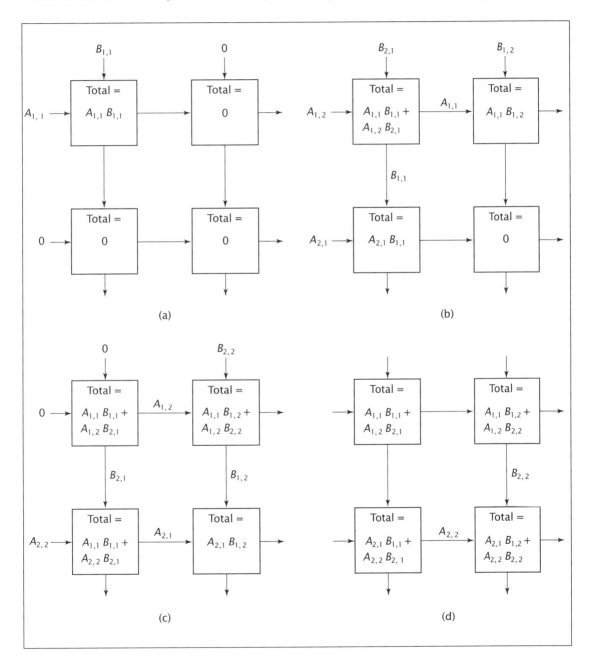

During the next clock cycle, several things happen. In processing element 1,1, we input $A_{1,2}$ to L and $B_{2,1}$ to U. This processing element multiplies them and adds the product to its running total, which becomes $A_{1,1}B_{1,1} + A_{1,2}B_{2,1}$, the final value of $C_{1,1}$. At the same time, $A_{1,1}$ is transmitted across to processing element 1,2. Since this processing element must calculate $A_{1,1}B_{1,2}$ to produce its final result, we input $B_{1,2}$ to its U input during this clock cycle. To ensure proper timing, we inserted a 0 to this input during the first clock cycle. Similarly, processing element 2,1 calculates $A_{2,1}B_{1,1}$. The results of these operations are shown in Figure 12.23(b).

Clock cycle 3 continues the matrix multiplication. Since $C_{1,1}$ has already been calculated, we input zeroes to the inputs of processing element 1,1 so the running total is not changed. The final values of $C_{1,2}$ and $C_{2,1}$ are calculated during this clock cycle, and the first part of $C_{2,2}$ is generated, as shown in Figure 12.23(c). The final value of $C_{2,2}$ is calculated during clock cycle 4, as shown in Figure 12.23(d); at this point, multiplication of the two matrices has been computed.

A standard way to illustrate a systolic array is to show the structure of the array with the data inputs in the order in which they enter the array. Figure 12.24 shows the array and its data inputs used to calculate the matrix product $C = A \times B$. The first data value on each input enters the array during the first clock cycle. The second enters the array during the second clock cycle, and so on.

Systolic architectures can perform specific functions very quickly, but they are limited to only one function per array. In general, systolic arrays can be used for specialized computational hardware but not for general purpose computing.

12.7.3   Neural Networks

Neural networks are vastly different from any other computing structure covered in this text. They may incorporate thousands or even millions of simple processing elements called **neurons,** named after the conductors of signals in the human nervous system. These neurons have far less processing power than even a simple CPU. There are a large number of direct interconnections between neurons, always between close neighboring neurons. These connections, along with the massive number of neurons, give the neural network its processing capabilities.

Unlike traditional computers, which are programmed, neural networks are **trained**. Training consists of defining system input data and defining the desired system outputs for that input data.

System outputs are generated as a function of the outputs of individual neurons. Each neuron's output, in turn, is a function of the outputs of the neurons to which it is connected. Consider a neuron, *N*, which is connected to several other neurons. For each of these other neurons, there is a **weighting factor**; the output of each neuron is mul-

FɪɢᴜʀᴇRE 12.24

A 2 × 2 systolic array to multiply two matrices with data values shown

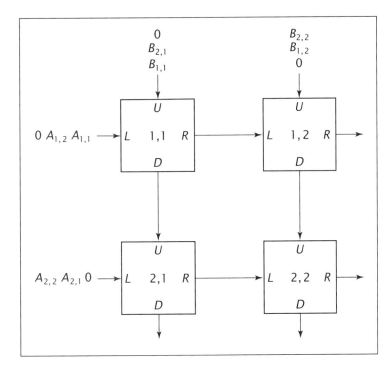

tiplied by its weighting factor. All of these weighted values are added together to generate a value for neuron N; however, this is not the output of neuron N. Instead, this value is compared to the **threshold value** for that neuron. (Each neuron can have a different threshold value.) If the weighted value is greater than or equal to the threshold value, the neuron outputs a logical value of 1; otherwise it outputs a 0. A neural network is trained by varying the weights on its connections.

To illustrate how this works, consider a neuron, N, which is connected to four other neurons, labeled 1, 2, 3, and 4, with weights of 0.1, 0.2, 0.3, and 0.4, respectively. Neuron N has a threshold value of 0.65. If the values of neurons 1, 2, 3, and 4 are 1, 1, 0, and 1, respectively, then the value input to neuron N is $(1 \cdot 0.1) + (1 \cdot 0.2) + (0 \cdot 0.3) + (1 \cdot 0.4) = 0.7$. Since this weighted value, 0.7, is greater than the threshold value for this neuron, 0.65, neuron N outputs a logical value of 1.

A neural network is not appropriate for general purpose computing; you won't find a neural network running Windows on a personal computer. Instead it has found applications in tasks that do not run well on conventional architectures, such as pattern recognition. Neural networks are also being used in control systems and artificial intelligence applications.

12.8 Summary

Parallel processing is commonly used to improve computer system performance. A uniprocessor system may incorporate parallelism using an instruction pipeline, a fixed or reconfigurable arithmetic pipeline, I/O processors, vectored arithmetic units, and multiport memory.

Multiprocessor systems can be classified using several attributes. Flynn's classification categorizes multiprocessor systems by their instruction and data streams. A system may also be classified by its topology, whether it uses a shared bus, ring, tree, mesh, hypercube, completely connected, or other topology. A topology is characterized by its diameter, total bandwidth, and bisection bandwidth. Systems may also be classified by their architectures, such as uniform memory access (UMA), nonuniform memory access (NUMA), cache coherent NUMA (CC-NUMA), cache only memory access (COMA), network or cluster of workstations (NOW or COW), or massively parallel processor (MPP). Some multiprocessors, including dataflow computers, systolic arrays, and neural networks, do not fit easily into any of these classifications.

Systems may use fixed communication connections, as in clustering, or reconfigurable connections. Reconfigurable communications systems are implemented using crossbar switches or multistage interconnection networks. Some MINs, such as the Beneš network, are rearrangeable but require a centralized routing unit. Others, such as the Omega network, are more limited but can use distributed, self-routing.

Multiprocessor systems often use shared memory. Memory interleaving is used to partition memory so that different modules can be accessed simultaneously. Each processor in a multiprocessor system may have its own cache memory. Protocols such as the MESI protocol are used to maintain coherence among data in the caches.

In addition to the functions performed in uniprocessor systems, a multiprocessor operating system must avoid memory deadlocks among the processes being executed by its different processors. It also implements load balancing to maximize system performance.

Programming languages implement parallelism by incorporating explicit parallel constructs or by using libraries with parallel implementations. Conditional branch instructions and data dependencies inhibit parallelism in programs. Properly mapping a parallel algorithm to the multiprocessor's topology and architecture maximizes system performance.

Problems

 What are the diameter, total bandwidth, and bisection bandwidth for 64-processor systems (63 for the tree) with the following topologies? The link bandwidth is 500 Mb/sec.

a) Shared bus
b) Ring
c) Tree (with 63 processors instead of 64)
d) Mesh without wraparound connections
e) Mesh with wraparound connections
f) Hypercube
g) Completely connected

2 Repeat Problem 1 for systems with 16 processors (15 for the tree) and a link bandwidth of 10 Mb/sec.

3 Find the number of processors for which the tree topology has a lower diameter than the ring topology of Figure 12.4.

4 Find the number of processors for which the mesh topology without wraparound connections has a lower diameter than the tree topology.

5 Find the number of processors for which the hypercube topology has a lower total bandwidth than the completely connected topology.

6 A 16-processor computer with a mesh topology and wraparound connections has a link bandwidth of 100 Mb/sec. What is the link bandwidth of 16-processor computers with the following topologies, such that they all have the same bisection bandwidth as this computer?

a) Completely connected topology
b) Hypercube topology
c) Mesh topology without wraparound connections

7 Show the 8×8 network created from the Clos network by setting $n = m = N/2$ and $k = 2$, and recursively decomposing any switches greater than 2×2 in size. What is the hardware complexity of this network?

8 A three-stage network is set so that $p(S_1) = \begin{pmatrix} 0\ 1\ 2\ 3\ 4\ 5\ 6\ 7 \\ 2\ 5\ 3\ 7\ 0\ 4\ 6\ 1 \end{pmatrix}$, $p(S_2) = \begin{pmatrix} 0\ 1\ 2\ 3\ 4\ 5\ 6\ 7 \\ 1\ 7\ 0\ 2\ 4\ 6\ 5\ 3 \end{pmatrix}$, and $p(S_3) = \begin{pmatrix} 0\ 1\ 2\ 3\ 4\ 5\ 6\ 7 \\ 7\ 5\ 3\ 6\ 4\ 2\ 0\ 1 \end{pmatrix}$. The network has $L_1 = L_2 = \begin{pmatrix} 0\ 1\ 2\ 3\ 4\ 5\ 6\ 7 \\ 0\ 4\ 1\ 5\ 2\ 6\ 3\ 7 \end{pmatrix}$. What permutation is realized by the network?

9 A three-stage network is set so that $p(S_1) = \begin{pmatrix} 0\ 1\ 2\ 3\ 4\ 5\ 6\ 7 \\ 7\ 5\ 3\ 6\ 4\ 2\ 0\ 1 \end{pmatrix}$, $p(S_2) = \begin{pmatrix} 0\ 1\ 2\ 3\ 4\ 5\ 6\ 7 \\ 1\ 7\ 0\ 2\ 4\ 6\ 5\ 3 \end{pmatrix}$, and $p(S_3) = \begin{pmatrix} 0\ 1\ 2\ 3\ 4\ 5\ 6\ 7 \\ 2\ 5\ 3\ 7\ 0\ 4\ 6\ 1 \end{pmatrix}$. The network has $L_1 = L_2 = \begin{pmatrix} 0\ 1\ 2\ 3\ 4\ 5\ 6\ 7 \\ 0\ 4\ 1\ 5\ 2\ 6\ 3\ 7 \end{pmatrix}$. What permutation is realized by the network?

10 For Problem 9, what value should $p(S_3)$ have for the network to realize the identity permutation, $\begin{pmatrix} 0\,1\,2\,3\,4\,5\,6\,7 \\ 0\,1\,2\,3\,4\,5\,6\,7 \end{pmatrix}$?

11 Show the settings of the switches in the 8×8 Beneš network generated by the Looping Algorithm for the following permutations.

a) $\begin{pmatrix} 0\,1\,2\,3\,4\,5\,6\,7 \\ 1\,3\,5\,2\,4\,6\,7\,0 \end{pmatrix}$

b) $\begin{pmatrix} 0\,1\,2\,3\,4\,5\,6\,7 \\ 0\,4\,6\,1\,2\,5\,7\,3 \end{pmatrix}$

c) $\begin{pmatrix} 0\,1\,2\,3\,4\,5\,6\,7 \\ 3\,1\,6\,4\,2\,0\,5\,7 \end{pmatrix}$

12 Show the settings of the switches in the 8×8 Omega network for the permutations of Problem 11. Denote any switches that are blocked.

13 Show the address ranges for the memory modules in the following systems. All systems use high-order interleaving.

a) A system with four processors, eight memory modules, and 64Mb of shared memory

b) A system with seven processors, four memory modules, and 128Mb of shared memory

c) A system with three processors, eight memory modules, and 32Mb of shared memory

14 Repeat Problem 13, with all systems using low-order interleaving.

15 Show the values and states in the caches of a four processor UMA system, which uses the MESI protocol, for the following sequence of events.

a) Processor 0 reads from location 1000H.
b) Processor 2 writes to location 1000H.
c) Processor 1 reads from location 1000H.
d) Processor 0 writes to location 1000H.
e) Processor 3 reads from location 1000H.
f) Processor 1 writes to location 1000H.
g) Processor 1 reads from location 1000H.

16 Repeat Problem 15 for the following sequence of events.

a) Processor 2 writes to location 1100H.
b) Processor 1 reads from location 1100H.
c) Processor 3 writes to location 1100H.
d) Processor 2 reads from location 1100H.

e) Processor 0 reads from location 1100H.

f) Processor 1 writes to location 1100H.

g) Processor 2 writes to location 1100H.

17 State the data dependencies, data antidependencies, and data output dependencies in the following code segment. For each dependency, give the statements involved, the type of dependency, and the dependent variable.

1: $A \leftarrow B + C$

2: $D \leftarrow E + F$

3: $G \leftarrow A + D$

4: $A \leftarrow D + E$

18 Repeat Problem 17 for the following code segment.

1: $A \leftarrow B + C$

2: $A \leftarrow A + D$

3: $D \leftarrow C + E$

4: $B \leftarrow D + F$

5: $G \leftarrow A + H$

6: $C \leftarrow F + H$

19 Repeat Problem 17 for the following code segment.

1: $A \leftarrow B + C$

2: $B \leftarrow A + C$

3: $C \leftarrow A + B$

4: $A \leftarrow B + D$

5: $D \leftarrow C + E$

6: $A \leftarrow A + F$

7: $E \leftarrow B + C$

8: $F \leftarrow A + E$

20 Show the trace of the modified parallel matrix multiplication algorithm

for $A = \begin{bmatrix} 1 & 0 & 1 \\ 1 & 2 & 1 \\ 2 & 2 & 0 \end{bmatrix}$ and $B = \begin{bmatrix} 2 & 1 & 2 \\ 1 & 2 & 0 \\ 2 & 0 & 1 \end{bmatrix}$.

21 Convert the following code segment so that it meets the requirements of the single assignment rule. Show its dataflow graph and I-structures.

1: $A \leftarrow B + C$ 4: $B \leftarrow D + F$

2: $A \leftarrow A + D$ 5: $G \leftarrow A + H$

3: $D \leftarrow C + E$

22   Repeat Problem 21 for the following code segment.

1: $A \leftarrow B + C$
2: $B \leftarrow A + A$
3: $C \leftarrow B + A$
4: $B \leftarrow C + D$
5: $B \leftarrow B + A$

Index